Lecture Notes in Computer Science   2567
Edited by G. Goos, J. Hartmanis, and J. van Leeuwen

Springer
Berlin
Heidelberg
New York
Barcelona
Hong Kong
London
Milan
Paris
Tokyo

Yvo G. Desmedt (Ed.)

Public Key Cryptography – PKC 2003

6th International Workshop
on Practice and Theory in Public Key Cryptography
Miami, FL, USA, January 6-8, 2003
Proceedings

 Springer

Series Editors

Gerhard Goos, Karlsruhe University, Germany
Juris Hartmanis, Cornell University, NY, USA
Jan van Leeuwen, Utrecht University, The Netherlands

Volume Editor

Yvo G. Desmedt
Florida State University
Department of Computer Science
253 Love Building, Tallahassee, FL 32306-4530, USA
E-mail: desmedt@cs.fsu.edu

Cataloging-in-Publication Data applied for

Bibliographic information published by Die Deutsche Bibliothek
Die Deutsche Bibliothek lists this publication in the DeutscheNationalbibliografie;
detailed bibliographic data is available in the Internet at <http://dnb.ddb.de>.

CR Subject Classification (1998): E.3, F.2.0, C.2.0, K.4.4, K.6.5

ISSN 0302-9743
ISBN 3-540-00324-X Springer-Verlag Berlin Heidelberg New York

Springer-Verlag Berlin Heidelberg New York
a member of BertelsmannSpringer Science+Business Media GmbH

http://www.springer.de

© Springer-Verlag Berlin Heidelberg 2002
Printed in Germany

Typesetting: Camera-ready by author, data conversion by DA-TeX Gerd Blumenstein
Printed on acid-free paper   SPIN 10871877   06/3142   5 4 3 2 1 0

Preface

PKC 2003 was the Sixth International Workshop on Practice and Theory in Public Key Cryptography and was sponsored by IACR, the International Association for Cryptologic Research (www.iacr.org). This year the workshop was organized in cooperation with the Department of Computer Science, Florida State University. The General Chair, Mike Burmester was responsible for local organization, registration, etc.

There were 105 submitted papers which were considered by the Program Committee. This is an increase of 52% compared to PKC 2002, which took place in Paris, France, February 2002, and which was incorrectly identified on the cover of the proceedings as being the fourth workshop. Due to the large number of submissions, some papers that contained new ideas had to be rejected. Priority was given to novel papers. Of the 105 submissions, 26 were selected for the proceedings. These contain the revised versions of the accepted papers. Each paper was sent to at least 3 members of the program committee for comments. Revisions were not checked for correctness of their scientific aspects and the authors bear full responsibility for the contents of their papers. Some authors will write final versions of their papers for publication in refereed journals.

I am very grateful to the members of the Program Committee for their hard work in the difficult task of selecting roughly 1 out of 4 of the submitted papers. Submissions to PKC 2003 were required to be anonymous. A Program Committee member could only present one accepted paper, or co-author at most two accepted papers without being allowed to present these. Papers submitted by members of the Program Committee were sent to at least 4 referees (and, of course, no Program Committee member reviewed his or her own paper).

The following external referees helped the Program Committee in reaching its decisions: Mehdi-Laurent Akkar, Joonsang Baek, Endre Bangerter, Régis Bevan, Daniel Bleichenbacher, Emmanuel Bresson, Eric Brier, Jan Camenisch, Matthew Campagna, Dario Catalano, Benoit Chevallier-Mames, Koji Chida, Nicolas Courtois, Annalisa De Bonis, Yevgeniy Dodis, Thomas Dübendorfer, Jacques Fournier, Atsushi Fujioka, Jun Furukawa, Clemente Galdi, Rosario Gennaro, Christophe Giraud, Louis Granboulan, Louis Goubin, Stuart Haber, Thomas Holenstein, Nick Howgrave-Graham, Stanislaw Jarecki, Antoine Joux, Jonathan Katz, Wataru Kishimoto, Erik Woodward Knudsen, Takeshi Koshiba, Hugo Krawczyk, Ben Lynn, Anna Lysyanskaya, Kazuto Matsuo, Patrick McDaniel, Phong Nguyen, Jesper Buus Nielsen, Satoshi Obana, Benny Pinkas, David Pointcheval, Bartosz Przydatek, Hervé Sibert, Francesco Sica, Nigel Smart, Markus Stadler, Martijn Stam, Reto Strobl, Koutarou Suzuki, Mike Szydlo, Tsuyoshi Takagi, Katsuyuki Takashima, Eran Tromer, Christophe Tymen, Salil Vadhan, Stefan Wolf, Jürg Wullschleger, and Akihiro Yamamura. (I apologize for any possible omission.) The Program Committee appreciates their efforts.

Thanks to Hoang Ha, Haizhi Chen, and Wayman E. Luy for secretarial work and for partially maintaining the WWW page of the conference, and to Wayne Sprague for setting up the e-mail addresses for PKC. Several people helped the General Chair with sending out the call for papers, registration, registration at the conference, etc.

Finally, I would like to thank everyone who submitted to PKC 2003, and IACR for its sponsorship.

October 2002   Yvo Desmedt

PKC 2003

Sixth International Workshop on Practice and Theory in Public Key Cryptography

Miami Convention Center, Miami, Florida, USA
January 6–8, 2003

Sponsored by the

International Association for Cryptologic Research
in cooperation with the
Department of Computer Science, Florida State University

General Chair

Mike Burmester, Florida State University, USA

Program Chair

Yvo Desmedt, Florida State University, USA

Program Committee

Masayuki Abe	NTT Laboratories, Japan
Feng Bao	Laboratories for Information Technology, Singapore
Giovanni Di Crescenzo	Telcordia, USA
Marc Joye	Gemplus, France
Kaoru Kurosawa	Ibaraki University, Japan
Arjen Lenstra	Citicorp, USA
Tal Malkin	AT&T Research, USA
Ueli Maurer	ETH, Zurich, Switzerland
Moni Naor	Weizmann Institute of Science, Israel
Tatsuaki Okamoto	NTT Laboratories, Japan
Jacques Patarin	Université de Versailles, France
Tal Rabin	IBM Research Lab., USA
Kazue Sako	NEC, Japan
Jacques Stern	École Normale Supérieure, France
Serge Vaudenay	ETH, Lausanne, Switzerland
Yongge Wang	University of North Carolina, USA
Michael Wiener	Canada
Moti Yung	Columbia University, USA
Yuliang Zheng	University of North Carolina, USA

Table of Contents

Specialized Multiparty Cryptography

Cryptanalysis I

Elliptic Curves: Implementation Attacks

Implementation and Hardware Issues

New Public Key Schemes

Elliptic Curves: General Issues

Cryptanalysis II

Efficient Construction
of (Distributed) Verifiable Random Functions

Yevgeniy Dodis

Department of Computer Science
New York University, USA
dodis@cs.nyu.edu

Abstract. We give the first simple and efficient construction of *verifiable random functions* (VRFs). VRFs, introduced by Micali et al. [13], combine the properties of regular pseudorandom functions (PRFs) (i.e., indistinguishability from a random function) and digital signatures (i.e., one can provide an unforgeable proof that the VRF value is correctly computed). The efficiency of our VRF construction is only slightly worse than that of a regular PRF construction of Naor and Reingold [16]. In contrast to our direct construction, all previous VRF constructions [13, 12] involved an expensive generic transformation from verifiable unpredictable functions (VUFs).

We also provide the first construction of *distributed* VRFs. Our construction is more efficient than the only known construction of distributed (non-verifiable) PRFs [17], but has more applications than the latter. For example, it can be used to distributively implement the random oracle model in a *publicly verifiable* manner, which by itself has many applications.

Our construction is based on a new variant of decisional Diffie-Hellman (DDH) assumption on certain groups where the regular DDH assumption does *not* hold [10, 9]. Nevertheless, this variant of DDH seems to be plausible based on our *current* understanding of these groups. We hope that the demonstrated power of our assumption will serve as a motivation for its closer study.

1 Introduction

As a motivating example for our discussion, consider the problem of implementing the *random oracle model* [2]. Recall that in this model one assumes the existence of a publicly verifiable random function $\mathcal{O}$ (over some suitable domain and range). Each value $\mathcal{O}(x)$ is random and independent from the other values, and evaluating $\mathcal{O}$ on the same input twice yields the same (random) output. This model has found numerous applications in cryptography, which we do not even attempt to enumerate. It was shown by Canetti et al. [5], though, that no fixed public function can generically replace the random oracle, so more elaborate solutions are needed.

Y.G. Desmedt (Ed.): PKC 2003, LNCS 2567, pp. 1–17, 2003.

PSEUDORANDOM FUNCTIONS. As the first attempt, we may assume the existence of a trusted (but computationally bounded) party T. Since a function is an exponential sized object, T cannot store it explicitly. While maintaining a dynamically growing look-up table is a possibility, it is very inefficient as it requires large storage and growing complexity. A slightly better option is to use a *pseudorandom function* (PRF) $F_{SK}(\cdot)$ [8]. As indicated, this function is fully specified and efficiently computable given its short secret key (or *seed*) SK. However, without the knowledge of SK it looks *computationally* indistinguishable from exponential-sized $\mathcal{O}$.

In terms of constructing PRFs, there are several options. The most relevant to this paper, however, is the number-theoretic construction due to Naor and Reingold [16], which is based on the decisional Diffie-Hellman (DDH) assumption. This assumption in some group $\mathbb{G}$ of prime order q states that given elements g, g^a and g^b of (where g is the generator of $\mathbb{G}$), it is hard to distinguish the value g^{ab} from a truly random value g^c (where a, b, c are random in $\mathbb{Z}_q$). The PRF of [16] is a tree-based construction similar to the PRF construction of [8] from a pseudorandom generator. Namely, the secret key $SK = (g, a_1, \ldots a_\ell)$ consists of a random generator g of $\mathbb{G}$ and ℓ random exponents in $\mathbb{Z}_q$ (where ℓ is the length of the input to our PRF $F_{SK} : \{0,1\}^\ell \to \mathbb{G}$). Given $x = x_1 \ldots x_\ell \in \{0,1\}^\ell$, the PRF is defined by:

$$F_{g,a_1,\ldots,a_\ell}(x_1 \ldots x_\ell) \stackrel{\text{def}}{=} g^{\prod_{\{i \mid x_i=1\}} a_i \bmod q} \tag{1}$$

VERIFIABLE RANDOM FUNCTIONS. Coming back to our motivating application, replacing random oracle with a PRF has several problems. The first one is the question of verifiability and transferability. Even if everybody trusts T (which we will revisit soon), T has to be contacted not only when the value of F has to be computed for the first time, but even if one party needs to verify that another party has used the correct value of F. Thus, it would be much nicer if each value of $F_{SK}(x)$ would come with a proof $\pi_{SK}(x)$ of correctness, so that the recipient and everybody else can use this proof without the need to contact T again. As a side product, the ability to give such proof will also ensure that T himself cannot "cheat" by giving inconsistent values of F, or denying a correctly computed value of the function. This leads to the notion of *verifiable (pseudo)random functions*, or VRFs [13]. Intuitively, such functions remain (pseudo)random when restricted to all inputs whose function values were not previously revealed (and proved). Notice, the pseudorandomness and verifiability of a VRF immediately imply that a VRF by itself is an unforgeable signature scheme secure against chosen message attack.

CONSTRUCTIONS OF VRFs. Unfortunately, VRFs are not very well studied yet. Currently, we have two constructions of VRFs: based on RSA [13], and based on a separation between computational and decisional Diffie-Hellman problems in certain groups [12]. Both of these constructions roughly proceed as follows. First, they construct a relatively simple and efficient verifiable *unpredictable* function (VUF) based on the corresponding assumption. Roughly, a VUF is the same verifiable object as a VRF, except each "new" value $F_{SK}(x)$ is only unpredictable (i.e., hard to compute) rather than pseudorandom. From VUFs, a generic construction to VRFs is given, as introduced by [13]. Unfortunately, this construction is very inefficient and also looses a very large factor in its exact security. Essentially, first one uses the Goldreich-Levin theorem [7] to construct a VRF with very small (slightly super-logarithmic) input size and output size 1 (and pretty dramatic security loss too!).[1] Then one makes enough such computations to amplify the output size to roughly match that of the input. Then one follows another rather inefficient tree-based construction on the resulting VRF to get a VRF with arbitrary input size and small output size. Finally, one evaluates the resulting convoluted VRF several times to increase the output size to the desired level. In some sense, the inefficiency of the above construction is expected given its generality and the fact that it has to convert pure unpredictability into a much stronger property of pseudorandomness. Still, this means that the resulting VRF constructions are very bulky and inelegant. In this work we present the first simple, efficient and "direct" VRF construction.

DISTRIBUTED PRFs. Returning to our target application of implementing the random oracle, the biggest problem of both PRF/VRF-based solutions is the necessity to fully trust the honest party T holding the secret key for F. Of course, VRFs slightly reduced this trust level, but T still singlehandedly knows all the values of F. Clearly, this approach (1) puts to much trust into T, (2) makes T is bottleneck of all the computations; (3) makes T is "single point of failure": compromising T will break the security of any application which depends on the random oracle assumption.

The natural solution to this problem is to distribute the role of T among n servers. This leads to the notion of *distributed* PRFs (DPRFs) and *distributed* VRFs (DVRFs). Since the latter concept was not studied prior to our work, we start with DPRFs, thus ignoring the issue of verifiability for now. Intuitively, DPRFs with threshold $1 \leq t < n$ allow any $(t + 1)$ out of n servers to jointly compute the function using their shares, while no coalition of up to t servers to be in a better situation that any outside party. Namely, the function remains pseudorandom to any such coalition.

DPRFs first originate in the work of Micali and Sidney [14]. However, their construction (later improved by [15]) can tolerate only a moderate number of servers or a small threshold, since its complexity is proportional to n^t. The next influential work is that of Naor et al. [15], who give several efficient constructions of certain weak variants of DPRFs. Ironically, one of the constructions (namely, that of distributed *weak* PRF) can be turned into an efficient DPRF by utilizing random oracles. Even though this is non-trivial (since nobody should compute the value of a DPRF without the cooperation of $t+1$ servers), we would certainly prefer a solution in the plain model, since elimination of the random oracle was one of the main motivation for DPRFs!

---

[1] The latter is the reason for such a small input size. One can make a very strong exponential assumption to increase the input size, like was done in [12], but the construction still loses a lot in security, and still goes through an intermediate VUF.

The first regular DPRF was recently constructed by Nielsen [17] by distributing a slightly modified variant of the Naor-Reingold PRF [16], given in Equation (1) (in the final version of their work, [16] also give essentially the same construction). Unfortunately, the resulting DPRF in highly *interactive* among the servers (while ideally the servers would only talk to the user requesting the function value) and requires a lot of rounds (proportional to the length of the input). In particular, the question of non-interactive DPRF construction remained open prior to this work.

DISTRIBUTED VRFs. Even though DVRFs were not explicitly studied prior to this work, they seem to provide the most satisfactory solution to our original problem of implementing the random oracle. Indeed, distributing the secret key ensures that no coalition of up to t servers can compromise the security (i.e., pseudorandomness) of the resulting random oracle. On the other hand, verifiability ensures that one does not need to contact the servers again after the random oracle was computed once: the proof can convince any other party of the correctness of the VRF value. For example, DVRFs by themselves provide an ordinary threshold signature scheme, which can be verified without further involvement of the servers. And, of course, using DVRFs are likely to enhance the security, robustness or functionality of many applications originally designed for plain PRFs, VRFs and DPRFs.

OUR CONTRIBUTIONS. We give the first simple and direct construction of VRFs, based on a new "DDH-like" assumption which seems to be plausible on certain recently proposed elliptic and hyper-elliptic groups (e.g., [10]). We call this assumption *sum-free decisional Diffie-Hellman* (sf-DDH) assumption. While we will discuss this assumption later, we mention that in the proposed groups the regular regular DDH assumption is *false* (in fact, this is what gives us verifiability!), and yet the sf-DDH or some similar assumption seems plausible. Our construction is similar to the Naor-Reingold (NR) construction given by Equation (1), except we utilize some carefully chosen encoding C before applying the NR-construction. Specifically, if $C : \{0,1\}^\ell \to \{0,1\}^L$ is some injective encoding, we consider the function of the form

$$F_{g,a_1,\dots,a_L}(x_1 \dots x_\ell) \stackrel{\text{def}}{=} g^{\prod_{\{i|C(x)_i=1\}} a_i \bmod q} \tag{2}$$

Identifying the properties of the encoding C and constructing C satisfying these properties will be one of the main technical challenges we will have to face. At the end we will achieve $L = O(\ell)$ (specifically, $L = 2\ell$ to get a regular PRF, and $L = 3\ell+2$ to get a VRF), making our efficiency very close to the NR-construction.

Our second main contribution is the first construction of a distributed VRF(DVRF). Namely, we show that our VRF construction can be made distributed and *non-interactive* (although multi-round). This is the first non-interactive construction of a distributed PRF (let alone VRF), since the only previous DPRF construction of [17, 16] is highly interactive among the servers. In fact, our DVRF construction is more efficient than the above mention DPRF construction, despite achieving the extra verifiability. We already mentioned the big saving in communication complexity (roughly, from $n^2\ell k$ to $n\ell k$, where k is the security parameter). Another important advantage, though, is that we dispense with the need to perform somewhat expensive (concurrently composable) zero knowledge proofs for the equality of discrete logs. This is because in our groups the DDH problem is easy, so it can be locally checked by each party without the need for the proof. In particular, even though we need to apply the encoding C to the message, while the construction of [17, 16] does not, the lack of ZK-proofs makes our round complexity again slightly better. Finally, we remark that the same distributed construction can be applied to distribute the VUF of Lysyanskaya [12] (which results in a threshold "unique signature" scheme under a different assumption than the one we propose).

2 Definitions

2.1 Verifiable Random Functions and Friends

Definition 1. *A function family* $F_{(\cdot)}(\cdot) : \{0,1\}^{\ell(k)} \rightarrow \{0,1\}^{m(k)}$ *is a family of* VRF*s, if there exists a probabilistic polynomial time algorithm* Gen *and deterministic algorithms* Prove *and* Verify *such that:* Gen(1^k) *outputs a pair of keys* (PK, SK); Prove$_{SK}(x)$ *outputs a pair* $\langle F_{SK}(x), \pi_{SK}(x) \rangle$, *where* $\pi_{SK}(x)$ *is the proof of correctness; and* Verify$_{PK}(x, y, \pi)$ *verifies that* $y = F_{SK}(x)$ *using the proof* π. *We require:*

1. *Uniqueness: no values* $(PK, x, y_1, y_2, \pi_1, \pi_2)$ *can satisfy* Verify$_{PK}(x, y_1, \pi_1) =$ Verify$_{PK}(x, y_2, \pi_2)$ *when* $y_1 \neq y_2$.
2. *Provability: if* $(y, \pi) =$ Prove$_{SK}(x)$, *then* Verify$_{PK}(x, y, \pi) = 1$.
3. *Pseudorandomness: for any PPT* $A = (A_1, A_1)$ *who did not call its oracle on* x *(see below), the following probability is at most* $\frac{1}{2} +$ negl(k) *(here and everywhere,* negl() *stands for some negligible function in the security parameter* k):

$$\Pr\left[b = b' \;\middle|\; \begin{array}{l} (PK, SK) \leftarrow \mathsf{Gen}(1^k); \; (x, st) \leftarrow A_1^{\mathsf{Prove}(\cdot)}(PK); \; y_0 = F_{SK}(x); \\ y_1 \leftarrow \{0,1\}^{m(k)}; \; b \leftarrow \{0,1\}; \; b' \leftarrow A_2^{\mathsf{Prove}(\cdot)}(y_b, st) \end{array} \right]$$

Intuitively, the definition states that no "new" value of the function can be distinguished from a random string, even after seeing any other function values together with the corresponding proofs. Regular PRFs form the non-verifiable analogs of VRFs. Namely, $PK = \emptyset$, $\pi_{SK}(\cdot) = \emptyset$, there is no algorithm Verify, no uniqueness and provability properties, and pseudorandomness is the only remaining property. We notice that the resulting definition is not the typical definition for PRFs [8]: namely, that no adversary can tell having oracle access to a truly random function from having oracle access to a pseudorandom function. However, it is easy to see that our definition is equivalent to that usual one, so will we use it as the more convenient in the context of VRFs.

2.2   Diffie-Hellman Assumptions

Assume $\mathsf{Setup}(1^k)$ outputs the description of some cyclic group $\mathbb{G}$ of prime order q together with its random generator g. Let $L = L(k)$ be some integer and $a_1 \ldots a_L$ be random elements of $\mathbb{Z}_q$. Let $[L]$ denote $\{1 \ldots L\}$, and given a subset $I \subseteq [L]$, we denote $a_I = \prod_{i \in I} a_i \bmod q$ (where $a_\emptyset = 1$), $G(I) = G_I = g^{a_I}$. Finally, we will often view an element $z \in \{0,1\}^L$ as either a subset $\{i \mid z_i = 1\}$, or an L-dimensional vector over $GF(2)$ (and vice versa).

GENERALIZED DIFFIE-HELLMAN ASSUMPTIONS. The security of ours, as well as the previous related constructions [16, 12], will rely on various assumptions of the following common flavor. The adversary A has oracle access to $G(\cdot)$, and tries to "obtain information" about some value $G(J)$. The meaning of obtaining information depends on whether we are making a computational or a decisional assumption. In the former case, A has to compute $G(J)$, while in the latter case A has to distinguish $G(J)$ from a random element of $\mathbb{G}$. While the decisional assumption is stronger, it has a potential of yielding a (verifiable) *pseudorandom* function, while the computational assumption can yield at best[2] a (verifiable) *unpredictable* function.

In either case, we require that it should be hard to any polynomial time adversary to succeed. Of course, one has to make some non-trivial restrictions on when the adversary is considered successful. Formally, given that the adversary called its oracle on subsets $I_1, \ldots, I_t$ and "obtained information" about $G(J)$, we can define a predicate $\mathcal{R}(J, I_1, \ldots I_t)$ which indicates whether the adversary's actions are "legal". For example, at the very least the predicate should be false if $J \in \{I_1 \ldots I_t\}$. We call any such predicate *non-trivial*. We will certainly restrict ourselves to non-trivial predicates, but may sometimes place some more restrictions on $\mathcal{R}$ in order to make a more plausible and weaker assumption (see below).

Definition 2. *Given $L = L(k)$, we say that the group $\mathbb{G}$ satisfies the* generalized decisional Diffie-Hellman *(gDDH) assumption of order L relative to a non-trivial predicate $\mathcal{R}$, if for any PPT adversary $A = (A_1, A_1)$ who called its oracle on subsets $I_1 \ldots I_t$ satisfying $\mathcal{R}(J, I_1, \ldots, I_t) = 1$, the probability below is at most $\frac{1}{2} + \mathsf{negl}(k)$:*

$$\Pr\left[\; b = b' \;\middle|\; \begin{array}{c} (\mathbb{G}, q, g) \leftarrow \mathsf{Setup}(1^k); \; (a_1 \ldots a_L) \leftarrow \mathbb{Z}_q, \; (J, st) \leftarrow A_1^{G(\cdot)}(\mathbb{G}, q); \\ y_0 = G(J); \; y_1 \leftarrow \mathbb{G}; \; b \leftarrow \{0,1\}; \; b' \leftarrow A_2^{G(\cdot)}(y_b, st) \end{array} \right]$$

Very similarly one can define the *generalized computational Diffie-Hellman* (gCDH) assumption of order L *relative to $\mathcal{R}$*, where the job of A is to *compute* $G(J)$. We notice that the more restrictions $\mathcal{R}$ places on the I_i's and the "target" set J, the harder it is for the adversary to succeed, so the assumption becomes weaker (and more preferable). Thus, the strongest possible assumption of the above type is to put no further restrictions on $\mathcal{R}$ other than non-triviality (i.e., $J \notin \{I_1, \ldots I_t\}$). We call the two resulting assumptions simply gDDH and gCDH (without specifying $\mathcal{R}$). A slightly weaker assumption results when we

---

[2] Unless a generic inefficient conversion is used, or one assumes random oracles.

require that the target set is equal to the full set $J = [L]$, i.e. the adversary has to obtain information about $g^{a_1 \cdots a_L}$. We call the resulting assumptions *full target* gDDH/gCDH (where $L = 2$ yields regular DDH/CDH). Finally, making L larger generally makes the assumption stronger, since the adversary can always choose to concentrate on some subset of L. Thus, it is preferable to base the security of some contsruction on as small L and as restrictive $\mathcal{R}$ as possible.

Before moving to our new sum-free gDDH assumption, let us briefly state some simple facts about gDDH/gCDH. It was already observed by [19] that gDDH assumption of any polynomial order $L(k)$ (with or without full target) follows from the regular DDH assumption (which corresponds to $L = 2$). Unfortunately, we do not know of the same result for the gCDH problem. The best analog of this result was implicitly obtained by [12], who more or less showed that the regular gCDH assumption of logarithmic order $O(\log k)$ (even with full target) implies the gCDH assumption of any polynomial order $L(k)$, *provided* in the latter we restrict the adversary to operate on the codewords of any good error-correcting code.

SUM-FREE gDDH. We already saw that the regular DDH assumption is a very strong security assumption in that it implies the gDDH assumption. This useful fact almost immediately implies, for example, that the Naor-Reingold construction in Equation (1) is a PRF under DDH, illustrating the power of DDH for proving pseudorandomness. Unfortunately, groups were DDH is true are not convenient for making *verifiable* random functions, since nobody can verify the equality of discrete logs. On the other hand, we will see shortly that it is very easy to obtain verifiability in groups where DDH is solvable in polynomial time (such as the group suggested by [10]). Unfortunately, such groups certainly do not satisfy the gDDH assumption too, which seems to imply that we have to settle for the computational assumption (like gCDH) in such groups, which in turn implies that we settle only for the VUF construction rather than the desired VRF. Indeed, obtaining such a VUF is exactly what was recently done by Lysyanskaya [12] in groups where DDH is easy but gCDH is hard.

However, we make the crucial observation that the easiness of regular DDH does *not* mean that no version of gDDH assumption can be true: it only means *we might have to put more restrictions on the predicate $\mathcal{R}$* in order to make it hard for the adversary to break the gDDH assumption relative to $\mathcal{R}$. Indeed, for the current elliptic groups for which we believe in a separation between DDH and CDH, we only know how to test if (h, u, v, w) is of the form $u = h^a, v = h^b, w = h^{ab}$ (this is called a DDH-tuple). This is done by means of a certain bilinear mapping (details are not important), for which we do not know a multi-linear variant. In fact, Boneh and Silverberg [4] observe that a multi-linear variant of such mapping seems unlikely to exist in the currently proposed groups, and pose as a major open problem to exhibit groups where such mappings exist. This suggests that many natural, but more restrictive flavors of DDH seem to hold in the currently proposed groups (where regular DDH is easy). For example, as was mentioned by Boneh and Franklin [3], it seems reasonable to assume that it is hard to distinguidh a tuple $(h, h^a, h^b, h^c, h^{abc})$ from a random tuple

(h, h^a, h^b, h^c, h^d). Put differently, when $a_1 \ldots a_L$ are chosen at random and given a sample $g = G(\emptyset), G(I_1) \ldots G(I_t)$, the only way we know how to distinguish $G(J)$ from a random element of such groups is by exhibiting three sets I_m, I_p, I_s (where $0 \leq m, p, s \leq t$, and I_0 denotes the empty set) such that $a_J \cdot a_{I_m} \equiv a_{I_p} \cdot a_{I_s} \bmod q$.[3] The last equation implies that "$J + I_m = I_p + I_s$", where we view the sets as L-bit 0/1-vectors, and the addition is bitwise over the integers. In other words, one has to explicitly find a DDH-tuple among the samples $G(I_i)$'s and the target $G(J)$.

We formalize this intuition into the following predicate $\mathcal{R}(J, I_1, \ldots, I_t)$. Let us denote $I_0 = \emptyset$. We say that J is DDH-*dependent* on $I_1 \ldots I_t$ if there are indices $0 \leq m, p, s \leq t$ satisfying $J + I_m = I_p + I_s$ (see explanation above). For example, 10101 is DDH-dependent on $01010, 00001$ and 11111, since $10101 + 01011 = 11111 + 00001 = 11112$. Then we define the DDH-*free* relation $\mathcal{R}$ to be true if and only if J is DDH-independent from $I_1 \ldots I_t$.

Definition 3. *Given $L = L(k)$, we say that the group $\mathbb{G}$ (where regular DDH is easy) satisfies the* sum-free decisional Diffie-Hellman *(sf-DDH) assumption of order L if it satisfies the gDDH assumption of order L relative to the DDH-free relation $\mathcal{R}$ above.*

For our purposes we notice that DDH-dependence also implies that $J \oplus I_m = I_p \oplus I_s$, where $\oplus$ indicates the bitwise addition moduo 2 (i.e., we make "2 = 0"), or $J \oplus I_m \oplus I_p \oplus I_s = 0$. Let us call J 4-*wise independent* from $I_1 \ldots I_t$ if no three sets I_m, I_p, I_s yield $J \oplus I_m \oplus I_p \oplus I_s = 0$. Hence, if we let $\mathcal{R}'(J, I_1, \ldots, I_t) = 1$ if and only if J is 4-wise independent from the I_i's, we get that $\mathcal{R}'$ is a stricter relation than our DDH-free $\mathcal{R}$. But this means that gDDH assumption relative to $\mathcal{R}'$ is a *weaker* assumption than sf-DDH, so we call it *weak* sf-DDH. Our actual construction will in fact be based on weak sf-DDH.

To summarize, sf-DDH is the strongest assumption possible in groups were regular DDH is false. We chose this assumption to get the simplest and most efficient VRF construction possible when DDH is false. However, even if the ambitious sf-DDH assumption we propose turns out to be false in the current groups where DDH is easy — which we currently have no indication of — it seems plausible that some reasonable weaker gDDH assumptions (relative to more restrictive $\mathcal{R}$) might still hold. And our approach seems to be general enough to allow some easy modification to our construction (at slight efficiency loss) meet many such weaker gDDH assumptions.

3   Constructions

Assume $\mathbb{G}$ is the group where DDH is easy while some version of sf-DDH holds. We consider the natural the type of functions given by Equation (2); in our new

---

[3] One can also try to find the additive relations, but since the a_i's are all random, it seems that the only such relations one can find would trivially follow from some multiplicative relations.

notation, $F_{g,a_1,\ldots,a_L}(x_1 \ldots x_\ell) = G(C(x))$,[4] where C is some currently unspecified (but efficiently computable) injective mapping from $\{0,1\}^\ell$ to $\{0,1\}^L$. To emphasize this dependence on C, we will sometimes denote the above function by $NR_C(\cdot)$.

3.1 Building PRFs

As a warm-up towards VRFs, we first determine the conditions on C and the kind of gDDH assumption we need in order to get a regular PRF.

Lemma 1. *Assume $\mathcal{R}$ and C are such that $\mathcal{R}(C(w), C(x_1), \ldots, C(x_t)) = 1$ for any $w \notin \{x_1, \ldots, x_t\}$. Then $NR_C(\cdot)$ is a PRF under the gDDH assumption of order L relative to $\mathcal{R}$.*

Proof. The proof follows almost immediately by comparing the deginition of gDDH relative to $\mathcal{R}$ (Definition 2) and the definition of PRF given in Section 2.1. Indeed, the adversary can query $NR_C(\cdot)$ at any points $x_1, \ldots x_t$, which corresponds to querying $G(\cdot)$ on $C(x_1) \ldots C(x_t)$, and has to distinguish $NR_C(w) = G(C(w))$ for some $w \notin \{x_1 \ldots x_t\}$. Since our assumption implies that $\mathcal{R}(C(w), C(x_1), \ldots, C(x_t)) = 1$, this adversary is legal for breaking gDDH (of order L) relative to $\mathcal{R}$.

As an immediate corollary, usual gDDH assumption implies that $NR_C(\cdot)$ is a PRF for any (injective) C, including the identity. This in turn gives the result of [16], since we mentioned that regular DDH implies gDDH [19].

More interestingly, we will now determine the properties of C which suffice to show that NR_C is a PRF under the much weaker sf-DDH assumption (for now, of the same large order L; we will reduce the order later). In the following, view every subset of $[L]$ (or element of $\{0,1\}^L$) as an L-dimensional vector over $GF(2)$. We say that the collection of vectors $I_1 \ldots I_t$ is *4-wise independent*, if no 4 or fewer vectors are linearly dependent. The proof of the theorem below is now obvious from Lemma 1.

Theorem 1. *Assume C is such that the collection $\{C(x) \mid x \in \{0,1\}^\ell\}$ is 4-wise independent. Then $NR_C(\cdot)$ is a PRF under the (weak) sf-DDH assumption of order L.*

CONSTRUCTING 4-WISE INDEPENDENT ENCODINGS. To get our PRF under the sf-DDH assumption, it thus suffices to construct a 4-wise independent encoding C. Naturally, the goal is to make L as close to ℓ as possible. Such encodings come up quite often in the theory of derandomization (see [1]), and are closely related to coding theory.[5] In our case, the well known construction is very simple

---

[4] Notice, we output a (pseudo)random element of $\mathbb{G}$ instead of a (pseudo)random m-bit string. However, standard hashing techniques imply we can extract an almost uniform string of length close to $\log |\mathbb{G}|$ from such an output. See [16].

[5] In particular, obtaining the 4-wise independent encoding C we need is equivalent to designing a parity check matrix of any linear code of distance 5. Our specific code gives such matrix for the famous (and optimal) BCH code of designed distance 5.

and efficient, so we present it in a self-contained manner. It will achieve (easily seen to be optimal) $L = 2\ell$.

Let us view any non-zero element $x \in \{0,1\}^\ell$ as an element of the field $GF(2^\ell)$, which can also be represented as an ℓ-dimensional vector over $GF(2)$. This gives us the same bitwise addition operation $\oplus$, but now we also have a multiplication operation. Then we set $L = 2\ell$ and define $C(x) = (x^3 \| x)$, which is interpreted as follows. We first cube x, which gives us another ℓ-dimentional vector x^3, and then we append x to it. Notice, the code C is explicit and extremely efficient to evaluate. Now, assume there are some *non-zero* distinct $x_1, x_2, x_3, x_4 \in GF(2^\ell)$ and constants $\alpha_1, \alpha_2, \alpha_3, \alpha_4 \in \{0,1\}$ such that $\sum_{i=1}^4 \alpha_i C(x_i) = 0$. We will show that $\alpha_1 = \alpha_2 = \alpha_3 = \alpha_4 = 0$, which yields 4-wise independence.

Since our bitwise addition is the same as in the field, we get $\sum_{i=1}^4 \alpha_i x_i = 0$ and $\sum_{i=1}^4 \alpha_i x_i^3 = 0$ over $GF(2^\ell)$. Next, we square the first equation. Since $GF(2^\ell)$ has characteristic 2 and $\alpha_i^2 = \alpha_i$, the only surviving terms are $\alpha_i x_i^2$, which gives us $\sum_{i=1}^4 \alpha_i x_i^2 = 0$. Similarly, raising the first equation to the power 4 gives $\sum_{i=1}^4 \alpha_i x_i^4 = 0$. We get a linear system (with unknowns $\alpha_1, \alpha_2, \alpha_3, \alpha_4$) saying that $\sum_{i=1}^4 \alpha_i x_i^j = 0$ for $j = 1, 2, 3, 4$. The system corresponds to the famous Vandermonde matrix whose determinant is $x_1 x_2 x_3 x_4 \cdot \prod_{i<j}(x_i - x_j) \neq 0$, since all the x_i's are distinct and non-zero. Thus, the only solution to the system is the trivial all-zero solution.

As a small technicality, we get the 4-wise independent encoding $C : \{0,1\}^\ell \setminus \{0^\ell\} \to \{0,1\}^{2\ell}$, i.e. we exclude the all-zero vector. This implies that we get the PRF whose input domain excludes the all-zero vector too. To summarize,

Theorem 2. *The encoding C above defines a* PRF *mapping ℓ bits (except 0^ℓ) to an element of $\mathbb{G}$, which is secure under the (weak)* sf-DDH *assumption of order 2ℓ.*

REDUCING THE ORDER. While Theorem 2 gives a simple PRF construction, it is based on the sf-DDH assumption of high polynomial order $2\ell(k)$. While this assumption is reasonable, we now show how to reduce the order to $O(\log k)$ at only a marginal efficiency loss. So let $C : \{0,1\}^\ell \to \{0,1\}^L$ be any 4-wise independet encoding satisfying Theorem 1 (like the one we constructied above). The idea, similar to that of [12], is to use an error-correcting code $E : \{0,1\}^L \to \{0,1\}^N$ on top of our encoding C. However, since we are dealing with linear dependence, we will have to restrict ourselves to *linear* codes (which was not needed in [12]), and the analysis will be slightly more involved. Thus, let E be a linear error correcting code of distance δN (where $\delta > 0$ and $N = O(L)$), and define $\tilde{C} = E \circ C : \{0,1\}^\ell \to \{0,1\}^N$. We get the following result, whose proof can be found in the full version [6].

Theorem 3. *Assume (weak)* sf-DDH *assumption holds for any order $p = O(\log k)$. Then $NR_{\tilde{C}}(\cdot)$ is a* PRF.

We remark that since error-correcting code can in principle approach a rate of 1, using Theorem 3 we can get a PRF construction with final expansion $N = (2+\varepsilon)\ell$.

3.2   Building VRFs

We now show how extend our ideas to get a VRF based of sf-DDH. As before, the construction is parameterized by some encoding $C : \{0,1\}^\ell \to \{0,1\}^L$. Recall also that we assume that testing regular DDH can be done in polynomial time.

- Gen(1^k): runs $(G, q, g) \leftarrow$ Setup(1^k), picks random $a_1, \ldots, a_{L+1} \in \mathbb{Z}_q$, sets $h = g^{a_{L+1}}$, $y_1 = h^{a_1}, \ldots, y_L = h^{a_L}$. Outputs public key $PK = (\mathbb{G}, q, g, h, y_1 = h^{a_1}, \ldots, y_L = h^{a_L})$, secret key $SK = (g, a_1, \ldots, a_L)$.
- Prove$_{SK}(x)$: outputs $(\sigma_1, \ldots \sigma_L)$, where $\sigma_j = g^{\prod_{\{i \leq j | C(x)=1\}} a_i}$ for $j = 1 \ldots L$. In particular, the value σ_L is $F_{SK}(x)$, while $(\sigma_1, \ldots, \sigma_{L-1})$ is the proof $\pi_{SK}(x)$.
- Verify$_{PK}(\sigma_1, \ldots, \sigma_L)$: sets $\sigma_0 = g$ and checks, for $i = 1 \ldots L$, that $(\sigma_{i-1}, \sigma_i, h, y_i)$ form a DDH-tuple (recall, DDH is easy!) when $C(x) = 1$, or that $\sigma_{i-1} = \sigma_i$ is $C(x)_i = 0$. Accept if all the tests pass.

To satisfy the definition of VRFs (Definition 1), we need to examine uniqueness, provability and pseudorandomness. The first two properties are very easy. Uniqueness follows from the fact that discrete logs are unique in $\mathbb{G}$ (and that our assumed algorithm for DDH will never accept an invalid tuple), while provability is obvious by construction.

Thus, we only need to examine pseudorandomness. Luckily, a lot of machinery has been already developed in Section 3.1. Essentially, the main difference we have is that when the adversary asks Prove(x), not only does he get $F(x) = G(C(x))$, but he also gets the proof values $G(I)$ for all $I \in$ Prefixes($C(x)$), where for a set $J \subseteq [L]$ we define Prefixes(J) $\overset{\text{def}}{=} \{\emptyset, J \cap [1], J \cap [2], \ldots, J \cap [L-1], J\}$. Additionally, the public key gives the adversary the values $G(\{L + 1\})$, $G(\{L + 1, 1\}), \ldots, G(\{L + 1, L\})$. We denote the latter $L + 1$ subsets of $[L + 1]$ involving element $L + 1$ by $Pub(L + 1)$. With these in mind, we easily get the following analog of Lemma 1.

Lemma 2. *Assume $\mathcal{R}$ and C are such that that for any $w \notin \{x_1, \ldots, x_t\}$ we have $\mathcal{R}(C(w), \text{Prefixes}(C(x_1)), \ldots, \text{Prefixes}(C(x_t)), Pub(L + 1)) = 1$. Then our construction is a VRF, under the gDDH assumption of order $L + 1$ relative to $\mathcal{R}$.*

Next, we can generalize the notion of 4-wise independence to that of 4-wise *prefix-independence*. Namely, a vector J is 4-wise prefix independent from vectors $I_1 \ldots I_t$ if there exist no $1 \leq p, r, s, \leq t$ and $I_p' \in$ Prefixes(I_p), $I_r' \in$ Prefixes(I_r), $I_s' \in$ Prefixes(I_s) such that $J \oplus I_p' \oplus I_r' \oplus I_s' = 0$. A collection $\{I_1 \ldots I_t\}$ is said to be 4-wise prefix independent if every vector I_i is 4-wise prefix independent from the remaining vectors. Finally, we will say that the above collection has *prefix-distance* at least 3, if for any $i \neq j$ and $I_j' \in$ Prefixes(I_j), we have that I_i and I_j' differ in at least 3 positions when viewed as binary vectors of length L. Then, we get the following analog of Theorem 1.

Theorem 4. *Assume C is such that the collection $\{C(x) \mid x \in \{0,1\}^\ell\}$ is 4-wise prefix-independent and has prefix-distance at least 3. Then our construction is a VRF under the weak (and thus regular) sf-DDH assumption of order $L + 1$.*

Proof. By Lemma 2, we only need to show that no vector $C(w)$ is linearly dependent on 3 vectors z_1, z_2, z_3 inside the sets $\mathsf{Prefixes}(C(x_1)), \ldots, \mathsf{Prefixes}(C(x_t))$, $Pub(L+1)$. Assuming the contrary, if none of z_1, z_2, z_3 comes from $Pub(L+1)$, we would exactly get that the collection $\{C(x) \mid x \in \{0,1\}^\ell\}$ is 4-wise prefix-dependent, a contradiction. Otherwise, some z_i's (say, z_1) is one of $\{\{L+1\}, \{L+1, 1\}, \ldots, \{L+1, L\}\}$. Since these are the only sets containing element $(L+1)$, in order to "cancel" $(L+1)$ one other z_i (say, z_2) also comes from this collection, which means that $z_1 \oplus z_2$ is some subset of I of $[L]$ or cardinality *at most* 2. The only way we can now have $C(w) \oplus I \oplus z_3 = 0$, is if some z_3 was a prefix of some $C(x_j)$ (where $x_j \neq w$) which differs from $C(w)$ in at most 2 coordinates. But this is exactly what is ruled out by the fact the collection $\{C(x) \mid x \in \{0,1\}^\ell\}$ has prefix-distance at least 3.

CONSTRUCTING THE ENCODING. It remains to construct a 4-wise prefix-independent encoding of prefix distance at least 3. We do it by giving a simple generic transformation from any regular 4-wise independent encoding $C : \{0,1\}^\ell \to \{0,1\}^L$, such as the encoding $(x^3\|x)$ considered in the previous section. We will assume without loss of generality that every two distinct elements $C(x)$ and $C(w)$ differ in at least two positions. For example, this is true with the 4-wise independent encoding $(x^3\|x)$ constructed in the previous section. However, even if originally false in C, one can always increase L by 1 by adding a "parity" bit to C (i.e., the XOR of all the bits of $C(x)$) and get the required distance at least 2 between distinct codewords. Also, for a technical reason we will exclude the zero vector 0^ℓ from the domain of our new encoding.

Lemma 3. *If C is 4-wise independent (and has distance at least 2), then $C'(x) = (C(x)\|1\|x\|1)$ is 4-wise prefix-independent and has prefix-distance at least 3.*

Proof. Below we will refer to the two 1's in the definition of C' as "middle" and "last". We start with showing the prefix distance. Take any $x \neq w$ and consider any prefix I of $C'(w)$. This prefix either "crosses" both the middle and the last 1, only the middle 1, or none of them. In the first case (i.e., we look at $C'(w)$ itself), we get distance three between $C'(x)$ and $C'(w)$ since $C(x)$ differs from $C(w)$ in at least two locations, and x differs from w in at least one more location. In the second case, $C(x)$ still differs from $C(w)$ in at least two locations, and now also I does not have the last 1 which $C'(x)$ has. Finally, in the last case (no 1's are crossed), I does not have both 1's that $C'(x)$ has, and also in between the 1's x is non-zero (this is where we exclude 0^ℓ) while the prefix I is zero, giving distance at least 3 again.

Next, we show the 4-wise prefix independence. Take any x, w_1, w_2, w_3 where $x \notin \{w_1, w_2, w_3\}$, and let z_1, z_2, z_3 be some prefixes of $C'(w_1), C'(w_2), C'(w_2)$ such that $(C(x)\|1\|x\|1) \oplus z_1 \oplus z_2 \oplus z_3 = 0$. Notice, in order to cancel the last 1 of $C'(x)$, at least one of the prefixes, say z_1, has to be full; i.e., $z_1 = C'(w_1) = C(w_1)\|1\|w_1\|1$. Since the middle 1's cancel out in $C'(x) \oplus C'(w_1)$, we have two possibilities for them to cancel in the full sum $C'(x) \oplus C'(w_1) \oplus z_2 \oplus z_3$. Either both prefixes z_2 and z_3 cross the middle 1, or none does. In the first case, taking the "C-prefixes" we get that $C(x) \oplus C(w_1) \oplus C(w_2) \oplus C(w_3) = 0$, which contradicts the fact that C is 4-wise independent. In the second case, we get that the identity parts between the 1's yield $x \oplus w_1 = 0$, i.e. $x = w_1$, which is again a contradiction.

Applying this Lemma to the encoding $C(x) = (x^3\|x)$ used in Theorem 2, we get:

Theorem 5. *The encoding $C'(x) = (x^3\|x\|1\|x\|1)$ defines a* VRF *mapping ℓ bits (except 0^ℓ) to an element of* $\mathbb{G}$, *under the (weak)* sf-DDH *assumption of order $3\ell + 3$.*

REDUCING THE ORDER. Similarly to Theorem 3, we apply an "outer" error-correcting code to reduce the order of the sf-DDH assumption we need for Theorem 5. However, we need to be sure that our construction preserves prefix-independence. Here is one direct way of doing it if we start — as in Lemma 3 — from any regular 4-wise independent (but perhaps not prefix-independent) $C : \{0,1\}^\ell \to \{0,1\}^L$ with minimum distance 2. Let $E_1 : \{0,1\}^L \to \{0,1\}^{N_1}$ and $E_2 : \{0,1\}^\ell \to \{0,1\}^{N_2}$ be two linear error correcting codes, both correcting some constant fraction of errors. We define the final encoding $\tilde{C}(x) = (E_1(C(x))\|1\|E_2(x)\|1)$ which maps ℓ non-zero bits to $N_1+N_2+2 = O(\ell)$ bits. By carefully combining the arguments in Theorem 3 with the technique in Lemma 3, we get the following corollary:

Theorem 6. *Assume (weak)* sf-DDH *assumption holds for any order $p - O(\log k)$. Then the code $\tilde{C}$ above defines a* VRF.

As earlier, using a very good code we can in principle construct a VRF with final expansion $N = (3 + \varepsilon)\ell$ based of the sf-DDH assumption of order $O(\log k)$.

Finally, we remark that with an extra overhead of 2 in the expansion of $\tilde{C}$ (and a large polynomial loss in exact security), we can reduce our PRF and VRF constructions in both Theorem 3 and Theorem 6 to using the *full target* sf-DDH assumption of order $O(\log k)$. We omit the details due to space constraints.

4   Distributed VRF

In this section we show that our VRF construction can be easily made distributed, which results in the first DVRF construction. Our construction is extremely simple and reminds DPRF construction of Nielsen [17] based on regular DDH. However, the fact that DDH is easy implies we can make our construction non-interactive (i.e., servers do not need to know about each other) and more efficient than that of Nielsen. We start by presenting our model, and then show our simple construction.

THE MODEL. We assume there are n servers $S_1, \ldots, S_n$ and that we have a regular VRF $V = (\mathsf{Gen}, \mathsf{Prove}, \mathsf{Setup})$ which we want to distribute. First, we define the syntax of the new generation algorithm $\mathsf{Gen}'(\cdot)$ run by the trusted party. $\mathsf{Gen}'(1^k)$ not only outputs the public/secret keys PK and SK for V, but also a pair of public/secret key (PK_i, SK_i) for each server S_i. The global secret key SK is then erased, each server S_i gets SK_i, and the values $(PK, PK_1, \ldots, PK_n)$ are published. When a user U approaches the server S_i with input x, the server determines if the user is qualified to learn the value/proof of $F(x)$. How this is done is specifed by the application at hand and is unimportant to us. If U is successful, though, we say that S_i was *initiated* on input x, and U and S_i engage in a possibly interactive protocol. To successfully complete this protocol, the user might have to simultaneously interact with several servers in some possibly predefined order (see below), but the servers do not need to interact to each other or know each other's state. Given a threshold t of the systems, the *robustness* property states that if U contacts s servers on input x, and at least at least $(t+1)$ of these servers are honest, then at the end of the protocol the user learns the unique correct output of $\mathsf{Prove}(x)$; i.e., the value $F(x)$ and the proof $\pi(x)$. This should hold even if the remaining $(s - t - 1)$ of the contacted servers are malicious. We notice also that while the user U needs to know the "local' public key PK_i of server i in order to interact with server S_i, any outside party only needs to know the "global" public key PK in order to verify the consistency of $F(x)$ and $\pi(x)$. In other words, the verification algortihm Verify does not have to be changed from the non-distributed setting.

The *security* property of the DVRF protocol states that for any t indices $i_1, \ldots, i_t$ and for any adversary $A = (A_1, A_2)$ who "breaks" the security of DVRF by "corrupting" servers $S_{i_1}, \ldots, S_{i_t}$ (see below), there exists an adversary $B = (B_1, B_2)$ which breaks the pseudorandomness property of our original VRF, as given by Definition 1. We now define what it means to break the security of DVRF. In addition to the public key $(PK, PK_1, \ldots, PK_n)$, A learns the values $SK_{i_1}, \ldots, SK_{i_t}$ of the corrupted servers. Then, A_1 runs in the first stage, in which it is given the ability to interact with any honest servers S_j on arbitrary inputs and in any manner that A_1 desires. However, we keep track of the set of inputs I which were initiated by A_1. At the end of the phase, A_1 outputs the challenge input x (and the state information for A_2). Then A_2 is given back a challenge y_b (for random b), which is either the value $y_0 = F(x)$ or a random element y_1 in the range of F. A_2 can then again interact with honest servers, just like A_1 did. At the end, A_2 outputs the guess $\tilde{b}$ and succeeds if $\tilde{b} = b$ and neither A_1 nor A_2 initiated the input x with any of the servers. A breaks the scheme if it succeeds with non-negligible advantage over $1/2$.

CONSTRUCTION. In Section 3.2 we defined a general candidate for VRF parametrized by any encoding C. We now show how to make such construction distributed for any C for which the basic construction is a VRF. The construction is quite simple, but it shows how convenient it is to have verifiability (given by the easiness of DDH) "for free". Recall that we had $SK = (g, a_1, \ldots, a_L)$;

$PK = (\mathbb{G}, q, g, h, y_1 = h^{a_1}, \ldots, y_L = h^{a_L})$; and $\mathsf{Prove}_{SK}(x) = (\sigma_1, \ldots \sigma_L)$, where $\sigma_0 = g$, $\sigma_j = \sigma_{j-1}^{a_j}$ if $C(x)_j = 1$ and $\sigma_j = \sigma_{j-1}$ otherwise.

To distribute this process, for every $j = 1 \ldots L$ we use Shamir's $(t + 1, n)$-secret sharing [18] over $\mathbb{Z}_q$ to split each a_j into n shares $(a_{j,1}, \ldots, a_{j,n})$, so that any $t + 1$ of these shares suffice to recover a_j, while t or fewer shares give no information about a_j. We set the secret key SK_i of server i to $(a_{1,i}, \ldots, a_{L,i})$, and its public key PK_i to $(y_{1,i} = h^{a_{1,i}}, \ldots, y_{L,i} = h^{a_{L,i}})$. To compute $\mathsf{Prove}(x)$, the user U needs to contact at least $(t + 1)$ honest servers. The protocol with the contacted S_i's proceeds in rounds. Assuming inductively that the value σ_{j-1} is known to both the user and the servers (with the base being $\sigma_0 = g$ which is known to everybody), we show how to compute σ_j. If $C(x)_j = 0$, $\sigma_j = \sigma_{j-1}$, so we are done. Otherwise, each server S_i sends the value $\sigma_{j,i} = \sigma_{j-1}^{a_{j,i}}$ to the user. The user locally checks that $(\sigma_{j-1}, \sigma_{j,i}, h, y_{j,i})$ form a proper DDH-tuple. If they do not, U discards the share and stops interacting with S_i. Upon receiving at least $(t + 1)$ correct shares, U uses the corresponding Lagrange interpolation in the exponent to compute the (necessarily correct) value σ_j, and sends σ_j to all the servers it is communicating with. Each server S_i, upon receiving σ_j, checks if $(\sigma_{j-1}, \sigma_j, h, y_j)$ form a valid DDH-tuple. If they do not, the server stops the interaction with U. Then the protocol proceeds to the next round until the entire output is computed.

SECURITY. The security of the above scheme is quite straightforward. Robustness is immediate since every share is checked for consistency. As for pseudorandomness, consider any successful distributed adversary $A = (A_1, A_2)$ who corrupts servers $i_1 \ldots i_t$. We build $B = (B_1, B_2)$ for our original VRF as follows. B picks random values $a_{j,i_s} \in \mathbb{Z}_q$ for every $j \in [L]$ and $s \in [t]$, and gives the resulting secret keys $SK_{i_1}, \ldots, SK_{i_t}$ to A. It then computes the induced public keys $PK_{i_1}, \ldots, PK_{i_t}$ and uses its own public key $h^{a_1}, \ldots, h^{a_L}$ to compute the remaining public keys PK_i for all non-corrupted users. This is done by performing the appropriate Lagrange interpolation in the exponent which computes the value $y_{j,i}$ from $y_j, y_{j,i_1}, \ldots, y_{j,i_t}$. It hands all these public keys to A, after which B_1 starts running A_1. When A_1 initiates any server on input x, B_1 asks for the value $\mathsf{Prove}(x)$, and uses the response $(\sigma_1, \ldots, \sigma_L)$, together with the knowledge of $SK_{i_1}, \ldots, SK_{i_t}$, to compute all the relevant shares $\sigma_{j,i}$ (by again doing straightforward Lagrange interpolation in the exponent; details are obvious and omitted). This allows B_1 to simulate all the responses to A_1. After B_1 outputs the same challenge x' as A_1, B_2 gets the output challenge y', which it forwards to A_2 as well. Then B_2 simulates A_2's interaction with the servers in exactly the same way B_1 did it for A_1. Finally, B_2 outputs the same guess $\tilde{b}$ as A_2, which completes the reduction and the proof of security.

EFFICIENCY. The above protocol is quite efficient. The communication complexity is $O(t\ell k)$, and the round complexity is $L = O(\ell)$.

Acknowledgments

I would like to thank Alexander Barg and Venkatesan Guruswami for useful discussions about BCH codes. I would also like to thank Dan Boneh and Don

Coppersmith for their preliminary (positive) evaluation of the sf-DDH assumption. Finally, I would like to thank Anna Lysyanskaya for inspiring this work.

References

[1] Noga Alon and Joel Spencer. *Probabilistic Method*. Wiley, John and Sons, 2000.
    9

[2] Mihir Bellare and Phillip Rogaway. Random oracles are practical: A paradigm for designing efficient protocols. In *Proceedings of the 1st ACM Conference on Computer and Communication Security*, pages 62–73, November 1993. Revised version appears in
    http://www-cse.ucsd.edu/users/mihir/papers/crypto-papers.html. 1

[3] Dan Boneh and Matthew Franklin. Identity based encryption from the weil pairing. In Kilian [11], pages 213–229. 7

[4] Dan Boneh and Alice Silverberg. Applications of multilinear forms to cryptography. IACR E-print Archive. Available from http://eprint.iacr.org/2002/080/, 2002. 7

[5] Ran Canetti, Oded Goldreich, and Shai Halevi. The random oracle methodology, revisited. In *Proceedings of the Thirtieth Annual ACM Symposium on Theory of Computing*, pages 209–218, Dallas, Texas, 23–26 May 1998. 1

[6] Yevgeniy Dodis. Efficient construction of (distributed) verifiable random functions. IACR E-print Archive. Available from
    http://eprint.iacr.org/2002/133/, 2002. 10

[7] O. Goldreich and L. Levin. A hard-core predicate for all one-way functions. In *Proceedings of the Twenty First Annual ACM Symposium on Theory of Computing*, pages 25–32, Seattle, Washington, 15–17 May 1989. 3

[8] Oded Goldreich, Shafi Goldwasser, and Silvio Micali. How to construct random functions. *Journal of the ACM*, 33(4):792–807, October 1986. 2, 5

[9] Antoine Joux. A one-round protocol for tripartite diffie-hellman. In *ANTS-IV Conference*, volume 1838 of *Lecture Notes in Computer Science*, pages 385–394. Spring-Verlag, 2000. 1

[10] Antoine Joux and Kim Nguyen. Separating decision Diffie-Hellman from Diffie-Hellman in cryptographic groups. IACR E-print Archive. Available from http://eprint.iacr.org/2001/003/, 2001. 1, 4, 7

[11] Joe Kilian, editor. *Advances in Cryptology—CRYPTO 2001*, volume 2139 of *Lecture Notes in Computer Science*. Springer-Verlag, 19–23 August 2001. 16

[12] Anna Lysyanskaya. Unique signatures and verifiable random functions from the dh-ddh separation. In Yung [21]. 1, 2, 3, 5, 6, 7, 10

[13] Silvio Micali, Michael Rabin, and Salil Vadhan. Verifiable random functions. In *40th Annual Symposium on Foundations of Computer Science*, pages 120–130, New York, October 1999. IEEE. 1, 2, 3

[14] Silvio Micali and Ray Sidney. A simple method for generating and sharing pseudo-random functions. In Don Coppersmith, editor, *Advances in Cryptology—CRYPTO '95*, volume 963 of *Lecture Notes in Computer Science*, pages 185–196. Springer-Verlag, 27–31 August 1995. 3

[15] Moni Naor, Benny Pinkas, and Omer Reingold. Distributed pseudo-random functions and KDCs. In Stern [20], pages 327–346. 3

[16] Moni Naor and Omer Reingold. Number-theoretic constructions of efficient pseudo-random functions. In *38th Annual Symposium on Foundations of Computer Science*, pages 458–467, Miami Beach, Florida, 20–22 October 1997. IEEE. 1, 2, 4, 5, 6, 9

[17] Jesper Nielsen. Threshold pseudorandom function construction and its applications. In Yung [21]. 1, 4, 5, 13

[18] Adi Shamir. How to share a secret. *Communications of the ACM*, 22(11):612–613, 1979. 15

[19] Michael Steiner, Gene Tsudik, and Michael Waidner. Diffie-hellman key distribution extended to group communicatio. In *Third ACM Conference on Computer and Communication Security*, pages 31–37. ACM, March 14–16 1996. 7, 9

[20] Jacques Stern, editor. *Advances in Cryptology—EUROCRYPT '99*, volume 1592 of *Lecture Notes in Computer Science*. Springer-Verlag, 2–6 May 1999. 16

[21] Moti Yung, editor. *Advances in Cryptology—CRYPTO 2002*, Lecture Notes in Computer Science. Springer-Verlag, 18–22 August 2002. 16, 17

An Identity-Based Signature
from Gap Diffie-Hellman Groups

Jae Choon Cha[1] and Jung Hee Cheon[2]

[1] Department of Mathematics
Korea Advanced Institute of Science and Technology
Taejon, 305–701, Korea
jccha@knot.kaist.ac.kr
http://knot.kaist.ac.kr/~jccha
[2] Information and Communications University (ICU)
Taejon, 305–732, Korea
jhcheon@icu.ac.kr
http://vega.icu.ac.kr/~jhcheon

Abstract. In this paper we propose an identity(ID)-based signature scheme using gap Diffie-Hellman (GDH) groups. Our scheme is proved secure against existential forgery on adaptively chosen message and ID attack under the random oracle model. Using GDH groups obtained from bilinear pairings, as a special case of our scheme, we obtain an ID-based signature scheme that shares the same system parameters with the ID-based encryption scheme (BF-IBE) by Boneh and Franklin [BF01], and is as efficient as the BF-IBE. Combining our signature scheme with the BF-IBE yields a complete solution of an ID-based public key system. It can be an alternative for certificate-based public key infrastructures, especially when efficient key management and moderate security are required.

Keywords: ID-based signature, GDH group, Elliptic curve, Weil pairing

1   Introduction

In 1984, Shamir asked for identity(ID)-based encryption and signature schemes to simplify key management procedures of certificate-based public key infrastructures (PKIs) [Sha84]. Since then, several ID-based encryption schemes and signature schemes have been proposed based on the integer factorization problem (IFP) [DQ86, Tan87, TI89, MY91]. Recently, Boneh and Franklin [BF01] proposed an ID-based encryption scheme (BF-IBE) based on bilinear maps on an elliptic curve. BF-IBE scheme is considered as the first practical ID-based encryption, but it was not reported whether it is possible to design a signature version of BF-IBE in [BF01]. Actually no concrete ID-based signature scheme was proposed on elliptic curves. We remark that an ID-based signature scheme based on pairings was proposed in [SOK01] but no security argument was given.

Y.G. Desmedt (Ed.): PKC 2003, LNCS 2567, pp. 18–30, 2003.

In this paper, we propose an ID-based signature scheme using gap Diffie-Hellman (GDH) groups. Its security is based on the hardness of computational Diffie-Hellman problem (CDHP). More precisely, under the random oracle model, our scheme is proved to be secure against existential forgery on adaptively chosen message and ID attack, which is a natural ID-based version of the standard adaptively chosen message attack (see Section 3 for details), assuming CDHP is intractable.

Using GDH groups obtained from bilinear pairings, as a special case of our scheme, we obtain an ID-based signature scheme that shares the same system parameters with BF-IBE. It is as efficient as BF-IBE. We remark that BF-IDE is indistinguishably secure against adaptively chosen ciphertext attack, assuming the hardness of the bilinear Diffie-Hellman problem (BDHP), which is believed to be more difficult than CDHP that our scheme is based on. BF-IBE and our scheme form a provably secure system which fully enjoys the functionals originally suggested by Shamir [Sha84].[1] Our scheme can also be used to realize proxy signatures by using the whole ID-based scheme for a single user, in a similar way to delegation of duties on encryption [BF01].

A problem of ID-based signatures is the difficulty of providing non-repudiation property. In all previous schemes based on IFP, one private key generator (PKG) knows the whole secret and so can generate valid signatures of any user. Thus non-repudiation property is obtained only when the PKG is completed trusted. On the other hand, in our scheme the secret can be shared to several parties through a threshold scheme. If we apply an (n, k)-threshold scheme to our scheme, at least k-parties out of n PKG's should collude to generate a valid signature and the number k can be as large as we want. That is, our scheme provides stronger non-repudiation property than previous ID-based schemes.

The rest of the paper is organized as follows: In Section 2, we introduce related mathematical problems and describe our scheme. In Section 3, we present a natural attack model and security proof of our signature scheme. In Section 4, we discuss the implementation issues of BF-IBE and our scheme. We conclude in Section 5.

2   Our Identity-Based Signature Scheme

In this section we propose an ID-based signature scheme that can be built on any group whose computational Diffie-Hellman problem is hard but decisional Diffie-Hellman problem is solved. We start with a formal definition of such groups.

---

[1] After we had submitted an earlier version[CC01] of this paper, some other schemes were also announced as preprints. Paterson's scheme [Pat02] was proposed with a brief security arguments but no rigorous proof. Hess's scheme [Hes02] was claimed to be provably secure with a proof in the case of fixed ID. It is interesting that all of the schemes are different. In this version of our paper, the security proof of the earlier version is extended to the case of adaptively chosen ID and the base problems are clarified.

2.1   Gap Diffie-Hellman (GDH) Groups

Let G be a cyclic group generated by P, whose order is a prime ℓ. We assume that multiplication and inversion in G can be computed in a unit time. We are interested in the following mathematical problems. View G as an additive group, and let a, b, and c be elements of $\mathbb{Z}/\ell$.

1. **Computation Diffie-Hellman Problem (CDHP).** Given (P, aP, bP), compute abP.
2. **Decisional Diffie-Hellman Problem (DDHP).** Given (P, aP, bP, cP), decide whether $c = ab$ in $\mathbb{Z}/\ell$. (If so, (P, aP, bP, cP) is called a valid Diffie-Hellman tuple.)

We call G a *GDH group* if DDHP can be solved in polynomial time but no probabilistic algorithm can solve CDHP with non-negligible advantage within polynomial time [OP01, BLS01].

2.2   The Scheme

Let G be a group of prime order ℓ in which DDHP can be solved.

1. **Setup.** Choose a generator P of G, pick a ramdom $s \in \mathbb{Z}/\ell$, set $P_{pub} = sP$, and choose cryptographic hash functions $H_1 \colon \{0,1\}^* \times G \to \mathbb{Z}/\ell$ and $H_2 \colon \{0,1\}^* \to G$. The system parameter is (P, P_{pub}, H_1, H_2). The master key is s. We remark that H_1 and H_2 will be viewed as random oracles in our security proof.
2. **Extract.** Given an identity ID, the algorithm computes $D_{\text{ID}} = sH_2(\text{ID})$ and output it as the private key associated to ID. We remark that $Q_{\text{ID}} = H_2(\text{ID})$ plays the role of the associated public key.
3. **Sign.** Given a secret key D_{ID} and a message m, pick a random number $r \in \mathbb{Z}/\ell$ and output a signature $\sigma = (U, V)$ where $U = rQ_{\text{ID}}$, $h = H_1(m, U)$, and $V = (r + h)D_{\text{ID}}$.
4. **Verify.** To verify a signature $\sigma = (U, V)$ of a message m for an identity ID, check whether $(P, P_{pub}, U + hQ_{\text{ID}}, V)$, where $h = H_1(m, U)$, is a valid Diffie-Hellman tuple.

This completes the description of our ID-based signature scheme. Consistency is easily proved as follows: If $\sigma = (U, V)$ is a valid signature of a message m for an identity ID, then $U = rQ_{\text{ID}}$ and $V = (r + h)D_{\text{ID}}$ for $r \in \mathbb{Z}/\ell$ and $h = H_1(m, U)$. Thus

$$(P, P_{pub}, U + hQ_{\text{ID}}, V) = (P, P_{pub}, (r + h)Q_{\text{ID}}, (r + h)D_{\text{ID}})$$
$$= (P, sP, (r + h)Q_{\text{ID}}, s(r + h)Q_{\text{ID}})$$

as desired.

We will prove that if G is a GDH group, i.e., if CDHP is hard, then our signature scheme is secure against existential forgery on a natural generalization of the standard adaptively chosen message attack for ID-based schemes, in Section 3 (see Theorems 3 and 5).

2.3   Relationship with BF-IBE

Although we described our scheme as one that is built on a given GDH-group, this can be easily transformed into one that can share the setup algorithm and resulting system parameters with BF-IBE [BF01] in a formal manner. Indeed, we will describe a variant of the **Setup** algorithm of our scheme and observe that we can view that of BF-IBE as a special case of this variant. For this we need to introduce a notion of a parameter generator which outputs GDH groups.

GDH Parameter Generator. A polynomial time probabilistic algorithm $\mathcal{IG}_{GDH}$ is called a *GDH parameter generator* if for a given positive integer k, which plays the role of a security parameter, it outputs (descriptions of) a cyclic group G of prime order and a polynomial time algorithm $\mathcal{D}$ which solves DDHP in G. We will always view G as an additive group. We denote the output of $\mathcal{IG}_{GDH}$ by $\mathcal{IG}_{GDH}(1^k)$.

Gap Diffie-Hellman Assumption. Let $\mathcal{IG}_{GDH}$ be a GDH parameter generator, and let $\mathcal{A}$ be an algorithm whose input consists of a group G of prime order ℓ, an algorithm $\mathcal{D}$ solving DDHP, a generator P of G, aP and bP $(a, b \in \mathbb{Z}/\ell)$ and whose output is an element of G that is expected to be abP. As usual, the advantage of $\mathcal{A}$ with respect to $\mathcal{IG}_{GDH}$ is defined to be

$$\Pr\left[\mathcal{A}(G, \mathcal{D}, P, aP, bP) = abP \ \Big| \ (G, \mathcal{D}) \leftarrow \mathcal{IG}_{GDH}(1^k), \ P \xleftarrow{R} G^*, \ a, b \xleftarrow{R} \mathbb{Z}/\ell\right].$$

$\mathcal{IG}_{GDH}$ is said to satisfy the *GDH assumption* if any polynomial time algorithm $\mathcal{A}$ has advantage $\leq 1/f(k)$ for all polynomial f, that is, no polynomial time algorithm can solve CDHP with non-negligible advantage.

A Variant of Setup. Let $\mathcal{IG}_{GDH}$ be a GDH parameter generator. We describe another setup algorithm for our scheme as follows.

Setup′. Given a security parameter k, it works as follows:
1. Run $\mathcal{IG}_{GDH}$ on input k and let $(G, \mathcal{D})$ be the output.
2. Choose P, s, H_1 and H_2 as in the **Setup** algorithm described above, and let $P_{pub} = sP$. The system parameter is $(G, \mathcal{D}, P, P_{pub}, H_1, H_2)$. The master key is s.

In [BF01], Boneh and Franklin used a *BDH parameter generator* to build an ID-based public key cryptosystem, which is defined to be an algorithm that runs in polynomial time in a given security parameter k, and outputs (descriptions of) two groups G_1, G_2 of prime order ℓ and a computable non-degenerated bilinear map $\hat{e} \colon G_1 \times G_1 \to G_2$. The scheme in [BF01] is proved to be secure if the *bilinear Diffie-Hellman problem (BDHP)*, which asks to compute $\hat{e}(P, P)^{abc}$ for a given (P, aP, bP, cP), is infeasible. Formally speaking, a BDH parameter generator

$\mathcal{IG}_{BDH}$ is said to satisfy the *bilinear Diffie-Hellman (BDH) assumption* if the advantage

$$\Pr\left[\mathcal{A}(G_1, G_2, \hat{e}, P, aP, bP, cP) = \hat{e}(P, P)^{abc} \;\middle|\; \begin{array}{l} (G_1, G_2, \hat{e}) \leftarrow \mathcal{IG}_{BDH}(1^k), \\ P \xleftarrow{R} G_1 - \{0\}, \\ a, b, c \xleftarrow{R} \mathbb{Z}/\ell \end{array}\right]$$

is negligible for any polynomial time algorithm $\mathcal{A}$.

We recall two well-known facts: (1) An algorithm $\mathcal{D}$ that solves DDHP in G_1 can be obtained using the non-degenerated bilinear map $\hat{e}$, since $\hat{e}(aP, bP) = \hat{e}(P, abP)$ implies that (P, aP, bP, cP) is a valid Diffie-Hellman tuple. (2) BDHP is solved if so is CDHP. An immediate consequence is that a BDH parameter generator $\mathcal{IG}_{BDH}$ satisfying the BDH assumption can also viewed as a GDH parameter generator $\mathcal{IG}_{GDH}$ satisfying the GDH assumption; $\mathcal{IG}_{GDH}$ runs $\mathcal{IG}_{BDH}$ on the same security parameter k and outputs $G(= G_1)$ and $\mathcal{D}$.

This shows that the setup algorithm of the ID-based encryption scheme described in [BF01] can be shared with our scheme; the system parameters G_1, P, P_{pub}, H_1, and H_2 generated by the setup algorithm of the scheme in [BF01] can also be used for our scheme without any loss of security.

3   Security Proof

In this section we prove the security of our signature scheme, assuming the hardness of CDHP.

3.1   Attack Model for ID-based Signature Schemes

The most general known notion of security of a non-ID-based signature scheme is security against existential forgery on adaptively chosen message attacks; in this model, an adversary wins the game if he outputs a valid pair of a message and a signature, where he is allowed to ask the signer to sign any message except the output. We consider the following natural generalization of this notion, which is acceptable as a standard model of security for ID-based signature schemes. We say that an ID-based signature scheme, which consists of four algorithms **Setup**, **Extract**, **Sign**, and **Verify** playing the same role as ours, is *secure against existential forgery on adaptively chosen message and* ID *attacks* if no polynomial time algorithm $\mathcal{A}$ has a non-negligible advantage against a challenger $\mathcal{C}$ in the following game:

1. $\mathcal{C}$ runs **Setup** of the scheme. The resulting system parameters are given to $\mathcal{A}$.
2. $\mathcal{A}$ issues the following queries as he wants:
   (a) Hash function query. $\mathcal{C}$ computes the value of the hash function for the requested input and sends the value to $\mathcal{A}$.
   (b) **Extract** query. Given an identity ID, $\mathcal{C}$ returns the private key corresponding to ID which is obtained by running **Extract**.

(c) **Sign** query. Given an identity ID and a message m, $\mathcal{C}$ returns a signature which is obtained by running **Sign**.

3. $\mathcal{A}$ outputs (ID, m, σ), where ID is an identity, m is a message, and σ is a signature, such that ID and (ID, m) are not equal to the inputs of any query to **Extract** and **Sign**, respectively. $\mathcal{A}$ wins the game if σ is a valid signature of m for ID.

For notational purposes, in the proof of the security of our scheme, the result of the **Sign** query (asked by $\mathcal{A}$ in Step 2) will be denoted by (ID, m, U, h, V) where (U, V) is the output of the signing algorithm of our scheme and $h = H_2(m, U)$, similarly to the convention of [PS00].

3.2 Our Signature Scheme and CDHP

Consider the following variant of the above game: First we fix an identity ID. In Step 1, $\mathcal{C}$ gives to $\mathcal{A}$ system parameters together with ID, and in Step 3, $\mathcal{A}$ must output the given ID (together with a message and a signature) as its final result. If no polynomial time algorithm $\mathcal{A}$ has non-negligible advantage in this game, we say that the signature scheme is secure under existential forgery on adaptively chosen message and *given* ID attacks. The first step of our proof is to reduce the problem to this case.

Lemma 1 *If there is an algorithm $\mathcal{A}_0$ for an adaptively chosen message and ID attack to our scheme with running time t_0 and advantage ϵ_0, then there is an algorithm $\mathcal{A}_1$ for an adaptively chosen message and given ID attack which has running time $t_1 \leq t_0$ and advantage $\epsilon_1 \leq \epsilon_0 (1 - \frac{1}{\ell}) / q_{H_2}$, where q_{H_2} is the maximum number of queries to H_2 asked by $\mathcal{A}_0$. In addition, the numbers of queries to hash functions, **Extract**, and **Sign** asked by $\mathcal{A}_1$ are the same as those of $\mathcal{A}_0$.*

Proof. We may assume that for any ID, $\mathcal{A}_0$ queries $G(ID)$ and **Extract**(ID) at most once, without any loss of generality. Our algorithm $\mathcal{A}_1$ is as follows:

1. Choose $r \in \{1, \ldots, q_{H_2}\}$ randomly. Denote by ID_i the input of the i-th query to H_2 asked by $\mathcal{A}_0$. Let ID'_i be ID if $i = r$, and ID_i otherwise. Define $H'_2(ID_i)$, **Extract**$'(ID_i)$, **Sign**$'(ID_i, m)$ to be $H_2(ID'_i)$, **Extract**(ID'_i), **Sign**(ID'_i, m), respectively.
2. Run $\mathcal{A}_0$ with the given system parameters. $\mathcal{A}_1$ responds to $\mathcal{A}_0$'s queries to H_1, H_2, **Extract**, and **Sign** by evaluating H_1, H'_2, **Extract**$'$, and **Sign**$'$, respectively. Let the output of $\mathcal{A}_0$ be (ID_{out}, m, σ).
3. If $ID_{out} = ID$ and (ID, m, σ) is valid, then output (ID, m, σ). Otherwise output `fail`.

Since the distributions produced by H'_2, **Extract**$'$, and **Sign**$'$ are indistinguishable from those produced by H_2, **Extract**, and **Sign** of our scheme, $\mathcal{A}_0$ learns nothing from query results, and hence

$$\Pr[(ID_{out}, m, \sigma) \text{ is valid}] \geq \epsilon.$$

Since H_2 is a random oracle, the probability that the output $(\text{ID}_{out}, m, \sigma)$ of $\mathcal{A}_0$ is valid without any query of $H_2'(\text{ID}_{out})$ is negligible. Explicitly,

$$\Pr[\text{ID}_{out} = \text{ID}_i \text{ for some } i \mid (\text{ID}_{out}, m, \sigma) \text{ is valid}] \geq 1 - \frac{1}{\ell}.$$

Since r is independently and randomly chosen, we have

$$\Pr[\text{ID}_{out} = \text{ID}_r \mid \text{ID}_{out} = \text{ID}_i \text{ for some } i] \geq \frac{1}{q_{H_2}}.$$

Combining these,

$$\Pr[\text{ID}_{out} = \text{ID}_r = \text{ID} \text{ and } (\text{ID}, m, \sigma) \text{ is valid}] \geq \epsilon \cdot \left(1 - \frac{1}{\ell}\right) \cdot \frac{1}{q_{H_2}}$$

as desired.

We remark that the algorithm $\mathcal{A}_1$ can be viewed as an adversary to the non-ID-based scheme obtained by fixing an ID in our ID-based scheme, which is allowed to access the extraction oracle to obtain secret keys associated to identities different from the fixed one, as well as the signing oracle and hash functions.

Now we are ready to construct an algorithm which solves CDHP, assuming the existence of $\mathcal{A}_1$.

Lemma 2 *If there is an algorithm $\mathcal{A}_1$ for an adaptively chosen message and given ID attack to our scheme which queries H_1, H_2, **Sign**, and **Extract** at most q_{H_1}, q_{H_2}, q_S, and q_E times, respectively, and has running time t_1 and advantage $\epsilon_1 \geq 10(q_S + 1)(q_S + q_{H_1})/\ell$, then CDHP can be solved with probability $\epsilon_2 \geq 1/9$ within running time $t_2 \leq 23 q_{H_1} t_1 / \epsilon_1$.*

Proof. We may assume that for any ID, $\mathcal{A}_1$ queries $H_2(\text{ID})$ and **Extract**(ID) at most once as before, and $\mathcal{A}_1$ queries $H_2(\text{ID})$ before ID is used as (part of) an input of any query to H_1, **Extract**, and **Sign**, by using a simple wrapper of $\mathcal{A}_1$. Our algorithm $\mathcal{A}_2$ described below computes abP for a randomly given instance (P, aP, bP) where P is a generator of G.

1. Fix an identity ID, and put $P_{pub} = aP$. Choose randomly $x_i \in \mathbb{Z}/\ell$, $y_j \in \mathbb{Z}/\ell$, and $h_j \in \mathbb{Z}/\ell$ for $i = 1, \ldots, q_G$, $j = 1, \ldots, q_S$. Denote by ID_i, ID_{i_k}, and (ID_{i_j}, m_j) the inputs of the i-th H_2 query, the k-th **Extract** query, and the j-th **Sign** query asked by $\mathcal{A}_1$, respectively. Define

$$H_2''(\text{ID}_i) = \begin{cases} bP, & \text{if } \text{ID}_i = \text{ID} \\ x_i P, & \text{otherwise}, \end{cases}$$

$$\textbf{Extract}''(\text{ID}_{i_k}) = x_{i_k}(bP),$$

$$\textbf{Sign}''(\text{ID}_{i_j}, m_j) = (\text{ID}_{i_j}, m_j, U_j, h_j, V_j)$$

$$\text{where } U_j = y_j P - h_j H_2''(\text{ID}_{i_j}), \; V_j = y_j(bP).$$

2. We apply the oracle replay attack which was invented by Pointcheval and Stern in [PS96, PS00]. As done in [PS00, Lemma 4 and Theorem 3] for adaptively chosen message attacks to non-ID-based signature schemes, a collusion of $\mathcal{A}_1$, H_2'', **Extract″**, and **Sign″** defines a machine $\mathcal{B}$ performing a "no-message attack" to the non-ID-based scheme obtained by fixing ID in the original scheme. ($\mathcal{B}$ is still allowed to ask queries to H_1.)

   We need to take care of a nasty problem of collisions of the query result of **Sign″** and H_1, as mentioned in [PS00, Proof of Lemma 4]. Whenever **Sign″**(ID_{i_j}, m_j) is queried, $\mathcal{B}$ stores the output h_j as the value of $H_1(m_j, U_j)$. This may cause some "collision"; a query result of **Sign″** may produce a value of H_1 that is inconsistent with other query results of **Sign″** or H_1. In this case $\mathcal{B}$ just outputs `fail` and exits.

3. If no collisions have appeared, $\mathcal{B}$ outputs a valid message-signature pair, which is expected to be valid for the fixed ID, without accessing any oracles except H_1. Here P and P_{pub} are used as system parameters for $\mathcal{A}_1$. By replays of $\mathcal{B}$ with the same random tape but different choices of H, as done in the *forking lemma* [PS00, Lemma 2], we obtain signatures $(\text{ID}, m, U, h, V))$ and $(\text{ID}, m, U, h', V')$ which are expected to be valid ones with respect to hash functions H_1 and H_1' having different values $h \neq h'$ on (m, U), respectively.

4. If both outputs are expected ones, then compute $(h - h')^{-1}(V - V')$ and output it. Otherwise, output `fail`.

It is straightforward to verify that **Extract″** and **Sign″** produce "valid" secret keys and signatures. Furthermore, since H_2'', **Extract″**, and **Sign″** generate random distribution and are indistinguishable from H_2, **Extract**, and **Sign** of the original scheme, $\mathcal{A}_1$ learns nothing from query results. Therefore $\mathcal{B}$ works as expected if no collisions appear in Step 2. Intuitively, since U_j is random, the possibility of collisions is negligible; in [PS00, Proof of Lemma 4], this probability was computed explicitly, and furthermore, it was proved that the oracle replay in Step 3 produces valid signatures $(\text{ID}, m, U, h, V))$ and $(\text{ID}, m, U, h', V')$ with expected properties such that that $m = m'$, $U = U'$, and $h \neq h'$ with probability $\geq 1/9$.

Now a standard argument for outputs of the forking lemma can be applied as follows: since both are valid signatures, $(P, P_{pub}, U + hH_2''(\text{ID}), V)$ and $(P, P_{pub}, U + h'H_2''(\text{ID}), V')$ are valid Diffie-Hellman tuples. In other words, $V = a(U + hbP)$ and $V' = a(U + h'bP)$. Subtracting the equations, $V - V' = (h - h')abP$ and $abP = (h - h')^{-1}(V - V')$ as desired.

The total running time t_2 of $\mathcal{A}_2$ is equal to the running time of the forking lemma [PS00, Lemma 4] which is bounded by $23q_{H_1}t_1/\epsilon_1$, as desired.

Combining the above lemma, we have

Theorem 3 *If there is an algorithm $\mathcal{A}_0$ for an adaptively chosen message and ID attack to our scheme which queries H_1, H_2, **Sign**, and **Extract** at most q_{H_1}, q_{H_2}, q_S, and q_E times, respectively, and has running time t_0 and advantage $\epsilon_0 \geq 10(q_S + 1)(q_S + q_{H_1})q_{H_2}/(\ell - 1)$, then CDHP can be solved with probability $\geq 1/9$ and within running time $\leq \dfrac{23q_{H_1}q_{H_2}t_0}{\epsilon_0(1 - \frac{1}{\ell})}$.*

Remark. Using another variant of the forking lemma [PS00, Theorem 3] instead of [PS00, Lemma 4], we have the following results:

Lemma 4 *If there is an algorithm $\mathcal{A}_1$ for an adaptively chosen message and given ID attack to our scheme which queries H_1, H_2, **Sign**, and **Extract** at most q_{H_1}, q_{H_2}, q_S, and q_E times, respectively, and has running time t_1 and advantage $\epsilon_1 \geq 10(q_S + 1)(q_S + q_{H_1})/\ell$, then CDHP can be solved within expected time $\leq 120686 q_{H_1} t_1 / \epsilon_1$.*

Theorem 5 *If there is an algorithm $\mathcal{A}_0$ for an adaptively chosen message and ID attack to our scheme which queries H_1, H_2, **Sign**, and **Extract** at most q_{H_1}, q_{H_2}, q_S, and q_E times, respectively, and has running time t_0 and advantage $\epsilon_0 \geq 10(q_S + 1)(q_S + q_{H_1})q_{H_2}/(\ell - 1)$, then CDHP can be solved within expected time $\leq \dfrac{120686 q_{H_1} q_{H_2} t_0}{\epsilon_0(1 - \frac{1}{\ell})}$.*

4 Implementation Issues

At the present time, no candidate for GDH group is known except some (hyper)elliptic curves, which are equipped with a bilinear map such as the Weil pairing or the Tate pairing. In this section, we discuss implementation issues for these groups.

4.1 Bilinear Maps

Let E be an elliptic curve over $\mathbb{F}_q$, $q = p^n$, p a prime. Let $E[\ell] = \{P \in E | \ell P = O\}$ denote the ℓ-torsion subgroup of E for a prime ℓ. The Weil pairing is a map $e\colon E[\ell] \times E[\ell] \to \mathbb{F}_{q^\alpha}^*$ for the least positive integer α, called an exponent, such that ℓ divides $q^\alpha - 1$. Assume ℓ divides $E(\mathbb{F}_q)$ with small cofactor. If we have a non-$\mathbb{F}_q$-rational map $\phi\colon E \to E$, then $G = E(\mathbb{F}_q)[\ell]$ is a group admitting an efficiently computable non-degenerated bilinear map $\hat{e}\colon G \times G \to \mathbb{F}_{q^\alpha}^*$, which is defined by $\hat{e}(P, Q) = e(P, \phi(Q))$. $\hat{e}$ is called a modified Weil pairing in [BF01]. The Tate pairing has similar properties (see [Gal01] for more details). DDHP in G can be solved using these pairings. In many cases, it is believed that CDHP is hard, i.e., G is a GDH group.

We summarize well-known classes of elliptic curves which may contain a GDH group in Table 1. Since the pairing computation becomes inefficient as the exponent α becomes large, we only consider supersingular curves with $\alpha \leq 6$. Note that the hardness of CDHP depends on the size of q^α due to MOV's attack as well as the largest prime divisor ℓ of $\#E(\mathbb{F}_q)$.

Any supersingular curve has the form $y^2 + y = x^3 + ax + b$ over a binary field. Due to the Weil descent attack, we consider only the case that m is odd. In this case, all supersingular elliptic curves are isomorphic to one of three curves [Men93]. The curves over trinary fields were introduced in [BLS01] and used for generation of short signatures. The reason they used is that the exponent is largest among supersingular curves. Over finite fields of characteristic

Table 1. Various curves and their properties

Char.	Ext. Deg.	Curve	Order	α	ϕ
$p = 2$	Odd m	$y^2 + y = x^3$	$p^m + 1$	2	ϕ_1
$p = 2$	$m \equiv \pm 1(8)$ $m \equiv \pm 3(8)$	$y^2 + y = x^3 + x$	$p^m + 1 + \sqrt{2p^m}$ $p^m + 1 - \sqrt{2p^m}$	4	ϕ_2
$p = 2$	$m \equiv \pm 1(8)$ $m \equiv \pm 3(8)$	$y^2 + y = x^3 + x + 1$	$p^m + 1 - \sqrt{2p^m}$ $p^m + 1 + \sqrt{2p^m}$	4	ϕ_2
$p = 3$	$m \equiv \pm 1(12)$ $m \equiv \pm 5(12)$	$y^2 = x^3 + 2x + 1$	$p^m + 1 + \sqrt{3p^m}$ $p^m + 1 - \sqrt{3p^m}$	6	ϕ_3
$p = 3$	$m \equiv \pm 1(12)$ $m \equiv \pm 5(12)$	$y^2 = x^3 + 2x - 1$	$p^m + 1 - \sqrt{3p^m}$ $p^m + 1 + \sqrt{3p^m}$	6	ϕ_4
$p > 3$ $(p \equiv 2(3))$	$m = 1$	$y^2 = x^3 + 1$	$p + 1$	2	ϕ_5
$p > 3$ $(p \equiv 2(3))$	$m = 1$	$y^2 = x^3 + x$	$p + 1$	2	ϕ_6

$\phi_1(x, y) = (\zeta x, y),$ $\zeta^2 + \zeta + 1 = 0$

$\phi_2(x, y) = (\zeta^2 x + \xi + 1, y + \zeta^2 \xi x + \eta),$ $\zeta^2 + \zeta + 1 = 0, \ \xi^4 + \xi + 1 = 0, \ \eta^2 + \eta = \xi^3$

$\phi_3(x, y) = (-x + r, iy),$ $r^3 + 2r + 2 = 0, \ i^2 + 1 = 0$

$\phi_4(x, y) = (-x + r, iy),$ $r^3 + 2r - 2 = 0, \ i^2 + 1 = 0$

$\phi_5(x, y) = (ix, y),$ $i^2 + 1 = 0$

$\phi_6(x, y) = (-x, iy),$ $i^2 + 1 = 0.$

> 3, we do not have a special form for supersingular elliptic curves. But certain curves are supersingular over almost half of primes (called a CM-curve). We have two well-known families that were suggested in [BF01]. A detailed discussion on the curves in Table 1 except the first and the last ones can be found in [Gal01].

4.2 Hash Functions

We used cryptographic hash functions H_1 and H_2 in our scheme and viewed them as random oracles in the security proof. Though it is a debating issue if currently-used cryptographic hash functions can be considered as random oracles, standard cryptographic hash functions onto fixed-length binary strings or a finite field are accepted as random oracles in general. For the case of H_2 whose range is a GDH group G, however, we need to be careful since the elements of the group might not be expressed uniformly as binary strings.

A known approach is to construct a hash function onto G from standard hash functions onto finite fields. In [BLS01], they constructed one called MapToGroup and showed that their short signature scheme with this hash function is secure provided so is the scheme with a cryptographic hash function onto G, for GDH groups given as subgroups of elliptic curves defined over a finite field with odd

Table 2. The number of operations for BF-IBE and our signature scheme

Algorithm	Bilinear map	Point mul.	Exp. in $\mathbb{F}_{p^2}$	Hash functions
Encrypt	1	1	1	2
Decrypt	1	0	0	1
Sign	0	2	0	1
Verify	2	1	0	2

characteristic. In [BF01, BKS02], similar results providing more efficiency were proved for some other hash functions onto G in more restricted cases.

The main technique of the proofs of these results is as follows: Given an adversary to a scheme with a (possibly non-cryptographic) hash function, to say H', from standard hash functions onto finite fields, an adversary to the scheme with a cryptographic hash function H can be constructed by simulating H' with the help of H. This argument is not specific to a particular scheme, and indeed the same conclusion can be drawn for our scheme: Our scheme with the hash functions described in [BLS01, BF01, BKS02] is secure provided so is the scheme with a cryptographic hash function.

4.3   Performance

We compare the performance of our scheme with BF-IBE in Table 2.

We can see that the verification is most expensive and the signing is least expensive assuming the pairing computation costs several times expensive than a point multiplication of $E(\mathbb{F}_q)$ or an exponentiation of an element of $\mathbb{F}_{q^\alpha}$. (Very recently, an efficient implementation of Tate pairing over an elliptic curve with odd characteristic was announced in [BKS02].)

Note that the security of the scheme depends on the size of q^α as long as ℓ has a small cofactor. Since the pairing computation is comparable to an exponentiation in $\mathbb{F}_{q^\alpha}$, the efficiency of all algorithms but Sign does not change as the curve changes. Since binary fields have more efficient implementations, we may expect that the curves over a binary field offer most efficient performance. Sign algorithm, that does not perform any pairing computation, is most efficient as the exponent is large. In this case, signature size also becomes small since the signature consists of two elliptic curve points.

5   Conclusion

In this paper, we proposed an ID-based signature scheme from gap Diffie-Hellman groups. Our scheme can share parameters with BF-IBE and is as efficient as BF-IBE. Our scheme is secure against existential forgery on adaptively chosen message and ID attacks, under the hardness assumption of CDHP, which is believed to be weaker than the BDH assumption of BF-IBE. Combining our scheme with BF-IBE gives a practical complete solution of an ID-based public key system.

The *ID-based PKI* obtained by combining BF-IBE and our scheme may be considered as an alternative for certificate-based PKI. This ID-based PKI can be used when we have an existing hierarchy for each users to distribute the secret key securely and confidence on the key generation center, and offers advantages such as simple key management procedure [Sha84] and built-in key recovery [BF01]. Applications may include email systems, cellular phone services, and groupwares in private company where the key escrow is required.

Acknowledgements

The authors thank Dooho Choi and Seungjoo Kim for helpful discussions and the anonymous referees their valuable comments.

References

[BF01]   D. Boneh and M. Franklin, *Identity Based Encryption from the Weil Pairing*, Proc. of Crypto '01, Lecture Notes in Computer Science, Vol. 2139, pp. 213-229, Springer-Verlag, 2001. (A full version is available from http://crypto.stanford.edu/ dabo/pubs.html)   18, 19, 21, 22, 26, 27, 28, 29

[BK02]   P. Barreto and H. Kim, *Fast Hashing onto Elliptic Curves over Fields of Characteristic 3*, Available from http://eprint.iacr.org, 2002.

[BKS02] P. Barreto, H Kim, and M. Scott, *Efficient Algorithms for Pairing-based Cryptosystems*, Available from http://eprint.iacr.org, 2002.   28

[BLS01] D. Boneh, B. Lynn, and H. Shacham, *Short Signatures from the Weil Pairing*, Proc. of Asiacrypt '01, Lecture Notes in Computer Sciences, Vol. 2248, pp. 514-532, Springer-Verlag, 2001.   20, 26, 27, 28

[CC01]   J. Cheon and J. Cha, *Identity-based Signatures from the Weil Pairing*, Available from http://vega.icu.ac.kr/ jhcheon/publications.html, 2001.   19

[DQ86]   Y. Desmedt and J. Quisquater, *Public-key Systems based on the Difficulty of Tampering*, Proc. of Crypto '86, Lecture Notes in Computer Sciences, Vol. 263, pp. 111-117, Springer-Verlag, 1987.   18

[FFS88] U. Feige, A. Fiat, and A. Shamir, *Zero-knowledge proofs of identity*, J. Cryptology, Vol. 1, pp. 77-94, 1988.

[FS86]   A. Fiat and A. Shamir, *How to prove youself: Practical solutions to identification and signature problems*, Proc. of Crypto '86, Lecture Notes in Computer Sciences, Vol. 263, pp. 186-194, Springer-Verlag, 1987.

[Hes02] F. Hess, *Exponent group signature schemes and efficient identity based signature schemes based on pairings*, Available from http://eprint.iacr.org, 2002.   19

[Gal01] S. Galbraith, *Supersingular curves in cryptography*, Proc. of Asiacrypt '01, Lecture Nores in Computer Sciences, Vol. 2248, pp. 495-513, Springer-Verlag, 2001.   26, 27

[Men93] A. Menezes, *Elliptic curve public key cryptosystems*, Kluwer Academic Publishers, 1993.   26

[MY91]   U. Maurer and Y. Yacobi, *Non-interective public-key cryptography*, Proc. of Eurocrypto '91, Lecture Nores in Computer Sciences, Vol. 547, pp. 498-507, Springer-Verlag, 1992. 18

[OP01]   T. Okamoto and D. Pointcheval, *The gap-problems: a new class of problems for the security of cryptographic Schemes*, Proc. of PKC '01, Lecture Nores in Computer Sciences, Vol. 1992, pp. 104-118, Springer-Verlag, 2001. 20

[Pat02]   K. Paterson, *ID-based signatures from pairings on elliptic curves*, Available from http://eprint.iacr.org, 2002. 19

[PS96]   D. Pointcheval and J. Stern, *Security proofs for signature schemes*, Proc. of Eurocrypt '96, Lecture Notes in Computer Sciences, Vol. 1070, pp. 387–398, Springer-Verlag, 1996. 25

[PS00]   D. Pointcheval and J. Stern, *Security arguments for digital signatures and blind signatures*, J. of Cryptology, Vol. 13, pp. 361-396, 2000. 23, 25, 26

[Sha84]   A. Shamir, *Identity-base cryptosystems and signature schemes*, Proc. of Crypto '84, Lecture Notes in Computer Science, Vol. 196, pp. 47-53, Springer-Verlag, 1985. 18, 19, 29

[SOK01]   R. Sakai, K. Ohgishi, and M. Kasahara, *Cryptosystems based on pairing*, Proc. of SCIS '00, Okinawa, Japan, Jan. pp. 26-28, 2001. 18

[Tan87]   H. Tanaka, *A realization scheme for the identity-based cryptosystem*, Proc. of Crypto '87, Lecture Nores in Computer Sciences, Vol. 293, pp. 341-349, Springer-Verlag, 1987. 18

[TI89]   S. Tsuji and T. Itoh, *An ID-based cryptosystem based on the discrete logarithm problem*, IEEE Journal of Selected Areas in Communications, Vol. 7, No. 4, pp. 467-473, 1989. 18

Threshold Signatures, Multisignatures and Blind Signatures Based on the Gap-Diffie-Hellman-Group Signature Scheme

Alexandra Boldyreva

Dept. of Computer Science & Engineering, University of California at San Diego,
9500 Gilman Drive, La Jolla, CA 92093, USA
aboldyre@cs.ucsd.edu
http://www-cse.ucsd.edu/users/aboldyre

Abstract. We propose a robust proactive threshold signature scheme, a multisignature scheme and a blind signature scheme which work in any Gap Diffie-Hellman (GDH) group (where the Computational Diffie-Hellman problem is hard but the Decisional Diffie-Hellman problem is easy). Our constructions are based on the recently proposed GDH signature scheme of Boneh et al. [8]. Due to the instrumental structure of GDH groups and of the base scheme, it turns out that most of our constructions are simpler, more efficient and have more useful properties than similar existing constructions. We support all the proposed schemes with proofs under the appropriate computational assumptions, using the corresponding notions of security.

1 Introduction

Recently Boneh, Lynn and Shacham [8] proposed a new signature scheme that uses groups where the Computational Diffie-Hellman (CDH) problem is hard but the Decisional Diffie-Hellman (DDH) problem is easy. (Recall that the CDH problem asks to compute $h = g^{\log_g u \cdot \log_g v}$ given the three random group elements (g, u, v) and the DDH problem asks to decide whether the four group elements (g, u, v, h) are all random or they are a valid Diffie-Hellman tuple, namely, they have the property that $\log_g u = \log_v h$.) Following [8] we will refer to such groups as Gap Diffie-Hellman (GDH) groups. The first example a GDH group is given in [29] and more details on the existence and composition of GDH groups can be found in [30, 6, 8]. Another signature scheme that works in GDH groups has been proposed by Lysyanskaya in [32]. Unlike the scheme of [8], it does not use random oracles but is less efficient.

Let G be a GDH group of prime order p and let g be a generator of G. Similarly to most discrete-log-based schemes, the secret key of the signature scheme GS of [8] is a random element $x \in Z_p^*$ and the public key is $y = g^x$. To sign a message $M \in \{0,1\}^*$ a signer who holds x computes the signature $\sigma = H(M)^x$, where H is a hash function mapping arbitrary strings to the elements of $G \setminus \{1\}$, where 1 denotes the identity element of G. Following [8] let us denote $G^* =$

Y.G. Desmedt (Ed.): PKC 2003, LNCS 2567, pp. 31–46, 2003.
© Springer-Verlag Berlin Heidelberg 2003

$G \setminus \{1\}$. In order to verify the validity of a candidate signature σ of a message M, a verifier simply checks whether $(g, y, H(M), \sigma)$ is a valid Diffie-Hellman tuple.

Boneh et al. [8] prove that signature scheme GS is secure against existential forgery under chosen message attack in the random oracle model assuming that the underlying group is GDH. They also show that using this signature scheme in some GDH groups leads to very short signatures of length approximately 160 bits. In this paper we show that besides this attractive property, GS gives rise to various efficient extensions. More precisely, we propose a robust threshold proactive signature scheme, a multisignature scheme and a blind signature scheme which are all based on the GS signature scheme. Thanks to the elegant structure of GDH groups and of the base scheme it turns out that most of our constructions are simpler, more efficient and have more useful properties than similar existing constructions. We support all the proposed schemes with proofs under the appropriate computational assumptions using the corresponding notions of security.

THE NEW GDH THRESHOLD SIGNATURE SCHEME. The idea behind the (t, n)-*thre-shold cryptography* approach [9, 14, 16, 43] is to distribute secret information (i.e. a secret key) and computation (i.e. signature generation or decryption) between n parties in order to remove single point of failure. The goal is to allow any subset of more than t parties to jointly reconstruct a secret and perform the computation while preserving security even in the presence of an active adversary which can corrupt up to t (a threshold) parties. A review of research on threshold cryptography is presented in [15].

In threshold signature schemes the secret key is distributed among n parties with the help of a trusted dealer or without it by running an interactive protocol among all parties. To sign a message M any subset of more than t parties can use their shares of the secret and execute an interactive signature generation protocol, which outputs a signature of M that can be verified by anybody using the unique fixed public key. The security notion for threshold signature schemes requires that no polynomial-time adversary that corrupts any t parties can learn any information about the secret key or can forge a valid signature on a new message of its choice. An important property of threshold signature schemes is *robustness*, which requires that even t malicious parties that deviate from the protocol cannot prevent it from generating a valid signature. Another useful property of a threshold signature scheme is *proactivness* [37, 13] (or periodic refreshment of shares of a secret) whose goal is to protect a system from an adversary that builds-up knowledge of a secret by several attempted break-ins to several locations. In general, the main goals of threshold signature constructions are to *provably* achieve the following properties: to support as high a threshold t as possible, to avoid use of a trusted dealer, to be robust, proactive and as efficient as possible in terms of computation, interaction and length of the shares.

THE NEW GDH THRESHOLD SIGNATURE SCHEME. In Section 3 we propose the thre-shold signature scheme TGS that works in any GDH group. It is based on the GDH signature scheme of [8]. Our threshold GDH group signature scheme can tolerate any $t < n/2$ malicious parties, which is an optimal result. Its key generation protocol does not require a trusted dealer. The signature generation protocol does not require interaction or any zero-knowledge proofs, and avoids other difficulties pertaining to various threshold schemes. The signature generation protocol has a minimal overhead compared to that of the base scheme. The shares are short and their length does not depend on the number of parties. The signature share generation protocol is basically the signing algorithm of the base scheme and the signature reconstruction requires only multiplication of shares. We state the security result in Theorem 2. The proof is in the random oracle model only because the latter is used in the proof of security of the base signature scheme. We also show how proactive security can be added to our scheme using general methods of [26, 25].

RELATED WORK. There exist many threshold signature scheme constructions, i.e. [16, 24, 17, 19, 41, 21, 44]. The proposals of [16, 24] lack security proofs, the schemes of [16, 17] are non-robust while those of [19, 41] are robust and proactive but require a lot of interaction. We compare our scheme with the threshold DSS signature scheme of Gennaro et al. [21] and with the threshold RSA scheme of Shoup [44].

The threshold DSS signature proposed in [21] is robust, does not require a trusted dealer and has a proof of security without the random oracle assumption. It deals with technical difficulties such as combining shares of two secrets into shares of the product of these secrets and producing shares of a reciprocal of a secret given shares of this secret. To achieve robustness, the authors use error-correction techniques of Berlekamp and Welch [4]. As a result, the threshold DSS can tolerate only $t < n/4$ malicious parties, the threshold signature-generation protocol requires a lot of interaction and the complexity of a threshold scheme increases considerably related to the base signature scheme. The scheme can be made proactive following the methods of [26, 25].

The robust threshold RSA signature scheme of [44] is proven secure in the random oracle model. It can tolerate $t < n/2$ malicious parties and its signature generation algorithm is non-interactive. It, however, requires a trusted dealer to run the key generation protocol. The public key uses an RSA modulus that is a product of two safe primes. The protocol utilizes zero-knowledge proofs in the random oracle model in order to achieve robustness. Proactivization is not considered in [44].

THE NEW GDH MULTISIGNATURE SCHEME. In order to gain intuition about what multisignature schemes are we first discuss this notion informally and compare it to other notions.

A multisignature scheme allows any subgroup of a group of players to jointly sign a document such that a verifier is convinced that each member of the subgroup participated in signing. The trivial solution which satisfies the above informal definition is as follows. The resulting multisignature is simply a concatenation of a description of the subgroup and of regular signatures computed by each member of the subgroup using its own secret key. In fact this simple scheme will meet the security requirements we formalize in Section 4 . Its main drawback, however, is that the signature length and verification time grows linearly with the number of users in the subgroup.

Multisignature schemes are different from threshold signatures for several reasons. The goal of a multisignature is to prove that each member of the stated subgroup signed the message and the size of this subgroup can be arbitrary, whereas in the latter setting the goal is to prove that *some* subgroup of *sufficient* size signed the message, and the minimal size is a parameter of the scheme and should be known in advance. As opposed to multisignatures, a threshold signature does not reveal identities of individual signers. Another difference is that the verification protocol of a threshold signature scheme does not depend on the current subgroup of signers. Multisignatures are also different from group signatures [13, 10] and ring signatures [42], where every *individual* member of the group can produce a valid signature on behalf of the whole group. In the latter two settings a signer remains anonymous with respect to a verifier. In the group signature setting there is also a third party called a group manager which can identify the identity of the signer.

RELATED WORK. Multisignatures have been introduced in [28] and have been the topic of many other works such as [24, 31, 27, 34, 35, 36, 33]. The schemes of [35, 36] do not support subgroups of signers, they allow only the case where each player of the group signs the document. The solutions of [28, 34] are not very efficient: multisignature generation and verification time grows linearly with the number of players. But most importantly, until recent works of Ohta and Okamoto and of Micali et al. [36, 33] there were no formal notions of security for multisignatures and therefore there were no provably secure multisignature schemes. As a result, the proposals of [31, 24] have been successfully attacked. The notion of security of [36] is not strong enough since it does not consider the possibility of adversarial attacks during key generation.

Micali et al. [33] first formalize the strong notion of security for multisignatures (they call them "accountable-subgroup multisignatures.") They modify the Schnorr-signature-based multisignature scheme originally proposed by Ohta and Okamoto in [36] and prove its security. The model of security and the multisignature scheme of [33] assume that the subset of signers L is known a priori. Each signer has to know all participants of the current subgroup of signers L, a description of which is hashed and signed along with a message. The authors of [33] state it as an interesting open problem to find a provably secure multisignature scheme where the composition of the subgroup can be decided after the signature shares are computed.

In their independent work Boneh et al. [7] propose a new aggregate signature scheme based on the GS signature scheme. Unlike multisignatures, aggregate signature schemes permit a group of users to aggregate multiple signatures of *different* messages. The scheme of [7] requires GDH groups with a special structure provided by bilinear maps.

THE NEW GDH MULTISIGNATURE SCHEME. In Section 4 we give precise definitions of multisignature schemes and their security. Our model of security is very similar to the simplified model of security of [33], but it is more general, it does not have the restriction that the subset of signers should be known in advance. We then propose the new GDH multisignature scheme MGS. It works in any GDH group. Our MGS scheme solves the open problem stated in [33]: it does not require a priori knowledge of a subgroup of signers and is provably secure. We state the security result and provide a proof in [5] . Moreover, MGS is more efficient than the one of [33] which requires three rounds of communication for the multisignature generation protocol, where MGS requires only one, it is basically non-interactive. Similarly to their scheme, the signature length and verification time for MGS is independent of the size of the subgroup and is almost the same as for the base signature scheme. In fact each signature share of our multisignature scheme is the standard GDH signature. In the scheme of [33] a signer is not allowed to begin a new signing protocol until the previous one has completed. This is because their proof of security uses rewinding which is incompatible with concurrency. Our scheme does not have such restriction not only because our proof does not use rewinding but mostly because the signing protocol is non-interactive.

We note that the approach underlying the construction of the multisignature scheme MGS can be used to achieve efficient batch verification of GDH signatures of the same message under different public keys.

THE NEW GDH BLIND SIGNATURE SCHEME. Blind signatures are the basic tool of digital cash schemes. Using a blind signature protocol a user can obtain from a bank a digital coin, that is a token properly signed by the bank. The goal of blind signature protocols is to enable a user to obtain a signature from a signer so that the signer does not learn information about the message it signed and so that the user cannot obtain more than one valid signature after one interaction with the signer. Chaum [11] first proposed the RSA-based blind signature scheme. However, it has been proved secure only recently by Bellare et al. [2]. The reason for this time gap is that it appears impossible to prove security of Chaum's scheme based on standard RSA assumptions. The approach taken by [2] is to introduce the new plausible computational assumption, namely, "chosen-target-one-more-RSA-inversion" and to prove security of Chaum's RSA blind signature based on this assumption. In [2] the authors suggest that an analogue of this assumption can be formulated for any family of one-way functions.

In Section 5 we define the new blind signature scheme BGS that works in GDH groups. The protocol is very similar to the RSA blind signature protocol. Namely, a user multiplies hash of the message with a random group element, submits it to the bank and later "derandomizes" the signature obtained from the bank using knowledge of the public key and of the random factor. In order to prove the security of BGS we follow the approach of [2] and define a new computational problem, the Chosen-target Computational-Diffie-Hellman problem. In [5] we prove the security of the blind signature BGS scheme under the Chosen-target CDH assumption.

2 Background

SIGNATURE SCHEMES AND THEIR SECURITY. A signature scheme S consists of three algorithms. The randomized *key generation* algorithm $\mathcal{K}$ takes a global information I and outputs a pair (sk, pk) of a secret and a public keys. The global information can contain, for example, a security parameter, a description of the group and its generator, and the description of the hash function. We do not focus on who generates these parameters and assume that they are publicly available. A (possibly) randomized *signature generation* algorithm S takes a message M to sign and global info I and a secret key sk and outputs M along with a signature σ. A deterministic verification algorithm $\mathcal{V}$ takes a public key pk, a message M and a signature σ and outputs 1 (accepts) if the signature is valid and 0 (rejects) otherwise. In the random oracle model [1] both signing and verification algorithms have access to the random hash oracle. Usually $M \in \{0, 1\}^*$. The common requirement is that $\mathcal{V}(pk, S(I, sk, M)) = 1$ for all $M \in \{0, 1\}^*$.

The widely-accepted notion of security for signature schemes is unforgeability under chosen-message attacks [23]. We recall this notion adjusted to the random oracle model in the full version of this paper [5].

We now recall the basic signature scheme of [8]. It uses Gap-Diffie-Hellman groups, so accordingly we first provide the definitions for the latter.

DIFFIE-HELLMAN PROBLEMS AND GDH GROUPS. Let G be a multiplicative group of the prime order p. We consider the following two problems in G.

Computational Diffie-Hellman (CDH) problem. Given (g, u, v), the three random elements of G, to compute $h = g^{\log_g u \cdot \log_g v}$.

Decisional Diffie-Hellman (DDH) problem. Given the four G elements (g, u, v, h), which with equal probability can be either all random elements of G or have the property that $\log_g u = \log_v h$, to output 0 in the former case and 1 otherwise.

We will refer to any four elements of G with the property defined above as a valid Diffie-Hellman (DH) tuple.

We now can define GDH groups. They are basically the groups where CDH problem is hard, while DDH problem is easy.

Definition 1. *A prime order group G is a GDH group if there exists an efficient algorithm $\mathcal{V}_{\mathcal{DDH}}()$ which solves the DDH problem in G and there is no polynomial-time (in $|p|$) algorithm which solves the CDH problem.*

For the details on the existence and composition of GDH groups see [6, 8, 29, 30].

THE GDH SIGNATURE SCHEME GS. Let G be a GDH group. Let $[\{0, 1\}^* \rightarrow G^*]$ be a hash function family, each member of which maps arbitrary long strings to G^* and H be a random member of this family. The global information I contains the generator g of G, p and a description of H. The algorithms of $GS[G] = (\mathcal{K}, S, \mathcal{V})$ are as follows.

- $\mathcal{K}(I)$: Parse I as (p, g, H). Pick random $x \xleftarrow{R} Z_p^*$ and compute $y \leftarrow g^x$. Return $(pk = (p, g, H, y), sk = x)$.
- $\mathcal{S}(I, sk, M)$: Parse I as (p, g, H). Compute $\sigma = H(M)^x$. Return (M, σ).
- $\mathcal{V}(pk, M, \sigma)$: Parse pk as (p, g, H, y). If $\mathcal{V}_{\mathcal{DDH}}(g, y, H(M), \sigma) = 1$ then return 1, else return 0.

In [8] the authors state and prove the following result.

Theorem 1. *Let G be a GDH group. Then $GS[G]$ is a secure signature scheme in the random oracle model.*

3 Robust Proactive Threshold GDH Signature Scheme

We present a threshold version of GDH signature scheme which is robust, proactive and does not require a trusted dealer. The construction is very simple, since the structure of the base scheme permits to avoid many difficulties one needs to overcome while making threshold versions of many standard signature schemes, such as RSA, DSS, etc.

We now recall the basic setting and notions of threshold signature schemes.

COMMUNICATION MODEL. As usual, the participants in our scheme are the set of n players $\{P_1, \ldots, P_n\}$. All players are connected by a broadcast channel as well as by secure point-to-point channels.

THRESHOLD SECRET SHARING. The set of values $(s_1, \ldots, s_n)$ is said to be a (t, n)-*threshold secret sharing* of the value s if any $k \le t$ values from this set does not reveal any information about s and there exists an efficient algorithm which takes as input any $t+1$ values from this set and outputs s. We write $(s_1, \ldots, s_n) \xrightarrow{(t,n)} s$.

THRESHOLD SIGNATURE SCHEMES AND THEIR SECURITY. Let $S = (\mathcal{K}, \mathcal{S}, \mathcal{V})$ be a signature scheme and let I be the associated global information. A corresponding (t, n)-*threshold signature scheme* $TS = (\mathcal{TK}, \mathcal{TS}, \mathcal{V})$ consists of three algorithms, where the verification algorithm is the same as of S. A randomized distributed *threshold key generation* algorithm $\mathcal{TK}$ is an interactive protocol that takes I and is run by the players $P_1, \ldots, P_n$. The protocol returns the public key pk, and the private output of each player P_i is a value x_i such that $(x_1, \ldots, x_n) \xrightarrow{(t,n)} sk$, where sk is a secret key corresponding to pk. $\mathcal{TK}$ is said to *complete successfully* if it outputs (sk, pk) having the distribution the same as the output of $\mathcal{K}$. The distributed possibly randomized *threshold signature generation* algorithm $\mathcal{TS}$ is an interactive protocol run by the subset of the players, where the input of each player P_i is a message M, the global info I and the player's private input x_i. The algorithm can be considered as consisting of two interactive protocols: a *signature share generation* and *signature reconstruction*. At the end of the signature share generation protocol each player outputs its signature share. All signature shares are then combined using the signature reconstruction protocol. The output of the algorithm is a message-signature pair (M, σ). $\mathcal{TS}$ is said to *complete successfully* if it outputs (M, σ) such that $(M, \sigma) = \mathcal{S}(I, sk, M)$, for all $M \in \{0, 1\}^*$.

Definition 2. *Let I be the global info, $S = (\mathcal{K}, \mathcal{S}, \mathcal{V})$ be a signature scheme and let $TS = (\mathcal{TK}, \mathcal{TS}, \mathcal{V})$ be the corresponding threshold signature scheme. TS is called secure robust threshold signature scheme if the following conditions hold:*

1. *Unforgeability. No polynomial-time adversary which is given I, is allowed to corrupt up to t players and given the view of the protocols $\mathcal{TK}, \mathcal{TS}$, the latter being run on the input messages of the adversary's choice, can produce the valid pair (M, σ) such that M has not been submitted by the adversary as public input to TS.*
2. *Robustness. For every polynomial-time adversary that is allowed to corrupt up to t players, the protocols $\mathcal{TK}, \mathcal{TS}$ complete successfully.*

In the above definition corruption means that an adversary chooses the players it wants to corrupt in advance and is allowed to alter the computation of the corrupted player in any way and to see their private inputs. If the above definition is adjusted to the random oracle model, then all the parties are given access to the random hash oracle.

TGS, THE THRESHOLD GDH SIGNATURE SCHEME. Let G be a GDH group, $I = (p, g, H)$ be the global info and let $GS[G] = (\mathcal{K}, \mathcal{S}, \mathcal{V})$ be the GDH signature scheme as defined in Section 2 . The algorithms $\mathcal{TK}, \mathcal{TS}$ of the corresponding threshold GDH signature scheme $TGS[G] = (\mathcal{TK}, \mathcal{TS}, \mathcal{V})$ are defined as follows.

$\mathcal{TK}$ is exactly the distributed key generation protocol DKG for discrete-log based systems of Gennaro et al. [22][1]. It is jointly executed by a set of paries $\{P_1, \ldots, P_n\}$ It takes as input I and outputs a public key y. The private output of each player P_i is a share x_i such that $(x_1, \ldots, x_n) \xrightarrow{(t,n)} x$, where $x = \log_g y$. Any subset R of $t + 1$ players can reconstruct x using well-known techniques of Lagrange interpolation: $x = \sum_{i \in R} L_i x_i$, where L_i is the appropriate Lagrange coefficient for the set R. As [22] shows, for each x_i, the value $B_i = g^{x_i}$ can be computed from publicly available information. Hence, we assume that these values are publicly available and will use them to achieve robustness.

In order to execute the signature share generation protocol of TS each player P_i in any subset of more than t players takes input a message M and its share x_i, computes the signature share $\sigma_i = H(M)^{x_i}$ and broadcasts σ_i. The signature reconstruction protocol can be performed by any player or a set of players. We will assume for simplicity that it is run by some *designated* player D. In order to achieve robustness D checks that $\mathcal{V}_{DDH}(g, B_i, H(M), \sigma_i) = 1$ for each i.

---

[1] We are interested in verifiable threshold key generation algorithms without a trusted dealer producing Shamir's secret sharing of a secret [43]. Some threshold signature scheme, e.g. threshold DSS proposed in [21] use the distributed key generation protocol (DKG) of Pedersen [38]. The intuition behind the latter protocol is to have n parallel executions of Feldman's verifiable secret sharing protocol [18], such that each player acts as a dealer. However, [22] point out the weakness of DKG of [38]. Namely, it is possible for a corruptive adversary to prevent the protocol from completing correctly by manipulating the distribution of the shared secret key. DKG protocol of [22] is based on the ideas similar to the protocol of [38], has comparable complexity, but provably fixes the weakness of the latter.

If this does not hold, new output requested from the corresponding player or it is assumed malicious. Assuming wlog that R is a set of $t+1$ honest players, D computes the resulting signature $\sigma = \Pi_{i \in R}(\sigma_i^{L_i})$, where L_i is the appropriate publicly known Lagrange coefficient for the set R. The output of the protocol is (M, σ).

Theorem 2. *Let G be a GDH group. Then $TGS[G]$ is a secure threshold signature scheme in the random oracle model against an adversary which is allowed to corrupt any $t < n/2$ players.*

The proof of the above theorem is in the full version of this paper [5].

ADDING PROACTIVE SECURITY. The idea of the proactive approach is to periodically renew shares of a secret such that information gained by an adversary learning some number of shares (less than a threshold) in one time period be useless for the adversary's next attacks in the future time periods when all shares are renewed. Proactive secret sharing algorithm PSS has been proposed in [26]. In order to simplify an application of PSS [25] state the requirements on a threshold signature scheme for proactivization with the help of the PSS protocol. Namely, the authors prove that the security of the robust threshold signature scheme will be preserved when used with PSS protocol if it is a discrete-log based robust threshold signature scheme, which threshold key generation protocol implements Shamir's secret sharing of the secret key x corresponding to the public key $y = g^x$ and outputs verification information $(g^{x_1}, \ldots, g^{x_n})$, where $(x_1, \ldots, x_n)$ are secret shares of the players and if the threshold signature protocol is simulatable. Note that TGS meets all these requirements (recall that the verification information mentioned above is not explicitly output by TK but can be computed using publicly available information.) Thus TGS can be proactivized using PSS and methods of [26, 25]. We add that PSS outputs the verification information after each share update, hence the verification of signature shares can be conducted as before.

We now briefly summarize the properties of TGS. It is robust and can tolerate any $t < n/2$ malicious parties. Its key generation protocol does not require a trusted dealer. Its signature share generation protocol is basically the signing algorithm of the base scheme and the signature reconstruction requires only multiplication of shares. Therefore the signature generation protocol does not require interaction or any zero-knowledge proofs, and has a minimal overhead compared to that of the base scheme. The shares are short and their length does not depend on the number of parties. We also showed how proactive security can be added to our scheme. We compared the new GDH threshold signature scheme with some other existing constructions in Section 1.

4   The GDH Multisignature Scheme

MULTISIGNATURE SCHEMES. Let $P = \{P_1, \ldots, P_n\}$ be a group of n players. Let I be the global information string. The algorithms of a multisignature scheme

$MS = (\mathcal{MK}, \mathcal{MS}, \mathcal{MV})$ are defined as follows. A randomized *key generation* algorithm $\mathcal{MK}$ takes a global information I and outputs a pair (sk, pk) of a secret and a public keys. Each player $P_i \in P$ runs $\mathcal{MK}$ and as a result obtains a pair of secret and public keys (sk_i, pk_i). A possibly randomized *multisignature generation* algorithm $\mathcal{MS}$ is an interactive protocol run by an arbitrary subset of players $L \subseteq P$. The input of each $P_i \in L$ is a message $M \in \{0,1\}^*$, the global info I and the player's secret key sk_i. The output of the algorithm is a triple $T = (M, L, \sigma)$ consisting of the message, description of the subgroup L and the multisignature. A deterministic *verification* algorithm $\mathcal{MV}$ takes M, L, σ and public keys of all players in L and T and outputs 1 (accepts) or 0 (rejects).

Note that it is up to a particular application to decide what subgroup is required to sign a message. A person who verifies the validity of a multisignature might reject it not because it's invalid but because she is not satisfied with the subgroup which signed the message. We leave it to applications to agree each time on the desired subgroup of signers and for the analysis we do not take this problem into account.

MGS, THE GDH MULTISIGNATURE SCHEME. We now describe the new multisignature scheme MGS which is based on the GS signature scheme of [8] we recalled in Section 2 . The construction is very simple and efficient, and it also solves an open problem stated in [33], namely, to find a provably secure multisignature scheme where the composition of the subgroup can be decided after the signature shares are computed by the signers.

Let G be a GDH group and let I be the global information that consists of a generator g of G, $p = |G|$ and a description H of a random member of the family of hash functions $[\{0,1\}^* \rightarrow G^*]$. Let $P = \{P_1, \ldots, P_n\}$ be the group of players. The key generation algorithm of $MGS[G] = (\mathcal{MK}, \mathcal{MS}, \mathcal{MV})$ is the same as the one of $GS[G]$. The rest of the algorithms are as follows.

$\mathcal{MS}$: Any player $P_j \in P$ with a secret key $sk_j = x_j$, that wishes to participate in signing takes M, computes and broadcasts $\sigma_j \leftarrow H(M)^{x_j}$. Let $L = \{P_{i_1}, \ldots, P_{i_l}\}$ be a subgroup of players contributed to the signing. Let $J = \{i_1, \ldots, i_l\}$ denote the set of indices of such players. The designated signer D (which can be implemented by any player) that we assume wlog knows the signer of each signature computes $\sigma = \Pi_{j \in J}(\sigma_j)$ and outputs $T = (M, L, \sigma)$.

$\mathcal{MV}$: The verifier takes $T = (M, L, \sigma)$ and the list of public keys of the players in L: $(pk_{i_1}, \ldots, pk_{i_l})$, where $pk_{i_j} = g^{x_{i_j}}$ for each $i_j \in J$. The verifier computes $pk_L = \Pi_{j \in J}(pk_j) = \Pi_{j \in J}(g^{x_j})$ and outputs $\mathcal{V}_{\mathcal{DDH}}(g, pk_L, H(M), \sigma)$.

The robustness property can be added to MGS if D verifies the validity of each signature it receives. We provided the comparison of MGS with other multisignature schemes in Section 1.

BATCH VERIFICATION OF GS SIGNATURES. The approach underlying the above multisignature scheme can easily be applied to provide efficient batch verification of several GS signatures of the same message under different public keys[2].

---

[2] This problem is orthogonal to the problem of batch verification of signatures of the different messages under the same key, which has been addressed in [3].

A verifier needs first to play the role of D above to multiply the given signatures and then continue the verification according to the verification algorithm above.

SECURITY OF MULTISIGNATURES. The notion of security for multisignatures has to capture the possibility of an adversary to "forge" a subgroup L and a multisignature of some message such that the latter is accepted by a verifier when not all players of the subgroup L did sign the message. In other words, no valid multisignature should keep an honest player that part of L accountable if it did not participate in signing.

In order to achieve its goal an adversary might corrupt players, send arbitrary messages during multisignature generation protocol, etc. We also allow an adversary to create arbitrary keys for corrupted players, possibly dependent on the keys of honest players, in order to model well-known rogue-key attacks. With respect to these attacks we put only one limitation on the adversary, namely we require it to prove knowledge of secret keys during the public key registration, which is (or should be) the standard practice. We model this for simplicity by asking the adversary to output public and secret key of corrupted users in key generation algorithm. Alternatively we could ask the adversary to provide proofs of knowledge so we be able to extract secret keys, however, this would unnecessary complicate the model. We allow an adversary to corrupt all but one player and its goal is to "frame" the honest player. We note that such a powerful adversary can always deviate from the protocol thus preventing generating a valid multisignature. Similarly to [33] we do not focus on the robustness property in this work. We will sketch, however, how our multisignature scheme can be made robust.

We now formalize the notion of security for multisignatures. It is similar to the one given in [33], however, our definition is more general in that an idividual signer does not have to know the subgroup of co-signers.

Definition 3. *An adversary A learns the global info I and a randomly generated public key pk_1 corresponding to a single honest player. Wlog we refer to the honest player P_1. A generates and outputs the rest of $n - 1$ pairs of public and secret keys and is allowed to run multisignature generation protocol with the honest player on behalf of $n - 1$ corrupted players on the messages chosen by the adversary. The advantage of the adversary $\mathsf{Adv}_{MS,I}^{mult}(A)$ is defined as the probability of A to output the valid message–subgroup–signature triple (M, L, σ), such that $P_1 \in L$, $\mathcal{MV}(M, L, \sigma) = 1$ and P_1 did not complete the multisignature generation protocol on the input message M.*

We say that a multisignature scheme MS is secure against existential forgery under chosen message attack (or just secure multisignature scheme) if there does not exist a polynomial-time adversary A with non-negligible advantage $\mathsf{Adv}_{MS,I}^{mult}(A)$.

As usual, in order to adjust the above definition to the random oracle model all parties and the signing oracle are given access to the random hash oracle.

SECURITY OF THE MGS MULTISIGNATURE SCHEME.

Theorem 3. *Let G be a GDH group. Then $MGS[G]$ is a secure multisignature scheme in the random oracle model.*

The proof of the above theorem is in the full version of this paper [5].

5   The Blind GDH Signature Scheme

The syntax of the key generation and verification algorithms $\mathcal{BK}, \mathcal{BV}$ of a blind signature scheme $BS = (\mathcal{BK}, \mathcal{BS}, \mathcal{BV})$ is the same as the one of the corresponding algorithms of a regular signature scheme. The *blind signing* algorithm $\mathcal{BS}$ is an interactive protocol between a *user* and a *signer*, where the former knows the public key and the latter is given the global info and the secret key. And the end of the protocol the user outputs a message-signature pair (M, σ). It is required that if (M, σ) is the output of the blind signing algorithm, then $\mathcal{V}(pk, M, \sigma) = 1$.

BGS, THE BLIND GDH SIGNATURE. We now propose a new blind signature scheme based on GDH signature scheme.

Let G be a GDH group. Let $I = (p, g, H)$ be the global info. Let $GS[G]$ be the GDH signature scheme of [8] we recalled in Section 2 . The blind GDH signature scheme $BGS[G] = (\mathcal{BK}, \mathcal{BS}, \mathcal{BV})$ is defined as follows. The algorithms $\mathcal{BK}, \mathcal{BV}$ are the same as those of GS. The blind signing protocol $\mathcal{BS}$ is defined as follows. The user holds a public key $pk = (p, g, H, y)$. In order to "blindly" sign a message $M \in \{0, 1\}^*$ the user picks a random number $r \xleftarrow{R} Z_p^*$, computes $\overline{M} = H(M) \cdot g^r$ and sends it to the signer. The signer knows $I = (p, g, H), sk = x$. The signer computes $\overline{\sigma} = (\overline{M})^x$ and sends it to the user. The latter computes $\sigma \leftarrow \overline{\sigma} \cdot y^{-r}$ and outputs (M, σ).

Note that above $\sigma = H(M)^x$, that is a valid signature on M.

SECURITY OF BLIND SIGNATURES. The notion of security of blind signatures captures two properties. The first property is *"blindness"*, meaning the signer in the blind signing protocol should not learn any information about the messages the user obtained signatures on. The second property is a special form of *unforgeability*, namely, the user that has been engaged in l runs of the blind signing protocol should not be able to obtain more than l signatures. The standard notion of unforgeability under chosen-message attack of digital signatures [23] cannot be used as a notion of unforgeability for blind signatures since by their construction a user has to be able to produce a valid signature of a previously unsigned message. The accepted formalization of security for blind signature is security *against one-more-forgery* [39, 40].

Definition 4. *Let S be a signature scheme and let $BS = (\mathcal{BK}, \mathcal{BS}, \mathcal{BV})$ be the corresponding blind signature scheme. An adversary A learns the public key pk randomly generated by $\mathcal{BK}$. A is allowed to play the role of a user in the runs of the blind signing protocol. After interactions with the signer A outputs some number of message-signature pairs. The advantage of the adversary $\mathsf{Adv}_{BS,I}^{blind}(A)$ is defined as the probability of A to output a set L of valid message-signature* *pairs, such that the number of invoked blind signing protocols with the signer is strictly less than the size of L.*

We say that the blind signature scheme BS is secure against one-more forgery under chosen message attack or just secure blind signature scheme if there does not exist a polynomial-time adversary A with non-negligible advantage $\mathsf{Adv}^{blind}_{BS,I}(A)$.

First we claim that BGS has the blindness property. This is because the signer receives only random elements in G which are independent of the outputs of the user.

CHOSEN TARGET CDH ASSUMPTION. Similarly to the proof of security of the Chaum's RSA-based blind signature scheme [11] given in [2] we reduce the security in the sense of unforgeability of the blind signature scheme to the *chosen-target* version of the appropriate computational assumption. Security of the RSA blind signature is proven secure assuming hardness of the chosen-target RSA inversion problem [2]. Namely, the assumption states that for a randomly generated RSA key pair $pk = (N, e), sk = (N, d)$[3] no polynomial time adversary which is given pk, the "target" oracle which outputs random target points in Z^*_N and the "helper" RSA inversion oracle $(\cdot)^d \bmod N$ can invert (compute $(\cdot)^d \bmod N$) any subset of the target points such that the number of queries to the helper RSA inversion oracle is strictly less than the number of queries to the target oracle. It is suggested in [2] that an analogue of this assumption can be formulated for any family of one-way functions. We propose the following analogous problem and the assumption.

Definition 5. *Let* $G = \langle y \rangle$ *be a group of a prime order* p. *Let* x *be a random element of* Z^*_p *and let* $y = g^x$. *Let* H *be a random instance of a hash function family* $[\{0,1\}^* \rightarrow G^*]$ *The adversary* B *is given* (p, g, H, y) *and has access to the target oracle* $\mathcal{T}_G$ *that returns random points* z_i *in* G *and the helper oracle* $(\cdot)^x$. *Let* q_t, *(resp.* q_h*) be the number of queries* B *made to the target (resp. helper) oracles. The advantage of the adversary attacking the chosen-target CDH problem* $\mathsf{Adv}^{ct-cdh}_G(B)$ *is defined as the probability of* B *to output a set* V *of, say,* l *pairs* $((v_1, j_1), \ldots (v_l, j_l))$, *where for all* $1 \leq i \leq l \; \exists \; 1 \leq j_i \leq q_t$ *such that* $v_i = z^x_{j_i}$, *all* v_i *are distinct and* $q_h < q_t$.

The chosen-target CDH assumption states that there is no polynomial-time adversary B *with non-negligible* $\mathsf{Adv}^{ct-cdh}_G(B)$.

Note that if the above adversary makes one query to the target oracle then the chosen-target CDH assumption is equivalent to the standard CDH assumption. We assume that the chosen-target CDH problem is hard for all groups where CDH problem is hard; this includes GDH groups.

---

[3] Here $N = pq$ is a product of two random primes, e is a random element of $Z^*_{\phi(N)}$ and $ed \equiv 1 \bmod \phi(N)$, where $\phi(\cdot)$ is a Euler's totient function.

SECURITY OF THE *BGS* BLIND SIGNATURE SCHEME.

Theorem 4. *If the chosen-target CDH assumption is true in G then BGS[G] is secure against one-more forgery under chosen message attack.*

The proof of the above theorem is in the full version of this paper [5].

6 Acknowledgements

We thank Mihir Bellare for the useful discussions, for suggesting to consider the topic of threshold signatures. We thank Daniele Micciancio and Adriana Palacio for their useful comments on the draft of this paper. We also thank Leonid Reyzin for clarifications on [33]. This research was supported in part by SDSC Graduate Student Diversity Fellowship, NSF Grant CCR-0098123 and NSF Grant ANR-0129617.

References

[1] M. BELLARE AND P. ROGAWAY, Random oracles are practical: a paradigm for designing efficient protocols. *First ACM Conference on Computer and Communications Security*, ACM, 1993.

[2] M. BELLARE, C. NAMPREMPRE, D. POINTCHEVAL AND M. SEMANKO, "The One-More-RSA-Inversion Problems and the security of Chaum's Blind Signature Scheme," *Financial Cryptography 01, Lecture Notes in Computer Science*, 2001. 36 35, 43

[3] M. BELLARE, J. GARAY AND T. RABIN, "Fast batch verification for modular exponentiation and digital signatures ," *Eurocrypt 98*, 1998. . 40

[4] E. BERLEKAMP AND L. WELCH, "Error correction of algebraic block codes," *US Patent 4,633,470.* 33

[5] A. BOLDYREVA "Threshold signatures, multisignatures and blind signatures based on the Gap-Diffie-Hellman-group signature scheme," Full version of this paper. Available at http://www-cse.ucsd.edu/users/aboldyre/. 35, 36, 39, 42, 44

[6] D. BONEH AND M. FRANKLIN. "Identity-based encryption from the Weil Pairing," *Crypto 01*, 2001.

[7] D. BONEH, C. GENTRY, B. LYNN AND H. SHACHAM, "Aggregate signatures from bilinear maps," Manuscript. 34

[8] D. BONEH, B. LYNN AND H. SHACHAM, "Short signatures from the Weil pairing," *Asiacrypt 01*, 2001. 31, 32, 36, 37, 40, 42

[9] C. BOYD, "Digital multisignatures," *Cryptography and Coding*, 1986 32

[10] J. CAMENISCH AND M. STADLER, "Efficient group signatures for large groups," *Crypto 97*, 1997. 34

[11] D. CHAUM, "Blind signatures for untreaceable payments," *Crypto 82*, 1982. 35, 43

[12] D. CHAUM AND E. VAN HEYST, "Group signatures," *Eurocrypt 91*, 1991.

[13] R. CANETTI AND A. HERZBERG, " Maintaining security in the presence of transient faults," *Crypto 94*, 1994. 32, 34

[14] Y. DESMEDT, "Society and group oriented cryptography," *Crypto 87*, 1987. 32

[15] Y. DESMEDT, "Threshold cryptography,", *European Transactions on Telecommunications*, 5(4), 1994. 32

[16] Y. DESMEDT AND Y. FRANKEL, "Threshold cryptosystems," *Crypto 89*, 1989. 32, 33

[17] Y. DESMEDT AND Y. FRANKEL, "Shared generation of authenticators and signatures," *Crypto 91*, 1991. 33

[18] P. FELDMAN "A practical scheme for non-interactive verifiable secret sharing," *FOCS 87*, 1987. 38

[19] Y. FRANKEL, P. GEMMAL, P. MACKENZIE AND M. YUNG, "Proactive RSA," *Crypto 97*, 1997. 33

[20] S. GALBRAITH, J. MALONE-LEE, N. P. SMART, "Public key signatures in the multi-user setting", *Information Processing Letters*, Vol. 83, Issue 5, 2002.

[21] R. GENNARO, S. JARECKI, H. KRAWCZYK AND T. RABIN, "Robust threshold DSS signatures," *Eurocrypt 96*, 1996. 33, 38

[22] R. GENNARO, S. JARECKI, H. KRAWCZYK AND T. RABIN, "Secure distributed key generation for discrete-log based cryptosystems", *Eurocrypt 99*, 1999. 38

[23] S. GOLDWASSER, S. MICALI AND R. RIVEST, "A digital signature secure against adaptive chosen-message attacks", *SIAM Journal on Computing*, 17(2):281-308, 1988. 36, 42

[24] L. HARN, "Group-oriented (t,n) threshold digital signature scheme and digital multisignature," *IEE Proc. Computers and Digital Techniques*, 141(5), 1994. 33, 34

[25] A. HERZBERG, M. JAKOBSSON, S. JARECKI, H. KRAWCZYK AND M. YUNG, "Proactive public key and signature systems," *ACM Conference on Computers and Communication Security*, 1997. 22:612-613, (1979). 33, 39

[26] A. HERZBERG, S. JARECKI, H. KRAWCZYK AND M. YUNG, "Proactive secret sharing, or: How to cope with perpetual leakage,", *Crypto 95*, 1995. 33, 39

[27] P. HORSTER, M. MICHELS AND H. PETERSEN, "Meta-multisignatures schemes based on the discrete logarithm problem," *IFIP/Sec 1995*. 34

[28] K. ITAKURA AND K. NAKAMURA, "A public key cryptosystem suitable for digital multisignatures," *NEC Research & Development*, 71:1-8, 1983. 34

[29] A. JOUX, "A one-round protocol for tripartite Diffie-Hellman," *ANTS-IV conference, vol. 1838*. 31, 36

[30] A. JOUX AND K. NGUYEN, "Separating Decision Diffie-Hellman from Diffie-Hellman in cryptographic groups," *e-print archive, report #2001/03*. 31, 36

[31] C. LI, T. HWANG AND N. LEE, "Threshold-multisignature schemes where suspected forgery implies traceability of adversarial shareholders," *Eurocrypt 94*, 1994. 34

[32] A. LYSYANSKAYA, "Unique signatures and verifiable random functions from the DH-DDH separation", *Crypto 02*, 2002. 31

[33] S. MICALI, K. OHTA AND L. REYZIN, "Accountable-subgroup multisignatures," *ACM Conference on Computer and Communications Security*, 2001. 34, 35, 40, 41, 44

[34] T. OKAMOTO, "A digital multisignature schema using bijective public-key cryptosystems," *ACM Transaction on Computer Systems*, 6(4): 432-441, 1988. 34

[35] K. OHTA AND T. OKAMOTO, "A digital multisignature scheme based on the Fiat-Shamir scheme", *Asiacrypt 91*, 1991. 34

[36] K. OHTA AND T. OKAMOTO, "Multi-signature scheme secure against active insider attacks", *IEICE Transactions on Fundamentals of Electronics Communications and Computer Sciences*, E82-A(1):21-31, 1999. 34

[37] R. OSTROVSKY AND M. YUNG, "How to withstand mobile virus attacks," *PODC*, 1991. 32

[38] T. PEDERSEN, "Non-interactive and information-theoretic secure verifiable secret sharing," *Eurocrypt 91*, 1991. 38

[39] D. POINTCHEVAL AND J. STERN, "Provably secure blind signature schemes," *Asiacrypt 96*, 1996. 42

[40] D. POINTCHEVAL AND J. STERN, "Security arguments for digital signatures and blind signatures," *Journal of Cryptology*, 13(3):361-396, 2000. 42

[41] T. RABIN, "A simplified approach to threshold and proactive RSA," *Crypto 98*, 1998. 33

[42] R. RIVEST, A. SHAMIR AND Y. TAUMAN, "How to leak a secret", *Asiacrypt 01*, 2001. 34

[43] A. SHAMIR, "How to share a secret," *Communications of the ACM*, 22:612-613, (1979). 32, 38

[44] V. SHOUP, "Practical threshold signatures", *Eurocrypt 00*, 2000.

An Efficient Two-Party Public Key Cryptosystem Secure against Adaptive Chosen Ciphertext Attack

Philip MacKenzie

Bell Laboratories, Lucent Technologies
Murray Hill, NJ 07974, USA
philmac@lucent.com

Abstract. We propose an efficient two-party public key cryptosystem that is secure against adaptive chosen ciphertext attack, based on the hardness of Decision Diffie-Hellman (DDH). Specifically, we show that the two parties together can decrypt ciphertexts, but neither can alone. Our system is based on the Cramer-Shoup cryptosystem. Previous results on efficient threshold cryptosystems secure against adaptive chosen ciphertext attack required either (1) a strict majority of uncorrupted decryption servers, and thus do not apply to the two-party scenario, or (2) the random oracle assumption, and thus were not proven secure in the "standard" model.

1 Introduction

In this paper we present an efficient and provably secure protocol by which alice and bob, each holding a share of a Cramer-Shoup [15] private key, can jointly decrypt a ciphertext, but such that neither alice nor bob can decrypt a ciphertext alone. Of course, protocols for generic secure two-party computation (e.g., [43]) could be used to perform this decryption operation, but here we present a more efficient protocol to solve this particular problem. To our knowledge, this is the first practical and provably secure protocol for a two-party Cramer-Shoup cryptosystem.

In addition to being an important theoretical question, our interest in a two-party Cramer-Shoup cryptosystem is motivated by some very practical applications. One is that it could be used for a secure distributed third-party decryption service, which requires the joint agreement by two parties to decrypt a ciphertext. For example, this may be used to provide added security to (1) a key recovery system by law enforcement (e.g., [37]), or (2) an "offline trusted third party" system in a fair exchange protocol (e.g., [2]).

Another application (and our main motivation) is related to the work of [35] on techniques by which a device that performs private key operations (signatures or decryptions) in networked applications, and whose local private key is activated with a password or PIN, can be immunized against offline dictionary

Y.G. Desmedt (Ed.): PKC 2003, LNCS 2567, pp. 47–61, 2003.
© Springer-Verlag Berlin Heidelberg 2003

attacks in case the device is captured. Briefly, this goal is achieved by involving a remote server in the device's private key computations, essentially sharing the cryptographic computation between the device and the server. The work of [35] showed how to accomplish this for the case of RSA functions and certain discrete-log-based functions, with DSA signatures and Cramer-Shoup decryptions being notable exceptions. These exceptions were due to the fact that there were no known provably secure protocols for a two-party DSA signature system or a two-party Cramer-Shoup cryptosystem. The work of [36] on two-party DSA signatures filled this gap for DSA signatures, although provable security was only obtained in the random oracle model based on the hardness of Decision Composite Residuosity [38] and Strong RSA [5], along with the standard security of DSA signatures.

The work in this paper fills this gap with respect to the Cramer-Shoup cryptosystem. Moreover, the cryptosystem presented here requires no extra assumptions beyond those required for the original Cramer-Shoup cryptosystem, and it is proven secure in the standard model (without random oracles). To achieve this we introduce some novel techniques, including the use of homomorphic encryptions of partial Cramer-Shoup decryption subcomputations (rather than encryptions of partial keys as in the two-party DSA signature system), and special three-move Σ-protocols for proving consistency (rather than non-interactive zero-knowledge proofs using random oracles as in the two-party DSA signature system). These Σ-protocols are especially noteworthy in that (1) they are not required to be (fully) zero-knowledge, and are used as proofs of consistency rather than proofs of knowledge, and thus they can be used in a concurrent setting (since neither simulation of provers nor extraction of witnesses is needed), and (2) their secure *use* relies in a fundamental way on the hardness of DDH, though their soundness and (honest-verifier) zero-knowledge properties do not. We will further discuss these technical issues in Section 5.

2   Related Work

The two-party Cramer-Shoup cryptosystem falls into the general category of threshold cryptography. Early work in the field is due to Boyd [7], Desmedt [19], Croft and Harris [17], Frankel [24], and Desmedt and Frankel [20]. Work in threshold cryptography for discrete-log based cryptosystems includes, for example, Desmedt and Frankel [20], Hwang [32], Pedersen [40], Cerecedo et al. [12], Harn [30], Langford [34], Gennaro et al. [29], Park and Kurosawa [39], Herzberg et al. [31], and Frankel et al. [26].

There have been previous proposals for threshold cryptosystems secure against adaptive chosen ciphertext attack, namely, Shoup and Gennaro [42], Canetti and Goldwasser [10], Abe [1], Jarecki and Lysyanskaya [33], and Fouque and Pointcheval [23]. They all assume the adversary corrupts t out of n decryption servers. Both the Shoup and Gennaro scheme and the Fouque and Pointcheval scheme may be used in the two-party case ($t = 1$, $n = 2$) if one is only concerned with security and not robustness, but they also both use the non-standard assumption that hashes are modeled as random oracles ([8, 11] give arguments for and against this assumption). In this paper we are concerned with schemes that may be proven secure without using random oracles.

The remaining proposals are all based on the Cramer-Shoup cryptosystem. Canetti and Goldwasser assume there are users that wish to have messages decrypted, and that the servers do not communicate with each other, but only with the users. Then they show a secure system for $n > 2t$, a secure and robust system for $n > t^2$, and a secure and robust system for $n > 2t$ if the users are given extra per-ciphertext robustness information. Abe, and Jarecki and Lysyanskaya allow the servers to communicate with each other and present secure and robust systems for $n > 2t$. Note that none of these results apply to the scenario of this paper, i.e., $t = 1$ and $n = 2$. In fact, it is often the case that threshold cryptosystems (assuming a strict minority of corrupted players) are developed before the corresponding two-party cryptosystems. For example, threshold DSA [12, 34, 29] was developed before two-party DSA [36], and threshold RSA key generation [4, 25] was developed before two-party RSA key generation [28, 41].

3 Preliminaries

Security parameter Let κ be the cryptographic security parameter used for, e.g., hash functions and discrete log group orders; reasonable values today may be $\kappa = 160$ or $\kappa = 256$.

Notation and definitions We use $(a, b) \times (c, d)$ to mean elementwise multiplication, i.e., (ac, bd). We use $(a, b)^r$ to mean elementwise exponentiation, i.e., (a^r, b^r). For a tuple V, the notation $V[j]$ means the jth element of V.

Let G_q denote a finite (cyclic) group of prime order q, where $|q| = \kappa$. Let g be a generator of G_q, and assume it is included in the description of G_q. Note that in the following definitions and descriptions, we will abuse notation slightly and let G_q denote its own description. For instance, when we say the input to a function is G_q, we mean that the input is the description of the group G_q.

Encryption schemes An *encryption scheme* $\mathcal{E}$ is a triple $(G_{\mathcal{E}}, E, D)$ of algorithms, the first two being probabilistic polynomial-time, and the last being deterministic polynomial time. $G_{\mathcal{E}}$ takes as input[1] G_q and outputs a public key pair (pk, sk), i.e., $(pk, sk) \leftarrow G_{\mathcal{E}}(G_q)$. E takes a public key pk and a message m as input and outputs an encryption c for m; we denote this $c \leftarrow E_{pk}(m)$. D takes a ciphertext c and a secret key sk as input and returns either a message m such that c is a valid encryption of m under the corresponding public key, if such an m exists, and otherwise returns an arbitrary value.

---

[1] For convenience, instead of using input 1^κ, we will simply use a fixed group G_q with $|q| = \kappa$ and define encryption schemes over this group.

Now we define the Cramer-Shoup encryption scheme [15, 16] using a fixed universal one-way hash function H and over a fixed group G_q, in which solving DDH is difficult.[2]

$G_{CS}(G_q)$: Let g be the generator of G_q (implicitly included in the description of G_q). Generate $g_2 \overset{R}{\leftarrow} G_q$ and $a, b, c, d, e \overset{R}{\leftarrow} \mathbb{Z}_q$, and set $U \leftarrow g^a(g_2)^b$, $V \leftarrow g^c(g_2)^d$, and $W \leftarrow g^e$. Let the public key be $<g, g_2, U, V, W>$ and the secret key be $<a, b, c, d, e>$.

$E_{<g,g_2,U,V,W>}(m)$: Generate $r \overset{R}{\leftarrow} \mathbb{Z}_q$ and compute $x \leftarrow g^r$, $y \leftarrow (g_2)^r$, $w \leftarrow W^r m$, $\sigma \leftarrow H(x, y, w)$, and $v \leftarrow U^r V^{r\sigma}$. Return $<x, y, w, v>$ as the ciphertext.

$D_{<a,b,c,d,e>}(<x, y, w, v>)$: Generate $\sigma \leftarrow H(x, y, w)$. If $v \neq x^{a+c\sigma}y^{b+d\sigma}$, return $\perp$, else return w/x^e.

Canetti and Goldwasser [10] give a variation of this protocol in which the decryption algorithm $D_{<a,b,c,d,e>}(<x, y, w, v>)$ generates σ as above, but then generates $s \overset{R}{\leftarrow} \mathbb{Z}_q$ and returns $w/(x^e(v/v')^s)$, where $v' = x^{a+c\sigma}y^{b+d\sigma}$. One can see that for invalid encryptions (those in which the original D function returns $\perp$) the new decryption function will return a completely random value, and for all other encryptions, the new decryption function returns the same value as the original. Our two-party protocol will actually perform the Canetti-Goldwasser variation of the decryption procedure.

System model Our system includes two parties, alice and bob, who obtain public and secret data through a trusted initialization procedure. Here we will simply assume alice and bob receive all their public and secret data from a trusted party. After initialization, communication between alice and bob occurs in *sessions* (or decryption protocol runs), one per ciphertext that they decrypt together. alice plays the role of session initiator in our decryption protocol. That is, alice receives requests to decrypt ciphertexts, and communicates with bob to decrypt these ciphertexts. We presume that each message between alice and bob is implicitly labeled with an identifier for the session to which it belongs. Multiple decryption sessions may be executed concurrently.

The adversary in our protocol controls the network, inserting and manipulating communication as it chooses. In addition, it takes one of two forms: an alice-compromising adversary that has perpetual read access to the private storage and computation of alice, and a bob-compromising adversary that has perpetual read access to the private storage and computation of bob.

We note that a proof of security in this two-party system extends to a proof of security in an n-party system in a natural way, assuming the adversary decides which parties to compromise before any session begins. The basic idea is to guess for which pair of parties the adversary decrypts a ciphertext without the assistance of the non-corrupted party, and focus the simulation proof on those

---

[2] Note that one possible group G_q may be found by generating a large prime p such that q divides $p - 1$, and letting G_q be the subgroup of order q in $\mathbb{Z}_p^*$.

two parties, running all other parties as in the real protocol. The only consequence is a factor of roughly n^2 lost in the reduction argument from the security of the encryption scheme.

Labeled ciphertexts Note that our scenario in which alice decides on which ciphertexts to decrypt is motivated by the systems in [35]. This removes the need to include in our model separate users that communicate with alice and bob to obtain decryptions, and allows us not to have to change the encryption scheme to use explicit labels (see [42]). Of course, the Cramer-Shoup encryption scheme does allow an easy way to introduce labels, and this could be done in our protocol also.

4   Definition and Basic Theory of Σ-Protocols

Our two-party decryption system in Section 5 uses special types of Σ-protocols to deal with malicious adversaries, so here we overview the basic definitions and properties of Σ-protocols [14, 13]. (This section may be skipped if one is only interested in the high-level design of our two-party decryption system, and in particular, a design that is only secure against so-called "honest-but-curious" adversaries.)

First we start with some definitions and notation. Let $R = \{(x, w)\}$ be a binary relation and assume that for some given polynomial $p(\cdot)$ it holds that $|w| \leq p(|x|)$ for all $(x, w) \in R$. Furthermore, let R be testable in polynomial time. Let $L_R = \{x : \exists w, (x, w) \in R\}$ be the *language* defined by the relation, and for all $x \in L_R$, let $W_R(x) = \{w : (x, w) \in R\}$ be the *witness set* for x. For any NP language L, note that there is a natural *witness relation* R containing pairs (x, w) where w is the witness for the membership of x in L, and that $L_R = L$.

Now we define a Σ-protocol (A, B) to be a three move interactive protocol between a probabilistic polynomial-time prover A and a probabilistic polynomial-time verifier B, where the prover acts first. The verifier is only required to send random bits as a challenge to the prover. For some $(x, w) \in R$, the common input to both players is x while w is private input to the prover. For such given x, let (a, c, z) denote the conversation between the prover and the verifier. To compute the first and final messages, the prover invokes efficient algorithms $a(\cdot)$ and $z(\cdot)$, respectively, using (x, w) and random bits as input. Using an efficient predicate $\phi(\cdot)$, the verifier decides whether the conversation is accepting with respect to x. The relation R, the algorithms $a(\cdot)$, $z(\cdot)$ and $\phi(\cdot)$ are public. The length of the challenges is denoted t_B, and we assume that t_B only depends on the length of the common string x. (In the following, we will always use challenges randomly drawn from $\mathbb{Z}_q$.)

We will need to broaden this definition slightly, to deal with cheating provers. We will define $\hat{L}_R$ to be the input language, with the properties that $L_R \subseteq \hat{L}_R$, and that membership in $\hat{L}_R$ may be tested in polynomial time. We implicitly assume B only executes the protocol if the common input $x \in \hat{L}_R$.

All Σ-protocols presented here will satisfy the following security properties:

1. *weak special soundness*: Let (a, c, z) and (a, c', z') be two conversations, that are accepting for some given x. If $c \neq c'$, then $x \in L_R$.[3] The pair of accepting conversations (a, c, z) and (a, c', z') with $c \neq c'$ is called a *collision* .
2. *special honest verifier zero knowledge* (special HVZK): There is a (probabilistic polynomial time) simulator M that on input $x \in L_R$ generates accepting conversations with the exact same distribution as when A and B execute the protocol on common input x (and A is given a witness w for x), and B indeed honestly chooses its challenges uniformly at random. The simulator is special in the sense that it can additionally take a random string c as input, and output an accepting conversation for x where c is the challenge. In fact, we will require the simulator to have this special property for not only $x \in L_R$, but also any $x \in \hat{L}_R$.

A simple but important fact (see [14]) is that if a Σ-protocol is HVZK, the protocol is perfectly *witness indistinguishable* (WI) [22]. Although HVZK by itself is defined with respect to a very much restricted verifier, i.e. an honest one, this means that if for a given instance x there are at least two witnesses w, then even an arbitrarily powerful and malicious verifier cannot distinguish which witness the prover uses.

In our results to follow, we need a particular, simple instance of the main theorem from [14]. Specifically, we use a slight generalization of a corollary in [14] which enables a prover, given two relations (R_1, R_2), values $(x_1, x_2) \in \hat{L}_{R_1} \times \hat{L}_{R_2}$, and corresponding 3-move Σ-protocols $((A_1, B_1), (A_2, B_2))$, to present a 3-move Σ-protocol (A_{or}, B_{or}) for proving the existence of a w such that either $(x_1, w) \in R_1$ or $(x_2, w) \in R_2$. We call this the "OR" protocol for $((A_1, B_1), (A_2, B_2))$,

For a relation R, let $\Sigma[R]$ denote a Σ-protocol over R. For a predicate P, let $\Sigma[P]$ denote $\Sigma[R]$ for the relation R defined by P, with public values defined by P. Furthermore, let $L_P = L_R$ and $\hat{L}_P = \hat{L}_R$, for the relation R defined by P. Let $\Sigma[X, Y]$ denote the "OR" protocol for $(\Sigma[X], \Sigma[Y])$.

5   S-CS System

In this section we present a new system called S-CS by which alice and bob can jointly decrypt Cramer-Shoup ciphertexts.

Our main motivating application naturally admits a trusted party for initializing the system (see [35]), so we will focus on that case.[4] Specifically, we

---

[3] Often these protocols are assumed to satisfy *special soundness*: On input x and those two conversations, a witness w such that $(x, w) \in R$ can be computed efficiently. We do not need special soundness for our results.

[4] Alternatively, one could build a distributed initialization protocol involving only alice and bob, and no trusted center. To achieve provable security, this initialization would have to be executed in a sequential manner prior to any decryption sessions, even though the decryption sessions themselves may be executed concurrently with respect to each other. Details are beyond the scope of this paper.

assume a trusted party is given a (public) group G_q with generator g and generates a Cramer-Shoup public key along with secret values for alice and bob to allow decryption:

$$g_2 \xleftarrow{R} G_q,$$

$$a_1, a_2, b_1, b_2, c_1, c_2, d_1, d_2, e_1, e_2 \xleftarrow{R} \mathbb{Z}_q,$$

$$<U_1, U_2> \leftarrow <g^{a_1}(g_2)^{b_2}, g^{a_2}(g_2)^{b_2}>,$$

$$<V_1, V_2> \leftarrow <g^{c_1}(g_2)^{d_2}, g^{c_2}(g_2)^{d_2}>,$$

$$<W_1, W_2> \leftarrow <g^{e_1}, g^{e_2}>,$$

$$\beta_1, \beta_2 \xleftarrow{R} \mathbb{Z}_q,$$

$$<h_1, h_2> \leftarrow <g^{\beta_1}, g^{\beta_2}>,$$

$$D_1, D_2, D_3, D'_1, D'_2, D'_3 \xleftarrow{R} G_q.$$

The trusted party gives alice the values $<a_1, b_1, c_1, d_1, e_1, \beta_1>$, gives bob the values $<a_2, b_2, c_2, d_2, e_2>$, and gives both alice and bob the values

$$<g, g_2, U_1, U_2, V_1, V_2, W_1, W_2, h_1, h_2, D_1, D_2, D_3, D'_1, D'_2, D'_3>.$$

Letting $U \leftarrow U_1 U_2$, $V \leftarrow V_1 V_2$ and $W \leftarrow W_1 W_2$, the Cramer-Shoup public key is $<g, g_2, U, V, W>$. Note that this public key is drawn from the same distribution as in the standard Cramer-Shoup key generation. Also note that only this public key is necessary for encryption, and not the partial public key values U_1, U_2, etc.

Here we give some intuition for this initialization. First, it is easy to see how the standard Cramer-Shoup private keys are split between alice and bob, with their associated public values. Next, the h_1 and h_2 values will be used as ElGamal [21] public keys for alice and bob, respectively. Note that it is not necessary for bob to receive β_2, since bob does not need to decrypt anything encrypted with h_2. Encryptions using h_2 will simply be used for consistency checking, as described below. Finally, the $D_1, D_2, D_3, D'_1, D'_2, D'_3$ values are used in order to make our consistency proofs work in the concurrent setting based on DDH, as explained later.

5.1   Decryption Protocol

The protocol by which alice and bob cooperate to decrypt ciphertexts with respect to the public key $<g, g_2, U, V, W>$ is shown in Figure 1. As input to this protocol, alice receives a ciphertext c to be decrypted. bob receives no input (but receives $c = <x, y, w, v>$ from alice in the first message). The predicates Ψ, Ψ', Γ, and Γ' used for consistency checking are displayed without their parameters in the figure for readability. We give their full descriptions below, with parameter names that correspond to the parameters in the S-CS protocol.

The decryption protocol proceeds as follows. Upon receiving c to decrypt, alice first generates a share s_1 of a random secret s as used in a Canetti-Goldwasser variant of Cramer-Shoup decryption. Then alice generates ElGamal encryptions of x^{s_1}, y^{s_1}, v^{s_1}, and $x^{-(a_1+c_1\sigma)}y^{-(b_1+d_1\sigma)}$. All of these values except v^{s_1} are needed by Bob to be able to perform his part of the decryption, but it is necessary to include v^{s_1} for consistency checking, and more specifically, for the protocol's proof of security. She generates these encryptions under the public key h_1, for which she knows the secret key. Finally, alice proves that she has generated these encryptions consistently.

Once bob receives c and the four encryptions from alice and accepts the proof, bob generates his own share s_2 of s. (Note that this is an intuitive description - s itself is actually determined by s_1 and s_2.) Next bob uses the homomorphic properties of the ElGamal encryption scheme used by alice to compute an encryption (still under the public key for which alice knows the secret key) of a partial decryption of c, using the first, second, and fourth encryptions sent by alice. Then bob generates ElGamal encryptions of x^{s_2}, y^{s_2}, v^{s_2}, and $x^{-s_2(a_2+c_2\sigma)}y^{-s_2(b_2+d_2\sigma)}$ under the public key h_2, for which the secret key is not known to alice. Finally, bob proves that he has generated these encryptions consistently. Note that the extra encryptions are not necessary for any computations of alice, but are used for consistency checking, and more specifically, for the protocol's proof of security.

When alice receives the encryptions from bob and accepts the proof, she decrypts the encryption containing bob's partial decryption of c, and then finishes the decryption of c using her local values.

Given g, g_2, $c = <x, y, w, v>$, and $\sigma = H(x, y, w)$, the predicates Ψ, Ψ', Γ, and Γ' are defined as follows.

$$\Psi[U_1, V_1, E_1, E_2, E_3, E_4] \overset{\text{def}}{=} \begin{bmatrix} \exists r_1, r_2, r_3, r_4, a_1, b_1, c_1, d_1, s_1 : \\ U_1 = g^{a_1}(g_2)^{b_1} \\ \wedge \qquad V_1 = g^{c_1}(g_2)^{d_1} \\ \wedge \qquad E_1 = (g^{r_1}, (h_1)^{r_1}x^{s_1}) \\ \wedge \qquad E_2 = (g^{r_2}, (h_1)^{r_2}y^{s_1}) \\ \wedge \qquad E_3 = (g^{r_3}, (h_1)^{r_3}v^{s_1}) \\ \wedge\, E_4 = (g^{r_4}, (h_1)^{r_4}x^{-(a_1+c_1\sigma)}y^{-(b_1+d_1\sigma)}) \end{bmatrix}$$

$\Psi'[U_2, V_2, W_2, E_5, E'_1, E'_2, E'_3, E'_4]$
$$\overset{\text{def}}{=} \begin{bmatrix} \exists r_5, r'_1, r'_2, r'_3, r'_4, a_2, b_2, c_2, d_2, e_2, s_2 : \\ U_2 = g^{a_2}(g_2)^{b_2} \\ \wedge \qquad V_2 = g^{c_2}(g_2)^{d_2} \\ \wedge \qquad W_2 = g^{e_2} \\ \wedge\, E_5 = (g^{r_5}, (h_1)^{r_5}x^{e_2}(vx^{-(a_2+c_2\sigma)}y^{-(b_2+d_2\sigma)})^{s_2}) \\ \times (E_1)^{-(a_2+c_2\sigma)} \times (E_2)^{-(b_2+d_2\sigma)} \times (E_4)^{s_2} \\ E'_1 = (g^{r'_1}, (h_2)^{r'_1}x^{s_2}) \\ \wedge \qquad E'_2 = (g^{r'_2}, (h_2)^{r'_2}y^{s_2}) \\ \wedge \qquad E'_3 = (g^{r'_3}, (h_2)^{r'_3}v^{s_2}) \\ \wedge \qquad E'_4 = (g^{r'_4}, (h_2)^{r'_4}) \times (E'_1)^{-(a_2+c_2\sigma)} \\ \times (E'_2)^{-(b_2+d_2\sigma)} \end{bmatrix}$$

$$\Gamma[D_1, D_2, D_3] \stackrel{\text{def}}{=} [\exists r : D_1 = g^r \wedge D_3 = (D_2)^r]$$

$$\Gamma'[D_1', D_2', D_3'] \stackrel{\text{def}}{=} [\exists r : D_1' = g^r \wedge D_3' = (D_2')^r]$$

The encryptions of alice are defined to be consistent if Ψ holds, but instead of simply constructing $\Sigma[\Psi]$ to prove consistency, alice constructs $\Sigma[\Psi, \Gamma]$, proving that either Ψ holds, or the triple (D_1, D_2, D_3) is a Diffie-Hellman triple. Obviously, since (D_1, D_2, D_3) was chosen randomly in initialization, most likely it will not be a Diffie-Hellman triple, and thus alice will essentially be proving that Ψ holds. The reason for including Γ is that we will be able to use it to simulate the Σ-protocols for alice, by having our simulator set (D_1, D_2, D_3) to be a Diffie-Hellman triple in the initialization protocol. By the hardness of DDH, this should not noticeably affect the adversary. Note that this technique only works in the case of static adversaries, and in particular, bob-compromising adversaries, since setting (D_1, D_2, D_3) to be a Diffie-Hellman triple may also allow an adversary to give a valid proof $\Sigma[\Psi, \Gamma]$ without Ψ holding. However, it is easy

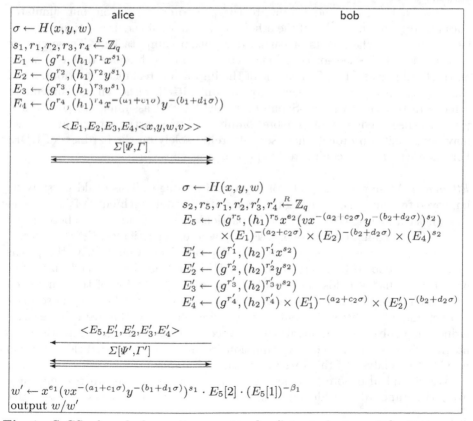

Fig. 1. S-CS shared decryption protocol: alice receives a ciphertext $c = <x, y, w, v>$ as input

to see (and follows from the proof) that a bob-compromising adversary gains no advantage from this.

The encryptions of bob are defined to be consistent if Ψ' holds, and the reasoning behind the $\Sigma[\Psi', \Gamma']$ construction is similar to the reasoning behind the $\Sigma[\Psi, \Gamma]$ construction of alice. $\Sigma[\Psi, \Gamma]$ and $\Sigma[\Psi', \Gamma']$ are similar to other protocols for proving relations among discrete logs, e.g., [9], and are omitted due to space limitations.

At this point, we have stated that E_3 and E_i' for $1 \leq i \leq 4$, as well as the two Σ-protocols, are used for consistency checking, and thus it may be tempting to believe that they could all be removed from the protocol if one were only to consider security against "honest-but-curious" adversaries. However, this does not seem to be true. The Σ-protocols and E_4' could in fact be removed, but the other values serve another purpose in our security proofs, namely, to allow a simulator for one of the parties to obtain the results of partial decryption computations from the other party. Thus if one were to consider the "simplified" protocol for honest-but-curious adversaries, only E_4' and the Σ-protocols would be removed, leaving alice and bob to send values to each other that are never actually used.[5]

As a final remark, and relating to the preceding discussion, our simulator does not require knowledge of the other party's share of the decryption randomizer s, but only the results of partial decryption computations. These can be encrypted and checked for consistency easily, using techniques that rely solely on the hardness of DDH. This is one of the important technical contributions of this paper, since having the simulator obtain s itself, although not difficult to achieve in threshold Cramer-Shoup protocols [10, 33] assuming an honest majority, seems to require a much more complicated two-party protocol, and in fact may not admit a protocol whose security relies solely on the hardness of DDH. For instance, it may requires techniques such as those in [36].

Efficiency As shown, our protocol requires 6 messages. This could possibly be improved to 4 messages by using the "committed proof" technique of Jarecki and Lysyanskaya [33] or Damgård [18]. In particular, one could replace bob's proof $\Sigma[\Psi', \Gamma']$ by a committed proof of $\Sigma[\Psi', \Gamma']$, where, in particular, E_5 is kept secret until the third message of the committed proof. This would allow the proofs by alice and bob to be interleaved, since E_5 would not be revealed until after bob verifies that Ψ holds. This would be a novel application of the committed proof technique, i.e., it would be used not for the purpose of obtaining security against adaptive adversaries, but for improving efficiency. However, the security reduction involved in the committed proof technique is neither as straightforward nor as efficient as the security reduction in our proofs. Nevertheless, we will provide the analysis of this variation in the full paper.

We should also note that our protocol could be reduced to two messages using the standard Fiat-Shamir technique [27] for making proofs non-interactive

---

[5] This would indeed be a "curious" protocol.

using a hash function to calculate a challenge, but then a proof of security would require the random oracle assumption, which we specifically want to avoid.

Turning to computational complexity, one can see that each party must perform roughly 90 exponentiations.[6] By comparison, the protocol of Shoup and Gennaro [42] only requires each party to perform about 7 exponentiations. However, the security of their protocol relies on the random oracle assumption, which, as stated above, we specifically want to avoid.

6   Security for S-CS

Due to space limitations, we will present our theorems, and briefly sketch our proofs. Details will be presented in the full paper.

First we informally define some notation. $\text{Adv}_{G_q}^{\text{DDH}}(t)$ is the maximum advantage of distinguishing a DH triple (g^x, g^y, g^{xy}) from a random triple (g^x, g^y, g^z), where the maximum is taken over all adversaries that run in time t. See [3] for details. For an encryption scheme $\mathcal{E} = (G_{\mathcal{E}}, E, D)$, $\text{Adv}_{\mathcal{E}, G_q}^{\text{ind-cca2}}(t, u)$ is the maximum advantage of distinguishing which of two messages was encrypted by a test oracle, where the maximum is taken over all adversaries that run in time t and make u queries to a decryption oracle (but not on the ciphertext returned by the test oracle). See [6, Property IND-CCA2] for details.

Finally, for an adversary $\mathcal{A}$ in the model described in Section 3 where two parties, alice and bob are running the S-CS protocol, $\text{Adv}_{\text{S-CS}, G_q}^{\text{ind-cca2}}(\mathcal{A})$ is the advantage of $\mathcal{A}$ in distinguishing which of two messages was encrypted by a test oracle, given that $\mathcal{A}$ cannot start an alice or bob session using the ciphertext returned by the test oracle. An "alice-compromising attacker" is additionally given perpetual read access to the private storage and computation of alice. A "bob-compromising attacker" has perpetual read access to the private storage and computation of bob. Recall that $\mathcal{A}$ is either an alice-compromising attacker or a bob-compromising attacker, but not both, and we assume this is statically fixed before initialization.

Now we state our theorems and give sketches of our proofs. The idea behind each proof is to construct a series of systems S-CS$_0$, S-CS$_1$, ..., related to S-CS, with S-CS$_0$ = S-CS, and such that we eventually come to a system S-CS$_i$ such that breaking S-CS$_i$ implies breaking the original Cramer-Shoup cryptosystem. We then show that for any attacker, the difference in the advantage of the attacker in breaking S-CS$_{i-1}$ and S-CS$_i$ is related to the maximum advantage of breaking DDH. For the following theorems, let t_{exp} be the time to perform an exponentiation in G_q.

---

[6] Although this number is somewhat high, most of the exponentiations are performed over one of a small number of bases, and thus preprocessing can be used to greatly reduce the computation time. Also, assuming that the group is of size q where $|q| = 160$, the exponents are reasonably small (roughly 160 bits each).

Theorem 1. *Fix an* alice-*compromising adversary* $\mathcal{A}$ *that runs in time* t. *Then for* $t' = O(t + (q_{\mathsf{alice}} + q_{\mathsf{bob}})t_{exp})$:

$$\mathsf{Adv}^{\mathrm{ind\text{-}cca2}}_{\mathrm{S\text{-}CS},G_q}(\mathcal{A}) \leq 4 \cdot \mathsf{Adv}^{\mathrm{DDH}}_{G_q}(t') + \mathsf{Adv}^{\mathrm{ind\text{-}cca2}}_{\mathrm{CS},G_q}(t', q_{\mathsf{bob}}) + \frac{2(q_{\mathsf{bob}} + 2)}{q}.$$

This is proven as follows. First simulate the initialization so that (D'_1, D'_2, D'_3) is a DH triple. The advantage gained by $\mathcal{A}$ is at most $O(\mathsf{Adv}^{\mathrm{DDH}}_{G_q}(t'))$. Then have bob instances generate E'_1, E'_2, E'_3, E'_4 randomly, and prove $\Sigma[\Psi', \Gamma']$ using Γ' (since (D'_1, D'_2, D'_3) is a DH triple). One can show that the advantage gained by $\mathcal{A}$ is $O(\mathsf{Adv}^{\mathrm{DDH}}_{G_q}(t'))$ plus a small amount related to Σ-protocols. Next set up a Cramer-Shoup decryption oracle (using the key from the simulated initialization) and have bob compute the encryption E_5 by taking the result of calling the decryption oracle on the input ciphertext and modifying it appropriately using E_1, E_2, E_3 (which can be decrypted with β_1 obtained from the simulated initialization). As long as E_1, E_2, E_3, E_4 are consistent, this does affect $\mathcal{A}$. Breaking this scheme can now be reduced to breaking the Cramer-Shoup scheme by taking a Cramer-Shoup key, along with a decryption and test oracle, simulating the private key shares of alice along with all public key shares, and having bob use the given decryption oracle to decrypt the input ciphertexts.

Theorem 2. *Fix a* bob-*compromising adversary* $\mathcal{A}$ *that runs in time* t. *Then for* $t' = O(t + (q_{\mathsf{alice}} + q_{\mathsf{bob}})t_{exp})$:

$$\mathsf{Adv}^{\mathrm{ind\text{-}cca2}}_{\mathrm{S\text{-}CS},G_q}(\mathcal{A}) \leq 4 \cdot \mathsf{Adv}^{\mathrm{DDH}}_{G_q}(t') + \mathsf{Adv}^{\mathrm{ind\text{-}cca2}}_{\mathrm{CS},G_q}(t', q_{\mathsf{bob}}) + \frac{6(q_{\mathsf{alice}} + 1) + 2}{q}.$$

This is proven as follows. First simulate the initialization so that (D_1, D_2, D_3) is a DH triple. The advantage gained by $\mathcal{A}$ is at most $O(\mathsf{Adv}^{\mathrm{DDH}}_{G_q}(t'))$. Then have alice instances generate E_1, E_2, E_3, E_4 randomly, prove $\Sigma[\Psi, \Gamma]$ using Γ (since (D_1, D_2, D_3) is a DH triple), and compute the decryption of the input ciphertext using E'_1, E'_2, E'_3 (which can be decrypted with β_2 obtained from the simulated initialization). One can show that the advantage gained by $\mathcal{A}$ is $O(\mathsf{Adv}^{\mathrm{DDH}}_{G_q}(t'))$ plus a small amount related to Σ-protocols. Next set up a Cramer-Shoup decryption oracle (using the key from the simulated initialization) and have alice output the result of calling the decryption oracle. Since E_1, E_2, E_3, E_4 are random, if $E_5, E'_1, E'_2, E'_3, E'_4$ are consistent, this does affect $\mathcal{A}$. Breaking this scheme can now be reduced to breaking the Cramer-Shoup scheme by taking a Cramer-Shoup key, along with a decryption and test oracle, simulating the private key shares of bob along with all public key shares, and having alice use the decryption oracle to decrypt the input ciphertexts.

References

[1] M. Abe. Robust distributed multiplication without interaction. In *CRYPTO '99* (LNCS 1666), pages 130–147, 1999. 48

[2] N. Asokan, M. Schunter, and M. Waidner. Optimistic protocols for fair exchange. In 3rd *ACM Conference on Computer and Communications Security*, pages 6–17, 1996. 47

[3] D. Boneh. The decision Diffie-Hellman problem. In *Proceedings of the Third Algorithmic Number Theory Symposium* (LNCS 1423), pp. 48–63, 1998. 57

[4] D. Boneh and M. Franklin. Efficient generation of shared RSA keys. In *CRYPTO '97* (LNCS 1294), pages 425–439, 1997. 49

[5] N. Barić and B. Pfitzmann. Collision-free accumulators and fail-stop signature schemes without trees. In *EUROCRYPT '97* (LNCS 1233), pages 480–494, 1997. 48

[6] M. Bellare, A. Desai, D. Pointcheval, and P. Rogaway. Relations among notions of security for public-key encryption schemes. In *CRYPTO '98* (LNCS 1462), pp. 26–45, 1998. 57

[7] C. Boyd. Digital multisignatures. In H. J. Beker and F. C. Piper, editors, *Cryptography and Coding*, pages 241–246. Clarendon Press, 1986. 48

[8] M. Bellare and P. Rogaway. Random oracles are practical: A paradigm for designing efficient protocols. In 1st *ACM Conference on Computer and Communications Security*, pages 62–73, November 1993. 49

[9] J. Camenisch and M. Stadler. Proof systems for general statements about discrete logarithms. Technical Report TR 260, Department of Computer Science, ETH Zurich, March 1997. 56

[10] R. Canetti and S. Goldwasser. An efficient threshold public key cryptosystem secure against adaptive chosen ciphertext attack. In *EUROCRYPT '99* (LNCS 1592), pages 90–106, 1999. 48, 50, 56

[11] R. Canetti, O. Goldreich, and S. Halevi. Random oracle methodology, revisited. In 30th ACM Symposium on Theory of Computing, pages 209–218, 1998. 49

[12] M. Cerecedo, T. Matsumoto, H. Imai. Efficient and secure multiparty generation of digital signatures based on discrete logarithms. *IEICE Trans. Fundamentals of Electronics Communications and Computer Sciences*, E76A(4):532–545, April 1993. 48, 49

[13] R. Cramer. Modular Design of Secure yet Practical Cryptographic Protocols. Ph.D. Thesis. CWI and University of Amsterdam, 1997. 51

[14] R. Cramer, I. Damgård, and B. Schoenmakers. Proofs of partial knowledge and simplified design of witness hiding protocols. In *CRYPTO '94* (LNCS 839), pages 174–187, 1994. 51, 52

[15] R. Cramer and V. Shoup. A practical public-key cryptosystem provably secure against adaptive chosen ciphertext attack. In *CRYPTO '98* (LNCS 1462), pages 13–25, 1998. 47, 50

[16] R. Cramer and V. Shoup. Universal hash proofs and a paradigm for adaptive chosen ciphertext secure public-key encryption. In *EUROCRYPT 2002* (LNCS 2332), pages 45–64, 2002. 50

[17] R. A. Croft and S. P. Harris. Public-key cryptography and reusable shared secrets. In H. Baker and F. Piper, editors, *Cryptography and Coding*, pages 189–201, 1989. 48

[18] I. Damgård. Efficient concurrent zero-knowledge in the auxiliary string model. In *EUROCRYPT 2000* (LNCS 1807), pages 418–430, 2000. 56

[19] Y. Desmedt. Society and group oriented cryptography: a new concept. In *CRYPTO '87* (LNCS 293), pages 120–127, 1987. 48

[20] Y. Desmedt and Y. Frankel. Threshold cryptosystems. In *CRYPTO '89* (LNCS 435), pages 307–315, 1989. 48

[21] T. ElGamal. A public key cryptosystem and a signature scheme based on discrete logarithms. *IEEE Transactions on Information Theory*, 31:469–472, 1985. 53

[22] U. Feige and A. Shamir. Witness indistinguishable and witness hiding protocols. In *22nd ACM Symposium on Theory of Computing*, pp. 416–426, 1990. 52

[23] P. Fouque and D. Pointcheval. Threshold Cryptosystems secure against Chosen-Ciphertext Attack. In *ASIACRYPT '01* (LNCS 2248), pages 351–368, 2001. 48

[24] Y. Frankel. A practical protocol for large group oriented networks. In *EURO-CRYPT '89* (LNCS 434), pages 56–61, 1989. 48

[25] Y. Frankel, P. MacKenzie, and M. Yung. Robust efficient distributed RSA-key generation. In 30th *ACM Symposium on Theory of Computing*, pages 663–672, 1998. 49

[26] Y. Frankel, P. MacKenzie, and M. Yung. Adaptively-secure distributed threshold public key systems. In *European Symposium on Algorithms* (LNCS 1643), pages 4–27, 1999. 48

[27] A. Fiat and A.Shamir. How to prove yourself: practical solutions to identification and signature problems. In *CRYPTO '86* (LNCS 263), pages 186–194, 1987. 56

[28] N. Gilboa. Two party RSA key generation. In *CRYPTO '99* (LNCS 1666), pages 116–129, 1999. 49

[29] R. Gennaro, S. Jarecki, H. Krawczyk, and T. Rabin. Robust threshold DSS signatures. In *EUROCRYPT '96* (LNCS 1070), pages 354–371, 1996. 48, 49

[30] L. Harn. Group oriented (t, n) threshold digital signature scheme and digital multisignature. *IEE Proc.-Comput. Digit. Tech.* 141(5):307–313, 1994. 48

[31] A. Herzberg, M. Jakobsson, S. Jarecki, H. Krawczyk, and M. Yung. Proactive public-key and signature schemes. In 4th *ACM Conference on Computer and Communications Security*, pages 100–110, 1997. 48

[32] T. Hwang. Cryptosystem for group oriented cryptography. In *EUROCRYPT '90* (LNCS 473), pages 352–360, 1990. 48

[33] S. Jarecki and A. Lysyanskaya. Adaptively secure threshold cryptography: Introducing concurrency, removing erasures. In *EUROCRYPT 2000* (LNCS 1807), pages 221–242, 2000. 48, 56

[34] S. Langford. Threshold DSS signatures without a trusted party. In *CRYPTO '95* (LNCS 963), pages 397–409, 1995. 48, 49

[35] P. MacKenzie and M. K. Reiter. Networked cryptographic devices resilient to capture. DIMACS Technical Report 2001-19, May 2001. Extended abstract in *2001 IEEE Symposium on Security and Privacy*, May 2001. 47, 48, 51, 52

[36] P. MacKenzie and M. K. Reiter. Two-party generation of DSA signatures. In *CRYPTO 2001* (LNCS 2139), pages 137–154, 2001. 48, 49, 56

[37] S. Micali. Fair public-key cryptosystems. In *CRYPTO '92* (LNCS 740), pages 113–138, 1992. 47

[38] P. Paillier. Public-key cryptosystems based on composite degree residuosity classes. In *EUROCRYPT '99* (LNCS 1592), pages 223–238, 1999. 48

[39] C. Park and K. Kurosawa. New ElGamal type threshold digital signature scheme. *IEICE Trans. Fundamentals of Electronics Communications and Computer Sciences*, E79A(1):86–93, January, 1996. 48

[40] T. Pedersen. A threshold cryptosystem without a trusted party. In *EURO-CRYPT '91* (LNCS 547), pages 522–526, 1991. 48

[41] G. Poupard and J. Stern. Generation of shared RSA keys by two parties. In *ASIACRYPT '98*, LNCS 1514, pages 11–24, 1998. 49

[42] V. Shoup and R. Gennaro. Securing threshold cryptosystems against chosen ciphertext attack. In *EUROCRYPT '98*, pp. 1–16, 1998. 48, 51, 57

[43] A. Yao. Protocols for secure computation. In 23rd *IEEE Symposium on Foundations of Computer Science*, pages 160–164, 1982. 47

On the Bit Security of NTRUEncrypt

Mats Näslund[1], Igor E. Shparlinski[2], and William Whyte[3]

[1] Ericsson Research
SE-16480 Stockholm, Sweden
mats.naslund@era.ericsson.se
[2] Department of Computing, Macquarie University
Sydney, NSW 2109, Australia
igor@ics.mq.edu.au
[3] NTRU Cryptosystems, Inc.
5 Burlington Woods, Burlington, MA 01803,USA
wwhyte@ntru.com

Abstract. We show that in certain natural computational models every bit of a message encrypted with the NTRUENCRYPT cryptosystem is as secure as the whole message.

1 Introduction

Whereas in the past cryptography used to be performed by national agencies running mainframe computers, today we see a trend towards the use of cryptography in thinner and thinner clients such as cellular phones, PDAs, etc. For public key cryptography to be widely deployed on these devices, we require high performance algorithms to obtain service behavior that is acceptable to the end-users. When designing faster and faster encryption schemes, there is of course always a risk that security is sacrificed, and new, high-performance schemes need to be thoroughly analyzed. One promising recent high-performance scheme is the NTRUENCRYPT cryptosystem [12].

It is quite natural that the performance, and more importantly, the security of NTRUENCRYPT is often compared to other schemes such as RSA, elliptic curves, etc. Unfortunately, like many other practical schemes, NTRUENCRYPT does not have a formal proof of security. On the other hand, the security appears to be closely based on some quite well-studied lattice problems, and to date, no serious attack on NTRUENCRYPT is known.

Still, it would be worthwhile to investigate whether new schemes such as NTRUENCRYPT enjoy security properties that are known to exist in the more "classical" schemes. For instance, it is known that RSA enjoys the property of *bit-security*: finding any single bit of the plaintext is (via polynomial time reductions) as hard as finding the whole plaintext, see [11]. Establishing the same property for NTRUENCRYPT would indicate a certain robustness in the scheme, and this is the problem we address in this paper.

Adopting a new (stronger) computational model, we answer the question positively. While it cannot be debated that our model makes the proof not seeming

Y.G. Desmedt (Ed.): PKC 2003, LNCS 2567, pp. 62–70, 2003.
© Springer-Verlag Berlin Heidelberg 2003

too hard, it far from trivializes the problem. Also, it is interesting to compare our methods and those previously used for the RSA scheme. In particular, the above mentioned results for RSA are obtained exploiting a quite undesirable property of "raw" RSA: multiplicativity; $x^e a^e \equiv (ax)^e \pmod{N}$. To obtain our results on NTRUENCRYPT we similarly make use of the basic scheme's malleability; given the NTRU encryption of x and one or more bits of x, it is possible to compute an encryption of x', corresponding to x with said bit(s) flipped.

Finally, in same classical model as that used in [11] we also obtain a bit-security result, though much weaker.

2   Preliminaries

We recall that in the NTRUENCRYPT cryptosystem [12], one selects integer parameters (N, q) and four sets $\mathcal{L}_f, \mathcal{L}_g, \mathcal{L}_\varphi, \mathcal{L}_m$ of polynomials f, g, φ, m in the ring $\mathcal{R} = \mathbb{Z}_q[X]/(X^N - 1)$. The coefficients of these polynomials are constrained by the choice of an additional parameter, p, a small integer or polynomial. In the original presentation of NTRUENCRYPT [12], p was taken to be the integer 3, and the polynomials f, g, φ, m were trinary. The authors of NTRUENCRYPT have since recommended [13] that p be taken to be the polynomial $2 + X$, and this is current practice in implementations [4]. This choice for p, along with other optimizations suggested in [13], leads to f, g, φ, m being constructed from binary polynomials. Of particular relevance to this paper is that it leads to the message representative polynomial m being binary.

We denote by $\odot$ the operation of multiplication in the ring $\mathcal{R}$.

We also recall the *key creation* procedure where the *receiver Alice* randomly selects polynomials $f \in \mathcal{L}_f$ and $g \in \mathcal{L}_g$ such that f has an inverse modulo q and modulo p (this issue has been discussed in [13,18] together with heuristic estimates for a polynomial $f \in \mathcal{L}_f$ to satisfy these conditions).

Then *Alice* computes inverses f_q^* and f_p^* that satisfy

$$f \odot f_q^* \equiv 1 \pmod{q}, \qquad f \odot f_p^* \equiv 1 \pmod{p},$$

and the product

$$h \equiv p \odot f_q^* \odot g \pmod{q}.$$

Alice publishes the polynomial h as her public key, retaining f as her private key. The polynomial f_p^* should also be stored for later use, and the polynomials f_q^*, g may be discarded. Note that the paper [13] recommends that f have the form $1 + p \odot F$ with $F \in \mathcal{R}$; in this case, of course, $f_p^* = 1$.

Suppose the *sender Bob* wants to *encrypt* and send a secret message to *Alice*. *Bob* selects a message m from the set of plaintexts $\mathcal{L}_m$. Next, *Bob* selects a random "blinding" polynomial $\varphi \in \mathcal{L}_\varphi$ and uses the public key h to compute

$$e \equiv \varphi \odot h + m \pmod{q}. \tag{1}$$

Bob then transmits e to *Alice*.

We do not discuss the decryption procedure and thus the structure on the sets $\mathcal{L}_f, \mathcal{L}_g, \mathcal{L}_\varphi, \mathcal{L}_m$ which maximizes the chance of unambiguous decryption (rather we refer to [12,13] for details). However the set $\mathcal{L}_m$ plays a crucial role and we recall that $\mathcal{L}_m$ consists of 2^N polynomials with $0, 1$-coefficients, that is

$$\mathcal{L}_m = \left\{ a_0 + a_1 X + \ldots + a_{N-1} X^{N-1} \mid a_0, a_1 \ldots, a_{N-1} \in \{0, 1\} \right\}.$$

Thus each coefficient of $m \in \mathcal{L}_m$ carries one bit of information. We also use the fact that the set $\mathcal{L}_\varphi$ is closed under multiplication by X^i for $i = 0, 1, \ldots, N-1$.

Here we prove that NTRUENCRYPT encryption has a very attractive bit security property. Namely, each coefficient of the encrypted message m is as secure as the whole message. Detailed surveys of bit security results are given in [6,8]; several more recent results can be found in [2,3,9,10,11,14,15,17]. Obviously any such results admit opposite points of view. One can express it as "a part is as hard as the whole" and say that this is an advantage of the corresponding cryptosystem. On the other hand, one can express the same property as "the whole is as weak as a part" and say that it is a weakness. We do not here favor either of the above points of view, but we note that the former one is more traditional and has been the main emphasis of prior work.

Our method is based on the following observation: Given an encryption e of a message m, we derive from (1) that

$$e_i = X^i e \equiv X^i \odot \varphi \odot h + X^i \odot m \pmod{q} \tag{2}$$

is a valid encryption of the message $m_i = X^i \odot m$ corresponding to the choice of the "blinding" polynomial $\varphi_i = X^i \odot \varphi \in \mathcal{L}_\varphi$. It is easy to see that m_i is just a cyclic shift of the message m and that since X^i is invertible modulo $X^N - 1$, φ_i is uniformly distributed in $\mathcal{L}_\varphi$. Thus given an oracle returning a prescribed coefficient of the message from a given encryption, one queries this oracle with the values of e_i, $i = 0, 1, \ldots, N-1$, to recover all bits of m one by one. This is a normally undesirable property since it means that the scheme is so-called malleable. We again note that similarly undesirable properties of RSA is the central ingredient in obtaining bit-security results for RSA, so this is not in any way strange. In fact, here we also use one other malleability aspect, see below.

Here we show that the same idea can be used for much weaker oracles which return the value of some coefficient of the message only for a very small proportion of the messages.

We remark that our arguments rely on the fact that the sets $\mathcal{L}_f, \mathcal{L}_g, \mathcal{L}_\varphi, \mathcal{L}_m$ which guarantee unambiguous decryption are public. In particular, this means that any "guess" for a message m can be efficiently verified by an attacker by checking whether $(e - m) \odot h^{-1} = \varphi$ with some $\varphi \in \mathcal{L}_\varphi$. We note that for the parameter sets given in [12,13] (see also [4]), the polynomial h (equivalently, g) is not invertible. However, because of the structure of φ, it is possible to use a "pseudo-inverse" of h to perform the check [16].

We say that an algorithm is polynomial time if its running time is bounded by $(N \log q)^{O(1)}$. In fact, typically q is of the same order as N, so this last expression can be replaced by simply $N^{O(1)}$. We do not evaluate the exact complexities (which depend on the accepted model of computation) but this is a very simple, although somewhat tedious task.

Finally, we use $\log z$ to denote the binary logarithm of $z > 0$.

3   Main Results

Earlier bit-security results, such as those referenced above, use the model of having access to an oracle that returns the ith bit of the message with probability $1/2 + \varepsilon$, for some small $\varepsilon > 0$ (which could be a function of some other parameters), where the probability is taken uniformly over the sample space of messages and auxiliary encryption parameters (and also, over the internal coinflips of the oracle). Here we use a somewhat different model.

Assume that we are given an oracle $\mathcal{NTRU}_\gamma$ which for any sequence of k *distinct* and *valid* encryptions $e_1, \ldots, e_k$, returns the leading coefficient of the corresponding messages $m_1, \ldots, m_k$ for at least $\lfloor \gamma k \rfloor$ queries and returns the error message symbol $*$ for the rest of the queries. We do not impose any restrictions on the behavior of this oracle on *invalid* inputs.

It is important to remark that repeatedly querying this oracle with the same message cannot help to extract any new information because it maintains the required rate of correct outputs only for distinct messages. In the same way, we do not specify the behavior of this oracle on invalid queries e which do not correspond to any valid message as we only require it to be correct on valid encryptions. For example, for such queries it can output 0 and 1 with probability $\gamma/2$ each, and output $*$ with probability $1 - \gamma$. Thus the oracle cannot be used to distinguish between valid and invalid encryptions.

On the other hand, we assume that it is a *Las Vegas* type oracle which never gives a wrong answer, although sometimes may give no answer at all. One can clearly argue that this model is qualitatively much stronger than the "classical" model, though on the other hand, it is quantitatively quite comparable as it only returns correct answers for some (non-negligible) γ-fraction of all queries. Moreover, the results obtained are stronger, since the reconstruction algorithm for the message m can be made fully deterministic.

It is known [5] that when N is composite then the whole scheme is not secure, thus we consider only the case of prime N.

For this and other algorithms our general strategy is to create several valid encryptions, by "flipping" already known (or "guessed") bits of m. In other words, we again exploit the malleability of basic NTRU. If all of them are distinct, then each time the oracle provides new information to us. On the other hand, if not all of them are distinct then, as the following statement shows, we can recover m without even using the oracle.

Lemma 1. *Let e be any* NTRUENCRYPT *encryption of a message $m \in \mathcal{L}_m$ and let $\{r_1, \ldots, r_k\} \subset \mathcal{R}$ be such that for all $i = 1, \ldots, k$, the polynomial $e + r_i$ is a valid encryption of $m + r_i \in \mathcal{L}_m$. Then, either*

   ○ *the polynomials $\{X^j \odot (m + r_i),\ j = 0, \ldots, N-1,\ i = 1, \ldots, k\}$ are all distinct,*

or,

   ○ *given the polynomials $r_1, \ldots, r_k$ one can recover m from e in polynomial time.*

Proof. We remark that if

$$X^{j_1} \odot (m + r_1) = X^{j_2} \odot (m + r_2), \tag{3}$$

for two distinct pairs $(j_1, r_1) \neq (j_2, r_2)$, then

$$\left(X^{j_1} - X^{j_2}\right) \odot m = X^{j_2} \odot r_2 - X^{j_1} \odot r_1.$$

If $j_1 = j_2$ then,

$$X^{j_1} \odot (r_2 - r_1) = 0$$

and because X and $X^N - 1$ are relatively prime, we obtain $r_1 = r_2$ which contradicts our assumption. For $j_1 \neq j_2$ we remark that the greatest common divisor of $X^{j_1} - X^{j_2}$ and $X^N - 1$ is $X - 1$. Therefore, each two distinct pairs $(j_1, r_1) \neq (j_2, r_2)$ uniquely define m modulo $(X^N - 1)/(X - 1)$. Because m has $0, 1$ coefficients there could be at most 2 possible values for m which can be found and verified by checking whether $(e - m) \odot h^{-1} \odot p^{-1} \in \mathcal{L}_\varphi$.   □

Theorem 1. *Let N be a prime. For any constant $A > 0$, given an oracle $\mathcal{NTRU}_\gamma$ with any*

$$\gamma \geq N^{-A},$$

there exists a deterministic polynomial time algorithm which, given a valid encryption e of a message $m \in \mathcal{L}_m$, makes $O(\gamma^{-2}N)$ calls to the oracle $\mathcal{NTRU}_\gamma$ and finds the message m.

Proof. The algorithm below calls the oracle $\mathcal{NTRU}_\gamma$ with valid encryptions of the form $X^j \odot (e + r)$ which correspond to some unknown messages of the form $X^j \odot (m + r)$ for some polynomial $r \in \mathcal{R}$ (chosen in such a way that $X^j \odot (m + r) \in \mathcal{L}_m$, and thus $X^j \odot (e + r)$ is its valid encryption).

By Lemma 1, in the algorithm below we always assume that each message (of the form $X^j \odot (m + r)$ where j and $r \in \mathcal{R}$ are known) it produces is distinct from all the previously generated messages, otherwise the above procedure finds m immediately. That is, each time a new message is produced we apply the above procedure (for this message and all previously used messages) and either find m or make sure this new message has never occurred before. Thus the corresponding encryptions are pairwise distinct as well.

We put $L = \lceil \log \gamma^{-1} \rceil$ and "guess" the L highest coefficients of m. For each guess we execute the below procedure. We remark that the total number of guesses $2^L = O(\gamma^{-1})$ and also it is enough to consider only the case when our guess is correct. Indeed, as we have already remarked, for each guess, the candidate for the message m produced by the below algorithm can easily be verified. Thus it is enough to find the right message m at least once (that is, for the right guess).

So we now assume that L highest coefficients $a_{N-1}, \ldots, a_{N-L+1}$ of m are known.

To find the coefficient a_{N-i}, $i = L+1, \ldots, N$, we consider the following 2^L valid messages (which are flips and cyclic shifts of m)

$$
m_i^{(\nu)} = X^{i-1} \odot \left(m - \sum_{j=N-L}^{N-1} (a_j - \nu_j) X^j \right)
$$

where $\nu = (\nu_{N-L}, \ldots, \nu_{N-1})$ runs over all L dimensional binary vectors, and compute the corresponding encryptions

$$
e_i^{(\nu)} = X^{i-1} \odot \left(e - \sum_{j=N-L}^{N-1} (a_j - \nu_j) X^j \right).
$$

For each $i = L+1, \ldots, N$, the algorithm makes 2^L calls of the oracle $\mathcal{NTRU}_\gamma$ with $e_i^{(\nu)}$. By the conditions on the oracle $\mathcal{NTRU}_\gamma$, because $2^L \gamma \geq 1$, it either returns correctly a_i at least once or we obtain an equation of the form (3).

To estimate the number of calls to the oracle $\mathcal{NTRU}_\gamma$, we remark that for each of the 2^L guesses the algorithm makes $O\left(2^L N\right)$ calls. Therefore the total number of calls is $O\left(2^{2L} N\right) = O\left(\gamma^{-2} N\right)$.   □

We now consider the more classical *Monte Carlo* type oracles, which always return a result which however is correct only with with probability bounded away from $1/2$. However, we make one additional assumption.

Namely, assume that we are given an oracle $\widetilde{\mathcal{NTRU}}_\varepsilon$ which for any sequence of k *distinct* and *valid* encryptions $e_1, \ldots, e_k$, returns the leading coefficient of the corresponding messages $m_1, \ldots, m_k$ for at least $(0.5 + \varepsilon)k + O(1)$ queries and returns an arbitrary value for other messages. Thus, the added assumption is that the advantage of the oracle is in a sense uniformly distributed over the sample space.

As before we assume that the oracle $\widetilde{\mathcal{NTRU}}_\varepsilon$ is consistent in its replies, it maintains the required rate of correct outputs only for distinct messages. Thus, asked several times with the same value of e, it returns the same value (correct or not) for the leading coefficient of the corresponding message m. Again, as before, we do not specify the behavior of this oracle on invalid queries e which do not correspond to any valid message. For example, for such queries it can output 1 with probability $0.5 + \varepsilon$ and 0 with probability $0.5 - \varepsilon$. As in the case of the previous oracle, this oracle cannot be used to distinguish valid from invalid encryptions either.

Theorem 2. *Let N be a prime. For any constant $A > 0$, given an oracle $\widetilde{\mathcal{NTRU}}_\varepsilon$ with any*

$$
\varepsilon \geq N^{-A},
$$

there exists a deterministic polynomial time algorithm which, given a valid encryption e of a message $m \in \mathcal{L}_m$, makes $O(\varepsilon^{-2}N)$ calls of the oracle $\widetilde{\mathcal{NTRU}}_\varepsilon$ and finds the message m.

Proof. Let C be a constant such that the oracle $\widetilde{\mathcal{NTRU}}_\varepsilon$ returns the correct answer for at least $(0.5 + \varepsilon)k - C$ pairwise distinct and correct queries (that is, C is the implicit constant in $O(1)$ in the definition of $\widetilde{\mathcal{NTRU}}_\varepsilon$).

Put $L = \lceil \log\left(C\varepsilon^{-1} + 2\right) \rceil$. We start with "guessing" the L highest coefficients of m. In fact, we repeat the below procedure with all $2^L = O(\varepsilon^{-1})$ possible "guesses" and remark that if our guess is correct, then the algorithm below finds the encrypted message correctly. Thus we just verify the obtained $2^L = O(\varepsilon^{-1})$ results in order to find which one corresponds to the encrypted message.

As in the proof of Theorem 1 we remark that by Lemma 1, all messages which appear in our algorithm are of the form $X^j \odot (m + r)$ where j and $r \in \mathcal{R}$ are known (and pairwise distinct). Thus we by checking polynomially many "suspects" we can assume that all valid encryptions used in our algorithm correspond to distinct messages.

Now, for each "guess" $(a_{N-L}, \ldots, a_{N-1})$ of the L highest coefficients of the message m we consider $2^L - 1$ "flips" of the L highest coefficients

$$m^{(\nu)} = m - \sum_{j=N-L}^{N-1} (a_j - \nu_j)X^j$$

and compute the corresponding encryptions

$$e^{(\nu)} = e - \sum_{j=N-L}^{N-1} (a_j - \nu_j)X^j$$

defined by an L-dimensional non-zero binary vector $\nu = (\nu_{N-L}, \ldots, \nu_{N-1})$.

Then for each $i = L+1, \ldots, N$ for which the corresponding coefficient a_{N-i} is still undefined, we query the oracle with $2^L - 1$ distinct encryptions $e_i^{(\nu)} = X^{i-1} \odot e^{(\nu)}$, getting (assuming our original guess of the L highest coefficients is correct) the value of a_{N-i} at least

$$(0.5 + \varepsilon)\left(2^L - 1\right) - C = 0.5\left(2^L - 1\right) + \varepsilon\left(2^L - 1\right) - C$$
$$\geq 0.5\left(2^L - 1\right) + \varepsilon\left(C\varepsilon^{-1} + 1\right) - C > 0.5\left(2^L - 1\right)$$

times. Thus we make the majority decision on the value of a_i. We remark that we make an odd number of queries thus the majority decision procedure is always correctly defined (even when our original guess of the coefficients is not correct). $\square$

Finally, we can indeed consider the classical model where the oracle gives us the leading coefficient of m with probability $0.5 + \delta$, where the probability is over random choices of m, φ and the (possible) internal random choices of the oracle. This complicates things since there could for example, be certain messages for which the oracle has no advantage at all. Still, we can obtain a (weak) non-trivial result as follows. Denote such an oracle $\widetilde{\mathcal{NTRU}}_\delta$.

Theorem 3. *Let $0 < \alpha < 1$ be a constant. If there is an oracle $\widehat{\mathcal{NTRU}}_\delta$ with*

$$\delta \geq \frac{1}{2} - \frac{\alpha}{N},$$

there exists a deterministic polynomial time algorithm which, given a valid, random, encryption e of a random message $m \in \mathcal{L}_m$, makes N calls of the oracle $\widehat{\mathcal{NTRU}}_\delta$ and finds the message m with probability $1 - \alpha$.

Proof. Querying $\widehat{\mathcal{NTRU}}_\delta$ on $X^i \odot e$, gives us a_{N-i-1} except with probability at most α/N. Proceeding with cyclic shifts we can extract all bits, but unfortunately, the queried inputs are highly dependent. Still, for randomly chosen m and φ, the probability that any of the N calls is wrong is at most α.   □

4   Concluding Remarks and Open Questions

It is obvious that similar algorithms work for an oracle producing any other fixed coefficient of the message m rather than just the leading coefficient.

Finally, one can probably consider an oracle which is a combination of the oracles $\widehat{\mathcal{NTRU}}_\gamma$ and $\widehat{\mathcal{NTRU}}_\varepsilon$, namely the oracle which for any sequence of k distinct and valid encryptions $e_1, \ldots, e_k$, returns $0, 1$ for at least $\gamma k + O(1)$ queries which is the correct value of the leading coefficient of the corresponding message for at least $(0.5 + \varepsilon)\gamma k + O(1)$ of them, while for the remaining queries it returns the error message symbol $*$.

It is easy to see that our approach applies to any choice of p, for example, to the original case $p = 3$, implying that finding any coefficient of the message m is as hard as finding the whole message.

It is hard to resist comparing our results to those known for other functions (in the classical model). While our results here are much weaker, the initial results for the RSA function, [7], were of the precisely the same strength as ours. Also, the best known results for Diffie-Hellman bits, [3,9], are (to date) not any stronger. In fact, they are obtained for much more powerful oracles (which return much longer bit strings and are always correct). Considering that it has taken quite some time before the "full" security of RSA bits was shown, [1], we hope that the methods developed in this paper in some form can eventually lead to an analogous result for NTRU. Unlike the RSA scheme, it is easy to see that NTRUENCRYPT has properties that guarantee that if any single bit is secure, then so are the others. Extending the results for the least significant bits of RSA, [1], to all bits, [11], on the other hand has taken almost twenty years.

Finally, it should be noted that whereas "a bit" is certainly a natural study-item for security, it is at the same time also a quite arbitrary concept. It would be of great interest to show security of *any* non-trivial predicate of an NTRU encrypted message.

References

1. W. Alexi, B. Chor, O. Goldreich and C.P. Schnorr, 'RSA and Rabin functions: Certain parts are as hard as the whole', *SIAM Journal on Computing*, **17** (1988), 194–209. 69
2. D. Boneh and I.E. Shparlinski, 'On the unpredictability of bits of the elliptic curve Diffie–Hellman scheme', *Lect. Notes in Comp. Sci.*, Springer-Verlag, Berlin, **2139** (2001), 201–212. 64
3. D. Boneh and R. Venkatesan, 'Hardness of computing the most significant bits of secret keys in Diffie–Hellman and related schemes', *Lect. Notes in Comp. Sci.*, Springer-Verlag, Berlin, **1109** (1996), 129–142. 64, 69
4. Consortium for Efficient Embedded Security, Efficient Embedded Security Standard #1, Draft 4. Available from http://www.ceesstandards.org. 63, 64
5. C. Gentry, 'Key recovery and message attack on NTRU-composite', *Lect. Notes in Comp. Sci.*, Springer-Verlag, Berlin, **2045** (2001), 182–194. 65
6. M. Goldman, M. Näslund and A. Russell, 'Complexity bounds on general hardcore predicates', *J. Cryptology*, **14** (2001), 177–195. 64
7. S. Goldwasser, S. Micali and P. Tong, 'Why and how to establish a private code on a public network (Extended abstract)', *Proc. 23rd Annual IEEE Symp. on Foundations of Comp. Sci.*, 1982, 134–144. 69
8. M.I. González Vasco and M. Näslund, 'A survey of hard core functions', *Proc. Workshop on Cryptography and Computational Number Theory*, Singapore 1999, Birkhäuser, 2001, 227–256. 64
9. M.I. González Vasco and I.E. Shparlinski, 'On the security of Diffie–Hellman bits', *Proc. Workshop on Cryptography and Computational Number Theory*, Singapore 1999, Birkhäuser, 2001, 257–268. 64, 69
10. M.I. González Vasco and I.E. Shparlinski, 'Security of the most significant bits of the Shamir message passing scheme', *Math. Comp.*, **71** (2002), 333–342. 64
11. J. Håstad and M. Näslund, 'The security of individual RSA and discrete log bits', *J. of the ACM*, (to appear). 62, 63, 64, 69
12. J. Hoffstein, J. Pipher and J.H. Silverman, 'NTRU: A ring based public key cryptosystem', *Lect. Notes in Comp. Sci.*, Springer-Verlag, Berlin, **1433** (1998), 267–288. 62, 63, 64
13. J. Hoffstein and J.H. Silverman, 'Optimizations for NTRU', *Proc. the Conf. on Public Key Cryptography and Computational Number Theory, Warsaw, 2000*, Walter de Gruyter, 2001, 77–88. 63, 64
14. N.A. Howgrave-Graham, P.Q. Nguyen and I.E. Shparlinski, 'Hidden number problem with hidden multipliers, timed-release crypto and noisy exponentiation', *Math. Comp.*, (to appear). 64
15. W.-C.W. Li, M. Näslund and I.E. Shparlinski, 'The hidden number problem with the trace and bit security of XTR and LUC', *Lect. Notes in Comp. Sci.*, Springer-Verlag, Berlin, **2442** (2002), 433–448. 64
16. P.Q. Nguyen and D. Pointcheval, 'Analysis and improvements of NTRU encryption paddings', *Lect. Notes in Comp. Sci.*, Springer-Verlag, Berlin, **2442** (2002, 210–225. 64
17. C.P. Schnorr, 'Security of almost all discrete log bits', *Electronic Colloq. on Comp. Compl.*, Univ. of Trier, **TR98-033** (1998), 1–13. 64
18. J.H. Silverman, 'Invertibility in truncated polynomial rings', *NTRU Cryptosystem Tech. Report 9*, 1998, 1–8. 63

Equivalence between Semantic Security and Indistinguishability against Chosen Ciphertext Attacks

Yodai Watanabe[1], Junji Shikata[2], and Hideki Imai[3]

[1] RIKEN Brain Science Institute
2-1 Hirosawa, Wako-shi, Saitama 351-0198, Japan
yodai@brain.riken.go.jp
[2] Graduate School of Environment and Information Sciences
Yokohama National University
79-7 Tokiwadai, Hodogaya-ku, Yokohama 240-8501, Japan
shikata@ynu.ac.jp
[3] Institute of Industrial Science, University of Tokyo
4-6-1 Komaba, Meguro-ku, Tokyo 153-8505, Japan
imai@iis.u-tokyo.ac.jp

Abstract. The aim of this work is to examine the relation between the notions of semantic security and indistinguishability against chosen ciphertext attacks. For this purpose, a new security notion called non-dividability is introduced independent of attack models, and is shown to be equivalent to each of the previous two notions. This implies the equivalence between semantic security and indistinguishability under any form of attack.

1 Introduction

The security of public key cryptosystems is usually classified from the point of view of their goals and attack models. The (currently known) standard goals of public key cryptosystems are as follows. (i)Semantic security (SS)[10]: In this security notion, any adversary (probabilistic polynomial-time Turing machine) cannot obtain any partial information about the plaintext of a given ciphertext. This notion corresponds to a computational version of the "perfect secrecy" introduced by Shannon[14]. (ii)Indistinguishability (IND)[10]: Here, given a ciphertext of one of two plaintexts any adversary cannot distinguish which one is encrypted. This notion is rather artificial, but in considering provable security of a public key cryptosystem it is usually convenient to employ this notion as the goal of the system. (iii)Non-malleability (NM)[6]: Given a ciphertext of a plaintext any adversary cannot construct another ciphertext whose plaintext is meaningfully related to the initial one.

On the other hand, the (currently known) standard attack models of public key cryptosystems are as follows. (a)Chosen plaintext attacks (CPA): In this model, an adversary has access to an encryption oracle. That is, she can choose

Y.G. Desmedt (Ed.): PKC 2003, LNCS 2567, pp. 71–84, 2003.

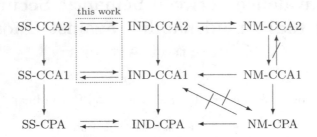

Fig. 1. Relations among security notions

a set of plaintexts and obtain the corresponding ciphertexts. (b)(Non-adaptive) chosen ciphertext attacks (CCA1)[12]: In this model, an adversary has, in addition to the ability of the CPA adversary, access to a decryption oracle before she obtains a challenge ciphertext. That is, she can choose a set of ciphertexts and obtain the corresponding plaintexts during this period. (c)Adaptive chosen ciphertext attacks (CCA2)[13]: In this model, an adversary has, in addition to the ability of the CCA1 adversary, access to a decryption oracle even after she obtains a challenge ciphertext. However, she is prohibited from asking the oracle to decrypt the challenge ciphertext itself.

Several security notions can be constructed by combining these goals and attack models, and, of course, there are relations between some of these notions. In fact, the following facts on such relations have been known so far (figure 1). First, regarding the attack models, the power of the adversaries gets stronger in the order CPA, CCA1 and CCA2, so does the strength of the security notions. Next, regarding the goals, it has been shown that NM implies IND in general, but, in CCA2 model, IND also implies NM[2]. On the other hand, SS is equivalent to IND in CPA model[7, 10], but, in CCA models, the equivalence has not been strictly verified so far (see [2]). Observe that, in proposing a public key cryptosystem, it is conventional to claim, based on the fact IND-CCA2⇔NM-CCA2 mentioned above, that the system has the strongest security by showing that it is secure in the sense of IND-CCA2 (see, e.g. [3, 5, 15]). However, in the background of this claim, it seems to be implicitly assumed that the equivalence between SS and IND holds under CCA models as well. Hence, formalizing and proving this equivalence under this stronger attack model (CCA) is of importance. In this paper, we show that this assumption is true, that is, SS and IND are equivalent under any attack model.[1]

The rest of this paper is organized as follows. We first extend the definition of semantic security to CCA models in section 2. In section 3, we introduce a new security notion called *non-dividability* which is equivalent to semantic security

---

[1] After the work of this paper had been completed, the authors were informed that Goldreich had independently shown the same result in a chapter of his book recently revised[8], which deals with wide-ranging subjects of encryption and contains several new results.

under any form of attack. In section 4, we show that this notion is equivalent to indistinguishability, which yields that semantic security is equivalent to indistinguishability under any form of attack. We devote section 5 to the conclusion of this paper.

2   Preliminaries

In this section, we consider two security notions, semantic security and indistinguishability. First, we provide the definition of indistinguishability according to Bellare et al.[2], and then that of semantic security according to Goldreich[7]. Note that the former is independent of attack models, while the latter supposes CPA model. Thus we next give an extended version of the definition of semantic security which is based on the framework by Bellare et al.[2], and so is independent of attack models. Finally, we show that the extended version of semantic security implies the original one (in CPA model), which ensures the validity of the extension.

We start with providing some definitions which will be used later.

Definition 1. *A public key encryption scheme is a triplet of algorithms, $\mathcal{PE} = (\mathcal{K}, \mathcal{E}, \mathcal{D})$, such that*

- *the key generation algorithm $\mathcal{K}$ is a probabilistic polynomial-time algorithm which takes a security parameter $k \in \mathbb{N}$ and outputs a pair (pk, sk) of matching public and secret keys,*
- *the encryption algorithm $\mathcal{E}$ is a probabilistic polynomial-time algorithm which takes a public key pk and a message x and outputs a ciphertext y,*
- *the decryption algorithm $\mathcal{D}$ is a deterministic polynomial-time algorithm which takes a secret key sk and a ciphertext y and outputs either a message x or a special symbol $\bot$ to indicate that the ciphertext is invalid,*

where $\mathcal{D}_{sk}(\mathcal{E}_{pk}(x)) = x$ for all x and (pk, sk).

Definition 2. *A function $\epsilon : \mathbb{N} \to \mathbb{R}$, $\epsilon(n) \geq 0$ for $n \in \mathbb{N}$, is called* negligible *if for every constant $c \geq 0$ there exists an integer k_c such that $\epsilon(k) < k^{-c}$ for all $k > k_c$.*

Now we consider the notion of indistinguishability. This notion was first introduced by Goldwasser and Micali[10], and later a version of this notion was provided by Bellare et al.[2]. We now describe the definition of this notion according to Bellare et al.[2]. Let $A = (A_1, A_2)$ be an adversary attacking an encryption scheme $\mathcal{PE} = (\mathcal{K}, \mathcal{E}, \mathcal{D})$. In the first stage of the attack by the adversary, algorithm A_1, given the public key pk, outputs a triplet (x_0, x_1, s), where the first two components are messages of the same length, and the last one is state information. A random one of x_0 and x_1, say x_b, is selected, and then x_b is encrypted to give a challenge ciphertext y. In the second stage of the attack by the adversary, algorithm A_2, given (x_0, x_1, s, y), guesses the bit b, i.e. which of the two messages is encrypted. If any adversary can guess the bit essentially no more than random guess, then $\mathcal{PE}$ is called secure in the sense of IND-ATK, where ATK represents the attack model of A, i.e. CPA, CCA1, or CCA2. The formal definition is as follows.

Definition 3 (Indistinguishability[2]). *Let* $\mathcal{PE} = (\mathcal{K}, \mathcal{E}, \mathcal{D})$ *be an encryption scheme and let* $A = (A_1, A_2)$ *be a polynomial-time adversary. For* $atk \in \{cpa, cca1, cca2\}$, $b \in \{0, 1\}$ *and* $k \in \mathbb{N}$, *consider*

$$\text{Experiment } \text{Exp}_{\mathcal{PE},A}^{ind-atk-b}(k)$$

$$(pk, sk) \xleftarrow{R} \mathcal{K}(k); \ (x_0, x_1, s) \leftarrow A_1^{\mathcal{O}_1(\cdot)}(pk); \ y \leftarrow \mathcal{E}_{pk}(x_b);$$

$$d \leftarrow A_2^{\mathcal{O}_2(\cdot)}(x_0, x_1, s, y);$$

$$\text{return } d$$

where $|x_0| = |x_1|$ *and*

$$\mathcal{O}_1(\cdot) = \epsilon \qquad \text{and } \mathcal{O}_2(\cdot) = \epsilon \qquad \text{for } atk = cpa$$

$$\mathcal{O}_1(\cdot) = \mathcal{D}_{sk}(\cdot) \text{ and } \mathcal{O}_2(\cdot) = \epsilon \qquad \text{for } atk = cca1$$

$$\mathcal{O}_1(\cdot) = \mathcal{D}_{sk}(\cdot) \text{ and } \mathcal{O}_2(\cdot) = \mathcal{D}_{sk}(\cdot) \text{ for } atk = cca2$$

with ϵ *being the function which, on any input, returns the empty string. In the case of CCA2,* A_2 *is prohibited from asking its oracle to decrypt* y. *Let*

$$\text{Adv}_{\mathcal{PE},A}^{ind-atk}(k) = \Pr[\text{Exp}_{\mathcal{PE},A}^{ind-atk-1}(k) = 1] - \Pr[\text{Exp}_{\mathcal{PE},A}^{ind-atk-0}(k) = 1],$$

where the probability is taken over the internal coin tosses of all the algorithms. Then $\mathcal{PE}$ *is said to be secure in the sense of IND-ATK if* $\text{Adv}_{\mathcal{PE},A}^{ind-atk}(k)$ *is negligible for any* A.

The notion of semantic security was first introduced by Goldwasser and Micali[10], and later refined by Goldreich[7]. The definitions formalize the intuition of privacy that whatever can be efficiently computed about a message from its ciphertext can also be computed without the ciphertext. This is a polynomially bounded version of "perfect secrecy" introduced by Shannon in the context of information theoretic security[14]. Now we describe the definition of this notion according to Goldreich[7]. Let A be an adversary attacking an encryption scheme $\mathcal{PE} = (\mathcal{K}, \mathcal{E}, \mathcal{D})$. First, a random message x is generated from a message space X_k samplable in polynomial time, and then x is encrypted to give a challenge ciphertext y. Given the public key pk, the length $|x|$ of the messages, a priori information $h(x)$ of x, and a challenge ciphertext y, the adversary A tries to extract partial information $f(x)$ of the message x. If for every A there exists its simulator A' which can guess $f(x)$ only from $(pk, |x|, h(x))$ (i.e. without y) essentially as well as A, then $\mathcal{PE}$ is called secure in the sense of SS_G-ATK. The formal definition is as follows.

Definition 4 (Semantic security under CPA model[7]). *Let* $\mathcal{PE} = (\mathcal{K}, \mathcal{E}, \mathcal{D})$ *be an encryption scheme. Let* A *be a polynomial-time adversary and* A' *be*

*a polynomial-time algorithm which simulates A (A′ is called a simulator of A).
For $k \in \mathbb{N}$, a polynomial-time samplable message space X_k, a polynomial-time
computable function h of X_k into $\{0,1\}^*$ and a function f of X_k into $\{0,1\}^*$,
consider*

Experiment $\mathrm{Exp}_{\mathcal{PE},A}^{ss_g-cpa-1}(k, X_k, f, h)$

$(pk, sk) \xleftarrow{R} \mathcal{K}(k); \ x \leftarrow X_k; \ y \leftarrow \mathcal{E}_{pk}(x); \ v \leftarrow A(k, pk, |x|, h(x), y);$

if $v = f(x)$ then $d \leftarrow 1$ else $d \leftarrow 0;$

return d

Experiment $\mathrm{Exp}_{\mathcal{PE},A'}^{ss_g-cpa-0}(k, X_k, f, h)$

$x \leftarrow X_k; \ v \leftarrow A'(k, |x|, h(x));$ if $v = f(x)$ then $d \leftarrow 1$ else $d \leftarrow 0;$

return d

where $|x| = |x'|$ for every $x, x' \in X_k$. Let

$$\mathrm{Adv}_{\mathcal{PE},A,A'}^{ss_g-cpa}(k, X_k, f, h) = \Pr[\mathrm{Exp}_{\mathcal{PE},A}^{ss_g-cpa-1}(k, X_k, f, h) = 1]$$
$$- \Pr[\mathrm{Exp}_{\mathcal{PE},A'}^{ss_g-cpa-0}(k, X_k, f, h) = 1].$$

Then $\mathcal{PE}$ is said to be secure in the sense of SS_G-CPA *if for every A there exists
A′ such that $\mathrm{Adv}_{\mathcal{PE},A,A'}^{ss_g-cpa}(k, X_k, f, h)$ is negligible for every X_k, f and h.*

Note that, in the above definition, there is neither restriction to the computability of f nor need for the adversary to know f.

The above definition of semantic security implicitly supposes CPA model. Thus, for our purpose, it is necessary first to extend the definition to CCA models. Now we give a definition of semantic security under any attack models based on the framework of of Bellare et al.[2]. Let $A = (A_1, A_2)$ be an adversary attacking an encryption scheme $\mathcal{PE} = (\mathcal{K}, \mathcal{E}, \mathcal{D})$. In the first stage of the attack by the adversary, algorithm A_1, given the public key pk, outputs a pair (M, s), where the first component is a message space samplable in polynomial time and the second one is state information. A random message x is generated from M and then encrypted to give a challenge ciphertext y. In the second stage of the attack by the adversary, algorithm A_2, given (M, s, y), tries to find a pair (v, f) such that $v = f(x)$. If for every A there exists a simulator A' which can find such a pair only from (M, s) (i.e. without y) essentially as well as A, then $\mathcal{PE}$ is called secure in the sense of SS-ATK. The formal definition is as follows.

Definition 5 (Semantic security under any attack models). *Let $\mathcal{PE} = (\mathcal{K}, \mathcal{E}, \mathcal{D})$ be an encryption scheme. Let A be a polynomial-time adversary and
A′ a polynomial-time simulator of A. For $k \in \mathbb{N}$, consider*

Experiment $\mathrm{Exp}_{\mathcal{PE},A}^{ss-atk-1}(k)$

$(pk, sk) \xleftarrow{R} \mathcal{K}(k); \ (M, s) \leftarrow A_1^{\mathcal{O}_1(\cdot)}(pk); \ x \leftarrow M; \ y \leftarrow \mathcal{E}_{pk}(x);$

$(v, f) \leftarrow A_2^{\mathcal{O}_2(\cdot)}(M, s, y);$ if $v = f(x)$ then $d \leftarrow 1$ else $d \leftarrow 0;$

return d

Experiment $\text{Exp}_{\mathcal{PE},A'}^{ss-atk-0}(k)$

$(pk, sk) \overset{R}{\leftarrow} \mathcal{K}(k);\ (M, s) \leftarrow A_1'(pk);\ x \leftarrow M;\ (v, f) \leftarrow A_2'(M, s);$

if $v = f(x)$ then $d \leftarrow 1$ else $d \leftarrow 0;$

return d

where $|x| = |x'|$ *for every* $x, x' \in M$, f *is a polynomial-time computable function (or a polynomial-time algorithm) of* M *into* $\{0,1\}^*$, $v \in f(M)$, *and* $\mathcal{O}_1(\cdot)$ *and* $\mathcal{O}_2(\cdot)$ *are as in definition 3. In the case of CCA2,* A_2 *is prohibited from asking its oracle to decrypt* y. *Let*

$$\text{Adv}_{\mathcal{PE},A,A'}^{ss-atk}(k) = \Pr[\text{Exp}_{\mathcal{PE},A}^{ss-atk-1}(k) = 1] - \Pr[\text{Exp}_{\mathcal{PE},A'}^{ss-atk-0}(k) = 1].$$

Then $\mathcal{PE}$ *is said to be* secure in the sense of SS-CPA *if for every* A *there exists* A' *such that* $\text{Adv}_{\mathcal{PE},A,A'}^{ss-atk}(k)$ *is negligible.*

To see the validity of the above formulation for CCA models, we show that, in CPA model, this one implies the original one, that is, this one provides a stronger security notion than the original one.

Theorem 1. *SS-CPA*$\Rightarrow$*SS$_G$-CPA*

Proof. Suppose that an encryption scheme $\mathcal{PE} = (\mathcal{K}, \mathcal{E}, \mathcal{D})$ is secure in the sense of SS-CPA. Then $\mathcal{PE}$ is shown to be secure in the sense of SS$_G$-CPA as follows.

Let B be an SS$_G$-CPA adversary, and let B' be a simulator of B defined as

Algorithm $B'(k, |x|, h(x))$

$(pk', sk') \leftarrow \mathcal{K}(k);\ x_1 \leftarrow X_k;\ y \leftarrow \mathcal{E}_{pk'}(x_1);\ v \leftarrow B(k, pk', |x_1|, h(x_1), y);$

return v

Now we show that $\text{Adv}_{\mathcal{PE},B,B'}^{ss_g-cpa}(k, X_k, f, h)$ is negligible for any B, X_k, f and h. For this purpose, we assume, towards contradiction, that there exists B such that $\text{Adv}_{\mathcal{PE},B,B'}^{ss_g-cpa}(k, X_k, f, h)$ is not negligible. By using such B, X_k, f and h, let us construct an SS-CPA adversary $A = (A_1, A_2)$ and its simulator $A' = (A_1', A_2')$ as follows.

Algorithm $A_1(pk)$
$M \leftarrow X_k;\ s \leftarrow \{pk\};$
return (M, s)

Algorithm $A_2(M, s, y)$
$v \leftarrow B(k, pk, |x|, h(x), y);$
$\tilde{f}(x) \leftarrow B(k, pk, |x|, h(x), \mathcal{E}_{pk}(x));$
return $(v, \tilde{f})$

Algorithm $A_1'(pk)$
$M \leftarrow X_k;\ s \leftarrow \{pk\};$
return (M, s)

Algorithm $A_2'(M, s)$
$(pk', sk') \leftarrow \mathcal{K}(k);\ x_1 \leftarrow M;\ y \leftarrow \mathcal{E}_{pk'}(x_1);$
$v \leftarrow B(k, pk', |x_1|, h(x_1), y);$
$\tilde{f}(x) \leftarrow B(k, pk', |x|, h(x), \mathcal{E}_{pk'}(x));$
return $(v, \tilde{f})$

It is clear from this construction that A and A' are polynomial-time. Now let us define $p(1)$, $p(0)$, $p'(1)$ and $p'(0)$ by

$$p(1) = \Pr[(pk, sk) \overset{R}{\leftarrow} \mathcal{K}(k); (M, s) \leftarrow A_1(pk); x_1 \leftarrow M; y \leftarrow \mathcal{E}_{pk}(x_1);$$
$$(v, \tilde{f}) \leftarrow A_2(M, s, y) : v = \tilde{f}(x_1)]$$
$$p(0) = \Pr[(pk, sk) \overset{R}{\leftarrow} \mathcal{K}(k); (M, s) \leftarrow A_1(pk); x_0 \leftarrow M;$$
$$(v, \tilde{f}) \leftarrow A_2'(M, s) : v = \tilde{f}(x_0)]$$
$$p'(1) = \Pr[(pk, sk) \overset{R}{\leftarrow} \mathcal{K}(k); x_1 \leftarrow X_k; y \leftarrow \mathcal{E}_{pk}(x_1);$$
$$v \leftarrow B(k, pk, |x_1|, h(x_1), y) : v = f(x_1)]$$
$$p'(0) = \Pr[x_0 \leftarrow X_k; v \leftarrow B'(k, |x_0|, h(x_0)) : v = f(x_0)]$$

respectively. It is now convenient to denote by E the experiment

Experiment E

$$(pk, sk) \overset{R}{\leftarrow} \mathcal{K}(k); x_0, x_1 \leftarrow X_k; y_0 \leftarrow \mathcal{E}_{pk}(x_0); y_1, y_1' \leftarrow \mathcal{E}_{pk}(x_1);$$
$$v_0 \leftarrow B(s_0, y_0); v_1 \leftarrow B(s_1, y_1); v_1' \leftarrow B(s_1, y_1');$$

where $s_b = \{k, pk, |x_b|, h(x_b)\}$ for $b \in \{0, 1\}$. Then it is straightforward to verify that

$$p'(1) = \Pr[E : v_0 = f(x_0)] = \Pr[E : v_1 = f(x_1)] = \Pr[E : v_1' = f(x_1)],$$
$$p'(0) = \Pr[E : v_0 = f(x_1)] = \Pr[E : v_1 = f(x_0)] = \Pr[E : v_1' = f(x_0)],$$

and

$$p(1) = \Pr[E : v_1 = v_1']$$
$$= \Pr[E : v_1 = f(x_1) \wedge v_1' = f(x_1)] + \Pr[E : v_1 = f(x_0) \wedge v_1' = f(x_0)]$$
$$\quad + \Pr[E : v_1 = v_1' \wedge v_1 \neq f(x_0) \wedge v_1 \neq f(x_1)]$$
$$\geq \Pr[E : v_1 = f(x_1) \wedge v_0 = f(x_0)] + \Pr[E : v_1 = f(x_0) \wedge v_0 = f(x_1)]$$
$$\quad + \Pr[E : v_1 = v_0 \wedge v_1 \neq f(x_0) \wedge v_1 \neq f(x_1)]$$
$$= p'(1)p'(1) + p'(0)p'(0) + \Pr[E : v_1 = v_0 \wedge v_1 \neq f(x_0) \wedge v_1 \neq f(x_1)],$$
$$p(0) = \Pr[E : v_1 = v_0]$$
$$= \Pr[E : v_1 = f(x_1) \wedge v_0 = f(x_1)] + \Pr[E : v_1 = f(x_0) \wedge v_0 = f(x_0)]$$
$$\quad + \Pr[E : v_1 = v_0 \wedge v_1 \neq f(x_0) \wedge v_1 \neq f(x_1)]$$
$$= p'(1)p'(0) + p'(0)p'(1) + \Pr[E : v_1 = v_0 \wedge v_1 \neq f(x_0) \wedge v_1 \neq f(x_1)].$$

It follows from the above equations that

$$\text{Adv}_{\mathcal{PE}, A, A'}^{ss-cpa}(k) = p(1) - p(0) \geq \left(p'(1) - p'(0)\right)^2 = \left(\text{Adv}_{\mathcal{PE}, B, B'}^{ss_g - cpa}(k)\right)^2.$$

Therefore, if $\text{Adv}_{\mathcal{PE}, B, B'}^{ss_g - cpa}(k, X_k, f, h)$ is non-negligible, then $\text{Adv}_{\mathcal{PE}, A, A'}^{ss-cpa}(k)$ is also non-negligible. This contradicts our supposition that $\mathcal{PE}$ is secure in the sense of SS-ATK, thus the theorem follows. □

It should be mentioned that the SS-CPA adversary can choose f at her will, while the SS_G-CPA adversary cannot. This indicates that the former has potentially stronger power of attack than the latter. In order that the converse of the above proposition holds as well, it would be necessary to modify f so that it is computable in polynomial time and also dependent on the outputs of an SS-CPA adversary $A = (A_1, A_2)$ (see [4]).

3   A New Security Notion: Non-dividability

In the previous section, we have provided the definitions of semantic security and indistinguishability. So far the equivalence between these two notions has been shown in CPA model[7, 10], but the equivalence is less clear at least by a direct comparison of their definitions. One obstacle to a clear understanding would be that semantic security is defined by use of an auxiliary function f. Thus, in this section, we introduce a new security notion called non-dividability which is equivalent to semantic security but is described only in terms of the message space.

Before describing the security notion non-dividability, we first prepare the following definition and proposition:

Definition 6. *Let M be a message space samplable in polynomial time. The membership problem of a subset $Z \subset M$ is a problem to test whether $x \in Z$ or not for a given $x \in M$. Let $\mathfrak{B}_p(M)$ denote the set of subsets of M whose membership problem is computable in polynomial time.*

Proposition 1. *Let M be a message space samplable in polynomial time, and f be a function defined on M computable in polynomial time. Then, for $v \in f(M)$, $f^{-1}(v) \in \mathfrak{B}_p(M)$.*

Proof. It is obvious that, for given $v \in f(M)$, $x \in f^{-1}(v)$ if and only if $f(x) = v$. It is thus clear that the membership problem of $f^{-1}(v)$ is computable in polynomial time by testing, for given $x \in M$, whether $f(x) = v$ or not.   □

The notion of non-dividability captures an adversary's inability to divide the message space into two parts in such a way that she can guess which part contains the message of a given ciphertext. We now describe the definition more precisely. Let $A = (A_1, A_2)$ be an adversary attacking an encryption scheme $\mathcal{PE} = (\mathcal{K}, \mathcal{E}, \mathcal{D})$. In the first stage of the attack by the adversary, algorithm A_1, given the public key pk, outputs a pair (M, s), where the first component is a message space samplable in polynomial time and the second one is state information. A random message x is generated from M and then encrypted to give a challenge ciphertext y. In the second stage of the attack by the adversary, algorithm A_2, given (M, s, y), tries to find a subset of M which contains the message x. If any adversary can find such a subset essentially no more than random guess, then $\mathcal{PE}$ is called secure in the sense of ND-ATK. The formal definition is as follows.

Definition 7 (Non-dividability). *Let* $\mathcal{PE} = (\mathcal{K}, \mathcal{E}, \mathcal{D})$ *be an encryption scheme and let* $A = (A_1, A_2)$ *be a polynomial-time adversary. For* $atk \in \{cpa, cca1, cca2\}$, $b \in \{0, 1\}$ *and* $k \in \mathbb{N}$, *consider*

Experiment $\mathrm{Exp}_{\mathcal{PE},A}^{nd-atk-b}(k)$

$$(pk, sk) \xleftarrow{R} \mathcal{K}(k); (M, s) \leftarrow A_1^{\mathcal{O}_1(\cdot)}(pk); x_0, x_1 \leftarrow M; y \leftarrow \mathcal{E}_{pk}(x_1);$$

$$Z \leftarrow A_2^{\mathcal{O}_2(\cdot)}(M, s, y); \texttt{if } x_b \in Z \texttt{ then } d \leftarrow 1 \texttt{ else } d \leftarrow 0;$$

$$\texttt{return } d$$

where $|x| = |x'|$ *for every* $x, x' \in M$, $Z \in \mathfrak{B}_p(M)$, *and* $\mathcal{O}_1(\cdot)$ *and* $\mathcal{O}_2(\cdot)$ *are as in definition 3. In the case of CCA2,* A_2 *is prohibited from asking its oracle to decrypt* y. *Let*

$$\mathrm{Adv}_{\mathcal{PE},A}^{nd-atk}(k) = \Pr[\mathrm{Exp}_{\mathcal{PE},A}^{nd-atk-1}(k) = 1] - \Pr[\mathrm{Exp}_{\mathcal{PE},A}^{nd-atk-0}(k) = 1].$$

Then $\mathcal{PE}$ *is said to be* secure in the sense of ND-ATK *if* $\mathrm{Adv}_{\mathcal{PE},A}^{nd-atk}(k)$ *is negligible for any A.*

Next we show that this notion is indeed equivalent to semantic security. The following proof may seem more complicated than expected. This is mostly because the definitions of these notions are based on different frameworks; the former is based on comparison, while the latter is based on simulator (see [4] for details of these frameworks). The essential point of the proof is merely that $v = f(x)$ if and only if $x \in f^{-1}(v)$ for given v and f; that is, what is leaked from the information $v = f(x)$ is that $x \in f^{-1}(v)$.

Theorem 2. *ND-ATK⇔SS-ATK*

Proof. (i) ND-ATK⇒SS-ATK

Suppose that an encryption scheme $\mathcal{PE} = (\mathcal{K}, \mathcal{E}, \mathcal{D})$ is secure in the sense of ND-ATK. Then $\mathcal{PE}$ is shown to be secure in the sense of SS-ATK as follows. Let $B = (B_1, B_2)$ be an SS-ATK adversary, and let $B' = (B_1', B_2')$ be a simulator of B defined as

Algorithm $B_1'(pk)$

    $(pk', sk') \leftarrow \mathcal{K}(k); (M, s) \leftarrow B_1^{\mathcal{O}_1'(\cdot)}(pk');$
    $s' \leftarrow \{s, pk', sk'\};$
    return (M, s')

Algorithm $B_2'(M, s')$

    $x_1 \leftarrow M; y \leftarrow \mathcal{E}_{pk'}(x_1);$
    $(v, f) \leftarrow B_2^{\mathcal{O}_2'(\cdot)}(M, s, y);$
    return (v, f)

Note that B' can answer queries from B because she knows the secret key sk'. Now we show that $\mathrm{Adv}_{\mathcal{PE},B,B'}^{ss-atk}(k)$ is negligible for any B. For this purpose, we assume, towards contradiction, that there exists B such that $\mathrm{Adv}_{\mathcal{PE},B,B'}^{ss-atk}(k)$ is non-negligible. By using such B, let us construct an ND-ATK adversary $A = (A_1, A_2)$ as follows.

Algorithm $A_1^{\mathcal{O}_1(\cdot)}(pk)$

    $(M, s) \leftarrow B_1^{\mathcal{O}_1(\cdot)}(pk);$
    return (M, s)

Algorithm $A_2^{\mathcal{O}_2(\cdot)}(M, s, y)$

    $(v, f) \leftarrow B_2^{\mathcal{O}_2(\cdot)}(M, s, y); Z \leftarrow f^{-1}(v);$
    return Z

Here, it is easy to see, on remembering proposition 1, that both A and B' are polynomial-time. Now, for $b \in \{0,1\}$, let us introduce $p(b)$, $p'(1)$ and $p'(0)$ by writing

$$p(b) = \Pr[(pk, sk) \overset{R}{\leftarrow} \mathcal{K}(k); (M, s) \leftarrow A_1^{\mathcal{O}_1(\cdot)}(pk); x_0, x_1 \leftarrow M;$$
$$y \leftarrow \mathcal{E}_{pk}(x_1); Z \leftarrow A_2^{\mathcal{O}_2(\cdot)}(M, s, y) : x_b \in Z]$$

$$p'(1) = \Pr[(pk, sk) \overset{R}{\leftarrow} \mathcal{K}(k); (M, s) \leftarrow B_1^{\mathcal{O}_1(\cdot)}(pk); x_1 \leftarrow M;$$
$$y \leftarrow \mathcal{E}_{pk}(x_1); (v, f) \leftarrow B_2^{\mathcal{O}_2(\cdot)}(M, s, y) : v = f(x_1)]$$

$$p'(0) = \Pr[(pk, sk) \overset{R}{\leftarrow} \mathcal{K}(k); (M, s) \leftarrow B_1'(pk); x_0 \leftarrow M;$$
$$(v, f) \leftarrow B_2'(M, s) : v = f(x_0)]$$

respectively. From these definitions, it is straightforward to verify that

$$p(1) = p'(1) \text{ and } p(0) = p'(0),$$

and so

$$\mathrm{Adv}_{\mathcal{PE}, A}^{nd-atk}(k) = p(1) - p(0) = p'(1) - p'(0) = \mathrm{Adv}_{\mathcal{PE}, B, B'}^{ss-atk}(k).$$

Since we have assumed that $\mathrm{Adv}_{\mathcal{PE}, B, B'}^{ss-atk}(k)$ is non-negligible, $\mathrm{Adv}_{\mathcal{PE}, A}^{nd-atk}(k)$ is also non-negligible. This contradicts our supposition that $\mathcal{PE}$ is secure in the sense of ND-ATK. Thus we have ND-ATK⇒SS-ATK.

(ii) ND-ATK⇐SS-ATK

Let $B = (B_1, B_2)$ be an ND-ATK adversary. By using B, let us construct an SS-ATK adversary $A = (A_1, A_2)$ and its simulator $A' = (A_1', A_2')$ in the same way as above:

Algorithm $A_1^{\mathcal{O}_1(\cdot)}(pk)$	Algorithm $A_2^{\mathcal{O}_2(\cdot)}(M, s, y)$
$(M, s) \leftarrow B_1^{\mathcal{O}_1(\cdot)}(pk);$	$Z \leftarrow B_2^{\mathcal{O}_2(\cdot)}(M, s, y);$
return (M, s)	$f \leftarrow f(x) = \begin{cases} 1 & \text{for } x \in Z, \\ 0 & \text{for } x \notin Z; \end{cases}$
	return $(1, f)$

Algorithm $A_1'(pk)$	Algorithm $A_2'(M, s')$
$(pk', sk') \leftarrow \mathcal{K}(k);$	$x_1 \leftarrow M; y \leftarrow \mathcal{E}_{pk'}(x_1);$
$(M, s) \leftarrow A_1^{\mathcal{O}_1'(\cdot)}(pk');$	$(v, f) \leftarrow A_2^{\mathcal{O}_2'(\cdot)}(M, s, y);$
$s' \leftarrow \{s, pk', sk'\};$	return (v, f)
return (M, s')	

Then we again obtain

$$\mathrm{Adv}_{\mathcal{PE}, A, A'}^{ss-atk}(k) = \mathrm{Adv}_{\mathcal{PE}, B}^{nd-atk}(k).$$

Therefore, if $\mathrm{Adv}_{\mathcal{PE}, B}^{nd-atk}(k)$ is non-negligible, then $\mathrm{Adv}_{\mathcal{PE}, A, A'}^{ss-atk}(k)$ is also non-negligible. This completes the presentation that ND-ATK⇐SS-ATK, so the theorem follows. □

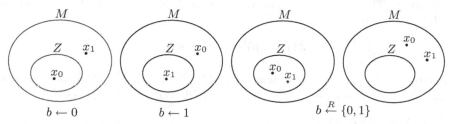

Fig. 2. Reduction of an ND-ATK adversary to an IND-ATK adversary

4   Equivalence among ND-ATK, SS-ATK and IND-ATK

In this section, we show that non-dividability is equivalent to indistinguishability under any attack model. The proof of the direct part is easy to show. Thus we now outline the proof of the converse part. Let x_0 and x_1 be two messages randomly generated from a message space M. A random one of x_0 and x_1, say x_b, is selected and then encrypted to give a challenge ciphertext y. Suppose that given y an ND-ATK adversary divides M into two parts. We wish, by using this adversary, to construct an IND-ATK adversary to guess the bit b. Observe that, if x_0 is in one of the two parts and x_1 is in the other, then the ND-ATK adversary can guess the bit b only by checking which part contains the message of y, i.e. x_b (see figure 2). Since this situation occurs with non-negligible probability, it follows that we can construct a required IND-ATK adversary. Below we describe this more precisely.

Theorem 3. *ND-ATK⇔IND-ATK*

Proof. (i) ND-ATK⇒IND-ATK

Let $B = (B_1, B_2)$ be an IND-ATK adversary. By using B, let us construct an ND-ATK adversary $A = (A_1, A_2)$ as follows.

Algorithm $A_1^{\mathcal{O}_1(\cdot)}(pk)$	Algorithm $A_2^{\mathcal{O}_2(\cdot)}(M, s', y)$
$(x_0, x_1, s) \leftarrow B_1^{\mathcal{O}_1(\cdot)}(pk);$	$b \leftarrow B_2^{\mathcal{O}_2(\cdot)}(x_0, x_1, s, y); \; Z \leftarrow x_b;$
$M \leftarrow \{x_0, x_1\}; \; s' \leftarrow \{x_0, x_1, s\};$	return Z
return (M, s')	

It is clear that A is polynomial-time. Here, for $b \in \{0, 1\}$, let us define $p(b)$ and $p'(b)$ as

$$p(b) = \Pr[(pk, sk) \overset{R}{\leftarrow} \mathcal{K}(k); \; (M, s) \leftarrow A_1^{\mathcal{O}_1(\cdot)}(pk); \; x_0, x_1 \leftarrow M;$$

$$y \leftarrow \mathcal{E}_{pk}(x_1); \; Z \leftarrow A_2^{\mathcal{O}_2(\cdot)}(M, s, y) : x_b \in Z]$$

$$= \Pr[(pk, sk) \overset{R}{\leftarrow} \mathcal{K}(k); \; (M, s) \leftarrow A_1^{\mathcal{O}_1(\cdot)}(pk); \; x_0, x_1 \leftarrow M;$$

$$y \leftarrow \mathcal{E}_{pk}(x_b); \; Z \leftarrow A_2^{\mathcal{O}_2(\cdot)}(M, s, y) : x_1 \in Z]$$

$$p'(b) = \Pr[(pk, sk) \overset{R}{\leftarrow} \mathcal{K}(k); \; (x_0, x_1, s) \leftarrow B_1^{\mathcal{O}_1(\cdot)}(pk);$$

$$y \leftarrow \mathcal{E}_{pk}(x_b); \; d \leftarrow B_2^{\mathcal{O}_2(\cdot)}(x_0, x_1, s, y) : d = 1]$$

respectively. Then it is clear from the construction of A that $p(b) = p'(b)$ for $b \in \{0, 1\}$, and so

$$\text{Adv}_{\mathcal{PE},A}^{nd-atk}(k) = p(1) - p(0) = p'(1) - p'(0) = \text{Adv}_{\mathcal{PE},B}^{ind-atk}(k).$$

Therefore, if $\text{Adv}_{\mathcal{PE},B}^{ind-atk}(k)$ is non-negligible, then $\text{Adv}_{\mathcal{PE},A}^{nd-atk}(k)$ is also non-negligible. This completes the presentation that ND-ATK$\Rightarrow$IND-ATK.

(ii) ND-ATK$\Leftarrow$IND-ATK

Let $B = (B_1, B_2)$ be an ND-ATK adversary. By using B, let us construct an IND-ATK adversary $A = (A_1, A_2)$ as follows.

Algorithm $A_1^{\mathcal{O}_1(\cdot)}(pk)$	Algorithm $A_2^{\mathcal{O}_2(\cdot)}(x_0, x_1, s', y)$
$\quad (M, s) \leftarrow B_1^{\mathcal{O}_1(\cdot)}(pk);$	$\quad Z \leftarrow B_2^{\mathcal{O}_2(\cdot)}(M, s, y);$
$\quad x_0, x_1 \leftarrow M; \ s' \leftarrow \{M, s\}$	$\quad \text{if } (x_0 \in Z \wedge x_1 \notin Z) \text{ then } d \leftarrow 0;$
$\quad \text{return } (x_0, x_1, s')$	$\quad \text{if } (x_1 \in Z \wedge x_0 \notin Z) \text{ then } d \leftarrow 1;$
	$\quad \text{else } d \xleftarrow{R} \{0, 1\};$
	$\quad \text{return } d$

It is clear that A is polynomial-time. Now, for $b \in \{0, 1\}$, let us define $p(b)$ and $p'(b)$ as

$$p(b) = \Pr[(pk, sk) \xleftarrow{R} \mathcal{K}(k); (x_0, x_1, s) \leftarrow A_1^{\mathcal{O}_1(\cdot)}(pk); y \leftarrow \mathcal{E}_{pk}(x_b);$$
$$d \leftarrow A_2^{\mathcal{O}_2(\cdot)}(x_0, x_1, s, y) : d = 1]$$

$$p'(b) = \Pr[(pk, sk) \xleftarrow{R} \mathcal{K}(k); (M, s) \leftarrow B_1^{\mathcal{O}_1(\cdot)}(pk); x_0, x_1 \leftarrow M; y \leftarrow \mathcal{E}_{pk}(x_1);$$
$$Z \leftarrow B_2^{\mathcal{O}_2(\cdot)}(M, s, y) : x_b \in Z]$$

$$= \Pr[(pk, sk) \xleftarrow{R} \mathcal{K}(k); (M, s) \leftarrow B_1^{\mathcal{O}_1(\cdot)}(pk); x_0, x_1 \leftarrow M; y \leftarrow \mathcal{E}_{pk}(x_b);$$
$$Z \leftarrow B_2^{\mathcal{O}_2(\cdot)}(M, s, y) : x_1 \in Z]$$

respectively. Here observe that A_2 outputs 1 not only when $x_1 \in Z \wedge x_0 \notin Z$ but also as a result of the coin flip $d \xleftarrow{R} \{0, 1\}$. With this observation in mind, we obtain

$$p(1) = p'(1)\big(1 - p'(0)\big) + \frac{1}{2}\big\{p'(1)p'(0) + \big(1 - p'(1)\big)\big(1 - p'(0)\big)\big\}$$
$$= \frac{1}{2} + \frac{1}{2}\big(p'(1) - p'(0)\big).$$

It thus follows that

$$\text{Adv}_{\mathcal{PE},A}^{ind-atk}(k) = p(1) - p(0) = 2p(1) - 1 = p'(1) - p'(0) = \text{Adv}_{\mathcal{PE},B}^{nd-atk}(k).$$

Therefore, if $\text{Adv}_{\mathcal{PE},B}^{nd-atk}(k)$ is non-negligible, then $\text{Adv}_{\mathcal{PE},A}^{ind-atk}(k)$ is also non-negligible. This completes the presentation that ND-ATK$\Leftarrow$IND-ATK, so the theorem follows. $\square$

This, together with the theorem in the previous section, at once yields the equivalence between semantic security and indistinguishability.[2]

Theorem 4. $SS\text{-}ATK \Leftrightarrow IND\text{-}ATK$

5 Conclusion

In this paper, we studied the relation between semantic security and indistinguishability against chosen ciphertext attacks. First, we extended the definition of semantic security to CCA models and confirmed that this extension is valid. Next, we introduced a new security notion called non-dividability which is independent of the attack model and is described only in terms of the message space. This notion is shown to be equivalent to both of the two notions, and hence we got that semantic security and indistinguishability are equivalent under any form of attack.

Acknowledgement

The first author acknowledges support from the Special Postdoctoral Researchers Program administered by RIKEN (The Institute of Physical and Chemical Research).

References

[1] J. H. An, Y. Dodis and T. Rabin, On the security of joint signature and encryption, In *Proceedings of Advances in Cryptology – Eurocrypt 2002*, Lecture Notes in Computer Science Vol. 2332, L. Knudsen ed., pp. 83–107, Springer-Verlag, 2002. 83

[2] M. Bellare, A. Desai, D. Pointcheval and P. Rogaway, Relations among notions of security for public-key encryption schemes. In *Proceedings of Advances in Cryptology – Crypto'98*, Lecture Notes in Computer Science Vol. 1462, H. Krawczyk ed., pp. 26–45, Springer-Verlag, 1998. The latest version is available from http://www-cse.ucsd.edu/users/mihir/ 72, 73, 74, 75

[3] M. Bellare and P. Rogaway, Optimal asymmetric encryption. In *Proceedings of Advances in Cryptology – Eurocrypt'94*, Lecture Notes in Computer Science Vol. 950, A. De Santis ed., pp. 92–111, Springer-Verlag, 1994. 72

[4] M. Bellare and A. Sahai, Non-Malleable Encryption: Equivalence between Two Notions, and an Indistinguishability-Based Characterization. In *Proceedings of Advances in Cryptology – Crypto'99*, Lecture Notes in Computer Science Vol. 1666, M. Wiener ed., pp. 519–536, Springer-Verlag, 1999. 78, 79

[5] R. Cramer and V. Shoup, A practical public key cryptosystem provably secure against adaptive chosen ciphertext attack. In *Proceedings of Advances in Cryptology – Crypto'98*, Lecture Notes in Computer Science Vol. 1462, H. Krawczyk, ed., pp. 13–25, Springer-Verlag 1998. 72

---

[2] We note that the result holds independent of attack models and the equivalence is also valid for generalized CCA, a slight relaxation of chosen ciphertext attacks (see, e.g., [1]).

[6] D. Dolev, D. Dwork and M. Naor, Non-malleable cryptography, In *Proceedings of the 23rd Annual ACM Symposium on Theory of Computing*, pp. 542–552, 1991; 71
     D. Dolev, D. Dwork and M. Naor, Non-malleable cryptography, *SIAM Journal on Computing* **30**, pp. 391–437, 2000.

[7] O. Goldreich, Foundations of cryptography: basic tools, Cambridge: New York, Cambridge University Press, 2001. The Volume II of this book is available from http://www.wisdom.weizmann.ac.il/~oded/PSBookFrag/enc2.ps 72, 73, 74, 78

[8] O. Goldreich, Foundations of cryptography, Volume II (third posted version), 2002.
     available from http://www.wisdom.weizmann.ac.il/~oded/PSBookFrag/enc.ps 72

[9] O. Goldreich, A uniform complexity treatment of encryption and zero-knowledge, Journal of Cryptology, Vol. 6, pp. 21–53, 1993.

[10] S. Goldwasser and S. Micali, Probabilistic encryption. *Journal of Computer and System Sciences* **28**, pp. 270–299, 1984. 71, 72, 73, 74, 78

[11] S. Micali, C. Rackoff and R. Sloan, The notion of security for probabilistic cryptosystems, *SIAM Journal on Computing* **17**, pp. 412–426, 1988.

[12] M. Naor and M. Yung, Public-key cryptosystems provably secure against chosen ciphertext attacks, In *Proceedings of the 22nd Annual ACM Symposium on Theory of Computing*, pp. 427–437, 1990. 72

[13] C. Rackoff and D. Simon, Non-interactive zero-knowledge proof of knowledge and chosen ciphertext attack, In *Proceedings of Advances in Cryptology – Crypto'91*, Lecture Notes in Computer Science Vol. 576, J. Feigenbaum ed., pp. 433–444, Springer-Verlag, 1991. 72

[14] C. E. Shannon, Communication theory of secrecy systems, *Bell System Technical Journal* **28**, pp. 656–715, 1949. 71, 74

[15] V. Shoup, OAEP Reconsidered, In *Proceedings of Advances in Cryptology – Crypto 2001*, Lecture Notes in Computer Science Vol. 2139, J. Kilian ed., pp. 239–259, Springer-Verlag, 2001. 72

[16] A. Yao, Theory and applications of trapdoor functions, In *Proceedings of the 23rd Symposium on Foundations of Computer Science*, pp. 80–91, IEEE, 1982.

Randomness Re-use in Multi-recipient Encryption Schemeas

Mihir Bellare[1], Alexandra Boldyreva[1], and Jessica Staddon[2]

[1] Dept. of Computer Science & Engineering
University of California at San Diego
9500 Gilman Drive, La Jolla, California 92093, USA
mihir@cs.ucsd.edu
http://www-cse.ucsd.edu/users/mihir
[2] Dept. of Computer Science & Engineering
University of California at San Diego
9500 Gilman Drive, La Jolla, California 92093, USA
aboldyre@cs.ucsd.edu
http://www-cse.ucsd.edu/users/aboldyre

Abstract. Kurosawa showed how one could design multi-receiver encryption schemes achieving savings in bandwidth and computation relative to the naive methods. We broaden the investigation. We identify new types of attacks possible in multi-recipient settings, which were overlooked by the previously suggested models, and specify an appropriate model to incorporate these types of attacks. We then identify a general paradigm that underlies his schemes and also others, namely the re-use of randomness: ciphertexts sent to different receivers by a single sender are computed using the same underlying coins. In order to avoid case by case analysis of encryption schemes to see whether they permit secure randomness re-use, we provide a condition, or test, that when applied to an encryption scheme shows whether or not the associated randomness re-using version of the scheme is secure. As a consequence, our test shows that randomness re-use is secure in the strong sense for asymmetric encryption schemes such as El Gamal, Cramer-Shoup, DHIES, and Boneh and Franklin's escrow El Gamal.

Keywords: Encryption, randomness, provable security, broadcast encryption.

1 Introduction

The standard setting for encryption is that a sender, in possession of the encryption key K of a receiver and a message M that it wants to send privately to this receiver, computes a ciphertext C by applying an encryption algorithm to K and M, and sends C to the receiver. We are interested in a setting where there is one sender but multiple receivers. The sender is in possession of encryption keys $K_1, \ldots, K_n$ of receivers $1, \ldots, n$ respectively, and of message $M_1, \ldots, M_n$ that it wants to send privately to receivers $1, \ldots, n$ respectively. A *multi-recipient*

Y.G. Desmedt (Ed.): PKC 2003, LNCS 2567, pp. 85–99, 2003.

encryption scheme is just like an encryption scheme except that the encryption algorithm is replaced by a (randomized) *multi-recipient encryption algorithm* which, given $K_1, \ldots, K_n$ and $M_1, \ldots, M_n$, outputs ciphertexts $C_1, \ldots, C_n$, with C_i an encryption of M_i under K_i.

There is of course a naive, or obvious way to build a multi-receiver encryption scheme: for each i simply encrypt M_i under K_i using the encryption algorithm of a standard scheme. However, viewing the task of producing multiple ciphertexts as being done by a single process allows one to explore reductions in cost that might arise from batching. In particular it enables different encryptions to be based on the same coins.

In this paper we introduce and define a subclass of multi-recipient encryption sche-mes that we call randomness-reusing multi-recipient encryption schemes. Let $\mathcal{E}$ denote the encryption algorithm of some standard encryption scheme. In the associated randomness-reusing multi-recipient encryption scheme, one picks at random coins r for $\mathcal{E}$, and then, for each i, computes $C_i = \mathcal{E}(K_i, M_i)$. In other words, the different ciphertexts are computed using the same coins.

MOTIVATING EXAMPLES. The definition of randomness-reusing multi-recipient encryption schemes was motivated by the work of Kurosawa [22]. Here is an example from his paper. Suppose a sender wants to send message M_i to receiver i encrypted under the latter's El Gamal public key g^{x_i} ($1 \leq i \leq n$). The naive procedure would be to separately encrypt each message with new coins, meaning pick $r_1, \ldots, r_n$ at random, let $C_i = (g^{r_i}, g^{x_i r_i} \cdot M_i)$, and send C_i to i for $1 \leq i \leq n$. Kurosawa [22] considers picking just one r at random and setting $C_i = (g^r, g^{x_i r} \cdot M_i)$ instead. Kurosawa's main motivation was to reduce bandwidth in the case that the ciphertexts were being broadcast or multi-cast by the sender, since in that case, the transmission would now be $\mathbf{C} = (g^r, g^{x_1 r} \cdot M_1, \ldots, g^{x_n r} \cdot M_n)$, which is about half as many bits as required to transmit the ciphertexts computed by the naive method. However, he also points out that his suggested scheme halves the computational cost (number of exponentiations), a more broadly applicable and perhaps more useful savings than the one in bandwidth. Kurosawa notes similar savings in using the Cramer-Shoup encryption scheme [13].

We note that the technique underlying Kurosawa's scheme is randomness re-use, specifically re-use of r as coins for El Gamal encryption of different messages under different public keys. Accordingly, we are considering randomness re-use at a more general level.

SECURITY ISSUES AND MODEL. Before we can meaningfully address the security of specific multi-recipient encryption schemes such as randomness-reusing ones, we need a model of security. We seek notions of security for multi-recipient encryption schemes, specifically appropriate definitions of IND-CPA and IND-CCA in this context.

Kurosawa [22] proposed such definitions based on a fairly direct adaptation of the definitions of encryption security in the multi-user setting [3, 1]. However, although the latter do explicitly consider the presence of many recipients, they assume all encryptions are produced under independent coins, which is not true for multi-recipient schemes. In particular, we show that Kurosawa's model and definitions fail to cover several practical attacks, and thus security proved under his definitions may not suffice for applications. We remedy this by providing a model that takes the new attacks into account. In Section 4 we specify the model and also provide examples of schemes that can be proven secure in the model of [22] but fall to practical attacks and can be (correctly) shown to be insecure in our model. Let us now highlight some of the new security issues for multi-recipient schemes that we consider.

First are rogue-key attacks. The framework is well-known, and consists of an adversary registering public keys created as a function of public keys of other, legitimate users. This can be particularly damaging in the context of random-string re-use, as we illustrate in Section 4 with a rogue-key attack on Kurosawa's El Gamal based scheme. It is important to be aware of this attack, but it is for such reasons that certification authorities require (or should require) that a user registering a public key prove knowledge of the corresponding secret key. (In that case, this attack fails.) The assumption we make in this paper is that the adversary cannot register a public key without knowing the corresponding secret key. The assumption is built into our formal model by requiring the adversary, at the time it corrupts a user, to supply not only a public key for that user, but also a corresponding secret key.

Second are insider attacks. An adversary who is one of the legitimate recipients can decrypt a received ciphertext, and might then obtain the coins r underlying the encryption. This is not a concern if, as in [1, 3], encryptions to other recipients use independent coins, and thus these works do not consider insider attacks. But in a multi-recipient scheme, the ciphertext sent to another recipient might be based on the same coins r, and thus the adversary might obtain information about the plaintext underlying this ciphertext too. Our model takes this into account, by allowing the adversary to corrupt some fraction of the users and choose secret and public keys for them. We present a variant of Kurosawa's El Gamal based randomness re-use scheme that is provably secure in his model but insecure under our model due to insider attacks. The attack is a practical one, highlighting the value of the enhanced model in capturing real attacks.

REPRODUCIBILITY PROPERTY AND THEOREM. Not all encryption schemes can securely re-use randomness. An example of a class of schemes that cannot are RSA embedding schemes such as PKCS#1: we illustrate in Section 3 how Håstad's attacks [19] can be exploited to break these schemes if randomness is re-used in generation of ciphertexts for three different receivers. Thus, an important issue is, given an encryption scheme, determine whether or not it permits secure randomness re-use.

Looking at the description of the existing encryption scheme it is easy to decide whether re-use of randomness will allow computational or bandwidth savings. However, it is not clear how to check whether this can be done securely. Case by case analysis of the many existing encryption schemes, e.g. following the proof techniques of [22] although possible, would be prohibitive. One of the main contributions of this paper is a way to establish that an encryption scheme permits secure randomness re-use based on existing security results about the scheme. It takes two parts: definition of a property of encryption schemes called *reproducibility*, and a theorem, called the *reproducibility theorem*. The latter says that if an encryption scheme is reproducible and is IND-CPA (resp. IND-CCA) in the standard, single-receiver setting, then the corresponding randomness re-using multi-recipient scheme is also IND-CPA (resp. IND-CCA) with respect to our notions of security for such schemes. It is usually easy to check whether a given encryption scheme is reproducible, and the test and theorem are valid for several asymmetric schemes, so numerous applications follow.

Reproducibility itself is quite simply explained. Focusing on the asymmetric case, let pk_1, pk_2 be public encryption keys, and let $C_1 = \mathcal{E}_{pk_1}(M_1, r)$ be a ciphertext of a message M_1 created under key pk_1 based on random string r. We say that the encryption scheme is *reproducible* if, given pk_1, pk_2, C_1, any message M_2, and the secret decryption key sk_2 corresponding to pk_2, there is a polynomial time *reproduction algorithm* that returns the ciphertext $C_2 = \mathcal{E}_{pk_2}(M_2, r)$. It might seem at first as a counter-intuitive property, exploiting some weakness of the encryption scheme. We show, however, that reproducibility itself does not compromise security and moreover, permits secure randomness re-use.

We now discuss applications of the reproducibility test and theorem to various asymmetric schemes.

EL GAMAL AND CRAMER-SHOUP. The corresponding randomness re-using schemes are those of Kurosawa [22], which he proved secure under the DDH (Decisional Diffie-Hellman) assumption. As noted above, however, his target notion of security is weak. Thus one needs to ask whether the schemes remain secure under our stronger notion of security. This is important because these are the schemes permitting the computation and broadcast ciphertext size-reductions noted above.

We show that the base El Gamal and Cramer-Shoup schemes are both reproducible, and our reproducibility theorem then says that indeed, Kurosawa's schemes remain secure with respect to our more stringent security notions. We then extend these results by providing reductions of improved concrete security. These improvements bypass the reproducibility theorem, instead directly exploiting the reproducibility property of the base schemes and, as in [3], using self-reducibility properties of the DDH problem [28, 24, 27].

DHIES. This is a Diffie-Hellman based asymmetric encryption scheme adopted by draft standards ANSI X9.63EC and IEEE P1363a. It has El Gamal-like cost in public-key operations while achieving Cramer-Shoup-like security (IND-CCA), although the proof [2] relies on significantly stronger assumptions than the DDH assumption used in [13]. Unlike El Gamal and Cramer-Shoup it does not assume the plaintext is a group element, but handles arbitrary plaintext strings via an integrated construction involving a symmetric encryption scheme. Randomness re-use for this scheme is attractive since it results in bandwidth and computational savings in various applications just as for the El Gamal scheme, so it is important to assess security.

We consider the case when the symmetric encryption scheme used in (asymmetric) DHIES scheme is CBC mode combined with any block cipher, e.g. AES (the most popular choice in practice) and show that then DHIES is reproducible. As usual, our reproducibility theorem then implies that the corresponding randomness re-using multi-recipient scheme is IND-CCA under the assumptions used to establish that DHIES is IND-CCA.

PAIRINGS-BASED ESCROW EL GAMAL. Boneh and Franklin [10] introduced an El Gamal like scheme with global escrow capabilities, based on the Weil pairing. We show that this scheme is reproducible. Our reproducibility theorem coupled with the result of [10] then implies that the corresponding randomness re-using multi-recipient scheme is IND-CPA in the random oracle model under the Bilinear Diffie-Hellman assumption. Our reproducibility algorithm exploits properties of the Weil pairing. Again, as for El Gamal scheme, re-using randomness permits computational and bandwidth savings.

RANDOMNESS RE-USE IN SYMMETRIC ENCRYPTION A novel element of our work compared to [22, 3] is consideration of the symmetric setting. In the full version of this paper [4] we show that reproducibility and the corresponding theorem apply in this setting too. We prove that CBC encryption with random IV, based on a given block cipher permits secure randomness re-use in the multi-recipient setting.

MINIMAL ASSUMPTIONS. In we determine minimal assumptions under which one can prove the existence of an encryption scheme permitting secure randomness re-use. We show that there exists an encryption scheme which under randomness re-use yields an IND-CPA multi-receiver encryption scheme if and only if there exists a standard IND-CPA encryption scheme. The analog holds for IND-CCA, and these results hold in both the symmetric and the asymmetric settings.

2   Definitions

We recall the standard definitions. An *asymmetric encryption scheme* $\mathcal{AE} = (\mathcal{G}, \mathcal{K}, \mathcal{E}, \mathcal{D})$ consists of four polynomial-time algorithms. The randomized *common-key generation* algorithm $\mathcal{G}$ takes as input a security parameter $k \in \mathbb{N}$ and returns a *common key* I; we write $I \stackrel{R}{\leftarrow} \mathcal{G}(k)$. I could include a prime number and a generator of a group, which all parties use to create their keys.) The randomized *key generation* algorithm $\mathcal{K}$ takes as input the common key I and returns a pair (pk, sk) consisting of a public key and a corresponding secret key; we write $(pk, sk) \stackrel{R}{\leftarrow} \mathcal{K}(I)$. In our context it is important to make explicit the random choices underlying the (randomized) *encryption* algorithm $\mathcal{E}$. On input a public key pk, a plaintext M, and coin tosses r, it returns the ciphertext $C = \mathcal{E}_{pk}(M; r)$. The notation $C \stackrel{R}{\leftarrow} \mathcal{E}_{pk}(M)$ is shorthand for $r \stackrel{R}{\leftarrow} \text{Coins}_{\mathcal{E}}(I, pk)$; $C \leftarrow \mathcal{E}_{pk}(M; r)$, where $\text{Coins}_{\mathcal{E}}(I, pk)$ is a set from which $\mathcal{E}$ draws its coins. The deterministic *decryption* algorithm $\mathcal{D}$ takes the secret key sk and a ciphertext C to return the corresponding plaintext or a special symbol $\perp$ indicating that the ciphertext was invalid; we write $x \leftarrow \mathcal{D}_{sk}(C)$. Associated to each common key I is a *message space* $\mathrm{MsgSp}(I)$ from which M is allowed to be drawn. We require that $\mathcal{D}_{sk}(\mathcal{E}_{pk}(M)) = M$ for all $M \in \mathrm{MsgSp}(I)$. We will use the terms "plaintext" and "message" interchangeably.

Let $\mathrm{Adv}_{\mathcal{AE}, A_{\mathrm{cpa}}}^{\mathrm{cpa}}(\cdot)$ (resp. $\mathrm{Adv}_{\mathcal{AE}, A_{\mathrm{cca}}}^{\mathrm{cca}}(\cdot)$) denote the advantage of adversary A_{cpa} (resp. A_{cca}) in breaking the scheme $\mathcal{AE}$ under a chosen-plaintext (resp. chosen-cipher-text) attack, as per the usual standard notions of security IND-CPA and IND-CCA. (We recall the formal definitions in [4]).

MULTI-RECIPIENT ENCRYPTION SCHEMES. In order to allow consideration of methods of producing multiple ciphertexts based on the same randomness, this paper introduces a primitive that we call a multi-recipient encryption scheme. Formally an *asymmetric multi-recipient encryption scheme* $\overline{\mathcal{AE}} = (\mathcal{G}, \mathcal{K}, \overline{\mathcal{E}}, \mathcal{D})$ consists of four algorithms. The common-key generation algorithm $\mathcal{G}$, the key generation algorithm $\mathcal{K}$, and the decryption algorithm $\mathcal{D}$ are as in a standard asymmetric encryption scheme above. On input a *public-key vector* $\mathbf{pk} = (\mathbf{pk}[1], \ldots, \mathbf{pk}[n])$, a *plaintext vector* $\mathbf{M} = (\mathbf{M}[1], \ldots, \mathbf{M}[n])$, and coin tosses r, the *multi-encryption* algorithm $\overline{\mathcal{E}}$ returns the *ciphertext vector* $\mathbf{C} = (\mathbf{C}[1], \ldots, \mathbf{C}[n]) = \overline{\mathcal{E}}_{\mathbf{pk}}(\mathbf{M})$. The notation $\mathbf{C} \xleftarrow{R} \overline{\mathcal{E}}_{\mathbf{pk}}(\mathbf{M})$ is shorthand for $r \xleftarrow{R} \mathrm{Coins}_{\overline{\mathcal{E}}}(I, \mathbf{pk})$; $\mathbf{C} \leftarrow \overline{\mathcal{E}}_{\mathbf{pk}}(\mathbf{M}; r)$, where $\mathrm{Coins}_{\overline{\mathcal{E}}}(I, \mathbf{pk})$ is a set from which $\mathcal{E}$ draws its coins. Associated with a common key I is a *message space* $\mathrm{MsgSp}(I)$ from which the components of $\mathbf{M}$ are allowed to be drawn. We require that for all $\mathbf{M}$ with components in the message space, the following experiment returns 1 with probability 1:

For $i = 1, \ldots, n$ do $(\mathbf{pk}[i], \mathbf{sk}[i]) \xleftarrow{R} \mathcal{K}(k)$ EndFor; $\mathbf{C} \xleftarrow{R} \overline{\mathcal{E}}_{\mathbf{pk}}(\mathbf{M})$;
$i \xleftarrow{R} \{1, \ldots, n\}$; If $(\mathcal{D}_{\mathbf{sk}[i]} \mathbf{C}[i]) = \mathbf{M}[i]$ then return 1 else return 0

SRS MUTLI-RECEIVER ENCRYPTION SCHEME. We are interested in a specific multi-receiver encryption scheme, obtained from a given asymmetric encryption scheme by using the same coins to encrypt the different messages in the message vector.

Definition 1. *The same random string (SRS) multi-receiver encryption scheme associated to a given asymmetric encryption scheme* $\mathcal{AE} = (\mathcal{G}, \mathcal{K}, \mathcal{E}, \mathcal{D})$ *is the multi-recipient encryption scheme* $\overline{\mathcal{AE}} = (\mathcal{G}, \mathcal{K}, \overline{\mathcal{E}}, \mathcal{D})$ *in which the common key generation, key generation algorithms and decryption algorithms are that of* $\mathcal{AE}$ *and the multi-recipient encryption algorithm is defined as follows:*

$\overline{\mathcal{E}}_{\mathbf{pk}}(\mathbf{M})$
        Let n be the number of components of $\mathbf{M}$ *[and also of* $\mathbf{pk}$*]*
        $r \xleftarrow{R} \mathrm{Coins}_{\mathcal{E}}(I, \mathbf{pk})$;
        For $i = 1, \ldots n$ do $\mathbf{C}[i] \leftarrow \mathcal{E}_{pk_i}(\mathbf{M}[i]; r)$ *EndFor Return* $\mathbf{C}$.
We refer to $\mathcal{AE}$ *as the base scheme of* $\overline{\mathcal{AE}}$.

We do not specify how $\mathbf{C}[i]$ is communicated to user i. It could be that the whole ciphertext vector $\mathbf{C}$ is sent via a broadcast or multi-cast channel and, if all $\mathbf{C}[i]$

have a common part due to a randomness re-use, this part can be sent only once. It could also be that $\mathbf{C}[i]$ is sent to party i directly. This issue depends on the specific application and is not relevant for security of the scheme. For examples of SRS schemes see Section 6.

3   Not Every SRS Scheme is Secure

We consider general embedding schemes which first apply a randomized invertible transform to a message and then apply a trapdoor permutation to the result. The example of such schemes is RSA-PKCS#1 [25] that has been proven to be IND-CCA secure (in the random oracle model) [16] and hence is also IND-CCA secure in a multi-user setting [1, 3]. Nonetheless, the associated SRS scheme is insecure. The attack is as follows. Let N_i be the public modulus of user i and assume all users have encryption exponent 3. Suppose the sender wants to send a single message M to three receivers, namely $\mathbf{M} = (M, M, M)$. Under the SRS scheme, it will pick a random string r, using M and a random r will compute a transform x, set $\mathbf{C}[i] = x^3 \bmod N_i$, and send $\mathbf{C}[i]$ to i. An adversary given $\mathbf{C}$ can use Håstad's attack (based on the fact that the modulii are relatively prime) to recover x, and them recover M by inverting the transform. The same attack applies regardless of embedding method, since the latter must be an invertible transform.

This indicates that secure randomness re-use is not possible for *all* base encryption schemes: there exist base encryption schemes that are secure, yet the associated the SRS multi-recipient encryption scheme is not secure. As we will see later, no encryption scheme where the random string used in encryption algorithm is a by-product of decryption can be a base of a secure SRS scheme,however, there are large classes of base encryption schemes for which the associated SRS scheme is secure. Before we can get there, we need to discuss what "secure" means.

4   Security of Multi-recipient Schemes

We provide the definition and follow it with a discussion illustrating how it takes into account the various security issues mentioned in the introduction.

MODEL AND DEFINITION. Let $\overline{\mathcal{AE}} = (\mathcal{G}, \mathcal{K}, \overline{\mathcal{E}}, \mathcal{D})$ be an asymmetric, multi-recipient encryption scheme. (We are particularly interested in the case where this is an SRS scheme, but the definition is not restricted to this case.) Let n be a polynomial. For atk $\in \{\mathrm{cpa}, \mathrm{cca}\}$ and for an adversary B attacking the scheme we define the experiment $\mathbf{Exp}_{\overline{\mathcal{AE}},B}^{n\text{-mr-atk-b}}(k)$ as follows. B runs in three stages. In the select stage the adversary is given an initial information string and outputs l such that $1 \leq l \leq n$, which indicates that it wants to corrupt $n - l$ users, assumed without loss of generality to be users $l + 1, \ldots, n$. In the find stage the adversary is given I and the public keys of the honest users $1, \ldots, l$. It outputs *two* l-vectors of messages corresponding to choices for the honest users;

one $(n - l)$-vector of messages corresponding to choices for the corrupted users;
a $(n - l)$-vector of public keys for the corrupted users; and a $(n - l)$-vector of
corresponding secret keys (see the discussion below.) Based on a challenge bit b,
one of the two l-vectors is selected, and the components of the $(n - l)$-vector of
messages are appended to yield a challenge n-vector of messages $\mathbf{M}$. The latter
is encrypted via the multi-encryption algorithm to yield a challenge ciphertext
$\mathbf{C}$ that is returned to the adversary, now in its guess stage. It wins if it returns
a bit d that equals the challenge bit b. In each stage the adversary will output
state information that is returned to it in the next stage. When atk = cca, the
adversary gets oracles $\mathcal{D}_{sk_i}(\cdot)$ for $1 \leq i \leq l$ with the restriction of not querying
them on the corresponding components of the challenge ciphertext vector.

Definition 2. *Let* $\overline{\mathcal{AE}} = (\mathcal{G}, \mathcal{K}, \overline{\mathcal{E}}, \mathcal{D})$ *be a multi-recipient encryption scheme,
let n be a polynomial and let* atk $\in$ {cpa, cca}. *Then for any security parameter k*
ind-*atk advantage of an adversary B is*

$$\mathsf{Adv}_{\overline{\mathcal{AE}},B}^{n\text{-}mr\text{-}atk}(k) \;=\; \Pr\left[\, \mathbf{Exp}_{\overline{\mathcal{AE}},B}^{n\text{-}mr\text{-}atk\text{-}0}(k) = 0 \right] - \Pr\left[\, \mathbf{Exp}_{\overline{\mathcal{AE}},B}^{n\text{-}mr\text{-}atk\text{-}1}(k) = 0 \right].$$

Definition 3. *Let* $\overline{\mathcal{AE}} = (\mathcal{G}, \mathcal{K}, \overline{\mathcal{E}}, \mathcal{D})$ *be a multi-recipient encryption scheme.
We say that it is IND-CPA (resp. IND-CCA) secure if the function*
$\mathsf{Adv}_{\overline{\mathcal{AE}},B}^{n\text{-}mr\text{-}cpa}(\cdot)$ *(respectively* $\mathsf{Adv}_{\overline{\mathcal{AE}},B}^{n\text{-}mr\text{-}cca}(\cdot)$*) is negligible for any polynomial-time
adversary B and any polynomial n.*

It is convenient to introduce a notion of security for base encryption schemes
based on the security of the corresponding SRS scheme. We stress that the
following is a notion of security for (standard) asymmetric encryption schemes,
not for multi-recipient encryption schemes.

Definition 4. *Let* $\mathcal{AE}$ *be an asymmetric encryption scheme. We say that it
is SRS-IND-CPA (resp. SRS-IND-CCA) secure (or, briefly SRSS) if the SRS
multi-recipient asymmetric encryption scheme* $\overline{\mathcal{AE}}$ *associated to* $\mathcal{AE}$ *is IND-CPA
(resp. IND-CCA) secure.*

DISCUSSION AND COMPARISON WITH THE MODEL OF SECURITY OF [22]. Previous works [1, 3, 22] only considered outsider attacks, meaning the adversary
was not one of the receivers. A novel element of our model relative to [1, 3, 22]
is the consideration of insider attacks. The adversary is allowed to corrupt some
fraction of the users and choose secret and public keys for them.

We argue that it is necessary for a model of security of multi-recipient schemes
to take into account insider attacks. The model of [22] does not address this
problem and we show that there exist multi-recipient encryption schemes which
can be proven secure using the model of [22] but are obviously insecure and can
easily be shown insecure using our model of security.

It is proved in [22] that El Gamal scheme permits secure randomness re-use
in the multi-recipient setting. Now consider a modified encryption scheme which
differs from El Gamal in that its encryption algorithm when invoked on one
particular public key (e.g. g^3) in addition to a ciphertext returns randomness

used to compute it. Assume this fact is known to the adversary. When this scheme used in a multi-recipient setting with randomness re-use the adversary can certify this public key and later after receiving a ciphertext can obtain the random string used to compute the ciphertexts of other users and thus break the scheme. Under our model the advantage of such adversary in breaking this scheme will be 1. But in the model of [22] all the public keys assumed to be random, and the scheme can be proven secure.

Consider another example which exploits a different weakness of the model of [22]. Let $\mathcal{AE}' = (\mathcal{G}', \mathcal{K}', \mathcal{E}', \mathcal{D}')$ be some IND-CPA secure encryption scheme. Consider a multi-recipient scheme $\overline{\mathcal{AE}}$ with user i's public key $pk_i = (g^{x_i}, pk'_i)$, where g^{x_i} is a public key for El Gamal encryption and pk'_i is a public key of $\mathcal{AE}'$. Let the encryption algorithm of $\mathcal{AE}'$ be as follows. It first draws a random value r at random. Then it computes $C[i]$ as $(g^r, (g^{x_i})^r M[i], C'[i])$ where $C'[i] = \mathcal{E}'_{pk'_i}(r)$. In other words each ciphertext consists of an El Gamal ciphertext computed with common randomness and of encryption of this common randomness under some fixed encryption scheme. We claim that there exists an attack on $\overline{\mathcal{AE}}$ but the scheme can be proven secure under the model of [22]. We first show that $\overline{\mathcal{AE}}$ is insecure in practice by presenting an attack. An adversary A "corrupts" the first user and chooses $pk_1 = (g^{x_1}, pk'_1)$ in normal way so that it knows x_1, sk'_1. When A receives a ciphertext vector $\mathbf{C}$ it decrypts $C'[1]$ using sk'_1 and obtains r. Now A can test whether particular messages were encrypted under the public keys of other users. Under our model of security A would have advantage 1. We now show that $\overline{\mathcal{AE}}$ is secure under the model of [22]. Let B be an adversary attacking $\overline{\mathcal{AE}}$ under the model of [22]. Then it is possible to construct an adversary D which attacks SRS El Gamal multi-recipient scheme. But [22] proves the latter scheme is secure, so this would imply that $\overline{\mathcal{AE}}$ is secure. D simply provides all the public keys it is given to B and outputs message vectors that B outputs. D then receives a challenge ciphertext vector $\mathbf{C}_D$, picks a random r' and computes a challenge $\mathbf{C}_B$ for B such that $\mathbf{C}_B[i] = (\mathbf{C}_D[i], \mathcal{E}'_{pk'_i}(r'))$. Since $\mathcal{AE}'$ is IND-CPA then the view of B in the simulated experiment is indistinguishable from the real experiment. Therefore the advantage of B is at most the advantage of D, but it is proven in [22] that the latter is negligible.

Moreover, the model of [22], as well as of [3, 1] do not take into account the possibility of rogue-key attack. This can be particularly damaging in the context of random-string re-use. For example, suppose the adversary registers public keys $(g^x)^2 = g^{2x}$ and $(g^x)^3 = g^{3x}$ where g^x is the key of a legitimate user. Suppose that symmetric session keys K_1, K, K are El Gamal encrypted with the same randomness r under public keys g^x, g^{2x}, g^{3x} and broadcast to the users. Thus the adversary sees the three corresponding ciphertexts $(g^r, g^{rx} \cdot K_1), (g^r, g^{2rx} \cdot K), (g^r, g^{3rx} \cdot K)$. From them it can compute $K_1 = [g^{rx} \cdot K_1] \cdot [g^{2rx} \cdot K] \cdot [g^{3rx} \cdot K]^{-1}$ and obtain the session key of the legitimate user. As a consequence, the adversary will be able to decrypt the secret information encrypted under this session key addressed to the legitimate user.

As we mentioned in the introduction, to prevent attacks of this type we put some limitation on the adversary in this regard, in particular to disallow it from creating public keys whose corresponding secret keys it does not know. The model incorporates this by requiring the adversary to supply, along with public keys for the corrupted users, corresponding secret keys. This models the effect of appropriate proofs of knowledge of the secret key that are assumed to be done as part of the key certification process. The alternative is to explicitly consider the certification process in the model, and then, in proofs of security, use the extractors, guaranteed by the proof of knowledge property [6], to extract the secret keys from the adversary. This being quite a complication of the model, we have chosen to build in the intended effects of the proofs of knowledge.

5   Reproducibility Test and Theorem

We provide a condition under which a given encryption scheme can be a base of the secure SRS scheme. Informally speaking, the condition is satisfied for those encryption schemes for which it is possible, using a public key and ciphertext of a random message, to create ciphertexts for arbitrary messages under arbitrary keys, such that all ciphertexts employ the same random string as that of the given ciphertext.

Definition 5. *Fix a public-key encryption scheme* $\mathcal{AE} = (\mathcal{G}, \mathcal{K}, \mathcal{E}, \mathcal{D})$. *Let n be polynomial in k, and let R be an algorithm that takes as input a public key and ciphertext of a random message, another random message together with a public-secret key pair, and returns a ciphertext. Consider the following experiment.*

Experiment $\mathbf{Exp}_{\mathcal{AE},R}^{repr}(k)$
$\quad I \xleftarrow{R} \mathcal{G}(k) \ ; \ (pk, sk) \xleftarrow{R} \mathcal{K}(I) \ ; \ M \xleftarrow{R} \mathrm{MsgSp}(I) \ ; \ r \xleftarrow{R} Coins_{\mathcal{E}}(I, pk)$
$\quad C \leftarrow \mathcal{E}_{pk}(M, r) \ ; \ (pk', sk') \xleftarrow{R} \mathcal{K}(I) \ ; \ M' \xleftarrow{R} \mathrm{MsgSp}(I)$
$\quad \mathit{If} \ (\mathcal{E}_{pk'}(M', r) = R(pk, C, M', pk', sk')) \ \mathit{then \ Return \ 1 \ else \ Return \ 0 \ EndIf}$

We say that $\mathcal{AE}$ is reproducible if for any k there exists a probabilistic, poly-time algorithm R called the reproduction algorithm such that $\mathbf{Exp}_{\mathcal{AE},R}^{repr}(k)$ *outputs 1 with the probability 1.*

Later we will show that many popular discrete-log-based encryption schemes are reproducible. It is an open question whether there exist reproducible encryption schemes of other types.

We now state the main reproducibility theorem. It implies that if an encryption scheme is reproducible and is IND-CPA (resp. IND-CCA) secure, then it is also SRS-IND-CPA (resp. SRS-IND-CCA) secure. The proof is in the full version of this paper [4].

Theorem 1. *Fix a public-key encryption scheme* $\mathcal{AE} = (\mathcal{G}, \mathcal{K}, \mathcal{E}, \mathcal{D})$ *and a polynomial $n(\cdot)$. Let $\overline{\mathcal{AE}} = (\mathcal{G}, \mathcal{K}, \overline{\mathcal{E}}, \mathcal{D})$ be the associated SRS scheme. If $\mathcal{AE}$ is reproducible then for any poly-time adversary B_{atk}, there exists a poly-time adversary A_{atk}, where $\mathrm{atk} = \{\mathrm{cpa}, \mathrm{cca}\}$, such that for any k*

$$\mathrm{Adv}_{\overline{\mathcal{AE}}, B_{\mathrm{atk}}}^{n\text{-}\mathrm{mr}\text{-}\mathrm{atk}}(k) \ \leq \ n(k) \cdot \mathrm{Adv}_{\mathcal{AE}, A_{\mathrm{atk}}}^{\mathrm{atk}}(k).$$

6   Analysis of Specific Schemes

In this section we show that many popular encryption schemes are reproducible. Using the known results about security of these schemes and the result of Theorem 1 this would imply that these schemes are also SRSS.

We first consider three DDH-based schemes which work over a group of prime order. A *prime-order-group generator* is a probabilistic algorithm that on input the security parameter k returns a pair (q, g) satisfying the following conditions: q is a prime with $2^{k-1} < q < 2^k$; $2q + 1$ is a prime; and g is a generator of G_q.

EL GAMAL. Let $\mathcal{G}$ be a prime-order-group generator. This is the common key generation algorithm of the El Gamal scheme $\mathcal{EG} = (\mathcal{G}, \mathcal{K}, \mathcal{E}, \mathcal{D})$, the rest of the algorithms are as follows:

$\mathcal{K}(q, g)$:	$\mathcal{E}_{pk}(M)$:	$\mathcal{D}_{sk}(Y, W)$:
$x \xleftarrow{R} Z_q$; $X \leftarrow g^x$	$r \xleftarrow{R} Z_q$; $Y \leftarrow g^r$	$T \leftarrow Y^x$
$pk \leftarrow (q, g, X)$; $sk \leftarrow (q, g, x)$	$T \leftarrow X^r$; $W \leftarrow TM$	$M \leftarrow WT^{-1}$
Return (pk, sk)	Return (Y, W)	Return M

Lemma 1. *The El Gamal encryption scheme* $\mathcal{EG} = (\mathcal{G}, \mathcal{K}, \mathcal{E}, \mathcal{D})$ *is reproducible.*

Proof. On input $(g^x, (g^r, g^{rx} \cdot M), M', g^{x'}, x')$ a polynomial time reproduction algorithm R returns $(g^r, (g^r)^{x'} \cdot M')$. It is easy to see that R always outputs a valid ciphertext which is created using the same random string as the given ciphertext and therefore the experiment $\mathbf{Exp}^{repr}_{\mathcal{EG}, R}(k)$ always outputs 1.

The El Gamal scheme in a group of prime order is known to be IND-CPA under the assumption that the decision Diffie-Hellman (DDH) problem is hard. (This is noted in [12, 24, 13, 29]). Let $\mathsf{Adv}^{ddh}_{\mathcal{G}, D}()$ denote the advantage of D in solving the Decisional Diffie-Hellman (DDH) problem for $\mathcal{G}$. We say that the DDH problem is hard for $\mathcal{G}$ if the function $\mathsf{Adv}^{ddh}_{\mathcal{G}, D}(\cdot)$ is negligible for every algorithm D whose time-complexity is polynomial in k. (We recall the full formal definition for the DDH problem in [3].) Theorem 1 and Lemma 1 imply that it is also SRS-IND-CPA or, equivalently, $\overline{\mathcal{EG}}$ is IND-CPA secure and the security degrades linearly as the number of users n increases. The following theorem shows that it is possible to obtain a tighter relation than the one implied by Theorem 1.

Theorem 2. *Let* $\mathcal{G}$ *be a prime-order-group generator,* $\mathcal{EG} = (\mathcal{G}, \mathcal{K}, \mathcal{E}, \mathcal{D})$ *the associated El Gamal encryption scheme, and* $\overline{\mathcal{EG}} = (\mathcal{G}, \mathcal{K}, \overline{\mathcal{E}}, \mathcal{D})$ *the associated SRS multi-recipient encryption scheme as per Construction 1. Let* n *be a polynomial. Then for any adversary* B *there exists a distinguisher* D *such that for any* k*

$$\mathsf{Adv}^{n\text{-}mr\text{-}cpa}_{\overline{\mathcal{EG}}, B}(k) \leq 2 \cdot \mathsf{Adv}^{ddh}_{\mathcal{G}, D}(k) + \frac{1}{2^{k-2}},$$

where the running time of D *is one of* B *plus* $O(n(k) \cdot k^3)$*.*

The proof of the above theorem is in the full version of this paper [4]. [22] proves a similar result but for a weaker notion of security of multi-recipient schemes.

$\mathcal{G}(k)$:

$(q, g_1) \xleftarrow{R} \overline{\mathcal{G}}$
$g_2 \xleftarrow{R} G_q$
$K \xleftarrow{R} \mathcal{GH}(k)$
Return $(q, g_1,$
$\quad g_2, K)$

$\mathcal{K}(q, g_1, g_2, K)$:

$x_1, x_2, y_1, y_2, z \xleftarrow{R} Z_q$
$c \leftarrow g_1^{x_1} g_2^{x_2} \ ; \ d \leftarrow g_1^{y_1} g_2^{y_2}$
$h \leftarrow g_1^z$
$pk \leftarrow (g_1, g_2, c, d, h, K)$
$sk \leftarrow (x_1, x_2, y_1, y_2, z)$
Return (pk, sk)

$\mathcal{E}_{pk}(M)$:

$r \xleftarrow{R} Z_q$
$u_1 \leftarrow g_1^r \ ; \ u_2 \leftarrow g_2^r$
$e \leftarrow h^r M$
$\alpha \leftarrow \mathcal{EH}_K(u_1, u_2, e)$
$v \leftarrow c^r d^{r\alpha}$
Return (u_1, u_2, e, v)

$\mathcal{D}_{sk}(u_1, u_2, e, v)$:

$\alpha \leftarrow \mathcal{EH}_K(u_1, u_2, e)$
If $u_1^{x_1 + y_1 \alpha} u_2^{x_2 + y_2 \alpha} = v$
$\quad$ then $M \leftarrow e/u_1^z$
$\quad$ else $M \leftarrow \perp$
EndIf
Return M

Fig. 1. Cramer-Shoup scheme

CRAMER-SHOUP. We now consider an SRS encryption scheme based on the Cramer-Shoup scheme [13] in order to get IND-CCA security properties. We first recall the Cramer-Shoup scheme. Let $\overline{\mathcal{G}}$ be a prime-order-group generator. The algorithms of the associated Cramer-Shoup scheme $\mathcal{CS} = (\mathcal{G}, \mathcal{K}, \mathcal{E}, \mathcal{D})$ are depicted in Figure 1. The proof of the following lemma is in [4].

Lemma 2. *The Cramer-Shoup encryption scheme* $\mathcal{CS} = (\mathcal{G}, \mathcal{K}, \mathcal{E}, \mathcal{D})$ *is reproducible.*

Let $\mathsf{Adv}_{\mathcal{H}, C}^{cr}(k)$ denote the advantage of an adversary C breaking collision-resistance of $\mathcal{H}$ (the full version [4] recalls the formal definition of collision resistance). If the DDH problem is hard for $\mathcal{G}$ and if $\mathcal{H}$ is collision-resistant then $\mathcal{CS}$ is IND-CCA secure [13]. Theorem 1 and Lemma 2 imply that it is also SRS-IND-CCA or, equivalently, $\overline{\mathcal{CS}}$ is IND-CCA secure. We match the result of [22] in getting a better security result than the one implied by Theorem 1 but we do it for a stronger notion of security of multi-recipient schemes. The following theorem states our improvement. The proof is in [4].

Theorem 3. *Let* $\mathcal{G}$ *be a prime-order-group generator,* $\mathcal{CS} = (\mathcal{G}, \mathcal{K}, \mathcal{E}, \mathcal{D})$ *the associated Cramer-Shoup encryption scheme and* $\overline{\mathcal{CS}} = (\mathcal{G}, \mathcal{K}, \overline{\mathcal{E}}, \mathcal{D})$ *the associated SRS multi-recipient encryption scheme as per Construction 1. Let* n *be a polynomial. Then for any adversary* B, *which makes* q_d *decryption oracle queries, there exists an adversary* A, *a distinguisher* D *and an adversary* C *such that for any* k

$$\mathsf{Adv}_{\overline{\mathcal{CS}}, B}^{n\text{-}mr\text{-}cca}(k) \leq 2\mathsf{Adv}_{\mathcal{G}, D}^{ddh}(k) + 2\mathsf{Adv}_{\mathcal{H}, C}^{cr}(k) + \frac{q_d(k) + 2}{2^{k-3}},$$

and the running time of D *and* C *is that of* B *plus* $O(n(k) \cdot k^3)$.

DHIES. We consider another DDH-based encryption scheme, DHIES [2], which is in several draft standards. It combines public and symmetric key encryption methods, a message authentication code and a hash function and provides security against chosen-ciphertext attacks. Let $\mathsf{SE} = (\mathrm{K}, \mathrm{E}, \mathrm{D})$ be a symmetric encryption scheme with key length kl and let $\mathsf{MAC} = (\mathcal{T}, \mathcal{V})$ be a message authentication code with key length ml, tagging algorithm $\mathcal{T}$ and verification algo-

$\mathcal{E}_{(q,g,X)}(M)$:

$r \xleftarrow{R} Z_q$; $Y \leftarrow g^r$; $K \leftarrow H(X^r)$
Let sk_m be the first ml bits of K
Let sk_e be the last kl bits of K
$C \xleftarrow{R} \mathsf{E}_{sk_e}(M)$; $T \leftarrow \mathcal{T}_{sk_m}(C)$
Return (Y, C, T)

$\mathcal{D}_x(Y, C, T)$:

$K \leftarrow H(Y^x)$
Let sk_m be the first ml bits of K
Let sk_e be the last kl bits of K
$M \leftarrow \mathsf{D}_{sk_e}(C)$
If $\mathcal{V}_{sk_m}(M, T) = 1$ then Return M
else Return $\perp$ EndIf

Fig. 2. DHIES

rithm $\mathcal{V}$. Let $H: \{0,1\}^{gl} \rightarrow \{0,1\}^{ml+kl}$ be a function. We assume MAC is deterministic. The common key and key generation algorithms of $\mathcal{DHIES}[\text{SE},H,\text{MAC}]$ $= (\mathcal{G}, \mathcal{K}, \mathcal{E}, \mathcal{D})$ are the same as the ones of El Gamal encryption scheme. The rest of the algorithms are in Figure 2. The proof of the following is in [4].

Lemma 3. *Let the symmetric encryption scheme used by DHIES scheme be any block cipher such as AES in CBC mode (we will refer to it as $\mathcal{CBC}$ encryption scheme.) Then $\mathcal{DHIES}[\mathcal{CBC}, H, \text{MAC}] = (\mathcal{G}, \mathcal{K}, \mathcal{E}, \mathcal{D})$ is reproducible.*

ESCROW EL GAMAL. Boneh and Franklin [10] suggested the El Gamal encryption scheme with global escrow capabilities. The $\mathcal{EEG} = (\mathcal{G}, \mathcal{K}, \mathcal{E}, \mathcal{D})$ scheme uses Weil pairing and is defined as follows. The algorithm $\mathcal{G}$ on input the security parameter k chooses a k-bit prime p such that $p \equiv 2 \mod 3$ and $p = 6q - 1$ for some prime $q \geq 3$. Let E be the elliptic curve defined by $y^2 = x^3 + 1$ over F_p. Then it chooses a random $P \in E/\mathsf{F}_p$ of order q, computes $Q = sP$ for a random $s \in Z_q^*$ and chooses a hash function $H: \mathsf{F}_{p^2} \rightarrow \{0,1\}^m$. The message space is $\{0,1\}^m$. The escrow key is s. $\mathcal{G}$ outputs (p, m, P, Q, H). The rest of the algorithms are as follows:

$\mathcal{K}(p, m, P, Q, H)$:

$x \xleftarrow{R} Z_q^*$; $X \leftarrow xP$
$pk \leftarrow (p, P, Q, X)$;
$sk \leftarrow (p, P, Q, x)$
Return (pk, sk)

$\mathcal{E}_{pk}(M)$:

$r \xleftarrow{R} Z_q^*$
$g \leftarrow \hat{e}(pk, Q)$
Return $(rP, M \oplus H(g^r))$

$\mathcal{D}_{sk}(U, V)$:

$M \leftarrow V \oplus H(\hat{e}(U, xQ))$
Return M

We do not define the decryption using the escrow key since it is not relevant for our goal. The proof is in [4].

Lemma 4. *The escrow El Gamal encryption scheme $\mathcal{EEG} = (\mathcal{G}, \mathcal{K}, \mathcal{E}, \mathcal{D})$ is reproducible.*

A standard argument shows that $\mathcal{EEG}$ is IND-CPA secure in the random oracle model assuming Bilinear Diffie-Hellman assumption (see [10] for proper definitions). The results of Theorem 1 and Lemma 4 can be easily adjusted for the random oracle model and they would imply that $\mathcal{EEG}$ is also SRS-IND-CPA or, equivalently, the corresponding multi-recipient scheme $\overline{\mathcal{EEG}}$ is IND-CPA secure, both in the random oracle model.

Acknowledgements

We thank Diana Smetters for useful discussions. Part of this research has been done when Alexandra Boldyreva was in PARC. Mihir Bellare and Alexandra Boldyreva were supported in part by NSF Grant CCR-0098123 and NSF Grant ANR-0129617. Alexandra was also supported by SDSC Graduate Student Diversity Fellowship.

References

[1] O. BAUDRON, D. POINTCHEVAL AND J. STERN, "Extended notions of security for multicast public key cryptosystems." *ICALP 2000* 86, 87, 91, 92, 93

[2] M. ABDALLA, M. BELLARE, AND P. ROGAWAY, "The Oracle Diffie-Hellman Assumptions and an Analysis of DHIES," *CT-RSA 01, Lecture Notes in Computer Science Vol. 2020, D. Naccache ed, Springer-Verlag, 2001.* 88, 96

[3] M. BELLARE, A. BOLDYREVA, AND S. MICALI, "Public-key Encryption in a Multi-User Setting: Security Proofs and Improvements," *Advances in Cryptology – Eurocrypt '00*, LNCS Vol. 1807, B. Preneel ed., Springer-Verlag, 2000 86, 87, 88, 89, 91, 92, 93, 95

[4] M. BELLARE, A. BOLDYREVA, AND J. STADDON "Randomness Re-Use in Multi-Recipient Encryption Schemes", Full version of this paper. Available at http:// www-cse.ucsd.edu/users/aboldyre 89, 90, 94, 95, 96, 97

[5] M. BELLARE, A. DESAI, D. POINTCHEVAL AND P. ROGAWAY, "Relations among notions of security for public-key encryption schemes," *Advances in Cryptology – Crypto '98*, LNCS Vol. 1462, H. Krawczyk ed., Springer-Verlag, 1998.

[6] M. BELLARE AND O. GOLDREICH, "On defining proofs of knowledge," *Advances in Cryptology – Crypto '92*, LNCS Vol. 740, E. Brickell ed., Springer-Verlag, 1992. 94

[7] S. BERKOVITS, "How to Broadcast a Secret", *Advances in Cryptology – Eurocrypt '91*, LNCS Vol. 547, D. Davies ed., Springer-Verlag, 1991.

[8] M. BLUM AND S. MICALI, "How to generate cryptographically strong sequences of pseudo-random bits," *SIAM J. on Computing* Vol. 13, No. 4, November 1984.

[9] D. BONEH. "Simplified OAEP for the RSA and Rabin Functions," *Advances in Cryptology – Crypto '01*, LNCS Vol. 2139, J. Kilian ed., Springer-Verlag, 2001.

[10] D. BONEH AND M. FRANKLIN. "Identity-based encryption from the Weil Pairing," *Advances in Cryptology – Crypto '01*, LNCS Vol. 2139, J. Kilian ed., Springer-Verlag, 2001. 89, 97

[11] J. CAMENISCH AND M. MICHELS, "Confirmer signature schemes secure against adaptive adversaries," *Advances in Cryptology – Eurocrypt '00*, LNCS Vol. 1807, B. Preneel ed., Springer-Verlag, 2000.

[12] R. CANETTI,, "Towards Realizing Random Oracles: Hash Functions that Hide All Partial Information,", *Advances in Cryptology – Crypto '97*, LNCS Vol. 1294, B. Kaliski ed., Springer-Verlag, 1997 95

[13] R. CRAMER AND V. SHOUP, "A practical public key cryptosystem provably secure against adaptive chosen ciphertext attack," *Advances in Cryptology – Crypto '98*, LNCS Vol. 1462, H. Krawczyk ed., Springer-Verlag, 1998. 86, 88, 95, 96

[14] T. ELGAMAL, "A public key cryptosystem and signature scheme based on discrete logarithms," *IEEE Transactions on Information Theory*, vol 31, 1985.

[15] A. FIAT AND M. NAOR, "Broadcast Encryption", *Advances in Cryptology – Crypto '93*, LNCS Vol. 773, D. Stinson ed., Springer-Verlag, 1993.

[16] E. FUJISAKI, T. OKAMOTO, D. POINTCHEVAL AND J. STERN, "RSA-OAEP is Secure under the RSA Assumption," *Advances in Cryptology – Crypto '01*, LNCS Vol. 2139, J. Kilian ed., Springer-Verlag, 2001. 91

[17] S. GOLDWASSER AND S. MICALI, "Probabilistic encryption," *Journal of Computer and System Science*, Vol. 28, 1984, pp. 270–299.

[18] O. GOLDREICH, S. GOLDWASSER AND S. MICALI, "How to construct random functions," *Journal of the ACM*, Vol. 33, No. 4, 210–217, (1986).

[19] J. HÅSTAD, "Solving simultaneous modular equations of low degree," *SIAM J. on Computing* Vol. 17, No. 2, April 1988. 87

[20] J. HÅSTAD, R. IMPAGLIAZZO, L. LEVIN, AND M. LUBY, "A pseudorandom generation from any one-way function ," *SIAM Journal on Computing*, Vol. 28, No. 4, 1364–1396, 1999.

[21] R. IMPAGLIAZZO AND M. LUBY, "One-way functions are essential for complexity based cryptography," *Proceedings of the* 30th *Symposium on Foundations of Computer Science*, IEEE, 1989

[22] K. KUROSAWA, "Multi-Recipient Public-Key Encryption with Shortened Ciphertext," *Proceedings of the Fifth International workshop on practice and theory in Public Key Cryptography (PKC'02)*. 86, 87, 88, 89, 92, 93, 95, 96

[23] S. MICALI, C. RACKOFF AND R. H. SLOAN, "The notion of security for probabilistic cryptosystems," *Advances in Cryptology – Crypto '86*, LNCS Vol. 263, A. Odlyzko ed., Springer-Verlag, 1986.

[24] M. NAOR AND O. REINGOLD, "Number-theoretic constructions of efficient pseudo-random functions," *Proceedings of the 38th Symposium on Foundations of Computer Science*, IEEE, 1997. 88, 95

[25] "PKCS-1," RSA LABS, http://www.rsasecurity.com/rsalabs/pkcs/pkcs-1/. 91

[26] C. RACKOFF AND D. SIMON, "Non-interactive zero-knowledge proof of knowledge and chosen-ciphertext attack," *Advances in Cryptology – Crypto '91*, LNCS Vol. 576, J. Feigenbaum ed., Springer-Verlag, 1991.

[27] V. SHOUP, "On formal models for secure key exchange, " Theory of Cryptography Library Record 99-12, http://philby.ucsd.edu/cryptolib/. 88

[28] M. STADLER, "Publicly verifiable secret sharing," *Advances in Cryptology – Eurocrypt '96*, LNCS Vol. 1070, U. Maurer ed., Springer-Verlag, 1996. 88

[29] Y. TSIOUNIS AND M. YUNG, "On the security of El Gamal based encryption," *Proceedings of the First International workshop on practice and theory in Public Key Cryptography (PKC'98)*, Lecture Notes in Computer Science Vol. 1431, H. Imai and Y. Zheng eds., Springer-Verlag, 1998. 95

[30] D. WALLNER, E. HARDER AND R. AGEE, "Key Management for Multicast: Issues and Architectures," Internet Request for Comments, **2627** (June 1999). Available at: ftp.ietf.org/rfc/rfc2627.txt.

[31] A. C. Yao. "Theory and application of trapdoor functions," *Proceedings of the* 23rd *Symposium on Foundations of Computer Science*, IEEE, 1982

Public Key Trace and Revoke Scheme Secure against Adaptive Chosen Ciphertext Attack*

Yevgeniy Dodis and Nelly Fazio

Computer Science Department, New York University, USA
{dodis,fazio}@cs.nyu.edu

Abstract. A (public key) Trace and Revoke Scheme combines the functionality of broadcast encryption with the capability of traitor tracing. Specifically, (1) a trusted center publishes a single public key and distributes individual secret keys to the users of the system; (2) anybody can encrypt a message so that all but a specified subset of "revoked" users can decrypt the resulting ciphertext; and (3) if a (small) group of users combine their secret keys to produce a "pirate decoder", the center can trace at least one of the "traitors" given access to this decoder.

We construct the first *chosen ciphertext* (CCA2) secure Trace and Revoke Scheme based on the DDH assumption. Our scheme is also the first *adaptively secure* scheme, allowing the adversary to corrupt players at any point during execution, while prior works (e.g., [14, 16]) only achieves a very weak form of non-adaptive security even against chosen plaintext attacks.

Of independent interest, we present a slightly simpler construction that shows a "natural separation" between the classical notion of CCA2-security and the recently proposed [15, 1] relaxed notion of gCCA2-security.

1 Introduction

A *broadcast encryption* scheme allows the sender to securely distribute data to a dynamically changing set of users over an insecure channel. Namely, it should be possible to selectively exclude (i.e., "revoke") a certain subset of users from receiving the data. In particular, each user should receive an individualized decoder which decrypts only the ciphertexts intended for the given user. Broadcast encryption has numerous applications, including pay-TV systems, distribution of copyrighted material, streaming audio/video and many others.

The formal study of broadcast encryption was initiated by Fiat and Naor [8], who showed a scheme with message overhead roughly $O(z^2 \log^2 z \log N)$, where z is the maximum number of excluded users (so called *revocation threshold*) and N is the total number of users. Subsequent works include [12, 10], and, more recently, [13, 11].

Most of the above works primarily concentrate on the centralized setting, where only the trusted center (the entity who generates all the secret keys) can

---

* This proceedings version lacks most proof details; for a complete version see [7].

Y.G. Desmedt (Ed.): PKC 2003, LNCS 2567, pp. 100–115, 2003.

send messages to the receivers. In the *public key* setting, studied in this paper, the center also prepares a fixed public key which allows any entity to play the role of the sender. The public key setting also allows the center to store secret keys in a secure place (e.g. off-line), and only use them when a new user join the system.

The only known public key Broadcast Encryption Schemes have been constructed by [14, 16] based on the DDH assumption, and achieve public key and message overhead $O(z)$. In fact, these schemes are essentially identical: in the following we will refer to the work of [16], who emphasize more the public key nature of their scheme.

Despite providing a simple and elegant scheme, the work of [16] has several noticeable shortcomings. First, the given (informal) notion of security makes little sense in a revocation setting. Indeed, to show the "security" of revocation, [16] show the following two claims: (1) the scheme is semantically secure when no users are revoked; (2) no set of z a-priori fixed users can compute the secret key of another user. Clearly, these properties do not imply the security notion we really care about and which informally states: (3) if the adversary controls some set $\mathcal{R}$ of up to z *revoked* users, then the scheme remains semantically secure. Actually, the scheme of [16] can be shown to satisfy (3) only when the set $\mathcal{R}$ is chosen by the adversary *non-adaptively*, and in fact only if it is chosen before the adversary learns the public key. Such weak non-adaptive security is clearly insufficient for realistic usages of a public key revocation scheme.

Most importantly, the extended scheme of [16] is proven to be CCA2-secure when none of the users is corrupted, but stops being such the moment just a single user is corrupted, even if this user is immediately revoked for the rest of the protocol. Again, this is too weak — the scheme should remain CCA2-secure *even after many users have been revoked*. As we will see, achieving this strong type of security is very non-trivial, and requires a much more involved scheme than the one proposed by [16].

OUR CONTRIBUTIONS. We construct the first *adaptive chosen ciphertext* (CCA2) secure public key Broadcast Encryption Scheme under the DDH assumption (with no random oracles). We remark that no CCA2 schemes were known even in the symmetric setting. Moreover, it doesn't seem obvious how to extend current symmetric schemes (e.g. [13]) to meet the CCA2 notion. Our public key scheme is based on the regular Cramer-Shoup encryption [5, 6], but our extension is non-trivial, as we have to resolve some difficulties inherent to Broadcast Encryption. Furthermore, we introduce for the first time a precise formalization of an appropriate notion of adaptive security for Broadcast Encryption (for both the CPA and the CCA2 setting). We also extend the CPA scheme of [16] to achieve such higher level of security, while maintaining essentially the same efficiency in all the parameters (up to a factor of 2).

Of independent interest, we also provide another scheme achieving a slightly weaker (but still very strong) notion of *generalized* CCA2 security (gCCA2) [15, 1]. As argued in [1], the gCCA2 security is much more robust to syntactic changes, while still sufficient for all known uses of CCA2-security. Interestingly, all the examples separating CCA2 and gCCA2-secure encryption were "artificial" in a sense that they made a more complicated scheme from an already existing CCA2-secure encryption. Our work shows the first "natural" separation, but for the *broadcast* public key encryption.

A NOTE ON TRAITOR TRACING. As first explicitly noticed by Gafni et al. [9], Broadcast Encryption is most useful when combined with a *Traitor Tracing* mechanism [4] by which the center can extract the identity of (at least one) "pirate" from any illegal decoder produced combining decryption equipments of a group of legal members (the "traitors"). By slightly modifying standard tracing algorithms from previous weaker schemes (e.g. [14, 16]), tracing algorithms can be added to our schemes, thus yielding fully functional *Trace and Revoke* schemes [14]. However, due to space limitations we omit the tracing part, focusing only on Broadcast Encryption (i.e. revocation), which is also the main novelty of this paper.

2   Notations and Basic Facts

LAGRANGE INTERPOLATION IN THE EXPONENT. Let q be a prime and $f(x)$ a polynomial of degree z over $\mathbb{Z}_q$; let $j_0, \ldots, j_z$ be distinct elements of $\mathbb{Z}_q$, and let $f_0 = f(j_0), \ldots, f_z = f(j_z)$. Using Lagrange Interpolation, we can express the polynomial as $f(x) = \sum_{t=0}^{z}(f_t \cdot \lambda_t(x))$, where $\lambda_t(x) = \prod_{0 \leq i \neq t \leq z} \frac{j_i - x}{j_i - j_t}$, $t \in [0, z]$. Now, define the Lagrange Interpolation Operator as: $\mathsf{LI}(j_0, \ldots, j_z; f_0, \ldots, f_z)(x) \doteq \sum_{t=0}^{z}(f_t \cdot \lambda_t(x))$.

Now, consider any cyclic group $\mathbb{G}$ of order q and a generator g of $\mathbb{G}$. For any distinct $j_0, \ldots, j_z \in \mathbb{Z}_q$ and (non necessarily distinct) $v_0, \ldots, v_z \in \mathbb{G}$, define the Lagrange Interpolation Operator in the Exponent as: $\mathsf{EXP\text{-}LI}(j_0, \ldots, j_z; v_0, \ldots, v_z)(x) \doteq g^{\mathsf{LI}(j_0, \ldots, j_z; \log_g v_0, \ldots, \log_g v_z)(x)} = \prod_{t=0}^{z} g^{(\log_g v_t \cdot \lambda_t(x))} = \prod_{t=0}^{z} v_t^{\lambda_t(x)}$. The last expression shows that the function $\mathsf{EXP\text{-}LI}$ is poly-time computable, despite being defined in terms of discrete logarithms (which are usually hard to compute). We also remark on another useful property of the above operator: $\mathsf{EXP\text{-}LI}(j_0, \ldots, j_z; v_0^r, \ldots, v_z^r)(x) = [\mathsf{EXP\text{-}LI}(j_0, \ldots, j_z; v_0, \ldots, v_z)(x)]^r$. In what follows, we will refer to a function of the form $g^{f(x)}$, where $f(x)$ is a polynomial, as an EXP-polynomial.

DDH ASSUMPTION. The security of our schemes will rely on the Decisional Diffie-Hellman (DDH) Assumption in the group $\mathbb{G}$: namely, it is computationally hard to distinguish a random tuple (g_1, g_2, u_1, u_2) of four independent elements in $\mathbb{G}$ from a random tuple satisfying $\log_{g_1} u_1 = \log_{g_2} u_2$ (for a survey, see [3]).

A PROBABILISTIC LEMMA. The following useful lemma states that to estimate the difference between two related experiments U_1 and U_2, it is sufficient to bound the probability of some event F which "subsumes" all the differences between the experiments.

Lemma 1. *If U_1, U_2 and F are events such that ($U_1 \wedge \neg F$) and ($U_2 \wedge \neg F$) are equivalent events, then $\left| \Pr[U_1] - \Pr[U_2] \right| \leq \Pr[F]$.*

3   Definition of Broadcast Encryption Scheme

Since a public-key broadcast encryption is typically used by encrypting a session key s for the privileged users (this encryption is called the *enabling block*), and then symmetrically encrypting the "actual" message with s, we will often say that the goal of a Broadcast Encryption Scheme is to *encapsulate* [6] a session key s, rather than to encrypt a message M.

Definition 1 (BROADCAST ENCRYPTION SCHEME).
A Broadcast Encryption Scheme BE *is a 4-tuple of* poly-*time algorithms* (KeyGen, Reg, Enc, Dec), *where:*

- KeyGen, *the* key generation algorithm, *is a probabilistic algorithm used by the center to set up all the parameters of the scheme.* KeyGen *takes as input a security parameter* 1^λ *and a revocation threshold* z *(i.e. the maximum number of users that can be revoked) and generates the public key* PK *and the master secret key* SK_{BE}.
- Reg, *the* registration algorithm, *is a probabilistic algorithm used by the center to compute the secret initialization data needed to construct a new decoder each time a new user subscribes to the system.* Reg *receives as input the master key* SK_{BE} *and a (new) index* i *associated with the user; it returns the user's secret key* SK_i.
- Enc, *the* encryption algorithm, *is a probabilistic algorithm used to encapsulate a given session key* s *within an enabling block* $\mathcal{T}$. Enc *takes as input the public key* PK, *the session key* s *and a set* $\mathcal{R}$ *of revoked users (with* $|\mathcal{R}| < z$ *) and returns the enabling block* $\mathcal{T}$.
- Dec, *the* decryption algorithm, *is a deterministic algorithm that takes as input the secret key* SK_i *of user* i *and the enabling block* $\mathcal{T}$ *and returns the session key* s *that was encapsulated within* $\mathcal{T}$ *if* i *was a legitimate user when* $\mathcal{T}$ *was constructed, or the special symbol* $\bot$.

3.1   Security of Revocation

Intuitively, we would like to say that even if a malicious *adversary* $\mathcal{A}$ learns the secret keys of at most z users, and these users are later revoked, then subsequent broadcasts do not leak any information to such adversary. The security threat posed by such adversary is usually referred to as *Chosen Plaintext Attack* (CPA), and a Broadcast Encryption Scheme withstanding such an attack is said to be *z-Resilient against* CPA.

For most realistic usages, however, it is more appropriate to consider the stronger *Chosen Ciphertext Attack* (CCA2), in which the adversary is allowed to "play" with the decryption machinery as she wishes, subject only to the condition that she doesn't ask about enabling blocks closely related to the "challenge" $\mathcal{T}^*$. In formalizing the notion of "close relationship", the usual treatment is to impose a minimal restriction to the adversary, forbidding just direct decryption of the challenge itself. As noted in [15, 1], such a mild constraint restricts too much the class of schemes that can be proven secure, excluding even schemes that ought to be considered secure under a more intuitive notion. For this reason, it seems more reasonable to consider a variant of the CCA2, to which we will refer to as *Generalized Chosen Ciphertext Attack* (gCCA2), following the terminology introduced in [1].

In a Generalized Chosen Ciphertext Attack, the set of enabling blocks the adversary is forbidden to ask about is defined in term of an efficiently computable equivalence relation $\Re(\cdot, \cdot)$. In fact, in the case of a broadcast (as opposed to ordinary) encryption, there is no unique decryption machinery, since the decryption algorithm can be used with the secret key of any legitimate user. Hence, we need to consider a *family* of efficient equivalence relations $\{\Re_i(\cdot, \cdot)\}$, one for each user i. As in the regular case [1], the equivalence relation $\Re_i(\cdot, \cdot)$ corresponding to each user i needs to be *i-decryption-respecting*: equivalent enabling blocks under $\Re_i$ are guaranteed to have exactly the same decryption according to the secret data of user i. Finally, this family should form an *explicit* parameter of the scheme (i.e., one has to specify some decryption-respecting family $\{\Re_i\}$ when proving the gCCA2-security of a given scheme).

FORMAL MODEL. We now formalize the above attack scenarios, starting with the CPA.

First, $(PK, SK_{BE}) \leftarrow$ BE.KeyGen$(1^\lambda, z)$ is run and the adversary $\mathcal{A}$ is given the public key PK. Then $\mathcal{A}$ enters the user corruption stage, where she is given oracle access to the *User Corruption Oracle* $\mathsf{Cor}_{SK_{BE}}(\cdot)$. This oracle receives as input the index i of the user to be corrupted, computes $SK_i \leftarrow$ BE.Reg(SK_{BE}, i) and returns the user's secret key SK_i. This oracle can be called *adaptively* for at most z times. Let us say that at the end of this stage the set $\mathcal{R}$ of at most z users is corrupted.

In the second stage, a random bit σ is chosen, and $\mathcal{A}$ can query the *Encryption Oracle* (sometimes also called the *left-or-right* oracle) $\mathcal{E}_{PK, \mathcal{R}, \sigma}(\cdot, \cdot)$ on any pair of session keys s_0, s_1.[1] This oracle returns $\mathsf{Enc}(PK, s_\sigma, \mathcal{R})$. Without loss of generality (see [2]), we can assume that the encryption oracle is called exactly once, and returns to $\mathcal{A}$ the *challenge enabling block* $\mathcal{T}^*$. At the end of this second stage, $\mathcal{A}$ outputs a bit σ^* which she thinks is equal to σ. Define the *advantage* of $\mathcal{A}$ as $\mathsf{Adv}_{BE, \mathcal{A}}^{CPA}(\lambda) \doteq |\Pr(\sigma^* = \sigma) - \frac{1}{2}|$.

Additionally, in the case of a Chosen Ciphertext Attack (generalized or not), $\mathcal{A}$ has also access to a *Decryption Oracle* $\mathcal{D}_{SK_{BE}}(\cdot, \cdot)$, which she can query on any pair $\langle i, \mathcal{T} \rangle$, where i is the index of some user and $\mathcal{T}$ is any enabling block of her choice. $\mathcal{A}$ can call this oracle at any point during the execution (i.e., both in the first and in the second stage, arbitrarily interleaved with her other oracle calls). To prevent the adversary from directly decrypting her challenge $\mathcal{T}^*$, the decryption oracle first checks whether $\Re_i(\mathcal{T}, \mathcal{T}^*)$ holds[2]: if so, $\mathcal{D}$ outputs $\perp$; if not, $\mathcal{D}$ computes $SK_i \leftarrow$ BE.Reg(SK_{BE}, i) and uses it to output BE.Dec$(i, \mathcal{T})$.

---

[1] For the sake of generality, we could have allowed $\mathcal{A}$ to interleave the calls to $\mathsf{Cor}_{SK_{BE}}(i)$ and $\mathcal{E}_{PK, \mathcal{R}, \sigma}$ (where $\mathcal{A}$ can choose any i's and $\mathcal{R}$'s only subject to $i \notin \mathcal{R}$). However, this clumsier definition is easily seen to be equivalent to the one we present.

[2] This preliminary check applies to the standard Chosen Ciphertext Attack as well, which corresponds to all the $\Re_i$'s being the equality relation.

As before, we define the corresponding advantages $\mathsf{Adv}_{\mathsf{BE},\mathcal{A}}^{\mathsf{gCCA2}}(\lambda)$ and $\mathsf{Adv}_{\mathsf{BE},\mathcal{A}}^{\mathsf{CCA2}}(\lambda)$.

Definition 2 (z-RESILIENCE OF A BROADCAST ENCRYPTION SCHEME).
Let $\mu \in \{\mathsf{CPA}, \mathsf{gCCA2}, \mathsf{CCA2}\}$. We say that a Broadcast Encryption Scheme BE is z-resilient against a μ-type attack if the advantage, $\mathsf{Adv}_{\mathsf{BE},\mathcal{A}}^{\mu}(\lambda)$, of any probabilistic poly-time algorithm $\mathcal{A}$ is a negligible function of λ.

4   Revocation Schemes

In this section, we present three Broadcast Encryption Schemes, achieving z-resilience in an adaptive setting for the case of a CPA, gCCA2 and CCA2 attack respectively. Subsequent schemes build on the previous one, in a incremental way, so that it is possible to obtain increasing security at the cost of a slight efficiency loss.

Considering the subtlety of the arguments, our proofs follow the structural approach advocated in [6] defining a sequence of attack games $\mathbf{G}_0$, $\mathbf{G}_1$, ..., all operating over the same underlying probability space. Starting from the actual adversarial game $\mathbf{G}_0$, we incrementally make slight modifications to the behavior of the oracles, thus changing the way the adversary's view is computed, while maintaining the view's distributions indistinguishable among the games. While this structural approach takes more space to write down, it is much less error-prone and much more understandable than a slicker "direct argument" (e.g., compare [5] and [6]).

4.1 z-Resilience against CPA Attack

As a warm-up before addressing the more challenging case of chosen ciphertext security, we describe a simpler CPA-secure scheme. Our scheme naturally builds upon previous works [14, 16], but achieves a much more appropriate notion of *adaptive* security, which those previous schemes do not enjoy.

THE KEY GENERATION ALGORITHM. The first step in the key generation algorithm $\mathsf{KeyGen}(1^\lambda, z)$ is to define a group $\mathbb{G}$ of order q, for a random λ-bit-long prime q such that $p = 2q + 1$ is also prime, in which the DDH assumption is believed to hold. This is accomplished selecting a random prime q with the above two properties and a random element g_1 of order q modulo p: the group $\mathbb{G}$ is then set to be the subgroup of $\mathbb{Z}_p^*$ generated by g_1, i.e. $\mathbb{G} = \{g_1^i \bmod p : i \in \mathbb{Z}_q\} \subset \mathbb{Z}_p^*$. A random $w \leftarrow_R \mathbb{Z}_q$ is then chosen and used to compute $g_2 = g_1^w$. (In what follows, all computations are mod q in the exponent, and mod p elsewhere.) Then, the key generation algorithm selects two random z-degree polynomials[3] $Z_1(\xi)$ and $Z_2(\xi)$ over $\mathbb{Z}_q$, and computes the values: $h_0 \doteq g_1^{Z_{1,0}} \cdot g_2^{Z_{2,0}}, \ldots, h_z \doteq g_1^{Z_{1,z}} \cdot g_2^{Z_{2,z}}$. Finally, the pair (PK, SK_{BE}) is given in output, where $PK \doteq \langle g_1, g_2, h_0, \ldots, h_z \rangle$ and $SK_{\mathsf{BE}} \doteq \langle Z_1, Z_2 \rangle$.

---

[3] For conciseness, we will use the following notation: $Z_{1,i} \doteq Z_1(i)$ and $Z_{2,i} \doteq Z_2(i)$.

Encryption algorithm $\mathsf{Enc}(PK, s, \mathcal{R})$	Decryption algorithm $\mathsf{Dec}(i, \mathcal{T})$
$E1.\ r_1 \leftarrow_R \mathbb{Z}_q$	$D1.\ H_i \leftarrow u_1^{Z_{1,i}} \cdot u_2^{Z_{2,i}}$
$E2.\ u_1 \leftarrow g_1^{r_1}$	$D2.\ s \leftarrow \dfrac{S}{\mathsf{EXP\text{-}LI}(j_1,..,j_z,i;H_{j_1},..,H_{j_z},H_i)(0)}$
$E3.\ u_2 \leftarrow g_2^{r_1}$	
$E4.\ H_t \leftarrow h_t^{r_1},\ t \in [0, z]$	
$E5.$ **for** $t = 1$ **to** z **do**	
$\qquad H_{j_t} \leftarrow \mathsf{EXP\text{-}LI}(0,..,z; H_0,..,H_z)(j_t)$	
$E6.$ **end for**	
$E7.\ S \leftarrow s \cdot H_0$	
$E8.\ \mathcal{T} \leftarrow \langle S, u_1, u_2, (j_1, H_{j_1}), .., (j_z, H_{j_z}) \rangle$	

Fig. 1. Encryption and decryption algorithms for the CPA scheme

THE REGISTRATION ALGORITHM. Each time a new user $i > z$ (in all our schemes, we reserve the indices $[0, z]$ for "special purposes") decides to subscribe to the system, the center provides him with a decoder box containing the secret key $SK_i \doteq \langle i, Z_{1,i}, Z_{2,i} \rangle$.

THE ENCRYPTION ALGORITHM. The encryption algorithm Enc is given in Fig. 1. It receives as input the public key PK, a session key s and a set $\mathcal{R} = \{j_1, \ldots, j_z\}$ of revoked users and returns the enabling block $\mathcal{T}$. If there are less than z revoked users, the remaining indices are set to $1 \ldots (z - |\mathcal{R}|)$, which are never given to any "real" user.

THE DECRYPTION ALGORITHM. To recover the session key embedded in the enabling block $\mathcal{T} = \langle S, u_1, u_2, (j_1, H_{j_1}), \ldots, (j_z, H_{j_z}) \rangle$ a legitimate user i can proceed as in Fig. 1. If i is a revoked user (i.e. $i \in \{j_1, \ldots, j_z\}$), the algorithm fails in step $D2$, since the interpolation points $j_1, \ldots, j_z, i$ are not pairwise distinct.

SECURITY. As shown in the theorem below, the z-resilience of the above scheme relies on the Decisional Diffie-Hellman (DDH) assumption.

Theorem 1. *If the* DDH *problem is hard in* $\mathbb{G}$, *then the above Broadcast Encryption Scheme is z-resilient against chosen plaintext attacks.*

Proof. We define a sequence of "indistinguishable" games $\mathbf{G}_0, \ldots$, where $\mathbf{G}_0$ is the original game, and the last game clearly gives no advantage to the adversary. **Game $\mathbf{G}_0$.** In game $\mathbf{G}_0$, $\mathcal{A}$ receives the public key PK and adaptively queries the corruption oracle $\mathsf{Cor}_{SK_{\mathsf{BE}}}(\cdot)$. Then, she queries the encryption oracle $\mathcal{E}_{PK, \mathcal{R}, \sigma}(\cdot, \cdot)$ on (s_0, s_1), where $\mathcal{R}$ must contain all users that $\mathcal{A}$ compromised through the oracle $\mathsf{Cor}_{SK_{\mathsf{BE}}}(\cdot)$; $\mathcal{A}$ receives back the enabling block $\mathcal{T}^*$. At this point, $\mathcal{A}$ outputs her guess $\sigma^* \in \{0, 1\}$. Let T_0 be the event that $\sigma = \sigma^*$ in game $\mathbf{G}_0$. **Game $\mathbf{G}_1$.** Game $\mathbf{G}_1$ is identical to game $\mathbf{G}_0$, except that step $E4$ of the encryption algorithm in Fig. 1, is changed in: $\boxed{E4'.\ H_t \leftarrow u_1^{Z_{1,t}} \cdot u_2^{Z_{2,t}},\ t \in [0, z]}$. By the properties of the Lagrange Interpolation in the Exponent, it is clear that step $E4'$ computes the same values $\{H_t\}_{t=0}^z$ as step $E4$. The point of this change is just to make explicit any functional dependency of the above quantities on u_1 and u_2. Let T_1 be the event that $\sigma = \sigma^*$ in game $\mathbf{G}_1$; clearly, it holds that $\Pr[T_0] = \Pr[T_1]$.

Game G_2. To turn game G_1 into game G_2 we again modify the encryption oracle used in G_1, replacing step $E1$ with $\boxed{E1'.\ r_1 \leftarrow_R \mathbb{Z}_q,\ r_2 \leftarrow_R \mathbb{Z}_q \setminus \{r_1\}}$ and step $E3$ with $\boxed{E3'.\ u_2 \leftarrow g_2^{r_2}}$. Let T_2 be the event that $\sigma = \sigma^*$ in game G_2. Notice that while in G_1 the values u_1 and u_2 are obtained using the same value r_1, in G_2 they are independent subject to $r_1 \neq r_2$. Therefore, using a standard reduction argument, any non-negligible difference in behavior between G_1 and G_2 can be used to construct a PPT algorithm $\mathcal{A}_1$ that is able to distinguish Diffie-Hellman tuples from totally random tuples with non negligible advantage. Hence, $\big|\Pr[T_2] - \Pr[T_1]\big| \leq \epsilon_1$ for some negligible ϵ_1.

Game G_3. To define game G_3, we make another change to the encryption oracle in game G_2, substituting step $E6$ with: $\boxed{E6'.\ e \leftarrow_R \mathbb{Z}_q,\ S \leftarrow g_1^e}$. Let T_3 be the event that $\sigma = \sigma^*$ in game G_3. Because of this last change, the challenge no longer contains σ, nor does any other information in the adversary's view; therefore, we have that $\Pr[T_3] = \frac{1}{2}$. Moreover, we can prove (see Lemma 3 in [7]), that the adversary has the same chances to guess σ in both games G_2 and G_3, i.e. $\Pr[T_3] = \Pr[T_2]$.

Finally, combining all the intermediate results together, we can conclude that adversary $\mathcal{A}$'s advantage is negligible; more precisely: $\mathsf{Adv}^{\mathsf{CPA}}_{\mathsf{BE}, \mathcal{A}}(\lambda) \leq \epsilon_1$.

4.2 z-Resilience against gCCA2 Attack

Once we have constructed a Broadcast Encryption Scheme z-resilient against CPA attacks, it is natural to try to devise an extension achieving adaptive chosen ciphertext security. This was already attempted by [16], but they do not elaborate (neither formally nor informally) on what an "adaptive chosen ciphertext attack" on a Broadcast Encryption Scheme exactly is. As a consequence, in their security theorem (Theorem 3 of [16]), the authors only show the security of their scheme against an adversary that does not participate to the system, while their scheme is certainly not CCA2-secure with respect to even a single malicious revoked user.

To achieve CCA2-security, we will first try to apply the standard technique of [5, 6] to the scheme presented in Section 4.1. Unfortunately, this natural approach does *not* completely solve the CCA2 problem; still it leads us to an interesting scheme that achieves the (sligthly weaker) notion of generalized chosen ciphertext security.

THE KEY GENERATION ALGORITHM. As before, the first task of the key generation algorithm is to select a random group $\mathbb{G} \subset \mathbb{Z}_p^*$ of prime order q and two random generators $g_1, g_2 \in \mathbb{G}$. Then, KeyGen selects six random z-degree polynomials[4] $X_1(\xi), X_2(\xi), Y_1(\xi), Y_2(\xi), Z_1(\xi)$ and $Z_2(\xi)$ over $\mathbb{Z}_q$, and computes the values $c_t \doteq g_1^{X_{1,t}} \cdot g_2^{X_{2,t}}$, $d_t \doteq g_1^{Y_{1,t}} \cdot g_2^{Y_{2,t}}$ and $h_t \doteq g_1^{Z_{1,t}} \cdot g_2^{Z_{2,t}}$, for $t \in [0, z]$.

Finally, KeyGen chooses at random a hash function $\mathcal{H}$ from a family $\mathcal{F}$ of collision resistant hash functions,[5] and outputs the pair (PK, SK_{BE}), where

---

[4] For conciseness, we will use the following notation: $X_{1,i} \doteq X_1(i), X_{2,i} \doteq X_2(i), Y_{1,i} \doteq Y_1(i), Y_{2,i} \doteq Y_2(i), Z_{1,i} \doteq Z_1(i)$ and $Z_{2,i} \doteq Z_2(i)$.

Encryption algorithm $\mathsf{Enc}(PK, s, \mathcal{R})$	Decryption algorithm $\mathsf{Dec}(i, \mathcal{T})$
$E1.\ r_1 \leftarrow_R \mathbb{Z}_q$	$D1.\ \alpha \leftarrow \mathcal{H}(S, u_1, u_2, (j_1, H_{j_1}), .., (j_z, H_{j_z}))$
$E2.\ u_1 \leftarrow g_1^{r_1}$	$D2.\ \bar{v}_i \leftarrow u_1^{X_{1,i}+Y_{1,i}\alpha} \cdot u_2^{X_{2,i}+Y_{2,i}\alpha}$
$E3.\ u_2 \leftarrow g_2^{r_1}$	$D3.\ v_i \leftarrow \mathsf{EXP\text{-}LI}(0, .., z; v_0, .., v_z)(i)$
$E4.\ H_t \leftarrow h_t^{r_1},\ t \in [0, z]$	$D4.\ \textbf{if } v_i = \bar{v}_i \textbf{ then}$
$E5.\ \textbf{for } t = 1 \textbf{ to } z \textbf{ do}$	$D5.\quad H_i \leftarrow u_1^{Z_{1,i}} \cdot u_2^{Z_{2,i}}$
$\qquad H_{j_t} \leftarrow \mathsf{EXP\text{-}LI}(0, .., z; H_0, .., H_z)(j_t)$	$D6.\quad s \leftarrow \dfrac{S}{\mathsf{EXP\text{-}LI}(j_1, .., j_z, i; H_{j_1}, .., H_{j_z}, H_i)(0)}$
$E6.\ \textbf{end for}$	$D7.\quad \textbf{return } s$
$E7.\ S \leftarrow s \cdot H_0$	$D8.\ \textbf{else return } \perp$
$E8.\ \alpha \leftarrow \mathcal{H}(S, u_1, u_2, (j_1, H_{j_1}), .., (j_z, H_{j_z}))$	$D9.\ \textbf{end if}$
$E9.\ v_t \leftarrow c_t^{r_1} \cdot d_t^{r_1 \alpha},\ t \in [0, z]$	
$E10.\mathcal{T} \leftarrow \langle S, u_1, u_2, (j_1, H_{j_1}), .., (j_z, H_{j_z}),$	
$\qquad\quad v_0, .., v_z \rangle$	

Fig. 2. Encryption and decryption algorithms for the gCCA2 scheme

$$PK \doteq \langle g_1, g_2, c_0, \ldots, c_z, d_0, \ldots, d_z, h_0, \ldots, h_z, \mathcal{H} \rangle \quad \text{and} \quad SK_{\mathsf{BE}} \doteq \langle X_1, X_2, Y_1, Y_2, Z_1, Z_2 \rangle.$$

THE REGISTRATION ALGORITHM. Each time a new user $i > z$ decides to subscribe to the system, the center provides him with a decoder box containing the secret key $SK_i \doteq \langle i, X_{1,i}, X_{2,i}, Y_{1,i}, Y_{2,i}, Z_{1,i}, Z_{2,i} \rangle$.

THE ENCRYPTION ALGORITHM. Using the idea of [5, 6], in order to obtain non-malleable ciphertexts, we "tag" each encrypted message so that it can be verified before proceeding with the actual decryption. In the broadcast encryption scenario, where each user has a different decryption key, the tag cannot be a single point — we need to distribute an entire EXP-polynomial $\mathcal{V}(x)$. This is accomplished appending $z + 1$ tags to the ciphertext: each user i first computes the tag v_i using his private key and then verifies the validity of the ciphertext by checking the interpolation of the $z + 1$ values in point i against its v_i.

The encryption algorithm Enc receives as input the public key PK, the session key s to be embedded within the enabling block and a set $\mathcal{R} = \{j_1, \ldots, j_z\}$ of revoked users. It proceeds as described in Fig. 2, and finally it outputs $\mathcal{T}$.

THE DECRYPTION ALGORITHM. To recover the session key embedded in the enabling block $\mathcal{T} = \langle S, u_1, u_2, (j_1, H_{j_1}), \ldots, (j_z, H_{j_z}), v_0, \ldots, v_z \rangle$, a legitimate user i can proceed as in Fig. 2. If i is a revoked user, the algorithm fails in step $D6$, since the interpolation points $j_1, \ldots, j_z, i$ are not pairwise distinct.

SECURITY. As mentioned above, the presence of many decryption keys leads to the use of an EXP-polynomial $\mathcal{V}(x)$ to tag the encryption of the message. This in turn makes the ciphertext malleable: since each user i can verify the value of $\mathcal{V}(x)$ only in one point, the adversary can modify the v_j's values and construct a different EXP-polynomial $\mathcal{V}'(x)$ intersecting $\mathcal{V}(x)$ at point i — thus fooling user i to accept as valid a corrupted ciphertext. In the next section we show a non-trivial solution to this problem; here, we assess the z-resilience of

---

[5] Recall, it is hard to find $x \neq y$ such that $\mathcal{H}(x) = \mathcal{H}(y)$ for a random member $\mathcal{H}$ of $\mathcal{F}$.

the Broadcast Encryption Scheme presented above against a gCCA2 attack. As already discussed in Section 3.1, to this aim it is necessary to introduce a family of equivalence relations $\{\Re_i\}$: intuitively, two ciphertexts $\mathcal{T}$ and $\mathcal{T}'$ are equivalent for user i if they have the same "data" components, and the tag "relevant to user i" is correctly verified, i.e. $v_i = v_i'$ (even though other "irrelevant" tags could be different). Clearly, this relation is efficiently computable and i-decryption-respecting.

Definition 3 (Equivalence Relation).
Consider the EXP-polynomials $\mathcal{V}(x) = \mathsf{EXP\text{-}LI}(0,\ldots,z;v_0,\ldots,v_z)(x)$ *and* $\mathcal{V}'(x) = \mathsf{EXP\text{-}LI}(0,\ldots,z;v_0',\ldots,v_z')(x)$. *Given a user i, and the two enabling blocks* $\mathcal{T} = \langle S, u_1, u_2, (j_1, H_{j_1}), \ldots, (j_z, H_{j_z}), v_0, \ldots, v_z \rangle$ *and* $\mathcal{T}' = \langle S, u_1, u_2, (j_1, H_{j_1}), \ldots,$
$(j_z, H_{j_z}), v_0', \ldots, v_z' \rangle$, *we say that $\mathcal{T}$ is* equivalent *to $\mathcal{T}'$ with respect to user i, and we write* $\Re_i(\mathcal{T}, \mathcal{T}')$, *if the two EXP-polynomials $\mathcal{V}(x)$ and $\mathcal{V}'(x)$ intersect at point i, i.e.* $v_i = \mathcal{V}(i) = \mathcal{V}'(i) = v_i'$.

Theorem 2. *If the DDH Problem is hard in $\mathbb{G}$ and $\mathcal{H}$ is chosen from a collision-resistant hash functions family $\mathcal{F}$, then the above Broadcast Encryption Scheme is z-resilient against generalized chosen ciphertext attacks, under the family of equivalence relations $\{\Re_i\}$.*

Proof. To prove this theorem, we pursue the same approach as in the proof of Theorem 1, where the starting scenario of the sequence of games is defined as in the definition of the adaptive gCCA2 attack.

Game $\mathbf{G}_0$. In game $\mathbf{G}_0$, $\mathcal{A}$ receives the public key PK and adaptively interleaves queries to the corruption oracle $\mathsf{Cor}_{SK_{\mathsf{BE}}}(\cdot)$ and to the decryption oracle $\mathcal{D}_{SK_{\mathsf{BE}}}(\cdot, \cdot)$. Then, she queries the encryption oracle $\mathcal{E}_{PK,\mathcal{R},\sigma}(\cdot, \cdot)$ on (s_0, s_1), where $\mathcal{R}$ must contain all users that $\mathcal{A}$ compromised through the oracle $\mathsf{Cor}_{SK_{\mathsf{BE}}}(\cdot)$; $\mathcal{A}$ receives back the enabling block $\mathcal{T}^*$. Then, $\mathcal{A}$ can again query the decryption oracle $\mathcal{D}_{SK_{\mathsf{BE}}}(i, \mathcal{T})$, restricted only in that $\neg\Re_i(\mathcal{T}, \mathcal{T}^*)$. Finally, she outputs her guess $\sigma^* \in \{0, 1\}$. Let T_0 be the event that $\sigma = \sigma^*$ in game $\mathbf{G}_0$.

Game $\mathbf{G}_1$. Game $\mathbf{G}_1$ is identical to game $\mathbf{G}_0$, except that steps $E4, E8$ of the encryption algorithm in Fig. 2, are changed in: $\boxed{E4'.\ H_t \leftarrow u_1^{Z_{1,t}} \cdot u_2^{Z_{2,t}},\ t \in [0, z]}$ and $\boxed{E8'.\ v_t \leftarrow u_1^{X_{1,t}+Y_{1,t}\alpha} \cdot u_2^{X_{2,t}+Y_{2,t}\alpha},\ t \in [0, z]}$. By the properties of the Lagrange Interpolation in the Exponent, it is clear that step $E4'$ computes the same values $\{H_{j_t}\}_{t=0}^{z}$ as steps $E4$; similarly, step $E8'$ computes the same values $\{v_t\}_{t=0}^{z}$ as step $E8$. The point of these changes is just to make explicit any functional dependency of the above quantities on u_1 and u_2. Let T_1 be the event that $\sigma = \sigma^*$ in game $\mathbf{G}_1$. Clearly, it holds that $\Pr[T_0] = \Pr[T_1]$.

Game $\mathbf{G}_2$. To turn game $\mathbf{G}_1$ into game $\mathbf{G}_2$ we again modify the encryption oracle used in $\mathbf{G}_1$, replacing step $E1$ with $\boxed{E1'.\ r_1 \leftarrow_R \mathbb{Z}_q,\ r_2 \leftarrow_R \mathbb{Z}_q \setminus \{r_1\}}$ and step $E3$ with $\boxed{E3'.\ u_2 \leftarrow g_2^{r_2}}$. Let T_2 be the event that $\sigma = \sigma^*$ in game $\mathbf{G}_2$. Notice that while in $\mathbf{G}_1$ the values u_1 and u_2 are obtained using the same value r_1, in $\mathbf{G}_2$ they are independent subject to $r_1 \neq r_2$. Therefore, using a standard reduction argument, any non-negligible difference in behavior between $\mathbf{G}_1$ and $\mathbf{G}_2$ can be used to construct a PPT algorithm $\mathcal{A}_1$ that is able to distinguish Diffie-Hellman tuples from totally random tuples with non negligible advantage. Hence, $\left| \Pr[T_2] - \Pr[T_1] \right| \leq \epsilon_1$ for some negligible ϵ_1.

Game $\mathbf{G}_3$. To define game $\mathbf{G}_3$ we modify the decryption oracle, changing steps $D2, D4, D5$ with

$$\boxed{D2'.\ \bar{v}_i \leftarrow u_1^{(X_{1,i}+Y_{1,i}\alpha)+(X_{2,i}+Y_{2,i}\alpha)\cdot w}}, \qquad \boxed{D4'.\ \text{if } (u_2 = u_1^w \wedge v_i = \bar{v}_i) \text{ then}},$$

$\boxed{D5'.\ H_i \leftarrow u_1^{Z_{1,i}+Z_{1,i}\cdot w}}$. The rationale behind these changes is that we want to strengthen the condition that the enabling block has to meet in order to be considered valid and hence to be decrypted. This will make it easier to show the security of the scheme; however, for these changes to be useful, there should be no observable difference in the way invalid enabling blocks are "caught" in games $\mathbf{G}_2$ and $\mathbf{G}_3$. To make it formal, let T_3 be the event that $\sigma = \sigma^*$ in game $\mathbf{G}_3$, and let R_3 be the event that $\mathcal{A}$ submits some decryption query that would have been decrypted in game $\mathbf{G}_2$ but is rejected in game $\mathbf{G}_3$; in other words, R_3 is the event that some decryption query that would have passed the test in step $D4$ of the decryption oracle used in $\mathbf{G}_2$, fails to pass the test in step $D4'$ used in $\mathbf{G}_3$. Clearly, $\mathbf{G}_2$ and $\mathbf{G}_3$ are identical until event R_3 occurs; hence, if R_3 never occurs, the adversary has the same chances to win in both the two games, i.e. (using Lemma 1) $T_3 \wedge \neg R_3 \equiv T_2 \wedge \neg R_3 \Rightarrow \left| \Pr[T_3] - \Pr[T_2] \right| \leq \Pr[R_3]$.

To bound the last probability, we consider two more games, $\mathbf{G}_4$ and $\mathbf{G}_5$.

Game $\mathbf{G}_4$. To define game $\mathbf{G}_4$, we change step $E6$ of the encryption oracle as follows: $\boxed{E6'.\ e \leftarrow_R \mathbb{Z}_q,\ S \leftarrow g_1^e}$. Let T_4 be the event that $\sigma = \sigma^*$ in game $\mathbf{G}_4$. Because of this last change, the challenge no longer contains the bit σ, nor does any other information in the adversary's view; therefore, we have that $\Pr[T_4] = \frac{1}{2}$.

Let R_4 be the event that $\mathcal{A}$ submits some decryption query that would have been decrypted in game $\mathbf{G}_2$ but is rejected in game $\mathbf{G}_4$; in other words, R_4 is the event that some decryption query that would have passed the test in step $D4$ of the decryption oracle used in $\mathbf{G}_2$, fails to pass the test in step $D4'$ used in $\mathbf{G}_4$. In [7], we prove (Lemma 4) that those events happen with the same probability as the corresponding events of $\mathbf{G}_3$, i.e. $\Pr[T_4] = \Pr[T_3]$ and $\Pr[R_4] = \Pr[R_3]$.

Game $\mathbf{G}_5$. We again modify the decryption algorithm, adding a *special rejection rule*, to prevent $\mathcal{A}$ from submitting illegal enabling blocks to the decryption oracle, once she has received her challenge $\mathcal{T}^* = \langle S^*, u_1^*, u_2^*, (j_1^*, H_{j_1^*}), \ldots, (j_z^*, H_{j_z^*}), v_0^*, \ldots, v_z^* \rangle$:

> After adversary $\mathcal{A}$ receives the challenge $\mathcal{T}^*$, the decryption oracle rejects any query $\langle i, \mathcal{T} \rangle$, with $\mathcal{T} = \langle S, u_1, u_2, (j_1, H_{j_1}), \ldots, (j_z, H_{j_z}), v_0, \ldots, v_z \rangle$ and $\langle S, u_1, u_2, (j_1, H_{j_1}), \ldots, (j_z, H_{j_z}) \rangle \neq \langle S^*, u_1^*, u_2^*, (j_1^*, H_{j_1^*}), \ldots, (j_z^*, H_{j_z^*}) \rangle$, but $\alpha = \alpha^*$, and it does so before executing the test in $D4'$.

Notice that in the gCCA2 setting the adversary is not allowed to query the decryption oracle $\mathsf{Dec}(i, \mathcal{T})$ on enabling blocks $\Re_i$-equivalent to the challenge $\mathcal{T}^*$.

Therefore, when the *special rejection rule* is applied, we already know that it holds $\neg\Re_i(\mathcal{T}, \mathcal{T}^*)$.

Let C_5 be the event that the adversary submits a decryption query that is rejected using the above *special rejection rule*; let R_5 be the event that $\mathcal{A}$ submits some decryption query that would have passed the test in step $D4$ of the decryption oracle used in $\mathbf{G}_2$, but fails to pass the test in step $D4'$ used in $\mathbf{G}_5$. Notice that this implies that such a query passed the $\Re_i$-equivalence test and the *special rejection rule*, because otherwise step $D4'$ wouldn't have been executed. Clearly, games $\mathbf{G}_4$ and $\mathbf{G}_5$ are identical until event C_5 occurs, i.e. by Lemma 1: $R_5 \wedge \neg C_5 \equiv R_4 \wedge \neg C_5 \Rightarrow \left| \Pr[R_5] - \Pr[R_4] \right| \leq \Pr[C_5]$.

Our final task is to show that events C_5 and R_5 occur with negligible probability: while the argument to bound event C_5 is based on the collision resistance assumption for the family $\mathcal{F}$ (using a standard reduction argument, we can construct a PPT algorithm $\mathcal{A}_2$ that breaks the collision resistance assumption with non negligible advantage), the argument to bound event R_5 hinges upon the fact that the adversary is not allowed to submit queries that are "$\Re_i$-related" to her challenge, and upon information-theoretic considerations (as proven in Lemma 5 of [7]). From these considerations, we obtain that $\Pr[C_5] \leq \epsilon_2$ and $\Pr[R_5] \leq \frac{Q_\mathcal{A}(\lambda)}{q}$, where ϵ_2 is a negligible quantity and $Q_\mathcal{A}(\lambda)$ is an upper bound on the number of decryption queries made by the adversary.

Finally, combining the intermediate results, we can conclude that adversary $\mathcal{A}$'s advantage is negligible; more precisely: $\mathsf{Adv}_{\mathsf{BE},\mathcal{A}}^{\mathsf{gCCA2}}(\lambda) \leq \epsilon_1 + \epsilon_2 + Q_\mathcal{A}(\lambda)/q$.

4.3 z-Resilience against CCA2 Attack

In Section 4.2, we saw how a direct application of the standard technique of [5, 6] does not provide a complete solution to the CCA2 problem, but only suffices for gCCA2 security. As proven in Lemma 5 of [7], the restriction imposed by the gCCA2 attack (namely, forbidding the adversary to submit decryption queries $\langle i, \mathcal{T} \rangle$ such that $\Re_i(\mathcal{T}, \mathcal{T}^*)$ holds) is essential for the security of the previous Broadcast Encryption Scheme. Indeed, given a challenge $\mathcal{T}^*$ with tag sequence $v_0 \ldots v_z$, it is trivial to come up with a different sequence $v_0' \ldots v_z'$ such that $v_i = v_i'$, resulting in a "different" enabling block $\mathcal{T}' \neq \mathcal{T}^*$: however, $\mathsf{Dec}(i, \mathcal{T}^*) = \mathsf{Dec}(i, \mathcal{T}')$, allowing the adversary to "break" the CCA2-security.

Although we feel that gCCA2-security is enough for most applications of Broadcast Encryption Schemes, it is possible to non-trivially modify the Broadcast Encryption Scheme presented in Section 4.2 to obtain CCA2 security (with only a slight efficiency loss). The modified scheme, presented in this section, maintains the same Key Generation and Registration algorithms described before; the essential modifications involve the operations used to construct the enabling block. In particular, to achieve CCA2 security, it is necessary to come up with some trick to make the tag sequence $v_0, \ldots, v_z$ non-malleable. To this aim, we will use any secure (deterministic) *message authentication code* (MAC) to guarantee the integrity of the entire sequence. In fact, we only need any *one-time* MAC, satisfying the following simple property: given a (unique) correct

Encryption algorithm $\mathsf{Enc}(PK, s, \mathcal{R})$	Decryption algorithm $\mathsf{Dec}(i, \mathcal{T})$
$E1.\ r_1 \leftarrow_R \mathbb{Z}_q$	$D1.\ \alpha \leftarrow \mathcal{H}(S, u_1, u_2, (j_1, H_{j_1}), .., (j_z, H_{j_z}))$
$E2.\ u_1 \leftarrow g_1^{r_1}$	$D2.\ \bar{v}_i \leftarrow u_1^{X_{1,i}+Y_{1,i}\alpha} \cdot u_2^{X_{2,i}+Y_{2,i}\alpha}$
$E3.\ u_2 \leftarrow g_2^{r_1}$	$D3.\ v_i \leftarrow \mathsf{EXP\text{-}LI}(0, .., z; v_0, .., v_z)(i)$
$E4.\ H_t \leftarrow h_t^{r_1},\ t \in [0, z]$	$D4.\ \textbf{if}\ v_i = \bar{v}_i\ \textbf{then}$
$E5.\ \textbf{for}\ t = 1\ \textbf{to}\ z\ \textbf{do}$	$D5.\quad H_i \leftarrow u_1^{Z_{1,i}} \cdot u_2^{Z_{2,i}}$
$E6.\quad H_{j_t} \leftarrow \mathsf{EXP\text{-}LI}(0, .., z; H_0, .., H_z)(j_t)$	$D6.\quad s \,\|\, k \leftarrow \dfrac{S}{\mathsf{EXP\text{-}LI}(j_1, .., j_z, i; H_{j_1}, .., H_{j_z}, H_i)(0)}$
$E7.\ \textbf{end for}$	$D7.\quad$ extract s and k from $s \,\|\, k$
$E8.\ k \leftarrow_R \mathcal{K}$	$D8.\quad \textbf{if}\ \tau \neq \mathsf{MAC}_k(v_0, .., v_z)\ \textbf{then}$
$E9.\ S \leftarrow (s \,\|\, k) \cdot H_0$	$D9.\qquad \textbf{return}\ \bot$
$E10.\ \alpha \leftarrow \mathcal{H}(S, u_1, u_2, (j_1, H_{j_1}), .., (j_z, H_{j_z}))$	$D10.\quad \textbf{else return}\ s$
$E11.\ v_t \leftarrow c_t^{r_1} \cdot d_t^{r_1\alpha},\ t \in [0, z]$	$D11.\quad \textbf{end if}$
$E12.\ \tau \leftarrow \mathsf{MAC}_k(v_0, .., v_z)$	$D12.\ \textbf{else return}\ \bot$
$E13.\ \mathcal{T} \leftarrow \langle S, u_1, u_2, (j_1, H_{j_1}), .., (j_z, H_{j_z}),$	$D13.\ \textbf{end if}$
$\qquad v_0, .., v_z, \tau \rangle$	

Fig. 3. Encryption and decryption algorithms for the CCA2 scheme

value $\mathsf{MAC}_k(M)$ for some message M (under key k), it is infeasible to come up with a correct (unique) value of $\mathsf{MAC}_k(M')$, for any $M' \neq M$.

THE ENCRYPTION ALGORITHM. The encryption algorithm Enc receives as input the public key PK, the session key s to be embedded within the enabling block and a set $\mathcal{R} = \{j_1, \ldots, j_z\}$ of revoked users. To construct the enabling block $\mathcal{T}$, the encryption algorithm (defined in Fig. 2) operates similarly to the gCCA2 encryption algorithm: the main difference is that now a MAC key k, randomly chosen from the MAC key space $\mathcal{K}$, is used to MAC the tag sequence $v_0, \ldots, v_z$, and is encapsulated within $\mathcal{T}$ along with the session key s.

THE DECRYPTION ALGORITHM. To recover the session key embedded in the enabling block $\mathcal{T} = \langle S, u_1, u_2, (j_1, H_{j_1}), \ldots, (j_z, H_{j_z}), v_0, \ldots, v_z, \tau \rangle$ a legitimate user i can proceed as in Fig. 3. If i is a revoked user, the algorithm fails in step $D6$, since the interpolation points $j_1, \ldots, j_z, i$ are not pairwise distinct.

SECURITY. The security analysis for this scheme is very subtle, because there is the risk of circularity in the use of the MAC key k. Namely, k is part of the ciphertext (since it is encapsulated, along with the session key s, within S); this means that α, the hash of the ciphertext, depends on k (at least Information-Theoretically), and thus the sequence of tags depends on k. In other words, we are MAC-ing something that depends on the MAC key k, which could be a problem. Luckily, the Information-Theoretic nature of the structural approach to the security analysis that we are pursuing (following [6]) allows us to prove that actually k is completely hidden within S, so that MAC-ing the resulting tag with k is still secure.

The solution to the CCA2 problem for Broadcast Encryption Schemes and the relative security analysis can be viewed as the main technical contribution of this paper; at the same time, the capability to resolve the apparent circularity in the use of the MAC demonstrates the importance of providing a formal model and precise definitions, without which it would have been much harder to devise a correct proof of security for the above scheme.

Theorem 3. *If the* DDH *Problem is hard in* $\mathbb{G}$, $\mathcal{H}$ *is chosen from a collision-resistant hash functions family* $\mathcal{F}$ *and* MAC *is a one-time message authentication code, then the above Broadcast Encryption Scheme is z-resilient against chosen ciphertext attacks.*

Proof. The proof proceeds defining a sequence of games similar to that presented in Theorem 2. The definition of games $\mathbf{G}_0, \ldots, \mathbf{G}_5$ closely follow the exposition given in Theorem 2: however, the statements of all lemmas (and their proofs) need to be changed to accommodate for the use of the MAC. In particular, we can easily state and prove a lemma analogous to Lemma 4 in [7], where the only difference is the presence of information about the MAC key k in the challenge (see Lemma 6 of [7]). More importantly, to bound the probability $\Pr[R_5]$ we introduce a new game $\mathbf{G}_6$ to deal with the use of the MAC in the enabling block, while a lemma similar to Lemma 5 is used to bound the probability of event R_6 defined in game $\mathbf{G}_6$ (see [7] for the details).

Game $\mathbf{G}_6$. We again modify the decryption algorithm, adding a *second special rejection rule* to detect illegal enabling blocks submitted by $\mathcal{A}$ to the decryption oracle, once she has received her challenge $T^* = \langle S^*, u_1^*, u_2^*, (j_1^*, H_{j_1^*}), \ldots, (j_z^*, H_{j_z^*}), v_0^*, \ldots, v_z^*, \tau^* \rangle$. Notice that, while the *special rejection rule*, defined in game $\mathbf{G}_5$, is used to reject adversary's queries aiming at exploiting any weakness in the collision-resistant hash family $\mathcal{F}$, the *second special rejection rule* is used to reject ciphertexts aiming at exploiting any weakness in the MAC scheme.

> After adversary $\mathcal{A}$ receives the challenge T^*, the decryption oracle rejects any query $\langle i, T \rangle$, with $T = \langle S, u_1, u_2, (j_1, H_{j_1}), \ldots, (j_z, H_{j_z}), v_0, \ldots, v_z, \tau \rangle$ and $\langle S, u_1, u_2, (j_1, H_{j_1}), \ldots, (j_z, H_{j_z}) \rangle = \langle S^*, u_1^*, u_2^*, (j_1^*, H_{j_1^*}), \ldots, (j_z^*, H_{j_z^*}) \rangle$ and $(v_0, \ldots, v_z) \neq (v_0^*, \ldots, v_z^*)$, but $\tau = \mathrm{MAC}_{k^*}(v_0, \ldots, v_z)$, and it does so before executing the test in $D4'$, and before applying the *special rejection rule*.

Let M_6 be the event that the adversary submits a decryption query that is rejected in game $\mathbf{G}_6$ using the *second special rejection rule*; let C_6 be the event that the adversary submits a decryption query that is rejected in game $\mathbf{G}_6$ using the *special rejection rule*; let R_6 be the event that $\mathcal{A}$ submits some decryption query that would have passed both the test in step $D4$ and in step $D8$ of the decryption oracle used in game $\mathbf{G}_2$, but fails to pass the test in step $D4'$ used in game $\mathbf{G}_6$. Notice that this implies that such a query passed both the *second special rejection rule* and the *special rejection rule*, because otherwise step $D4'$ wouldn't have been executed at all.

Event M_6 is closely related to the security of the one time MAC used in the scheme; in particular, any difference in behavior between game $\mathbf{G}_5$ and game $\mathbf{G}_6$ can be used to construct a PPT algorithm $\mathcal{A}_3$ that is able to forge a legal authentication code under a one-message attack with non-negligible probability, thus breaking the MAC scheme. Hence, $\Pr[M_6] \leq \epsilon_3$, for some negligible ϵ_3.

Moreover, since $\mathbf{G}_5$ and $\mathbf{G}_6$ are identical until event M_6 occurs, if it doesn't occur at all, they will proceed identically; by Lemma 1: $C_6 \wedge \neg M_6 \equiv C_5 \wedge \neg M_6 \Rightarrow \left| \Pr[C_6] - \Pr[C_5] \right| \leq \Pr[M_6]$ and $R_6 \wedge \neg M_6 \equiv R_5 \wedge \neg M_6 \Rightarrow \left| \Pr[R_6] - \Pr[R_5] \right| \leq \Pr[M_6]$.

Our final task is to bound the probability that events C_6 and R_6 occur: the argument to bound $\Pr[C_6]$ is based on the collision resistance assumption for the family $\mathcal{F}$, while the argument to bound $\Pr[R_6]$ hinges upon information-theoretic considerations (as proven in Lemma 7 of [7]). From those facts, we obtain that $\Pr[C_6] \leq \epsilon_2$ and $\Pr[R_6] \leq \frac{Q_{\mathcal{A}}(\lambda)}{q}$, where ϵ_2 is a negligible quantity and $Q_{\mathcal{A}}(\lambda)$ is an upper bound on the number of decryption queries made by the adversary.

Finally, combining the intermediate results, we can conclude that adversary $\mathcal{A}$'s advantage is negligible; more precisely: $\mathsf{Adv}_{\mathsf{BE},\mathcal{A}}^{\mathsf{CCA2}}(\lambda) \leq \epsilon_1 + \epsilon_2 + 2\epsilon_3 + Q_{\mathcal{A}}(\lambda)/q$.

Acknowledgments

We wish to thank Jonathan Katz, Yevgeniy Kushnir, Antonio Nicolosi and Victor Shoup for helpful observations on an preliminary version of the paper and the anonymous referees for useful comments.

References

[1] J. H. An, Y. Dodis, and T. Rabin. On the Security of Joint Signature and Encryption. In *Advances in Cryptology - EuroCrypt '02*, pages 83–107, Berlin, 2002. Springer-Verlag. LNCS 2332. 100, 101, 103, 104

[2] M. Bellare, A. Desai, E. Jokipii, and P. Rogaway. A Concrete Security Treatment of Symmetric Encryption: Analysis of the DES Modes of Operation. In *Proceedings of the 38th Annual Symposium on Foundations of Computer Science - FOCS '97*, pages 394–403, 1997. 104

[3] D. Boneh. The Decision Diffie-Hellman Problem. In *Algorithmic Number Theory - ANTS-III*, pages 48–63, Berlin, 1998. Springer-Verlag. LNCS 1423. 102

[4] B. Chor, A. Fiat, and N. Naor. Tracing Traitors. In *Advances in Cryptology - Crypto '94*, pages 257–270, Berlin, 1994. Springer-Verlag. LNCS 839. 102

[5] R. Cramer and V. Shoup. A Practical Public Key Cryptosystem Provably Secure Against Adaptive Chosen Ciphertext Attack. In *Advances in Cryptology - Crypto '98*, pages 13–25, Berlin, 1998. Springer-Verlag. LNCS 1462. 101, 105, 107, 108, 111

[6] R. Cramer and V. Shoup. Design and Analysis of Practical Public-Key Encryption Scheme Secure against Adaptive Chosen Ciphertext Attack. Manuscript, 2001. 101, 103, 105, 107, 108, 111, 112

[7] Y. Dodis and N. Fazio. Public Key Trace and Revoke Scheme Secure against Adaptive Chosen Ciphertext Attack. Full version of this paper, available at http://eprint.iacr.org/, 2002. 100, 107, 110, 111, 113, 114

[8] A. Fiat and M. Naor. Broadcast Encryption. In *Advances in Cryptology - Crypto '93*, pages 480–491, Berlin, 1993. Springer-Verlag. LNCS 773. 100

[9] E. Gafni, J. Staddon, and Y. L. Yin. Efficient Methods for Integrating Traceability and Broadcast Encryption. In *Advances in Cryptology - Crypto '99*, pages 372–387, Berlin, 1999. Springer-Verlag. LNCS 1666. 102

[10] A Garay, J. Staddon, and A. Wool. Long-Lived Broadcast Encryption. In *Advances in Cryptology - Crypto 2000*, pages 333–352, Berlin, 2000. Springer-Verlag. LNCS 1880. 100

[11] D. Halevy and A. Shamir. The LSD Broadcast Encryption Scheme. In *Advances in Cryptology - Crypto '02*, pages 47–60, Berlin, 2002. Springer-Verlag. LNCS 2442. 100

[12] M. Luby and J. Staddon. Combinatorial Bounds for Broadcast Encryption. In *Advances in Cryptology - EuroCrypt '98*, pages 512–526, Berlin, 1998. Springer-Verlag. LNCS 1403. 100

[13] D. Naor, M. Naor, and J. Lotspiech. Revocation and Tracing Schemes for Stateless Receivers. In *Advances in Cryptology - Crypto '01*, pages 41–62, Berlin, 2001. Springer-Verlag. LNCS 2139. 100, 101

[14] M. Naor and B. Pinkas. Efficient Trace and Revoke Schemes. In *Financial Cryptography - FC 2000*, pages 1–20, Berlin, 2000. Springer-Verlag. LNCS 1962. 100, 101, 102, 105

[15] V. Shoup. A Proposal for an ISO Standard for Public-Key Encryption. Manuscript, 2001. 100, 101, 103

[16] W. G. Tzeng and Z. J. Tzeng. A Public-Key Traitor Tracing Scheme with Revocation Using Dynamics Shares. In *Public Key Cryptography - PKC '01*, pages 207–224, Berlin, 2001. Springer-Verlag. LNCS 1992. 100, 101, 102, 105, 107

The Cramer-Shoup Strong-RSA
Signature Scheme Revisited

Marc Fischlin

Fraunhofer-Institute Secure Telecooperation (SIT)
Security and Smart Card Technologies (SICA)
marc.fischlin@sit.fraunhofer.de
http://www.sit.fraunhofer.de/~fischlin/

Abstract. We discuss a modification of the Cramer-Shoup strong-RSA signature scheme. Our proposal also presumes the strong RSA assumption, but allows faster signing and verification and produces signatures of roughly half the size. Then we present a stateful version of our scheme where signing (but not verifying) becomes almost as efficient as with RSA-PSS. We also show how to turn our signature schemes into "lightweight" anonymous yet linkable group identification protocols without random oracles.

1   Introduction

Existential unforgeability under adaptive chosen-message attacks has become the salient security criterion for signature schemes. For instance, the well-known RSA-PSS scheme [4, 17] meets this requirement under the RSA assumption in the random oracle model. But only very few efficient schemes are known to achieve this security level without relying on random oracles. One of these schemes is the Cramer-Shoup signature scheme [10] which is provably secure under the strong RSA (aka. flexible RSA) assumption.

Here, we present an improvement of the Cramer-Shoup scheme which also forgos random oracles and is merely based on the strong RSA assumption (and a collision-intractable hash function for long messages). In the original Cramer-Shoup scheme each signature requires the signer to generate a prime and to compute two exponentiations, one exponentiation with a full-fledged exponent and the other one with a smaller exponent. Our solution eliminates the "small" exponentiation which, according to the implementation figures of the Cramer-Shoup scheme [10, 18], saves almost one third of the time for signature generation (when standard speed-up methods like preprocessing and Chinese remainder are used).

Additionally, our proposal almost halves the size of a signature, e.g., for a 1024-bit RSA modulus a signature now has 1350 bits instead of 2200 bits as in the original scheme. The size of the public key in our case marginally grows, but verification too becomes slightly faster and the key generation times are essentially identical.

Y.G. Desmedt (Ed.): PKC 2003, LNCS 2567, pp. 116–129, 2003.

We then present a stateful variation of our signature system. The state information consists of a short prime, typically less than 60 bits long. But this state information buys us another efficiency improvement for the signer while keeping the effort for the verifier unchanged. Namely, the expensive prime generation for each signature almost vanishes, such that the signer mainly has to compute a full-fledged exponentiation. Therefore, signing becomes almost as efficient as for RSA-PSS (yet, in our case, additional preprocessing techniques apply). Moreover, the signature size in our stateful variant is decreased even further, by approximately 100 bits, making it comparable to the size of RSA-PSS signatures. Still, RSA-PSS is significantly superior with respect to key generation and verification, and is of course stateless.

At the end of this paper, we touch anonymous group identification protocols in which users can prove membership in a group without disclosing their identity. We discuss how to construct a "lightweight" anonymous (yet linkable) group identification scheme from our signature schemes. Our solution does not need random oracles, and the group's common public key as well as the performance of a single identification is independent of the number of users.

2   A Modification of the Cramer-Shoup Protocol

In this section we recall the original Cramer-Shoup scheme, introduce our modification and prove it to be secure, and compare our proposal to the original protocol.

We adhere to the notation in [10]; still, the protocol description should be intelligible without [10]. We remark that the strong RSA assumption (introduced by Barić and Pfitzmann [2] as well as Fujisaki and Okamoto [13]) says that for a random RSA modulus n and a random element $z \in \mathbb{Z}_n^*$ it is infeasible to find an integer $e \geq 2$ and the e-th root of z in $\mathbb{Z}_n^*$. Hence, compared to the ordinary RSA assumption where the exponent is given, a solution for the strong RSA problem allows to come up with a self-determined exponent.

Recently, Damgård and Koprowski [11] have generalized the Cramer-Shoup signature scheme to generic groups for which the strong root assumption, the counterpart to the strong RSA assumption in $\mathbb{Z}_n^*$, holds. We note that our improvements here also apply to the model of Damgård and Koprowski.

2.1   Original Cramer-Shoup Signature Scheme

The original Cramer-Shoup scheme works as follows:

Key Generation: Generate $n = pq$, where $p = 2p' + 1$ and $q = 2q' + 1$ for primes p, q, p', q'. Also pick two quadratic residues $h, x \in \mathrm{QR}_n$ and a random $(l + 1)$-bit prime e'. The public verfication key is (n, h, x, e') and the private key is (p, q).

Signing: To sign a message m compute the l-bit hash value $H(m)$ with a collision-intractable hash function $H(\cdot)$. Pick a random $(l+1)$-bit prime $e \neq e'$ and a random $y' \in \mathrm{QR}_n$, compute x' where

$$(y')^{e'} = x'h^{H(m)} \bmod n$$

as well as y with

$$y^e = xh^{H(x')} \bmod n.$$

Computing this e-th root is easy given the factorization of n. The signature equals (e, y, y').

Verification: First check that e is an odd $(l+1)$-bit integer different from e', then compute $x' = (y')^{e'} h^{-H(m)}$ and verify that $x = y^e h^{-H(m)}$.

Note that computing the e-th root of $xh^{H(x')}$ corresponds to an exponentiation with a full-fledged exponent $e^{-1} \bmod \varphi(n)$, while the computation of y' solely involves "small" l-bit exponents. If these exponentiations are performed in $\mathbb{Z}_n^*$ then the running times differ significantly. However, when using the Chinese remainder and appropriate preprocessing methods, the implementation results in [10, 18] show that both exponentiations roughly need the same time. Specifically, according to [10, 18] the prime generation and the exponentiations then each take approximately one third of the total signing time.

2.2   Modified Cramer-Shoup Signature Scheme

One can view the value $H(x')$ as a trapdoor commitment of the message m, using the RSA trapdoor commitment scheme. Therefore, as pointed out in [10], one may replace this part with any other appropriate trapdoor commitment. Indeed, [10, Sec. 5] suggest as an example a trapdoor commitment based on the discrete-log assumption. By this, the signature length shrinks to almost half of the original size. Unfortunately, this advantage disappears again if one switches to other trapdoor commitments based on the RSA or factoring assumption, or even general one-way functions.

The second part of the signature generation can be thought of as a representation problem. That is, a representation of x with respect to h, e, n is a pair (α, y) such that $h^\alpha y^e = x \bmod n$. In this sense, a signature in the original protocol requires that one finds a representation of x involving the hash value $-H(x')$ and a self-determined exponent e. In the modified signature scheme here, we assimilate the trapdoor commitment to the representation problem:

Key Generation: Generate $n = pq$, where $p = 2p' + 1$ and $q = 2q' + 1$ for primes p, q, p', q'. Also pick three quadratic residues $h_1, h_2, x \in \mathrm{QR}_n$. The public verfication key is (n, h_1, h_2, x) and the private key is (p, q).

Signing: To sign a message m calculate the l-bit hash value $H(m)$ with a collision-intractable hash function $H(\cdot)$. Pick a random $(l+1)$-bit prime e, a random l-bit string α and compute a representation $(-\alpha, -(\alpha \oplus H(m)), y)$ of x with respect to h_1, h_2, e, n, i.e.,

$$y^e = x h_1^{\alpha} h_2^{\alpha \oplus H(m)} \bmod n.$$

Computing this e-th root y from $x h_1^{\alpha} h_2^{\alpha \oplus H(m)}$ is easy given the factorization of n. The signature is given by (e, α, y).

Verification: Check that e is an odd $(l+1)$-bit integer, that α is l bits long, and that $y^e = x h_1^{\alpha} h_2^{\alpha \oplus H(m)} \bmod n$.

The idea of splitting $H(m)$ into random (but dependent) parts α and $\alpha \oplus H(m)$ is not new. It has already been applied for the well-known protocol for proving knowledge of one out of two discrete logarithms [9] and for security amplification reducing chosen-message attacks to random-message attacks [8]. As we will discuss below, it also gives the desired trapdoor information for proving security here.

We remark that we may instead select α at random in $\mathbb{Z}_e$ and split the message into α and $\alpha + H(m) \bmod c$. Moreover, we may alternatively define y in the signature generation as the unique value such that $x = h_1^{\alpha} h_2^{\alpha \oplus H(m)} y^e \bmod n$, i.e., rearrange the equation to derive a "well-formed" representation problem. Our security proof also works for these variations, even when combined.

2.3 Performance Comparison

Compared to the original scheme with signature size $2|n| + l + 1$, both the modification here as well as the one using the discrete-log trapdoor commitment produce signatures of size $|n| + 2l + 1$. Disadvantegeously, both modifications slightly increase the size of the public key, e.g., adding $|n| - l$ bits in our case. However, this is outweighed by the shorter signatures.

The same speedup techniques as in [10, Sec. 3, 6 and 7] apply here (e.g., computation via Chinese remainder, faster prime number generation, taking e-th roots efficiently, precomputation techniques, etc.). In particular, selecting $x = h_1^a$ and $h_2 = h_1^{a'}$ for appropriate a, a' and storing a, a' in the secret key, the effort to compute the e-th root of $x h_1^{\alpha} h_2^{\alpha \oplus H(m)} = h_1^{\alpha + a + a'(\alpha \oplus H(m))}$ is (almost) the same as in the original scheme for $x h^{H(x')} = h^{a + H(x')}$. That is, the signer first computes $f = e^{-1}(a + H(x')) \bmod \varphi(n)$ in the original scheme or, in our case, $f = e^{-1}(\alpha + a + a'(\alpha \oplus H(m))) \bmod \varphi(n)$ with a few more operations. Then the signer calculates $h^f \bmod n$ resp. $h_1^f \bmod n$, possibly using the Chinese remainder method and preprocessing techniques. In summary, since our proposal does not require the computation of the separate trapdoor commitment we eliminate the "small" exponentiation almost for free.

For signature verification, the cost for the verifier for checking the single equation in our scheme with two generators h_1, h_2 is only marginally higher than the cost of checking the equation $y^e = xh^{H(x')}$ with a single generator h in the original scheme. The reason is that, using standard methods, such exponentiations can be carried out with roughly the same effort as in the single generator case. Yet, in our case the additional verification of the trapdoor commitment disappears.

Unfortunately, all solutions share the expensive prime generation of e. A profound algorithm to generate e has been presented in [10, Sec. 6] (see also the corresponding implementation results in [18]). Another possible improvement is to decrease the length of e at the cost of a larger public key. Namely, if we put, say, three values h_1, h_2, h_3 into the public key, then we can divide the hash value $H(m)$ into halves $H_1(m), H_2(m)$ of 80 bits each, and choose α and e to be 80 and 81 bits, respectively. A signature is then described by the equation $xh_1^\alpha h_2^{\alpha \oplus H_1(m)} h_3^{\alpha \oplus H_2(m)} = y^e$, and the signature length is about 80 bits shorter. The security proof in the next section straightforwardly extends to this case.

If we choose three generators h_1, h_2, h_3, then the effort for the signer to compute the e-th root y given stored values a, a', a'' does not change significantly in comparison to the case of two generators. But an 81-bit prime e is much easier to find than a 161-bit one. The verifier now has to perform a faster to compute "quadruple" exponentiation $h_1^\alpha h_2^{\alpha \oplus H_1(m)} h_3^{\alpha \oplus H_2(m)} y^e$ with 81-bit exponents instead of a "triple" exponentiation $h_1^\alpha h_2^{\alpha \oplus H(m)} y^e$ with 161-bit exponents.

Our signature scheme also has the feature that for short messages, e.g., of 80 bits, a collision-intractable hash function becomes obsolete and the signer may choose e also as a shorter prime, e.g., 81 bits or even 41 bits with the trick above. Moreover, signing and verifying become slightly faster. This may be interesting for identification protocols, where users identify by signing short random messages.

2.4 Security Proof

We discuss that the modified signature scheme is secure against adaptive chosen-message attacks. Basically, the proof follows the one in [10].

Note that in an adaptive chosen-message attack the adversary is given the public key of the signer and can ask the signer to sign arbitrary messages. The choice of the next message submitted to this signature oracle is adaptively determined by the data gathered before. Finally, the adversary outputs a message that has not been signed by the oracle, together with a putative signature for this message.

Let m_i be the i-th query to the signer and (e_i, α_i, y_i) denote the answer. Let m and (e, α, y) be the putative forgery of the adversary. We assume that all e_i chosen by the signer during an attack are distinct (yet, the adversary's choice e may equal some e_j), and that $H(m) \neq H(m_i)$ for all m_i (otherwise we have found a collision $m \neq m_i$).

There are two types of forgers (dubbed according to [10]):

Type II: The adversary outputs $e = e_j$ for some j.

Type III: The adversary outputs a new e, different from all e_i.

Type I forgers as in [10] disappear due to our modification. We show that type II forgers contradict the (ordinary) RSA assumption, whereas type III forgers refute the strong RSA assumption.

Type II Forger

We assume that we know j, otherwise we can guess it. Since $H(m_j) \neq H(m)$ we have $\alpha_j \neq \alpha$ or $\alpha_j \oplus H(m_j) \neq \alpha \oplus H(m)$. With probability $1/2$ we can guess in advance which case will happen, and we assume for simplicity that $\alpha_j \neq \alpha$ here. The other case is treated analogously.

We are given n, $z \in \mathbb{Z}_n^*$ and an odd prime r and are supposed to output $z^{1/r}$. To do so, we invoke the type II forger on the following public key and signature oracle: Set $e_j = r$ and for all $i \neq j$ choose a random $(l+1)$-bit prime e_i (where i is bounded by the number of queries to the signature oracle in the attack). Let

$$h_1 = z^{2 \cdot \prod_{i \neq j} e_i}, \quad h_2 = v^{2 \cdot \prod_i e_i}, \quad x = h_1^{-\beta} \cdot w^{2 \cdot \prod_i e_i}$$

for random $v, w \in \mathbb{Z}_n^*$ and a random l-bit string β. The "prepared" public key is (n, h_1, h_2, x).

To sign the i-the message on behalf of the signer, $i \neq j$, select an l-bit string α_i and compute

$$y_i = w^{2 \cdot \prod_{k \neq i} e_k} \cdot \left(z^{2 \cdot \prod_{k \neq j, k \neq i} e_k} \right)^{\alpha_i - \beta} \cdot \left(v^{2 \cdot \prod_{k \neq i} e_k} \right)^{\alpha_i \oplus H(m_i)}$$

$$= \left(x h_1^{\alpha_i} h_2^{\alpha_i \oplus H(m_i)} \right)^{1/e_i}$$

For the j-th signature query set $\alpha_j = \beta$ and compute y_j as[1]

$$y_j = w^{2 \cdot \prod_{k \neq j} e_k} \cdot \left(v^{2 \cdot \prod_{k \neq j} e_k} \right)^{\alpha_j \oplus H(m_j)} = \left(x h_1^{\alpha_j} h_2^{\alpha_j \oplus H(m_j)} \right)^{1/e_j}$$

It is not hard to see that the data in this simulation is identically distributed to the one in a real attack. In particular, x and the signatures for $i \neq j$ are distributed independently of β, and therefore α_j in this simulation has the same distribution as in an actual attack.

The adversary's output yields another representation of x with respect to n, h_1, h_2 and $e_j = r$. More precisely,

$$h_1^{-\alpha_j} h_2^{-(\alpha_j \oplus H(m_j))} y_j^r = x = h_1^{-\alpha} h_2^{-(\alpha \oplus H(m))} y^r \mod n.$$

And, plugging in the preselected values,

$$h_1^{\alpha - \alpha_j} = h_2^{(\alpha_j \oplus H(m_j)) - (\alpha \oplus H(m))} \cdot (yy_j^{-1})^r$$

$$z^{2 \cdot \prod_{i \neq j} e_i \cdot (\alpha - \alpha_j)} = \left(v^{2 \cdot \prod_{i \neq j} e_i \cdot ((\alpha_j \oplus H(m_j)) - (\alpha \oplus H(m)))} \cdot yy_j^{-1} \right)^r$$

---

[1] If we had bet on $\alpha_j \oplus H(m_j) \neq \alpha \oplus H(m)$ then we would have basically swapped the roles of h_1 and h_2 and would now set $\alpha_j = \beta \oplus H(m_j)$.

Since $|\alpha - \alpha_j| \in \mathbb{Z}_r - \{0\}$ and all e_k are relatively prime, we can compute an r-th root of z by standard procedures (see, for instance, [10]).

Type III Forger

This case is almost identical to the one discussed in [10]. Namely, given n, z preselect all e_i and set

$$h_1 = z^{2 \cdot \prod_i e_i}, \quad x = h_1^a, \quad h_2 = h_1^{a'}$$

for random $a, a' \in \{1, \ldots, n^2\}$. As h_1 is a generator of QR_n with high probability and since $a, a' \bmod p'q'$ are statistically close to the uniform distribution on $\mathbb{Z}_{p'q'}$, the values x, h_2 are almost uniformly distributed quadratic residues. Also, we can sign any query m_i since we know the e_i-th roots of $xh_1^{\alpha_i} h_2^{\alpha_i \oplus H(m_i)}$ for any α_i. On the other side, the forgery yields the equation

$$y^e = xh_1^\alpha h_2^{\alpha \oplus H(m)} = z^m$$

where

$$m = 2 \cdot \prod_i e_i \cdot (a + \alpha + a'(\alpha \oplus H(m))).$$

The fact that $e \nmid m$ with non-negligible probability and that we can compute a non-trivial $e/\gcd(e, m)$-th root of z now follows as in [10]. Specifically, if r is a prime dividing e, then r clearly does not divide $2 \cdot \prod_i e_i$. Write a as $a = bp'q' + c$ for $0 \leq c < p'q'$ and note that the adverary's view is essentially independent of b, even if given c. Hence, $b \bmod r$ is almost uniform on $\mathbb{Z}_r$ and the probability that $r | (a + \alpha + a'(\alpha \oplus H(m)))$ or, equivalently, that $a + \alpha + a'(\alpha \oplus H(m)) = 0 \bmod r$ is negligibly close to $1/r$.

We conclude that with probability close to $1 - 1/r$ for the smallest prime factor r of e we have $e \nmid m$. Once more, in this case it is easy to compute a non-trivial $e/\gcd(e, m)$-th root of z by standard techniques.

3   Efficient Stateful Signatures

In this section we present a stateful variation of our signature scheme above. This modification here removes the necessity to generate a 161-bit prime for each signature. Instead, the signer uses a smaller prime number, e.g., up to 60 bits, which he must update after each signing.

3.1   Description

Our stateful scheme can be outlined as follows. Instead of using random $(l + 1)$-bit primes e (such that $e \geq 2^l - 1$) as before, the signer here uses shorter primes e and the smallest power e^t such that $e^t \geq 2^l - 1$. The signer starts with $e_1 = 3$ or, for security reasons [6], rather with $e_1 = 2^{16} + 1$. After signing with this prime, he proceeds to the next prime e_2 after e_1. Having used e_2 the signer then picks e_3 for the next signature and so on. More generally, for the j-th signature the signer uses the j-th prime e_j (after the offset $2^{16} + 1$). For this, the signer stores the current prime e and, after signing, updates it with algorithm nextprime(e) which generates the closest prime after e.

Key Generation: Generate $n = pq$, where $p = 2p' + 1$ and $q = 2q' + 1$ for primes p, q, p', q'. Also pick three quadratic residues $h_1, h_2, x \in \mathrm{QR}_n$ and initialize $e = 2^{16} + 1$. The public verfication key is (n, h_1, h_2, x) and the private key is (p, q) and the state information is given by e.

Signing: To sign a message m calculate the l-bit hash value $H(m)$ with a collision-intractable hash function $H(\cdot)$. Find the smallest integer t such that $e^t \geq 2^l - 1$. Then pick a random l-bit string α and compute a representation $(-\alpha, -(\alpha \oplus H(m)), y)$ of x with respect to h_1, h_2, e^t, n, i.e.,

$$y^{e^t} = x h_1^\alpha h_2^{\alpha \oplus H(m)} \bmod n.$$

Computing this e^t-th root y from $x h_1^\alpha h_2^{\alpha \oplus H(m)}$ is easy given the factorization of n. The signature is given by (e, α, y). Finally, update e as nextprime(e).

Verification: Given a putative signature (e, α, y) check that α is l bits long, that $e \geq 2^{16} + 1$ is odd, and that $y^{e^t} = x h_1^\alpha h_2^{\alpha \oplus H(m)} \bmod n$, where t is the smallest integer such that $e^t > 2^l - 1$.

3.2   Performance Comparison

In comparison to the modified Cramer-Shoup scheme in the previous section, in this stateful scheme here the signer needs to generate a much shorter prime. In fact, if the signer signs at most 2^{50} messages, then less than 60 bits are enough to store the current prime.

We remark that short primes are easier to generate. For example, using an observation by Bleichenbacher [5], reported in [15] and also pointed out in [10], there is a determinsitic primality test for short numbers. Bleichenbacher has shown that it suffices to run the Miller-Rabin primality test with fixed bases $\mathcal{B} = \{2, 3, 5, 7, 11, 13, 23\}$ in order to identify primes up to 53 bits. Additionally, for shorter primes, e.g., of 30 bits, an even smaller base suffices (see [5, Chap. 3]). Together with standard trial division, this gives a very efficient way to generate the primes (up to the approximately first 2^{45} signatures).

In summary, the signing time is now dominated by the computation of the e^t-th root y. Thus, the overall effort for signing is pretty close to the one for RSA signatures where one also computes an e-th root. Yet, in contrast to RSA where the exponent and its inverse are fixed, here we must first compute the inverse of e^t when signing. But in favor of our scheme we observe that preprocessing for the computation of the root y is applicable.

Surprisingly, the gain in efficiency compared to the stateless version also comes with a decrease in signature size. Namely, instead of 161-bit primes, a signature now contains the j-th smallest prime after $2^{16}+1$. As noted above, 60 bits are usually sufficient to append this prime to the signature, thus saving another 100 bits.

3.3 Security Proof

Once more, assume that an adversary successfully runs an adaptive chosen-message attack. Denote the i-th submission to the signer by m_i and let (e_i, α_i, y_i) be the answer. We also denote by t_i the corresponding exponent such that $e_i^{t_i} \geq 2^l - 1$. The putative forgery is given by m and (e, α, y). For simplicity, assume again that $H(m) \neq H(m_i)$ for all m_i.

The two types of forgers are:

Type II: The adversary outputs e such that $e_j | e$ for some j.
Type III: The adversary outputs e such that no prime e_j divides e.

In a sense, these types generalize the ones of the proof in the previous section. It is therefore not surprising that the proof carries over immediately: Type II forgers will contradict the RSA assumption (for a small given exponent $r = e_j$, that is, the j-th prime e_j after $2^{16}+1$), whereas type III forgers refute the strong RSA assumption.

Type II Forger

This part of the proof is similar to the case of type II forgers before. Suppose that we know j with $e_j | e$ in advance. Again, from $H(m_j) \neq H(m)$ it follows $\alpha_j \neq \alpha$ or $\alpha_j \oplus H(m_j) \neq \alpha \oplus H(m)$, and, to simplify, we only treat the case $\alpha_j \neq \alpha$ here.

Given n, $z \in \mathbb{Z}_n^*$ and the j-th prime e_j after $2^{16}+1$, we feed the adversary the following data: For all $i \neq j$ compute the i-th prime e_i and the exponent t_i and set

$$h_1 = z^{2 \cdot \prod_{i \neq j} e_i^{t_i}}, \quad h_2 = v^{2 \cdot \prod_i e_i^{t_i}}, \quad x = h_1^{-\beta} \cdot w^{2 \cdot \prod_i e_i^{t_i}}$$

for random $v, w \in \mathbb{Z}_n^*$ and a random l-bit string β. These values make up the public key (n, h_1, h_2, x).

To simulate the signing process for the i-the message, $i \neq j$, choose a random l-bit value α_i and compute

$$y_i = w^{2 \cdot \prod_{k \neq i} e_k^{t_k}} \cdot \left(z^{2 \cdot \prod_{k \neq j, k \neq i} e_k^{t_k}} \right)^{\alpha_i - \beta} \cdot \left(v^{2 \cdot \prod_{k \neq i} e_k^{t_k}} \right)^{\alpha_i \oplus H(m_i)}$$

$$= \left(x h_1^{\alpha_i} h_2^{\alpha_i \oplus H(m_i)} \right)^{1/e_i^{t_i}}$$

For the j-th signature query set $\alpha_j = \beta$ and compute y_j as

$$y_j = w^{2 \cdot \prod_{k \neq j} e_k^{t_k}} \cdot \left(v^{2 \cdot \prod_{k \neq j} e_k^{t_k}} \right)^{\alpha_j \oplus H(m_j)} = \left(x h_1^{\alpha_j} h_2^{\alpha_j \oplus H(m_j)} \right)^{1/e_j^{t_j}}$$

A successful forgery of the adversary yields another representation of x with respect to n, h_1, h_2 and $e_j^{t_j}$. Specifically,

$$h_1^{-\alpha_j} h_2^{-(\alpha_j \oplus H(m_j))} y_j^{e_j^{t_j}} = x = h_1^{-\alpha} h_2^{-(\alpha \oplus H(m))} y^{e_j^{t_j}} \bmod n.$$

Therefore,

$$h_1^{\alpha - \alpha_j} = h_2^{(\alpha_j \oplus H(m_j)) - (\alpha \oplus H(m))} \cdot \left(y y_j^{-1}\right)^{e_j^{t_j}}$$

$$z^{2 \cdot \Pi_{i \neq j} e_i^{t_i} \cdot (\alpha - \alpha_j)} = \left(v^{2 \cdot \Pi_{i \neq j} e_i^{t_i} \cdot ((\alpha_j \oplus H(m_j)) - (\alpha \oplus H(m)))} \cdot y y_j^{-1}\right)^{e_j^{t_j}}$$

Because $\alpha \neq \alpha_j$ and $e_j^{t_j} \geq 2^l - 1$ there is some integer $k < t_j$ such that

$$\alpha = \alpha_j \bmod e_j^k \quad \text{and} \quad \alpha \neq \alpha_j \bmod e_j^{k+1}$$

Applying well-known techniques (see again [10], for example) we can compute an $e_j^{t_j}$-th root a of $h_1^{e_j^k}$. Since raising elements to the e_j-th power is a permutation, it follows that $a^{e_j^{t_j - k - 1}}$ is an e_j-th root of $h_1 = z^{2 \cdot \Pi_{i \neq j} e_i^{t_i}}$. Once more, this gives us straightforwardly an e_j-th root of the given value z.

Type III Forger

Observing that the smallest prime factor r of the adversary's choice e does not divide any $e_i^{t_i}$ (by assumption), this part of the proof is identical to the previously given proof. We thus omit this part and note that this completes the proof.

Remark

The devil's advocate may object that, in this scheme here, type II adversaries need to break RSA for a small exponent $e \geq 2^{16} + 1$ only, whereas in the stateless version the adversary must use a large $(l + 1)$-bit prime. However, we remark that for low public exponents $e \geq 2^{16} + 1$ no better attacks than the ones for large exponents are known [6]. Additionally, our scheme supports a flexible offset and one may start with larger primes, for example, $e_1 \geq 2^{40}$. But this also means a slight loss in efficiency.

4   "Lightweight" Anonymous Group Identification

With an anonymous group identification scheme each user of a group is able to prove membership in the group while hiding his identity among the group members. Below, we present an anonymous group identification scheme which does not rely on random oracles, and where both the size of the group's public key as well as the computational effort for an identification are independent of the number of users in the group. For convenience we only present the protocol based on our stateless signature scheme; it is easy to adapt it to the case of stateful signatures.

Unfortunately, our protocol is linkable in the sense that a verifier is able to decide if two identifications have been carried out by the same user (although the verifier is unable to specify the user among the group members). An obvious countermeasure against this problem is to frequently refresh one's membership and receive new keys (as in the case of pseudonyms).

Also note that the group manager is able to identify on behalf of any user (besides the fact that the manager can issue keys for fake users). Still, our protocol enjoys other strong security characteristics: it is for instance secure against any number of users that actively coorperate to intrude as another honest user; details follow.

Several anonymous group identification schemes (which can be derived for example from group signature schemes) have been constructed in the past, e.g., [12, 7, 1, 14], each with different security and performance features. Our solution seems to exceed all these protocols in performance, but at the cost of unlinkability.

4.1 Description

The group manager in our anonymous identification scheme picks an RSA modulus $n = pq$ of strong primes $p = 2p' + 1, q = 2q' + 1$, and a random element $x \in QR_n$ together with a generator h_1 of QR_n. The values (n, x, h_1) make up the group's public key. If a user u wants to join, then the manager picks a random $(l + 1)$-bit prime e_u and a random l-bit value α_u, and computes y_u such that $h_1^{\alpha_u} y_u^{e_u} = x \bmod n$. The manager hands the pair (α_u, y_u) and e_u to the user.[2]

Next, we describe the identification protocol; it is also depicted in Figure 1. If a user u wants to identify as a group member to some verifier, both parties run Okamoto's RSA identification protocol [16] on the user's key and the group's public key. That is, the user picks $a \in \mathbb{Z}_{e_u}$, $z \in \mathbb{Z}_n^*$ in order to calculate $A = h_1^a z^{e_u} \bmod n$ and sends this value A with e_u to the verifier.[3] The verifier answers with a random challenge $c \in \mathbb{Z}_{e_u}$ and the user conclusively transmits b, B where $b = a + c\alpha_u \bmod e_u$ and $B = zx^c h_1^{\lfloor (a+c\alpha_u)/e_u \rfloor} \bmod n$. The verifier checks that e_u is an odd $l + 1$-bit number and the correctness condition $Ax^c = h_1^b B^{e_u} \bmod n$ of the identification protocol.

Note that we can add "threshold admittance levels" to our identification protocol almost for free. That is, each user u is assigned a privilege number l_u

---

[2] For ease of notation we switch to a "well-formed" representation problem as explained at the end of Section 2.2. Also for simplicity we have chosen the version with "large" $(l + 1)$-bit primes e_u. The protocol can be easily adapted to work with shorter primes e_u and powers $e_u^{t_u} \geq 2^l - 1$ instead.

[3] Okamoto's protocol does not require to send the exponent e_u as the exponent is already part of the public key. Here, the group's public key does not contain the users' exponents, so we let the user append it to the protocol data. Indeed, this is what makes our protocol linkable.

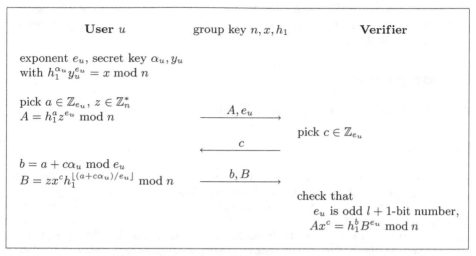

Fig. 1. Anonymous Identification Protocol

and this user is only allowed to enter (by means of identification) level ℓ areas for $\ell_u \geq \ell$. This feature is easy to accomplish in our scheme by demanding that, in order to enter level ℓ, the user u must identify with respect to an $(l+1+\ell)$-bit (or larger) number e_u, and by letting the group manager distribute corresponding exponents to the users when joining.

4.2 Security

Basically, our identification protocol inherits security from our signature scheme. Think of the group manager giving each new user u a signature for random message α_u. Note that this message α_u is chosen by the group manager, i.e., this setting corresponds to a random-message attack. Therefore, we do not need a trapdoor commitment nor a random splitting.

If some malicious user u^*, either a member or not, successfully identifies as another member using an exponent e_u of an honest user u, then, by the proof-of-knowledge property of Okamoto's scheme, we can extract a representation (α^*, y^*) of x with respect to e_u from this identification attempt. As Okamoto's identification is witness-independent, we have $\alpha_u \neq \alpha^*$ with probability $1 - 2^{-l}$ for the user's secret key (α_u, y_u). In this case, party u^* thus forges a signature of a new message α^* which is infeasible under the RSA assumption. Similarly, if u^* chooses a new e_{u^*} and successfully proves membership, we obtain a successful signature forgery for message α^* for this e_{u^*}, contradicting the strong RSA assumption.

We remark that security even holds with respect to any adversary that controls all corrupted users and who may adaptively decide to join further malicious users, to corrupt existing parties, and to run protocols with the honest users before trying to intrude. Using techniques developed in [3], one can even extend it to the case that some dishonest user u^* tries to intrude in the name of a user u while executing the identification protocol with that user u (in the presence of so-called session IDs).

Acknowledgments

We thank Ronald Cramer and Victor Shoup for comments.

References

[1] G. ATENIESE, J. CAMENISCH, M. JOYE, G. TSUDIK: A Practical and Provably Secure Coalition-Resistant Group Signature Scheme, *Advances in Cryptology—Crypto 2000, Lecture Notes in Computer Science, Vol. 1880, pp. 255–270, Springer-Verlag*, 2000. 126

[2] N. BARIĆ, B. PFITZMANN: Collision-free Accumulators and Fail-Stop Signature Schemes Without Trees, *Advances in Cryptology—Eurocrypt '97, Lecture Notes in Computer Science, Vol. 1233, pp. 480–495, Springer-Verlag*, 1997. 117

[3] M. BELLARE, M. FISCHLIN, S. GOLDWASSER, S. MICALI: Identification Protocols Secure Against Reset Attacks, *Advances in Cryptology—Eurocrypt 2001, Lecture Notes in Computer Science, Vol. 2045, pp. 495–511, Springer-Verlag*, 2001. 127

[4] M. BELLARE, P. ROGAWAY: The Exact Security of Digital Signatures — How to Sign with RSA and Rabin, *Advances in Cryptology—Eurocrypt '96, Lecture Notes in Computer Science, Vol. 1070, pp. 399–416, Springer-Verlag*, 1996. 116

[5] D. BLEICHENBACHER: Efficiency and Security of Cryptosystems Based on Number Theory, *Ph.D. thesis, Swiss Federal Institute of Technology, Zürich*, 1996. 123

[6] D. BONEH: Twenty Years of Attacks on the RSA Cryptosystem, *Notices of the American Mathematical Society (AMS), Vol. 46, No. 2, pp. 203–213*, 1999. 122, 125

[7] D. BONEH, M. FRANKLIN: Anonymous Authentication with Subset Queries, *Proceedings of the 6th ACM Conference on Computer and Communication Security, pp. 113-119*, 1999. 126

[8] R. CRAMER, I. DAMGÅRD, T. PEDERSEN: Efficient and Provable Security Amplification, *CWI Reports, Computer Science, CS-R9529*, 1995. 119

[9] R. CRAMER, I. DAMGÅRD, B. SCHOENMAKERS: Proofs of Partial Knowledge and Simplified Design of Witness Hiding Protocols, *Advances in Cryptology—Crypto'94, Lecture Notes in Computer Science, Vol. 839, pp. 174–187, Springer-Verlag*, 1994. 119

[10] R. CRAMER, V. SHOUP: Signature Schemes Based on the Strong RSA Assumption, *ACM Transactions on Information and System Security (ACM TISSEC), 3(3), pp. 161–185*, 2000. 116, 117, 118, 119, 120, 121, 122, 123, 125

[11] I. DAMGÅRD, M. KOPROWSKI: Generic Lower Bounds for Root Extraction and Signature Schemes in General Groups, *Advances in Cryptology—Eurocrypt 2002, Lecture Notes in Computer Science, Springer-Verlag*, 2002. 117

[12] A. DE SANTIS, G. DI CRESCENZO, G. PERSIANO: Communication-Efficient Anonymous Group Identification, *Proceedings of the 5th ACM Conference on Computer and Communication Security, pp. 73-82*, 1998. 126

[13] E. FUJISAKI, T. OKAMOTO: Statistical Zero Knowledge Protocols to Prove Modular Polynomial Relations, *Advances in Cryptology—Crypto '97, Lecture Notes in Computer Science, vol. 1294, pp. 16–30, Springer Verlag*, 1997. 117

[14] C. LEE, X. DENG, H. ZHU: Desing and Security Analysis of Anonymous Group Identifcation Protocols, *Public Key Cryptography (PKC) 2002, Lecture Notes in Computer Science, Springer-Verlag*, 2002. 126

[15] U. MAURER: Fast Generation of Prime Numbers and Secure Public-Key Cryptographic Parameters, *Journal of Cryptology, vol. 8, pp. 123–155, Springer-Verlag*, 1995.

[16] T. OKAMOTO: Provable Secure and Practical Identification Schemes and Corresponding Signature Schemes, *Advances in Cryptology—Crypto '92, Lecture Notes in Computer Science, vol. 740, pp. 31–53, Springer Verlag*, 1993. 126

[17] RSA CRYPTOGRAPHY STANDARD: PKCS #1 v2.1, *available at* www.rsa.security.com/rsalabs/pkcs, June 2002. 116

[18] T. SCHWEINBERGER, V. SHOUP: ACE — The Advanced Cryptographic Engine, *available at* www.shoup.net, August 2002.

Strong Key-Insulated Signature Schemes

Yevgeniy Dodis[1], Jonathan Katz[2] *, Shouhuai Xu[3], and Moti Yung[4]

[1] Department of Computer Science, New York University, USA
dodis@cs.nyu.edu
[2] Department of Computer Science, University of Maryland (College Park), USA
jkatz@cs.umd.edu
[3] Department of Information and Computer Science
University of California at Irvine, USA
shxu@ics.uci.edu
[4] Department of Computer Science, Columbia University, USA
moti@cs.columbia.edu

Abstract. Signature computation is frequently performed on insecure
devices — e.g., mobile phones — operating in an environment where
the private (signing) key is likely to be exposed. Strong key-insulated
signature schemes are one way to mitigate the damage done when this
occurs. In the key-insulated model [6], the secret key stored on an insecure device is refreshed at discrete time periods via interaction with
a physically-secure device which stores a "master key". All signing is still
done by the insecure device, and the public key remains fixed throughout
the lifetime of the protocol. In a strong (t, N)-key-insulated scheme, an
adversary who compromises the insecure device and obtains secret keys
for up to t periods is unable to forge signatures for any of the remaining
$N-t$ periods. Furthermore, the physically-secure device (or an adversary
who compromises only this device) is unable to forge signatures for *any*
time period.

We present here constructions of strong key-insulated signature schemes
based on a variety of assumptions. First, we demonstrate a generic construction of a strong $(N-1, N)$-key-insulated signature scheme using
any standard signature scheme. We then give a construction of a strong
(t, N)-signature scheme whose security may be based on the discrete
logarithm assumption in the random oracle model. This construction offers faster signing and verification than the generic construction, at the
expense of $O(t)$ key update time and key length. Finally, we construct
strong $(N-1, N)$-key-insulated schemes based on any "trapdoor signature scheme" (a notion we introduce here); our resulting construction in
fact serves as an identity-based signature scheme as well. This leads to
very efficient solutions based on, e.g., the RSA assumption in the random
oracle model.

1 Introduction

Security of cryptographic primitives typically relies on the assumption that secret keys are kept "perfectly secure"; standard cryptosystems provide no secu-

---

* Work done in part while at DIMACS.

Y.G. Desmedt (Ed.): PKC 2003, LNCS 2567, pp. 130–144, 2003.
© Springer-Verlag Berlin Heidelberg 2003

rity guarantees in case secret keys are ever exposed. In practice, however, the assumption that keys are never exposed is often unwarranted. In many cases, it is easier to obtain a secret key from a stolen device (or by otherwise tricking an unsuspecting user) than to break the computational assumption on which the security of the system is based. Clearly, methods of effectively dealing with key exposure are needed.

A recently-proposed method of minimizing the damage caused by secret key exposures is that of *key-insulated cryptography* [6]. In this model, physical security (and hence secrecy of stored data) is guaranteed for a single device that holds a "master" secret key SK^* corresponding to a fixed public key PK. Day-to-day cryptographic operations, however, are performed by an insecure device which "refreshes" its key periodically by interacting with the secure device. In a (t, N)-key-insulated cryptosystem (informally) an adversary who compromises the insecure device and obtains keys for up to t time periods is unable to violate the security of the cryptosystem for any of the remaining $N - t$ periods; we elaborate for the specific case of digital signatures below. In a *strong* key-insulated scheme, security is additionally guaranteed with respect to the secure device itself or compromises thereof; this is vital when the secure device may be untrusted. Strong key-insulated public-key encryption schemes have been defined and constructed recently [6]; here, we provide definitions and constructions for strong key-insulated signature schemes.

OVERVIEW OF THE MODEL. We review the informal description of the key-insulated model as given in [6], adapted here for the case of digital signatures. As in a standard signature scheme, the user begins by registering a single public key PK; this key will remain fixed for the lifetime of the protocol. A master secret key SK^*, generated along with PK, is stored on a device which is physically secure and hence resistant to compromise. All signing, however, is done by the user on an insecure device for which key exposures may occur. The lifetime of the protocol is divided into distinct periods $1, \ldots, N$; at the beginning of period i, the user interacts with the secure device to derive a temporary secret key SK_i which will be used by the insecure device to sign messages during that period. Signatures are labeled with the time period during which they were generated; thus, signing message M during period i results in signature $\langle i, s \rangle$.

As mentioned above, the user's insecure device is assumed to be vulnerable to repeated key exposures; specifically, we assume that up to $t < N$ periods can be compromised. Our goal is to minimize the effect such compromises will have. Of course, when a key SK_i is exposed an adversary will be able to sign messages of his choice for period i. Our notion of security is that this is the best an adversary can do. In particular, the adversary will be unable to forge a signature on a new message for any of the remaining $N - t$ periods. We call a scheme satisfying this notion (t, N)-*key-insulated*.

If the physically-secure device is completely trusted, it may generate (PK, SK^*) itself, keep SK^*, and publish PK on behalf of the user. When the user requests a key for period i, the device may compute SK_i and send it. More involved methods are needed when the physically-secure device is *not* trusted by the user. In this, more difficult case (which we consider here), a solution is to have the user generate (PK, SK), publish PK, and then derive keys SK^*, SK_0. The user then sends SK^* to the device and stores SK_0 himself on the insecure device. When the user wants to update his key to that of period j (and the user currently holds the key for period i) the physically-secure device computes and sends "partial" key $SK'_{i,j}$ to the user, who may then compute the "actual" key SK_j using SK_i and $SK'_{i,j}$. If designed appropriately, the user's security may be guaranteed during *all* time periods with respect to the device itself. Schemes meeting this level of security are termed *strong*. As noted previously [6], strong key-insulation is essential when a single device serves many different users. Here, users may trust the device to update their keys but may not want the device to be able to sign on their behalf.

Clearly, some form of authentication between the user and the physically-secure device is necessary. Note that if a key K used for this authentication is stored on the insecure device, an adversary who exposes keys even *once* obtains K and can then impersonate the user during subsequent key updates (thus obtaining signing keys for subsequent time periods). As in previous work, however, we assume that authentication is handled by an underlying protocol (outside the scope of this work) which is immune to such attacks. As one possible example, K might never be stored on the insecure device but will instead be obtained directly from the user each time authentication is needed (e.g., K may be a password or a key derived from biometric information).

OUR CONTRIBUTIONS. The initial work on key-insulated cryptosystems [6] focused primarily on the case of public-key encryption; here, we focus on the complementary case of digital signatures. Adapting a "folklore" result (see [1]), we first show a generic construction of a strong $(N - 1, N)$-key-insulated signature scheme from any standard signature scheme. We then give a more efficient strong (t, N)-key-insulated signature scheme whose security may be reduced to the discrete logarithm assumption in the random oracle model. This construction offers faster signing and verification than the generic construction, at the expense of $O(t)$ key update time and key length. Finally, we construct strong $(N - 1, N)$-key-insulated signature schemes based on any "trapdoor signature scheme" (a term we introduce here); this results in very efficient solutions based on, e.g., the RSA assumption in the random oracle model. Our construction (which may be viewed as a generalization of recent independent work [4, 14, 24, 25]) may also be used as an identity-based signature scheme; we believe this is of independent interest since no rigorous proofs of security for ID-based signature schemes were previously known.

RELATED WORK. Girault [10] investigates a notion similar to key-insulated digital signatures in the context of smart-card research. However, this preliminary work contained no formal model or proofs of security. Key-insulated public-key encryption was considered by Tzeng and Tzeng [30] and also by Lu and Shieh [19], but these works only consider security against a weak, non-adaptive adversary. Key-insulated public-key encryption was first formally defined in [6], and schemes with rigorous proofs of security are given there.

Somewhat related to key insulation is the problem of signature delegation [11]. In this model, a user wants to delegate use of a signing key in a particular way. For example (to place it in our setting), a user may delegate the right to sign messages for a single day. Here, one seeks to prevent exposure of the "master" signing key when a small number of delegated keys are exposed. On the other hand, to prevent excessive delegation it is required that exposure of many delegated keys completely reveals the master key. The key-insulated model makes no such requirement, and this allows for greater efficiency and flexibility. We also note that the existing practical delegation schemes [11] are not provably-secure against an *adaptive* adversary who chooses which keys to expose at any point during its execution. Finally, our *strong* schemes also protect against forgeries by the physically-secure device itself; this has no counterpart in the context of signature delegation.

Besides the key-insulated model, many alternate approaches have been proposed to address the risks associated with key exposure. The first such example is that of forward security [2, 3]. In this model no external device is present, and the entire secret key is stored on — and updated by — the insecure device itself. Clearly, any exposure now compromises *all future* time periods; forward-secure signature schemes, however, prevent compromise of *prior* time periods. A consequence of this model (which is not present in our model) is that even the valid user is unable to recover keys for prior time periods once the appropriate secret key has been erased.

More recently — and subsequent to the present work — the key-insulated model has been extended and strengthened to yield the notion of intrusion-resilience [16]. This model adds to our notion a proactive refresh capability which may be performed more frequently than key updates; hence, intrusion-resilient schemes can tolerate multiple corruptions of both the user and the physically secure device (called the "home base") while maintaining security of the scheme for all time periods during which the user's device remained uncorrupted. Furthermore, if both user and home base are corrupted simultaneously, the scheme remains secure for all prior time periods (as in forward-secure schemes).

Each of these models may be appropriate for use in different contexts. Forward-secure schemes are advantageous in that the user need not interact with any other device. On the other hand, when interaction with such a device may be assumed, key-insulated and intrusion-resilient schemes provide a stronger level of security. Finally, although intrusion-resilience represents a stronger level of security than key-insulation, the assumption of physically-secure storage confers other benefits in the key-insulated model. For example, the key-insulated model enables the honest user to request "old" keys thereby allowing, e.g., the signing of documents for prior time periods when needed. This is impossible in the forward-secure or intrusion-resilient settings. Also, known intrusion-resilient schemes [16, 15] are (thus far) less efficient than the key-insulated schemes presented here, suggesting that one use the latter when physical security of the "home base" can be guaranteed.

Independent of the present work, we have become aware of related work in the context of re-keyed digital signatures [1]. Recasting this work in our model, one may observe that they construct $(N-1, N)$-key-insulated signature schemes based on either (1) generic signature schemes or (2) the factoring assumption. Their generic construction is essentially identical to ours except that we additionally ensure that our scheme is *strong* key-insulated. Our discrete logarithm scheme has no counterpart in [1]. Our scheme based on trapdoor signatures and specialized for RSA may be viewed as the "Guillou-Quisquater" [13] analogue to their "Ong-Schnorr" [23] factoring-based scheme, where again we additionally ensure strong security of our construction. The notion of random access to keys is unique to our treatment.

Finally, we mention that an identity-based signature scheme [28] immediately gives an $(N-1, N)$-key-insulated signature scheme (ensuring *strong* security requires some additional work). However, we are not aware of any previous formal definitions or proofs of security for identity-based signature schemes. Our proof of security for the construction of Section 5 (which is based on earlier work [28]) may be easily adapted to show that this construction is in fact an identity-based signature scheme as well.

2   The Model

For completeness, we provide a formal definition of key-insulated signature schemes and their security (based on [6]). We begin with the definition of a key-updating signature scheme, which generalizes the notion of a key-evolving signature scheme [3]. In a key-updating signature scheme there is some data (namely, SK^*) that is never erased; this data will be stored on a physically-secure device and hence is never exposed.

Definition 1. *A key-updating signature scheme is a 5-tuple of poly-time algorithms* (Gen, Upd*, Upd, Sign, Vrfy) *such that:*

- Gen, *the* key generation algorithm, *is a probabilistic algorithm taking as input a security parameter* 1^k *and the total number of time periods* N. *It returns a public key* PK, *a master key* SK^*, *and an initial key* SK_0.
- Upd*, *the* device key-update algorithm, *is a probabilistic algorithm taking as input indices* i, j *for time periods (throughout, we assume* $1 \leq i, j \leq N$*) and the master key* SK^*. *It returns a partial secret key* $SK'_{i,j}$.
- Upd, *the* user key-update algorithm, *is a deterministic algorithm taking as input indices* i, j, *a secret key* SK_i, *and a partial secret key* $SK'_{i,j}$. *It returns the secret key* SK_j *for time period* j.
- Sign, *the* signing algorithm, *is a probabilistic algorithm taking as input an index* i *of a time period, a message* M, *and a secret key* SK_i. Sign$_{SK_i}(i, M)$ *returns a signature* $\langle i, s \rangle$ *consisting of the time period* i *and a signature* s.
- Vrfy, *the* verification algorithm, *is a deterministic algorithm taking as input the public key* PK, *a message* M, *and a pair* $\langle i, s \rangle$. Vrfy$_{PK}(M, \langle i, s \rangle)$ *returns a bit* b, *where* $b = 1$ *means the signature is accepted.*

If $\mathsf{Vrfy}_{PK}(M, \langle i, s \rangle) = 1$, *we say that* $\langle i, s \rangle$ *is a* valid *signature of M for period i.* *We require that all signatures output by* $\mathsf{Sign}_{SK_i}(i, M)$ *are accepted as valid by* Vrfy.

In a key-updating signature scheme, a user begins by generating $(PK, SK^*, SK_0) \leftarrow \mathsf{Gen}(1^k, N)$, registering PK in a central location (just as he would for a standard public-key scheme), storing SK^* on a physically-secure device, and storing SK_0 himself. When the user — who currently holds SK_i — wants to obtain SK_j, the user requests $SK'_{i,j} \leftarrow \mathsf{Upd}^*(i, j, SK^*)$ from the secure device. Using SK_i and $SK'_{i,j}$, the user computes $SK_j = \mathsf{Upd}(i, j, SK_i, SK'_{i,j})$; this key may be then used to sign messages during time period j without further access to the device. After computation of SK_j, the user erases SK_i and $SK'_{i,j}$. Note that verification is always performed with respect to a fixed public key PK which is never changed.

Remark 1. The above definition corresponds to schemes supporting random-access key updates [6]; that is, schemes in which one can update SK_i to SK_j in one "step" for any i, j. A weaker definition allows $j = i + 1$ only. All schemes presented in this paper support random-access key updates.

BASIC KEY INSULATION. The adversary we consider is extremely powerful: (1) it may request signatures on messages of its choice during time periods of its choice, adaptively and in any order (i.e., we do not restrict the adversary to making its queries in chronological order); (2) it may expose the secrets contained on the insecure device for up to ℓ adaptively-chosen time periods (alternately, it may choose to expose the secrets stored on the physically-secure device); and (3) it can compromise the insecure device during a key-update phase, thus obtaining partial keys in addition to full-fledged secret keys. The adversary is considered successful if it can forge a valid signature $\langle i, s \rangle$ on message M such that the adversary never requested a signature on M for period i and furthermore the adversary never exposed the insecure device at time period i.

We model each of these attacks by defining appropriate oracles to which the adversary is given access. To model key exposures, we define a *key exposure oracle* $\mathsf{Exp}_{SK^*, SK_0}(\cdot)$ that does the following on input i: (1) The oracle first checks whether period i has been "activated"; if so, the oracle returns the value already stored for SK_i. Otherwise, (2) the oracle runs $SK'_i \leftarrow \mathsf{Upd}^*(0, i, SK^*)$ followed by $SK_i = \mathsf{Upd}(0, i, SK_0, SK'_i)$, returns and stores the value SK_i, and labels period i as "activated". We also give the adversary access to a *signing oracle* $\mathsf{Sign}_{SK^*, SK_0}(\cdot, \cdot)$ that does the following on input i, M: (1) The oracle first checks whether period i has been "activated"; if so, the oracle returns $\mathsf{Sign}_{SK_i}(i, M)$ (where a value for SK_i is already stored). Otherwise, (2) the oracle runs $SK'_i \leftarrow \mathsf{Upd}^*(0, i, SK^*)$ followed by $SK_i = \mathsf{Upd}(0, i, SK_0, SK'_i)$, stores SK_i, returns $\mathsf{Sign}_{SK_i}(i, M)$, and labels period i as "activated".

Remark 2. Storing the values of the secret keys for "activated" periods is only necessary when Upd^* is probabilistic; when it is deterministic, the oracle may simply run Upd^* "from scratch" whenever needed to answer an oracle query. To be fully general, one could allow the adversary to access a "reissuing oracle" which on input i re-computes the secret key SK_i via $SK_i \leftarrow$

$\mathsf{Upd}(0, i, SK_0, \mathsf{Upd}^*(0, i, SK^*))$. The schemes presented here all remain secure under a more complex definition of this form.

Definition 2. *Let Π be a key-updating signature scheme and fix t. For any adversary A, we may perform the following experiment:*

$$(PK, SK^*, SK_0) \leftarrow \mathsf{Gen}(1^k, N); \quad (M, \langle i, s \rangle) \leftarrow A^{\mathsf{Sign}_{SK^*, SK_0}(\cdot, \cdot), \mathsf{Exp}_{SK^*, SK_0}(\cdot)}(PK).$$

We say that A succeeds if $\mathsf{Vrfy}_{PK}(M, \langle i, s \rangle) = 1$, (i, M) was never submitted to the signing oracle, i was never submitted to the key exposure oracle, and A made at most t calls to the key-exposure oracle. Denote the probability of A's success by $\mathsf{Succ}_{A,\Pi}(k)$. We say that Π is (t, N)-key-insulated if for any PPT A, $\mathsf{Succ}_{A,\Pi}(k)$ is negligible. We say Π is perfectly key-insulated if Π is $(N-1, N)$-key-insulated.

We remark that we allow the adversary to interleave signing requests and key exposure requests, and in particular the key exposure requests of the adversary may be made adaptively (based on the entire transcript of the adversary's execution) and in any order.

SECURE KEY UPDATES. For the purposes of meeting Definition 2, we could let $SK'_{i,j} = SK^*$ for all i, j; the user could then run Upd^* and Upd by himself to derive SK_i (and then erase SK^*). Of course, one reason for not doing so is the realistic concern that an adversary who gains access to the insecure device is likely to have access for several consecutive time periods (i.e., until the user detects or re-boots) including the *key update steps*. In this case, an adversary attacking the scheme above would obtain SK^* and we would not be able to achieve even $(1, N)$-key-insulated security.

To address this problem, we consider attacks in which an adversary compromises the user's storage while a key is being updated from SK_i to SK_j; we call this a *key-update exposure at (i, j)*. When this occurs, the adversary receives $SK_i, SK'_{i,j}$, and SK_j (actually, the latter can be computed from the former). We say a scheme has *secure key updates* if a key-update exposure at (i, j) is of no more help to the adversary than key exposures at both periods i and j. More formally:

Definition 3. *A key-updating signature scheme Π has* secure key updates *if the view of any adversary A making a key-update exposure at (i, j) can be perfectly simulated by an adversary A' making key exposure requests at periods i and j.*

STRONG KEY INSULATION. Finally, we address attacks that compromise the physically-secure device (this includes attacks by the device itself, in case it is untrusted). Our definition is similar to Definition 2 except that instead of having access to the key exposure oracle, the adversary is simply given the master key SK^*. Schemes which are secure in this sense — and also (t, N)-key-insulated — are termed *strong (t, N)-key-insulated*. We do not protect against adversaries who compromise *both* the physically-secure device and the user's storage; in our model, this is impossible to achieve. (Intrusion-resilient schemes [16] partially protect against such attacks by allowing the insecure device to interact with the secure device even when not updating its key.)

Definition 4. *Let* $\Pi = (\mathsf{Gen}, \mathsf{Upd}, \mathsf{Upd}^*, \mathsf{Sign}, \mathsf{Vrfy})$ *be a signature scheme which is* (t, N)*-key-insulated. For adversary* B*, we perform the following experiment:*

$$(PK, SK^*, SK_0) \leftarrow \mathsf{Gen}(1^k, N); \quad (M, \langle i, s \rangle) \leftarrow B^{\mathsf{Sign}_{SK^*,SK_0}(\cdot,\cdot)}(PK, SK^*).$$

We say that B *succeeds if* $\mathsf{Vrfy}_{PK}(M, \langle i, s \rangle) = 1$ *and* (i, M) *was never submitted to the signing oracle. Denote the probability of* B*'s success by* $\mathsf{Succ}_{B,\Pi}(k)$*. We say that* Π *is* strong (t, N)*-key-insulated if for any* PPT B*,* $\mathsf{Succ}_{B,\Pi}(k)$ *is negligible.*

3   Generic, Perfectly Key-Insulated Signature Scheme

We demonstrate a perfectly key-insulated signature scheme that can be constructed from any existentially unforgable (standard) signature scheme $\Theta = (G, S, V)$. Rather than repeating the standard definition of security, we may view Θ as as $(0, 1)$-key-insulated scheme in the natural way. Thus, our construction can be viewed as amplifying a $(0, 1)$-key-insulated scheme to a perfectly key-insulated scheme for larger N. We later show how to achieve strong key insulation with minimal additional cost.

The basic construction achieving perfect $(N-1, N)$-key-insulation is folklore. Gen generates a pair of keys $(PK, SK^*) \leftarrow G(1^k)$, sets the public key to PK, sets $SK_0 = \perp$, and stores SK^* on the physically-secure device. At the beginning of time period i, the device generates a fresh pair of keys $(pk_i, sk_i) \leftarrow G(1^k)$ and certifies pk_i for time period i by signing it as follows: $\mathsf{cert}_i = (pk_i, S_{SK^*}(pk_i\|i))$. It then sets $SK_i = \langle sk_i, \mathsf{cert}_i \rangle$ and sends SK_i to the user, who erases the previous key. The user signs a message M at time period i by using the "temporary" key sk_i and appending the certificate cert_i; that is, $\mathsf{Sign}_{sk_i}(i, M) = \langle i, \sigma, \mathsf{cert}_i \rangle$, where $\sigma \leftarrow S_{sk_i}(M)$. To verify, one first verifies correctness of the cerificate and then uses the period verification key pk_i to verify the signature σ, accepting only if both are valid. We remark that it is crucial to sign the time period i along with pk_i since this prevents an adversary from re-using the same certificate at a different time.

Signing requires computation equivalent to the original (basic) signature scheme, while the cost of signature verification is increased by a factor of two. In practice, verifying the validity of cert_i need only be done once per period when multiple signatures are verified. Security of the scheme is given by the following lemma.

Lemma 1. *If* Θ *is existentially unforgeable under a chosen message attack, then* Π *as described is* $(N-1, N)$*-key-insulated. Furthermore,* Π *has secure key updates.*

Proof. That Π has secure key updates is trivial. We therefore focus on the proof of perfect key insulation. Let A attack Π. A forgery occurs when the adversary forges a valid signature $\langle i, \sigma, (pk, \tau) \rangle$ of some message M at time period i such that: (1) τ is a vaild signature of $(pk\|i)$ w.r.t. PK; (2) σ is a valid signature of M w.r.t. pk; (3) period i was not exposed; and (4) (i, M) was not submitted to the signing oracle.

Denote the event of a forgery by F. Wlog, we assume that the period i is "activated" (cf. Section 2), so that the value of pk_i is well defined. We let Eq be the event that $pk = pk_i$. Clearly, $\Pr(\mathsf{F}) = \Pr(\mathsf{F} \wedge \mathsf{Eq}) + \Pr(\mathsf{F} \wedge \overline{\mathsf{Eq}})$.

Case 1: In case events F and Eq both occur then $pk = pk_i$. Assume that A makes at most $q(k) = \mathsf{poly}(k)$ queries to the signing oracle overall. We construct A' attacking Θ as follows: A' has as input a verification key pk' for which it does not know the corresponding secret key sk', and also has oracle access to the signing oracle $S_{sk'}(\cdot)$. A' chooses a random index $r \in \{1, \ldots, q(k)\}$, generates a random key pair $(PK, SK^*) \leftarrow G(1^k)$, and runs A on input PK. Let i^* be the period for which the rth signing query of A was made. If a previous signing query was made for that same period i^*, the experiment is aborted. Otherwise, adversary A' implicitly uses (pk', sk') to respond to the query by making use of its signing oracle $S_{sk'}(\cdot)$. For signature queries $r + 1, \ldots, q(k)$, if A requests a signature for period i^* the signature is computed using $S_{sk'}(\cdot)$. Additionally, if A ever makes a key exposure query for period i^*, the experiment is aborted. All other oracle queries are answered by A' in the expected manner; namely, by generating fresh temporary keys and using the corresponding secret keys to answer signing and key exposure requests. If the final output of A is $(M, \langle i, \sigma, (pk, \tau) \rangle)$ and the experiment was never aborted, then A' simply outputs (M, σ).

With probability at least $1/q(k)$, the experiment is not aborted and $i^* = i$ (recall, i is the period for which a forgery is made). The success probability of A' in forging a signature for Θ is thus at least $\Pr[\mathsf{F} \wedge \mathsf{Eq}]/q(k)$. By the assumed security of Θ, this quantity must be negligible. Since $q(k)$ is polynomial in k, it must be that $\Pr[\mathsf{F} \wedge \mathsf{Eq}]$ is negligible as well.

Case 2: In case events F and $\overline{\mathsf{Eq}}$ both occur, then either period i is not "activated" or else $pk \neq pk_i$. We construct A' attacking Θ as follows: A' has as input a verification key pk' for which it does not know the corresponding secret key sk', and has access to a signing oracle $S_{sk'}(\cdot)$. A' sets $PK = pk'$ and implicitly sets the master key $SK^* = sk'$. A' then simulates the entire run of A by generating (on its own) all the temporary keys as needed, and using its signing oracle $S_{sk'}(\cdot)$ to produce the needed certificates. If the final output of A is $(M, \langle i, \sigma, (pk, \tau) \rangle)$ then A' simply outputs $(pk\|i, \tau)$. The success probability of A' in forging a signature for Θ is then exactly $\Pr[\mathsf{F} \wedge \overline{\mathsf{Eq}}]$. By the assumed security of Θ, this quantity is negligible.   □

ACHIEVING STRONG KEY INSULATION. The above construction is extensively used in practice. However, the scheme assumes a fully-trusted device on which to store SK^* since, as described, the device can sign messages without the user's consent. We now present a simple method to achieve strong security for *any* key-insulated scheme (i.e., not just the folklore scheme above).

Let $\Pi = (\mathsf{Gen}, \mathsf{Upd}^*, \mathsf{Upd}, \mathsf{Sign}, \mathsf{Vrfy})$ be a (l, N)-key-insulated signature scheme and let $\Theta = (G, S, V)$ be a standard signature scheme. We construct a scheme Π' as follows. $\mathsf{Gen}'(1^k)$ runs $(PK, SK^*, SK_0) \leftarrow \mathsf{Gen}(1^k, N)$ followed by $(pk, sk) \leftarrow G(1^k)$. It sets $PK' = (PK, pk)$, $SK^{*\prime} = SK^*$ and $SK_0' = (SK_0, sk)$. In other words, the user get "his own" signing key sk. The key updating algorithms are modified in the expected way, so that at all times the user stores a key of the form (SK_i, sk). When signing, the user computes both the signature of M w.r.t. Π and the signature of $(M\|i)$ w.r.t. S. Formally, $\mathsf{Sign}'_{(SK_i, sk)}(i, M) = \langle \mathsf{Sign}_{SK_i}(i, M), S_{sk}(M\|i)\rangle$. To verify, simply check the validity of both signatures.

The modified scheme is obviously (t, N)-key-insulated as before (a formal proof is immediate). Strong security also follows as long as Θ is secure, since an adversary who has only the master key SK^* can never forge a signature on a "new" message $(M\|i)$ with respect to Θ. We remark that it is crucial that the period i be signed along with M using sk. To summarize:

Lemma 2. *If Π is (t, N)-key-insulated and Θ is existentially unforgeable, then Π' as described is strong (t, N)-key-insulated.*

4 (t, N)-Key Insulation under the DLA

While the scheme of the previous section is asymptotically optimal in all parameters, in practice one might hope for more efficient solutions, especially for strong security. In particular, one might hope to avoid the doubling (tripling) of signature/verification time and also to reduce the length of a signature. In the following sections, we provide schemes based on specific assumptions in which signing and verifying require only a single application of the signing/verification algorithm of the underlying scheme. The signature length will also be essentially the same as that of the underlying scheme.

In this section, we present a (t, N)-key-insulated scheme which may be proven secure under the discrete logarithm assumption. Unfortunately, the lengths of the public key and the master key grow linearly with t (yet they are independent of N). Thus, while practical for small values of t, it does not completely solve the problem for $t \approx N$. We defer such a solution to the following section.

Our scheme builds on the Okamoto-Schnorr signature scheme [22, 26] which we review here. Let p, q be primes such that $p = 2q + 1$ and let $\mathcal{G}$ be the subgroup of $\mathbb{Z}_p^*$ of order q. Fix generators $g, h \in \mathcal{G}$. A public key is generated by choosing $x, y \in_R \mathbb{Z}_q$ and setting $v = g^x h^y$. To sign message M, a user chooses random $r_1, r_2 \in \mathbb{Z}_q$ and computes $w = g^{r_1} h^{r_2}$. Using a hash function H (modeled as a random oracle), the user then computes $t = H(M, w)$, where t is interpreted as an element of $\mathbb{Z}_q$. The signature is: $(w, r_1 - tx, r_2 - ty)$. A signature (w, a, b) on message M is verified by computing $t = H(M, w)$ and then checking that $w \stackrel{?}{=} g^a h^b v^t$. It can be shown [22, 21] that signature forgery is equivalent to computing $\log_g h$.

Our construction achieving strong (t, N)-key-insulated security appears in Figure 1. We stress that the scheme achieves *strong* security without additional modifications, yet the time required for signing and verifying is essentially the same as in the basic Okamoto-Schnorr scheme. Furthermore, using two generators enables a proof of security for an *adaptive* adversary who can choose which time periods to expose at any point during its execution. A proof of the following theorem appears in the full version of this paper.

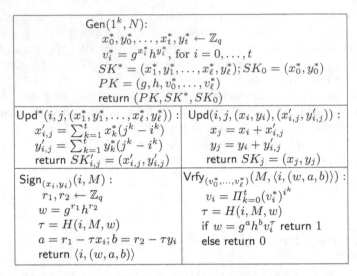

Fig. 1. A strong (t, N)-key-insulated signature scheme

Theorem 1. *Under the discrete logarithm assumption, the scheme of Figure 1 is strong (t, N)-key-insulated and has secure key updates in the random oracle model.*

5 Perfectly Key-Insulated Signature Schemes

We now construct a strong, *perfectly* key-insulated scheme whose security (in the random oracle model) is based on what we call *trapdoor signatures*. This scheme is more efficient than the generic signature scheme presented in Section 3, and results in a variety of specific perfectly key-insulated signatures; e.g., an efficient perfectly key-insulated scheme based on ordinary RSA (in the random oracle model).

Informally, we say that signature scheme $\Theta = (G, S, V)$ is a *trapdoor signature scheme* if the following hold: (1) Key generation consists of selecting a permutation (f, f^{-1}) from some family of trapdoor permutations, choosing random y, and computing $x = f^{-1}(y)$; and (2) the public key is $\langle f, y \rangle$ and the private key is x. It is essential that it is *not* necessary to include f^{-1} as part of the private key.

Given any trapdoor signature scheme, we construct a perfectly key-insulated signature scheme Π as follows (methods for achieving strong security are discussed below): Gen chooses trapdoor permutation (f, f^{-1}) and publishes $PK = \langle f, H \rangle$ for some hash function H (which will be treated as a random oracle in our analysis). The long-term secret key is $SK^* = f^{-1}$. The key SK_i for time period i is computed as $SK_i = f^{-1}(H(i))$, and a signature on message M during period i is computed (using the basic scheme) via $\sigma \leftarrow S_{SK_i}(M)$. Verification of signature $\langle i, M \rangle$ is done using the basic verification algorithm and "period public key" $PK_i \stackrel{\text{def}}{=} \langle f, H(i) \rangle$. The security of this scheme is given by the following:

Theorem 2. *If Θ is a secure trapdoor signature scheme, then Π (as constructed above) is perfectly key-insulated and has secure key updates.*

Proof. That Π has secure key updates is obvious. Given an adversary A attacking the security of Π, we construct an adversary B attacking the security of Θ. Adversary B is given public key $\langle f, y \rangle$ for an instance of Θ as well as access to a signing oracle $S_x(\cdot)$. Assume that A makes $q(k) = \text{poly}(k)$ queries to hash function $H(\cdot)$. Adversary B chooses a random index $i \in \{1, \dots, q(k)\}$ and runs A on input $PK = f$. We assume without loss of generality that for any index I, A queries $H(I)$ before querying $\text{Exp}(I)$ or $\text{Sign}(I, *)$ and also before outputting a forgery of the form $(M, \langle I, \sigma \rangle)$; if not, we can have B perform these queries on its own. To answer the jth query of A to $H(\cdot)$ for $j \neq i$, B chooses a random x_j, computes $y_j = f(x_j)$, and returns y_j. To answer the ith query of A to $H(\cdot)$, B simply returns y. Let $I_1, \dots, I_{q(k)}$ represent the queries of A to $H(\cdot)$. Note that B can answer honestly all oracle queries of the form $\text{Sign}(I_j, *)$ for $1 \leq j \leq q(k)$: when $j \neq i$ then B has the necessary secret key and when $j = i$ then B can make use of its own signing oracle to answer the query. Furthermore, B can answer honestly all oracle queries of the form $\text{Exp}(I_j)$ as long as $j \neq i$; on the other hand, B aborts the simulation if the query $\text{Exp}(I_i)$ is ever asked. When A outputs a forgery $(M, \langle I_j, \sigma \rangle)$, if $j \neq i$ then B aborts; otherwise, B outputs forgery (M, σ). Note that the probability that B does not abort is exactly $1/q(k)$ and therefore $\Pr[\text{Succ}_{B,\Theta}] = 1/q(k) \cdot \Pr[\text{Succ}_{A,\Pi}]$. Since this quantity must be negligible, the success probability of A must be negligible as well. $\qquad\square$

This conversion of Θ to a perfectly key-insulated scheme is quite efficient. The length of PK is roughly equal to the length of the public key in Θ, and temporary keys SK_i require as much storage as secret keys in the original scheme. Signing and verifying times in Π are essentially identical to those in Θ. As for concrete instantiations of Θ, the Guillou-Quisquater scheme [13] provides a trapdoor signature scheme based on the RSA assumption (in the random oracle model). However, a number of additional schemes satisfy this requirement as well (e.g., [8, 20, 23, 29, 27]). Thus our technique is quite flexible and allows for adaptation of a number of standard (and previously analyzed) schemes.

We also note that the loss of a factor $q(k) = q_{\text{hash}}$ (where this represents the number of hash queries) in the concrete security reduction above can be improved for schemes based on specific trapdoor permutations. In particular, when the trapdoor permutation is induced by a claw-free permutation (see [7] for a definition) and Θ is constructed via the Fiat-Shamir transform [8] (i.e., the signature corresponds to a proof of knowledge of $f^{-1}(y)$), we can obtain a security bound losing only a factor $O(q_{\text{exp}})$, where q_{exp} denotes the number of key exposures. In particular, we can achieve this tighter security reduction for the RSA-based Guillou-Quisquater scheme mentioned above.

ACHIEVING STRONG SECURITY. Strong security for any scheme following the above construction can be achieved immediately using the "generic" conversion outlined in Section 3 and proven secure in Lemma 2. This increases the cost of signature computation and verification. For specific schemes, however, we can often do better: in particular, when computation of f^{-1} can be done in a 2-out-of-2 threshold manner by the user and the device. As an example, for the RSA-based scheme in which $f_{N,e}(x) \stackrel{\text{def}}{=} x^e \bmod N$ and $f_{N,d}^{-1}(y) \stackrel{\text{def}}{=} y^d \bmod N$ (for $ed = 1 \bmod \varphi(N)$), the user and the device can share d *additively* using standard threshold techniques (e.g., [9]). Here, the user stores (at all times) d_1 and the physically-secure device stores d_2 such that $d_1 + d_2 = d \bmod \varphi(N)$. To compute the key SK_i for period i, the device sends $x_{i,2} = H(i)^{d_2}$ to the user who then computes $SK_i = x_{i,2} \cdot H(i)^{d_1} = H(i)^d$. We note that similar threshold techniques are available for computing f^{-1} in 2^t-root signature schemes [18], showing that the scheme based on Ong-Schnorr signatures can be efficiently made strong as well.

6   Relation to Identity-Based Signature Schemes

An *ID-based signature scheme* [28] allows a trusted center to publish a system-wide public key PK while keeping secret a "master" key SK^*, and to then use SK^* to extract signing keys SK_I corresponding to *any identity I*. The security of ID-based signatures roughly states that no coalition of users can sign on behalf of any other user. By identifying time periods with identities, we see that any ID-based signature scheme yields a perfectly (but not necessarily strong) key-insulated signature scheme. Although the converse does not necessarily hold, we note that our construction of the previous section *does* yield an identity-based signature scheme as well. Indeed, when our construction is instantiated with the Guillou-Quisquater scheme, the resulting scheme is essentially equivalent to the original ID-based signature scheme of Shamir [28]. We mention, however, that prior to our work no formal proofs of security for any identity-based signature scheme have appeared. We believe that it is extremely important to provide such formal treatment due to the practical relevance of both ID-based and key-insulated signatures.

We also remark that very recently (and independently from this work) several proposals [25, 24, 4, 14] for ID-based signatures have been given. (Among these, only [4] provides formal definitions and analysis; indeed, one of the schemes of [14] was recently broken [5].) Interestingly, they all can be viewed as applying our methodology above to various trapdoor signature schemes using the same function f^{-1}. Roughly, the corresponding function (considered in a "gap Diffie-Hellman" group; see [17]) has the form $f_{g,g^a}^{-1}(g^b) = g^{ab}$. This (inverse) function can be efficiently computed given the trapdoor a. Even though f itself is not efficiently computable given only g, g^a, one can easily see that all we need in Theorem 2 is to efficiently sample random pairs of the form (g^b, g^{ab}) (in order to respond to the random oracle queries), which is easy to do for the above f.

Thus, our approach encompasses a variety of proposed schemes, and almost immediately yields a simple proof of security in each case.

We note that these proposals for ID-based schemes in gap Diffie-Hellman groups may be efficiently converted to *strong* key-insulated schemes. In particular, they can be made strong by randomly splitting $a = a_1 + a_2$ and noticing that $f_{g,g^a}^{-1}(H(i)) = (H(i))^a = (H(i))^{a_1}(H(i))^{a_2}$, so that the device can compute $(H(i))^{a_2}$ and the user can then multiply it by $(H(i))^{a_1}$ to get the key for the current period.

References

[1] M. Abdalla and M. Bellare. Rekeyed Digital Signature Schemes: Damage-Containment in the Face of Key Exposure. Manuscript. July, 2001. 132, 134
[2] R. Anderson. Invited lecture, CCCS '97. 133
[3] M. Bellare and S. K. Miner. A Forward-Secure Digital Signature Scheme. Crypto '99. 133, 134
[4] J. Cha and J. Cheon. An Identity-based Signature Scheme from Gap Diffie-Hellman Groups. Available at http://eprint.iacr.org/2002/018/. 132, 142
[5] J. Cheon. A Universal Forgery of Hess's Second ID-based Signature against the Known-message Attack. Available at http://eprint.iacr.org/2002/028/. 142
[6] Y. Dodis, J. Katz, S. Xu and M. Yung. Key-Insulated Public-Key Cryptosystems. Eurocrypt 2002. 130, 131, 132, 134, 135
[7] Y. Dodis and L. Reyzin. On the Power of Claw-Free Permutations. SCN 2002. 141
[8] A. Fiat and A. Shamir. How to Prove Yourself: Practical Solutions to Identification and Signature Problems. Crypto '86. 141
[9] R. Gennaro, T. Rabin, S. Jarecki, and H. Krawczyk. Robust and Efficient Sharing of RSA Functions. J. Crypto 13(2): 273–300 (2000). 142
[10] M. Girault. Relaxing Tamper-Resistance Requirements for Smart Cards Using (Auto)-Proxy Signatures. CARDIS '98. 132
[11] O. Goldreich, B. Pfitzmann, and R. L. Rivest. Self-Delegation with Controlled Propagation — or — What if You Lose Your Laptop? Crypto '98. 133
[12] S. Goldwasser, S. Micali, and R. L. Rivest. A Digital Signature Scheme Secure Against Adaptive Chosen-Message Attacks. SIAM J. Computing 17(2): 281–308 (1988).
[13] L. C. Guillou and J.-J. Quisquater. A Practical Zero-Knowledge Protocol Fitted to Security Microprocessors Minimizing Both Transmission and Memory. Eurocrypt '88. 134, 141
[14] F. Hess. Exponent Group Signature Schemes and Efficient Identity Based Signature Schemes Based on Pairings. Available at http://eprint.iacr.org/2002/012/. 132, 142
[15] G. Itkis. Intrusion-Resilient Signatures: Generic Constructions, or Defeating Strong Adversary with Minimal Assumptions. SCN 2002. 133
[16] G. Itkis and L. Reyzin. SiBIR: Signer-Base Intrusion-Resilient Signatures. Crypto 2002. 133, 136
[17] A. Joux and K. Nguyen. Separating Decision Diffie-Hellman from Diffie-Hellman in Cryptographic Groups. Available at http://eprint.iacr.org/2001/003/. 142
[18] J. Katz and M. Yung. Threshold Cryptptosystems Based on Factoring. Asiacrypt 2002. 142

[19] C.-F. Lu and S. W. Shieh. Secure Key-Evolving Protocols for Discrete Logarithm Schemes. RSA 2002. 132

[20] S. Micali. A Secure and Efficient Digital Signature Algorithm. Technical Report MIT/LCS/TM-501, MIT, 1994. 141

[21] K. Ohta and T. Okamoto. On Concrete Security Treatment of Signatures Derived from Identification. Crypto '98. 139

[22] T. Okamoto. Provably Secure and Practical Identification Schemes and Corresponding Signature Schemes. Crypto '92. 139

[23] H. Ong and C. Schnorr. Fast Signature Generation with a Fiat-Shamir-Like Scheme. Eurocrypt '90. 134, 141

[24] K. Paterson. ID-based Signatures from Pairings on Elliptic Curves. Available at http://eprint.iacr.org/2002/004/. 132, 142

[25] R. Sakai, K. Ohgishi, M. Kasahara. Cryptosystems based on pairing. SCIC 2001. 132, 142

[26] C. P. Schnorr. Efficient Signature Generation by Smart Cards. J. Crypto 4(3): 161–174 (1991). 139

[27] C. P. Schnorr. Security of 2^t-root Identification and Signatures. Crypto '96. 141

[28] A. Shamir. Identity-Based Cryptosystems and Signature Schemes. Crypto '84. 134, 142

[29] V. Shoup. On the Security of a Practical Identification Scheme. J. Crypto 12(4): 247–160 (1999). 141

[30] W.-G. Tzeng and Z.-J. Tzeng. Robust Key-Evolving Public Key Encryption Schemes. Available at http://eprint.iacr.org/2001/009/. 132

A Verifiable Secret Shuffle of Homomorphic Encryptions

Jens Groth[1,2]

[1] Cryptomathic A/S, Denmark
www.cryptomathic.com
[2] BRICS, University of Aarhus, Denmark*
jg@brics.dk

Abstract. We show how to prove in honest verifier zero-knowledge the correctness of a shuffle of homomorphic encryptions (or homomorphic commitments.) A shuffle consists in a rearrangement of the input ciphertexts and a reencryption of them so that the permutation is not revealed. Our scheme is more efficient than previous schemes both in terms of communication complexity and computational complexity. Indeed, in the case of shuffling ElGamal encryptions, the proof of correctness is smaller than the encryptions themselves.

1 Introduction

A shuffle of ciphertexts $E_1, \ldots, E_n$ is a new set of ciphertexts $E_1', \ldots, E_n'$ so that both sets of ciphertexts have the same plaintexts. If we are working with a homomorphic cryptosystem with encryption algorithm $E_{pk}(\cdot)$, we may shuffle $E_1, \ldots, E_n$ by selecting a permutation $\pi \in \Sigma_n$ and letting $E_1' = E_{\pi(1)} E_{pk}(0), \ldots, E_n' = E_{\pi(n)} E_{pk}(0)$. If the cryptosystem is semantically secure it is not possible for somebody else to see which permutation we used in the shuffle. On the other hand this also means that somebody else cannot check directly if we did make a correct shuffle. Our goal in this paper is to construct a proof system that enables us to prove that indeed we have made a correct shuffle.

Shuffling encrypted elements and proving the correctness of the shuffle play an important part in mix-nets. A mix-net is a multi-party protocol to shuffle elements so that neither of the parties knows the permutation linking the input and output. To shuffle ciphertexts we may let the parties one after another make a shuffle with a random permutation and prove correctness of it. The proofs of correctness allow us to catch any cheater, and if at least one party is honest, it is impossible to link the input and output. In this indirect fashion, shuffling plays an important role in anonymization protocols and voting schemes.

Currently the two most efficient proof systems, both public coin honest verifier zero-knowledge, for proving the correctness of a shuffle of ElGamal encryptions are the schemes by Furukawa and Sako [4] and Neff [6]. The proof system

---

* Basic Research in Computer Science (www.brics.dk), funded by the Danish National Research Foundation.

Y.G. Desmedt (Ed.): PKC 2003, LNCS 2567, pp. 145–160, 2003.
© Springer-Verlag Berlin Heidelberg 2003

in [4], the most efficient scheme of the two, requires the prover to make $8n$ exponentiations and the verifier to make $10n$ exponentiations. In the case where the ElGamal cryptosystem is based on a 1024-bit prime p with the operations taking place in a group of order q, where q is a 160-bit prime so that $q|p-1$, their proofs require the prover to send $5280n$ bits. Jakobsson, Juels and Rivest take a different approach in [5] and provide a global structure for creating an efficient mix-net. In their scheme, however, a cheating prover does have non-negligible chance of succeeding, the scheme only ensures that only a very small fraction of the ciphertexts may be substituted for something else. Furthermore, it does not hide the permutation completely.

Our scheme, unlike those of [4] and [6], is not restricted to proving shuffles of ElGamal ciphertexts but can be used with any homomorphic cryptosystem. However, for the sake of comparison with the previous schemes we consider what happens when we use our scheme on an ElGamal cryptosystem with the primes p, q chosen as above. The prover uses around $6n$ exponentiations to make a proof, the verifier uses roughly $6n$ exponentiations to verify a proof, and the proofs themselves are of size around $1184n$ bits. In some cases, for instance in connection with electronic voting, the encrypted data may have to remain uncompromised several years into the future and then a key length of 1024 bits cannot be considered adequate. We gain an additional advantage in comparison with [4] and [6] when the key size increases since the groups in which we do the exponentiations may be smaller than the groups used in the cryptosystem. Our proof system uses 7 rounds just as that of [6], whereas that of [4] only uses 3 rounds. The proof system we construct is public coin honest verifier zero-knowledge,[1] just as [4] and [6].

The main ideas in our proof system are quite general and, while we only consider homomorphic encryptions in this paper, can be used for proving the correctness of shuffles of both homomorphic encryptions and homomorphic commitments. When considering homomorphic commitments, where we may have only computational binding, the proof takes on the nature of a proof of knowledge of the permutation and the modifications done to the commitments, with knowledge error that can be the inverse of any polynomial in the security parameter. Indeed, also when working with encryptions, the proof system we present proves knowledge of the shuffle being correct. This does have some interest in its own right for achieving non-malleability of the secret shuffle. Consider for instance a party doing one of the shuffles in a mix-net. Surely, the global properties of the mix-net are unsatisfactory if a corrupt party can shuffle all the elements back again right after this shuffle! Some degree of non-malleability is therefore needed.

Let us give a brief introduction to our proof system and the tools we use. The shuffle can be done by selecting a permutation π at random, selecting randomizers $r'_1, \ldots, r'_n$ at random, and setting $E'_1 = E_{\pi(1)} E_{pk}(0; r'_1), \ldots, E'_n =$

---

[1] Actually it is special honest verifier zero-knowledge, see [1]. Special honest verifier knowledge says that given any challenges it is possible to simulate a proof with those challenges.

$E_{\pi(n)}E_{pk}(0; r'_n)$. The task for the prover is now to prove that some permutation π exists so that the plaintexts of $E'_1, \ldots, E'_n$ and $E_{\pi(1)}, \ldots, E_{\pi(n)}$ are identical.

As a first step, we think of the following naïve proof system. The prover informs the verifier of the permutation π. The verifier picks at random $t_1, \ldots, t_n$, computes $E_1^{t_1} \cdots E_n^{t_n}$ and $(E'_1)^{t_{\pi(1)}} \cdots (E'_n)^{t_{\pi(n)}}$. Finally, the prover proves that the two resulting ciphertexts have the same plaintext in common. Unless π really corresponds to a pairing of ciphertexts with identical plaintexts the prover will be caught with overwhelming probability.

The obvious problem with the above scheme is the lack of zero-knowledge. We remedy this in the following way:

1. The prover commits to the permutation π by choosing different elements $s_1, \ldots, s_n$ and setting $c_{s,1} = commit(s_{\pi(1)}), \ldots, c_{s,n} = commit(s_{\pi(n)})$. He sends, in that order, $s_1, \ldots, s_n, c_{s,1}, \ldots, c_{s,n}$ to the verifier. Additionally he proves that indeed $s_1, \ldots, s_n$ are inside the commitments. This fixes a permutation π.

2. The verifier selects at random $t_1, \ldots, t_n$ and the prover sends $c_{t,1} = commit(t_{\pi(1)}), \ldots, c_{t,n} = commit(t_{\pi(n)})$ to the verifier. He proves that he has committed to $t_1, \ldots, t_n$, and he proves that the pairs (s_i, t_i) match in the commitments, i.e., for all i the pair $(c_{s,i}, c_{t,i})$ contains a pair (s_j, t_j), where $1 \leq j \leq n$. This ensures that $t_1, \ldots, t_n$ are committed to in the sequence specified by π.

3. Finally, the prover uses multiplication proofs and equivalence proofs to show that the products $E_1^{t_1} \cdots E_n^{t_n}$ and $(E'_1)^{t_{\pi(1)}} \cdots (E'_n)^{t_{\pi(n)}}$ have equivalent contents without revealing anything else. This last step corresponds to carrying out the naïve proof system in zero-knowledge.

The remaining problem is to convince the verifier that $c_{s,1}, \ldots, c_{s,n}$ contain a shuffle of $s_1, \ldots, s_n$, that $c_{t,1}, \ldots, c_{t,n}$ contain a shuffle of $t_1, \ldots, t_n$, and finally that the two sequences of elements have been shuffled in the same way. It seems like we have just traded one shuffle problem with another. The difference is that the supposed contents of the commitments are known to both the prover and the verifier, whereas we cannot expect either to know the contents of the ciphertexts being shuffled. Following an idea from [6] we can prove efficiently a shuffle when the contents are known and we are using a homomorphic commitment scheme.[2]

To see that the pairs match we let the verifier pick λ at random, and let the prover demonstrate that $c_{s,1}c_{t,1}^\lambda, \ldots, c_{s,n}c_{t,n}^\lambda$ contain a shuffle of $s_1 + \lambda t_1, \ldots, s_n + \lambda t_n$. If a pair (s_i, t_i) is not contained in a pair of commitments as required, then with high likelihood over the choice of λ the shuffle proof will be impossible. We shall see later that we can combine the proofs associated with step 1 and 2 into one combined proof.

---

[2] See Section 3.

2   Homomorphic Commitments and Encryption

2.1   Commitments

We start by specifying the type of commitments we are using. First there is the key generation phase in which a public key, K, is generated. The key generation procedure is not of concern in this article so we will just assume whenever we use a key in the article that it has been appropriately generated and publicized. In general, we use the letter K to signify such a key. With each key there is an associated message space $\mathcal{M}_K$, a randomizer space $\mathcal{R}_K$, an opening space $\mathcal{B}_K \supset \mathcal{R}_K$, a commitment space $\mathcal{C}_K$, a commitment function $com_K(\cdot, \cdot) : \mathcal{M}_K \times \mathcal{R}_K \to \mathcal{C}_K$ and a verification function $ver_K(\cdot, \cdot, \cdot) : \mathcal{M}_K \times \mathcal{B}_K \times \mathcal{C}_K \to \{0, 1\}$.

Given the key we can commit to an element $m \in \mathcal{M}_K$ by selecting at random, according to some distribution specified by the commitment scheme and the key, $r \in \mathcal{R}_K$, and letting the commitment be $c = com_K(m; r) \in \mathcal{C}_K$. This (m, r, c)-triple satisfies $ver_K(m, r, c) = 1$.

To open a commitment we reveal $m \in \mathcal{M}_K, r \in \mathcal{B}_K$ such that $ver_K(m, r, c) = 1$. Note that we do allow openings not corresponding to correctly formed commitments since the opening space and the randomizer space do not need to be identical.[3] However, we still require the binding property to be satisfied, i.e., nobody can find a commitment in $\mathcal{C}_K$ and two correct openings of it with different messages m_1 and m_2.

The spaces associated with the commitment scheme shall be abelian groups[4]. We write the commitment space with multiplicative notation and the other groups with additive notation, so we have groups $(\mathcal{M}_K, +), (\mathcal{R}_K, +) \leq (\mathcal{B}_K, +)$ and $(\mathcal{C}_K, \cdot)$. In this paper the message space will be $\mathbf{Z}_N$ for some suitable large integer N, and the randomizer space will be some finite group where elements are chosen uniformly at random. See, however, Section 5 for a possible use of integer commitments.

Homomorphic property: The commitment schemes we look at must be homomorphic, meaning that for all $m_1, m_2 \in \mathcal{M}_K$ and all $r_1, r_2 \in \mathcal{B}_K$:

$$com_K(m_1; r_1)com_K(m_2; r_2) = com_K(m_1 + m_2; r_1 + r_2) \ .$$

Root opening: We demand that if we can find $c \in \mathcal{C}_K, e \neq 0$ with $\gcd(e, |\mathcal{M}_K|) = 1$[5] and $m \in \mathcal{M}_K, z \in \mathcal{B}_K$ such that $com_K(m; z) = c^e$ then we can compute an opening of c.

---

[3] See [2] for an example of an integer commitment scheme where the randomizer space and the opening space are different.

[4] Throughout the paper we assume that both the groups and the elements in the groups we work with can be represented in a suitable manner, the binary operations and inversions can be computed efficiently, and that we can recognize whether an element belongs to a particular group.

[5] If $\mathcal{M}_K$ is infinite we define $\gcd(e, |\mathcal{M}_K|) = 1$ for all e.

Few polynomial roots: For any non-zero polynomial $p(T) \in \mathcal{M}_K[T]$ of low degree[6], the probability that a randomly picked element from $\mathcal{M}_K$ is a root is negligible.

For future use, we note that the few polynomial roots assumption implies that the order of $\mathcal{M}_K$, if finite, does not have small divisors. This in turn means that when picking an integer at random from a sufficiently large interval it is with overwhelming probability prime to $|\mathcal{M}_K|$, a useful fact to bear in mind in connection with the root opening assumption.

We give the following example of a homomorphic commitment scheme. The key is $K = (p, q, g, h)$, where p, q are large primes, $q|p - 1$, g, h are generators of a group $G \leq \mathbf{Z}_p^*$ and $\log_g h, \log_h g$ are both unknown. We have $\mathcal{M}_K = \mathbf{Z}_q, \mathcal{C}_K = <g>$ and $\mathcal{B}_K = \mathcal{R}_K = \mathbf{Z}_q$. Commitment to m is done by selecting $r \in \mathbf{Z}_q$ at random and letting $com_K(m; r) = g^r h^m \bmod p$. Verifying a commitment opening (m, r) of $c \in \mathcal{C}_K$ is done by letting $ver_K(m, r, c) = 1$ if and only if $m, r \in \mathbf{Z}_q$ and $c = g^r h^m \bmod p$.

2.2 Multicommitments

In the commitment scheme described above the elements in the message space have a natural description as integers. However, there are circumstances where we do not really need this property but we just need the message space to have a structure as an abelian group. Potentially, having fewer restrictions on the commitment scheme allows for faster generation of commitments.

In our case, what we will need is a way to commit to a tuple of elements. We therefore describe what we in the paper shall call multicommitments. A multicommitment scheme works just as a commitment scheme, except we may commit to a k-tuple from the message space $\mathcal{M}_{MK}$, where k is specified in the key MK.

An example of a multicommitment scheme is the following variant of the commitment scheme mentioned previously. The key consists of large primes p, q so that $q|p - 1$, and randomly chosen generators $g, h_1, \ldots, h_k$ of a group $G \leq \mathbf{Z}_p^*$ of order q. The sender of the commitment does not have knowledge about the generation of the keys, in particular, he does not know discrete logarithms of the generators with respect to other generators. The message space is $\mathcal{M}_{(p,q,g,h_1,\ldots,h_k)} = \mathbf{Z}_q$, the randomizer and opening spaces are $\mathcal{R}_{(p,q,g,h_1,\ldots,h_k)} = \mathcal{B}_{(p,q,g,h_1,\ldots,h_k)} = \mathbf{Z}_q$ and the commitment space is $\mathcal{C}_{(p,q,g,h_1,\ldots,h_k)} = <g>$. The commitment function is defined as follows: $mcom_{(p,q,g,h_1,\ldots,h_k)}(m_1, \ldots, m_k; r) = g^r h_1^{m_1} \cdots h_k^{m_k} \bmod p$. Opening of the commitment is done by revealing $m_1, \ldots, m_k, r$.

2.3 Encryptions

In this paper, we use pk to denote a public key for a semantically secure homomorphic public key cryptosystem. Associated with such a key is a message

---

[6] More precisely of degree less than n, the number of elements we want to shuffle.

space $\mathcal{M}_{pk}$, a randomizer space $\mathcal{R}_{pk}$ and a ciphertext space $\mathcal{C}_{pk}$. Furthermore, we have an encryption function $E_{pk}(\cdot;\cdot) : \mathcal{M}_{pk} \times \mathcal{R}_{pk} \rightarrow \mathcal{C}_{pk}$. We restrict ourselves to cryptosystems with errorless decryption, i.e., it is infeasible to find $m \in \mathcal{M}_{pk}, r \in \mathcal{R}_{pk}$ so that $E_{pk}(m;r)$ does not decrypt to m. We also require that we have stable decryption in the sense that we cannot find an element $E \in \mathcal{C}_{pk}$ that decrypts to anything but a message in the message space or can decrypt to two different messages with significant[7] probability.

We require that the message space, the randomizer space and the ciphertext space are large finite groups. In other words we have groups $(\mathcal{M}_{pk}, +), (\mathcal{R}_{pk}, +)$ and $(\mathcal{C}_{pk}, \cdot)$. We will also assume a couple of properties that correspond to those of the commitments:

Homomorphic properties: The cryptosystem is homomorphic, meaning that for all $m_1, m_2 \in \mathcal{M}_{pk}$ and for all $r_1, r_2 \in \mathcal{R}_{pk}$:

$$E_{pk}(m_1; r_1)E_{pk}(m_2; r_2) = E_{pk}(m_1 + m_2; r_1 + r_2) \ .$$

In addition, if $E_1, E_2 \in \mathcal{C}_{pk}$ are two ciphertexts decrypting to m_1, m_2 respectively then $E_1 E_2$ decrypts to $m_1 + m_2$.

When dealing with a shuffle of ciphertexts $E_1, \ldots, E_n$ and $E'_1, \ldots, E'_n$ we will typically not be interested in whether they have been formed correctly, i.e., there exists a permutation π and $r'_1, \ldots, r'_n$ so that $E'_1 = E_{\pi(1)}E_{pk}(0; r'_1), \ldots, E'_n = E_{\pi(n)}E_{pk}(0; r'_n)$. What we really want to know is whether they decrypt correctly, i.e., there exists a permutation π so that for all i we have that E'_i and $E_{\pi(i)}$ decrypt to the same.

This difference means that when dealing with commitments we typically want to prove knowledge of openings of commitments satisfying some property. When dealing with ciphertexts we typically want to prove knowledge that their contents satisfy some property. Accordingly, we modify the root opening assumption to something that will be more suitable when talking about ciphertexts later in the article.

Root decryption: We demand that if we can find $E \in \mathcal{C}_{pk}, e \neq 0$ so that $\gcd(e, |\mathcal{M}_{pk}|) = 1$ and $m \in \mathcal{M}_{pk}, z \in \mathcal{R}_{pk}$ so that $E_{pk}(m;z) = E^e$, then m can be written uniquely as em', where $m' \in \mathcal{M}_{pk}$, and E decrypts to m'.

We mention two examples of cryptosystems that satisfy our requirements. The ElGamal cryptosystem may be set up with the same kind of key as in the commitment scheme example. This time the message space is $\mathcal{M}_{(p,q,g,h)} = <g>$. We encrypt by letting $E_{(p,q,g,h)}(m;r) = (g^r \bmod p, h^r m \bmod p)$. Decryption can be done if the secret exponent x so that $h = g^x \bmod p$ is known. The ciphertext (u, v) decrypts to $m = vu^{-x} \bmod p$.

Another example of a homomorphic cryptosystem is the generalization of Paillier's cryptosystem [7] invented by Damgård and Jurik [3]. Here the pub-

---

[7] By significant we mean not negligible.

lic key is an RSA-modulus N together with a small integer s. The encryption function takes a message $m \in \mathbf{Z}_{N^s}$ and a randomizer $r \in \mathbf{Z}_N^*$ as input and sets $E_{(N,s)}(m;r) = (1+n)^m r^{N^s} \bmod N^{s+1}$.

2.4   Compatibility of Commitments, Multicommitments and Encryptions

From now on, we will simply assume that we have some commitment scheme with key K, some multicommitment scheme with key MK and a cryptosystem with key pk. The keys may or may not overlap so that elements from one key are also included in another key. For instance, we could imagine the cryptosystem were an ElGamal scheme with primes $p, q | p - 1$ and generators g, h and that the commitment scheme used the exact same elements.

We require that the keys be selected so that the message spaces are compatible in the following way. The message spaces of the commitment scheme and the multicommitment scheme are identical, i.e., $\mathcal{M}_K = \mathcal{M}_{MK}$. Furthermore, the message space for the cryptosystem, $\mathcal{M}_{pk}$ is a module over $\mathcal{M}_K$.

3   Proof of a Shuffle of Known Contents

Before going into the general protocol for proving a correct shuffle let us build some intuition by presenting, without proof, a proof system for a shuffle where the contents are known.

Say we have commitments $c_1, \ldots, c_n$ and want to prove that they contain $m_1, \ldots, m_n$ without revealing which commitment contains what. If the message space is an integral domain, we can, following [6], use the fact that an n'th degree non-zero polynomial has at most n roots. Let x be any element in the message space and set $c_x = com_K(x; 0)$. In case $c_1, \ldots, c_n$ do not contain a shuffle of $m_1, \ldots, m_n$ there can at most be n challenges x where the product of the contents of $c_1 c_x^{-1}, \ldots, c_n c_x^{-1}$ is the same as $\prod_{i=1}^n (m_i - x)$. By choosing x at random, the verifier can therefore give the cheating prover a challenge he only has negligible chance to answer.

Proof of commitments containing a shuffle of known contents
Common input: $c_1, \ldots, c_n \in \mathcal{C}_K$ and $m_1, \ldots, m_n \in \mathcal{M}_K$.
Prover's input: A permutation $\pi \in \Sigma_n$ and $r_1, \ldots, r_n \in \mathcal{R}_K$ so that $c_1 = com_K(m_{\pi(1)}; r_1), \ldots, c_n = com_K(m_{\pi(n)}; r_n)$.

Initial challenge: Prover receives x chosen at random from $\mathcal{M}_K$.
Multiplication Proof: Make a 3-move proof using a multiplication proof of knowledge[8] that the product of the contents of $c_1 c_x^{-1}, \ldots, c_n c_x^{-1}$ equals the content in $com_K(\prod_{i=1}^n (m_i - x); 0)$.

---

[8] Such 3-move proofs are standard tools in cryptography. See for instance [3] for an example of such proofs.

Theorem 1. *The scheme is a public coin 4-move proof system for proving that the prover knows π and $r_1, \ldots, r_n$ so that $c_1 = com_K(m_{\pi(1)}; r_1), \ldots, c_n = com_K(m_{\pi(n)}; r_n)$. The proof system is special honest verifier zero-knowledge.*

The condition that the message space is an integral domain can be relaxed. In the assumptions on the commitment scheme, we only required that given some polynomial it should be unlikely that a randomly chosen element in $\mathcal{M}_K$ is a root, unless the polynomial is the zero-polynomial.

4   Proof of a Shuffle

Let us go back to the idea in the introduction for proving a shuffle this time having firmer grasp of the concepts. There are ciphertexts $E_1, \ldots, E_n, E'_1, \ldots, E'_n$, and the prover knows a permutation π and randomizers $r'_1, \ldots, r'_n$ so that $E'_1 = E_{\pi(1)} E_{pk}(0; r'_1), \ldots, E'_n = E_{\pi(n)} E_{pk}(0; r'_n)$. His aim is to convince the verifier that a permutation π exists so that for each $i = 1, \ldots, n$ the ciphertexts E'_i and $E_{\pi(i)}$ decrypt to the same.

The prover selects different elements $s_1, \ldots, s_n$ and creates commitments $c_{s,1} = com_K(s_{\pi(1)}), \ldots, c_{s,n} = com_K(s_{\pi(n)})$. He sends all of this to the verifier.

The verifier responds with $t_1, \ldots, t_n$ chosen at random in the message space. The prover sends $c_{t,1} = com_K(t_{\pi(1)}), \ldots, c_{t,n} = com_K(t_{\pi(n)})$ back.

The verifier sends a random λ to the prover. The prover demonstrates by using a shuffle proof of known contents that he knows that $c_{s,1} c_{t,1}^\lambda, \ldots, c_{s,n} c_{t,n}^\lambda$ contain a shuffle of $s_1 + \lambda t_1, \ldots, s_n + \lambda t_n$.

Unless indeed $(c_{s,1}, c_{t,1}), \ldots, (c_{s,n}, c_{t,n})$ contain a shuffle of the pairs $(s_1, t_1), \ldots, (s_n, t_n)$ there is overwhelming probability over the choices of λ that this proof will fail. In other words, we get three pieces of information from this proof: The commitments $c_{s,1}, \ldots, c_{s,n}$ sent in the first round did contain $s_1, \ldots, s_n$. The commitments $c_{t,1}, \ldots, c_{t,n}$ sent in the third round did contain $t_1, \ldots, t_n$. The s_i's and t_i's were shuffled using the same permutation.

What we have so far is that we can get the prover to commit to a permutation through the choices of $c_{s,1}, \ldots, c_{s,n}$, and subsequently we can ensure that he commits to $t_1, \ldots, t_n$ permuted in the same way. Let us call this permutation π.

The prover can conclude his proof by computing $E''_1 = (E'_1)^{t_{\pi(1)}} E_{pk}(0), \ldots, E''_n = (E'_n)^{t_{\pi(n)}} E_{pk}(0)$. Using basic multiplication proofs, he can demonstrate to the verifier that this set of ciphertexts has been correctly formed. Finally, he can show through an equality proof that $E''_1 \cdots E''_n$ has the same content as $E_1^{t_1} \cdots E_n^{t_n}$.

From the verifier's point of view, this demonstrates that $(E'_1)^{t_{\pi(1)}} \cdots (E'_n)^{t_{\pi(n)}}$ has the same content as $E_1^{t_1} \cdots E_n^{t_n}$. With overwhelming probability over the choice of $t_1, \ldots, t_n$ this is only possible if each of the pairs $(E'_1, E_{\pi(1)}), \ldots, (E'_n, E_{\pi(n)})$ are pairs of ciphertexts with the same plaintext. We have thus proven the shuffle without revealing π.

To optimize the proof we note the following. First, we only use $E_1'', \ldots, E_n''$ temporarily. We may as well prove that $(E_1')^{t_{\pi(1)}} \cdots (E_n')^{t_{\pi(n)}}$ has the same content as $E_1^{t_1} \cdots E_n^{t_n}$ directly if possible, and indeed this is possible. This way we save n encryptions.

Another optimization comes from the use of multicommitments. When making a shuffle proof for $c_{s,1}c_{t,1}^\lambda, \ldots, c_{s,n}c_{t,n}^\lambda$ containing a shuffle of $s_1 + \lambda t_1, \ldots, s_n + \lambda t_n$ we need to make multiplications and prove them done correctly. However, up to this point we only use additions. Therefore we can instead make multicommitments to $s_1, \ldots, s_n$ and $t_1, \ldots, t_n$ and from this create multicommitments to $s_1 + \lambda t_1 - x, \ldots, s_n + \lambda t_n - x$, where x is the randomly chosen challenge to be used in the shuffle proof with known contents. First now do we begin to prove that the product of the contents in the multicommitments matches the product $\prod_{i=1}^n (s_i + \lambda t_i - x)$.

When starting to make this proof we use the fact that we can combine the multiplication proof used in the shuffle proof of known contents and the multiplication proofs used with the encryptions. Instead of raising the ciphertexts to $t_1, \ldots, t_n$ we can raise them to $s_1 + \lambda t_1 - x, \ldots, s_n + \lambda t_n - x$. Since $t_1, \ldots, t_n, \lambda$ and x are all chosen by the verifier these values have the same random distribution as the original $t_1, \ldots, t_n$. But in the basic multiplication proofs used on the ciphertexts we create the values $f_1 = e(s_{\pi(1)} + \lambda t_{\pi(1)} - x) + d_1, \ldots, f_n = e(s_{\pi(n)} + \lambda t_{\pi(n)} - x) + d_n$ and reveal them. Having those values helps us create an efficient proof of the shuffle of known contents. The idea here is that we can compute $e^n \prod_{i=1}^n (s_i + \lambda t_i - x)$ as $f_1 \cdots f_n - d_1 f_2 \cdots f_n - (f_1 - d_1)d_2 f_3 \cdots f_n - \cdots - (f_1 - d_1) \cdots (f_{n_1} - d_{n-1})d_n$.

Let us now write down the proof system for proving a shuffle that we have been aiming for throughout the paper. For simplicity and without loss of generality we assume $k|n$.

Proof of shuffle of ciphertexts
Common input: $E_1, \ldots, E_n, E_1', \ldots, E_n' \in \mathcal{C}_{pk}$.
Prover's input: A permutation $\pi \in \Sigma_n$ and randomizers $r_1', \ldots, r_n' \in \mathcal{R}_{pk}$ satisfying $E_1' = E_{\pi(1)}E_{pk}(0; r_1'), \ldots, E_n' = E_{\pi(n)}E_{pk}(0; r_n')$.

Initial message: Select $s_1, \ldots, s_n$ as different elements from $\mathcal{M}_K$.
    Select $r_{s,1}, \ldots, r_{s,\frac{n}{k}}$ at random from $\mathcal{R}_{MK}$.
    Let $c_{s,1} = mcom_{MK}(s_{\pi(1)}, \ldots, s_{\pi(k)}; r_{s,1}), \ldots,$
    $c_{s,\frac{n}{k}} = mcom_{MK}(s_{\pi(n-k+1)}, \ldots, s_{\pi(n)}; r_{s,\frac{n}{k}})$.
    Send $s_1, \ldots, s_n, c_{s,1}, \ldots, c_{s,\frac{n}{k}}$ to the verifier.
First challenge: $t_1, \ldots, t_n$ chosen at random from $\mathcal{M}_K$.
First answer: Select $r_{t,1}, \ldots, r_{t,\frac{n}{k}}$ at random from $\mathcal{R}_{MK}$.
    Set $c_{t,1} = mcom_{MK}(t_{\pi(1)}, \ldots, t_{\pi(k)}; r_{t,1}), \ldots,$
    $c_{t,\frac{n}{k}} = mcom_{MK}(t_{\pi(n-k+1)}, \ldots, t_{\pi(n)}; r_{t,\frac{n}{k}})$.
    Send $c_{t,1}, \ldots, c_{t,\frac{n}{k}}$ to the verifier.
Second challenge: Choose λ, x at random from $\mathcal{M}_K$.
Second answer: For $j = 1, \ldots, n$ let $a_j = \prod_{i=1}^j (s_{\pi(i)} + \lambda t_{\pi(i)} - x)$.

Select $d_1, \ldots, d_n$ at random from $\mathcal{M}_{MK}$. Select $r_{d,1}, \ldots, r_{d,\frac{n}{k}}$ at random from $\mathcal{R}_{MK}$. Set $c_{d,1} = mcom_{MK}(d_1, \ldots, d_k; r_{d,1}), \ldots, c_{d,\frac{n}{k}} = mcom_{MK}(d_{n-k+1}, \ldots, d_n; r_{d,\frac{n}{k}})$.

Select $r_1, \ldots, r_n$ at random from $\mathcal{R}_K$. Select r at random from $\mathcal{R}_K$. Set $c_1 = com_K(d_1; r_1), c_2 = com_K(a_1 d_2; r_2), \ldots, c_n = com_K(a_{n-1} d_n; r_n)$. Set $c = com_K(0; r)$.[9]

Select r' at random from $\mathcal{R}_{pk}$. Set $E' = (E_1')^{d_1} \cdots (E_n')^{d_n} E_{pk}(0; r')$.

Send $c_{d,1}, \ldots, c_{d,\frac{n}{k}}, c_1, \ldots, c_n, c, E'$ to the verifier.

Third challenge: Select at random $e \in \mathcal{M}_K$.

Final answer: Set $f_1 = e(s_{\pi(1)} + \lambda t_{\pi(1)} - x) + d_1, \ldots, f_n = e(s_{\pi(n)} + \lambda t_{\pi(n)} - x) + d_n$. Set $z_1 = e(r_{s,1} + \lambda r_{t,1}) + r_{d,1}, \ldots, z_{\frac{n}{k}} = e(r_{s,\frac{n}{k}} + \lambda r_{t,\frac{n}{k}}) + r_{d,\frac{n}{k}}$.

Set $z = r - ef_2 \cdots f_n r_1 - \cdots - e^n r_n$.

Set $z' = r' - (e(s_{\pi(1)} + \lambda t_{\pi(1)} - x) + d_1)r_1' - \cdots - (e(s_{\pi(n)} + \lambda t_{\pi(n)} - x) + d_n)r_n'$.

Send $f_1, \ldots, f_n, z_1, \ldots, z_{\frac{n}{k}}, z, z'$ to the verifier.

Verification: Check that $f_1 \ldots, f_n \in \mathcal{M}_K$. Check that $c_{s,1}, \ldots, c_{s,\frac{n}{k}}, c_{t,1}, \ldots, c_{t,\frac{n}{k}}, c_{d,1}, \ldots, c_{d,\frac{n}{k}} \in \mathcal{C}_{MK}$. Check that $z_1, \ldots, z_{\frac{n}{k}} \in \mathcal{R}_{MK}$. Check that $c_1, \ldots, c_n, c \in \mathcal{C}_K$. Check that $z \in \mathcal{R}_K$. Check that $E' \in \mathcal{C}_{pk}$. Check that $z' \in \mathcal{R}_{pk}$.

Let $c_x = mcom_{MK}(x, \ldots, x; 0)$.

Check that $mcom_{MK}(f_1, \ldots, f_k; z_1) = (c_{s,1} c_{t,1}^\lambda c_x^{-1})^e c_{d,1}, \ldots,$
$mcom_{MK}(f_{n-k+1}, \ldots, f_n; z_{\frac{n}{k}}) = (c_{s,\frac{n}{k}} c_{t,\frac{n}{k}}^\lambda c_x^{-1})^e c_{d,\frac{n}{k}}$.

Check that $com_K(e^{n+1} a_n - ef_1 \cdots f_n; z) = c_1^{-ef_2 \cdots f_n} \cdots c_n^{-e^n} c$.

Check that $(E_1')^{f_1} \cdots (E_n')^{f_n} E_{pk}(0; z') = (E_1^{s_1 + \lambda t_1 - x} \cdots E_n^{s_n + \lambda t_n - x})^e E'$.

Theorem 2. *The scheme is a public coin 7-move proof system for a correct shuffle. It is complete, sound and special honest verifier zero-knowledge. If the commitments are statistically hiding, then the entire proof is statistical special honest verifier zero-knowledge.*

Proof. It is easy to see that we are dealing with a 7-move public coin protocol. Completeness follows by straightforward verification. Soundness follows from Lemma 1. Special honest verifier zero-knowledge follows from Lemma 2.   □

Lemma 1. *The proof system is sound.*

Proof. We will assume that the proof system is not sound and derive a contradiction with the assumptions made on the commitment schemes and the cryptosystem that we use. Therefore, let us assume there is some adversary $\mathcal{A}$ that has a significant probability of succeeding in the following game. Public keys for the schemes are generated and given to the adversary. It then produces two sets of encryptions $E_1, \ldots, E_n$ and $E_1', \ldots, E_n'$ and engages in a proof with the verifier. It is succesful if the verifier accepts the proof. By the definition of significant this means that there is some inverse polynomial, $\epsilon(l)$, in the security parameter l where $\mathcal{A}$ is succesful with probability $\epsilon(l)$ for an infinite number of possible security parameters.

---

[9] The a_j's can be computed recursively using the formula $a_j = a_{j-1}(s_{\pi(j)} + \lambda t_{\pi(j)} - x)$.

From the adversary $\mathcal{A}$ we will construct an algorithm $\mathcal{B}$ that is capable of violating the assumptions made on the schemes we use. Basically $\mathcal{B}$ will run $\mathcal{A}$ to get two sets of ciphertexts $E_1, \ldots, E_n$ and $E'_1, \ldots, E'_n$ and then use rewinding techniques to find witnesses for these decrypting to the same plaintexts. If they do not decrypt to the same plaintexts then the root decryption assumption has been violated.

Sampling of proofs

$\mathcal{B}$ works in the following way. It runs $\mathcal{A}$ to get ciphertexts $E_1, \ldots, E_n$ and $E'_1, \ldots, E'_n$. By the assumption we have $\epsilon(l)$ probability for these ciphertexts not decrypting to the same families of plaintexts, yet $\mathcal{A}$ being succesful in the proof. Let $p(l)$ be an easily computable polynomial in the security parameter that is sufficiently larger[10] than $\text{time}_{\mathcal{A}}(l)/\epsilon(l)$. $\mathcal{B}$ lets $\mathcal{A}$ send the initial message of the proof, and then selects at random $p(l)$ first challenges $t_1, \ldots, t_n$. On each such challenge $t_1, \ldots, t_n$ it runs the adversary $p(l)$ times to receive $p(l)$ answers to the first challenge. For each such answer it selects at random $p(l)$ second challenges λ, x. It splits $\mathcal{A}$ further into $p(l)$ copies and lets each copy produce an answer to one of the second challenges λ, x. For each of these answers it selects $p(l)$ final challenges e. It runs $\mathcal{A}$ to the end to see if it gets acceptable final answers to some of these final challenges.

All in all $\mathcal{B}$ runs $p(l)^3$ copies of $\mathcal{A}$. We hope to find n sets of challenges $t_1, \ldots, t_n$ so that for each of those sets we have 2 sets of challenges λ, x, where we in turn have $n + 2$ sets of challenges c with acceptable answers. All in all, we hope to end up with $2n(n + 2)$ related proofs. With overwhelming probability this happens if we have set $p(l)$ to be a large enough polynomial and the probability of $\mathcal{A}$ for succeeding after having sent the initial message is larger than $\epsilon(l)$.

With overwhelming probability these acceptable proofs include n linearly independent vectors $(s_1 + \lambda t_1 - x, \ldots, s_n + \lambda t_n - x)$. We also have with overwhelming probability that the two second challenges λ, x have different λ's. Finally, we have with overwhelming probability that the vectors $e = (1, e, \ldots, e^{n+1})$ are linearly independent. To see the latter note that vectors of such a form can be seen as rows in a Vandermonde matrix and with high probability the Vandermonde matrix has determinant different from 0.

We now go backwards through the conversations that constitute the acceptable proofs we have found and see what we can conclude. First we look at a conversation that has been completed up to the point where the verifier is about to pick the final challenge e and give it to the prover. We see what can be deduced from the $n + 2$ answers to this challenge. Next we take a step back and look at a conversation where the verifier is about to pick the second challenge λ, x. Again we see what we can conclude from the $2(n + 2)$ acceptable continuations of a proof from this point. Finally, we step back to the point where the verifier is picking the first challenge, consisting of $t_1, \ldots, t_n$, and see what we can conclude

---

[10] We leave it to the reader to use Chernoff bounds to estimate exactly what sufficiently larger means.

from the n sets of initial challenges that are succesfully answered $2(n+2)$ times each.

We start out by looking at the situation where a conversation has been conducted up to the point where the verifier is selecting the final challenge.

The final challenge

Given acceptable answers $f_1, \ldots, f_n, z_1, \ldots, z_{\frac{n}{k}}, z, z'$ and $\widetilde{f}_1, \ldots, \widetilde{f}_n$, $\widetilde{z}_1, \ldots, \widetilde{z}_{\frac{n}{k}}, \widetilde{z}, \widetilde{z}'$ to two different challenges $e, \widetilde{e}$, we have for $i = 1, \ldots, \frac{n}{k}$:

$$mcom_{MK}(f_{ik-k+1}, \ldots, f_{ik}; z_i) = (c_{s,i}c_{t,i}^\lambda c_x^{-1})^e c_{d,i}$$
$$\wedge mcom_{MK}(\widetilde{f_{ik-k+1}}, \ldots, \widetilde{f_{ik}}; \widetilde{z}_i) = (c_{s,i}c_{t,i}^\lambda c_x^{-1})^{\widetilde{e}} c_{d,i} . \qquad (1)$$

This implies that

$$mcom_{MK}(f_{ik-k+1} - \widetilde{f_{ik-k+1}}, \ldots, f_{ik} - \widetilde{f_{ik}}; z_i - \widetilde{z}_i) = (c_{s,i}c_{t,i}^\lambda c_x^{-1})^{e-\widetilde{e}}.$$

By the root opening assumption, this means that we can find an opening of $c_{s,i}c_{t,i}^\lambda c_x^{-1}$. The binding property of the multicommitment scheme implies that this is the only way we can open the multicommitments. We call the contents of $c_{s,i}c_{t,i}^\lambda c_x^{-1}$ for $m_{ki-k+1}, \ldots, m_{ki}$. We can now go back and find an opening of $c_{d,i}$ too. We write $d_{ki-k+1}, \ldots, d_{ki}$ for the content of this commitment. We have $f_i = em_i + d_i$, for $i = 1, \ldots, n$.

Looking at the encryptions we get from the answers to two challenges $e, \widetilde{e}$ that

$$(E_1')^{f_1-\widetilde{f}_1} \cdots (E_n')^{f_n-\widetilde{f}_n} E_{pk}(0; z' - \widetilde{z}') = (E_1^{s_1+\lambda t_1-x} \cdots E_n^{s_n+\lambda t_n-x})^{e-\widetilde{e}}.$$

Plugging in the f_i's and the corresponding m_i's we conclude that

$$E_{pk}(0; z' - \widetilde{z}') = (E_1^{s_1+\lambda t_1-x} \cdots E_n^{s_n+\lambda t_n-x}(E_1')^{-m_1} \cdots (E_n')^{-m_n})^{e-\widetilde{e}}.$$

The root decryption assumption then tells us that $E_1^{s_1+\lambda t_1-x} \cdots E_n^{s_n+\lambda t_n-x}$ and $(E_1')^{m_1} \cdots (E_n')^{m_n}$ decrypt to the same.

A prover having significant chance of answering the last challenge can also be used to to conclude that $a_n = m_1 \cdots m_n$, where $a_n = \prod_{i=1}^n (s_{\pi(i)} + \lambda t_{\pi(i)} - x)$.

By writing out the f_i's we see that an answer to a challenge e satisfies

$$com_K(e^{n+1}(m_1 \cdots m_n - a_n) + e^n(d_1 m_2 \cdots m_n + \cdots + m_1 \cdots m_{n-1}d_n) + \cdots$$
$$+e(d_1 \cdots d_n); -z)c = (c_1^{m_2 \cdots m_n} \cdots c_n^1)^{e^n} \cdots (c_1^{d_2 \cdots d_n})^e.$$

From a linear combination of $n + 2$ linearly independent vectors on the form $(1, \ldots, e^{n+1})$ we can get a vector on the form $(0, \ldots, 0, \gamma)$, where γ with overwhelming probability is prime to $|\mathcal{M}_K|$. From answers to $n + 2$ different e's that satisfy (1) this linear combination gives us an element $z_\gamma \in \mathcal{R}_K$ so that

$$com_K(\gamma(m_1 \cdots m_n - a_n); z_\gamma) = 1 .$$

This in turn shows that $z_\gamma = 0$ and $a_n = m_1 \cdots m_n$.

Going a step back in the proof we now look at a situation where the prover is about to receive the two challenges λ and x.

The second challenge

We first look at the challenge x. For such challenges we have seen that the contents $m_1, \ldots, m_n$ of $c_{s,1} c_{t,1}^\lambda c_x^{-1}, \ldots, c_{s,\frac{n}{k}} c_{t,\frac{n}{k}}^\lambda c_x^{-1}$ satisfy

$$a_n = \prod_{i=1}^{n}(s_i + \lambda t_i - x) = m_1 \ldots m_n = \prod_{i=1}^{n}(m_i' - x) \ ,$$

where $m_1', \ldots, m_n'$ are the contents of $c_{s,1} c_{t,1}^\lambda, \ldots, c_{s,\frac{n}{k}} c_{t,\frac{n}{k}}^\lambda$. We have an evaluation of an n'th degree polynomial on both sides and by the few polynomial roots assumption the two evaluations must be equal if the prover has to have a significant chance of answering the challenges x and e. This in turn means that the two polynomials we evaluate have identical roots. Therefore the elements $m_1', \ldots, m_n'$ are some permutation of $s_1 + \lambda t_1, \ldots, s_n + \lambda t_n$.

We proceed to look at the challenge λ. Being able to answer two different challenges λ and $\widetilde{\lambda}$ gives us openings of $c_{s,i} c_{t,i}^\lambda c_x^{-1}$ and $c_{s,i} c_{t,i}^{\widetilde{\lambda}} c_x^{-1}$ for $i = 1, \ldots, \frac{n}{k}$. By the homomorphic property of the multicommitment scheme this gives us openings of $c_{t,1}^{\lambda - \widetilde{\lambda}}, \ldots, c_{t,\frac{n}{k}}^{\lambda - \widetilde{\lambda}}$. By the root opening assumption we can therefore open $c_{t,1}, \ldots, c_{t,\frac{n}{k}}$. We call the contents for $\hat{t}_1, \ldots, \hat{t}_n$. We are now also able to open $c_{s,1}, \ldots, c_{s,\frac{n}{k}}$. We call the contents for $\hat{s}_1, \ldots, \hat{s}_n$.

Let us look at $s_1 + \lambda t_1$. With overwhelming probability over the choices of $s_1, \ldots, s_n$ and $t_1, \ldots, t_n$ there are at most n different values of λ where it would correspond to one of $\hat{s}_1 + \lambda \hat{t}_1, \ldots, \hat{s}_n + \lambda \hat{t}_n$, unless there exists $i \in \{1, \ldots, n\}$ where $\hat{s}_i = s_1$ and $\hat{t}_i = t_1$. Arguing similarly for the pairs $(s_2, t_2), \ldots, (s_n, t_n)$ we deduce that there is a unique permutation π so that $\hat{s}_i = s_{\pi(i)}$ and $\hat{t}_i = t_{\pi(i)}$ for $i = 1, \ldots, n$. Since the prover committed to $s_1, \ldots, s_n$ in the initial message the permutation was fixed already then.

We take another step back in the conversation and see what we can conclude from the answers following the first challenge.

The first challenge

Since $s_1 + \lambda t_1 - x, \ldots, s_n + \lambda t_n - x$ are linearly indendent we can for $i = 1, \ldots, n$ find linear combinations of the vectors $(s_1 + \lambda t_1 - x, \ldots, s_n + \lambda t_n - x)$ giving us the vector $(0, \ldots, 0, \gamma_i, 0, \ldots, 0)$, where γ_i is prime to $|\mathcal{M}_{pk}|$. Returning to the encryptions we can therefore for $i = 1, \ldots, n$ find z_{γ_i}' so that $E_{pk}(0; z_{\gamma_i}') = (E_i')^{\gamma_i} E_{\pi(i)}^{-\gamma_i}$. This by the root decryption assumption implies that $E_{\pi(i)}$ and E_i' decrypt to the same.

This means that we have in polynomial time found witnesses on the form $E_{pk}(0; z_{\gamma_i}') = (E_i' E_{\pi(i)}^{-1})^{\gamma_i}$ for the plaintexts of $E_1, \ldots, E_n$ and $E_1', \ldots, E_n'$ decrypting to the same. But this contradicts the root decryption assumption if the ciphertexts are to decrypt to different plaintexts. We must therefore conclude that the adversary has negligible chance of cheating with the proof.   □

Lemma 2. *The proof system is special honest verifier zero-knowledge. If the commitments and multicommitments are statistically or perfectly hiding then the proof system is statistical or perfect special honest verifier zero-knowledge.*

Proof. We first describe the simulator. Afterwards, we argue that its output is indistinguishable from a real proof.

The simulation

We are given $t_1, \ldots, t_n, \lambda, x, e$ as input, and wish to produce something that is indistinguishable from a real proof.

We let $c_{s_1} = mcom_{MK}(0, \ldots, 0), \ldots, c_{s,\frac{n}{k}} = mcom_{MK}(0, \ldots, 0)$.

We let $c_{t,1} = mcom_{MK}(0, \ldots, 0), \ldots, c_{t,\frac{n}{k}} = mcom_{MK}(0, \ldots, 0)$.

We let $c_1 = com_K(0), \ldots, c_n = mcom_K(0)$.

We select $f_1, \ldots, f_n$ at random from $\mathcal{M}_{MK}$, $z_1, \ldots, z_{\frac{n}{k}}$ at random from $\mathcal{R}_{MK}$, z at random from $\mathcal{R}_K$ and z' at random from $\mathcal{R}_{pk}$.

We let $c_x = mcom_{MK}(x, \ldots, x; 0)$.

We set $c_{d,1} = mcom_{MK}(f_1, \ldots, f_k; z_1)(c_{s,1} c_{t,1}^{\lambda} c_x^{-1})^{-e}, \ldots,$

$c_{d,\frac{n}{k}} = mcom_{MK}(f_{n-k+1}, \ldots, f_n; z_{\frac{n}{k}})(c_{s,\frac{n}{k}} c_{t,\frac{n}{k}}^{\lambda} c_x^{-1})^{-e}$.

We set $c = com_K(e^{n+1} a_n - e f_1 \cdots f_n; z) c_1^{e f_2 \cdots f_n} \cdots c_n^{e^n}$.

Finally we let $E' = E_{pk}(0; z')(E_1')^{f_1} \cdots (E_n')^{f_n}(E_1^{s_1 + \lambda t_1 - x} \cdots E_n^{s_n + \lambda t_n - x})^{-e}$.

The simulated proof is $(s_1, \ldots, s_n, c_{s,1}, \ldots, c_{s,\frac{n}{k}}, t_1, \ldots, t_n, c_{t,1}, \ldots, c_{t,\frac{n}{k}}, \lambda, x,$
$c_{d,1}, \ldots, c_{d,\frac{n}{k}}, c_1, \ldots, c_n, c, E', e, f_1, \ldots, f_n, z_1, \ldots, z_{\frac{n}{k}}, z, z')$.

Proof that the simulation works

Let us argue that this simulated proof is indistinguishable from a real proof. We define the following sequence of experiments:

Exp_1: We carry out a real proof with challenges $t_1, \ldots, t_n, \lambda, x, e$.

Exp_2: First we pick $d_1, \ldots, d_n, r_{d,1}, \ldots, r_{d,\frac{n}{k}}, r, r'$. Then we carry out a real proof using these values.

Exp_3: We pick $f_1, \ldots, f_n, z_1, \ldots, z_{\frac{n}{k}}, z, z'$. We then carry out a real proof, except when making the second answer. In that step the values $d_1, \ldots, d_n, r_{d,1}, \ldots, r_{d,\frac{n}{k}}, r, r'$ are fitted to the uniquely determined values that will make the entire proof acceptable.

Exp_4: We pick as in Exp_3 the elements $f_1, \ldots, f_n, z_1, \ldots, z_{\frac{n}{k}}, z, z'$ first. Afterwards we fit $c_{d,1}, \ldots, c_{d,\frac{n}{k}}, c, E'$ to the other commitments and ciphertexts, as we do in the simulation.

Exp_5: We carry out Exp_4 this time committing to zeros when making $c_{s,1}, \ldots, c_{s,\frac{n}{k}}, c_{t,1}, \ldots, c_{t,\frac{n}{k}}, c_1, \ldots, c_n$.

Exp_6: We make a simulated proof.

Exp_1 and Exp_2 are the same experiments where we have only changed the order in which we pick some elements. They are therefore perfectly indistinguishable.

Exp_2 and Exp_3 are perfectly indistinguishable since the elements we pick get the same distribution either way.

Exp_3 and Exp_4 are perfectly indistinguishable since we get the same $c_{d,1}, \ldots, c_{d,\frac{n}{k}}, c, E'$ no matter which method we use.

Exp_4 and Exp_5 are indistinguishable due to the hiding property of the commitment scheme. If the commitment scheme is statistically or perfectly hiding, the two experiments are statistically respectively perfectly indistinguishable.

Exp_5 and Exp_6 are the same experiments except for the order in which we pick some of the elements.

From this, we deduce that Exp_1 and Exp_6 are indistinguishable, in other words real proofs and simulated proofs are indistinguishable. Furthermore, when the commitment schemes are statistically or perfectly hiding, then the real proof and the simulated proof are statistically, respectively perfectly, indistinguishable.

$\square$

While this proof system is intended for proving correctness of a shuffle of encryptions, we can use a virtually identical proof if we wish to prove a shuffle of commitments $c_1, \ldots, c_n, c'_1, \ldots, c'_n$. When making the proof for commitments the root opening property of commitment schemes allows us to extract in polynomial time with high probability a witness for a shuffle consisting of a permutation π and openers $r_1, \ldots, r_n$ so that the commitments satisfy $c'_i = c_{\pi(i)} com_K(0; r_i)$ for $i = 1, \ldots, n$.

5   Speed, Space and Tricks

We start by mentioning a speedup. As $s_1, \ldots, s_n$ we may as well use the values $0, \ldots, n-1$. With this convention, the prover does not need to send $s_1, \ldots, s_n$ to the verifier. Furthermore, by choosing $s_1, \ldots, s_n$ as small as possible we may save some computation when making the multicommitments to $s_1, \ldots, s_n$. We use this speedup in the following estimate of the computational and communicational effort involved in making a proof of a shuffle.

We look at the special case of an ElGamal cryptosystem built over a 1024-bit prime p and a 160-bit prime q as in the introduction, and using the commitment scheme we have looked at before with these parameters as well as the suggested generalization to a multicommitment scheme. The prover makes $6n + 3\frac{n}{k} + 3$ exponentiations, the verifier makes $6n + 3\frac{n}{k} + 6$ exponentiations. The prover sends $1184n + 3232\frac{n}{k} + 3392$ bits during the proof. For optimal efficiency of the shuffle we select $k = n$. However, in cases where n is not known in advance, or where the public keys may need to be computed using a complicated multi-party computation protocol, we may wish to use a smaller k.

When comparing our scheme with that of [4] we have achieved significant improvements, in particular in the communication complexity. However, in many settings 1024-bit ElGamal encryption is not sufficiently strong, in particular not when long-term protection of data is needed. Here we may take advantage of the fact that we can use any commitment and multicommitment schemes, as long as the message spaces are compatible with the message space of the cryptosystem, and get further improvements. Let us say for instance that we have set up an ElGamal cryptosystem with a 3000-bit prime p and a 300-bit prime $q|p-1$. We may then use another 1500-bit prime p' for the commitment schemes instead of p

if $q|p'-1$. This speeds up the group operations considerably when computing the commitments, and because the proof system is statistical zero-knowledge it does not compromise the systems ability to hide the underlying permutation used in the shuffle.

An approach along the same lines that can be used quite generally is to use an integer commitment scheme as a virtual $\mathbf{Z}_N$ commitment scheme, where N is some appropriate integer in connection with the message space of the cryptosystem. This works by simply computing with the contents of the commitment schemes modulo N. However, some care must be taken not to accidentally leak information.

In the proof above, we picked the challenges $t_1, \ldots, t_n, \lambda, x, e$ from the message space $\mathcal{M}_K$. When the message space is small, such as $\mathbf{Z}_q$, where q is a 160-bit prime this is reasonable enough. However, when the message space is large we can make the protocol more efficient by picking the challenges from some suitable small subset of $\mathcal{M}_K$, say for instance $\{0, \ldots, 2^t - 1\}$ where t is a secondary security parameter of, say, 160 bits.

Finally, we mention that if we have several lists of ciphertexts that we need to shuffle according to the same permutation π, then we do not have to pay much extra for each additional π-shuffle. Almost all of the protocol can be reused.

References

[1] R. Cramer, I. Damgård and B. Schoenmakers, "Proofs of Partial Knowledge and Simplified Design of Witness Hiding Protocols", CRYPTO '94, LNCS series, volume 893: p. 174-187, 1994 146

[2] I. Damgård and E. Fujisaki, "An Integer Commitment Scheme based on Groups with Hidden Order", Cryptology ePrint Archive, Report 2001/064, 2001 148

[3] I. Damgård and M. J. Jurik, "A Generalisation, a Simplification and Some Applications of Paillier's Probabilistic Public-Key System", PKC 2001, LNCS series, volume 1992: p. 119-136, 2001 150, 151

[4] J. Furukawa and K. Sako, "An Efficient Scheme for Proving a Shuffle", CRYPTO '01, LNCS series, volume 2139: p. 368-387, 2001 145, 146, 159

[5] M. Jakobson, A. Juels and R. L. Rivest, "Making Mix Nets Robust for Electronic Voting by Randomized Partial Checking", USENIX Security '02, 2002 146

[6] A. Neff, "A Verifiable Secret Shuffle and its Application to E-Voting", ACM CCS '01: p. 116-125, 2001 145, 146, 147, 151

[7] P. Paillier, "Public-key cryptosystems based on composite residuosity classes", EUROCRYPT '99, LNCS series, volume 1592: p. 223-239, 1999 150

Round-Optimal Contributory Conference Key Agreement

Colin Boyd and Juan Manuel González Nieto

Information Security Research Centre
Queensland University of Technology, Brisbane, Australia
{boyd,juanma}@isrc.qut.edu.au

Abstract. Becker and Wille derived a lower bound of only one round for multi-party contributory key agreement protocols. Up until now no protocol meeting this bound has been proven secure. We present a protocol meeting the bound and prove it is secure in Bellare and Rogaway's model. The protocol is much more efficient than other conference key agreement protocols with provable security, but lacks forward secrecy.

1 Introduction

Communications efficiency is concerned with the number and length of messages that need to be sent and received during a protocol. As well as minimising the number of individual messages, it can be important to have as few *rounds* as possible in the protocol. One round includes all the messages that can be sent in parallel during the protocol. Protocols where the messages are independent of each other require fewer rounds than those where messages include fields received in previous protocol messages.

Most published key agreement protocols are based on Diffie-Hellman's famous key exchange protocol. A number of generalisations of the Diffie-Hellman protocol have been devised which allow many parties to agree jointly on a session key. With the exception of a recent protocol proposed by Joux for three parties in a special setting [19], all these generalisations require multiple rounds of communications in order to complete.

In 1998, Becker and Wille [3] derived several bounds on multi-party key agreement protocols. Amongst these was the bound on the number of rounds which is only one, no matter what is the number of users involved. A protocol that meets this bound would allow all messages to be sent simultaneously in one time unit, as long as parallel messages are possible. No Diffie-Hellman generalisation is able to meet this bound and Becker and Wille leave as an open question whether any contributory key agreement scheme can meet this bound.

The purpose of this paper is to describe a protocol which meets the bound of Becker and Wille. In addition we present a new proof of the security of the protocol under the assumption that standard secure cryptographic primitives exist for encryption and signature, and using ideal hash functions (random oracles). Although Becker and Wille considered only unauthenticated key agreement protocols, which are insecure against active adversaries, we provide a proven secure

Y.G. Desmedt (Ed.): PKC 2003, LNCS 2567, pp. 161–174, 2003.

authenticated key agreement which is secure in the usual understanding of key establishment protocols. Despite this extra security we still meet the bound. The protocol is simple and very efficient in comparison with previously published conference key agreement protocols. Its only significant limitation is that it does not provide forward secrecy. We regard the following as the main contributions.

- A new conference key agreement protocol is proven secure in the random oracle model.
- The computational requirements for the protocol are smaller than those for any existing provable secure conference key protocol.
- The first proven secure protocol that meets the bound of Becker and Wille for a single round protocol.

1.1 Related Work

Conference Key Agreement Most conference key agreement protocols are based on generalisations of Diffie and Hellman's famous key exchange protocol [15]. Examples include a set of protocols by Ingemarsson, Tang and Wong [18], a protocol by Burmester and Desmedt [14] and three protocols of Steiner, Tsudik and Waidner [23].

In their basic form none of these protocols provides authentication of the users so they do not protect against active attacks. Ateniese *et al.* [1, 2] propose two ways to extend one of the protocols of Steiner *et al.* to provide authenticated group key agreement. However, Pereira and Quisquater [21] have described a number of potential attacks, highlighting the need for ways to obtain greater assurance in the security of such protocols.

The protocol of Joux [19] is the only example currently known of a group key agreement protocol that can be run in a single round and still provide forward secrecy; however the protocol can only work with three parties. Joux's protocol works in elliptic curve groups and exploits pairings of group points.

Provable Security for Protocols An important direction in cryptographic protocol research was pioneered by Bellare and Rogaway in 1993 [7] when they published the first mathematical proof that a simple entity authentication protocol was secure. This work, which covered only the two-party case, was followed up with a paper on server-based protocols [4] and various authors have extended the same idea to include public-key based key transport [8], key agreement protocols [9], password-based protocols [6, 10], and conference key protocols [13, 11, 12].

The general approach is to produce a mathematical model that defines a protocol in which a powerful adversary plays a central role. The adversary essentially controls all the principals and can initiate protocol runs between any principals at any time. Insider attacks are modelled by allowing the adversary to corrupt any principals, and the adversary can also obtain previously used keys. Cryptographic algorithms are modelled in an idealised manner. Security of protocols is defined in terms of matching conversations (for authentication) and indistinguishability (for confidentiality of keys). The proofs follow the style of most proofs in modern cryptography by reducing the security of the protocol to the security of some underlying primitive.

Up until now the only conference key protocols which carry a reduction proof are those of Bresson *et al.* [13, 11, 12]. Based on the generalised Diffie-Hellman protocols of Steiner *et al.* [23], these protocols are (relatively) computationally expensive. In addition they require a number of rounds equal to the number of principals in the conference. The advantage they have over the protocol examined in this paper is the provision of forward secrecy.

1.2 Protocols of Tzeng and Tzeng

Two new round-efficient conference key agreement protocols were presented by Tzeng and Tzeng [24]. Although they claim that their protocols can be completed in one round and are proven secure, we would like to point out the following limitations of their protocols.

- Their protocols require a session identifier to be known by all participating principals. Unless this session identifier is agreed beforehand their protocols cannot be completed in one round.
- Although they claim that their protocol provides authentication and does not leak information, they provide no reduction proof for a powerful adversary.

Like our protocol, the protocols of Tzeng and Tzeng do not provide forward secrecy. A feature of their protocols is a proof of knowledge that each party has been sent the same inputs. The purpose of these proofs is to provide fault detection and exclude principals who deviate from the protocol. However, such a proof is only useful on the strong assumption that the broadcast channel which they use provides integrity of all messages; otherwise a malicious insider can send different proofs to different principals.

The first protocol of Tzeng and Tzeng uses a conventional type of signature to provide authentication of signatures. However, their second protocol attempts to provide authentication implicitly by including the private key of the sender in the proof. Unfortunately this proof is not sound and consequently the protocol can be broken. The details are presented in Appendix A.

1.3 Outline of Paper

Sections 2 and 3 present the communications model and definitions of security which we use. These follow quite closely the definitions of Bellare and Rogaway [4] with modifications required for the special situation of conference keys. Section 4 presents our new protocol and explains the differences from other related protocols. Section 5 presents the proof of security.

2   Communications Model

We follow closely the model established by Bellare and Rogaway [7, 4] incorporating later updates [6]. In particular we use the later form of *partnering* which seems more suitable for the multi-party environment.

The adversary $\mathcal{A}$ is a probabilistic machine that controls all the communications that take place and does this by interacting with a set of *oracles*, each of which represents an instance of a principal in a specific protocol run. Each principal has an identifier U from a finite set $\{U_1, \ldots, U_n\}$. Oracle Π_U^s represents the actions of principal U in the protocol run indexed by integer s. The number of principals n is polynomial in the security parameter k. Each user has a long-lived key, obtained at the start of the protocol using a key distribution algorithm $\mathcal{G}_L$. Interactions with the adversary are called oracle *queries* and the list of allowed queries is summarised in Table 1. We now describe each one informally.

Send(U, s, m) This query allows the adversary to make the principal U run the protocol normally. The oracle Π_U^s will return to the adversary the same next message that an honest principal U would if sent message m according to the conversation so far. (This includes the possibility that m not be of the expected format in which case Π_U^s may simply halt.) If Π_U^s accepts the session key or halts this is included in the response. The adversary can use this query to initiate a new protocol instance by sending a flag message $m = \mathsf{Initiator}$ or $m = \mathsf{Responder}$ indicating the role that the principal plays.

Reveal(U, s) This query models the adversary's ability to find session keys. If a session key K_s has previously been accepted by Π_U^s then it is returned to the adversary. An oracle can only accept a key once (of course a principal can accept many keys modelled in different oracles). An oracle is called *opened* if it has been the object of a Reveal query.

Corrupt(U, K) This query models insider attacks by the adversary. The query returns the oracle's internal state and sets the long-term key of U to be the value K chosen by the adversary. The adversary can then control the behaviour of U with Send queries. A principal is called *corrupted* if it has been the object of a Corrupt query.

Test(U, s) Once the oracle Π_U^s has accepted a session key K_s the adversary can attempt to distinguish it from a random key as the basis of determining security of the protocol. A random bit b is chosen; if $b = 0$ then K_s is returned while if $b = 1$ a random string is returned from the same distribution as session keys. This query is only asked once by the adversary.

Table 1. Queries available to the adversary

Send(U, s, m)	Send message m to oracle Π_U^s
Reveal(U, s)	Reveal session key (if any) accepted by Π_U^s
Corrupt(U, K)	Reveal state of U and set long-term key of U to K
Test(U, s)	Ask for test key to distinguish session key accepted by oracle Π_U^s

3   Security

Definitions of security in the Bellare-Rogaway model depend on the notion of the *partner* oracles to any oracle being tested. The way of defining partner oracles has varied in different papers using the technique. In the more recent research partners have been defined by having the same session identifier (SID) which consists of a concatenation of the messages exchanged between the two. Partners must both have accepted the same session key and recognise each other as partners. Bresson *et al.* [13] defined a set of session IDs for an oracle so that oracles in the same session should share session IDs pairwise. However, since all messages in our protocol are broadcast we can expect all oracles in the same session to derive the same session ID. Therefore we define $SID(\Pi_U^s)$ as the concatenation of all (broadcast) messages that oracle Π_U^s has sent and received.

Definition 1. *A set of oracles are* partnered *if:*

- *they have accepted with the same session ID,*
- *they agree on the set of principals, and*
- *they agree on the initiator of the protocol.*

Note that an oracle only 'knows' which principals it is communicating with but not which instance of the principals is involved.

Definition 2. *An oracle Π_U^s is* fresh *at the end of its execution if:*

- *Π_U^s has accepted with set of partners Π^*;*
- *Π_U^s and all oracles in Π^* are unopened;*
- *All principals of oracles in Π^* (including U) are uncorrupted.*

The security of the protocol is defined by the following game played between the adversary and an infinite collection of oracles Π_U^s for $U \in \{U_1, \ldots, U_n\}$ and $s \in \mathbb{N}$. Firstly, long-lived keys are assigned to each user by running the key distribution algorithm $\mathcal{G}_L$ on input of the security parameter. Then, the adversary $\mathcal{A}(1^k)$ is run. $\mathcal{A}$ will interact with the oracles through the queries defined above. At some stage during the execution a Test query is performed by the adversary to a fresh oracle. The adversary may continue to make other queries and eventually outputs a bit b' and terminates. Success of the adversary $\mathcal{A}$ in this game is measured in terms of its *advantage* in distinguishing the session key of the Test query from a random key, i.e. its advantage in outputting $b' = b$. This advantage must be measured in terms of the security parameter k. If we define Good-Guess to be the event that $\mathcal{A}$ guesses correctly whether $b = 0$ or $b = 1$ then

$$\text{Advantage}^{\mathcal{A}}(k) = 2 \cdot \Pr[\text{Good-Guess}] - 1.$$

To define validity of a conference key agreement protocol, we use the concept of a *benign adversary* as an adversary that faithfully relays flows between participants [7].

Definition 3. *A protocol P is a* secure conference key agreement scheme *if the following two properties are satisfied:*

- Validity: *in the presence of a benign adversary partner oracles accept the same key.*
- Indistinguishability: *for every probabilistic polynomial time adversary $\mathcal{A}$,* Advantage$^{\mathcal{A}}(k)$ *is negligible.*

In the literature [20] it is often stated that a requirement of any key establishment protocol is *key authentication*, which means that each principal should have assurance that no other party has possession of the session key. A superficial examination of the above definition (or any of the several related ones in papers using the Bellare-Rogaway model) indicates that key authentication is ignored since the definition only refers to the adversary gaining information about the session key and not the identity of principals holding the key. In reality key authentication is implicitly included through the notion of partnering. If an oracle should accept a session key that is shared with an unknown principal then that principal is *not* the partner of the accepting oracle and can therefore be opened by the adversary and so the adversary does indeed gain an advantage.

Security of a protocol is proved by finding a reduction to some well known computational problem whose intractability is assumed. For the new protocol that we present in this paper, this reduction is to the security of the underlying public key encryption and signature schemes. Thus, we require notions of secure encryption and signature which are by now quite standard.

3.1   Secure Encryption Schemes

Let k denote the security parameter. A *public-key encryption scheme* $\mathcal{PE} = (\mathcal{K}, \mathcal{E}, \mathcal{D})$ consists of three algorithms.

- The *key generation* algorithm $\mathcal{K}$ is a probabilistic algorithm which, on input 1^k, outputs a pair (e, d) of matching public and private keys, respectively.
- The *encryption* algorithm $\mathcal{E}$ is a probabilistic algorithm which takes a public key e and a message m drawn from a message space M associated to e and returns a ciphertext c. This is denoted as $c \xleftarrow{R} \mathcal{E}_e(m)$.
- The *decryption* algorithm $\mathcal{D}$ is a deterministic algorithm which takes a private key d and a ciphertext c and returns the corresponding plaintext m. This is denoted as $m \leftarrow \mathcal{D}_d(m)$. We require that $\mathcal{D}_d(\mathcal{E}_e(m)) = m$ for every $(e, d) \leftarrow \mathcal{K}(1^k)$.

For security we use the standard definition of *semantic security* due to Goldwasser and Micali [16]. For any probabilistic polynomial time adversary $\mathcal{A}$, the security is defined in terms of the following game.

1. Choose a key pair $(e, d) \leftarrow \mathcal{K}(1^k)$.
2. Given e, the adversary outputs two messages of equal length $m_0, m_1 \in M$ of her choice.

3. Compute $c_b \overset{R}{\leftarrow} \mathcal{E}_e(m_b)$ where $b \overset{R}{\leftarrow} \{0,1\}$. The bit b is kept secret from the adversary.
4. The adversary is then given c_b and has to output a guess b' for b.

We define the advantage of the adversary playing the above game as Advantage$^{\mathcal{A}}(k) = 2 \cdot \Pr[b' = b] - 1$. The encryption scheme $\mathcal{PE}$ is secure if the adversary's advantage is negligible.

3.2   Secure Signature Scheme

Let k be the security parameter. A *digital signature scheme* $\Sigma = (\mathcal{K}, \mathcal{S}, \mathcal{V})$ consists of the following three algorithms.

- The *key generation algorithm* $\mathcal{K}$ is a probabilistic algorithm that takes as input 1^k and outputs a pair of matching keys (e, d). The string e is the (public) *verification key*, and d the corresponding (private) *signing key*.
- The *signing algorithm* $\mathcal{S}$ takes as input a signing key d and a plaintext message m and outputs a signature σ.
- The *verification algorithm* $\mathcal{V}$ takes as input a verification key e, a message m and a signature σ, and outputs 1 if the signature is valid, and 0 otherwise.

For a signature scheme to be secure we require that it be computationally impossible for any adversary to forge a signature on any message (*existential forgery*) even *under adaptive chosen-message attacks* [17].

4   The Protocol

We now define the protocol that we shall prove secure. All parameter choices depend on a security parameter k. The protocol that we analyse involves the set of n users, $\mathcal{U} = \{U_1, U_2, \ldots, U_n\}$. The protocol has associated a secure public key encryption scheme $\mathcal{PE} = (\mathcal{K}, \mathcal{E}, \mathcal{D})$, where $\mathcal{K}$ is the key generation algorithm, and $\mathcal{E}, \mathcal{D}$ are the encryption and decryption algorithms, respectively. The protocol also uses a secure signature scheme $\Sigma = (\overline{\mathcal{K}}, \mathcal{S}, \mathcal{V})$, with $\overline{\mathcal{K}}$ the key generation algorithm, $\mathcal{S}$ the signing algorithm and $\mathcal{V}$ the verification algorithm. The key distribution algorithm $\mathcal{G}_L$ assigns to each user U_i an encryption/decryption key pair $(e_i, d_i) \leftarrow \mathcal{K}(1^k)$ and a signing/verification key pair $(\overline{e}_i, \overline{d}_i) \leftarrow \overline{\mathcal{K}}(1^k)$. The key distribution algorithm $\mathcal{G}_L$ also provides each user with an authentic copy of the public keys of all other users.

Each user, U_i, chooses a *nonce* (a random value, N_i, of size k bits). One user, say U_1, will be distinguished and will send its value N_1 to each other user in an authenticated and confidential way. We call this distinguished user the *initiator* of the protocol and the other users the *responders*. In an implementation there is no need for the messages of U_1 to be sent before the other messages, so it is perfectly possible for all messages to be sent together in one round.

The responders only have to broadcast their nonces so that all users in $\mathcal{U}$ receive all the N_i values. U_1 will encrypt N_1 for each other user U_i using U_i's

$$\overline{\begin{array}{l} 1.\ U_1 \rightarrow * : \mathcal{U}, \mathcal{S}_{d_1}(\mathcal{U}, \mathcal{E}_{e_2}(N_1), \mathcal{E}_{e_3}(N_1), \dots, \mathcal{E}_{e_n}(N_1)) \\ 2.\ U_1 \rightarrow * : \mathcal{E}_{e_i}(N_1) \text{ for } i \leq 2 \leq n \\ 3.\ U_i \rightarrow * : U_i, N_i \\ \qquad K_\mathcal{U} = h(N_1 || N_2 || N_3 \dots || N_n) \end{array}}$$

Fig. 1. Protocol execution with a benign adversary

public encryption key e_i. U_1 will then sign the encrypted values of N_1 together with the names of all users in the conference. Since this message is the same for every user it only needs to be formed and sent once in a broadcast to all users. The value of N_1 is sent to user U_i encrypted with that user's public key, e_i. Thus, the protocol has three stages, all of which broadcast a message; in some communications scenarios each broadcast constitutes $n-1$ messages.

Figure 1 shows the message flows in a protocol run without any disruption from the adversary. In the communications model this corresponds to the situation in which the adversary is benign, i.e. simply passes messages between principals. The asterisk is used to denote broadcast messages. The conference key should then be defined as follows, where h is a one-way function which will be modelled as a random oracle in the proof.

$$K_\mathcal{U} = h(N_1 || N_2 || N_3 \dots || N_n) \tag{1}$$

Let us consider the computational requirements for each user. U_1 has to perform $n-1$ public key encryptions and generate one signature. The other $n-1$ users have only to check one signature and decrypt one message, so for them the computational requirements are the same as for the two user case. The computational burden of U_1 can be reduced substantially by careful choice of public key cryptosystem. The computations required are substantially less than in the proven secure generalised Diffie-Hellman protocols of Bresson *et al.* [13, 11, 12], which require U_i to perform $i+1$ exponentiations in addition to generating and verifying a signature.

In common with most conference key protocols, we provide no confirmation to principals that others principals have obtained the session key. It is not possible to be sure whether some participants have been 'excluded' by an adversary who cuts off their incoming communications. Providing such assurances seems difficult and expensive to achieve.

5   Security Proof

The proof follows that of Bellare and Rogaway [4]; differences include the number of entities involved and the different partnering function used. The validity of the protocol is straightforward to verify. Thus, it remains to prove that the protocol satisfies the indistinguishability requirement. The general idea of the security proof is to assume that the adversary can gain a non-negligible advantage in distinguishing test keys, and use this to break the assumption about the security of the underlying encryption scheme or the signature scheme. Since the adversary relies on its oracles to run we simulate the oracles so that we can supply the answers to all the queries the adversary might ask.

In our protocol we assume that the principals involved in each conference are the same. We do *not* assume that the same principal acts as the initiator. The case where the set of principals is chosen dynamically is easily handled too. The effect on the security proof is to make the reduction less tight.

Following Bellare and Rogaway [4] we need to extend the definition of a secure encryption scheme to allow the adversary to obtain encryptions of the same plaintext under multiple different independent encryption keys. Such an adversary is termed a *multiple eavesdropper*. We can bound the advantage of a multiple eavesdropper by considering it as a special case of the multi-user setting analysed by Bellare *et al.* [5]. In their notation we have the case of $q_e = 1$, meaning that the eavesdropper can only obtain one encryption for each public key. Let r be the number of encryptions of the same plaintext message seen by a multiple eavesdropper. Specialising their main theorem gives the following.

Lemma 1 ([5]). *Suppose that an adversary has advantage at most $\epsilon(k)$ for encryption scheme $\mathcal{PE} = (\mathcal{K}, \mathcal{E}, \mathcal{D})$. Then a multiple eavesdropper has advantage not more than $r \cdot \epsilon(k)$.*

We follow Bresson *et al.* [13] in dividing the proof into two cases. Firstly we consider the case in which the adversary $\mathcal{A}$ gains her advantage by forging a signature with respect to some user's signing key. In this case we construct a simple signature forging algorithm $\mathcal{F}$ against Σ that uses $\mathcal{A}$. In the second case, $\mathcal{A}$ gains her advantage without forging a signature. Then, we can construct an algorithm $\mathcal{X}$ that uses $\mathcal{A}$ against the security of the encryption algorithm.

5.1   Signature Forger

Assume that $\mathcal{A}$ gains an advantage by forging a signature for some principal. We use $\mathcal{A}$ to construct a forger $\mathcal{F}$ for the signature scheme Σ. When $\mathcal{F}$ runs, it receives a public key $\bar{e}$ generated by $\overline{\mathcal{K}}(1^k)$ and access to a signing oracle for the corresponding signing key. The objective of $\mathcal{F}$ is to output a valid signature for a message which was not previously asked of the signing oracle.

In order to obtain the forgery $\mathcal{F}$ runs $\mathcal{A}$ with the following setting. Firstly, $\mathcal{F}$ chooses at random a principal $\overline{U}$ from $\mathcal{U}$. $\overline{U}$ is $\mathcal{F}$'s guess at which principal $\mathcal{A}$ will choose for the forgery. The adversary assigns $\bar{e}$ as the public key of $\overline{U}$. For all other principals, $\mathcal{F}$ generates the signing keys using the signature key generation algorithm $\overline{\mathcal{K}}$. $\mathcal{F}$ also generates the encryption keys for all the principals using $\mathcal{K}$. This allows $\mathcal{F}$ to answer all the oracle queries from $\mathcal{A}$ as follows.

Send(U, s, m) Assume $m = $ Initiator. According to the protocol specification, a random nonce is generated and encrypted under the keys of the responders. Since all encryption keys are known, all the ciphertexts can be formed. If $U \neq \overline{U}$ then the signing key is available too, otherwise the signature is obtained by querying the signing oracle. The ciphertexts and signature are returned to the adversary. If $m \neq \mathsf{Initiator}$ then this query can be answered normally as per protocol specification.

Reveal(U, s) Since all the session keys are known from the $\mathsf{Send}(U, s, m)$ queries, the query can be trivially answered with the correct session key (if available).

Corrupt(U, K) As long as $U \neq \overline{U}$ all the private information is available and the query can be answered. In the case $U = \overline{U}$ then the query cannot be properly answered, and fails.

Test(U, s) Since all the accepted session keys are known from running the send queries, the query can be trivially answered by identifying the correct session key.

If during the execution of $\mathcal{A}$, $\mathcal{A}$ makes a query that includes a forged signature, then $\mathcal{F}$ returns the forgery and halts. Otherwise, $\mathcal{F}$ halts when $\mathcal{A}$ does and outputs fail. Notice that when a Corrupt query fails, this means that the guess of $\overline{U}$ as the user whose signature was to be forged by $\mathcal{A}$ was wrong. (Recall that we are assuming that $\mathcal{A}$ gets her advantage by forging a signature.) Suppose that $\mathcal{A}$ succeeds by forging a signature with probability at least $\nu_s(k)$. The probability that this is a forgery for $\overline{e}$ is at least $1/n$. Therefore the signature forger succeeds with probability

$$\mathsf{Succ}_{\Sigma}(k) \geq \nu_s(k)/n.$$

In other words, the success probability of an adversary attacking the protocol in this case is at most n times the probability of signature forgery. Since n is polynomial in the security parameter, k, if $\nu_s(k)$ is non-negligible, then so is $\mathsf{Succ}_{\Sigma}(k)$.

5.2 Encryption Attacker

Now assume that $\mathcal{A}$ gains an advantage without forging a signature. This time we use $\mathcal{A}$ to form an algorithm $\mathcal{X}$ which has an advantage against the underlying encryption scheme $\mathcal{PE} = (\mathcal{K}, \mathcal{E}, \mathcal{D})$ in the multi-user setting.

The input to $\mathcal{X}$ consists of the following.

- Public keys $e_2, \ldots e_n$ generated by $\mathcal{K}(1^k)$.
- Two randomly chosen values σ_0 and σ_1 of equal bit length k.
- Encryptions $\alpha_2 = \mathcal{E}_{e_2}(\sigma_\theta), \ldots, \alpha_n = \mathcal{E}_{e_n}(\sigma_\theta)$, where θ is randomly chosen in $\{0, 1\}$.

The goal of $\mathcal{X}$ is to gain an advantage in guessing whether $\theta = 0$ or $\theta = 1$.

Algorithm $\mathcal{X}$ runs as follows. Firstly, $\mathcal{X}$ chooses at random a principal from $\mathcal{U}$. Without loss of generality we assume this principal to be U_1. $\mathcal{X}$ then proceeds to distribute long-lived keys to all principals. $\mathcal{X}$ assigns signature keys $(\overline{e}_i, \overline{d}_i) \leftarrow \overline{\mathcal{K}}(1^k)$ to each user U_i for $i \in [1, n]$. In order to distribute encryption keys, $\mathcal{X}$ assigns $(e_1, d_1) \leftarrow \mathcal{K}(1^k)$ to U_1 and the public encryption keys $e_2, \ldots, e_n$ to principals $U_2, \ldots, U_n$, respectively. $\mathcal{X}$ also chooses a random session identifier, $t \in [1, S]$, where S is the maximum number of sessions that the adversary

$\mathcal{A}$ is allowed to instantiate. S is polynomial in the security parameter k. The identifier t is used to decide when the initiator will give the input ciphertexts to $\mathcal{A}$. Algorithm $\mathcal{X}$ answers all the oracle queries from $\mathcal{A}$ as follows.

Send(U, s, m) If the query is to start a new protocol run, we have the following two cases.

1. Suppose that (U, s) is to be the initiator of the protocol. If $s = t$ and $U = U_1$, then $\alpha_2, \ldots, \alpha_n$ are used as the encrypted values for the other $n-1$ principals and signed using U_1's signing key. The ciphertexts $\alpha_2, \ldots, \alpha_n$ and signature are returned to the adversary.

   Otherwise, a nonce is chosen randomly of k bits, and is then encrypted under the public encryption keys of the rest of the principals. Since all encryption keys are known, all the ciphertexts can be formed. Similarly, since all signing keys are available to $\mathcal{X}$ the signature of U on these encryptions can also be computed. The ciphertexts and signature are returned to $\mathcal{A}$.

   Algorithm $\mathcal{X}$ should record that (U, s) is the initiator and the nonce and ciphertext values chosen.

2. Now suppose that (U, s) is the responder. Then a nonce is chosen randomly of k bits. The nonce is returned to the adversary. Algorithm $\mathcal{X}$ should record that (U, s) is the responder and the nonce value chosen.

If the query is not to start a new protocol run, then we get the following two cases.

1. If (U, s) is the initiator, then Π_U^s accepts a new conference key provided m is of the expected form (a set of $n-1$ nonces of the correct length); otherwise, it fails. The outcome of whether it accepts or fails is returned to $\mathcal{A}$. Algorithm $\mathcal{X}$ records the nonces received by (U, s).

2. If (U, s) is a responder then m must consist of a signature, $n-1$ ciphertexts and $n-2$ nonces of correct size. If the format is correct and the signature is verified correctly then Π_U^s accepts and this information is returned to $\mathcal{A}$. Otherwise it outputs 'fail'. Algorithm $\mathcal{X}$ records the signature, ciphertexts and nonces received by (U, s).

Reveal(U, s) Since session keys are modelled as the output of a random oracle, we only need to keep track of which keys have been revealed before. If a key has not been revealed then a random string is returned. If it has been revealed then the same value as used before is returned. Let us assume Π_U^s has accepted (otherwise the query fails).

If (U, s) is a responder then it must have received and accepted signed ciphertexts. Since the adversary cannot forge signatures, the ciphertexts must have been formed in a Send query and are known to $\mathcal{X}$. (They were either formed by $\mathcal{X}$ or they are the α_i values.) If (U, s) is an initiator then $\mathcal{X}$ knows which nonces were received by (U, s) and also which ciphertexts were output by $(U, s$ to intitiate the protocol run. Therefore, in either case, $\mathcal{X}$ knows if the key have been revealed before and can respond correctly.

Corrupt(U, K) As long as $U = U_1$ then all the private information is available and the query can be answered. Otherwise the query cannot be answered and $\mathcal{A}$ will fail.

Test(U, s) If $s \neq t$ or the initiator of the conference for session s is not U_1 then the algorithm fails. Otherwise, $\mathcal{X}$ outputs a random string.

At some stage, $\mathcal{A}$ completes and returns a value b. We need to show how the prediction of the session key allows prediction of the plaintext chosen as input for $\mathcal{X}$. To do this we make use of the random oracle to model the hash function. Therefore we assume that whenever $\mathcal{A}$ makes a query of the hash function the value is returned randomly except if the same query was previously asked. The oracle keeps a list of all previously asked queries, and if the same query is asked again then the response is the same as the first time. Because of the random output of the oracle, $\mathcal{A}$ can gain no advantage in guessing any key for which the oracle is not queried. Therefore $\mathcal{X}$ examines all queries made by $\mathcal{A}$ of the form $h(N_1, N_2, \ldots, N_n)$. If there exists a query with $N_1 = \sigma_0$ then $\mathcal{X}$ returns $\theta = 0$. Otherwise it returns $\theta = 1$. Let $\nu_e(k)$ be the success probability of $\mathcal{A}$. Since the probability that during $\mathcal{X}$ execution the test query does not fail is $\frac{1}{nS}$, $\mathcal{X}$'s success probability is

$$\mathsf{Succ}_{n\mathcal{PE}}(k) \geq \frac{\nu_e(k)}{nS}.$$

Thus, on the assumption that $\mathcal{A}$ does not perform a signature forgery, we have shown that a non-negligible (in k) advantage in attacking the indistinguishability property of the conference key agreement scheme can be turned into a non-negligible advantage to attack the encryption scheme in the multiple-user setting, and by virtue of Lemma 1 into a non-negligible advantage to attack it in the single-user setting.

6   Conclusion

We have described the first known conference key agreement protocol that can be completed in one round and provided a proof of its security. It remains an open question whether it is possible to design a multi-party contributory key agreement scheme which completes in one round of communication and also provides forward security.

References

[1] Giuseppe Ateniese, Michael Steiner, and Gene Tsudik. Authenticated group key agreement and friends. In *5th Conference on Computer and Communications Security*, pages 17–26. ACM Press, 1998. 162
[2] Giuseppe Ateniese, Michael Steiner, and Gene Tsudik. New multi-party authentication services and key agreement protocols. *IEEE Journal on Selected Areas in Communications*, 18(4):628–639, April 2000. 162
[3] Klaus Becker and Uta Wille. Communication complexity of group key distribution. In *5th Conference on Computer and Communications Security*, pages 1–6. ACM Press, 1998. 161

[4] M. Bellare and P. Rogaway. Provably secure session key distribution – the three party case. In *Proceedings of the 27th ACM Symposium on the Theory of Computing*, 1995. 162, 163, 164, 168, 169

[5] Mihir Bellare, Alexandra Boldyreva, and Silvio Micali. Public-key encryption in a multi-user setting: Security proofs and improvements. In B. Preneel, editor, *Advances in Cryptology – Eurocrypt 2000*, volume 1807 of *LNCS*. Springer-Verlag, 2000. Full version at http://www-cse.ucsd.edu/users/mihir/papers/key-distribution.html. 169

[6] Mihir Bellare, David Pointcheval, and Phillip Rogaway. Authenticated key exchange secure against dictionary attacks. In *Advances in Cryptology - Eurocrypt 2000*, pages 139–155. Springer-Verlag, 2000. 162, 164

[7] Mihir Bellare and Phillip Rogaway. Entity authentication and key distribution. In *Advances in Cryptology – CRYPTO'93*, pages 232–249. Springer-Verlag, 1993. Full version at www-cse.ucsd.edu/users/mihir. 162, 164, 165

[8] S. Blake-Wilson and A. Menezes. Security proofs for entity authentication and authenticated key transport protocols employing asymmetric techniques. In *Security Protocols Workshop*. Springer-Verlag, 1997. 162

[9] Simon Blake-Wilson and Alfred Menezes. Authenticated Diffie-Hellman key agreement protocols. In *Selected Areas in Cryptography*, pages 339–361. Springer-Verlag, 1999. 162

[10] Victor Boyko, Philip MacKenzie, and Sarvar Patel. Provably secure password-authenticated key exchange using Diffie-Hellman. In *Advanced in Cryptology - Eurocrypt 2000*. Springer-Verlag, 2000. 162

[11] Emmanuel Bresson, Olivier Chevassut, and David Pointcheval. Provably authenticated group Diffie-Hellman key exchange – the dynamic case. In *Advances in Cryptology - Asiacrypt 2001*, pages 290–309. Springer-Verlag, 2001. 162, 163, 168

[12] Emmanuel Bresson, Olivier Chevassut, and David Pointcheval. Dynamic group Diffie-Hellman key exchange under standard assumptions. In *Advances in Cryptology - Eurocrypt 2002*. Springer-Verlag, 2002. 162, 163, 168

[13] Emmanuel Bresson, Olivier Chevassut, David Pointcheval, and Jean-Jacques Quisquater. Provably authenticated group Diffie-Hellman key exchange. In *CCS'01*, pages 255–264. ACM Press, November 2001. 162, 163, 165, 168, 169

[14] Mike Burmester and Yvo Desmedt. A secure and efficient conference key distribution system. In *Advances in Cryptology – Eurocrypt'94*, pages 275–286. Springer-Verlag, 1995. 162

[15] W. Diffie and M. Hellman. New directions in cryptography. *IEEE Transaction on Information Theory*, 22:644–654, 1976. 162

[16] Shafi Goldwasser and Silvio Micali. Probabilistic encryption. *Journal of Computer Security*, 28:270–299, 1984. 166

[17] Shafi Goldwasser, Silvio Micali, and Ronald Rivest. A digital signature scheme secure against adaptive chosen-message attacks. *SIAM J. Comput.*, 17(2), 1988. 167

[18] Ingemar Ingemarsson, Donald T. Tang, and C. K.Wong. A conference key distribution system. *IEEE Transactions on Information Theory*, IT-28(5):714–720, September 1982. 162

[19] Antoine Joux. A one round protocol for tripartite Diffie-Hellman. In W. Bosma, editor, *Algorithmic Number Theory, 4th International Symposium, ANTS-IV*, volume 1838 of *LNCS*, pages 385–393. Springer-Verlag, 2000. 161, 162

[20] A. Menezes, P. van Oorschot, and S. Vanstone. *Handbook of Applied Cryptography*. CRC Press, 1996. 166

[21] Olivier Pereira and Jean-Jacques Quisquater. A security analysis of the Cliques protocol suites. In *Computer Security Foundations Workshop*, pages 73–81. IEEE Computer Society Press, 2001. 162

[22] Charles Rackoff and Daniel R. Simon. Non-interactive zero-knowledge proof of knowledge and chosen ciphertext attack. In Joan Feigenbaum, editor, *Advances in Cryptology – CRYPTO '91*, volume 576 of *Lecture Notes in Computer Science*, pages 433–444. Springer-Verlag, Berlin, Germany, 1992.

[23] Michael Steiner, Gene Tsudik, and Michael Waidner. Diffie-Hellman key distribution extended to group communication. In *3rd ACM Conference on Computer and Communications Security*, New Delhi, March 1996. ACM Press. 162, 163

[24] Wen-Guey Tzeng and Zhi-Jha Tzeng. Round-efficient conference key agreement protocols with provable security. In T. Okamoto, editor, *Advances in Cryptology – Asiacrypt 2000*, volume 1976 of *LNCS*, pages 614–627. Springer-Verlag, 2000. 163, 174

A   Attack on Tzeng and Tzeng's Second Protocol

Tzeng and Tzeng's second protocol [24] relies on a proof of knowledge to provide authentication of the principals. In this appendix we show that this proof is not sound so that the protocol provides no authentication.

In the conference key protocol a non-interactive version of the proof is used, but to explain the idea the authors use a conventional interactive description which we will review now. The prover is one member of the conference which has n users with public keys y_j for $1 \leq j \leq n$. The prover has public key $\tilde{y}$ and corresponding private key $\tilde{x}$ so that $\tilde{y} = g^{\tilde{x}}$. The prover chooses $k \in_R \mathbb{Z}_q$ and calculates $u_j = y_j^k$ for $1 \leq j \leq n$.

$$
\begin{array}{ccc}
P & & V \\
r_1, r_2 \in_R \mathbb{Z}_q & & \\
b_j = y_j^{r_1} g^{r_2}, 1 \leq j \leq n & & \\
& \xrightarrow{\quad b_1, b_2, \ldots, b_n \quad} & \\
& & c \in_R [0..2^t - 1] \\
& \xleftarrow{\qquad c \qquad} & \\
w_1 = r_1 - ck & & \\
w_2 = r_2 - c\tilde{x} & \xrightarrow{\quad w_1, w_2 \quad} & b_j \stackrel{?}{=} y_j^{w_1} g^{w_2} (\tilde{y} u_j)^c
\end{array}
$$

The purpose of the proof is to show that:

– the values $\log_{y_j} u_j$ are equal for all j and known to P.
– P knows the secret $\tilde{x}$.

We now show that an adversary A can masquerade as the prover without knowing the value $\tilde{x}$. First A chooses $v_j \in_R \mathbb{Z}_q$ and chooses the values u_j by solving $u_j \tilde{y} = g^{v_j}$. (In the protocol the u_j values are sent together with the non-interactive proof.) Then A can choose the commitments in the usual way as $b_j = y_j^{r_1} g^{r_2}$ for randomly chosen r_1, r_2. Now when A receives the challenge c he can compute $w_1 = r_1$ and $w_2 = -v_j c + r_2$ and the checks by V will succeed.

Security Analysis of the MOR Cryptosystem

Christian Tobias

Justus Liebig University Giessen, Department of Mathematics
Arndtstrasse 2, 35392 Giessen, Germany
christian.tobias@math.uni-giessen.de

Abstract. The paper cryptanalyses a new public key cryptosystem that
has been recently proposed by Paeng, Ha, Kim, Chee and Park [5].
The scheme works on finite non-abelian groups. We focus on the group
$SL(2, \mathbb{Z}_p) \times_\theta \mathbb{Z}_p$ which was discussed in [5] extensively.

Keywords: MOR Cryptosystem, Public Key Cryptosystem, Cryptanalysis, Conjugacy Problem, Finite Non Abelian Groups

1 Introduction

In [5] Paeng, Ha, Kim, Chee and Park presented a new public key encryption
scheme based on the difficulty of the discrete log problem in the inner automorphism
group of a non-abelian group G. This scheme was later called MOR cryptosystem
[6]. As underlying group the authors propose the semi-direct product
group $SL(2, \mathbb{Z}_p) \times_\theta \mathbb{Z}_p$ and discuss the resulting encryption scheme in detail.
In [5] the authors do not give a formal proof of security for their system. They
rather informally argue why an attacker should not be able to derive the secret
key from the public key.
Our analysis of the MOR system comprises several attacks that enable an attacker
to determine the plaintext message under certain conditions without compromising
the secret key.

The security of the MOR system is closely related to the hardness of the conjugacy
problem in the underlying group G. Given $x, y \in G$ the conjugacy problem
is to find $w \in G$ such that $y = wxw^{-1}$. In MOR using $G = SL(2, \mathbb{Z}_p) \times_\theta \mathbb{Z}_p$
the situation is slightly different. If $m \in G$ is the plaintext message, ciphertexts
are of the form $C(m) = x^{ab} m x^{-ab}$. The special situation of MOR using
$SL(2, \mathbb{Z}_p) \times_\theta \mathbb{Z}_p$, that we use in our attacks, is that the value x can easily be
calculated from the public information (an element from the centralizer of x is
already sufficient). We will see that in this case an attacker can collect valuable
information about m in a ciphertext-only attack.

To increase the efficiency of their scheme in $SL(2, \mathbb{Z}_p) \times_\theta \mathbb{Z}_p$ the authors
further propose some modifications to the original scheme. The first proposal is
to use $SL(2, \mathbb{Z}_p) \times_\theta \{0\} \cong SL(2, \mathbb{Z}_p)$ instead of $SL(2, \mathbb{Z}_p) \times_\theta \mathbb{Z}_p$.
In its basic form the MOR system is a probabilistic encryption scheme: The
sender has to choose a random encryption exponent for every message he wants

Y.G. Desmedt (Ed.): PKC 2003, LNCS 2567, pp. 175–186, 2003.
© Springer-Verlag Berlin Heidelberg 2003

to encrypt. For $G = SL(2, \mathbb{Z}_p) \times_\theta \mathbb{Z}_p$ the authors propose to fix the encryption exponent and use it for multiple encryptions. A randomised algorithm that maps plaintext messages in $\mathbb{Z}_p$ to matrices in $SL(2, \mathbb{Z}_p)$ is used to get a probabilistic encryption scheme. We will present and discuss the drawbacks of these modifications.

The rest of this paper is organised as follows. In section 2 we give a short summary of the MOR cryptosystem and its underlying constructions. For a more detailed description of the MOR system we refer to [5]. The sections 3 and 4 discuss the security of the MOR system. In section 3.1 we show that MOR using $SL(2, \mathbb{Z}_p) \times_\theta \mathbb{Z}_p$ is not harder than MOR using $SL(2, \mathbb{Z}_p)$. We further show that the parameter selection from [5] is not secure. In section 3.2 we present two ciphertext-only attacks for MOR using $SL(2, \mathbb{Z}_p) \times_\theta \mathbb{Z}_p$ that enable an attacker given one component of the plaintext to determine the whole plaintext message. In section 4 we investigate the security of the MOR cryptosystem when the encryption exponent is fixed. As we will see, MOR with fixed encryption exponent is vulnerable to known-plaintext attacks. Only one resp. two plaintext-ciphertext pairs are sufficient to decrypt all ciphertexts that were encrypted using the same exponent. In the appendix useful results about the matrix groups $SL(2, \mathbb{Z}_p)$ and $GL(2, \mathbb{Z}_p)$ are summarised.

Related Work: The conjugacy problem is considered a hard problem in braid groups. There is no known polynomial time algorithm which solves the decisional or the computational conjugacy problem in braid groups. For a detailed discussion of cryptography on braid groups we refer to [1, 3, 4].

Other cryptosystems using the conjugation map on matrix groups have been published by Yamamura [7, 8]. The systems later were broken by Blackburn and Galbraith [2].

2 Framework and Definitions

2.1 The MOR System

Definition 1 (Semi-direct Product Group). *Let G and H be given groups and $\theta : H \to Aut(G)$ be a homomorphism. Then the semi-direct product $G \times_\theta H$ is the set*

$$G \times H = \{(g, h) \mid g \in G, h \in H\}$$

together with the multiplication map

$$(g_1, h_1)(g_2, h_2) = (g_1\theta(h_1)(g_2), h_1h_2)$$

The semi-direct product $G \times_\theta H$ is also a group.

Definition 2 (The Mapping Inn). *Let G be a group. Then the mapping*

$$Inn : G \to Aut(G)$$
$$g \mapsto Inn(g)$$

is given by $Inn(g)(h) = ghg^{-1}$.

We call $Inn(g)$ an inner automorphism and $Inn(G) = \{Inn(g) \mid g \in G\}$ the inner automorphism group. If G is an abelian group then $Inn(g)$ is the identity map for all $g \in G$ and $Inn(G)$ is trivial. Let $\{\gamma_i\}$ be a set of generators of G. Since $Inn(g)$ is a homomorphism, $Inn(g)$ is totally specified for all $m \in G$ if the values $\{Inn(g)(\gamma_i)\}$ are given.

Definition 3 (Center, Centralizer). *Let G be a group. The center $Z(G)$ of G is defined as $Z(G) := \{g \in G \mid xg = gx \; \forall x \in G\}$.*
The centralizer $Z(g)$ of a group element $g \in G$ is defined as $Z(g) := \{h \in G \mid hg = gh\}$.
Note that $Z(G) = \bigcap_{g \in G} Z(g)$.

Definition 4 (Conjugacy Problem). *Let G be a group. For arbitrary $x, y \in G$ the conjugacy problem (CP) is to find $w \in G$ such that $wxw^{-1} = y$.*

Let $w \in G$ be a solution for the instance (x, y) of the CP, i.e. $wxw^{-1} = y$. Then $w \cdot Z(x)$ is the solution set for (x, y).

Definition 5 (Special Conjugacy Problem). *For a given $Inn(g)$ the special conjugacy problem is to find a group element $\bar{g} \in G$ satisfying $Inn(g) = Inn(\bar{g})$.*

The solution set for the special conjugacy problem is $g \cdot Z(G)$.

In $GL(2, \mathbb{Z}_p)$ the conjugacy problem is easy. To solve the special conjugacy problem in $GL(2, \mathbb{Z}_p)$ two pairs $(A_1, Inn(A_1))$ and $(A_2, Inn(A_2))$ with $A_1 \notin Z(A_2)$ are needed (see appendix A.2 for details).

The MOR cryptosystem: MOR is an asymmetric cryptosystem with a random value a as secret and the two mappings $Inn(g)$ and $Inn(g^a)$ (given as $\{Inn(g)(\gamma_i)\}$ and $\{Inn(g^a)(\gamma_i)\}$ for a generator set $\{\gamma_i\}$ of G) as corresponding public key.

The encryption process works as follows:

1. Alice expresses the plaintext $m \in G$ as a product of the γ_i.
2. Alice chooses an arbitrary b and computes $(Inn(g^a))^b$, i.e. $\{(Inn(g^a))^b(\gamma_i)\}$.
3. Alice computes $E = Inn(g^{ab})(m) = (Inn(g^a))^b(m)$.
4. Alice computes $\Phi = Inn(g)^b$, i.e. $\{Inn(g^b)(\gamma_i)\}$.
5. Alice sends (E, Φ).

Decryption Process:

1. Bob expresses E as a product of the γ_i.
2. Bob computes Φ^{-a}, i.e. $\{\Phi^{-a}(\gamma_i)\}$.
3. Bob computes $\Phi^{-a}(E)$.

In [5] no formal proof of security is given for the MOR cryptosystem. The authors state that the security of the MOR cryptosystem relies on the discrete log problem in the inner automorphism group of G. They argue that even an adversary that is able to calculate discrete logs in G is not able to determine the secret exponent a since the conjugacy problem does not have a unique solution and if G has a center of appropriate size, the attacker gets a vast number of DLP instances and is not able to figure out the correct one.

2.2 MOR Using $SL(2, \mathbb{Z}_p) \times_\theta \mathbb{Z}_p$

In [5] the authors propose to use the group

$$G = SL(2, \mathbb{Z}_p) \times_\theta \mathbb{Z}_p$$

where

$$\theta = Inn \circ \theta_1 : \mathbb{Z}_p \to Aut(SL(2, \mathbb{Z}_p))$$

and θ_1 is an isomorphism from $\mathbb{Z}_p$ to $\langle \alpha \rangle$ with $\alpha \in SL(2, \mathbb{Z}_p)$ of order p. Thus we get $\theta(y)(x) = \theta_1(y)x\theta_1(y)^{-1}$.

Let $g = (x, y) \in G$. The conjugate of $(a, b) \in G$ is

$$(x, y)(a, b)(x, y)^{-1} = (x\theta(y)(a)\theta(b)(x^{-1}), b)$$
$$= (x\ \theta_1(y)a(\theta_1(y))^{-1}\ \theta_1(b)x^{-1}(\theta_1(b))^{-1}, b)$$

Since $(x, y)^n = ((x\theta_1(y))^n\theta_1(y)^{-n}, ny)$ we get

$$(x, y)^n(a, b)(x, y)^{-n} = ((x\theta_1(y))^na\ \theta_1(b)(x\theta_1(y))^{-n}\theta_1(-b), b)$$

The two matrices $T = \begin{pmatrix} 1 & 1 \\ 0 & 1 \end{pmatrix}$ and $S = \begin{pmatrix} 0 & -1 \\ 1 & 0 \end{pmatrix}$ are generating $SL(2, \mathbb{Z}_p)$ and thus $\{(T, 0), (S, 0), (I, 1)\}$ is a generator set for $SL(2, \mathbb{Z}_p) \times_\theta \mathbb{Z}_p$. Given $g \in SL(2, \mathbb{Z}_p)$ with non-zero (2,1)-component a decomposition $g = T^{j_1}ST^{j_2}ST^{j_3}$ can be calculated efficiently (see [5]).

3 Attacking MOR Using $SL(2, \mathbb{Z}_p) \times_\theta \mathbb{Z}_p$

In this section we reveal several vulnerabilities of MOR using $SL(2, \mathbb{Z}_p) \times_\theta \mathbb{Z}_p$ and demonstrate how they can be exploited. In a first step we show that MOR using $SL(2, \mathbb{Z}_p) \times_\theta \mathbb{Z}_p$ is not more secure than MOR using $SL(2, \mathbb{Z}_p)$.

MOR using $SL(2, \mathbb{Z}_p)$ suffers from the big disadvantage that the ciphertext already reveals valuable information about the encrypted plaintext. If $\bar{M} = XMX^{-1}$ for $X, M \in SL(2, \mathbb{Z}_p)$ then $det(\bar{M}) = det(M)$ and $trace(\bar{M}) = trace(M)$. A MOR ciphertext is of the form $C(M) = g^{ab}Mg^{-ab}$. We present two simple but powerful attacks that can be carried out if g or any element of the centralizer of g is known to the attacker. Both attacks are ciphertext-only. The first attack uses the above mentioned properties of $G = SL(2, \mathbb{Z}_p)$, whereas the second may be used for arbitrary groups G where the conjugacy problem is easy.

3.1   MOR Using $SL(2, \mathbb{Z}_p) \times_\theta \mathbb{Z}_p$ is not Harder than MOR Using $SL(2, \mathbb{Z}_p)$

We know that $Inn(g) = Inn(g \cdot z)$ if and only if $z \in Z(G)$. Let $G = SL(2, \mathbb{Z}_p) \times_\theta \mathbb{Z}_p$. Since $Z(G) = \{(x, y) \mid y \in \mathbb{Z}_q, x = \pm\theta_1(-y)\}$ we get $g \cdot Z(G) = \{(\pm x \cdot \theta_1(-z), y + z) \mid z \in \mathbb{Z}_q\}$ for $g = (x, y) \in G$.

Thus every $\hat{g} = (\hat{x}, \hat{y}) \in g \cdot Z(G)$ can be written as $\hat{g} = (\pm x\theta_1(-z), y + z)$ for a $z \in \mathbb{Z}_q$ and $\hat{x}\theta_1(\hat{y})$ is of the form

$$\hat{x}\theta_1(\hat{y}) = \pm x\theta_1(-z)\theta_1(y + z)$$
$$= \pm x\theta_1(y)$$

It follows that the value $x\theta_1(y)$ is (apart from its sign) invariant for all elements of $g \cdot Z(G)$.

The encryption function of MOR using $SL(2, \mathbb{Z}_p) \times_\theta \mathbb{Z}_p$ is of the form

$$Inn(g^n)(m) = (x, y)^n (m_1, m_2)(x, y)^{-n}$$
$$= ((x\theta_1(y))^n m_1 \theta_1(m_2)(x\theta_1(y))^{-n}\theta_1(-m_2), m_2)$$

where $g = (x, y), m = (m_1, m_2) \in SL(2, \mathbb{Z}_p) \times_\theta \mathbb{Z}_p$. By calculating $Inn(g^n)(m_i)$ for several messages $m_i \in SL(2, \mathbb{Z}_p) \times_\theta \mathbb{Z}_p$ and solving the conjugacy problem in $SL(2, \mathbb{Z}_p)$ an attacker is able to extract $(\pm x\theta_1(y))^n$.

For MOR using $SL(2, \mathbb{Z}_p) \times_\theta \mathbb{Z}_p$ that means that an attacker is able to calculate $\pm x\theta_1(y)$ and $(\pm x\theta_1(y))^n$ from the receiver's public key and $(\pm x\theta_1(y))^b$ from the ciphertext.

Thus MOR using $SL(2, \mathbb{Z}_p) \times_\theta \mathbb{Z}_p$ is not harder than MOR using $SL(2, \mathbb{Z}_p)$. In particular, recovering the plaintext m in a ciphertext-only attack in MOR using $SL(2, \mathbb{Z}_p) \times_\theta \mathbb{Z}_p$ is not harder than the computational Diffie-Hellman problem in $SL(2, \mathbb{Z}_p)$.

In [5] the authors propose to choose $g = (x, y) \in SL(2, \mathbb{Z}_p) \times_\theta \mathbb{Z}_p$ satisfying $x\theta_1(y) = A(I + c\delta_{12})A^{-1}$ for some $c \in \mathbb{Z}_p$ and $A \in SL(2, \mathbb{Z}_p)$ (where δ_{ij} is the matrix whose entries are all zero except the (i, j)-entry which is 1).

This is a really unfortunate choice since the authors themselves showed in [5], remark 1, that the discrete log problem is easy for matrices of this special form which means that the secret key a can be calculated easily in this case. In fact, the value $g = (x, y) \in G$ has to be chosen such that the discrete log problem is hard in the subgroup generated by $x\theta_1(y)$.

In the following sections we will concentrate on MOR using $SL(2, \mathbb{Z}_p)$, but with the techniques presented in this section the described attacks can easily be applied to attack MOR using $SL(2, \mathbb{Z}_p) \times_\theta \mathbb{Z}_p$ also.

3.2   Ciphertext-Only Attacks with Known Centralizer Elements

In this section we present two ciphertext-only attacks on MOR using $GL(2, \mathbb{Z}_p)$ and MOR using $SL(2, \mathbb{Z}_p)$.

Our attacker is given a ciphertext $\hat{M} = Inn(X^k)(M) = X^k M X^{-k}$. We assume that the attacker knows X or any element from the centralizer of X (Since the CP is easy in $SL(2, \mathbb{Z}_p)$, X can be computed given $Inn(X) = \{Inn(X)(\gamma_i)\}$ which is part of the receiver's public key.).

In our first attack we use the centralizer element $\hat{X} \in Z(X)$ to transform the given ciphertext $\hat{M}$ to a ciphertext $\hat{X} \cdot \hat{M} = X^k (\hat{X} \cdot M) X^{-k}$ of $\hat{X} \cdot M$. Using the invariance of the trace and the determinant under conjugation we get three equations in the components of M which enables us to derive the structure of the encrypted plaintext M. In particular, if one component of M is known, the whole plaintext matrix M can be reconstructed.

In the second attack the centralizer element $\hat{X} \in Z(X)$ is used to calculate $Inn(\hat{M})(\hat{X}) = (X^k \cdot M)\hat{X}(X^k \cdot M)^{-1}$. Since the conjugacy problem is easy in $GL(2, \mathbb{Z}_p)$ one gets information about the structure of $X^k \cdot M$.

This simple lemma will be very useful in the following sections:

Lemma 1. *Let* $M = \begin{pmatrix} a & b \\ c & d \end{pmatrix}, X = \begin{pmatrix} x & y \\ w & z \end{pmatrix}$ *and* $\hat{M} = XMX^{-1} = \begin{pmatrix} \hat{a} & \hat{b} \\ \hat{c} & \hat{d} \end{pmatrix}$ *be in* $GL(2, \mathbb{Z}_p)$. *Then* $tr(M) = tr(\hat{M})$.

Proof. Since $X^{-1} = \begin{pmatrix} \frac{z}{detX} & \frac{-y}{detX} \\ \frac{-w}{detX} & \frac{x}{detX} \end{pmatrix} \in GL(2, \mathbb{Z}_p)$ we get $\hat{a} = \frac{1}{detX}(axz + cyz - bxw - dyw)$ and $\hat{d} = \frac{1}{detX}(bwx + dzx - awy - czy)$. It follows that $tr(\hat{M}) = \hat{a} + \hat{d} = \frac{1}{detX}((a + d)(xz - wy)) = \frac{1}{detX}((a + d)(detX)) = a + d = tr(M)$. $\square$

Attack 1:
Using the notation of the lemma we know that $tr(\hat{M}) = tr(M) = a + d$. Let $\hat{X} = \begin{pmatrix} \hat{x} & \hat{y} \\ \hat{w} & \hat{z} \end{pmatrix} \in Z(X)$. We now compute $\bar{M} = \hat{X} \cdot \hat{M} = X^k(\hat{X} \cdot M)X^{-k}$ and get $tr(\bar{M}) = tr(\hat{X} \cdot M) = a\hat{x} + c\hat{y} + b\hat{w} + d\hat{z}$, i.e. a second linear equation for the desired values a, b, c, d.

Unfortunately, this trick only works once. If we do the same trick again with another centralizer element $\bar{X} = \begin{pmatrix} \bar{x} & \bar{y} \\ \bar{w} & \bar{z} \end{pmatrix} \in Z(X)$ and set $\widetilde{M} = \bar{X} \cdot \hat{M} = X^k(\bar{X} \cdot M)X^{-k}$, we get a system of three linear equations:

$$a + \qquad\qquad\quad d \quad = \quad tr(\hat{M})$$
$$\hat{w} \cdot b + \hat{y} \cdot c + (\hat{z} - \hat{x}) \cdot d = tr(\bar{M}) - \hat{x} \cdot tr(\hat{M})$$
$$\bar{w} \cdot b + \bar{y} \cdot c + (\bar{z} - \bar{x}) \cdot d = tr(\widetilde{M}) - \bar{x} \cdot tr(\hat{M})$$

We further know that $\hat{x} = \hat{z} + \frac{a-d}{c}\hat{w}$, $\hat{y} = \frac{b}{c}\hat{w}$, $\bar{x} = \bar{z} + \frac{a-d}{c}\bar{w}$ and $\bar{y} = \frac{b}{c}\bar{w}$ (see appendix A.1). Setting $k := \frac{\hat{w}}{\bar{w}}$ it follows that $k \cdot \bar{y} = \hat{y}$ and $k \cdot (\bar{z} - \bar{x}) = \hat{z} - \hat{x}$, i.e. our third equation differs from the second equation only by a constant factor.

The two linear equations allow us to express a and b in terms of c and d. If we further use that $det(\hat{M}) = det(M) = ad - bc$ we can also express c in terms of d and know that the searched plaintext has the structure $M = \begin{pmatrix} f_1(d) & f_2(d) \\ f_3(d) & d \end{pmatrix}$ where the functions f_1, f_2 and f_3 are known.

Attack 2:
Let again $\hat{M} = Inn(X^k)(M) = X^k M X^{-k}$. The aim of the second attack is to calculate the value $X^k \cdot M$.

Let $\hat{X} = \begin{pmatrix} \hat{x} & \hat{y} \\ \hat{c} & \hat{d} \end{pmatrix} \in Z(X)$ and $\bar{X} = \begin{pmatrix} \bar{x} & \bar{y} \\ \bar{c} & \bar{d} \end{pmatrix} = \hat{M}\hat{X}\hat{M}^{-1} = (X^k \cdot M)\hat{X}(X^k \cdot M)^{-1}$.

By solving the conjugacy problem for the instance $(\hat{X}, \bar{X})$ one gets that $X^k \cdot M = \begin{pmatrix} \frac{\hat{w}}{\bar{w}}t + \frac{\hat{x}-\bar{z}}{\bar{w}}s & \frac{\hat{y}}{\bar{w}}s + \frac{\bar{z}-\bar{z}}{\bar{w}}t \\ s & t \end{pmatrix}$ for some $s, t \in \mathbb{Z}_p$.

Unfortunately, performing this attack multiple times does not lead to more data about $X^k \cdot M$ (see appendix A.2).

If $X \in SL(2, \mathbb{Z}_p)$, we know that $det(X^k M) = det(M)$ and can further express s in terms of t.

4   Attacks when Exponents are Used Multiple Times

To make MOR using $SL(2, \mathbb{Z}_p) \times_\theta \mathbb{Z}_p$ more efficient the authors propose to fix the encryption exponent b and use it for multiple encryptions.
The problem with that approach is that given one plaintext-ciphertext pair an attacker is able to calculate $(x\theta_1(y))^{ab}$ which can be used to decrypt all ciphertexts that were encrypted using the same b[1].

In [5] remark 4 the authors therefore propose to choose $\mathbb{Z}_p$ as message space and use some randomised padding technique:

Let $m \in \mathbb{Z}_p$ with $m \neq 0$ be the plaintext message. Choose random $r_1, r_2 \in_R \mathbb{Z}_p$ and encrypt $M = \begin{pmatrix} m & r_1 \\ r_2 & \frac{1+r_1 r_2}{m} \end{pmatrix} \in SL(2, \mathbb{Z}_p)$ with the MOR cryptosystem.

In this section we will present two attacks that show that this padding technique is highly insecure. Both attacks are known plaintext attacks, i.e. the attacker knows pairs of ciphertext and corresponding plaintext. We show that an attacker that knows one resp. two plaintext-ciphertext pairs is able to decrypt all ciphertexts that are encrypted using the same encryption exponent b.

Our attacks work in $SL(2, \mathbb{Z}_p)$ as well as in $GL(2, \mathbb{Z}_p)$. Since $GL(2, \mathbb{Z}_p)$ is the more general case, we concentrate on $GL(2, \mathbb{Z}_p)$ (though the MOR system was originally presented using $SL(2, \mathbb{Z}_p)$). In our case, if a plaintext message $m \in \mathbb{Z}_p$ with $m \neq 0$ is given, we encrypt $M = \begin{pmatrix} m & r_1 \\ r_2 & r_3 \end{pmatrix} \in GL(2, \mathbb{Z}_p)$,

---

[1] If no element from the centralizer of $(x\theta_1(y))$ is known, two plaintext-ciphertext pairs are needed (see also appendix A.2).

where $r_1, r_2, r_3 \in_R \mathbb{Z}_p$ with the MOR cryptosystem. Since $det(M)$ is known, the value r_3 can be expressed as $r_3 = \frac{det(M)+r_1 r_2}{m}$.

Let $\bar{M} = XMX^{-1}$ be a MOR encryption of a message $m \in \mathbb{Z}_p$. This equation can also be written as $X^{-1}\bar{M}X = M$. If the plaintext m is known the attacker gets one equation over $\mathbb{Z}_p$ on the unknown entries of X per known plaintext-ciphertext-pair. In our attacks we further use the invariance of trace and determinant under conjugation and the homomorphic property of mapping $Inn(g)$, i.e. multiplying two ciphertexts $Inn(g)(m_1)$ and $Inn(g)(m_2)$ results in a ciphertext $Inn(g)(m_1 \cdot m_2)$ of $m_1 \cdot m_2$ (this property only holds if the exponent b is fixed for multiple encryption).

In the first attack we assume that the attacker knows an element $X \in Z(x\theta_1(y))$, i.e. we are in the situation of section 3.2. In fact our attack is very similar to section 3.2 attack 1 which enables an attacker to determine the whole plaintext message if only one component is known. We will see that one plaintext-ciphertext pair is sufficient to solve the special conjugacy problem in $GL(2, \mathbb{Z}_p)$, i.e. to find a value $\bar{X} \in GL(2, \mathbb{Z}_p)$ with $Inn(\bar{X}) = Inn((x\theta_1(y))^{ab})$.

In the second attack we assume that the attacker does not know any elements from the centralizer of $x\theta_1(y)$. This might be the case when the mapping $Inn(g)$ is represented in a different way. We show that in this case two plaintext-ciphertext pairs are sufficient to decrypt all future ciphertexts.

This attack also demonstrates that the special conjugacy problem might also be easy in $GL(2, \mathbb{Z}_p)$ if pairs $(A_i, Inn(A_i))$ are given, but only parts of the matrices A_i are known.

4.1   Attack with Known Centralizer

The attacker is given a message $m \in \mathbb{Z}_p$ and the corresponding ciphertext

$$C = (C_1, 0) = (x, y)^{ab}(M, 0)(x, y)^{-ab} = ((x\theta_1(y))^{ab}M(x\theta_1(y))^{-ab}, 0)$$

where $M = \begin{pmatrix} m & r \\ s & t \end{pmatrix} \in GL(2, \mathbb{Z}_p)$ with $r, s, t \in_R \mathbb{Z}_p$. We further assume that

the attacker knows an element $X = \begin{pmatrix} x & y \\ w & z \end{pmatrix} \in Z(x\theta_1(y))$ with $X \notin Z(M)$.

Since $tr(M) = tr(C_1)$ and $det(M) = det(C_1)$ the attacker can compute t and $r \cdot s$. We now use the trick of section 3.2 attack 1: $C_1 \cdot X = (x\theta_1(y))^{ab}(M \cdot X)(x\theta_1(y))^{-ab}$ and $tr(C_1 \cdot X) = tr(M \cdot X) = mx + rw + sy + tz$. This is sufficient to calculate r and s. [2]

With (M, C_1) and $(X \cdot M, X \cdot C_1)$ we get two instances of the conjugacy problem in $GL(2, \mathbb{Z}_p)$. From $X \notin Z(M)$ we get that $M \notin Z(X \cdot M)$. Thus,

---

[2] The matrix M can also be completely reconstructed if the semi-direct product group is used, i.e. if $C = (C_1, \bar{m}) = (x, y)^{ab}(M, \bar{m})(x, y)^{-ab} = ((x\theta_1(y))^{ab}(M\theta_1(\bar{m}))(x\theta_1(y))^{-ab}\theta_1(-\bar{m}), \bar{m})$. Since $\theta_1(\bar{m})$ and m are known, the evaluation of $tr(C_1\theta_1(\bar{m}))$ and $tr(XC_1\theta_1(\bar{m}))$ results in two linear equations in the variables r, s and t. We further know that $det(M) = det(C_1)$ which is sufficient to derive matrix M.

the two instances (M, C_1) and $(X \cdot M, X \cdot C_1)$ are sufficient to solve the special conjugacy problem in $GL(2, \mathbb{Z}_p)$, i.e. to find a matrix $\bar{X} \in GL(2, \mathbb{Z}_p)$ with $Inn(x\theta_1(y)) = Inn(\bar{X})$ (see appendix A.2).

This value $\bar{X}$ can be used to decrypt all following ciphertexts that where encrypted using the same encryption exponent b.

4.2   Attack without Centralizer Elements

We now assume that the attacker is given two plaintext messages $m_1, m_2 \in \mathbb{Z}_p$ and $\bar{A} = XAX^{-1} = \begin{pmatrix} \bar{a} & \bar{b} \\ \bar{c} & \bar{d} \end{pmatrix}$ and $\bar{B} = XBX^{-1} = \begin{pmatrix} \hat{a} & \hat{b} \\ \hat{c} & \hat{d} \end{pmatrix}$ where $A = \begin{pmatrix} m_1 & r_1 \\ r_2 & r_3 \end{pmatrix}$ and $B = \begin{pmatrix} m_2 & s_1 \\ s_2 & s_3 \end{pmatrix}$ and $r_1, r_2, r_3, s_1, s_2, s_3 \in_R \mathbb{Z}_p$.[3]

From the traces of $\bar{A}$ and $\bar{B}$ the attacker gets $tr(\bar{A}) = tr(A) = m_1 + r_3$ and $tr(\bar{B}) = tr(B) = m_2 + s_3$. Using the plaintexts m_1 and m_2 he is able to calculate r_3 and s_3. Evaluating the determinant $det(\bar{A}) = det(A) = m_1 \cdot r_3 - r_1 \cdot r_2$ the attacker is further able to compute $r_1 \cdot r_2$ resp. $s_1 \cdot s_2$.

We now use the homomorphic property of the conjugation map. Since $tr(\bar{A}\bar{B}) = tr(XABX^{-1}) = tr(AB) = m_1 m_2 + r_1 s_2 + r_2 s_1 + r_3 s_3$, we get $r_1 s_2 + r_2 s_1$.

By solving the quadratic equation

$$x^2 - (r_1 s_2 + r_2 s_1)x + s_1 s_2 r_1 r_2 = 0$$

we get the two values $r_1 \cdot s_2$ and $r_2 \cdot s_1$ (we have to guess which of the two solutions equals $r_1 \cdot s_2$ and which equals $r_2 \cdot s_1$).

We now take a closer look at equation $\bar{A}X = X A$ which is equivalent to $\bar{A} = XAX^{-1}$ and describe it as a system of linear equations:

$$
\begin{array}{rcl}
(m_1 - \bar{a})x + \quad r_2 y \quad - \quad \bar{b}w \quad\quad\quad\quad & = 0 \\
r_1 x \quad + (r_3 - \bar{a})y \quad\quad\quad - \quad \bar{b}z & = 0 \\
-\bar{c}x \quad\quad\quad + (m_1 - \bar{d})w + \quad r_2 z & = 0 \\
- \quad \bar{c}y \quad + \quad r_1 w \quad + (r_3 - \bar{d})z & = 0
\end{array}
$$

By adding the linear equations resulting from $\bar{B}X = XB$ and simplifying the system by removing redundant equations we get:

$$
\begin{array}{rl}
x + & \dfrac{s_2(\bar{d}-m_1) - r_2(\hat{d}-m_2)}{\bar{c}(\hat{d}-m_2) - \hat{c}(\bar{d}-m_1)} z \quad = 0 \\[3mm]
y + & \left(\dfrac{\bar{d}-r_3}{\bar{c}} + \dfrac{\hat{c}r_1 r_2 - \bar{c}r_1 s_2}{\bar{c}(\bar{c}(\hat{d}-m_2) - \hat{c}(\bar{d}-m_1))}\right) z = 0 \\[3mm]
w + & \dfrac{\hat{c}r_2 - \bar{c}s_2}{\bar{c}(\hat{d}-m_2) - \hat{c}(\bar{d}-m_1)} z \quad = 0
\end{array}
$$

---

[3] If the two MOR ciphertexts $C(m_1) = (\bar{A}, 0) = ((x\theta_1(y))^{ab} A(x\theta_1(y))^{-ab}, 0)$ and $C(m_2) = (\bar{B}, 0) = ((x\theta_1(y))^{ab} B(x\theta_1(y))^{-ab}, 0)$ are given, we get this form by setting $X = (x\theta_1(y))^{ab}$.

Since we know the values $r_1 \cdot r_2$ and $r_1 \cdot s_2$, we are able to express s_2 as $s_2 = k \cdot r_2$ for a $k \in \mathbb{Z}_p$. Thus we get $x = c_1 r_2 z$, $y = c_2 z$ and $w = c_3 r_2 z$ where $c_1 = \frac{(\hat{d}-m_2)-k(\hat{d}-m_1)}{\hat{c}(\hat{d}-m_2)-\hat{c}(\hat{d}-m_1)}$, $c_2 = \frac{r_3 - \hat{d}}{\hat{c}} + \frac{\hat{c} r_1 s_2 - \hat{c} r_1 r_2}{\hat{c}(\hat{c}(\hat{d}-m_2)-\hat{c}(\hat{d}-m_1))}$ and $c_3 = \frac{k\hat{c}+\hat{c}}{\hat{c}(\hat{d}-m_2)-\hat{c}(\hat{d}-m_1)}$.

Since $\bar{a} = \frac{1}{detX}(m_1 xz + r_2 yz - r_1 xw - r_3 yw) = \frac{1}{detX} r_2 z^2 (m_1 c_1 + c_2 - r_1 r_2 c_1 c_3 - r_3 c_2 c_3)$ we get $r_2 z^2 = \frac{\bar{a} \cdot detX}{m_1 c_1 + c_2 - r_1 r_2 c_1 c_3 - r_3 c_2 c_3} =: c_4 \cdot detX$.

The values c_1, c_2, c_3 and c_4 are all that is necessary to decrypt arbitrary ciphertexts that are encrypted using the same matrix X. Assume that we are given a matrix $XCX^{-1} = \bar{C} = \begin{pmatrix} \tilde{a} & \tilde{b} \\ \tilde{c} & \tilde{d} \end{pmatrix}$ where $C = \begin{pmatrix} m_3 & t_1 \\ t_2 & t_3 \end{pmatrix}$ is completely unknown. We know that

$$m_3 = \frac{1}{detX}(\tilde{a}xz - \tilde{c}xy + \tilde{b}wz - \tilde{d}xy)$$
$$= \frac{1}{detX} r_2 z^2 (\tilde{a}c_1 - \tilde{c}c_1 c_2 + \tilde{b}c_3 - \tilde{d}c_2 c_3)$$
$$= c_4 (\tilde{a}c_1 - \tilde{c}c_1 c_2 + \tilde{b}c_3 - \tilde{d}c_2 c_3)$$

and get the desired cleartext message by using the components of the ciphertext in combination with the precomputed constants c_1, c_2, c_3 and c_4. In a similar way all other components of C can be calculated.

5   Conclusion

In section 3.1 we showed that $x\theta_1(y)$ and $(x\theta_1(y))^a$ can be extracted from $Inn((x,y))$ and $Inn((x,y)^a)$. Hence, for the security of MOR using $G = SL(2, \mathbb{Z}_p) \times_\theta \mathbb{Z}_p$ it is necessary to choose $(x,y) \in G$ such that the discrete log problem is hard in the subgroup generated by $(x\theta_1(y))$. In particular, (x,y) must not be chosen such that $x\theta_1(y) = A(I + c\delta_{12})A^{-1}$ where $c \in \mathbb{Z}_p$ and $A \in SL(2, \mathbb{Z}_p)$ as proposed in [5].

With the ciphertext-only attacks from section 3.2 it is possible to determine the whole plaintext message if only one component is known. This attacks works in $SL(2, \mathbb{Z}_p)$ as well as in $SL(2, \mathbb{Z}_p) \times_\theta \mathbb{Z}_p$. To prevent this attack we recommend to use padding. Using the padding technique from [5] remark 4 (see section 4) and choosing the encryption exponent b randomly for every ciphertext is a good countermeasure against the presented attack.

The most critical point we discussed is fixing the encryption exponent b and using it for multiple encryptions. Without padding the resulting system is vulnerable to known plaintext attacks. If one plaintext-ciphertext pair is known all following ciphertexts can be decrypted. In section 4 we showed that the padding technique from [5] does not make the system more secure. It is an open question whether the MOR system (with fixed exponent) can be made secure by using an appropriate padding technique.

If MOR is used with $SL(2, \mathbb{Z}_p) \times_\theta \mathbb{Z}_p$, an appropriate padding technique and the encryption exponent is chosen uniformly and independently for every plaintext to be encrypted, the resulting system seems to offer a reasonable amount of security (though there still is no formal proof). On the other hand calculating $Inn(g^b)$ and $Inn(g^{ab})$ from $Inn(g)$ and $Inn(g^a)$ which then is necessary for every single encryption process is computationally very expensive which makes the system less efficient than RSA and ElGamal.

References

[1] I. Anshel, M. Anshel, D. Goldfeld, "An Algebraic Method for Public-Key Cryptography", Mathematical Research Letters, 6 (1999), pp.287-291   176
[2] S. Blackburn, S. Galbraith, "Cryptanalysis of two cryptosystems based on group action", Advances in Cryptology - Asiacrypt 1999, LNCS 1716   176
[3] K. H. Koo, S. J. Lee, J. H. Cheon, J. W. Han, J. Kang, C. Park, "New Public-Key Cryptosystem Using Braid Groups", Advances in Cryptology - Crypto 2000, LNCS 1880, pp. 166-183   176
[4] E. Lee, S. J. Lee, S. G. Hahn, "Pseudorandomness from Braid Groups", Advances in Cryptology - Crypto 2001, LNCS 2139   176
[5] Seong-Hun Paeng, Kil-Chan Ha, Jae Heon Kim, Seongtaek Chee, Choonsik Park, "New Public Key Cryptosystem Using Finite Non Abelian Groups", Advances in Cryptology - Crypto 2001, LNCS 2139   175, 176, 177, 178, 179, 181, 184
[6] Seong-Hun Paeng, Daesung Kwon, Kil-Chan Ha, Jae Heon Kim "Improved public key cryptosystem using finite non abelian groups", IACR EPrint-Server, Report 2001/066, http://eprint.iacr.org/2001/066   175
[7] A. Yamamura, "Public key cryptosystems using the modular group", 1st International Public Key Cryptography Conference PKC 1998, LNCS 1431   176
[8] A. Yamamura, "A functional cryptosystem using a group action", 4th Australian Information Security and Privacy Conference ACISP 1999, LNCS 1587   176

A   General Results for Matrix Groups

A.1   Computing Centralizers in $GL(2, \mathbb{Z}_p)$

Let $A = \begin{pmatrix} a & b \\ c & d \end{pmatrix} \in GL(2, \mathbb{Z}_p)$ with $c \neq 0$. Then centralizer elements $C \in Z(A)$ are of the form

$$C = \begin{pmatrix} z + \frac{a-d}{c}w & \frac{b}{c}w \\ w & z \end{pmatrix} = \begin{pmatrix} \frac{a-d}{c}w & \frac{b}{c}w \\ w & 0 \end{pmatrix} + z \cdot \begin{pmatrix} 1 & 0 \\ 0 & 1 \end{pmatrix}$$

for arbitrary $w, z \in \mathbb{Z}_p$.

A.2   The Conjugacy Problem in $GL(2, \mathbb{Z}_p)$ and $SL(2, \mathbb{Z}_p)$

Let $A = \begin{pmatrix} a & b \\ c & d \end{pmatrix}$ and $\hat{A} = \begin{pmatrix} \hat{a} & \hat{b} \\ \hat{c} & \hat{d} \end{pmatrix}$ be a given instance of the conjugacy problem,

i.e. a matrix $X = \begin{pmatrix} x & y \\ w & z \end{pmatrix}$ satisfying $\hat{A} = X \cdot A \cdot X^{-1}$ has to be found.

If we write $\hat{A} = X \cdot A \cdot X^{-1}$ as $\hat{A} \cdot X = X \cdot A$, we get the following system of linear equations:

$$
\begin{aligned}
(a - \hat{a}) \cdot x + & \quad c \cdot y & - & \quad \hat{b} \cdot w & & = 0 \\
b \cdot x & + (d - \hat{a}) \cdot y & & - & \hat{b} \cdot z & = 0 \\
-\hat{c} \cdot x & & + (a - \hat{d}) \cdot w + & \quad c \cdot z & & = 0 \\
& - \quad \hat{c} \cdot y & + & \quad b \cdot w & + (d - \hat{d}) \cdot z & = 0
\end{aligned}
$$

By removing redundant equations one gets:

$$
\begin{aligned}
x & + \left(\tfrac{\hat{d}-a}{\hat{c}}\right) \cdot w - \tfrac{c}{\hat{c}} \cdot z & = 0 \\
y & - \tfrac{b}{\hat{c}} \cdot w + \tfrac{\hat{d}-d}{\hat{c}} \cdot z & = 0
\end{aligned}
$$

(Note that we only considered the case that $\hat{c} \neq 0$. The case $\hat{c} = 0$ is analogue.)

That means that the matrices that solve the conjugacy problem are of the form
$$
\bar{X} = \begin{pmatrix} \tfrac{c}{\hat{c}} \cdot z + \tfrac{a-\hat{d}}{\hat{c}} \cdot w & \tfrac{b}{\hat{c}} \cdot w + \tfrac{d-\hat{d}}{\hat{c}} \cdot z \\ w & z \end{pmatrix} \text{ where } w, z \in \mathbb{Z}_p.
$$
In $SL(2, \mathbb{Z}_p)$ we further know that $det(\bar{X}) = 1$ and can replace w by a term depending only on z.

Let $G \in \{GL(2, \mathbb{Z}_p), SL(2, \mathbb{Z}_p)\}$. Given only one instance of the conjugacy problem in G, i.e. $M, \bar{M} = XMX^{-1} \in G$, the solution set for the CP is $L = X \cdot Z(M)$.

If more than one instance is given, i.e. $M_1, M_2, \bar{M}_1 = XM_1X^{-1}, \bar{M}_2 = XM_2X^{-1} \in G$ that does not necessarily imply that the solution set can further be narrowed. If $M_1 \in Z(M_2)$ the solution set is still $L = X \cdot Z(M)$. If $M_1 \notin Z(M_2)$ the solution set is $L = X \cdot Z(G)$.

Since $Inn(g) = Inn(g \cdot z)$ for $z \in Z(G)$ and for all $g \in G$ we are able to solve the special conjugacy problem in the latter case.

Remark: If $(M_1, \bar{M}_1 = XM_1X^{-1})$ with $M_1 \notin Z(X)$ is an instance of the conjugacy problem and an element $\hat{X} \in Z(X)$ with $\hat{X} \notin Z(M_1)$ is known, we can easily construct a second instance $(M_2, \bar{M}_2)$ with $M_1 \notin Z(M_2)$ of the conjugacy problem by setting $M_2 = \hat{X}M_1$ and $\bar{M}_2 = \hat{X}\bar{M}_1 = X(\hat{X}M_1)X^{-1}$.

A Practical Attack on Some Braid Group Based Cryptographic Primitives

Dennis Hofheinz and Rainer Steinwandt

IAKS, Arbeitsgruppe Systemsicherheit, Prof. Dr. Th. Beth
Fakultät für Informatik, Universität Karlsruhe
Am Fasanengarten 5, 76 131 Karlsruhe, Germany

Abstract. A simple heuristic approach to the conjugacy problem in braid groups is described. Although it does not provide a general solution to the latter problem, it demonstrates that various proposed key parameters for braid group based cryptographic primitives do not offer acceptable cryptographic security. We give experimental evidence that it is often feasible to reveal the secret data by means of a normal PC within a few minutes.

Keywords: braid groups, cryptanalysis

1 Introduction

Within the last years various attempts have been made to derive cryptographic primitives from problems originating in combinatorial group theory (see, e. g., [WM85, Wag90, GZ91, AAG99, KLC+00, AAFG01]). One theoretically rather appealing family of schemes is derived from braid groups. These finitely presented groups are well-studied (e. g., [Gar69, Bir74]), and various proposals have been made for deriving cryptographic primitives from the conjugacy problem in these groups.

No general efficient solution for the conjugacy problem in braid groups is known so far, but the attacks from [LL02, Hug02] exhibit weaknesses in the key agreement scheme considered in [AAG99, AAFG01]. The attacks of J. Hughes, S.J. Lee and E. Lee focus on the so-called *multiple simultaneous conjugacy problem* in braid groups, and they propose a modification of the original specification to avoid their attack on the scheme of [AAG99, AAFG01].

In this contribution we demonstrate that the modification considered there is not sufficient for saving the scheme in [AAG99, AAFG01]. Moreover, we demonstrate the vulnerability of the key exchange scheme and the public key cryptosystem from [KLC+00] with respect to a simple heuristic procedure for the conjugacy problem. This procedure does by no means provide a general efficient method for solving the conjugacy problem in braid groups, but our experimental results demonstrate that with the proposed parameter choices both the key agreement and the encryption scheme from [KLC+00] do not offer acceptable cryptographic security.

Y.G. Desmedt (Ed.): PKC 2003, LNCS 2567, pp. 187–198, 2003.

In more detail our contribution is organized as follows: in the next section we recall some basic terminology concerning braid groups with the main focus on some algorithmic aspects of the word and conjugacy problem. Thereafter we describe our heuristic approaches for tackling the variants of the conjugacy problem underlying the proposals in [AAG99, KLC⁺00, AAFG01]. We recall the set-up of these proposals to the extent necessary for describing our attack and give experimental results that illustrate the cryptographic relevance of our approach. Finally, some conclusions are given.

2   Braid Groups

The *braid group* B_n $(n \in \mathbb{N})$ is a finitely presented group that is defined through the following presentation (cf. [Art25]):

$$\left\langle \sigma_1, \ldots, \sigma_{n-1} \middle| \begin{array}{ll} \sigma_i \sigma_j \sigma_i = \sigma_j \sigma_i \sigma_j & \text{if } |i - j| = 1 \\ \sigma_i \sigma_j = \sigma_j \sigma_i & \text{if } |i - j| > 1 \end{array} \right\rangle$$

We refer to $\sigma_1, \ldots, \sigma_{n-1}$ as *(Artin) generators* and to arbitrary elements of B_n as *braids*. If we refer to a concrete representation of a braid in terms of Artin generators, we use the term *braid word*. A braid is said to be *positive* iff it can be written as a product of generators σ_i, i.e., in this case no negative powers of the σ_i are involved. Here the identity $\varepsilon \in B_n$ is also regarded as positive, and it can be shown that the positive braids in B_n form a *monoid* B_n^+ which embeds into B_n (cf. [Gar69]).

2.1   The Δ-Normal Form

Setting inductively $\Delta_1 := \sigma_1$ and $\Delta_i = \sigma_1 \cdots \sigma_i \cdot \Delta_{i-1}$ for $1 < i < n$, we define the *fundamental braid* $\Delta \in B_n$ as $\Delta := \Delta_{n-1}$. Next, we establish a partial ordering $\leq$ on the elements of B_n by setting $v \leq w$ iff there are positive braids $\alpha, \beta \in B_n^+$ such that $w = \alpha v \beta$. Now any braid $\alpha \in B_n$ which satisfies $\varepsilon \leq \alpha \leq \Delta$ is called a *canonical factor*. There is a *canonical homomorphism* $\pi : B_n \to S_n$ from the braid group B_n into the symmetric group S_n which maps σ_i onto the transposition interchanging i and $i + 1$ and whose restriction to the set of canonical factors in B_n induces a bijection; see [EM94].

A factorization $\gamma = \alpha \beta$ of a positive braid γ into a canonical factor α and a positive braid β is said to be *left-weighted* iff α has the maximal length among all such decompositions. A *right-weighted* factorization is defined analogously. For any braid $w \in B_n$ we denote the greatest $i \in \mathbb{Z}$ with $\Delta^i \leq w$ by inf w; analogously, sup w stands for the smallest $i \in \mathbb{Z}$ with $w \leq \Delta^i$. With this notation every braid $w \in B_n$ can be written *uniquely* as

$$w = \Delta^r W_1 \cdots W_s \tag{1}$$

with $r = \inf w$, $s = \sup w - \inf w$ and canonical factors $\varepsilon < W_i < \Delta$ such that $W_i W_{i+1}$ is left-weighted for $1 \leq i < s$ (cf. [Gar69]). In this context, we refer to s as the *canonical length* of w.

The explicit decomposition (1) is called the Δ-*normal form* or simply the *normal form* of w. Note here that the W_i are canonical factors, so each of them can be represented uniquely by the corresponding permutation $\pi(W_i)$ in the symmetric group S_n. For a given braid word $w \in B_n$, its normal form can be computed in time $\mathcal{O}(|w|^2 n \log n)$ with $|\cdot|$ denoting the word length (see [CKL+01] for details).

2.2   The Conjugacy Problem in B_n

For convenience, we introduce the notion of a *tail*: $\gamma \in B_n^+$ is said to be a *tail* of some braid $\alpha \in B_n^+$, iff there is a factorization $\alpha = \beta\gamma$ with $\beta \in B_n^+$. Also we define the automorphism τ of B_n through $\tau(w) := \Delta^{-1}w\Delta$ $(w \in B_n)$. With this terminology we can formulate a lemma that is of importance for the heuristic approach to the conjugacy problem discussed below; the first part of this result has already been stated in [LL02]:

Lemma 1. *Let* $v, w \in B_n$ *be two positively conjugate braid words such that* $w = \alpha^{-1}v\alpha$ *for some* $\alpha \in B_n^+$. *Let* $\Delta^r W_1 \cdots W_s$ *be the normal form of* w. *Then the following relations hold:*

- *If* $\inf w < \inf v$, *then the canonical factor* $\Delta\tau^r(W_1^{-1})$ *is a tail of* α.
- *If* $\sup w > \sup v$, *then* W_s *is a tail of* α.

Proof. A proof of the first claim can be found in the proof of Lemma 4.3 in [EM94]; using the terminology from [EM94], the second part follows immediately by noticing that 'reverse cycling' some braid word $w \in B_n$ can be achieved by cycling its inverse w^{-1}. $\square$

Note that the restriction to *positively* conjugated braids is not really a restriction: suppose we have $v, w \in B_n$ with $w = x^{-1}vx$ for some braid word $x \in B_n$, whose normal form is $\Delta^r X_1 \cdots X_s$, with $r \in \mathbb{Z}$ possibly non-zero. Since Δ^2 lies in the centre of B_n (cf. [Gar69]), then also for $\tilde{x} := \Delta^{r \bmod 2} X_1 \cdots X_s$ we find $w = \tilde{x}^{-1}v\tilde{x}$, and $\tilde{x}$ is obviously positive.

Lemma 1 tells us for any given braid word $w \in B_n$ how to eventually find a word with minimal canonical length in w's conjugacy class. (To see this, note that minimal canonical length is equivalent to minimal sup and maximal inf.) The set of all words with minimal canonical length in w's conjugacy class is called the *super summit set* $\mathcal{S}(w)$ of w and can be shown to be finite; moreover, there is an algorithm for computing $\mathcal{S}(w)$ for any given braid word $w \in B_n$ (cf. [EM94]). Of course, two super summit sets $\mathcal{S}(v), \mathcal{S}(w)$ of braid words $v, w \in B_n$ are either equal or disjoint. So we eventually obtain an algorithm for the conjugacy problem in the braid group B_n: given $v, w \in B_n$, we compute $\mathcal{S}(v)$ and *one* element w' of $\mathcal{S}(w)$. Then v and w are conjugate iff $w' \in \mathcal{S}(v)$. This approach cannot only be used to decide whether v and w are conjugated; it can also be used to obtain a positive braid word $\alpha \in B_n^+$ with $w = \alpha^{-1}v\alpha$. Unfortunately, the complexity of this algorithm is not clear, since no precise estimate for the cardinality of $\mathcal{S}(v)$ is known.

Remark There is another presentation for the braid group B_n due to Birman, Ko, and Lee [BKL98]. In this presentation, we may find a unique normal form for any braid word $w \in B_n$ in time $\mathcal{O}(|w|^2 n)$.

3   A Heuristic Approach to the Conjugacy Problem

Given two conjugate braid words $v, w \in B_n$, we would like to find a conjugating braid $\alpha \in B_n$ so that $w = \alpha^{-1} v \alpha$. Actually, for certain proposed parameters $n \in \mathbb{N}$ and specific braids $v, w \in B_n$, this problem is hoped to be computationally intractable and has been suggested as a tool for deriving cryptographic primitives (see, e.g., [KLC+00, AAFG01]). In the sequel, we present an algorithm using Lemma 1 and some additional heuristics which tries to solve the conjugacy problem for the parameter sizes considered in proposals for cryptographic primitives. We do not aim at providing a general efficient solution for the conjugacy problem in braid groups. Nevertheless, the heuristic approach described below exhibits security problems in several cryptographic proposals based on braid groups.

3.1   The Algorithm

Consider Algorithm A (shown in Figure 1) for tackling an instance of the conjugacy problem in B_n (the function `GuessPermutation` is discussed in the next section).

Algorithm A:

   – Input: $v, w \in B_n$ with $w = x^{-1} v x$ for some unknown $x \in B_n^+$ with $\inf x = 0$.
   – Output: either $\alpha \in B_n^+$ with $w = \alpha^{-1} v \alpha$ or '`failed`'.

     1. Initialize α as the empty word ε.
     2. Put v and w in normal form, so that $w = \Delta^r W_1 \cdots W_s$.
     3. While $\inf w < \inf v$ do
           Let $\gamma := \Delta \tau^r (W_1^{-1})$, $\alpha := \gamma \alpha$, $w := \gamma w \gamma^{-1}$,
           Put w in normal form as in 2.
     4. While $\sup w > \sup v$ do
           Let $\gamma := W_s$, $\alpha := \gamma \alpha$, $w := \gamma w \gamma^{-1}$,
           Put w in normal form as in 2.
     5. Let $\mu :=$`GuessPermutation`(v, w), $\alpha := \mu \alpha$, $w := \mu w \mu^{-1}$.
     6. If $v = w$, then
           Return α,
        else
           Return '`failed`'.

Fig. 1. Algorithm A

As mentioned already, the restriction to inputs $v, w \in B_n$ that are *positively* conjugated is not relevant. Requiring the conjugating braid $x = \Delta^r X_1 \cdots X_s$ to fulfill the condition $r(= \inf x) = 0$ is of no practical relevance, either: if $w = x^{-1}vx$ holds, then also $w = \tilde{x}^{-1}v\tilde{x}$ for $\tilde{x} := \Delta^{r \bmod 2} X_1 \ldots X_s$ holds. But either $\tilde{x}$ or $\Delta^{-1}\tilde{x}$ is a positive braid with zero inf. So in the general case it suffices to run Algorithm A *twice* (maybe in parallel): once with inputs v, w and once with inputs $\Delta^{-1}v\Delta, w$.

3.2   Discussion of the Algorithm

Let us take a closer look at the behaviour of Algorithm A: in Step 1 and Step 2 our guess α for the conjugating element x is initialized and the words $v, w \in B_n$ are prepared. Steps 3 and 4 conjugate w in a way that after completion of these steps the canonical length of our new w is not greater than the canonical length of v. Using Lemma 1, at the beginning of Step 5 we therefore have $w = x'^{-1}vx'$ with $x = x'\alpha$ and $x' \in B_n^+$.

Now we assume that in this situation, the 'not yet uncovered' part x' of the conjugating word x is 'essentially determined' by its induced permutation $\pi(x')$. Consequently, in Step 5, we *guess* the permutation $\pi(x')$, i. e., the function GuessPermutation(v,w) is to return a canonical factor μ with $\pi(\mu) = \pi(x')$. To find such a braid word μ in the general case, we would have to solve the conjugacy problem $\pi(w) = \pi(x')^{-1}\pi(v)\pi(x')$ in the symmetric group S_n; also there might be a vast number of possible solutions for $\pi(x')$ when we consider *pure* braids v, i. e., braids $v \in B_n$ satisfying $\pi(v) = \text{id}$. We'll discuss this 'pure case' below. For non pure braids v, experimentally it turned out that in many cases $\pi(x')$ is a sufficiently 'simple' permutation and that the simple implementation of GuessPermutation shown in Figure 2 works fine (it exploits that in cycle notation conjugating a permutation σ by a permutation τ means applying τ to the 'entries' of σ).

Of course, in the case of pure braid words v we have to modify the function GuessPermutation accordingly. A promising heuristic approach seems then to be the following: supposing that $v = \Delta^{r_v} V_1 \cdots V_{s_v}$ and $w = \Delta^{r_w} W_1 \cdots W_{s_w}$ are in their normal forms, chances are good that $\mu = \pi^{-1}\left(\pi(V_1 W_1^{-1})\right)$ or $\mu = \pi^{-1}\left(\pi(V_{s_v}^{-1}W_{s_w})\right)$. For our experiments, we optimized this strategy a little: in case neither one of these candidates for μ solves our conjugation problem in B_n, we then guess the *right meet* of these candidates as only a *tail* of μ; here by a *right meet* of two positive braid words α, β we mean a tail of *both* α and β with maximal length in generators.

Back to Algorithm A, in Step 6 we return α in case it actually is a conjugating element.

Note that neither Algorithm A nor the function GuessPermutation is probabilistic, so there is no chance that, once one of them has failed, successive applications might improve this result. In particular, there is lots of room for improving and adding heuristics to Algorithm A. E. g., in our experiments with the following variation we were able to solve the conjugacy problem in certain cases in which at the beginning of Step 5 no canonical factor μ alone satisfied

---

Function GuessPermutation:

- Input: $v, w \in B_n$ with $w = x^{-1}vx$, for some unknown $x \in B_n^+$ with $\inf x = 0$.
- Output: a canonical factor $\mu \in B_n^+$, such that $\pi(\mu) = \pi(x)$.

    1. Let $\tau \in S_n$ be the identity permutation.
    2. Let $(\chi_1, \ldots, \chi_n) := (\text{false}, \ldots, \text{false})$.
    3. For i from n downto 1 do
        Let $r := i$, $s := i$,
        While $\chi_r = \text{false}$ do
            Let $\chi_r := \text{true}$,
            Let $r := \pi(v)(r)$, $s := \pi(w)(s)$,
            If $r \neq s$, then
                Let $\tau(r) := s$.
    4. Let $(\xi_1, \ldots, \xi_n) := (\text{false}, \ldots, \text{false})$.
    5. For i from n downto 1 do
        If $\xi_i = \text{false}$, then
            Let $\xi_i := \text{true}$, $r := i$,
            While $\xi_{\tau(r)} = \text{false}$ and $\tau(r) \neq r$ do
                Let $r := \tau(r)$, $\xi_r := \text{true}$.
            Let $\tau(r) := i$.
    6. Return $\pi^{-1}(\tau)$.

Fig. 2. The function GuessPermutation

$w = \mu^{-1}v\mu$: instead of guessing the *whole* braid word μ in Step 5, one guesses only a *tail* of some canonical factor μ satisfying $\pi(\mu) = \pi(x)$. Then in Step 6, if we are not yet finished (i.e., if $v \neq w$), we repeat Steps 3–5 until we are.—Of course, here we rely on the assumption that the tails of μ we guess in Step 5 are indeed tails of x.

3.3 The Multiple Simultaneous Conjugacy Problem

Algorithm A can be modified to work for an instance of the *multiple simultaneous conjugacy problem*: given $m \geq 1$ braid words $v_i, w_i \in B_n$ with $w_i = x^{-1}v_ix$ ($1 \leq i \leq m$) for some unknown braid $x \in B_n$, we are looking for some $\alpha \in B_n$ which also satisfies $w_i = \alpha^{-1}v_i\alpha$ for all i. Consider the modification of Algorithm A shown in Figure 3, which can be regarded as an extension to the algorithm used in [LL02, Theorem 2].

Here the function GuessSimultPerm takes as input pairs $(v_i, w_i) \in B_n^2$ of braid words such that $w_i = x^{-1}v_ix$ for all i, and yields a guess for a canonical factor β with $\pi(\beta) = \pi(x)$ as a result. For implementing this function, similar ideas as for the function GuessPermutation can be used; we skip a detailed discussion of this topic and do not give a sample implementation of GuessSimultPerm here.

However, it is worthwhile to remark that—just like in the case of Algorithm A—sometimes it may be helpful to use a variation of Algorithm B which in Step 5 only guesses some *tail* of μ and then repeats Steps 3–6 as necessary.

Algorithm B:

- Input: $m \geq 1$ pairs $(v_i, w_i) \in B_n^2$ such that $w_i = x^{-1} v_i x$ $(1 \leq i \leq m)$ for some unknown $x \in B_n^+$ with $\inf x = 0$.
- Output: either $\alpha \in B_n^+$ with $w_i = \alpha^{-1} v_i \alpha$ for all i or 'failed'.

```
1. Initialize α as the empty word ε.
2. Put all vᵢ and all wᵢ in normal form,
```
$$\text{so that } w_i = \Delta^{r_i} W_1^{(i)} \cdots W_{s_i}^{(i)}.$$
```
3. While inf wⱼ < inf vⱼ for some j ∈ {1,...,m} do
```
$$\text{Let } \gamma := \Delta \tau^r ((W_1^{(j)})^{-1}), \quad \alpha := \gamma \alpha,$$
$$\text{Let } w_i := \gamma w_i \gamma^{-1} \text{ for all } i \in \{1,\ldots,m\},$$
```
        Put all wᵢ in normal form as in 2.
4. While sup wⱼ > sup vⱼ for some j ∈ {1,...,m} do
```
$$\text{Let } \gamma := W_s^{(j)}, \quad \alpha := \gamma \alpha,$$
$$\text{Let } w_i := \gamma w_i \gamma^{-1} \text{ for all } i \in \{1,\ldots,m\},$$
```
        Put all wᵢ in normal form as in 2.
5. Let μ :=GuessSimultPerm((v₁,w₁),...,(vₘ,wₘ)).
6. Let α := μα, and  wᵢ := μwᵢμ⁻¹ for all i ∈ {1,...,m}.
7. If vᵢ = wᵢ for all i, then
        Return α,
    else
        Return 'failed'.
```

Fig. 3. Algorithm B

Also another heuristic step turned out to be helpful: after Step 4, it can be worthwhile to 'combine' pairs of braid words v_i, w_i to extend the set of these pairs. Namely, if $w_i = x^{-1} v_i x$ for $i = 1, \ldots, m$, then also $w' = x^{-1} v' x$, where $v' = v_i^{-1} v_j v_i$ and $w' = w_i^{-1} w_j w_i$ for any $i, j \in \{1, \ldots, m\}$. In particular, new found pairs v', w' with $\inf w' < \inf v'$ or $\sup w' > \sup v'$ are interesting in view of a re-application of Steps 3–4.

4   Braid Groups in Cryptography

Several suggestions have been put forward for deriving cryptographic primitives from the conjugacy problem in braid groups. In the sequel we shortly recall the key agreement schemes from [KLC+00, AAFG01] and the public key encryption scheme from [KLC+00]; all of these schemes are based on variants of the conjugacy problem in braid groups. We do not give all details of these proposals and put our main focus on the suggested parameters of the underlying variant of the conjugacy problem. Then we apply the techniques described above to concrete instances of these systems with realistic parameter sizes to get an idea of the practical significance of our approach. For our experiments we used Linux PCs with a clock rate of 1.8 GHz and the CBraid package of [Cha01]. The concrete running times varied in dependence on the actual parameter choice and the type of the conjugacy problem: while for individual conjugacy problems usually a few seconds were sufficient, instances of the multiple simultaneous conjugacy problem typically required some (less than 30) minutes of CPU time.

4.1   Commutator Based Key Agreement Protocol

In [AAG99], a key agreement protocol has been proposed that is based on the multiple simultaneous conjugacy problem. In [AAFG01], the addition of a so-called *key extractor* is suggested. But as the latter modification does not affect our attack, we omit the details on the key extractor in our description:

Public information:
  - braid index $n \in \mathbb{N}$
  - a subgroup $G_A = \langle a_1, \ldots, a_r \rangle \leq B_n$
  - a subgroup $G_B = \langle b_1, \ldots, b_s \rangle \leq B_n$

Private key:
  - Alice selects $a \in G_A$
  - Bob selects $b \in G_B$

Public key:
  - Alice publishes $[a^{-1}b_1a, \ldots, a^{-1}b_sa]$
  - Bob publishes $[b^{-1}a_1b, \ldots, b^{-1}a_rb]$

Shared key: derived from $a^{-1}b^{-1}ab$

In [AAG99], no concrete parameter choices for the above scheme are suggested. So for our experiments we used the parameters suggested in [AAFG01]. Namely, we chose the braid index $n = 80$ and public subgroups G_A, $G_B \leq B_n$ with $r = s = 20$ generators each. Each of the generators a_i resp. b_i of the public subgroups was comprised of $5 \leq \ell \leq 10$ Artin generators. The private keys a and b were made up of 100 public generators each.

Using Algorithm B and some of the techniques described in Section 3.3 to attack the multiple simultaneous conjugacy problem with these parameters, we obtained the following success rates for our attack on the secret key of Alice (resp. Bob):

n	$r = s$	ℓ	number of samples	success rate
80	20	5	1000	99.0%
80	20	10	1000	98.9%

To prevent the attack described in [LL02], in [LL02] S. J. Lee and E. Lee suggest to take *pure* braid words a_i, resp. b_i as public generators. More precisely, they suggest to raise any one of the already created generators a_i (resp. b_i) to a suitable power, so that the induced permutation becomes the identity. We implemented this construction and applied Algorithm B with some additional ideas from Sections 3.2 and 3.3. Our results are shown below:

n	$r = s$	ℓ	number of samples	success rate
80	20	5	1000	100.0%
80	20	10	1000	100.0%

Based on a reference to a private communication with one of the authors of [AAFG01], in [Hug02] J. Hughes describes a slightly different parameter choice. Namely, the public generators a_i resp. b_i are words of length 5 comprised of Artin generators and their inverses. Also, when Alice resp. Bob forms the secret word a resp. b, the description of [Hug02] suggests to use a word of length 100 in the public generators a_i resp. b_i and their inverses.

We've also done a few experiments with such a modified parameter choice, but these parameters also turned out to be vulnerable with respect to our attack, and at the moment it is unclear how a practical parameter choice for the schemes from [KLC+00, AAFG01] should look like.

4.2   A Diffie-Hellman Type Key Agreement Protocol and a Public Key Cryptosystem

The following key agreement protocol has been proposed in [KLC+00]. Analogously as in the commutator based scheme just described, in [AAFG01] a modification by means of a so-called key extractor is suggested. This modification does not affect our attack and is therefore not discussed in the sequel.

We denote by LB_ℓ resp. RB_r $(1 < \ell, r < n)$ the subgroup of B_n generated by $\sigma_1, \ldots, \sigma_{\ell-1}$ resp. $\sigma_{n-r+1}, \ldots, \sigma_{n-1}$. Now a key agreement scheme can be described as follows:

Public information:
  – braid index $n \in \mathbb{N}$
    integers $\ell, r \in \mathbb{N}$ with $\ell + r = n$
  – a braid word $x \in B_n$
Private key:
  – Alice selects $a \in LB_\ell$
  – Bob selects $b \in RB_r$
Public key:
  – Alice publishes $a^{-1}xa$
  – Bob publishes $b^{-1}xb$
Shared key: derived from $(ab)^{-1}x(ab)$

The parameters considered in [KLC+00, AAFG01] for this key exchange protocol coincide with those for a public key cryptosystem also described in [KLC+00]. Hence, we recall the description of this encryption scheme before giving our experimental results. For this we denote by $H : B_n \longrightarrow \{0,1\}^k$ an ideal hash function from the braid group B_n to the message space $\{0,1\}^k$.

Public information:
  – braid index $n \in \mathbb{N}$
  – integers $\ell, r \in \mathbb{N}$ with $\ell + r = n$
Private key: Alice chooses $a \in LB_\ell$
Public key:
  – Alice publishes a braid word $x \in B_n$, and
  – she publishes $y := a^{-1}xa$

Encryption: To transmit $m \in \{0,1\}^k$ to Alice,
  – Bob chooses $b \in RB_r$ at random, and
  – he sends $(c,d) := (b^{-1}xb, H(b^{-1}yb)$ XOR $m)$ to Alice
Decryption: Alices computes $m = H(a^{-1}ca)$ XOR d

For our experiments we used the parameters that have also been considered in [KLC+00, AAFG01]. Namely, we used braid groups of index $n \geq 45$ and chose $\ell = \lfloor n/2 \rfloor, r = n-\ell$. For x and a (resp. b) we used braid words of canonical length $p \geq 3$. In [KLC+00] the braid word x is required to be 'sufficiently complicated'. Lacking a specification on how to determine such a 'sufficiently complicated' $x \in B_n$, we decided to pick such a braid word in the same manner as proposed in [CKL+01] for generating 'random braid words'. Then we attacked so-obtained instances $y = a^{-1}xa$ of the *generalized conjugacy problem* in B_n by Algorithm A. Below are the results of our experiments for some proposed parameters n and p, where p denotes the canonical length of both x and a (resp. b):

n	p	Total samples	Success rate
45	3	1000	78.1%
50	5	1000	79.1%
70	7	1000	79.0%
90	12	1000	80.0%

Without further specification, in [KLC+00] it is also suggested to use pure braid words x. We decided to generate pure braids as follows: after generating a 'random' braid word x of canonical length p as above, we appended to x the (simple) braid word $\pi^{-1}\left(\pi\left(x^{-1}\right)\right)$, and attacked the so-obtained instances of the system with Algorithm A and the variant of `GuessPermutation` discussed in section 3.2. The figures below show the results of these attacks:

n	p	Total samples	Success rate
45	3	1000	76.9%
50	5	1000	82.4%
70	7	1000	87.5%
90	12	1000	88.9%

So from a cryptographic point of view the parameters in [KLC+00, AAFG01] look rather worrisome, and it remains open how to generate practical instances of the above schemes.

5   Conclusion

We have described a heuristic algorithm for the conjugacy problem in braid groups. This algorithm does not solve the conjugacy problem in the general case, yet it applies in most of the cases considered for public key cryptosystems. We have run various experiments with parameters proposed for braid group cryptosystems to back this result; indeed, we do not know of any public key cryptosystem based on the conjugacy problem in braid groups whose proposed parameters yield hard instances of this problem with respect to our algorithm.

Furthermore, we believe that our algorithm can be improved to succeed for some parameters not considered yet for cryptographic applications. So it remains unclear how to efficiently find hard instances of the conjugacy problem in braid groups for such purposes.

References

[AAFG01]   Iris Anshel, Michael Anshel, Benji Fisher, and Dorian Goldfeld. New Key Agreement Protocols in Braid Group Cryptography. In David Naccache, editor, *"Topics in Cryptology — CT-RSA 2001"*, volume 2020 of *Lecture Notes in Computer Science*, pages 13–27. Springer, 2001. 187, 188, 190, 193, 194, 195, 196

[AAG99]   Iris Anshel, Michael Anshel, and Dorian Goldfeld. An Algebraic Method for Public-Key Cryptography. *Mathematical Research Letters*, 6:287–291, 1999. 187, 188, 194

[Art25]   Emil Artin. Theorie der Zöpfe. *Hamb. Abh.*, 4:47–72, 1925. 188

[Bir74]   Joan S. Birman. *Braids, Links, And Mapping Class Groups*. Number 82 in Annals of Mathematics Studies. Princeton University Press and University of Tokyo Press, Princeton, New Jersey, 1974. 187

[BKL98]   Joan S. Birman, Ki Hyoung Ko, and Sang Jin Lee. A new approach to the word and conjugacy problems in the braid groups. *Advances in Mathematics*, 139:322–353, 1998. 190

[Cha01]   Jae Choon Cha. CBraid: a C++ library for computations in braid groups, 2001. At the time of writing available electronically at http://knot.kaist.ac.kr/~jccha/cbraid/. 193

[CKL⁺01]   Jae Choon Cha, Ki Hyoung Ko, Sang Jin Lee, Jae Woo Han, and Jung Hee Cheon. An Efficient Implementation of Braid Groups. In Colin Boyd, editor, *Advances in Cryptology — ASIACRYPT 2001*, volume 2248 of *Lecture Notes in Computer Science*, pages 144–156. Springer, 2001. 189, 196

[EM94]   Elsayed A. Elrifai and H. R. Morton. Algorithms for positive braids. *Quarterly Journal of Mathematics Oxford*, 45:479–497, 1994. 188, 189

[Gar69]   F. A. Garside. The Braid Group and Other Groups. *Quarterly Journal of Mathematics Oxford*, 20:235–254, 1969. 187, 188, 189

[GZ91]   Max Garzon and Yechezkel Zalcstein. The Complexity of Grigorchuk groups with application to cryptography. *Theoretical Computer Science*, 88:83–98, 1991. 187

[Hug02]   Jim Hughes. A Linear Algebraic Attack on the AAFG1 Braid Group Cryptosystem. In Lynn Batten and Jennifer Seberry, editors, *Information Security and Privacy. 7th Australasian Conference, ACISP 2002*, volume 2384 of *Lecture Notes in Computer Science*, pages 176–189. Springer, 2002. 187, 195

[KLC⁺00]   Ki Hyoung Ko, Sang Jin Lee, Jung Hee Cheon, Jae Woo Han, Ju sung Kang, and Choonsik Park. New Public-Key Cryptosystem Using Braid Groups. In Mihir Bellare, editor, *Advances in Cryptology — CRYPTO 2000*, volume 1880 of *Lecture Notes in Computer Science*, pages 166–183. Springer, 2000. 187, 188, 190, 193, 195, 196

[LL02]   Sang Jin Lee and Eonkyung Lee. Potential Weaknesses of the Commutator
           Key Agreement Protocol Based On Braid Groups. In Lars Knudsen, editor,
           Advances in Cryptology – EUROCRYPT 2002, volume 2332 of *Lecture
           Notes in Computer Science*, pages 14–28. Springer, 2002. 187, 189, 192,
           194

[Wag90]   Neal R. Wagner. Searching for Public-Key Cryptosystems. In *Proceedings
           of the 1984 Symposium on Security and Privacy (SSP '84)*, pages 91–98,
           Los Angeles, Ca., USA, 1990. IEEE Computer Society Press. 187

[WM85]   Neal R. Wagner and Marianne R. Magyarik. A Public Key Cryptosystem
           Based on the Word Problem. In G. R. Blakley and D. Chaum, editor,
           Advances in Cryptology. Proceedings of CRYPTO 1984, volume 196 of
           Lecture Notes in Computer Science, pages 19–36. Springer, 1985. 187

A Refined Power-Analysis Attack on Elliptic Curve Cryptosystems

Louis Goubin

CP8 Crypto Lab, SchlumbergerSema
36-38 rue de la Princesse, BP45, 78430 Louveciennes Cedex, France
lgoubin@slb.com

Abstract. As Elliptic Curve Cryptosystems are becoming more and more popular and are included in many standards, an increasing demand has appeared for secure implementations that are not vulnerable to side-channel attacks. To achieve this goal, several generic countermeasures against Power Analysis have been proposed in recent years.

In particular, to protect the basic scalar multiplication – on an elliptic curve – against Differential Power Analysis (DPA), it has often been recommended using "random projective coordinates", "random elliptic curve isomorphisms" or "random field isomorphisms". So far, these countermeasures have been considered by many authors as a cheap and secure way of avoiding the DPA attacks on the "scalar multiplication" primitive. However we show in the present paper that, for many elliptic curves, such a DPA-protection of the "scalar" multiplication is not sufficient. In a *chosen message* scenario, a Power Analysis attack is still possible even if one of the three aforementioned countermeasures is used. We expose a new Power Analysis strategy that can be successful for a large class of elliptic curves, including most of the sample curves recommended by standard bodies such as ANSI, IEEE, ISO, NIST, SECG or WTLS.

This result means that the problem of randomizing the basepoint may be more difficult than expected and that "standard" techniques have still to be improved, which may also have an impact on the performances of the implementations.

Keywords: Public-key cryptography, Side-channel attacks, Power Analysis, Differential Power Analysis (DPA), Elliptic curves, Smartcards.

1   Introduction

Since their introduction by V. Miller [21] and N. Koblitz [15], elliptic curve cryptosystems have been included in many international standards. One of their advantages is the small size of their keys, compared to those of RSA and ElGamal-type cryptosystems. Therefore, there has been a growing interest in implementing such cryptographic schemes in low-cost cryptographic devices such as smartcards.

Whereas the mathematical aspects of the security of such elliptic curve cryptosystems have been scrutinized for years now, a new threat appeared in 1998

Y.G. Desmedt (Ed.): PKC 2003, LNCS 2567, pp. 199–211, 2003.

when P. Kocher *et al.* [16, 17] introduced attacks based on power analysis. The idea of this new class of attacks is to monitor the power consumption of the electronic device while it is performing the cryptographic computation and then to use a statistical analysis of the measured consumption curves to deduce some information about the secret key stored in the device. The initial focus was on symmetric cryptosystems such as DES but public key cryptosystems were also shown vulnerable, including RSA [20] and elliptic curve cryptosystems [7].

The simple power analysis (SPA) only uses a single observed information. Two main stategies have been suggested to avoid this SPA attack.

The first strategy consists in hiding the fact that, during the computation of a scalar multiplication $d.P$ (d being an integer and P a point of the elliptic curve), the nature of the basic operations (*e.g.* addition or doubling) executed at each step depends on the value of the secret exponent d. Following this strategy, J.S. Coron proposed the "double-and-add-always" method [7]. The "Montgomery" method [23] also proved useful, giving a natural way of avoiding both timing and SPA attacks [25, 27]. For binary fields $GF(2^m)$ a trick allows the computation of the scalar multiplication to be performed without using the y-coordinates [1, 19]. This property was extended to the case of prime fields $GF(p)$ for elliptic curves which have "Montgomery-form" [28, 22] and then for any elliptic curve on $GF(p)$ [12, 4, 8].

The second strategy consists in using indistinguishable addition and doubling in the scalar multiplication [5]. This has been shown feasible for some classes of curves over a prime field $GF(p)$: Hesse-type [29, 13] and Jacobi-type [18] elliptic curves give a unified formula for computing both addition and doubling. A unified formula was recently proposed by E. Brier and M. Joye [4] to achieve the same indistinguishability for any elliptic curve on $GF(2^m)$ or $GF(p)$. For the binary field case, the insertion of dummy operations is also possible [3] to build an indistinguishable adding and doubling.

As pointed out in [7, 27, 14], these anti-SPA methods are not sufficient to prevent DPA attacks. However, many countermeasures have been proposed to transform an SPA-resistant scheme into a DPA-resistant scheme.

In [7], J.S. Coron suggested three anti-DPA methods: randomizing the secret exponent d, adding a random point R to P and using randomized projective homogeneous coordinates. The first two methods have been considered with skepticism in [27] and [12], but the third one is widely accepted: see [25], [27] or [18].

In the same spirit, M. Joye and C. Tymen [14] proposed two other generic methods: performing the computations in another elliptic curve which is deduced from the usual one through a random isomorphism, and performing the basic field operations with another representation of the field which is deduced from the usual one though a random field isomorphism. Note that [14] also gives a specific method for ABC curves (see also [9]).

Hence [7, 14] propose three generic methods ("random projective coordinates", "random elliptic curve isomorphisms" and "random field isomorphisms"), which so far have been considered by many authors as a cheap and secure way of thwarting the DPA attacks: see *e.g.* [26], [3], [12]. For example it is stated in [4] that DPA attacks are not really a threat for elliptic curve cryptography since they are easily avoided by randomizing the inputs.

However, in the present paper we prove that, for a large class of elliptic curves, a Power Analysis attack can still work, even if we apply one of the three countermeasures above (together with an SPA countermeasure, such as "Add-and-double always", the Montgomery method, or a unified add/double formula).

In our scenario, the attacker can choose the message, *i.e.* the input of the "scalar multiplication" primitive. The only way the sensitive data are blinded is by using random projective coordinates (for the input), random elliptic curve isomorphisms (for the curve itself) or random field isomorphism (for the algebraic structure).

The paper is organized as follows. In section 2, we give the mathematical background about elliptic curves and scalar multiplication. In section 3, we describe our new strategy of attack, for each of the three DPA-countermeasures of [7, 14]. In section 4, we study more precisely the necessary conditions on the elliptic curve for our attack to work, and show that most of the sample curves proposed by standardization bodies [2, 10, 11, 24, 30, 31] verify these conditions.

2   Mathematical Background

2.1   Parametrizations of Elliptic Curves

General (affine) Weierstraß Form We consider the elliptic curve defined over a field K by its Weierstraß equation:

$$E : y^2 + a_1 xy + a_3 y = x^3 + a_2 x^2 + a_4 x + a_6.$$

We denote by $E(K)$ the set of points $(x, y) \in K^2$ satisfying this equation. If we introduce a formal "point at infinity" denoted by $\mathcal{O}$, the set $E(K) \bigcup \mathcal{O}$ can be equiped with an operation $+$ which makes it an abelian group whose identity element is $\mathcal{O}$.

Projective Coordinates To avoid costly inversions, it is convenient to use projective coordinates. Among many possibilities developed in [6], we describe *homogeneous* and *Jacobian* projective coordinates.

Homogeneous projective coordinates are obtained by setting $x = X/Z$ and $y = Y/Z$, so that the general Weierstraß equation becomes

$$E : Y^2 Z + a_1 XYZ + a_3 YZ^2 = X^3 + a_2 X^2 Z + a_4 XZ^2 + a_6 Z^3.$$

The point at infinity $\mathcal{O}$ is then represented by $(0, \theta, 0)$ for some $\theta \in K^*$, the affine point (x, y) is represented by a projective point $(\theta x, \theta y, \theta)$ for some $\theta \in K^*$ and a projective point $(X, Y, Z) \neq \mathcal{O}$ corresponds to the affine point $(X/Z, Y/Z)$.

Jacobian projective coordinates are obtained by setting $x = X/Z^2$ and $y = Y/Z^3$, so that the general Weierstraß equation becomes

$$E : Y^2 + a_1 XYZ + a_3 YZ^3 = X^3 + a_2 X^2 Z^2 + a_4 XZ^4 + a_6 Z^6.$$

The point at infinity $\mathcal{O}$ is then represented by $(\theta^2, \theta^3, 0)$ for some $\theta \in K^*$, the affine point (x, y) is represented by a projective point $(\theta^2 x, \theta^3 y, \theta)$ for some $\theta \in K^*$ and a projective point $(X, Y, Z) \neq \mathcal{O}$ corresponds to the affine point $(X/Z^2, Y/Z^3)$.

Simplified (affine) Weierstraß Forms When $\text{Char}(K) \neq 2, 3$, the general Weierstraß equation can be simplified to

$$E : y^2 = x^3 + ax + b$$

and the addition formulas, giving $P + Q = (x_3, y_3)$ from $P = (x_1, y_1)$ and $Q = (x_2, y_2)$, become

$$\begin{cases} x_3 = \lambda^2 - x_1 - x_2 \\ y_3 = \lambda(x_1 - x_3) - y_1 \end{cases} \text{ with } \lambda = \begin{cases} \frac{y_1 - y_2}{x_1 - x_2} & \text{if } P \neq Q \\ \frac{3x_1^2 + a}{2y_1} & \text{if } P = Q \end{cases}$$

When $\text{Char}(K) = 2$ and the curve is non-supersingular, the general Weierstraß equation can be simplified to

$$E : y^2 + xy = x^3 + ax^2 + b$$

and the addition formulas to

$$\begin{cases} x_3 = \lambda^2 + \lambda + a + x_1 + x_2 \\ y_3 = \lambda(x_1 + x_3) + x_3 + y_1 \end{cases} \text{ with } \lambda = \begin{cases} \frac{y_1 - y_2}{x_1 - x_2} & \text{if } P \neq Q \\ x_1 + \frac{y_1}{x_1} & \text{if } P = Q \end{cases}$$

Montgomery Form In order to ease the additions, P.L. Montgomery considered in [23] the family of elliptic curves of the following form (on a field K of characteristic $\neq 2$):

$$E : By^2 = x^3 + Ax^2 + x \quad \text{with } B(A^2 - 4) \neq 0.$$

As noticed in [27], on such elliptic curves, the point $(0, 0)$ is of order 2 and the cardinality of $E(K)$ is always divisible by 4.

Hessian Form The Hessian-type elliptic curves were considered because they provide a unified formula for adding and doubling. Defined as the intersection of two quadrics, they can be given in the following form (on a field $K = \text{GF}(q)$ with $q \equiv 2 \bmod 3$)

$$E : x^3 + y^3 + 1 = 3Dxy \quad \text{with } D \in K, D^3 \neq 1.$$

As mentioned in [29, 13], point $(-1, 0)$ has order 3, that implies that the cardinality of $E(K)$ is always divisible by 3.

2.2 Usual SPA Countermeasures

To compute the scalar multiplication $d.P$, where $d = d_{n-1}2^{n-1} + d_{n-2}2^{n-2} + ... + d_1 2 + d_0$, with $d_{n-1} = 1$ and $P \in E(K)$, the following generic schemes have been proposed.

Classical Binary Method This method (see Algorithm 1) is analogous to the "square-and-multiply" principle used in RSA. Note that an analogous method exists, which is from the least significant bit. As noticed in [7], both are vulnerable to SPA attacks. That is why two other methods were introduced: the "Double-and-add-always" and the "Montgomery" methods.

Algorithm 1 Binary method (from the most significant bit)

Require: d, P
Ensure: $Q = d.P$
  $Q := P$
  for $i = n - 2$ down to 0 **do**
    $Q := 2.Q$
    if $d_i = 1$ **then**
      $Q := Q + P$
    end if
  end for
  Return Q

Double-and-Add-Always This method (Algorithm 2) was proposed in [7]. Note that an analogous method also exists, which is from the least significant bit [7, 12]. Both are SPA-resistant.

Algorithm 2 Double-and-add-always (from the most significant bit)

Require: d, P
Ensure: $Q_0 = d.P$
  $Q_0 := P$
  for $i = n - 2$ down to 0 **do**
    $Q_0 := 2.Q_0$
    $Q_1 := Q_0 + P$
    $Q_0 := Q_{d_i}$
  end for
  Return Q_0

Montgomery Method This method (Algorithm 3) was originally proposed in [23] and then elaborated in [1, 19, 25, 27, 28, 28, 22, 12, 4, 8]. It is SPA-resistant.

Algorithm 3 Montgomery's method

Require: d, P
Ensure: $Q_0 = d.P$
  $Q_0 := P$
  $Q_1 := 2.P$
  for $i = n - 2$ down to 0 **do**
    $Q_{1-d_i} := Q_0 + Q_1$
    $Q_{d_i} := 2.Q_{d_i}$
  end for
  Return Q_0

---

3   Our New Power Analysis Attack

We present here a Power Analysis attack that can work on many elliptic curves, even if an SPA-countermeasure (such as *Double-and-add-always* or the *Montgomery* method) is used, together with one of three aforementioned DPA-countermeasures (*Random projective coordinates*, *Random elliptic curve isomorphisms* or *Random field isomorphisms*).

3.1   The Strategy of the Attack

In this section, we describe the generic attack on an elliptic curve scalar multiplication, SPA-protected with *Double-and-add-always* or the *Montgomery* method. Note however that the attack is not limited to the case of binary methods (such as Algorithm 2 or Algorithm 3) and can be extended to the case of other addition chains.

Suppose the attacker already knows the highest bits d_{n-1}, ..., d_{i+1} of the secret multiplier d. We illustrate below how he can find the next bit d_i.

Let us suppose that the elliptic curve $E(K)$ contains a "special" point $P_0 \neq \mathcal{O}$, i.e. a point $P_0 \neq \mathcal{O}$ such that one of the (affine or projective) coordinates equals 0 in K.

Note that, for each of the three aforementioned DPA-countermeasures, the randomization does not affect the "special" property of the point P_0 (see section 3.2).

Double-and-Add-Always In Algorithm 2, for any given input point P, the value Q_0 obtained at the end of the i-th step of the loop is

$$Q_0 = \Big(\sum_{j=i+1}^{n-1} d_j 2^{j-i} + d_i \Big).P.$$

We then have two cases:

- If $d_i = 0$, the values that appear during the $(i+1)$-st step of the loop are
$$\Big(\sum_{j=i+1}^{n-1} d_j 2^{j-i+1} \Big).P \text{ and } \Big(\sum_{j=i+1}^{n-1} d_j 2^{j-i+1} + 1 \Big).P.$$
- If $d_i = 1$, the values that appear during the $(i+1)$-st step of the loop are
$$\Big(\sum_{j=i+1}^{n-1} d_j 2^{j-i+1} + 2 \Big).P \text{ and } \Big(\sum_{j=i+1}^{n-1} d_j 2^{j-i+1} + 3 \Big).P.$$

We consider the point P_1 given by

$$P_1 = \Big[\Big(\sum_{j=i+1}^{n-1} d_j 2^{j-i+1} + 1 \Big)^{-1} \bmod |E(K)| \Big].P_0$$

if $\Big(\sum_{j=i+1}^{n-1} d_j 2^{j-i+1} + 1 \Big)$ is coprime to $|E(K)|$ (this corresponds to the guess $d_i = 0$), or

$$P_1 = \Big[\Big(\sum_{j=i+1}^{n-1} d_j 2^{j-i+1} + 3 \Big)^{-1} \bmod |E(K)| \Big].P_0$$

if $\Big(\sum_{j=i+1}^{n-1} d_j 2^{j-i+1} + 3 \Big)$ is coprime to $|E(K)|$ (this corresponds to the guess $d_i = 1$). In many cases, both possibilities can be chosen.

Let us now denote by C_r, for $1 \leq r \leq R$, the power consumption curves associated to r distinct computations of $d.P_1$. Because of the randomization performed before each computation, two curves corresponding to the same input value can be different.

We then consider the mean curve

$$\mathcal{M}_{P_1} = \frac{1}{R} \sum_{r=1}^{R} C_r.$$

If the guess for d_i (i.e. the choice for the point P_1) is incorrect, then $\mathcal{M}_{P_1} \simeq 0$, since the values appearing in the $(i+1)$-st step of the loop in Algorithm 2, are correctly randomized.

On the contrary, if the guess for d_i is correct, the mean curve $\mathcal{M}_{P_1}$ shows appreciable consumption "peaks" (compared to the mean power consumption of random points), corresponding to the treatment of the zero value in the $(i+1)$-st step of the loop.

Once d_i is known, the remaining bits $d_{i-1}, ..., d_0$ are recovered recursively, in the same way.

The Montgomery Method In Algorithm 3, for any given input point P, the values Q_0 and Q_1 obtained at the end of the i-th step of the loop are

$$Q_0 = \Big(\sum_{j=i+1}^{n-1} d_j 2^{j-i} + d_i \Big).P$$

$$Q_1 = \Big(\sum_{j=i+1}^{n-1} d_j 2^{j-i} + d_i + 1 \Big).P$$

We then have two cases:

- If $d_i = 0$, the values that appear during the $(i+1)$-st step of the loop are $\Big(\sum_{j=i+1}^{n-1} d_j 2^{j-i+1} + 1 \Big).P$ on the one hand, and $\Big(\sum_{j=i+1}^{n-1} d_j 2^{j-i+1} \Big).P$ or $\Big(\sum_{j=i+1}^{n-1} d_j 2^{j-i+1} + 2 \Big).P$ on the other hand.

- If $d_i = 1$, the values that appear during the $(i+1)$-st step of the loop are $\Big(\sum_{j=i+1}^{n-1} d_j 2^{j-i+1} + 3 \Big).P$ on the one hand, and $\Big(\sum_{j=i+1}^{n-1} d_j 2^{j-i+1} + 2 \Big).P$ or $\Big(\sum_{j=i+1}^{n-1} d_j 2^{j-i+1} + 4 \Big).P$ on the other hand.

We then consider then point P_1 given by

$$P_1 = \Big[\Big(\sum_{j=i+1}^{n-1} d_j 2^{j-i+1} + 1 \Big)^{-1} \bmod |E(K)| \Big].P_0$$

if $\Big(\sum_{j=i+1}^{n-1} d_j 2^{j-i+1} + 1 \Big)$ is coprime to $|E(K)|$ (the guess is $d_i = 0$), or

$$P_1 = \Big[\Big(\sum_{j=i+1}^{n-1} d_j 2^{j-i+1} + 3 \Big)^{-1} \bmod |E(K)| \Big].P_0$$

if $\Big(\sum_{j=i+1}^{n-1} d_j 2^{j-i+1} + 3 \Big)$ is coprime to $|E(K)|$ (the guess is $d_i = 1$).

The rest of the attack is then exactly the same as for the "Double-and-add-always" method: the bit d_i is found by power analysis, and the remaining bits d_{i-1}, ..., d_0 in the same way.

3.2   Application to Three Usual DPA-Countermeasures

Random Projective Coordinates The basic idea of this method is the following. The computation $Q = d.P$ is performed in projective coordinates. The basepoint $P = (x, y)$ can be represented by $(\theta x, \theta y, \theta)$ (*homogeneous* projective coordinates) or $(\theta^2 x, \theta^3 y, \theta)$ (*Jacobian* projective coordinates) for some $\theta \in K^*$.

Thus the computation is performed in 3 steps:

1. Choose a random $\theta \in K^*$ and let $P' = (\theta x, \theta y, \theta)$ (homogeneous projective coordinates) or $P' = (\theta^2 x, \theta^3 y, \theta)$ (Jacobian projective coordinates).
2. Compute $Q' = (X', Y', Z') = d.P'$.
3. Compute $Q = (X'/Z', Y'/Z')$ (homogeneous projective coordinates) or $Q = (X'/Z'^2, Y'/Z'^3)$ (Jacobian projective coordinates).

It is easy to see that the "special" point mentioned in section 3.1 remains of the form $(X, 0, Z)$ or $(0, Y, Z)$, whatever the random value θ may be. This shows that the above strategy applies.

Random Elliptic Curve Isomorphisms This method applies for an elliptic curve $E : y^2 = x^3 + ax + b$ on a field K of characteristic $\neq 2, 3$. For $P = (x, y)$, the computation of $Q = d.P$ is performed as follows:

1. Choose a random $\theta \in K^*$ and let $P' = (\theta^2 x, \theta^3 y, 1)$, $a' = \theta^{-4} a$ and $b' = \theta^{-6} b$.
2. Compute $Q' = (X', Y', Z') = d.P'$ in $E' : Y^2 Z = X^3 + a' X Z^2 + b' Z^3$ (homogeneous projective coordinates).
3. Compute $Q = (\theta^2 X'/Z', \theta^3 Y'/Z')$.

A variant consists in computing $Q' = d.P'$ in $E' : Y^3 = X^3 + a' X Z^4 + b' Z^6$ (Jacobian projective coordinates). It is easy to see that the "special" point mentioned in section 3.1 remains of the form $(X, 0, Z)$ or $(0, Y, Z)$, whatever the random value θ may be. This shows that the strategy of section 3.1 applies again.

Random Field Isomorphisms This method applies for an elliptic curve over a field $K = \mathrm{GF}(2^m) = \mathrm{GF}(2)[X]/\Pi(X)$, where Π is an irreducible polynomial of degree m over $\mathrm{GF}(2)$. The idea is that there are many such irreducible polynomials, so that K can be replaced (randomly) by an isomorphic field K'. The computation of $Q = d.P$ is performed as follows:

1. Choose a random irreducible polynomial Π' of degree m over $\mathrm{GF}(2)$ and let $K' = \mathrm{GF}(2)[X]/\Pi'(X)$.
2. Let φ be the field isomorphism between K and K' and $P' = \varphi(P)$.
3. Compute $Q' = d.P' \in K'^2$ in $E_{/K'}$.
4. Compute $Q = \varphi^{-1}(Q') \in K^2$.

Again, the "special" point mentioned in section 3.1 remains of the form $(x, 0)$ or $(0, y)$ (with the usual representation of the zero value), whatever the random polynomial Π' may be, so that the strategy of section 3.1 also applies.

4 Practical Applications

4.1 Computation of the "Special" Point

Special Points $(0, y)$ For a non-singular binary elliptic curve, whose reduced Weierstraß form is $E : y^2 + xy = x^3 + ax^2 + b$ over $K = \mathrm{GF}(2^m)$, we can choose $P_0 = (0, b^{2^{m-1}})$ as the "special" point.

For an elliptic curve $E : y^2 = x^3 + ax + b$ over a prime field $K = \mathrm{GF}(p)$ ($p > 3$), a special point of the form $(0, y)$ exists if and only if b is a quadratic residue modulo p, i.e. $\left(\frac{b}{p} \right) = 1$, where $\left(\frac{\cdot}{\cdot} \right)$ is the Legendre symbol.

Among the standardized curves over a prime field satisfying the condition are: four curves proposed in FIPS 186-2 [24], the basic curve (curve number 7) proposed in WTLS [31], the seven curves proposed in ANSI X9.62 [2] (Annex J5), and two curves proposed in the working draft ISO/IEC 15946-4 [11] (Annexes A2.1 and A3.1). Only one curve of FIPS 186-2 (P224) and four curves of ISO/IEC 15946-4 (Annexes A1.1[1], A4.1, A5.1 and A6.1) have no special point $(0, y)$.

Special Points $(x, 0)$ For an elliptic curve $E : y^2 = x^3 + ax + b$ over a prime field $K = \mathrm{GF}(p)$ ($p > 3$), a special point of the form $(x, 0)$ exists if and only if the equation $x^3 + ax + b = 0$ has at least one root α in K.

Note that $P_0 = (\alpha, 0)$ is then a point of order 2 in $E(K)$. At first glance, it may seem that the strategy of section 3.1 fails, because P_1 does not depend on the guess made on d_i (P_1 is always equal to P_0). However, the successive values of Q that appear during Algorithm 2, for $i = n - 2, ..., 0$ are either $\mathcal{O}$ (if $d_i = 0$) or P (if $d_i = 1$). Therefore the mean curve $\mathcal{M}_{P_1}$ shows in fact many peaks: for instance if Algorithm 2 is applied, with random homogeneous projective coordinates, the chip instructions manipulating $\mathcal{O} = (0, \theta, 0)$ are likely to create 2 such peaks (one for each 0), whereas the instructions manipulating $(\theta x, 0, \theta)$ are likely to create only 1 peak. This allows the attacker to recover all the bits d_i of the secret exponent d with only one application of the strategy of 3.1.

Some particular classes of curves automatically have such points of order 2. As mentioned in section 2.1, for all Montgomery-form elliptic curves, $(0, 0)$ is of order 2: its double is $\mathcal{O} = (0, 1, 0)$. For the Hessian form, all (x, x) are of order 2: their double is $\mathcal{O} = (-1, 1, 0)$.

4.2   Cardinality of the Elliptic Curve

Another condition for our strategy of attack to work is the fact that at least one of the values $\left(\sum_{j=i+1}^{n-1} d_j 2^{j-i+1} + 1 \right)$ and $\left(\sum_{j=i+1}^{n-1} d_j 2^{j-i+1} + 3 \right)$ is coprime to $|E(K)|$.

Over a prime field, FIPS 186-2 [24] or SECG [30] recommend to use elliptic curves of prime cardinality, and binary curves of cardinality $2q$ or $4q$ (q prime). All the curves proposed by WTLS [31] and ISO/IEC 15946-4 [11] have cardinality q, $2q$, $4q$, $6q$ (q prime). It is also true for most of the curves of ANSI X9.62 [2].

This shows that the condition above is true for most standardized elliptic curves.

---

[1] This curve however has a point of order 2, hence a special point $(x, 0)$.

5   Conclusion

This attack we present here shows that the problem of randomizing the base-point may be more difficult than expected and that "standard" techniques for securing the "scalar multiplication" primitive still have to be improved. Evaluating the performances of secure implementations of elliptic curve cryptosystems will require to take those improvements into account. The results of this paper also highlight the necessity to choose a message blinding method (before entering the "scalar multiplication" primitive) that prevents an attacker from choosing the messages.

References

[1] G. B. Agnew, R. C. Mullin, S. A. Vanstone, *An Implementation of Elliptic Curve Cryptosystems over* $\mathbf{F}_{2^{155}}$. IEEE Journal on Selected Areas in Communications, vol. 11, n. 5, pp 804-813, 1993. 200, 204

[2] ANSI X9.62, Public Key Cryptography for the Financial Services Industry, *The Elliptic Curve Digital Signature Algorithm (ECDSA)*, 1999. 201, 208

[3] A. Bellezza, *Countermeasures against Side-Channel Attacks for Elliptic Curve Cryptosystems.* IACR, Cryptology ePrint Archive, 2001/103, 2001. Available from http://eprint.iacr.org/2001/103/ 200, 201

[4] E. Brier, M. Joye, *Weierstraß Elliptic Curves and Side-Channel Attacks.* In Proceedings of PKC'2002, LNCS 2274, pp. 335-345, Springer-Verlag, 2002. 200, 201, 204

[5] C. Clavier, M. Joye, *Universal Exponentiation Algorithm – A First Step towards Provable SPA-Resistance.* In Proceedings of CHES'2001, LNCS 2162, pp. 300-308, Springer-Verlag, 2001. 200

[6] H. Cohen, A. Miyaji, T. Ono, *Efficient Elliptic Curve Exponentiation Using Mixed Coordinates.* In Proceedings of ASIACRYPT'98, LNCS 1514, pp. 51-65, Springer-Verlag, 1998. 201

[7] J.-S. Coron, *Resistance Against Differential Power Analysis for Elliptic Curve Cryptosystems.* In Proceedings of CHES'99, LNCS 1717, pp. 292-302, Springer-Verlag, 1999. 200, 201, 203

[8] W. Fischer, C. Giraud, E. W. Knudsen, J.-P. Seifert, *Parallel Scalar Multiplication on General Elliptic Curves over* $\mathbf{F}_p$ *hedged against Non-Differential Side-Channel Attacks.* IACR, Cryptology ePrint Archive, 2002/007, 2002. Available from http://eprint.iacr.org/2002/007/ 200, 204

[9] M. A. Hasan, *Power analysis attacks and algorithmic approaches to their countermeasures for Koblitz curve cryptosystems.* In Proceedings of CHES'2000, LNCS 1965, pp. 93-108, Springer-Verlag, 2000. 200

[10] IEEE P1363, *Standard Specifications for Public-Key Cryptography*, 2000. Available from http://groupe.ieee.org/groups/1363/ 201

[11] ISO/IEC 15946-4, *Information technology - Security techniques – Cryptographic techniques based on elliptic curves - Part 4: Digital signatures giving message recovery.* Working Draft, JTC 1/SC 27, December 28th, 2001. 201, 208

[12] T. Izu, T. Takagi, *A Fast Parallel Elliptic Curve Multiplication Resistant against Side Channel Attacks.* In Proceedings of PKC'2002, LNCS 2274, pp. 280-296, Springer-Verlag, 2002. 200, 201, 203, 204

[13] M. Joye, J.-J. Quisquater, *Hessian Elliptic Curves and Side-Channel Attacks*. In Proceedings of CHES'2001, LNCS 2162, pp. 412-420, Springer-Verlag, 2001. 200, 202

[14] M. Joye, C. Tymen, *Protections against Differential Analysis for Elliptic Curve Cryptography – An Algebraic Approach*. In Proceedings of CHES'2001, LNCS 2162, pp. 377-390, Springer-Verlag, 2001. 200, 201

[15] N. Koblitz, *Elliptic curve cryptosystems*. Mathematics of Computation, Vol. 48, pp. 203-209, 1987. 199

[16] P. Kocher, J. Jaffe, B. Jun, *Introduction to Differential Power Analysis and Related Attacks*. Technical Report, Cryptography Research Inc., 1998. Available from http://www.cryptography.com/dpa/technical/index.html 200

[17] P. Kocher, J. Jaffe, B. Jun, *Differential Power Analysis*. In Proceedings of CRYPTO'99, LNCS 1666, pp. 388-397, Springer-Verlag, 1999. 200

[18] P.-Y. Liardet, N. P. Smart, *Preventing SPA/DPA in ECC system using the Jacobi Form*. In Proceedings of CHES'2001, LNCS 2162, pp. 401-411, Springer-Verlag, 2001. 200

[19] J. López, R. Dahab, *Fast Multiplication on Elliptic Curves over $GF(2^m)$ without Precomputation*. In Proceedings of CHES'99, LNCS 1717, pp. 316-327, Springer-Verlag, 1999. 200, 204

[20] T. S. Messerges, E. A. Dabbish, R. H. Sloan, *Power Analysis Attacks of Modular Exponentiation in Smartcards*. In Proceedings of CHES'99, pp. 144-157, Springer-Verlag, 1999. 200

[21] V. Miller, *Uses of elliptic curves in cryptography*. In Proceedings of CRYPTO'85, LNCS 218, pp. 417-426, Springer-Verlag, 1986. 199

[22] B. Möller, *Securing Elliptic Curve Point Multiplication against Side-Channel Attacks*. In Proceedings of ISC'2001, LNCS 2200, pp. 324-334, Springer-Verlag, 2001. 200, 204

[23] P. L. Montgomery, *Speeding the Pollard and Elliptic Curve Methods for Factorizations*. Mathematics of Computation, vol. 48, pp. 243-264, 1987. 200, 202, 204

[24] National Institute of Standards and Technology (NIST), *Recommended Elliptic Curves for Federal Government Use*. In the appendix of FIPS 186-2, available from http://csrc.nist.gov/publications/fips/fips186-2/fips186-2.pdf 201, 208

[25] K. Okeya, H. Kurumatani, K. Sakurai, *Elliptic Curve with the Montgomery Form and their cryptographic Applications*. In Proceedings of PKC'2000, LNCS 1751, pp. 238-257, Springer-Verlag, 2000. 200, 204

[26] K. Okeya, K. Miyazaki, K. Sakurai, *A Fast Scalar Multiplication Method with Randomized Projective Coordinates on a Montgomery-form Elliptic Curve Secure against Side Channel Attacks*. In Pre-proceedings of ICICS'2001, pp. 475-486, 2001. 201

[27] K. Okeya, K. Sakurai, *Power Analysis Breaks Elliptic Curve Cryptosystem even Secure against the Timing Attack*. In Proceedings of INDOCRYPT'2000, LNCS 1977, pp. 178-190, Springer-Verlag, 2000. 200, 202, 204

[28] K. Okeya, K. Sakurai, *Efficient Elliptic Curve Cryptosystems from a Scalar Multiplication Algorithm with Recovery of the y-coordinate on a Montgomery-form Elliptic Curve*. In Proceedings of CHES'2001, LNCS 2162, pp. 126-141, Springer-Verlag, 2001. 200, 204

[29] N. P. Smart, *The Hessian Form of an Elliptic Curve*. In Proceedings of CHES'2001, LNCS 2162, pp. 118-125, Springer-Verlag, 2001. 200, 202

[30] Standards for Efficient Cryptography Group (SECG), *Specification of Standards for Efficient Cryptography*, Ver. 1.0, 2000. Available from `http://www.secg.org/secg_docs.htm` 201, 208

[31] Wireless Application Protocol (WAP) Forum, *Wireless Transport Layer Security (WTLS) Specification*. Available from `http://www.wapforum.org` 201, 208

Validation of Elliptic Curve Public Keys

Adrian Antipa[1], Daniel Brown[1], Alfred Menezes[2],
René Struik[1], and Scott Vanstone[2]

[1] Certicom Research, Canada
{aantipa,dbrown,rstruik}@certicom.com
[2] Dept. of Combinatorics and Optimization, University of Waterloo, Canada
{ajmeneze,savansto}@uwaterloo.ca

Abstract. We present practical and realistic attacks on some standard-ized elliptic curve key establishment and public-key encryption protocols that are effective if the receiver of an elliptic curve point does not check that the point lies on the appropriate elliptic curve. The attacks combine ideas from the small subgroup attack of Lim and Lee, and the differen-tial fault attack of Biehl, Meyer and Müller. Although the ideas behind the attacks are quite elementary, and there are simple countermeasures known, the attacks can have drastic consequences if these countermea-sures are not taken by implementors of the protocols. We illustrate the effectiveness of such attacks on a key agreement protocol recently pro-posed for the IEEE 802.15 Wireless Personal Area Network (WPAN) standard.

1 Introduction

The purpose of public key validation, as enunciated by Johnson [16, 17], is to verify that a public key possesses certain arithmetic properties. Public key val-idation is especially important in Diffie-Hellman protocols where an entity B derives a shared secret k by combining his private key with a public key received from A, and subsequently uses k in some symmetric-key protocol (e.g., encryp-tion or message authentication) with A. A dishonest A might select an invalid public key in such a way that the use of k reveals information about B's pri-vate key. Lim and Lee [20] demonstrated the importance of public key validation by presenting so-called *small subgroup attacks* on some discrete logarithm key agreement and encryption protocols that are effective if the receiver of a group element does not verify that the element belongs to the desired group of high order (e.g., a subgroup of prime order q of $\mathbb{Z}_p^*$).

Although public key validation has become recognized as prudent practice, many cryptographic standards do not mandate that it be performed. In this paper, we present attacks on some standardized elliptic curve key establishment and public-key encryption protocols that are effective if the receiver of an el-liptic curve point does not check that the point lies on the appropriate elliptic curve. We argue with considerable care that, despite their simplicity, the attacks are practical and realistic. We illustrate their effectiveness on a key agreement

Y.G. Desmedt (Ed.): PKC 2003, LNCS 2567, pp. 211–223, 2003.

protocol recently proposed for the IEEE 802.15 WPAN standard. The attacks provide further evidence for the necessity of performing public key validation.

The remainder of this paper is organized as follows. Section 2 describes several standardized elliptic curve cryptographic schemes that will be used to demonstrate the attacks. Validation of elliptic curve public keys is defined in Section 3. The invalid-curve attacks are presented and analyzed in Section 4. Some countermeasures are proposed in Section 5. Finally, we draw our conclusions in Section 6.

2   Elliptic Curve Cryptographic Schemes

We present some elliptic curve schemes that have been included in several standards and draft standards. The schemes are presented in sufficient detail to convince the reader that the assumptions made in our attacks are plausible, and that the attacks can indeed be a significant threat in practice.

In any public-key cryptographic system, the entities may share common data called *domain parameters*, and they have *key pairs* each consisting of a *public key* and a corresponding *private key*. A key pair may be *static* (long-term) if it is intended to be used for an extended period of time, or *ephemeral* (short-term) if it is only intended to be used for a single run of a protocol.

Domain parameters. For elliptic curve cryptographic schemes, the domain parameters D include the following:

1. The *order* q of the underlying finite field $\mathbb{F}_q$.
2. An indication of the *representation* used for elements of $\mathbb{F}_q$ (e.g., the irreducible reduction polynomial if the field has characteristic 2 and a polynomial basis representation is used).
3. The *defining equation* of the elliptic curve E over $\mathbb{F}_q$.
4. A *base point* $P = (x_P, y_P) \in E(\mathbb{F}_q)$ of prime order.
5. The *order* n of P.
6. The *cofactor* $h = \#E(\mathbb{F}_q)/n$.

We assume throughout this paper that elliptic curve domain parameters D have been selected so that the elliptic curve discrete logarithm problem resists all known attacks, and that n^2 does not divide $\#E(\mathbb{F}_q)$ whence $\langle P \rangle$ is the unique subgroup of $E(\mathbb{F}_q)$ having order n. Examples of such parameters are the *NIST domain parameters* specified in the FIPS 186-2 standard [10]. We shall assume that all entities have an authentic copy of D.

Key pairs. A user A now selects $w_A \in_R [1, n-1]$ and computes $W_A = w_A P$. A's static key pair is (W_A, w_A), where W_A is the static public key and w_A is the static private key. B's static key pair is denoted (W_B, w_B). We assume that A and B can obtain authentic copies of each others static public keys, e.g., via certificates.

Notation and terminology. If a discrete logarithm protocol takes place in a subgroup G_1 of prime order of a group G_2, then G_1 is called the *main group*, while G_2 is called the *supergroup*. For example, in the elliptic curve setting, $E(\mathbb{F}_q)$ is the supergroup while $\langle P \rangle$ is the main group. The point at infinity is denoted by ∞, H denotes a cryptographic hash function, and $x(R)$ denotes the x-coordinate of a point R. In the ECMQV protocol, if R is a finite point then $\overline{R}$ is defined to be the integer $(\overline{x} \bmod 2^{\lceil f/2 \rceil}) + 2^{\lceil f/2 \rceil}$ where $\overline{x}$ is the integer representation of $x(R)$, and $f = \lfloor \log_2 n \rfloor + 1$.

2.1   One-Pass ECDH

One-pass ECDH is a basic elliptic curve Diffie-Hellman protocol that combines the sender's ephemeral public key and the receiver's static public key. Although it provides very limited authentication, it might be useful in scenarios where only unilateral authentication is needed, e.g., in the widely deployed SSL/TLS protocol (see the ECDH_ECDSA protocol in [11]) and in SMIME (see [8]). ECDH is fully specified in ANSI X9.63 [4] and IEEE 1363-2000 [12].

1. A selects $r_A \in_R [1, n-1]$, and computes $R_A = r_A P$, $K = r_A W_B$ and $k = H(x(K))$. A sends R_A to B.
2. B computes $K = w_B R_A$ and $k = H(x(K))$.
3. The shared secret key is k.

2.2   ECIES

The elliptic curve integrated encryption scheme (ECIES) is due to Bellare and Rogaway [6] who proposed the scheme in the general setting of a group of prime order. ECIES has been included in several standards and draft standards including ANSI X9.63 [4], IEEE P1363a [13], and ISO/IEC 15946-3 [15]. It can be used to transport a session key (to be used subsequently in some symmetric-key protocol) or to transmit a confidential message of arbitrary length. ECIES uses a hash function H, a message authentication algorithm MAC, and a symmetric encryption scheme SYM. Abdalla, Bellare and Rogaway [1] proved that ECIES is semantically secure against adaptive chosen-ciphertext attacks under some variants of the computational Diffie-Hellman assumption, and the assumptions that MAC and SYM are secure.

Encryption. To send a message m to B, A does:

1. Select $r_A \in_R [1, n-1]$ and compute $R_A = r_A P$ and $K = r_A W_B$.
2. Derive symmetric keys (k_1, k_2) from $H(x(K))$.
3. Compute $c = \text{SYM}_{k_1}(m)$ and $t = \text{MAC}_{k_2}(c)$.
4. Send (R_A, c, t) to B.

Decryption. To decrypt (R_A, c, t), B does:

1. Compute $K = w_B R_A$.
2. Derive symmetric keys (k_1, k_2) from $H(x(K))$.
3. Compute $t' = \text{MAC}_{k_2}(c)$ and reject the ciphertext if $t' \neq t$.
4. Compute $m = \text{SYM}_{k_1}^{-1}(c)$.

2.3   One-Pass ECMQV

The one-pass ECMQV key agreement protocol [18] differs from one-pass ECDH and ECIES in that it combines the static key of the receiver with both the ephemeral and static keys of the sender. The protocol is specified in the ANSI X9.63 [4], IEEE 1363-2000 [12] and ISO 15946-3 [15] standards.

1. A selects $r_A \in_R [1, n-1]$, computes $R_A = r_A P$, and sends this to B.
2. A computes $s_A = (r_A + \overline{R}_A w_A) \bmod n$ and $K = h s_A (W_B + \overline{W}_B W_B)$. If $K = \infty$, then A terminates the protocol run with failure; otherwise A computes $k = H(x(K))$.
3. B computes $s_B = (w_B + \overline{W}_B w_B) \bmod n$ and $K = h s_B (R_A + \overline{R}_A W_A)$. If $K = \infty$, then B terminates the protocol with failure; otherwise B computes $k = H(x(K))$.
4. The shared secret key is k.

2.4   ECDSA

The elliptic curve digital signature algorithm (ECDSA) is specified in the ANSI X9.62 [3], IEEE 1363-2000 [12], FIPS 186-2 [10] and ISO 15946-2 [14] standards.

Signature generation. To sign a message m, A does:

1. Select $k \in_R [1, n-1]$ and compute $r = x(kP)$. (Check that $r \neq 0$.)
2. Compute $e = H(m)$ and $s = k^{-1}(e + w_A r) \bmod n$. (Check that $s \neq 0$.)
3. A's signature on m is (r, s).

Signature verification. To verify A's signature (r, s) on m, B does:

1. Reject the signature if $r \notin [1, n-1]$ or if $s \notin [1, n-1]$.
2. Compute $e = H(m)$, $u_1 = s^{-1} e \bmod n$ and $u_2 = s^{-1} r \bmod n$.
3. Compute $V = u_1 P + u_2 W_A$ and $v = x(V) \bmod n$.
4. Accept the signature iff $v = r$.

3   Public Key Validation

Validation of an elliptic curve public key W ensures that W is a point of order n in $E(\mathbb{F}_q)$, where $\mathbb{F}_q$, E and n are specified by the associated domain parameters.

Definition 1 A point $W = (x_W, y_W)$ (static or ephemeral) associated with a set of domain parameters D is *valid* if the following four conditions are satisfied:

1. $W \neq \infty$.
2. x_W and y_W are properly represented elements of $\mathbb{F}_q$ (e.g., integers in the interval $[0, q-1]$ if $\mathbb{F}_q$ has prime order).
3. W satisfies the defining equation of the elliptic curve E.
4. $nW = \infty$.

If any one of these conditions is violated, then W is *invalid*.

There may be ways of verifying condition 4 of Definition 1 that are much faster than performing an expensive point multiplication nW. For example, if $h = 1$ (which is usually the case for elliptic curves over prime fields that are used in practice), then condition 4 is implied by the other three conditions. In some protocols the check that $nW = \infty$ may either be embedded in the protocol computations or replaced by the check that $hW \neq \infty$ (which guarantees that W is not in a small subgroup of $E(\mathbb{F}_q)$ of order dividing h).

Small subgroup attacks. Lim and Lee [20] presented attacks on some discrete logarithm key agreement and encryption protocols to demonstrate the importance of checking that group elements received from another entity belong to the main group, and not to some small subgroup of the supergroup. Their attacks are effective if the cofactor h (the index of the main group in the supergroup) has many small factors—the attacker can then determine the victim's static key modulo these small factors and combine the results using the Chinese remainder theorem. This is often the case in the ordinary discrete logarithm setting where the main group is a subgroup of prime order q of the multiplicative group $\mathbb{Z}_p^*$. In practice, one may have $q \approx 2^{160}$ and $p \approx 2^{1024}$, and the cofactor $h = (p-1)/q$ may have many small factors.

In the elliptic curve setting, the cofactor h is typically very small, (e.g., $h \in \{1, 2, 4\}$ for the 15 elliptic curves in FIPS 186-2 [10]). In this case, the small subgroup attacks are not effective in determining private keys since an adversary has very limited choices for small subgroup elements and therefore can learn at most a few bits of the victim's private key.

Differential fault analysis. Biehl, Meyer and Müller [7] presented several differential fault attacks [9] on elliptic curve cryptographic schemes. The main observation in their attacks is that the usual formulae for adding points (in either affine coordinates or in projective coordinates) on an elliptic curve given by the general Weierstrass equation

$$y^2 + a_1 xy + a_3 y = x^3 + a_2 x^2 + a_4 x + a_6 \tag{1}$$

do not involve a_6. Similarly, the addition formulae given in IEEE 1363-2000 [12] for elliptic curves over prime fields with reduced equation

$$y^2 = x^3 + ax + b \qquad (2)$$

and for non-supersingular elliptic curves over characteristic two finite fields with reduced equation

$$y^2 + xy = x^3 + ax^2 + b \qquad (3)$$

do not involve b. Thus the addition formulae are the same for two curves of the form (2) (or of the form (3)) whose defining equations have the same a coefficient but different b coefficients. In the attack, the adversary sends a point Q that has small order l on some elliptic curve whose defining equation has a different coefficient b (but the same coefficient a) as the victim's elliptic curve. Now, if the victim does not check whether Q is a point on his elliptic curve, then the victim would proceed to compute wQ where w is her private key. Since wQ has order dividing l, subsequent use of wQ may reveal $w \bmod l$ to the adversary. By repeating the attack with points Q of orders l that are pairwise relatively prime, the adversary can eventually recover w by the Chinese Remainder Theorem. Biehl, Meyer and Müller [7] described their attack on the basic ElGamal encryption scheme which was already known to be insecure against active attacks.

4   Invalid-Curve Attacks

In this section, we combine the small subgroup attack of Lim and Lee and the differential fault attack of Biehl, Meyer and Müller to obtain attacks that are effective on the one-pass ECDH, ECIES, and one-pass ECMQV protocols if the receiver of an elliptic curve point does not verify that the point does indeed lie on the elliptic curve specified by the domain parameters. In essence, the attacks use the observations of Biehl, Meyer and Müller to extend the small subgroup attacks to elliptic curves different from the one specified by the domain parameters. We call these attacks *invalid-curve attacks*. We illustrate the effectiveness of such attacks on a key agreement protocol that was recently proposed for the IEEE 802.15 WPAN standard.

The invalid-curve attacks we are going to describe fail if the receiver of a point W checks that $nW = \infty$ by performing a point multiplication operation. We argue, however, that it is plausible that an implementor may have elected not to perform this operation. First, in the case where the cofactor is small, it is not known how small subgroup attacks on the one-pass ECDH, ECIES, and one-pass ECMQV protocols can be effectively mounted to determine static private keys and hence the check $nW = \infty$ might have been omitted. Second, an implementor may have elected to verify that $nW = \infty$ using a faster method, e.g., simply checking that $W \neq \infty$ in the case that $h = 1$ (and neglected to check that W is on the curve). Indeed, none of the ANSI X9.63, IEEE 1363-2000, IEEE P1363a, ISO 15946-2 and ISO 15946-3 standards mandate that public key validation be performed. ANSI X9.63 does mandate that *some* form of public key validation be performed, but this can include simply receiving the assurance (in some unspecified way) that the owner generated the public key itself using trusted routines; hence *explicit* public key validation as specified in Definition 1 is not mandated. We note, however, that some standards such as ANSI X9.63 specify a conversion routine from octet strings to elliptic curve points that explicitly verifies that the recovered point is on the elliptic curve. Thus, if public keys are represented using octet strings and these conversion routines are used, then the invalid-curve attacks we are going to describe are thwarted.

Definition 2 Let E be an elliptic curve defined over the finite field $\mathbb{F}_q$ with defining equation (1) in Weierstrass form. Then an *invalid curve* (relative to E) is an elliptic curve E' defined over $\mathbb{F}_q$ whose Weierstrass equation differs from E's only in the coefficient a_6.

Note that $E(\mathbb{F}_q) \cap E'(\mathbb{F}_q) = \{\infty\}$. If $Q \in E'(\mathbb{F}_q)$ and $Q \neq \infty$, then a private key w such that $Q = wP$ does not exist. We assume henceforth that the addition formulae used for E do not involve a_6. Hence, if $Q \in E'(\mathbb{F}_q)$, t is an integer, and the addition formulae for E are used in any point multiplication algorithm to compute $R = tQ$, then R is indeed equal to tQ as points in $E'(\mathbb{F}_q)$.

4.1 Invalid-Curve Attack on One-Pass ECDH

Suppose that one-pass ECDH is used by A to establish a shared secret k with B, and that k is subsequently used by B to send messages authenticated with a message authentication algorithm MAC to A. A selects an invalid curve E' such that $E'(\mathbb{F}_q)$ contains a point Q of small order l, and sends Q to B. B computes $K = w_B Q$ and $k = H(x(K))$. Later, when B sends A a message m and its tag $t = \mathrm{MAC}_k(m)$, A can determine the correct K up to sign[1] by finding a $K' \in \langle Q \rangle$ satisfying $t = \mathrm{MAC}_{k'}(m)$, where $k' = H(x(K'))$. Since Q has order l, the expected number of trials before A succeeds is $l/2$, whereafter A has determined $w_l = \pm w_B \bmod l$. Hence A knows that $w_l^2 \equiv w_B^2 \pmod{l}$. By repeating the attack with points Q (on perhaps different invalid curves) having orders that are pairwise relatively prime, A can eventually recover $z = w_B^2 \bmod N$ for some $N > n^2$ by the Chinese Remainder Theorem. Since $w_B^2 < n^2 < N$, we have $z = w_B^2$, and hence A can compute $w_B = \sqrt{z}$. Observe that B is unaware that the attack has taken place.

In many applications, such as email, the sender A will send its ephemeral public key R_A together with a message encrypted or authenticated with k. In this scenario, an invalid-curve attack similar to the one on ECIES described in Section 4.2 can be mounted.

4.2 Invalid-Curve Attack on ECIES

The attack on ECIES is somewhat more complicated than the attack on one-pass ECDH since the attacker A has to demonstrate possession of the shared

---

[1] Recall that two points on an elliptic curve have the same x-coordinate if and only if they are negatives of each other.

secret point K by producing the proper MAC tag t on the ciphertext c. As with the attack on ECDH, A selects a point Q of order l on an invalid curve E'. A then makes a guess $w_l \in [0, l-1]$ for w_B mod l and computes $K = w_l Q$ (instead of $K = r_B W_A$). A transmits Q (instead of R_A) to B, who computes $K' = w_B Q$. With overwhelming probability, the key k'_2 derived from K' satisfies $t = \mathrm{MAC}_{k'_2}(c)$ if and only if $w_l \equiv \pm w_B \pmod{l}$. If A is able to determine whether or not B accepted the ciphertext, then A is expected to determine $\pm w_B$ mod l after about $l/4$ iterations. As before, the attack can be repeated to recover w_B. Unlike the case of one-pass ECDH, the victim B may be aware than an invalid-curve attack on ECIES is being launched if he notices that he is receiving many invalid ciphertexts from A.

We comment that this invalid-curve attack on ECIES does not contradict its provable security since the protocol and proof in [1] assume that received points are always in the main group.

4.3 Invalid-Curve Attack on One-Pass ECMQV

As with one-pass ECDH, suppose that one-pass ECMQV is used by A to establish a shared secret k with B, and that k is subsequently used by B to send messages authenticated with a message authentication algorithm MAC to A. The attack on one-pass ECMQV is more complicated than the attack on one-pass ECDH since the victim B uses A's static and ephemeral public keys to derive the shared secret.

A selects an invalid curve E' such that $E'(\mathbb{F}_q)$ contains a point Q_A of small prime order l with $\gcd(l, h) = 1$. A selects Q_A as its static public key and obtains a certificate for it (see below). A next selects $T_A \in \langle Q_A \rangle$, $T_A \neq \infty$, such that $T_A + \overline{T}_A Q_A \neq \infty$, and sends T_A to B (instead of R_A). Since $T_A + \overline{T}_A Q_A \in \langle Q_A \rangle$, the point K that B computes is also in $\langle Q_A \rangle$. (If $K = \infty$ and B terminates the protocol then it must be the case that $s_B \equiv 0 \pmod{l}$.) As with the attack on one-pass ECDH, A can deduce $\pm s_B$ mod l. Repeating the attack gives s_B and $w_B = s_B (1 + \overline{W}_B)^{-1}$ mod n.

Certifying invalid public keys. Suppose that A wishes to have a point Q of (small) order l that is on an invalid curve E' certified by a Certification Authority (CA). In practice, as dictated by PKI standards such as [2, Section 2.3] and [22, Section 4], the CA does not validate Q. Rather, the CA performs a proof of possession (POP) of a private key test whereby A has to submit a signature generated with respect to Q on some message m of a predetermined format (perhaps chosen by the CA), and the signature is thereafter verified by the CA. We show that if the signature scheme used is ECDSA (Section 2.4), then A is able to generate a signature on m that is accepted by the CA. A does the following:

1. Select arbitrary $s, u'_2 \in [1, n-1]$.
2. Compute $e = H(m)$ and $u_1 = s^{-1} e$ mod n.
3. Compute $T_1 = u_1 P \in E(\mathbb{F}_q)$, $T_2 = u'_2 Q \in E'(\mathbb{F}_q)$, $V = T_1 + T_2$, and $r = x(V)$. (Note that V is computed using the addition formulae for E, and is in neither $E(\mathbb{F}_q)$ nor $E'(\mathbb{F}_q)$.)

4. Compute $u_2 = s^{-1}r \bmod n$.
5. If $u_2 \not\equiv u_2' \pmod{l}$ then go to step 1.
6. Output the signature (r, s).

A straightforward heuristic argument shows that the expected number of iterations of the main loop before A terminates is about l. The CA will accept the signature since $u_2 \equiv u_2' \pmod{l}$ and hence $u_2 Q = u_2' Q$.

4.4   Analysis

We first note that the restriction that a is fixed in equations (2) and (3) is without much loss of generality since approximately half of all isomorphism classes of elliptic curves over $\mathbb{F}_q$ will have a representative with the given a coefficient. Since the orders of elliptic curves over $\mathbb{F}_q$ are almost uniformly distributed among the admissible orders in the Hasse interval $[q + 1 - 2\sqrt{q}, q + 1 + 2\sqrt{q}]$ (see [19]), we can expect to quickly find an elliptic curve E where $\#E(\mathbb{F}_q)$ is divisible by a specified small prime l. Table 1 lists some elliptic curves defined over the prime field $\mathbb{F}_p$, where $p = 2^{192} - 2^{64} - 1$, that have points of small prime order l. This field is the smallest of the five prime fields recommended by NIST [10]. The curves in Table 1, and also the NIST curve over $\mathbb{F}_p$, all have $a = -3$ in their defining equations (2).

Let p_i denote the ith prime number, and suppose that the attacker uses points of orders $l = p_1, p_2, p_3, \ldots, p_s$. The attacker needs $N > n^2 \approx q^2$, so s should be the smallest positive integer such that

$$N = \prod_{i=1}^{s} p_i > q^2.$$

Let $T = \sum_{i=1}^{s} p_i / 4$. Then the attack on one-pass ECDH requires about s interactions (partial protocol runs) with the victim, and about $2T$ MAC computations by the attacker. The attack on ECIES requires about T interactions with the victim. The attack on one-pass ECMQV requires certification of about s invalid public keys, s interactions with the victim, and about $2T$ MAC computations by the attacker. The parameters s and T for the five NIST prime fields in FIPS 186-2 are presented in Table 2.

Optimizations of the invalid-curve attacks. By selecting larger primes p_i, the attacker in the one-pass ECDH and one-pass ECMQV scenarios can decrease the number of interactions with the victim at the expense of an increased number of MAC computations. The number of interactions with the victim can also be decreased by using elliptic curves having points whose orders are divisible by powers of small primes. Consider, for example, an implementation of ECIES using the NIST elliptic curve over $\mathbb{F}_p$ where $p = 2^{521} - 1$. Now, if p is a prime satisfying $p \equiv 3 \pmod{4}$, and if a is a quadratic residue modulo p, then it is known that the (supersingular) elliptic curve

$$E : y^2 = x^3 + ax$$

Table 1. Elliptic curves $E : y^2 = x^3 - 3x + b$ over $\mathbb{F}_p$ where $p = 2^{192} - 2^{64} - 1$ having points of small prime order l

b	l	$\#E(\mathbb{F}_p)$
7	17	6277101735386680763835789423152579575769728003507816940176
8	29	6277101735386680763835789423134254969503970241284573199712
12	7, 103	6277101735386680763835789423330235564423778417310050448358
20	11	6277101735386680763835789423241857284589896488855666951129
21	53,83	6277101735386680763835789423280657011091039330875664478827
24	109	6277101735386680763835789423333887568524621161433609724057
25	2,3,23,79	6277101735386680763835789423122144658648828167097184768836
28	131	6277101735386680763835789423268748257445578040429701148868
30	127	6277101735386680763835789423210775104109650069520558949736
31	37, 107	6277101735386680763835789423204441525191330010353698233123
32	43	6277101735386680763835789423258617709088937800879867650520
34	19	6277101735386680763835789423250038640299327488215705493600
35	41	6277101735386680763835789423231000109287096932320643629080
39	31	6277101735386680763835789423184749274510329350288277847727
40	5, 47	6277101735386680763835789423336243740890007819730551142808
42	97	6277101735386680763835789423100126242413526789909842794735
43	71	6277101735386680763835789423348140981991719874891656011856
59	13, 59	6277101735386680763835789423214305021449488084661039666632
68	101	6277101735386680763835789423152535895119425594340719306505
69	73	6277101735386680763835789423316686344024991599507825887793
74	89	6277101735386680763835789423207521611646327664801082254174
82	151	6277101735386680763835789423205224777875334437065750522006
104	139	6277101735386680763835789423352646215168136324998796285949
107	113	6277101735386680763835789423073056697678061416724633187404
119	137	6277101735386680763835789423312863477238674670518689754010
142	61	6277101735386680763835789423320128694158340103743426909958
166	67	6277101735386680763835789423259116488526354652819809060300
201	149	6277101735386680763835789423174207583130851129966653984609

over $\mathbb{F}_p$ has order $p + 1$ and $E(\mathbb{F}_p)$ is cyclic [21, Example 2.18]. For the case of the NIST prime $p = 2^{521} - 1$, we have $p \equiv 3 \pmod 4$ and $a = -3$ is a quadratic residue modulo p. Thus the group of $\mathbb{F}_p$-rational points on

$$E : y^2 = x^3 - 3x$$

is cyclic of order 2^{521}. This group can be used in the invalid-curve attack with the attacker iteratively querying the victim with points of order $2, 4, 8, \ldots$. Only about 521 interactions with the victim are needed, versus the 11548 interactions in Table 2.

Table 2. Attack parameters for the five NIST prime fields $\mathbb{F}_p$

prime p	s	T
$2^{192} - 2^{64} - 1$	61	1996
$2^{224} - 2^{96} + 1$	68	2548
$2^{256} - 2^{224} + 2^{192} + 2^{96} - 1$	76	3275
$2^{384} - 2^{128} - 2^{96} + 2^{32} - 1$	105	6735
$2^{521} - 1$	134	11548

4.5   Invalid-Curve Attack on a Key Agreement Protocol Proposed to IEEE 802.15

IEEE 802.15 is a working group developing standards for Wireless Personal Area Networks (WPANs) for short-distance wireless networks. A WPAN can be comprised of as many as 256 *devices*, one of which is designated by the devices as the *controller*. One of the controller's tasks is to consider requests from new devices to enter the network. If the controller approves the request, then it securely transports data keys to the device. The data keys can then be used by the device to securely communicate with other devices in the WPAN.

Bailey, Singer and Whyte [5] proposed the following key agreement protocol based on ECIES for this purpose. The elliptic curve chosen is the NIST curve over the prime field $\mathbb{F}_p$ with $p = 2^{256} - 2^{224} + 2^{192} + 2^{96} - 1$. Suppose that each legitimate device has a certificate for its elliptic curve public key. If a device A wishes to enter the network, it transports a session key k_A to the controller B using ECIES (and B's public key). Similarly, the controller transports a session key k_B to A using ECIES (and A's public key). Both devices now derive two shared keys from k_A and k_B, one of which is used in a key confirmation stage and the other to transport data keys.

The proposal [5] explicitly mentions that public key validation is optional. If validation if not performed, then a rogue device A, using some other device's public key certificate, can launch the invalid-curve attack for ECIES on the controller. Since B terminates the run of the key agreement protocol if ciphertext received from A is not valid, A easily learns whether its guess w_l for w_B mod l is correct. The roughly 3275 (see Table 2) interactions required with B is quite feasible given that the controller is expecting frequent interactions with the many other devices in the network. We conclude that the attack is very effective in this scenario.

5   Preventing Invalid-Curve Attacks

The simplest way to prevent the invalid-curve attacks is to check that a received point does indeed lie on the legitimate elliptic curve.

There are many other techniques that can potentially guard against the invalid-curve attacks. For example, one may use formulas for the addition law that use both coefficients a and b of the equation of the legitimate elliptic curve—it is then unlikely that the addition law is valid for any other elliptic curve. The invalid-curve attacks may also fail on some classes of elliptic curves that use special, faster forms of point multiplication. For example, the fast point multiplication algorithms [23] for Koblitz curves (elliptic curves whose coefficients belong to $\mathbb{F}_2$) repeatedly apply the Frobenius map $\tau : (x, y) \mapsto (x^2, y^2)$. If $Q \in E'(\mathbb{F}_{2^m})$ where E' is not a Koblitz curve, then $\tau(Q)$ is generally not in $E'(\mathbb{F}_{2^m})$. Hence the fast point multiplication algorithms with inputs an integer k and $Q \in E'(\mathbb{F}_{2^m})$ generally will not compute kQ.

6   Conclusions

We have presented invalid-curve attacks on some elliptic curve key establishment and public-key encryption protocols. The simplest and most effective way to prevent these attacks is to check that a received point Q indeed lies on the right elliptic curve. Preferably, the receiver should perform a full validation on Q. The attacks reinforce the importance of performing validation on public keys in protocols where a public key is combined with the receiver's static private key.

References

[1] M. ABDALLA, M. BELLARE AND P. ROGAWAY, "The oracle Diffie-Hellman assumptions and an analysis of DHIES", *Topics in Cryptology—CT-RSA 2001*, Lecture Notes in Computer Science, vol. 2020 (2001), 143-158. 213, 218

[2] C. ADAMS AND S. FARRELL, *Internet X.509 Public Key Infrastructure: Certificate Management Protocols*, RFC 2510, March 1999. Available from http://www.ietf.org. 218

[3] ANSI X9.62, *Public Key Cryptography for the Financial Services Industry: The Elliptic Curve Digital Signature Algorithm (ECDSA)*, American National Standards Institute, 1999. 214

[4] ANSI X9.63, *Public Key Cryptography for the Financial Services Industry: Key Agreement and Key Transport using Elliptic Curve Cryptography*, American National Standards Institute, 2001. 213, 214

[5] D. BAILEY, A. SINGER AND W. WHYTE, "IEEE P802-15_TG3 NTRU full security text proposal", submission to the IEEE P802.15 Working Group for Wireless Personal Area Networks (WPANs), April 22, 2002. Available from http://grouper.ieee.org/groups/802/15/pub/2002/May02/02210r0P802-15_TG3-NTRU-Full-Security-Text-Proposal.pdf. 221

[6] M. BELLARE AND P. ROGAWAY, "Minimizing the use of random oracles in authenticated encryption schemes", *Information and Communications Security*, Lecture Notes in Computer Science, vol. 1334 (1997), 1-16. 213

[7] I. BIEHL, B. MEYER AND V. MÜLLER, "Differential fault analysis on elliptic curve cryptosystems", *Advances in Cryptology—CRYPTO 2000*, Lecture Notes in Computer Science, vol. 1880 (2000), 131-146. 215, 216

[8] S. BLAKE-WILSON, D. BROWN AND P. LAMBERT, *Use of Elliptic Curve Cryptography (ECC) Algorithms in Cryptographic Message Syntax (CMS)*, RFC 3278, April 2002. Available from http://www.ietf.org. 213

[9] D. BONEH, R. DEMILLO AND R. LIPTON, "On the importance of checking crypto-graphic protocols for faults", *Advances in Cryptology—EUROCRYPT '97*, Lecture Notes in Computer Science, vol. 1233 (1997), 37-51. 215

[10] FIPS 186-2, *Digital Signature Standard (DSS)*, Federal Information Processing Standards Publication 186-2, National Institute of Standards and Technology, 2000. 212, 214, 215, 219

[11] V. GUPTA, S. BLAKE-WILSON, B. MOELLER AND C. HAWK, *ECC Ci-pher Suites for TLS*, IETF Internet-Draft, August 2002. Available from http://www.ietf.org. 213

[12] IEEE STD 1363-2000, *IEEE Standard Specifications for Public-Key Cryptogra-phy*, 2000. 213, 214, 216

[13] IEEE P1363A, *Draft Standard Specifications for Public-Key Cryptography — Amendment 1: Additional Techniques*, working draft 10.5, April 26 2002. Avail-able from http://grouper.ieee.org/groups/1363/tradPK/P1363a/draft.html. 213

[14] ISO/IEC 15946-2, *Information Technology — Security Techniques — Crypto-graphic Techniques Based on Elliptic Curves — Part 2: Digital Signatures*, draft, February 2001. 214

[15] ISO/IEC 15946-3, *Information Technology — Security Techniques — Crypto-graphic Techniques Based on Elliptic Curves — Part 3: Key Establishment*, draft, February 2001. 213, 214

[16] D. JOHNSON, Contribution to ANSI X9F1 working group, 1997. 211

[17] D. JOHNSON, "Key validation", Contribution to IEEE P1363 working group, 1997. 211

[18] L. LAW, A. MENEZES, M. QU, J. SOLINAS AND S. VANSTONE, "An efficient protocol for authenticated key agreement", *Designs, Codes and Cryptography*, to appear. 214

[19] H. LENSTRA, "Factoring integers with elliptic curves", *Annals of Mathematics*, 126 (1987), 649-673. 219

[20] C. LIM AND P. LEE, "A key recovery attack on discrete log-based schemes using a prime order subgroup", *Advances in Cryptology—CRYPTO '97*, Lecture Notes in Computer Science, vol. 1294 (1997), 249-263. 211, 215

[21] A. MENEZES, *Elliptic Curve Public Key Cryptosystems*, Kluwer Academic Pub-lishers, 1993. 220

[22] M. MYERS, C. ADAMS, D. SOLO AND D. KEMP, *Internet X.509 Cer-tificate Request Message Format*, RFC 2511, March 1999. Available from http://www.ietf.org. 218

[23] J. SOLINAS, "Efficient arithmetic on Koblitz curves", *Designs, Codes and Cryp-tography*, 19 (2000), 195-249. 222

Exceptional Procedure Attack
on Elliptic Curve Cryptosystems

Tetsuya Izu[1] and Tsuyoshi Takagi[2]

[1] FUJITSU LABORATORIES Ltd.
4-1-1, Kamikodanaka, Nakahara-ku, Kawasaki, 211-8588, Japan
izu@flab.fujitsu.co.jp
[2] Technische Universität Darmstadt, Fachbereich Informatik
Alexanderstr.10, D-64283 Darmstadt, Germany
ttakagi@cdc.informatik.tu-darmstadt.de

Abstract. The scalar multiplication of elliptic curve based cryptosystems (ECC) is computed by repeatedly calling the addition formula that calculates the elliptic curve addition of two points. The addition formula involves several exceptional procedures so that implementers have to carefully consider their treatments. In this paper we study the exceptional procedure attack, which reveals the secret scalar using the error arisen from the exceptional procedures. Recently new forms of elliptic curves and addition formulas for ECC have been proposed, namely the Montgomery form, the Jacobi form, the Hessian form, and the Brier-Joye addition formula. They aim at improving security or efficiency of the underlying scalar multiplications. We analyze the effectiveness of the exceptional procedure attack to some addition formulas. We conclude that the exceptional procedure attack is infeasible against the curves whose order are prime, i.e., the recommended curves by several standards. However, the exceptional procedure attack on the Brier-Joye addition formula is feasible, because it yields non-standard exceptional points. We propose an attack that reveals a few bits of the secret scalar, provided that this multiplier is constant and fixed. By the experiment over the standard elliptic curves, we have found many non-standard exceptional points even though the standard addition formula over the curves has no exceptional point. When a new addition formula is developed, we should be cautious about the proposed attack.

Keywords: Elliptic curve cryptosystem (ECC), scalar multiplication, exceptional procedure attack, exceptional point, side channel attack

1   Introduction

The scalar multiplication of the elliptic curve cryptosystem (ECC) is implemented using the addition formula assembled by arithmetics of a definition field. The addition formula involves exceptional procedures that cause an error (0^{-1} of the definition field) at the end of the scalar multiplication. Implementers should carefully deal with the exceptional procedures. Recently new forms of elliptic curves and addition formulas have been proposed, namely the Montgomery

Y.G. Desmedt (Ed.): PKC 2003, LNCS 2567, pp. 224–239, 2003.

form [OKS00], the Jacobi form [LS01, BiJ02], the Hessian form [JQ01, Sma01], and the Brier-Joye addition formula [BrJ02]. These new curves and formulas aim at improving security or efficiency of their scalar multiplications.

In this paper we study a possible attack using the error arisen from the exceptional procedures of the addition formula, called the *exceptional procedure attack*. Two points are called the exceptional points if they cause the exceptional procedure. The goal of the attack is to reveal the secret key d. The attack tries to produce the exceptional point of the elliptic curve E during the scalar multiplication by manipulating the base point $P \in E$ to the appropriate point $P' \in E$. If an error occurs in the scalar multiplication $d * P' \in E$, the attack can know a few significant bits of d depending on the underlying addition chain. A basic principal of the proposed attack is different from that of the fault based attacks [BDL97, BMM00] or the small subgroup attack [LMQSV98]. The fault attacks usually analyze the scalar multiplication $d * P^* \in E^*$ with the point P^* over the different curve E^*, which need a physical fault in order to generate a failure point P^*. The small subgroup attack performs a calculation of $d*P$ over the subgroup $\mathrm{Tor}(E) \subset E$ with small order, and the order of the elliptic curve must be divisible by a small integer. The exceptional procedure attack essentially requires neither the physical fault nor the curves with the small subgroup.

We first discuss the exceptional procedure attack against the standard addition formula. We observe necessary and sufficient conditions that two points are exceptional points, that is P_1 or P_2 is contained in the torsion subgroups of the underlying group. When the order of the elliptic curve is divisible by a small integer, the curve has several exceptional points. In other words, the curves whose order are prime are secure against the proposed attack, namely the recommended curves in several standards [ANSI, IEEE, SEC].

Next we analyze the exceptional procedure attack against the non-standard addition formula proposed by Brier-Joye [BrJ02]. This addition formula is designed for enhancing security of the scalar multiplication, namely resistant against the side channel attack [KJJ99]. Their exceptional points are two points $P_1 = (x_1, y_1), P_2 = (x_2, y_2)$, which only satisfy $y_1 + y_2 = 0$. Some of these points are non-trivial exceptional points. Especially, a point P is called the m-th collision point if two points mP, P are exceptional points. We show necessary and sufficient conditions that a point P is the m-th collision point. We demonstrate that there exist many m-th collision points over the recommended curves by the international standards [ANSI, IEEE, SEC]. Moreover, we analyze a possible attack against the plain ElGamal cryptosystem using the collision points.

The attack proposed in this paper is independent from the characteristic of the definition field. However, just for a simplicity, we only discuss prime field cases in the following.

2   Elliptic Curves

In this section we briefly review basic properties of elliptic curves. The standard addition formula and its variants over different coordinate systems are described. We then explain how the scalar multiplication provides an error.

2.1   Standard Addition Formula

Let $\mathbb{F}_p$ be a finite field with p elements, where $p > 3$ is a prime. Let E be an elliptic curve over $\mathbb{F}_p$ defined by Weierstrass-form equation

$$E : y^2 = x^3 + a\,x + b \quad (a, b \in \mathbb{F}_p, \ 4a^3 + 27b^2 \neq 0). \tag{1}$$

A point of E is uniquely represented as (x, y) that is the pair in the basic field $\mathbb{F}_p$. It is called the affine coordinate representation. A set of all points on curve E, including the point of infinity $\mathcal{O}$, is denoted by $E(\mathbb{F}_p)$. This set has a commutative additive group structure with the neutral element $\mathcal{O}$. We denote by $+$ the addition of the $E(\mathbb{F}_p)$. Especially we have $P + \mathcal{O} = P$ and $P + (-P) = \mathcal{O}$, where $-P = (x, -y)$ for point $P = (x, y) \in E(\mathbb{F}_p) \setminus \{\mathcal{O}\}$.

In order to algorithmically describe the addition rule arisen from the addition group $E(\mathbb{F}_p)$, we employ the arithmetic of the definition field $\mathbb{F}_p$, namely additions, subtractions, multiplications, and inversions. The addition rule is called the addition formula.

We explain the standard addition formula in the following. Let $P_1 = (x_1, y_1)$, $P_2 = (x_2, y_2)$ be points on $E(\mathbb{F}_p)$ that are different from $\mathcal{O}$. The standard addition formula calculates the point $P_3 = (x_3, y_3)$ of the addition $P_3 = P_1 + P_2$. The standard addition formula is as follows:

$$\begin{cases} x_3 = \lambda^2 - x_1 - x_2, \\ y_3 = -\lambda x_3 - \mu, \end{cases}$$

where

$$(\lambda, \mu) = \begin{cases} \left(\frac{y_2 - y_1}{x_2 - x_1}, \frac{y_1 x_2 - y_2 x_1}{x_2 - x_1} \right), & x_1 \neq x_2 \\ \left(\frac{3x_1^2 + a}{2y_1}, \frac{-x_1^3 + a\,x_1 + 2b}{2y_1} \right), & (x_1 = x_2) \wedge (P_2 \neq -P_1) \end{cases}$$

We remark that there are two formulas for (λ, μ) based on the condition of two points P_1, P_2. The first one is used for the case $P_1 \neq P_2$ and it is called ECADD. The second one is used for the case $P_1 = P_2$ and is called ECDBL. Note that the standard addition formula does not support the points P_1, P_2 with $P_1 + P_2 = \mathcal{O}$, $P_1 = \mathcal{O}$, $P_2 = \mathcal{O}$ for ECADD and $P = (x, 0)$ for ECDBL. It is called the exceptional procedure of the standard addition formula, because they require exceptional treatment in the formula.

2.2   Coordinate System

The standard addition formula described in the previous section is designed for the affine representation of points. It possesses one inversion of the definition field, which is relatively expensive in most computing environments. Fortunately the elliptic curve has different coordinate systems which do not need inversions. The projective coordinate and the Jacobian coordinate are examples [CMO98]. Using these coordinates we can avoid computing inversions in $\mathbb{F}_p$. In the following we represent the standard addition formula using the projective coordinate and the Jacobian coordinate, which are widely employed in elliptic curve cryptosystems.

In the projective coordinate, a point is represented by a tuple $(X : Y : Z)$, where two points $(X : Y : Z)$ and $(rX : rY : rZ)$ $(r \in \mathbb{F}_p^*)$ are identified as the same point. The curve equation is given by substituting $x = X/Z$, $y = Y/Z$ into (1). The identity point $\mathcal{O}$ is represented by $(0 : 1 : 0)$; this is the only point with its Z-coordinate equal to 0. Setting $x = X/Z$, $y = Y/Z$ in the affine equation, we obtain the projective Weierstrass equation $E_\mathcal{P} : Y^2 Z = X^3 + a\, X Z^2 + b Z^3$. The inverse of $P = (X : Y : Z)$ is $-P = (X : -Y : Z)$. Let $P_1 = (X_1 : Y_1 : Z_1)$, $P_2 = (X_2 : Y_2 : Z_2)$ and $P_1 + P_2 = P_3 = (X_3 : Y_3 : Z_3)$, then the addition formulas are as follows:

ECADD in Projective Coordinate $(P_1 \neq \pm P_2)$: $X_3 = vA$, $Y_3 = u(v^2 X_1 Z_2 - A) - v^3 Y_1 Z_2$, $Z_3 = v^3 Z_1 Z_2$ with $u = Y_2 Z_1 - Y_1 Z_2$, $v = X_2 Z_1 - X_1 Z_2$, $A = u^2 Z_1 Z_2 - v^3 - 2v^2 X_1 Z_2$

ECDBL in Projective Coordinate $(P_1 = P_2)$: $X_3 = 2hs$, $Y_3 = w(4B - h) - 8Y_1^2 s^2$, $Z_3 = 8s^3$ with $w = aZ_1^2 + 3X_1^2$, $s = Y_1 Z_1$, $B = X_1 Y_1 s$, $h = w^2 - 8B$

If $Z_1 = 0$, then $Z_3 = 0$ for both ECADD and ECDBL. Thus the point $P = (X : Y : 0)$ is the exceptional points of the standard addition formula using the projective coordinate.

The Jacobian coordinate system offers a faster computation of the addition formula. In this coordinate, a point on the curve is represented as a tuple $(X : Y : Z)$. Two points $(X : Y : Z)$ and $(r^2 X : r^3 Y : rZ)$ $(r \in \mathbb{F}_p^*)$ are identified as the same point. The identity point $\mathcal{O}$ is represented by $(0 : 1 : 0)$; this is again the only point with its Z-coordinate equal to 0. Setting $x = X/Z^2$, $y = Y/Z^3$ in the affine equation, we obtain the Jacobian equation $E_\mathcal{J} : Y^2 = X^3 + a\, X Z^4 + b Z^6$. The inverse of $P = (X : Y : Z)$ is $-P = (X : -Y : Z)$. Let $P_1 = (X_1 : Y_1 : Z_1)$, $P_2 = (X_2 : Y_2 : Z_2)$ and $P_1 + P_2 = P_3 = (X_3 : Y_3 : Z_3)$, then the addition formulas are as follows:

ECADD in Jacobian Coordinate $(P_1 \neq \pm P_2)$: $X_3 = -H^3 - 2U_1 H^2 + r^2$, $Y_3 = -S_1 H^3 + r(U_1 H^2 - X_3)$, $Z_3 = Z_1 Z_2 H$ with $U_1 = X_1 Z_2^2$, $U_2 = X_2 Z_1^2$, $S_1 = Y_1 Z_2^3$, $S_2 = Y_2 Z_1^3$, $H = U_2 - U_1$, $r = S_2 - S_1$

ECDBL in Jacobian Coordinate $(P_1 = P_2)$: $X_3 = T$, $Y_3 = -8Y_1^4 + M(S - T)$, $Z_3 = 2Y_1 Z_1$ with $S = 4X_1 Y_1^2$, $M = 3X_1^2 + aZ_1^4$, $T = -2S + M^2$

As we discuss for the projective coordinate, if $Z_1 = 0$, then $Z_3 = 0$ for both ECDBL and ECDBL. Thus the point $P_1 = (X : Y : 0)$ is the exceptional points of the standard addition formula using the Jacobian coordinate.

2.3   Scalar Multiplication

Let d be an n-bit integer and P be a point on the elliptic curve $E(\mathbb{F}_p)$. The scalar multiplication is to compute the point $d * P = P + P + \cdots + P$ ($d -$ 1 additions). This is the dominant computation of all ECC algorithms, including the encryption/decryption and the signature generation/verification.

The standard algorithm for computing the scalar multiplication is the binary method. Let $d = d[0]2^0 + d[1]2^1 + \ldots + d[n-1]2^{n-1}$ be the binary representation of the scalar d, where $d[n - 1]$ is the most significant bit of d and $d[n - 1] = 1$. Then the binary addition chain computes the scalar multiplication $d * P$ for given $d[0], d[1], ..., d[n-1]$ and point P as follows. We first assign $T = P$. For $i = n - 2$ down to 0 we compute $T = \mathrm{ECDBL}(T)$ and $T = \mathrm{ECADD}(T, P)$ if $d[i] = 1$. Finally T is returned as the value of the scalar multiplication $d * P$.

With the projective coordinate, a scalar multiplication $d * P = (x_d, y_d)$ of $P = (x, y)$ is computed as follows:

1. Set $(X : Y : Z) = (x : y : 1)$.
2. Compute $(X_d : Y_d : Z_d) = d * (X : Y : Z)$.
3. Convert $(X_d : Y_d : Z_d)$ to $(x_d, y_d) = (X_d/Z_d, Y_d/Z_d)$.

Note that if $Z_d = 0$ in Step 3, the conversion fails. Similarly, the conversion fails using the Jacobian coordinate if the Z-coordinate is zero in Step 3. Once the Z-coordinate of the projective (or Jacobian) coordinate becomes zero during the scalar multiplication, the error will be occurred in Step 3. The error is usually returned as the system error and we can observe that the exceptional procedure of the addition formula has caused during the scalar multiplication.

3   Exceptional Procedure Attack

In this section, we propose the exceptional procedure attack by using the exceptional procedure in the addition formula and we analyze its effectiveness for the standard addition formula. This section aims at proposing the general idea of the exceptional procedure attack using the standard addition formula. The analysis of this attack against the other addition formulas (or the addition formula for hyper-elliptic curves) strongly depend on their explicit formula. Details of the analysis for each addition formula must be independently considered. Indeed we deeply analyze the Brier-Joye addition formula in the next section.

3.1   Basic Idea

Let P be a base point of an elliptic curve E and d be a secret scalar. The exceptional procedure attack tries to reveal (part of) the secret key d. An idea of the attack is to produce the exceptional point over E, which causes an error $(0^{-1} \in \mathbb{F}_p)$ at the end of the scalar multiplication. The secret key d is guessed from the error of the scalar multiplication $d * Q$ for different base points Q of the curve E. For example the replacement can be accomplished by the chosen ciphertext attack. The attacker uses the scalar multiplication $d * Q$ for chosen point Q as a black box.

Base Point $Q \in E \longrightarrow$ | **Black Box of computing** $d * Q \in E$ | $\longrightarrow$ Error

In order to achieve this scenario, we assume the following two assumptions for our attack setting.

1. (Base Point Replacement) In the beginning of the scalar multiplication $d * P \in E$, the attacker can replace the base point P to another point Q of the elliptic curve E.
2. (Error Detection) The attacker can detect the error caused by the final inversion $(0^{-1} \in \mathbb{F}_p)$ of the scalar multiplication.

Instead of outputting the error $(0^{-1} \in \mathbb{F}_p)$, one can return 0 (or some other value) for Z-coordinate. However, one can still detect the error, because the returned point is not a correct value of the scalar multiplication $d * Q \in E$ and thus it causes an error of the cryptographic primitive in the decryption process.

One of the main theme of our attack is how to produce these exceptional points. We first investigate the occurrence criteria of exceptional points.

3.2   Exceptional Procedure in Standard Formula

We investigate conditions with which the standard formula has the exceptional procedures, namely the Z-coordinate of the addition $P_1 + P_2$ becomes zero. We consider the standard formula using the projective coordinate and the Jacobian coordinate.

First, we look at the standard formula using the projective coordinate. Let $P_1 = (X_1 : Y_1 : Z_1)$, $P_2 = (X_2 : Y_2 : Z_2)$ with $P_1 \neq P_2$. Then, from the standard formula using the projective coordinate, the Z-coordinate of the addition $P_3 = (X_3 : Y_3 : Z_3) = P_1 + P_2$ is computed by $Z_3 = v^3 Z_1 Z_2$ for $v = X_2 Z_1 - X_1 Z_2$. If $Z_3 = 0$, we have three cases, (1) $v = 0$, (2) $Z_1 = 0$, or (3) $Z_2 = 0$. Suppose $v = X_2 Z_1 - X_1 Z_2 = 0$. If $(X_2 = 0) \wedge (X_1 = 0)$, $P_1 = \pm P_2$. If $(X_2 = 0) \wedge (Z_2 = 0)$, $P_2 = \mathcal{O}$. If $(Z_1 = 0) \wedge (X_1 = 0)$, $P_1 = \mathcal{O}$. If $(Z_1 = 0) \wedge (Z_2 = 0)$, $P_1 = P_2 = \mathcal{O}$. Suppose $v \neq 0$. Then we have $P_1 = \mathcal{O}$ $(Z_1 = 0)$ or $P_2 = \mathcal{O}$ $(Z_2 = 0)$. These observations are summarized as follows: $Z_3 = 0$ iff $P_1 = \pm P_2$ or (at least) one of P_1, P_2 is $\mathcal{O}$. These points coincide the exceptional points in the standard addition formula except $P_1 = P_2$. If $P_1 = P_2$, we use the formula ECDBL. The Z-coordinate of $\text{ECDBL}(P_1)$ becomes zero iff $Y_1 = 0$ or $Z_1 = 0$ holds. We can compute all points P with $Y_1 = 0$ using the definition equation $x^3 + ax + b = 0$. This equation has solutions over $\mathbb{F}_p$ iff the order of the curve is divisible by 2.

Next we consider the Jacobian case. Let Z_3 be the Z-coordinate of the addition $P_1 + P_2$ using the Jacobian coordinate, where $P_1 = (X_1 : Y_1 : Z_1)$, $P_2 = (X_2 : Y_2 : Z_2)$ with $P_1 \neq P_2$. We have $Z_3 = Z_1 Z_2 H$, where $H = X_2 Z_1^2 - X_1 Z_2^2$. If $Z_3 = 0$, we have three cases, (1) $H = 0$, (2) $Z_1 = 0$, or (3) $Z_2 = 0$. By a similar calculation, we obtain the conditions of the exceptional points which are same as the projective case.

Thus, we have the following theorem.

Theorem 1. *The standard addition formula using the projective (or Jacobian) coordinate for computing $P_1 + P_2$ returns the zero Z-coordinate if and only if one of the following condition satisfies: (1)$P_1 + P_2 = \mathcal{O}$, (2)$P_1 = \mathcal{O}$, (3)$P_2 = \mathcal{O}$ for ECADD(P_1, P_2), or P has order 2 for ECDBL(P).*

3.3   Exceptional Procedure Attack against Standard Formula

We explain the exceptional procedure attack based on the exceptional procedure.

For the sake of simplicity, we assume that the scalar multiplication is computed by the binary method in section 2.3. The scalar multiplication produces the sequence $a_0 Q, a_1 Q, a_2 Q, \ldots, a_n Q$ for the given base point Q, which are generated by ECDBL and ECADD. a_0 is always 2 because of $a_0 Q = \text{ECDBL}(Q)$. Then $a_1 = 3$ holds if and only if the second most significant bit $d[n-2]$ is one. If the curve has the point Q with order 3, we can break the second significant bit $d[n-2]$ because of the error $3Q = \mathcal{O}$. Generally the information $a_i (i > 3)$ are able to provide the lower bits $d[n-3], d[n-4]$, and so on.

From Theorem 1, in order to cause the error in the sequence, the attacker has to find the point Q that satisfies one of the following condition (I) ECADD($Q, d_1 * Q$) $= \mathcal{O}$ for some integers d_1, (II) $d_2 * Q = \mathcal{O}$ for some integers d_2, or (III) ECDBL(Q) $= \mathcal{O}$. These cases are equivalent to the problems that find the $(d_1 + 1)$-th division points, d_2-th division points, and the 2-nd division points, respectively. The a-th division points are defined by the points Q that satisfies $a * Q = \mathcal{O}$. It is well-known that the a-th division points exist over the elliptic curve, if and only if $\#E$ is a multiple of a, where $\#E$ is the order of the elliptic curve E [Sil86]. The points with small order can be efficiently generated by the division polynomial. If the order of the curve is divisible by small integers, the curve involves the exceptional points.

The elliptic curves over prime fields recommended in the several standards has prime order [ANSI, IEEE, SEC]. In these cases there are no non-trivial division points and the exceptional point attack against the standard addition formula is not feasible. However, in the next section we show the exceptional procedure attack over the standard curves is effective against a non-standard addition formula from [BrJ02].

3.4   Relation to Other Attacks

Here we examine differences of our attack to other similar attacks.

The Fault Attack (FA) or the Differential Fault Attack (DFA) [BDL97], [BMM00], which is sophisticated from FA, are very similar to our attack. The attack model and the aim are almost same. FA/DFA use special points which are not on the curve. We show a simple example. The attacker changes the curve E and the base point $P \in E$ to E^* and $Q^* \in E^*$ where the order of E^* is smooth. The result of the scalar multiplication $d * Q^*$ is contained in curve E^*. Thus the attacker can easily recover the secret scalar d by the Pohlig-Hellman algorithm. However, these points are easily detected by checking whether the base point satisfies the curve equation of E or not. On the other hand, our attack uses points on the original curve. The checking process cannot reject the manipulated points. Another difference is the means of the attack. FA/DFA enforce bit errors from outside of the device, while our attack is able to be achieved by a chosen ciphertext attack and we don't need such physical tools.

Other similar attack is the Subgroup Attack (SA) [LMQSV98], which uses a special point on the curve whose order is small. For example, if we use the base point P with the small order $h > 1$, the possible values of the scalar multiplication $d * P$ are at most h. If the attacker can change the base point of the Diffie-Hellman protocol to the smooth order point, then the attack can guess the shared key by the brute-force attack with the size h. SA succeeds only when the order of the curve is divisible by small integer and, if the order is prime, SA has no effectiveness. When we use the standard addition formula, our attack is successful only when the curve has points of order 2. From this point, our attack seems weaker than SA. However, as we will discuss in the next section, our attack is successful for Brier-Joye's addition formula even if the order is prime, while SA has no effectiveness on this curve. Thus our attack is different property from that of SA.

4   Brier-Joye's Addition Formula

In this section, we investigate the security of the non-standard addition formula proposed by Brier and Joye [BrJ02]. The addition formula is designed in order to prevent side channel attacks [KJJ99]. It can computes both ECADD and ECDBL using only one formula. We do not have to switch pairs (λ, μ) of the addition formula depending on inputs. However the addition formula has non-standard exceptional points that have not appeared in the standard addition formula. We analyze these non-standard exceptional points and apply these points to the exceptional procedure attack described in the previous section.

4.1   Brier-Joye's Addition Formula

Let $y(P)$ denote the y-coordinate value of a point P.

Proposition 1 (Indistinguishable Addition Formula, [BrJ02]). *Let E be an elliptic curve over a finite field $\mathbb{F}_p$ ($p > 3$ a prime) defined by $y^2 = x^3 + a\,x + b$ and let $P_1 = (x_1, y_1)$ $P_2 = (x_2, y_2)$ be points on the curve with $y(P_1) \neq y(-P_2)$. Then (λ, μ) in the addition formula is given by*

$$(\lambda, \mu) = \left(\frac{x_1^2 + x_1 x_2 + x_2^2 + a}{y_1 + y_2}, y_1 - \lambda x_1 \right).$$

Brier-Joye also proposed an efficient algorithm to compute $P_1 + P_2$ in the projective coordinate system as follows:

Proposition 2 ([BrJ02]). *Let E be an elliptic curve over a finite field $\mathbb{F}_p$ ($p > 5$ a prime) defined by $Y^2 Z = X^3 + a\, X Z^2 + b Z^3$ (the projective coordinate system) and let $P_1 = (X_1 : Y_1 : Z_1)$ and $P_2 = (X_2 : Y_2 : Z_2)$ be points on the curve. Then, $P_3 = (X_3 : Y_3 : Z_3) = P_1 + P_2$ is given by*

$$X_3 = 2FW, \ Y_3 = R(G - 2W) - L^2, \ Z_3 = 2F^3, \qquad (2)$$

where $U_1 = X_1 Z_2$, $U_2 = X_2 Z_1$, $T = U_1 + U_2$, $R = T^2 - U_1 U_2 + a\, Z^2$, $M = Y_1 Z_2 + Y_2 Z_1$, $F = Z_1 Z_2 M$, $L = MF$, $G = TL$ and $W = R^2 - G$.

4.2   Exceptional Procedure in Brier-Joye's Formula

Let $P_1 = (X_1 : Y_1 : Z_1)$, $P_2 = (X_2 : Y_2 : Z_2)$, $P_3 = (X_3 : Y_3 : Z_3) = P_1 + P_2$ be points on the curve represented in the projective coordinate. If $Z_3 = 0$, from (2), we have three cases, (1) $Y_1 Z_2 + Y_2 Z_1 = 0$, (2) $Z_1 = 0$, or (3) $Z_2 = 0$. The latter two cases are reduced to trivial conditions $P_1 = \mathcal{O}$ or $P_2 = \mathcal{O}$. However the first condition is worth to investigate. The condition implies $y_1 + y_2 = 0$. If $P_1 + P_2 = \mathcal{O}$, we have $y_1 + y_2 = 0$, but this is not interesting. Conversely, even if $y_1 + y_2 = 0$, $P_1 + P_2$ does not always equal to $\mathcal{O}$. That is, we can pick up points P_1, P_2 such that $x_1 \neq x_2$, $y_1 + y_2 = 0$. Once such "exceptional points" are added in the scalar multiplication, we have $Z_d = 0$ and the conversion from the projective to the affine fails. In this case, we cannot obtain the correct result of $d * P = (x_d, y_d)$ and we can observe that an error has occurred in the scalar multiplication.

4.3   Finding Collision Points

Next, we discuss the criteria $y_1 + y_2 = 0$, which are exceptional cases of the Brier-Joye's addition formula. We call two points $P_1 = (x_1, y_1)$, $P_2 = (x_2, y_2)$ satisfy the *DZ condition* if

$$x_1 \neq x_2, \ y_1 + y_2 = 0$$

holds, and in this case, we call P_1, P_2 as a *collision pair*. The necessary condition for the DZ condition is $x_1^3 + a\, x_1 + b = x_2^3 + a\, x_2 + b$, namely $x_1^2 + x_1 x_2 + x_2^2 + a = 0$. From the condition we can generate a collision pair P_1, P_2, which satisfies the DZ condition. A point P is called the *m-th self-collision point* if P and $m * P$ is the collision pair.

We explain how to find a collision pair (P_1, P_2) in the following. For a given elliptic curve $E : y^2 = x^3 + ax + b$ and a base point $P_1 = (x_1, y_1)$ on the curve, determining whether P_1 has collision points or not is easy. For simplicity, we assume the order of the elliptic cure E is prime. If (P_1, P_2) is a collision pair, an intuitive relation of P_1 and P_2 is in Fig. 1. So, P_1 has collision points if the equation $x^2 + x_1 x + (x_1^2 + a) = 0$ has roots in $\mathbb{F}_p$ and this evaluation

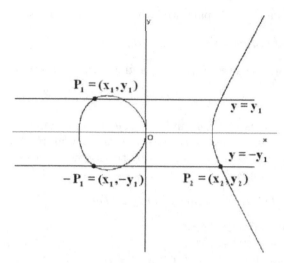

Fig. 1. A geometric relation of collision points

is done quite easily. However, we need a relation between P_1 and P_2 in the attack, namely we have to solve the discrete logarithm $P_2 = u * P_1$ on the curve (the *Collision-ECDLP*). This problem might be easier than the general discrete logarithm problem over elliptic curves because we have the constrained condition $x_1 \neq x_2$ and $y_1 + y_2 = 0$. However there is no evidence of the difference between these problems and this is an open problem.

Thus we have to change the approach. Assume we have an elliptic curve E and an integer m. The next approach is to find a point P_1 such that $(P_1, m * P_1)$ is a collision pair. Such P_1 satisfies a certain equation – the *self-collision polynomial*, which will be defined in the next section – and finding P_1 is equivalent to solve this equation. Roughly speaking, computing the m-th self-collision polynomial is not easier than computing the m-th division polynomial at the moment. However, computing the m-th self-collision points is feasible for small m, which are enough for our attack.

4.4   Self-Collision Polynomial

We discuss how to find the m-th self-collision points for a randomly chosen curve. We denote the m-th division polynomial as $\psi_m = \psi_m(x, y)$. If a point $P = (x, y)$ is in the m-torsion group, namely $m * P = \mathcal{O}$, then (x, y) satisfies $\psi_m(x, y) = 0$. Let denote $P = (x, y)$ and $m * P = (x_m, y_m)$. Then, x_m and y_m are written as in the following by the division polynomials [BSS99]:

$$(x_m, y_m) = \left(x - \frac{\psi_{m-1}\psi_{m+1}}{\psi_m^2}, \frac{\psi_{m+2}\psi_{m-1}^2 - \psi_{m-2}\psi_{m+1}^2}{4y\psi_m^3} \right). \tag{3}$$

If P and $m * P$ is a collision pair, we have $y + y_m = 0$ and so

$$F_m(x, y) = 4y^2\psi_m^3 + \psi_{m+2}\psi_{m-1}^2 - \psi_{m-2}\psi_{m+1}^2 = 0. \tag{4}$$

On the other hand, because of $y^2 = y_m^2$ and $x - x_m \neq 0$, we have

$$G_m(x, y) = (3x^2 + a)\psi_m^4 - 3x\psi_m^2\psi_{m-1}\psi_{m+1} + \psi_{m-1}^2\psi_{m+1}^2 = 0. \tag{5}$$

Here the two equations $F_m(x, y)$ and $G_m(x, y)$ have a common polynomial divisor $f_m(x, y)$. Small examples of $f_m(x)$ are in the appendix. A concrete relation between $F_m(x, y)$ and $G_m(x, y)$ is given by the following proposition. The proof is described in the appendix.

Proposition 3. *Let m be an integer $m \geq 2$. Then,*

1. $F_m(x, y) = 4y f_m(x, y)\psi_{m+1}(x, y)$,
2. $G_m(x, y) = f_m(x, y)f_{m+1}(x, y)$.
3. $f_m(x, y) = f_m(x)$, *i.e.* $f_m \in \mathbb{Z}[x]$
4. $f_m(x) = (m^2 - m + 1)x^{m^2-m} +$ *lower terms of x*

We call the polynomial $f_m(x)$ as the *m-th self-collision polynomial*. As in the above discussion, if a point $P = (x, y)$ is the m-th self-collision point, $x = x(P)$ should satisfy $f_m(x) = 0$. However all roots of $f_m(x) = 0$ does not lead to the points on the curve. So what we want is roots of $f_m(x) = 0$ such that $x^3 + ax + b$ is quadratic residue. Thus we have the following Theorem:

Theorem 2. *Let $P = (x, y)$ be a point on an elliptic curve. Then, $f_m(x) = 0$ iff P is the m-th self-collision point.*

Corollary 1. *Let $E : y^2 = x^3 + ax + b$ be an elliptic curve. Then, $f_m(x) = 0$ and $x^3 + ax + b$ is square iff E has the m-th self-collision points whose x-coordinate value is x.*

We made an experiment of finding the m-the self-collision points for small m $(2 \leq m \leq 9)$ using the polynomial $f_m(x)$. We used several standard elliptic curves in the draft of SECG [SEC]. Then we have found several m-th self-collision points. Therefore our proposed attack is feasible for several standard curves with the Brier-Joye's addition formula. These results are summarized in the appendix.

4.5 Attack to the ElGamal-Type Encryption

We shortly explain the exception point attack against the ElGamal-type encryption. The attacker chooses a k-th self-collision point Q on the underlying curve. The point Q is sent to the decryption primitive that computes the scalar multiplication $d * P$ using the secret key d. If the attacker receives the error from the decryption oracle, he/she knows the scalar multiplication has calculated the addition $Q + k * Q$.

We assume that the scalar multiplication is computed by the binary method in section 2. If the attacker wants to guess the 2-nd most significant bit, the attacker asks the 3-rd self collision point to the decryption oracle, which is computed during the scalar multiplication if and only if the second most significant bit is one. We can recursively apply this process to lower bits.

Note that the k-th self-collision point Q is not a division point such that $Q + k*Q = (k+1)*Q = \mathcal{O}$. Therefore the attack is feasible for the curves with prime order, namely standard curves [ANSI, IEEE, SEC].

5   Concluding Remarks

This paper studied the exceptional procedure attack that uses the exceptional procedure of the addition formula. We show the attack is effective against the addition formula proposed by Brier-Joye. Partial bits of the secret key can be revealed by our proposed attack. We demonstrated the feasibility of our attack against the recommended curves in the international standards [ANSI, IEEE, SEC] and found enough curves for which our attack works. However, the attack discussed in Section 4.5 is restricted to the ElGamal-type systems, in particular it is not relevant to ECDSA because the base point of ECDSA is usually fixed as the system parameter. An application to other cryptosystems will be our future work.

When a new addition formula is designed, the designers should be careful for the exceptional procedure attack. Even though the new formula is secure against previously known attacks, it might be insecure against the exceptional procedure attack or similar attacks based on the exceptional procedures in the formula. This attack can be essentially extended to the attacks against hyperelliptic curve cryptosystems. The security analysis of the attack strongly depends on their explicit formulas.

Acknowledgments

We would like to thank Marc Joye and anonymous referees for their valuable comments.

References

[ANSI]   ANSI X9.62, Public Key Cryptography for the Financial Services Industry: The Elliptic Curve Digital Signature Algorithm (ECDSA), draft, 1998. 225, 230, 235

[BMM00]   I. Biehl, B. Meyer, and V. Müller, "Differential Fault Attacks on Elliptic Curve Cryptosystems", *CRYPTO 2000*, LNCS 1880, pp.131-146, Springer-Verlag, 2000. 225, 230

[BiJ02]   O. Billet and M. Joye, "The Jacobi Model of an Elliptic Curve and Side-Channel Analysis", Cryptology ePrint Archive, Report 2002/125, 2002. 225

[BDL97]   D. Boneh, R. DeMillo, and R. Lipton, "On the Importance of Checking Cryptographic Protocols for Faults", *Eurocrypt'97*, LNCS 1233, pp.37-51, Springer-Verlag, 1997. 225, 230

[BrJ02]   E. Brier and M. Joye, "Weierstraß Elliptic Curves and Side-Channel Attacks", *PKC 2002*, LNCS 2274, pp.335-345, Springer-Verlag, 2002. 225, 230, 231, 232

[BSS99]   I. Blake, G. Seroussi, and N. Smart, *Elliptic Curves in Cryptography*, Cambridge University Press, 1999. 233

[CMO98]   H.Cohen, A.Miyaji and T.Ono, "Efficient Elliptic Curve Exponentiation using Mixed Coordinates", *Asiacrypt'98*, LNCS 1514, Springer-Verlag, pp.51-65, 1998. 227

[IEEE]   IEEE P1363, Standard Specifications for Public-Key Cryptography, 2000. Available from http://groupe.ieee.org/groups/1363/ 225, 230, 235

[IT02]   T. Izu and T. Takagi, "On the Security of Brier-Joye's Addition Formula for Weierstrass-form Elliptic Curves", Technical Report, No. TI-3/02, Technische Universität Darmstadt, 2002.

[JQ01]   M. Joye and J. Quisqiater, "Hessian Elliptic Curves and Side-Channel Attacks", *CHES 2001*, LNCS 2162, pp.412-420, Springer-Verlag, 2001. 225

[KJJ99]   C. Kocher, J. Jaffe, and B. Jun, "Differential Power Analysis", *Crypto'99*, LNCS 1666, pp.388-397, Springer-Verlag, 1999. 225, 231

[LMQSV98]   L. Law, A. Menezes, M. Qu, J. Solinas, and S. Vanstone, "An Efficient Protocol for Authenticated Key Agreement", Technical report CORR 98-05, University of Waterloo, 1998. 225, 231

[LS01]   P. Liardet and N. Smart, "Preventing SPA/DPA in ECC System using the Jacobi Form", *CHES 2001*, LNCS 2162, pp.401-411, Springer-Verlag, 2001. 225

[OKS00]   K. Okeya, H. Kurumatani, and K. Sakurai, "Elliptic Curves with the Montgomery Form and their cryptographic Applications", *PKC 2000*, LNCS 1751, pp.446-465, Springer-Verlag, 2000. 225

[SEC]   Standards for Efficient Cryptography Group (SECG), Specification of Standards for Efficient Cryptography. Available from http://www.secg.org 225, 230, 234, 235, 236

[Sil86]   J. Silverman, *The Arithmetic of Elliptic Curves*, GMT 106, Springer-Verlag, 1986. 230

[Sma01]   N. Smart, "The Hessian Form of an Elliptic Curve", *CHES 2001*, LNCS 2162, pp.118-125, Springer-Verlag, 2001. 225

A   Numerical Examples

In this appendix, we show numerical examples of polynomial $f_m(x)$ and the m-th self-collision points on standardized curves over a prime field in [SEC].

A.1   Self-Collision Points

Table 1 shows the number of the m-th self-collision points ($2 \leq m \leq 9$) on the elliptic curves standardized in [SEC].

Table 1. The number of the m-th self-collision points

m	2	3	4	5	6	7	8	9
secp112r1	2	-	-	2	2	-	-	2
secp112r2	-	-	-	2	-	-	2	4
secp128r1	-	2	4	-	-	2	4	-
secp128r2	2	-	-	-	2	-	2	2
secp160k1	-	-	-	-	-	-	-	-
secp160r1	-	-	-	-	-	-	-	2
secp160r2	-	-	2	-	-	-	-	-
secp192k1	-	-	-	-	-	-	-	-
secp192r1	2	-	-	2	2	-	4	-
secp224k1	-	-	-	-	-	-	-	-
secp224r1	-	2	4	-	-	2	2	2
secp256k1	-	-	-	-	-	-	-	-
secp256r1	-	-	-	-	4	2	-	-
secp384r1	2	-	-	2	2	2	-	-
secp521r1	4	-	2	-	-	-	-	-

In the following, the numerical data of self-collision points on the standardized curve secp128r1 are listed. All data are described in hexadecimal.

$$p = \text{0xfffffffdffffffffffffffffffffffff}$$
$$a = \text{0xfffffffdfffffffffffffffffffffffc}$$
$$b = \text{0xe87579c11079f43dd824993c2cee5ed3}$$

The 3rd self-collision points (2 points)

(0xa2b4652401379e1e3ff1f915e64ca2c8, 0xea7c93c0989bb3d2d4611a81df3032b)
(0xa2b4652401379e1e3ff1f915e64ca2c8, 0xf15836c1f67644c2d2b9ee57e20cfcd4)

The 4-th self-collision points (4 points)

(0xfc34bdc223c2601307ad0b8b21e1c8be, 0xc4e0ed0ac0db88cf58ee1806bc2621e)
(0xfc34bdc223c2601307ad0b8b21e1c8be, 0xf3b1f12d53f247730a711e7f943d9de1)
(0x28a53b1ca02fdb170f2330225b05cab6, 0xdfed12d13ceba387b3695ef16010f0f7)
(0x28a53b1ca02fdb170f2330225b05cab6, 0x2012ed2cc3145c784c96a10e9fef0f08)

The 7-th self-collision points (2 points)

(0x3e420615cdb89fc6b57989b0661d13a8, 0x23dc8dd9995872ba72a1cbccfbffe4ff)
(0x3e420615cdb89fc6b57989b0661d13a8, 0xdc23722466a78d458d5e343304001b00)

The 8-th self-collision points (4 points)

(0x95f75d5e09789632c30aa23aadebd9f7, 0xbe80ab797a9e63f4a687f081f670e439)
(0x95f75d5e09789632c30aa23aadebd9f7, 0x417f548485619c0b59780f7e098f1bc6)
(0x9a8034c28924315a96fc0a0c4f69c358, 0x9b3a46c0fcce148116e4be42bff777c9)
(0x9a8034c28924315a96fc0a0c4f69c358, 0x64c5b93d0331eb7ee91b41bd40088836)

A.2 Self-Collision Polynomial $f_m(x)$

Here are small examples of $f_m(x)$. The definition of $f_m(x)$ is in section 4.3.

$f_2(x) = 3x^2 + a$

$f_3(x) = 7x^6 + 11a\,x^4 - 4bx^3 + 13a^2x^2 + 20a\,bx + a^3 + 16b^2$

$f_4(x) = 13x^{12} + 70a\,x^{10} + 52bx^9 + 231a^2x^8 + 912a\,bx^7 + (100a^3 + 1536b^2)x^6$

$\qquad + 408a^2bx^5 + (43a^4 + 1776a\,b^2)x^4 + (-176a^3b + 1024b^3)x^3$

$\qquad + (54a^5 + 96a^2b^2)x^2 + (84a^4b + 448a\,b^3)x + a^6 + 48a^3b^2 + 256b^4$

$f_5(x) = 21x^{20} + 298a\,x^{18} + 828bx^{17} + 1917a^2x^{16} + 16224a\,bx^{15}$

$\qquad + (-360a^3 + 43920b^2)x^{14} + 3024a^2bx^{13} + (938a^4 + 88368a\,b^2)x^{12}$

$\qquad + (-31200a^3b + 42432b^3)x^{11} + (11484a^5 + 42768a^2b^2)x^{10}$

$\qquad + (-600a^4b + 113600a\,b^3)x^9 + (13794a^6 + 26928a^3b^2 + 101376b^4)x^8$

$\qquad + (45216a^5b + 127872a^2b^3)x^7 + (4312a^7 + 104496a^4b^2 + 252672a\,b^4)x^6$

$\qquad + (16464a^6b + 169344a^3b^3 + 129024b^5)x^5 + (225a^8 + 38160a^5b^2 + 276480a^2b^4)x^4$

$\qquad + (-1056a^7b + 28352a^4b^3 + 254976a\,b^5)x^3$

$\qquad + (138a^9 - 720a^6b^2 + 768a^3b^4 + 86016b^6)x^2 + (252a^8b + 1728a^5b^3)x$

$\qquad + a^{10} + 144a^7b^2 + 1536a^4b^4 + 4096a\,b^6$

$f_6(x) = 31x^{30} + 967a\,x^{28} + 5332bx^{27} + 10431a^2x^{26} + 162252a\,bx^{25}$

$\qquad + (-37737a^3 + 651744b^2)x^{24} - 233640a^2bx^{23} + (-2373a^4 + 1471536a\,b^2)x^{22}$

$\qquad + (-1775928a^3b - 458304b^3)x^{21} + (755427a^5 + 382896a^2b^2)x^{20}$

$\qquad + (-119844a^4b + 596928a\,b^3)x^{19} + (2161515a^6 + 6446544a^3b^2 + 7594752b^4)x^{18}$

$\qquad + (9080100a^5b + 22216320a^2b^3)x^{17} + (2480643a^7 + 39949488a^4b^2 + 69276672a\,b^4)x^{16}$

$\qquad + (13109904a^6b + 106820352a^3b^3 + 491673600b^5)x^{15}$

$\qquad + (1514205a^8 + 55841760a^5b^2 + 272943360a^2b^4)x^{14}$

$\qquad + (6809520a^7b + 124271232a^4b^3 + 347083776a\,b^5)x^{13}$

$\qquad + (705045a^9 + 34703328a^6b^2 + 295451904a^3b^4 + 1588222400b^6)x^{12}$

$\qquad + (482124a^8b + 62178432a^5b^3 + 527431680a^2b^5)x^{11}$

$\qquad + (491997a^{10} + 7532448a^7b^2 + 68961024a^4b^4 + 461328384a\,b^6)x^{10}$

$\qquad + (360276a^9b + 25187328a^6b^3 + 141441024a^3b^5 + 136445952b^7)x^9$

$\qquad + (273573a^{11} - 1545408a^8b^2 + 15061248a^5b^4 + 225533952a^2b^6)x^8$

$\qquad + (1294488a^{10}b + 827136a^7b^3 - 30200832a^4b^5 + 132857856a\,b^7)x^7$

$\qquad + (34569a^{12} + 2980080a^9b^2 + 11748096a^6b^4 - 40587264a^3b^6 + 20643840b^8)x^6$

$\qquad + (190728a^{11}b + 4920768a^8b^3 + 19031040a^5b^5 - 35979264a^2b^7)x^5$

$\qquad + (a^{13} + 486768a^{10}b^2 + 7898880a^7b^4 + 26443776a^4b^6 - 31260672a\,b^8)x^4$

$\qquad + (-5756a^{12}b + 511424a^9b^3 + 8380416a^6b^5 + 29884416a^3b^7 - 10747904b^9)x^3$

$\qquad + (313a^{14} - 3696a^{11}b^2 + 265728a^8b^4 + 4767744a^5b^6 + 18284544a^2b^8)x^2$

$\qquad + (572a^{13}b + 7040a^{10}b^3 + 135168a^7b^5 + 1622016a^4b^7 + 5767168a\,b^9)x$

$\qquad + a^{15} + 304a^{12}b^2 + 5888a^9b^4 + 61440a^6b^6 + 393216a^3b^8 + 1048576b^{10}$

B   Proof of Proposition 3

Proposition 3. *Let m be an integer $m \geq 2$. Then,*

1. $F_m(x, y) = 4y f_m(x, y) \psi_{m+1}(x, y)$,
2. $G_m(x, y) = f_m(x, y) f_{m+1}(x, y)$.
3. $f_m(x, y) = f_m(x)$, *i.e. $f_m \in \mathbb{Z}[x]$*
4. $f_m(x) = (m^2 - m + 1)x^{m^2 - m} +$ *lower terms of x*

Proof. The division polynomial ψ_m is a polynomial in $\mathbb{Z}[x]$ if m is odd, and $\psi_m/(2y)$ is a polynomial in $\mathbb{Z}[x]$ if m is even. 1. If a point $P = (x, y)$ satisfies $\psi_{m+1} = 0$, then P is the m-th self-collision. So, we have $\psi_{m+1}(x, y) | F_m(x, y)$. If m is odd, we have $4y^2 | \psi_{m+2} \psi_{m-1}^2$, $4y^2 | \psi_{m-2} \psi_{m+1}^2$ and $4y | F_m(x, y)$. It is the same for even m. 2. If $P = (x, y)$ is the $(m+1)$-th self-collision, then, $-P = (x, -y)$ is the m-th self-collision. So we have $f_{m+1}(x, y) | G_m(x, y)$. 3. If m is odd, $F_m(x, y) \in \mathbb{Z}[x]$. On the other hand, ψ_{m+1} can be factored into the form $2yg(x)$. So $f_m = F_m/(8y^2 g(x)) \in \mathbb{Z}[x]$. It's the same for even m. 4. We know $\psi_m(x, y) = mx^{(m^2-1)/2} +$ lower term of x, where we weight x as 1 and y as 3/2.

On Montgomery-Like Representations
for Elliptic Curves over $GF(2^k)$

Martijn Stam [*],[**]

Technische Universiteit Eindhoven
P.O.Box 513, 5600 MB Eindhoven, The Netherlands
stam@win.tue.nl

Abstract. This paper discusses representations for computation on non-supersingular elliptic curves over binary fields, where computations are performed on the x-coordinates only. We discuss existing methods and present a new one, giving rise to a faster addition routine than previous Montgomery-representations. As a result a double exponentiation routine is described that requires 8.5 field multiplications per exponent bit, but that does not allow easy y-coordinate recovery. For comparison, we also give a brief update of the survey by Hankerson et al. and conclude that, for non-constrained devices, using a Montgomery-representation is slower for both single and double exponentiation than projective methods with y-coordinate.

Keywords: ECC, Montgomery, point multiplication, Lucas chains

1 Introduction

Since the introduction of elliptic curve cryptography in the mid 1980s, many proposals have been made to speed up the group arithmetic. There are essentially three ways to achieve this: speed up the arithmetic in the underlying field (e.g., binary, prime, optimal extension fields [3]), pick a convenient representation of the group elements (e.g., affine, projective, Chudnovsky, 'mixed coordinates' [7]), or choose a short addition chain (e.g., non-adjacent form, Frobenius-expansions).

The effects of the three possible choices are certainly not independent as demonstrated by for instance [3, 7, 11]. This is in particular the case if the so-called Montgomery representation is used [21]. This representation was introduced in 1987 to speed up implementation of the elliptic curve integer factoring method, but has been relatively uncommon in cryptographic applications. For the Montgomery representation the general elliptic curve equation

$$E : Y^2 + a_1 XY + a_3 Y = X^3 + a_2 X^2 + a_4 X + a_6$$

---

[*] The author is sponsored by STW project EWI.4536.
[**] Part of the work was done while visiting BRICS, Center of the Danish National Research Foundation, Aarhus University, Denmark.

Y.G. Desmedt (Ed.): PKC 2003, LNCS 2567, pp. 240–254, 2003.

over any finite field is replaced by

$$E_M : BY^2 = X^3 + AX^2 + X$$

over finite fields of odd characteristic. Because of its intended application in the elliptic curve integer factoring method, the Montgomery representation was specifically designed to speed up the calculation of the x-coordinate of nP, for large integers n and points P on the curve E_M. Montgomery's representation is characterized not so much by the particular form of the curve-equation, but mostly by the facts that to add two points their difference must be known and that the y-coordinate is absent. Furthermore, the order of the elliptic curve group must be divisible by 4 [24]. These facts have to be taken into account when one tries to take advantage of the fast Montgomery representation based computation of nP in a cryptographic context. For instance, the divisibility by 4 rules out the so-called NIST curves [23].

It is well known that for most cryptographic protocols a y-coordinate is not really needed; for instance, in Diffie-Hellman it adds only a single bit and ECDSA [10] can be run with just x-coordinates. Nevertheless, if the y-coordinate of some point P is needed, it can be computed if P's x-coordinate is known along with the x-coordinate of some other point Q and both the x and y coordinates of $P - Q$. Whether or not these data are available depends on the way P is computed. In the Montgomery representation, and assuming P is the result of a scalar multiplication, P is computed using a second order recurrence in the x-coordinate known as a Lucas chain, because to add two points their difference must be known. If a binary Lucas chain is used the difference is fixed (and known), so that the y-coordinate can be recovered [21, 25]; it has the additional benefit that the addition cost can be reduced by choosing some of the denominators as one.

The difference is not fixed (and in general not known) if a continued fraction based Lucas chain is used. As a result it is no longer possible to recover the y-coordinate in an efficient manner, but such chains give rise to a very fast double exponentiation algorithm [20, 27]. Slower double exponentiation with y-coordinate recovery can be achieved using an algorithm due to Akishita [2].

For elliptic curves over fields of characteristic two, the traditional Montgomery representation based on the curve equation E_M does not work, because the curve isomorphism requires a division by 2. Adaptation of Montgomery's representation to fields of characteristic two based on the ordinary shortened Weierstrass form for non-supersingular curves is considered in [1, 17, 30], resulting in a reasonably fast single exponentiation routine without precomputation.

In this paper we further optimize the method from [17] by introducing an alternative curve equation. We show that it saves a finite field multiplication for general point addition.[1] Compared to [17] this leads to a speedup of about 15% for double exponentiation. Furthermore, we investigate the consequences for

---

[1] This situation is reminiscent of [6, 9] where Lucas chains are given for x-coordinates of general Weierstrass curves (including the NIST curves). It leads to relatively slow scalar multiplication. Optimization of those formulae leads to Montgomery's results

single exponentiation with precomputation, y-coordinate recovery, and two simultaneous exponentiations. Our methods apply to all non-supersingular curves over $\mathbf{F}_{2^k}$, irrespective of the group order.

The Montgomery representation is said to have three possible advantages: it is fast, requires only few registers in memory and can serve as a hedge against timing and power analysis attacks. From our results and comparison with other work, we conclude that in the binary case the Montgomery representation is not as fast as regular methods, both for single and double exponentiation. Furthermore, the fastest Montgomery representation approach to either type of exponentiation uses continued fraction based Lucas chains; as a consequence the protection against timing and power analysis attacks is lost. So, despite the fact that our results improve on previous results in this area, we conclude that the use of Montgomery representations for elliptic curves over binary fields can hardly be recommended, unless our results can be improved upon. Only if memory usage or timing and power analysis are of serious concern, the Montgomery representations regain their attractiveness.

In Section 2 we review the traditional way of doing elliptic curve arithmetic by means of projective coordinates. In Section 3 we review known Montgomery representations and introduce a new one, that requires one field multiplication fewer for a point addition. In Section 4 exponentiation routines suitable for the Montgomery representation are analyzed and compared. In Section 5 we present our conclusions.

2   Elliptic Curves over $\mathbf{F}_{2^k}$

Before discussing curves over $\mathbf{F}_{2^k}$, we briefly discuss field arithmetic of $\mathbf{F}_{2^k}$ itself. The additive group can usually be implemented using the exclusive or of two elements. The runtime of an algorithm is typically determined by the number of multiplicative operations required. There are three important multiplicative operations, namely squaring of an element, multiplication of two elements, and inversion of an element. Squarings are so cheap that they are not counted and inversions are so expensive that they are as much as possible avoided. The cost is measured by the number of $\mathbf{F}_{2^k}$-multiplications, and it is assumed that an inversion costs the same as 10 multiplications to ease comparison with [8].

2.1   Curve Definition

An elliptic curve over $\mathbf{F}_{2^k}$ is the set of points $(X, Y) \in (\mathbf{F}_{2^k})^2$ satisfying the long Weierstrass equation

$$E : Y^2 + a_1 XY + a_3 Y = X^3 + a_2 X^2 + a_4 X + a_6 \tag{1}$$

together with a point at infinity, denoted $\mathcal{O}$. The coefficients $a_i, i \in \{1, 2, 3, 4, 6\}$, are taken from $\mathbf{F}_{2^k}$. An elliptic curve forms an abelian finite group under the

---

from [21] with the same restriction on the curve group order (but slightly more freedom in the curve equation).

addition operation also known as the chord-tangent process. The point at infinity, $\mathcal{O}$, serves as group identity and the negation of a point (X, Y) is given by $(X, -Y - a_1X - a_3)$.

In the literature several constants related to the a_i are defined; we recall the following three:

$$b_8 = a_1^2 a_6 + a_1 a_3 a_4 + a_2 a_3^2 + a_4^2 ;$$
$$\Delta = a_1^4 b_8 + a_3^4 + a_1^3 a_3^3 ;$$
$$j = a_1^{12}/\Delta .$$

Here Δ is called the discriminant and the j stands for j-invariant. A curve is singular iff $\Delta = 0$; henceforth we will assume $\Delta \neq 0$. The j-invariant characterizes isomorphism classes over $\bar{\mathbf{F}}_{2^k}$: Two curves are isomorphic over $\bar{\mathbf{F}}_{2^k}$ if and only if their j-invariants are the same. A curve is supersingular iff $\Delta \neq 0$ and $j = 0$.

Often the long Weierstrass equation is replaced by the following short Weierstrass equation for non-supersingular curves over fields of binary characteristic:

$$E : Y^2 + XY = X^3 + a_2 X^2 + a_6 . \tag{2}$$

For every curve of the form (1) there is an isomorphic curve of the form (2). Moreover, if the extension degree k is odd, a_2 in (2) can be taken either 0 or 1. Hence multiplications by a_2 may be neglected. A curve of the form (2) has discriminant a_6 and j-invariant $1/a_6$.

We assume we are working in a cyclic subgroup of size q with generator P and $\log_2 q \approx k$. As customary we use additive notation for the group operation.

2.2   Curve Arithmetic

Throughout this article, we let P_i for $0 < i \leq 5$ be points on the curve and assume that $P_3 = P_1 + P_2, P_4 = P_1 - P_2$, and $P_5 = 2P_1$. Moreover, we assume that $\mathcal{O}$ is not among the P_i. This allows us to write $P_i = (X_i, Y_i)$ in affine coordinates or $P_i = (x_i, y_i, z_i)$ in projective coordinates, usually with $X_i = x_i/z_i$ and $Y_i = y_i/z_i$. Note that upper case characters are used for affine coordinates, and lower case ones for projective coordinates. The following relations hold (see e.g., [4]):

$$X_3 = \left(\frac{Y_1 + Y_2}{X_1 + X_2}\right)^2 + a_1\left(\frac{Y_1 + Y_2}{X_1 + X_2}\right) + X_1 + X_2 + a_2 \tag{3}$$

$$X_4 = \left(\frac{Y_1 + Y_2 + a_1X_2 + a_3}{X_1 + X_2}\right)^2 + a_1\left(\frac{Y_1 + Y_2 + a_1X_2 + a_3}{X_1 + X_2}\right) + X_1 + X_2 + a_2 \tag{4}$$

$$X_5 = \frac{X_1^4 + a_1a_3X_1^2 + b_8}{(a_1X_1 + a_3)^2} . \tag{5}$$

Fast arithmetic on elliptic curves has been well studied. A nice overview can be found in [8]. Skewed projective coordinates $(x/z, y/z^2)$ are the most efficient

Table 1. Expected number of field multiplications for point multiplication given a k-bit exponent

Type	Method	Given in [8]	Improvement
single	windowed NAF, $w = 4$	$5.8k + 60$	$5.6k + 60$
fixed single	fixed base comb, $w = 4$	$3.11k + 8$	$2.88k + 9$
semi-fixed double	comb+Montgomery	$9.11k + 40$	n.a.
semi-fixed double	Möller, $w = 4$	n.a.	$7.24k + 60$
double	Möller, $w = 4$	n.a.	$7.24k + 108$
double	Solinas	n.a.	$8k + 36$

representation known [16, 11]. Using skewed projective coordinates, a general additions costs 14 field multiplications. However, if one of the points is given in affine coordinates, this drops to 9 field multiplications. Doubling a point costs 4 field multiplications. King [11] notes that, if the resulting point of an addition is subsequently doubled, a multiplication can be saved at the cost of a squaring. For a large class of popular exponentiation routines, this effectively reduces the cost of an addition to 8 field multiplications.

2.3   Exponentiation (or Scalar Multiplication)

The survey [8] contains several exponentiation routines. Three different settings are examined: single exponentiation with a fixed base; single exponentiation with an arbitrary base and double exponentiation with one base fixed and the other arbitrary. This choice seems motivated by the facts that signature generation is a fixed base exponentiation and signature verification is a double exponentiation with one base fixed. However, with the introduction of fast point counting algorithms it becomes more realistic to deviate from the NIST curves, which is why we also consider double exponentiations with both bases arbitrary. Having a fixed base can ease computation by precomputing certain values.

For single exponentiation [8] proposes a windowed NAF with window size 4 (note that using Montgomery representation is reported to be faster). This results in approximately 1 point doubling and $\frac{1}{5}$ point additions per exponent bit. Moreover, 3 points have to be precomputed, namely $3P, 5P$, and $7P$. This has to be done affinely and costs 8 multiplications and 4 inversions. If the base is fixed, [8] proposes a fixed base comb of size 4. An exponentiation will cost $\frac{1}{4}$ point doublings and $\frac{15}{64}$ point additions per exponent bit on average. The number of precomputed points is 14. Note that this method does not exploit cheap point negation. The double exponentiation routine presented assumes one base is fixed and simply consists of two separate single exponentiation routines and multiplying the result (using a fixed base comb and Montgomery respectively).

A double exponentiation without any fixed bases is not addressed in [8]. However, using Solinas' trick, it will require 1 point doubling and $\frac{1}{2}$ point additions per bit of the longest exponent. Interestingly, this method already outperforms the double exponentiation routine with fixed base given in [8]. Möller [19] proposes to interleave two windowed NAF routines thereby saving one set of point doublings. For window size 4 this results in 8 points to be precomputed affinely and 1 point doubling and $\frac{2}{5}$ point additions per exponent bit.[2] Note that King's improvement does not apply in approximately $\frac{1}{25}$ of the additions. Of the 8 points to be precomputed, half can be done in advance if the base is fixed.

Table 1 summarizes these results. We give the number of field multiplications for a k-bit exponent, according to [8] and with inclusion of the known speedups just described. We use the same ratio, that one inversion costs the same as 10 multiplications. The extra costs needed at the end to convert back to affine coordinates are also included. For $k = 163$, compare with [8, Table 6].

3   The Montgomery Representation

The Montgomery representation was introduced as part of a speedup of the elliptic curve factoring method. Hence it was specifically tailored for curves over large prime fields. (Actually, over large rings $\mathbf{Z}_n^*$, where failure to invert would constitute a factoring success.) The connection with elliptic curve cryptography was made later.

We first review known methods of computing without y-coordinates for curves over binary fields. Interestingly, these methods are all based on a relationship for $X_3 + X_4$, hence the name additive Montgomery formulae. Next, we analyse methods based on a relationship for $X_3 X_4$, called multiplicative Montgomery formulae. The terminology additive and multiplicative method is also used in [9] for curves over large prime fields. We conclude with a small word on recovering the y-coordinate based on [17].

3.1   Additive Montgomery Formulae

Agnew et al. [1] mention computing with x-coordinates only for non-supersingular curves over large extension fields of characteristic two. By using the curve equation (1) it is possible to rewrite (3) as

$$X_3 = \frac{Y_1(a_1 X_2 + a_3) + Y_2(a_1 X_1 + a_3) + (X_1 + X_2)(a_4 + X_1 X_2)}{(X_1 + X_2)^2}. \qquad (6)$$

For X_4 a similar formula can be obtained by replacing Y_2 in (6) with $Y_2 + a_1 X_2 + a_3$, the y-coordinate of $-P_2$. This shows that

$$X_3 + X_4 = \frac{(a_1 X_1 + a_3)(a_1 X_2 + a_3)}{(X_1 + X_2)^2}. \qquad (7)$$

For the shortened Weierstrass form the above is simplified by setting $a_1 = 1$ and $a_3 = 0$. The projective version presented in [1] based on these formulae is incorrect.

---

[2] Apparently [8] and [19] use different definitions for window sizes. We adhere to the first.

In 1999 correct projective versions for non-supersingular curves appeared in [17] and [30], both using the short Weierstrass form. In both works the following formulae are given, easily verified by (7) and (5):

$$\frac{x_3}{z_3} = \frac{x_4(x_1z_2 + x_2z_1)^2 + z_4(x_1z_2)(x_2z_1)}{z_4(x_1z_2 + x_2z_1)^2} \; ; \tag{8}$$

$$\frac{x_5}{z_5} = \frac{x_1^4 + a_6z_1^4}{x_1^2z_1^2} .$$

Both [17] and [30] emphasize on an addition where the difference P_4 is fixed, and hence z_4 in (8) is set to 1. Such a fixed difference addition takes 4 field multiplications and 1 squaring.[3] It seems that for an ordinary addition one needs 6 field multiplications and 1 squaring. A point doubling takes 2 multiplications and, if $a_6^{1/4}$ is precomputed, 3 squarings.[4] It is also noted that having a small $a_6^{1/4}$ can reduce the cost of multiplication with $a_6^{1/4}$ considerably, and therefore of a point doubling. A similar argument holds for fixed difference addition if x_4 is small.

Affine versions are also presented, but not worked out in full since the inversions seem to deter. It is said that a point addition takes 2 multiplications, a squaring and an inversion, whereas a doubling takes one multiplication less.

3.2 Multiplicative Montgomery Formulae

Originally, Montgomery derived his formula for curves over large prime characteristic by multiplying X_3 and X_4, not by considering their difference. Not surprisingly, a multiplicative version of Montgomery's trick also proves possible for curves over binary characteristic. For a non-supersingular curve, taking $a_3 = 0$, one obtains:

$$\frac{x_3x_4}{z_3z_4} = \frac{x_1^2x_2^2 + b_8z_1^2z_2^2}{(x_1z_2 + x_2z_1)^2} \; ;$$

$$\frac{x_5}{z_5} = \frac{x_1^4 + b_8z_1^4}{(a_1x_1z_1)^2} .$$

In the short Weierstrass form a_1 will be 1, but b_8 can be any field element. Hence, computing x_3 and z_3 will take 6 field multiplications,[5] one less if P_4 is fixed and $z_4 = 1$. Setting $b_8 = 1$ will reduce these costs to 5 respectively 4 field multiplications, while at the same time keeping the costs for a point doubling the same. As an alternative, one could consider using the representation (x, z, xz). This requires the same number of multiplications though, so should therefore not be recommended.

---

[3] For some reason [30] report 2 squarings.

[4] And here [17] use 5 squarings, which is more than needed even without precomputation of $a_6^{1/4}$.

[5] Compute $(x_1z_2 + x_2z_1)$ as $(x_1 + z_1)(x_2 + z_2) - x_1x_2 - z_1z_2$.

If $a_3 = 0$, then $b_8 = a_1^2 a_6 + a_4^2$. Hence, $b_8 = 1$ can be achieved by setting $a_4 = 0$ and $a_6 = 1/a_1^2$. We therefore propose working on elliptic curves of the form

$$E : Y^2 + a_1 XY = X^3 + a_2 X^2 + 1/a_1^2 , \tag{9}$$

where a_1 and a_2 are in $\mathbf{F}_{2^k}$. To ensure we do not exclude any interesting curves we present the following lemma.

Lemma 1 *Any non-supersingular curve over $\mathbf{F}_{2^k}$ is isomorphic to a curve over $\mathbf{F}_{2^k}$ of the form (9).*

Proof. Recall that all non-supersingular curves have a representation of the form (2), having j-invariant $1/a_6$. A curve of the form (9) has j-invariant equal to a_1^8. Squaring is a permutation on $\mathbf{F}_{2^k}$ whence all elements have a unique eighth root in $\mathbf{F}_{2^k}$. Set $a_1 = a_6^{-1/8}$ and let $s \in \mathbf{F}_{2^k}$. Consider the admissible change of variables given by

$$x = X/a_1^2,$$
$$y = sX/a_1^2 + Y/a_1^3 .$$

This gives an isomorphism over $\mathbf{F}_{2^k}$ of the curve given by (2) and

$$1/a_1^2 + a_1^2(a_2 + s + s^2)x^2 + x^3 - a_1xy + y^2 . \tag{10}$$

It is easily verified that (10) is of the form (9).

3.3   Recovery of the y-Coordinate

The curve equation provides a way to determine the y-coordinate of a given point using a square root computation. This method is relatively expensive and one still needs to address the square root ambiguity. An alternative is presented in [17]. If two points P_1 and P_2 are given by x-coordinate only and their difference P_4 is fully specified, either unknown y-coordinate can be retrieved in a small number of field multiplications. Moreover, there is no square root ambiguity. The method from [17] to recover the y-coordinate is described in more detail below (slightly generalized).

Given X_1, X_2, X_4 and Y_4, it is possible to determine Y_2 efficiently. From formula (3) it follows how to determine Y_1 if X_1, X_2, X_3 and Y_2 are given, by using the curve equation (1) to get rid of the quadratic term Y_1^2. However, since the values $(P, Q, P - Q)$ have the same additive relation to each other as the values $(P + Q, P, Q)$, the desired result follows from a suitable re-indexing:

$$Y_1 = \frac{(X_2 + X_4)(a_4 + X_2 X_4 + X_1 X_2 + X_1 X_4) + (a_3 + a_1 X_2)Y_4}{a_3 + a_1 X_4} .$$

Note that $a_3 + a_1 X_4 = 0$ iff $P_4 = \mathcal{O}$, which we assumed not to be the case.

For $a_3 = 0$ and $a_4 = 0$ and projective coordinates, the formula in [17] can be generalized to

$$X_1 = \frac{a_1 z_4 x_4 z_2 x_1}{a_1 z_4 x_4 z_2 z_1} \; ; \tag{11a}$$

$$Y_1 = y_4 + \frac{(x_2 z_4 + x_4 z_2)((x_1 z_4 + x_4 z_1)(x_2 z_4 + x_4 z_2) + z_1 z_2 x_4^2 + a_1 z_1 z_2 z_4 y_4)}{a_1 z_1 z_2 x_4 z_4} \; . \tag{11b}$$

Simultaneous recovery of X_1 and Y_1 will therefore cost at most 15 multiplications and 1 inversion. If $z_4 = 1$, this reduces to 11 multiplications and 1 inversion. A further reduction to 10 multiplications and 1 inversion is achieved if $a_1 = 1$, which is the case for the shortened Weierstrass form.

4   Exponentiation, Aka Scalar Multiplication

4.1   Lucas Chains

Suppose we are given a point P and we want to determine nP, where n is a random element in $\mathbf{Z}_q$. Using a traditional curve representation this can efficiently be done using short addition-subtraction chains. An addition-subtraction chain for an integer $n > 0$ is a sequence $a_0, a_1, \ldots, a_l$ with $a_0 = 1, a_l = n$ and for all $0 < k \leq l$ there should exist $0 \leq i, j < k$ such that $a_k = a_i + a_j$ or $a_k = a_i - a_j$. There is extensive literature concerning addition chains [12] and addition-subtraction chains.

Using the Montgomery form allows us to add two points only if their difference is known. Let R_1 and R_2 be two points in the same cyclic subgroup generated by P. Without loss of generality the points can be denoted $R_1 = \kappa P$ en $R_2 = \lambda P$, their difference is $(\kappa - \lambda)P$ and their sum $(\kappa + \lambda)P$. The computation of a scalar multiple nP of P requires as intermediate values $a_0 P, a_1 P, \ldots, a_l P$ with $a_0 = 1, a_l = n$, and for all $0 < k \leq l$ there should be $0 \leq i, j < k$ such that $a_k = a_i + a_j$ and $a_i - a_j$ occurs somewhere in the chain before a_k. Such a chain is known as a Lucas chain. Although Lucas chains are much less studied than addition chains there is some literature concerning them [20, 5].

There are two types of Lucas chains, those based on a binary algorithm and those based on the extended Euclidean algorithm.

4.2   The Binary Algorithm

Single Exponentiation For ordinary exponentiation the square-and-multiply algorithm (here double-and-add) is very well known. Let $n = \sum_{i=0}^{k-1} n_i 2^i$ be an exponent and let $a = \sum_{i=j}^{k-1} n_i 2^{i-j}$ and $A = aP$ be invariant. Initialization with $j = k, a = 0$, and $A = \mathcal{O}$ poses no problems and if $j = 0$ we also have $a = n$ and hence $A = nP$ as required. Decreasing j by 1 requires replacing a by $2a + n_{j-1}$ to maintain the invariant. For A this constitutes a point doubling and, depending on whether the bit n_{j-1} is set or not, addition by P.

The binary algorithm for addition chains can easily be adapted[6] for Lucas chains if the invariant is strengthened with $b = a + 1$ and $B = bP$. Decreasing j by 1 requires replacing (a, b) by $(2a + 1, 2a + 2) = (a + b, 2b)$ if the bit n_{j-1} is set and by $(2a, 2 + 1) = (2a, a + b)$ otherwise. Note that A and B have P as known fixed difference and hence can be added.

Contrary to the binary algorithm for addition chains, in this algorithm the operations performed per step do not depend on the value of the exponent bit. This property can serve as a hedge against timing and power analysis [6, 9]. It also implies that the algorithm always requires one doubling and one fixed difference addition on the curve. In both the old and the new representation this adds up to 6 multiplications in $\mathbf{F}_{2^k}$ per exponent bit.

The binary algorithm produces not only nP, but also $(n+1)P$. Assuming that the y-coordinate of P was also known, it is easy to reconstruct the y-coordinate of nP as well, according to (11).

Double Exponentiation For ordinary addition chains there is a generalization of the binary method to multi-exponentiation due to Straus [28]. For double exponentiation, i.e., the problem of determining $nP + mQ$ given n, m, P, and Q, this method is known as Shamir's trick. Basically, one starts with $A = \mathcal{O}$ and reads both exponents from left to right simultaneously. In a single step first compute $2A$ and depending on the two bits being read, add in either nothing, P, Q, or $P + Q$.

This technique can also be exploited for Lucas-chains, as shown by Schoenmakers [26]. In this case, not only A has to be recorded, but also $A + P$ and $A + Q$ (not $A + P + Q$, since then any efficiency gain is lost). Unless both bits are set, a step will cost one point doubling and two fixed difference additions. If both bits are set a step will cost three fixed difference additions and two ordinary additions. Using the new curve representation, a double exponentiation will on average cost 13 field multiplications per exponent bit. The relatively expensive ordinary additions make this method more expensive than the straightforward method of using two single exponentiations, recovering the y-coordinates and adding the two, costing 12 field multiplications per exponent bit.

Nevertheless, an improvement to the above is possible, due to Akishita [2]. By doing some lookahead, the cost of the most expensive step is reduced to three fixed difference additions. As a result, one step takes on average $2\frac{1}{4}$ fixed difference additions and $\frac{3}{4}$ doublings. A double exponentiation will then cost 10.5 field multiplications per bit exponent for both the old and the new representation.

4.3   Montgomery's Euclidean Algorithm

Double Exponentiation The algorithm below first appeared as a single exponentiation routine in [20] under the name PRAC, the adaptation to double exponentiation was pointed to in [22]. Let R_1 and R_2 be two points in the same

---

[6] It is unclear who should receive credit for this adaptation, possibly Lehmer [15].

Table 2. Substitution rules for Montgomery's Euclidean Lucas algorithm

No.	Condition	Substitution(d, e)	Costs	Dual costs
M1	$d \leq \frac{5}{4}e, d \equiv -e \mod 3$	$((2d - e)/3, (2e - d)/3)$	3α	3α
M2	$d \leq \frac{5}{4}e, d \equiv e \mod 6$	$((d - e)/2, e)$	$\alpha + \delta$	$2\alpha + \delta$
M3	$d \leq 4e$	$(d - e, e)$	α	α
M4	$d \equiv e \mod 2$	$((d - e)/2, e)$	$\alpha + \delta$	$2\alpha + \delta$
M5	$d \equiv 0 \mod 2$	$(d/2, e)$	$\alpha + \delta$	$\alpha + \delta$
M6	$d \equiv 0 \mod 3$	$(d/3 - e, e)$	$3\alpha + \delta$	$4\alpha + \delta$
M7	$d \equiv -e \mod 3$	$((d - 2e)/3, e)$	$3\alpha + \delta$	4α
M8	$d \equiv e \mod 3$	$((d - e)/3, e)$	$3\alpha + \delta$	$3\alpha + \delta$
M9	$e \equiv 0 \mod 2$	$(d, e/2)$	$\alpha + \delta$	$\alpha + \delta$

order q subgroup generated by P. There exist unique κ and λ in $\mathbf{Z}_q$ satisfying $R_1 = \kappa P$ and $R_2 = \lambda P$. Given two exponents n and m, one faces the task of computing $nR_1 + mR_2 = (n\kappa + m\lambda)P$. Introduce auxiliary variables a, b, d and e and auxiliary points A, B and C. The variables a and b are kept only for explanatory purposes and should not be implemented (hence κ and λ need not be known). Keep as invariant $A = aP, B = bP$, and $C = A - B$, as well as $0 < d \leq e, ad + be = n\kappa + m\lambda$ and $\gcd(d, e) = \gcd(n, m)$. This invariant can be initialized with $a = \kappa, b = \lambda, d = n, e = m$, and accordingly $A = \kappa P$ and $B = \lambda P$. In the main body of the algorithm, the pair (d, e) is decreased step by step, until eventually both d and e equal the greatest common divisor of n and m. At this point $d(A + B) = nR_1 + mR_2$, so a single exponentiation routine should be called to perform the scalar multiplication $d(A + B)$.

Table 2 contains the list of substitutions for (d, e) proposed by Montgomery. One is supposed to perform the first applicable rule from the table. The costs per step are denoted in point additions (α) and point doublings (δ). As an alternative the ternary steps (M1, M2, M6, M7, and M8) can be left out to simplify the algorithm.

Simulation shows that a double exponentiation with two k-bit exponents takes on average slightly less than 1.5 ordinary additions and 0.5 doublings per exponent bit. Using the additive Montgomery version, this would yield 10 field multiplications per exponent bit for a double exponentiation. Using the new multiplicative representation, a double exponentiation costs only 8.5 field multiplications per exponent bit.

As always, single exponentiation can be sped up by precomputing $2^{k/2}P$, effectively transforming a k-bit single exponentiation into a $k/2$-bit double exponentiation. The result is a single exponentiation routine taking, on average, 4.2 field multiplications per exponent bit. A minor detail is that $(2^{k/2} - 1)P$ is also required, being the difference between $2^{k/2}P$ and P. Fortunately, the binary algorithm returns both. Variations with other values instead of $2^{k/2}$ are possible.

Single Exponentiation without Precomputation Although the algorithm in [20] actually describes a double exponentiation, it was only used there for sin-

Table 3. Overview of asymptotic costs of scalar multiplication based on Montgomery representation

	Y	General	Old	New
Single exponentiation				
Binary	Yes	$\dot\alpha + \delta$	6	6
Montgomery	No	$1.5\alpha + 0.25\delta$	9.5	8
Precomp. Montgomery	No	$0.75\alpha + 0.25\delta$	5	4.3
Double exponentiation				
Schoenmakers	Yes	$\frac{3}{4}(2\dot\alpha + \delta) + \frac{1}{4}(3\dot\alpha + 2\alpha)$	13.5	13
Akishita	Yes	$\frac{3}{4}(2\dot\alpha + \delta) + \frac{3}{4}\dot\alpha$	10.5	10.5
Montgomery	No	$1.5\alpha + 0.5\delta$	10	8.5
Twofold exponentiation				
Montgomery	No	$1.5\alpha + 0.5\delta$	10	8.5

gle exponentiations by computing nP as $(n - r)P + rP$. Montgomery proposed setting $(n - r)/r \approx \phi$, where $\phi = \frac{1+\sqrt{5}}{2}$ is the golden ratio. This will result in $\log_\phi \sqrt{n}$ Fibonacci steps (type M3) costing one ordinary addition each, which will be followed by what looks like a random double exponentiation with exponents of magnitude about $\sqrt{n}$ [27]. Putting the pieces together, this results in approximately 8 field multiplications per exponent bit using the new representation and 9.5 field multiplications using the old. This difference is completely irrelevant, since both are outperformed by the binary algorithm (Section 4.2): it is both faster and easier; moreover it allows easy recovery of the y-coordinate and helps to thwart timing and power analysis.

Twofold Exponentiation Montgomery's algorithm can also be used to compute both nP and mP at the same time for relatively low costs by reversing the order. More precisely, go through the entire algorithm, but only keeping track of d and e. At the end, $d = 1$ and $e = 1$. Now work your way back up to $d = n$ and $e = m$ by performing the inverse of each step, but also keeping as invariant $D = dP, E = eP$, and $C = D - E$. Initialization is easy and when $(d, e) = (n, m)$ the pair (D, E) gives the desired powers. The only point of concern is whether the steps can be performed backwards. Inspection of the 9 steps shows this is indeed possible. In Table 2 the costs for performing a step backwards are listed under 'dual costs', referring to the notion of duality for addition chains [14]. Note that the costs for a step and its dual are not always the same.

Tsuruoka [29] gives a recursive version of the dual algorithm, but does not seem to realize that his algorithm is actually Montgomery's dual. Tsuruoka gives a slightly different set of transformation rules (even when taking into account duality), giving a negligible speedup (fine-tuning Montgomery's algorithm is a rather complicated business, as demonstrated by [27, Appendix A]).

Summary In Table 3 an overview is given of the various methods based on Montgomery representation. Once again, α stands for a point addition and δ

for a point doubling. The notation $\dot{\alpha}$ is used for a point addition with a fixed difference, since these are cheaper. Old refers to [17] and [30]'s additive version, new refers to the multiplicative version presented in this paper. The column Y denotes whether easy y-coordinate recovery using (11) is possible or not.

5   Conclusion

Comparing Table 1 with Table 3 shows that the Montgomery representation is considerably slower than traditional methods, both for single and for double exponentiation. However, for single exponentiation using the Montgomery form can still have two advantages. First of all, the uniformity of the steps in the binary algorithm provides a hedge against timing and power analysis. Using ordinary projective in conjunction with the Lucas binary algorithm is substantially slower. Secondly, the Montgomery method requires less memory during a computation.

For double exponentiation timing and power analysis are seldom of any concern, but if they were, the fast double exponentiation routines by Akishita and Montgomery would not provide a hedge. Of course one could run two single exponentiations, recover the y-coordinates and add the result. As for memory requirements, here the Montgomery representation clearly stands out. During computation three points have to be stored, each consisting of two $\mathbf{F}_{2^k}$-elements. Moreover d and e, elements in $\mathbf{Z}_q$, need to be stored. All in all $8k$ bits. On the other hand, Solinas' method precomputes four points of two $\mathbf{F}_{2^k}$-elements each (this includes the two bases). During computation, one point of three $\mathbf{F}_{2^k}$-elements is used. The exponents need to be recoded and stored as well. In total, this costs $13k$ bits. The method based on interleaving two windowed NAFs requires even more memory.

Acknowledgements

The author would like to thank Arjen K. Lenstra for his encouragement, advice, and careful reading of several early drafts, Berry Schoenmakers for fruitful discussions and his kind permission of inclusion of his method, and Peter Beelen and an anonymous referee for useful comments.

References

[1] G. Agnew, R. Mullin, and S. Vanstone. An implementation of elliptic curve cryptosystems over $F_{2^{155}}$. *IEEE J-SAC*, 11(5):804–813, 1993. 241, 245

[2] T. Akishita. Fast simultaneous scalar multiplication on elliptic curve with Montgomery form. *SAC'01*, LNCS **2259**, pages 255–268. 241, 249

[3] D. Bailey and C. Paar. Efficient arithmetic in finite field extensions with application in elliptic curve cryptography. *Journal of Cryptology*, 14(3):153–176, 2001. 240

[4] I. Blake, G. Seroussi, and N. Smart. *Elliptic Curves in Cryptography*. Cambridge University Press, 1999. 243

[5] D. Bleichenbacher. *Efficiency and Security of Cryptosystems based on Number Theory*. PhD thesis, ETH Zürich, 1996. 248

[6] É. Brier and M. Joye. Weierstraß elliptic curves and side-channel attacks. *PKC'02*, LNCS **2274**, pages 335–345. 241, 249

[7] H. Cohen, A. Miyaji, and T. Ono. Efficient elliptic curve exponentiation using mixed coordinates. *Asiacrypt'98*, LNCS **1514**, pages 51–65. 240

[8] D. Hankerson, J. López Hernandez, and A. Menezes. Software implementation of elliptic curve cryptography over binary fields. *CHES'00*, LNCS **1965**, pages 1–24. 242, 243, 244, 245

[9] T. Izu and T. Takagi. A fast parallel elliptic curve multiplication resistant against side channel attacks. *PKC'02*, LNCS **2274**, pages 280–296. 241, 245, 249

[10] D. Johnson and A. Menezes. The elliptic curve digital signature algorithm (ECDSA). CACR Technical report CORR 99-31, University of Waterloo, 1999. 241

[11] B. King. An improved implementation of elliptic curves over $GF(2^n)$ when using projective point arithmetic. *SAC'01*, LNCS **2259**, pages 134–150. 240, 244

[12] D. E. Knuth. *Seminumerical Algorithms*, volume 2 of *The Art of Computer Programming*. Addison Wesley, 3 edition, 1997. 248

[13] D. E. Knuth, editor. *Selected papers on analysis of algorithms*. CSLI Publications, Stanford, 2000. 253

[14] D. E. Knuth and C. H. Papadimitriou. Duality in addition chains. *Bull. Eur. Assoc. Theor. Comput. Sci EATCS*, 13:2–4, 1981. Reprinted in [13, Chapter 31]. 251

[15] D. H. Lehmer. Computer technology applied to the theory of numbers. *Studies in Number Theory*, volume 6 of *MAA Studies in Mathematics*, pages 117–151, 1969. 249

[16] J. López and R. Dahab. Improved arithmetic for elliptic curve arithmetic in $GF(2^m)$. *SAC'98*, LNCS **1556**, pages 201–212. 244

[17] J. López and R. Dahab. Fast multiplication on elliptic curves over $GF(2^m)$ without precomputation. *CHES'99*, LNCS **1717**, pages 316 327. 241, 245, 246, 247, 248, 252

[18] A. J. Menezes and S. A. Vanstone. Elliptic curve cryptosystems and their implementation. *Journal of Cryptology*, 6(4):209–224, 1993.

[19] B. Möller. Algorithms for multi-exponentiation. *SAC'01*, LNCS **2259**, pages 165–180. 244, 245

[20] P. L. Montgomery. Evaluating recurrences of form $X_{m+n} = f(X_m, X_n, X_{m-n})$ via Lucas chains. Available from ftp.cwi.nl: /pub/pmontgom/Lucas.ps.gz, 1983. 241, 248, 249, 250

[21] P. L. Montgomery. Speeding the Pollard and elliptic curve methods of factorization. *Mathematics of Computation*, 48(170):243–264, 1987. 240, 241, 242

[22] P. L. Montgomery, Aug. 2000. Private communication: *expon2.txt, Dual elliptic curve exponentiation*. 249

[23] National Institute of Standards and Technology. *Digital Signature Standard*, 2000. FIPS Publication 186-2. 241

[24] K. Okeya, H. Kurumatani, and K. Sakurai. Elliptic curves with the Montgomery-form and their cryptographic applications. *PKC'00*, LNCS **1751**, pages 238–257. 241

[25] K. Okeya and K. Sakurai. Efficient elliptic curve cryptosystems from a scalar multiplication algorithm with recovery of the y-coordinate on a Montgomery-form elliptic curve. *CHES'01*, LNCS **2162**, pages 126–141. 241

[26] B. Schoenmakers, Aug. 2000. Personal communication. 249

[27] M. Stam and A. K. Lenstra. Speeding up XTR. *Asiacrypt'01*, LNCS **2248**, pages 125–143. 241, 251

[28] E. G. Straus. Problems and solutions: (5125) addition chains of vectors. *American Mathematical Monthly*, 71:806–808, 1964. 249

[29] Y. Tsuruoka. Computing short Lucas chains for elliptic curve cryptosystems. *IEICE Trans. Fundamentals*, E84-A(5):1227–1233, 2001. 251

[30] S. A. Vanstone, R. C. Mullin, A. Antipa, and R. Gallant. Accelerated finite field operations on an elliptic curve. WO 99/49386, Patent Cooperation Treaty, 1999. 241, 246, 252

A Dedicated Sieving Hardware

Willi Geiselmann and Rainer Steinwandt

IAKS, Arbeitsgruppe Systemsicherheit, Prof. Dr. Th. Beth
Fakultät für Informatik, Universität Karlsruhe
Am Fasanengarten 5, 76 131 Karlsruhe, Germany

Abstract. We describe a hardware device for supporting the sieving step in integer factoring algorithms like the quadratic sieve or the number field sieve. In analogy to Bernstein's proposal for speeding up the linear algebra step, we rely on a mesh of very simple processing units. Manufacturing the device at moderate cost with current hardware technology on standard wafers with 200 mm or 300 mm diameter should not provide any major obstacle.
A preliminary analysis of the parameters for factoring a 512-bit number with the number field sieve shows that the design considered here might outperform a TWINKLE device.

Keywords: factorization, number field sieve, RSA

1 Introduction

Current factoring algorithms like the quadratic sieve (QS) or the number field sieve (NFS) involve a so-called *sieving step* that is usually considered to be the most time-consuming part of the whole algorithm. Consequently, the question arises whether a specialized hardware can be used to achieve a significant speed-up in this step. For the QS a proposal for such a specialized hardware is due to Pomerance, Smith and Tuler [8]; according to [7] this special-purpose quadratic sieve processor "was built but never functioned properly. The point later became moot due to the exponential spread of low-cost, high-quality computers."

A more recent proposal for a dedicated sieving hardware, due to Shamir, is the TWINKLE device [10]. In [5] Lenstra and Shamir analyze this proposal in more detail and discuss the use of such a hardware in conjunction with the NFS. A major practical drawback of the TWINKLE device is the fact that it relies on the use of (expensive) Gallium Arsenide technology with optoelectronic components; a satisfactory silicon based approach without optical components seems not to be known.

Recently, Bernstein [1] proposed the use of a 'classical' mesh-architecture, which does not rely on the use of optoelectronic components, for the *linear algebra step* of the NFS. For a discussion of this approach we refer to [6]. Here we want to dwell on the question whether a hardware design similar to the one considered by Bernstein can be used for speeding-up the sieving step. It turns out that this approach seems possible indeed, and that it might be more efficient than using TWINKLE devices.

Y.G. Desmedt (Ed.): PKC 2003, LNCS 2567, pp. 254–266, 2003.

Our contribution is organized as follows: after recalling the sieving step of the NFS to the extent necessary for the sequel, we describe the algorithm we want to use for sieving, along with the corresponding hardware requirements. Thereafter we give a rough analysis of the occurring parameter sizes when dealing with 512-bit numbers. Some remarks on possible improvements and further work conclude the paper.

2   The Sieving Step in the NFS

For an introduction to the number field sieve we refer to [4]; here we recall only those aspects of the relation collection/sieving step relevant for the sequel. The importance of this step is illustrated by the following comment from [6], for instance: "We conclude that from a practical standpoint, the security of RSA relies exclusively on the hardness of the relation collection step of the number field sieve."

In the first step of the NFS two univariate polynomials $f_1(x), f_2(x) \in \mathbb{Z}[x]$ are chosen that share a common root m modulo n. Typically, $f_1(x)$ is of degree 5 and $f_2(x)$ is monic and linear:

$$f_1(x) = a_5 x^5 + a_4 x^4 + a_3 x^3 + a_2 x^2 + a_1 x + a_0$$
$$f_2(x) = x - m$$

where $f_1(m) = f_2(m) = 0$ (mod n). From these two polynomials two bivariate and homogeneous polynomials $F_1(x, y), F_2(x, y) \in \mathbb{Z}[x, y]$ are derived via $F_1(x, y) := y^5 \cdot f_1(x/y)$ resp. $F_2(x, y) := y \cdot f_2(x/y)$. Now everything related to $f_1(x)$ resp. $F_1(x, y)$ is said to belong to the *algebraic side*, and everything related to $f_2(x)$ resp. $F_2(x, y)$ is referred to as the *rational side*. In particular, we refer to the sets

$$P_i := \{(p, r) : f_i(r) \equiv 0 \pmod{p}, p \text{ prime}, p < 2^{24}, 0 \le r < p\} \subseteq \mathbb{N}^2 \ (i = 1, 2)$$

as algebraic and rational *factor base*, respectively. The upper bound 2^{24} used here aims at the factorization of a 512-bit number and is taken from [5].

The aim of the relation collection step is to find pairs of coprime integers $(a, b) \in \mathbb{Z}^2$ such that b is positive and the values $F_1(a, b)$ and $F_2(a, b)$ are *smooth*. Having in mind 512-bit numbers, according to [5] a sensible definition of 'smoothness' is the following:

Algebraic Side: $F_1(a, b)$ factors over the primes $< 2^{24}$, except for possibly 3 primes $< 10^9$

Rational Side: $F_2(a, b)$ factors over the primes $< 2^{24}$, except for possibly 2 primes $< 10^9$

Of course, these parameter choices are debatable: e. g., in [2] a significantly larger algebraic factor base along with only two (instead of three) large primes is used. Also, it is common to exclude small primes from the factor bases to speed up the sieving step (cf., e. g., [3]). In Section 3 we shall see that for the approach to sieving considered in this paper, such variations also prove useful.

For finding pairs (a, b) with $F_1(a, b)$ and $F_2(a, b)$ being smooth, typically some kind of sieving process is applied to a rectangular region $-A \leq a < A$, $0 < b \leq B$ where $A, B \in \mathbb{N}$. Different techniques are available for organizing this sieving process. For sake of simplicity, here we focus on so-called *line sieving*; some comments on *special q sieving* are given in Section 5. Denoting by T_1, T_2 appropriate threshold values for the algebraic and rational side, respectively, a rough outline of line sieving reads as follows:

$b \leftarrow 0$
repeat
$\quad b \leftarrow b + 1$
$\quad$**for** $i \leftarrow [1, 2]$
$\quad\quad s_i(a) \leftarrow 0 \quad (\forall a : -A \leq a < A)$
$\quad\quad$**for** $(p, r) \leftarrow P_i$
$\quad\quad\quad s_i(br + kp) \leftarrow s_i(br + kp) + \log_2(p) \quad (\forall k : -A \leq br + kp < A)$
$\quad$**for** $a \leftarrow \{-A \leq a < A : \gcd(a, b) = 1, \ s_1(a) > T_1, \text{ and } \ s_2(a) > T_2\}$
$\quad\quad$check if both $F_1(a, b)$ and $F_2(a, b)$ are smooth
until enough pairs (a, b) with both $F_1(a, b)$ and $F_2(a, b)$ smooth are found

E. g. in [5] it is pointed out that in the last step of the main loop, i. e., when testing $F_1(a, b)$ and $F_2(a, b)$ for being smooth, it is computationally too expensive to use a simple trial-division over the primes in the factor base. The sieving device described below takes this problem into consideration: when reporting that some $F_1(a, b)$ and $F_2(a, b)$ values are smooth, also prime factors hereof that have been found during sieving are reported.

3   A Sieving Device

3.1   Schimmler's Sorting Algorithm

An essential algorithmic tool we will use for sieving is Schimmler's sorting algorithm: assume we are given an $M \times M$ mesh of processing units $(Q_{i,j})_{1 \leq i,j \leq M}$ where $M := 2^n$ and each processing unit Q_{ij} stores some integer $q_{i,j}$. Then Schimmler's sorting algorithm can sort these M^2 numbers in $8M - 8$ 'steps' according to any of the following orders on the indices (i, j) of the processing units $Q_{i,j}$:

left-to-right: $(1, 1) \leq (1, 2) \leq \ldots \leq (1, M) \leq (2, 1) \leq \ldots \leq (M, M)$
right-to-left: $(1, M) \leq (1, M - 1) \leq \ldots \leq (1, 1) \leq (2, M) \leq \ldots \leq (M, 1)$
snakelike: $(1, 1) \leq (1, 2) \leq \ldots \leq (1, M) \leq (2, M) \leq (2, M - 1) \leq \ldots \leq (M, 1)$

A detailed explanation of this algorithm is given in [9, 1], for instance. Here it is sufficient to recall an elementary 'step' of the algorithm: in analogy to the well-known odd-even transposition sorting, in a single step each processing unit Q_{ij} communicates with exactly one of its horizontal or vertical neighbours. So let

$\hat{Q}$, $\tilde{Q}$ be two communicating processing units, and denote by $\hat{q}$, $\tilde{q}$ the integers stored in $\hat{Q}$, $\tilde{Q}$, respectively. At the end of one 'elementary step' one of the two processing units, say $\hat{Q}$, must hold $\min(\hat{q}, \tilde{q})$ while the other one has to store the value $\max(\hat{q}, \tilde{q})$. To achieve this we can proceed as follows:

1. $\hat{Q}$ sends $\hat{q}$ to $\tilde{Q}$, and $\tilde{Q}$ sends $\tilde{q}$ to $\hat{Q}$. E. g., if the stored integers represent natural numbers $< 2^{24}$, this operation can be completed in one clock cycle via a unidirectional 24-bit bus in each direction.
2. Both $\hat{Q}$ and $\tilde{Q}$ compute the boolean value $exchange := (\tilde{q} < \hat{q})$. E. g., if $\hat{q}$ and $\tilde{q}$ are 24-bit numbers, this comparison can be done in one clock cycle.
3. If $exchange$ evaluates to true, then $\hat{Q}$ stores $\tilde{q}$ and deletes $\hat{q}$. Analogously, $\tilde{Q}$ keeps $\hat{q}$ and deletes $\tilde{q}$, in this case. If $exchange$ evaluates to false, then both $\hat{Q}$ and $\tilde{Q}$ keep their old values and delete the values received in the first step. Again, for 24-bit integers this operation does not require more than one clock cycle. In fact it is feasible to integrate this step into the previous one without requiring an additional clock cycle.

In summary, when dealing with natural numbers $< 2^{24}$, Schimmler's sorting algorithm enables us to sort M^2 numbers in less than $8M$ steps where each step takes 2 clock cycles. If pairs of integers (q, r) have to be sorted according to the size of q, this can easily be done within the same time. In Step 2 and Step 3 the bus is not used and thus can transmit r. On behalf of $exchange$ this value is stored or ignored by the appropriate unit.

Before applying these observations to the sieving step of the NFS, for sake of completeness, we would like to point out that the idea of making use of Schimmler's sorting algorithm within the sieving step is also mentioned (without further explanation) in [1, Section 5, 'Plans.'].

3.2   Sieving with a Fast Sorting Hardware

For the ease of exposition we first describe the basic outline of our algorithm and postpone a more detailed discussion of the hardware requirements and the resulting performance to a separate paragraph.

The Sieving Algorithm Assume that in a precomputation step the factor bases P_1 and P_2 have been computed. For the moment we also assume that all primes that do not exceed some bound S are excluded from the two factor bases; for 512-bit numbers we may think of $S = 2^{22}$, i. e., the 295,947 smallest primes do not occur in P_1 and P_2—of course we must not ignore that many small primes, and we will discuss later how to lower the bound S.

Now we load into each processing unit of the sorting network one of the $|P_1| + |P_2|$ tuples $(p, r, i) \in \mathbb{N}^2 \times \{1, 2\}$ with $(p, r) \in P_i$. In other words, each processing unit holds an element from one of the factor bases along with a flag i that indicates to which of the two factor bases the stored value belongs. For sake of simplicity let us assume that $|P_1| + |P_2|$ coincides with the number M^2 of processing units.

For the actual sieving of an interval $-A \leq a < A$ (with b fixed), at first we divide this interval into $2A/S$ subintervals, each of size S (throughout we assume that $S \mid 2A$). Then we know that for $(p,r) \in P_1 \cup P_2$ arbitrary, each of these subintervals contains no more than one element $\tilde{r}$ with $r \equiv \tilde{r} \pmod{p}$. Further on, for $\tilde{a}$ an arbitrary number from a given subinterval and $(p,r) \in P_i$, the value $\lfloor \log_2(p) \rfloor$ is added to $s_i(\tilde{a})$ during line sieving if and only if $\tilde{a} \equiv br \pmod{p}$ ($i = 1, 2$). The initial values stored in the processing units correspond to $b = 1$, and to identify potentially useful $(a, 1)$-pairs we first apply Schimmler's algorithm to 'collect equal residues', namely we perform the following computation:

(I) Sort the triples (p, r, i) in snakelike order (smaller values first) according to the following order: $(p_0, r_0, i_0) < (p_1, r_1, i_1) \iff r_0||i_0 < r_1||i_1$, where $r_j||i_j$ denotes the value obtained by concatenating the registers where r_j and i_j are stored.

Now all pairs (p, r) that share the same r- and i-values are neighbours of each other. Thus, all (p, r)-pairs that belong to the same factor base and that contribute a value $\log_2(p)$ to the same counter $s_i(-A+1\cdot r)$ during line sieving are neighbours. In Step (II)–(VI) we determine (by means of local computations) whether for both factor bases the value $\sum_{p|(-A+r)} \lfloor \log_2(p) \rfloor$ (with p ranging over P_1 resp. P_2) exceeds the corresponding threshold value T_1 resp. T_2. Within each sequence of identical r-values an ok-flag will be set if and and only if both threshold values are exceeded.

To do so, first of all each processing unit determines the approximate bit length of the currently stored prime number:

(II) Each processing unit initializes an internal counter c to $\lfloor \log_2(p) \rfloor$ by counting the leading zeroes in p (where (p, r, i) is the currently stored value).

Next, for each sequence of equal r-values referring to the same factor base, we want to identify the first resp. last element of the sequence—in dependence of the stored factor base index i. The processing units holding these values play a distinguished role in the sequel.

(III) Each processing unit sends $r||i$ to its two neighbours in the snakelike order. A processing unit with $i = 1$ receives an $r||i$-value different from its own (from its successor) if and only if it is the last one in a sequence of equal $r||i$-values. Analogously, processing units with $i = 2$ can decide whether they are at the beginning of a sequence of equal r-values with $i = 2$.

For each sequence of r-values we want to compute $\sum_{p|(-A+r)} \lfloor \log_2(p) \rfloor$ for p ranging over the primes in the algebraic and the rational factor base, respectively:

(IV) Each processing unit not at the end of an r-sequence ($i = 1$) or not at the beginning of an r-sequence ($i = 2$), sends its $\lfloor \log_2(p) \rfloor$-value c to its neighbours in the snakelike order. Further on, these processing units receive and store the c-value from their predecessor ($i = 1$) resp. successor ($i = 2$). Processing units at the end of an r-sequence ($i = 1$) or at the beginning of an r-sequence ($i = 2$) send 0 and add the value received from their predecessor resp. successor to their current counter c.

Depending on the expected maximal number of prime divisors of the $F_i(a, b)$ within a factor base, this step is repeated several times (for 512-bit numbers say ≈ 10).

Due to the order used during sorting in Step (I), for an r-value that occurs both with factor base index $i = 1$ and $i = 2$, the two processing units storing $\sum_{p|(-A+r)} \lfloor \log_2(p) \rfloor$ with p ranging over P_1 and P_2 respectively, are neighbours. Consequently, for deciding whether the value $-A + r$ belongs to a potentially useful $(a, 1)$-pair, these two processing units compare their counter c with the corresponding 'smoothness threshold' T_i; these threshold values are identical for all processing units and adapted for new a-subintervals (through an external signal) if required.

(V) The processing units that summed up the $\lfloor \log_2(p) \rfloor$-values in their counter c compare c with the corresponding threshold value T_i. If $c > T_i$ then a flag ok is set to 1, otherwise ok is set to 0.

Thereafter, in case of factor base index $i = 1$, the stored $ok\|r$-value is sent to the successor. Dually, for $i = 2$ the stored $ok\|r$-value is sent to the predecessor. Finally, the stored ok-value is left unaltered, if the stored $ok\|r$-value coincides with the received one, otherwise ok is set to 0.

Hereafter, the ok-flags of the two processors 'in the middle of an r-sequence' are set if and only if both smoothness conditions are met, i. e., a potentially useful $(a, 1)$-pair has been found. As we do not want to loose the prime factors found during sieving, we next broadcast these (identical) ok-flags to all elements of the corresponding r-sequence:

(VI) Repeating Step (III) with the roles of $i = 1$ and $i = 2$ interchanged, the processing units with $i = 1$ notice whether they are at the beginning of an r-sequence. Dually, for $i = 2$ the end is recognized.

These 'border units' send 0 in the sequel to ensure that only the correct prime factors are marked. The other processing units send their ok-flag. The processing units with $i = 1$ receive and store the ok-flag from their successor and those processing units with $i = 2$ from their predecessor. Similarly as in Step (V), in dependence on the number of expected prime factors, this operation is repeated several times.

At the end of Step (VI) exactly those (p, r, i)-triples are marked with $ok = 1$ that we want to have as output to examine the smoothness of $F_1(-A + r, 1)$ and $F_2(-A + r, 1)$ in more detail:

(VII) To output the marked triples, we sort in snakelike[1] order (larger values first) according to the following order: $(p_0, r_0, i_0, ok_0) < (p_1, r_1, i_1, ok_1)$ $\Longleftrightarrow$

---

[1] left-to-right or right-to-left would work as well here

$ok_0 \| r_0 < ok_1 \| r_1$. Then, depending on the maximal number of 'hits' expected, a fixed part of the processing units writes their (p, r, i, ok)-values in parallel into the output buffer.

As there are only very few hits expected within one subinterval of size S, this step can be simplified: first sort the columns according to the order above; thereafter with high probability all marked triples are within the first few rows (for 512-bit numbers say $\approx 4)^2$. Next, we sort these first few rows left-to-right, and write them into an output buffer—possibly several rows in parallel.

The output will serve as basis for more precise smoothness tests discussed in Section 4. Here we focus on the problem of how to continue with the sieving of the next subinterval once the first subinterval $[-A, \ldots, -A + S - 1]$ has been sieved as described above. For passing to the next subinterval each processing unit must adapt its r-values to the new start $-A + S$ of the sieve subinterval. This can be done with simple 'local' computations, i.e., *there is no need to load new data into the mesh*. At this we exploit that all processed prime numbers are larger than the length S of the sieving interval:

(VIII) Each processing unit performs the following operation: r is replaced by $r - S$, and in case of $r - S < 0$ the prime p is added.

Now we are in essentially the same position as before Step (I), but now the processing units are initialized for sieving an interval of length S that starts at $-A + S$. Consequently, we apply the Steps (I)–(VIII) again, and continue in this way until the complete interval $-A \leq a < A$ of a-values has been sieved.— Without having to load new data into the mesh. Once the complete interval has been processed, the current value of b must be increased by 1. For doing so, new data is loaded into the network: in analogy to the case $b = 1$, each processing unit is initialized with a triple of the form $(p, b \cdot r \pmod{p}, i)$ where $(p, r) \in P_i$. In this way the sieving is continued until enough coprime values a, b with $F_1(a, b)$ and $F_2(a, b)$ being smooth are found.

We are still left to explain in more detail how the smoothness testing is actually done; in particular all prime numbers $\leq S$ have not been taken into account so far. But before dwelling onto this topic, we take a more detailed look on the hardware characteristics and the possible performance of the above device when dealing with 512-bit numbers.

Hardware Requirements To analyze the technical limits of the above algorithm we first estimate the number of transistors required for one processing unit when dealing with 512-bit numbers. Each of these units requires

2 registers with 24 bit each (p, r),

---

2 For the very few subintervals with $|a|$, $|b|$ very small a different procedure should be used, as otherwise too many useful candidates might be lost. This part is so small, however, that even a few hours on a normal PC are sufficient to take care hereof.

1 adder/compare unit for 25-bit numbers,

2 registers with 1 bit each (i, ok),

3 registers with 8 bit each (c, T_1, T_2), and

2 unidirectional 25-bit connections with each of the 4 neighbours; one to send and one to receive data

to perform the algorithm above. One D Flip-Flop can be realized with 8 transistors, and an adder of the appropriate size with about 40 transistors per bit. In total, around 1600 transistors are required for these basic elements. Together with 4 multiplexers for the 25-bit connections (4 transistors per bit each) and the additional program-logic, e. g., to store internal states like first/last unit in a sequence of equal r-values, we estimate the number of transistors required per processing unit as 2500 transistors. (In [6] a slightly simpler unit was assumed to need 2000 transistors.) Within each cell only a very small program logic is required; most commands determine how to set the multiplexers and are identical within one row resp. column. These commands can be generated outside the square area of processing units and distributed through a couple of connections. The only part of the procedure that requires more logic within the units is the calculation of $\lfloor \log_2(p) \rfloor$; it might be more efficient to store and communicate this 8-bit value through the complete calculation.

With current 0.13 μm technology (used for the Intel Pentium 4 "Northwood" processor) more than 400,000 transistors and thus at least 160 processing units fit on 1 mm². On the square area of a wafer with 200 mm diameter 3.2 million units can be placed; on a 300 mm wafer, as used for the Pentium 4 'Northwood' processor, 7.2 million processing units fit. Thus it is certainly possible to produce a mesh of $2^{11} \times 2^{11}$ processing units with current technology.

This estimation does not take into account the problem of defective cells. Additional rows and columns and some logic have to be added to the layout to bypass complete rows and columns with defective units. On a 300 mm wafer there should be enough space left to take care of this problem.

Performance If a mesh with $M^2 = 2^{22}$ processing units is given we want to analyze its use for the sieving step in the NFS for a 512-bit number. The size of the factor bases and the regions to be sieved are taken from [5] to easily compare the suggested hardware with the version of the TWINKLE device adapted for the NFS.

With subintervals of length $S = 2^{22}$, on a mesh with 2^{22} processors a large part of the factor bases, namely all pairs $(p, r) \in P_i$ $(i = 1, 2)$ with $2^{17} < p < 2^{24}$, can be processed in the form described in Section 4: for all these primes the triples $(k \cdot p, r + (l-1) \cdot p, i)$ with $1 \leq l \leq k := \lceil 2^{22}/p \rceil$ are stored. In summary, then $2,025,624$ processors are needed for the rational factor base and about the same number for the algebraic factor base. The $12,251$ primes smaller 2^{17} have to be processed by the trial division pipeline described in Section 4.

With a conservative estimation the mesh can be expected to work at a clock rate of 500 MHz; the communication across the border of the wafer is slower by a factor 4. Using a 48-bit I/O bus for loading the data for the 2^{22} cells sequentially onto the wafer requires 2^{24} clock cycles or 0.034 seconds; with $4 \cdot 48$ I/O pins this initialization can be finished in less than 0.01 seconds.—If an additional powerful (standard) processor and 32 MB of memory are placed on the remaining $\approx 35\%$ of the wafer outside the square area, this operation can be speeded up significantly.

Schimmler's sorting algorithm has to be performed in Step (I) and requires about $8M$ steps with 2 clock cycles each. The reduced version in Step (VII) works with about $2M$ steps. The rest of the algorithm, Steps (II)–(VI) and (VIII) require a small fixed number of clock cycles (less than 100) and are neglected for the following estimations.

For $M = 2^{11}$ an interval of length $S = 2^{22}$ can be sieved within $20 \cdot 2^{11}$ clock cycles. A line of the sieving region required for factoring a 512-bit number with the NFS has a length of $1.8 \cdot 10^{10}$; it can be sieved in 4292 runs of the above algorithm within 0.36 seconds. The modified TWINKLE device with 2 LEDs per cell, working at a clock rate of 10 GHz, requires 1.8 seconds for the same interval or 18 seconds, when working at the lower speed of 1 GHz; there are about 10 wafers with 6 inches (≈ 152 mm) required for this TWINKLE architecture.

To sieve the complete region necessary for the 512-bit factorization, $9 \cdot 10^5$ such lines are required and can be processed in less than 4 days with the device described here.

Alternatively, a different (slower) setting of the parameters can be chosen to reduce the false alarms by allowing only two large primes on the algebraic side instead of three (cf. [2]). In this case the computing time of the further processing (like trial division and checking for large primes) is reduced. To find still enough relations one has to increase the size of the algebraic factor base. This can be achieved if the size of the subinterval in the above procedure is reduced to $S := 2^{21}$: in the 2^{22} processing units the part of the factor bases related to the primes p with $2^{16} < p < 2^{24}$ can be stored analogously as above. Then $1,577,786$ processors are required for the rational factor base and about the same number for the algebraic factor base related to the primes $< 2^{24}$. The remaining $1,030,000$ processors can be used to deal with the $985,818$ primes up to 2^{25}. In this setting only 6542 primes smaller 2^{16} have to be taken into account for the trial division pipeline, and the size of the algebraic factor base has nearly doubled. Compared to the previous parameters the time for sieving has increased by a factor 2 to less than 8 days.

4 Handling Small Primes and Testing Smoothness

The assumption that the mesh handles only primes $p > S$ is overnecessarily restrictive. If we are willing to dedicate more than one processing unit to a pair $(p, r) \in P_1 \cup P_2$, then at least primes that are not 'much' smaller than S can be dealt with: let $(p, r) \in P_1 \cup P_2$ and $k \in \mathbb{N}$ minimal with $k \cdot p > S$. Then we use k processing units for representing the triple (p, r, i) where the lth unit ($1 \leq l \leq k$) holds the value $(k \cdot p, r + (l - 1) \cdot p, i)$. Note here that this approach introduces an inaccuracy into the summation of the $\lfloor \log_2(p) \rfloor$-values: if we proceed during the summation as described in Section 3.2, we essentially add $\lfloor \log_2(kp) \rfloor$ instead of $\lfloor \log_2(p) \rfloor$. If one is not willing to accept this inaccuracy, one may think of adding a fourth component to the triples $(k \cdot p, r + (l-1) \cdot p, i)$ to store the value $\lfloor \log_2(p) \rfloor$. Of course, whenever two processing units exchange their currently stored values throughout Schimmler's sorting algorithm, the additional fourth component must also be taken care of then. To do so without sacrificing time, one can use a broader bus between the processing units. E. g., if $\lfloor \log_2(p) \rfloor$ is represented with 8 bits, then 4 extra bits on the bus are sufficient to transmit this value within two clock cycles.—Step (II), and therewith also parts of the program logic, obviously become superfluous when $\lfloor \log_2(p) \rfloor$ is stored explicitly.

Using $S = 2^{22}$, on the rational side all 1,065,620 primes p with $2^{17} < p < 2^{24}$ can be represented with 2,025,624 processing units in this way.—And analogously on the algebraic side. Using $S = 2^{21}$, the 1,071,329 primes p with $2^{16} < p < 2^{24}$ on the rational side can be handled with 1,577,786 processing units. But even with the modification just described, for $S = 2^{22}$ resp. $S = 2^{21}$ so far we still ignore the smallest 12,251 resp. 6,542 prime numbers; these remaining primes can be dealt with in a 'trial division pipeline':

Once the sieving of a subinterval is completed, the output of the sieving device tells us promising (a, b)-pairs (note that the a-value corresponding to a (p, r, i)-triple of the output is given by $a = -A + (u-1) \cdot S + r$ with $u \geq 1$ denoting the number of the subinterval sieved). A separate processor reads the output buffer of the sieving device and stores a and b along with the corresponding (p, i)-values found during sieving, if $\gcd(a, b) = 1$ holds.

If in the earlier $\lfloor \log_2(p) \rfloor$-summation the inaccuracies— due to multiples $j \cdot p$— have not been taken into account, this processor can also recompute the sum of the logarithms of the potential prime factors in each factor basis and compare them with the corresponding threshold value T_i. In this way the number of candidates that have to be explored in more detail can be reduced. For all (a, b)-pairs that passed the tests so far, the result of the two $\lfloor \log_2(p) \rfloor$-summations is appended to the already stored list of prime factors of the $F_i(a, b)$. The values $F_1(a, b)$ and $F_2(a, b)$ are also stored and passed to a 'trial division pipeline' that divides out small prime factors (in the above example with $S = 2^{22}$ resp. $S = 2^{21}$ the first 12,251 resp. 6,542 primes have to be dealt with here): this device has a simple pipeline structure where in each step of the pipeline a small prime factor is divided out if this divisor is actually present, and the result is passed on to the next stage of the pipeline. For very small primes one may also devote several stages of the pipeline to one prime factor; e. g., to divide out all powers of 2 up to 2^7 one can use three division units that try to divide out 2^4, 2^2, and 2^1, respectively.

The output of this pipeline is forwarded to a processor that determines the bit length of the result and subtracts the corresponding $\lfloor \log_2(p) \rfloor$-sum hereof. (Note that by construction the output of the division pipeline alternately refers to the algebraic and rational side, and the algebraic and rational $\lfloor \log_2(p) \rfloor$-sum have been stored right before passing $F_1(a, b)$, $F_2(a, b)$ into the division pipeline.) If the obtained value is too large for being the length of a number consisting of two resp. three large primes, the candidate pair (a, b) is not processed any further—in the corresponding table entry a 'to do' flag will be set to zero in this case. Otherwise the factors $\tilde{F}_1$ and $\tilde{F}_2$ of $F_1(a, b)$ and $F_2(a, b)$ obtained from the division pipeline are appended to the table entry for (a, b) and the table entry is marked by setting a 'to do' flag.

While the two processors before and after the division pipeline fill the table row by row in this way, the entries marked with 'to do' will be processed by several additional processors (working in parallel) as explained in a moment. In particular the processing of these entries—which might, e. g., be done by a PC network—has to be fast enough so that at the time when the table would be full, a wrap around is possible; entries already processed will then have a reset 'to do' flag.

As indicated already, the actual factorization of $F_1(a, b)$ and $F_2(a, b)$ is performed by several additional processors. These processors are assumed to be able to do long integer arithmetics: they look for set 'to do' flags in the table, read out the table entry and reset the 'to do' flag. Now the $\tilde{F}_i$ values are divided by all prime factors that have been found during sieving. Finally, the resulting cofactor is checked for being composed of only two or three primes. If this is the case, the small factors removed by the division pipeline will have to be recovered—say by factoring the values $F_i(a, b)/\tilde{F}_i$ $(i = 1, 2)$ with trial division. Once a complete (a, b)-pair has been processed (and if necessary the resulting factorizations been written in an output buffer), the next table entry with set 'to do' flag is looked for and processed.

Although several details are ignored in the above discussion, we think it gives ample evidence that neglecting smaller prime values during the actual sieving does not provide fundamental difficulties. In fact, for 512-bit numbers one might think about locating the division pipeline and the supporting processors (possibly including the hardware that provides the $(p, (b \cdot r) \bmod p, i)$-triples to be loaded into the processing units) on the same 300 mm wafer as the actual sieving circuit.

5   Improvements and Further Work

The sieving device described above is certainly not optimal, and several questions seem worth to be explored. We would like to mention some interesting issues here:

- A crucial point is the reinitialization of the device when incrementing b. In particular, if one thinks about implementing so-called q sieving (instead of line sieving) this point becomes important, as here the a-intervals are shorter. If one is willing to store the initial r-values and to add some additional hardware for an externally controlled shift-and-add procedure, updating the b-values should be possible within ≈ 100 clock cycles (in parallel in each processing unit). Of course, the additionally stored r-value also has to be taken care of during the sorting.

- A well-known optimization of the line-sieving procedure that is exploited in normal PC implementations is to exclude sieving regions with both a and b even. Assuming w.l.o.g. the numbers A and S to be even one can think of increasing the bit size of the processed numbers by one and using a similar trick in the above device: whenever b is even, we subtract S twice (and if necessary add $2p$) to get into the next subinterval.
- Also the question of scalability should be explored further, as the above design exploits that the complete sieving circuit is located on a single wafer.

6 Conclusions

We have described a dedicated hardware for supporting the sieving step in factoring algorithms like the NFS. The given rough analysis for the case of 512-bit numbers gives evidence that it might be feasible to manufacture such a circuit on the basis of a standard wafer, and that such an approach could possibly be preferable to the optoelectronic approach used for the TWINKLE device.

Acknowledgement

We are indebted to an anonymous referee for various valuable comments on the original manuscript.

References

[1] Daniel J. Bernstein. Circuits for Integer Factorization: a Proposal. At the time of writing available electronically at http://cr.yp.to/papers.html#nfscircuit, 2001. 254, 256, 257

[2] Stefania Cavallar, Bruce Dodson, Arjen K. Lenstra, Walter Lioen, Peter L. Montgomery, Brian Murphy, Herman te Riele, Karen Aardal, Jeff Gilchrist, Gérard Guillerm, Paul Leyland, Joël Marchand, François Morain, Alec Muffet, Chris Putnam, Craig Putnam, and Paul Zimmermann. Factorization of a 512-bit RSA Modulus. In Bart Preneel, editor, *Advances in Cryptology — EUROCRYPT 2000*, volume 1807 of *Lecture Notes in Computer Science*, pages 1–18. Springer, 2000. 255, 262

[3] Marije Elkenbracht-Huizing. An Implementation of the Number Field Sieve. *Experimental Mathematics*, 5(3):231–253, 1996. 256

[4] Arjen K. Lenstra and Jr. Hendrik W. Lenstra, editors. *The development of the number field sieve*, volume 1554 of *Lecture Notes in Mathematics*. Springer, 1993. 255

[5] Arjen K. Lenstra and Adi Shamir. Analysis and Optimization of the TWINKLE Factoring Device. In Bart Preneel, editor, *Advances in Cryptology — EUROCRYPT 2000*, volume 1807 of *Lecture Notes in Computer Science*, pages 35–52. Springer, 2000. 254, 255, 256, 261

[6] Arjen K. Lenstra, Adi Shamir, Jim Tomlinson, and Eran Tromer. Analysis of Bernstein's Factorization Circuit. At the time of writing available electronically at http://www.cryptosavvy.com/mesh.pdf, 2002. 254, 255, 261

[7] Carl Pomerance. A Tale of Two Sieves. *Notices of the AMS*, 43(12):1473–1485, 1996. 254

[8] Carl Pomerance, J. W. Smith, and Randy Tuler. A pipeline architecture for factoring large integers with the quadratic sieve algorithm. *SIAM Journal on Computing*, 17:387–403, 1988. 254

[9] Manfred Schimmler. Fast sorting on the instruction systolic array. Technical Report 8709, Christian Albrecht Universität Kiel, Germany, 1987. 256

[10] Adi Shamir. Factoring Large Numbers with the TWINKLE Device. In Çetin K. Koç and Christof Paar, editors, *Cryptographic Hardware and Embedded Systems. First International Workshop, CHES'99*, volume 1717 of *Lecture Notes in Computer Science*, pages 2–12. Springer, 1999. 254

A Fast and Secure Implementation of Sflash[*]

Mehdi-Laurent Akkar, Nicolas T. Courtois, Romain Duteuil, and Louis Goubin

SchlumbergerSema, CP8 Crypto Lab
36-38 rue de la Princesse, 78430 Louveciennes, France
{MAkkar,NCourtois,RDuteuil,LGoubin}@slb.com

Abstract. Sflash is a multivariate signature scheme, and a candidate for standardisation, currently evaluated by the European call for primitives Nessie. The present paper is about the design of a highly optimized implementation of Sflash on a low-cost 8-bit smart card (without coprocessor). On top of this, we will also present a method to protect the implementation protection against power attacks such as Differential Power Analysis.

Our fastest implementation of Sflash takes 59 ms on a 8051 based CPU at 10MHz. Though the security of Sflash is not as well understood as for example for RSA, Sflash is apparently the fastest signature scheme known. It is suitable to implement PKI on low-cost smart card, token or palm devices. It allows also to propose secure low-cost payment/banking solutions.

Keywords: Digital Signatures, PKI, Addition Chains, Multivariate Cryptography, Matsumoto-Imai cryptosystem C^*, C^{*--} trapdoor function, HFE, portable devices, Smart cards, Power Analysis, SPA, DPA.

1 Introduction

The design of Flash and Sflash signature schemes is due to Courtois, Patarin and Goubin [17, 18]. Sflash is based on a so called C^{*--} multivariate signature scheme, the name of C^{*--} being due to Patarin [14]. The idea goes back to the Matsumoto-Imai cryptosystem proposed at Eurocrypt'88, also called C^* in [12], that is a remote cousin of RSA, that uses a power function over an extension of a finite field. At the time the Matsumoto-Imai or C^* cryptosystem was believed very secure, and were amazingly fast. At the same time, in France, the smart cards become a great success: they allow to divide by ten the fraud figures in the payment systems. However RSA is too slow to be used on a smart card, and this keeps the security achieved by smart cards solutions insufficient: unable to implement a real public key signature. From this arises the motivation to find a signature scheme that could be implemented on low-cost smart cards. Unfortunately, at Crypto'95 Patarin shows Matsumoto-Imai is insecure[1], see [13, 10]. Subsequently Patarin studied many other variants and

---

[*] The work described in this paper has been supported by the French Ministry of Research under RNRT Project "Turbo-signatures".

[1] Note that H. Dobbertin claims to have independently found this attack in 93/94.

Y.G. Desmedt (Ed.): PKC 2003, LNCS 2567, pp. 267–278, 2003.
© Springer-Verlag Berlin Heidelberg 2003

generalizations of Matsumoto-Imai (or C*) (for example the Dragons). Most of them are broken, and very few remain. Among these, C^{*-} is particularly simple, and remains unbroken. It is simply the original scheme combined with the idea of preventing structural attacks by simply removing some of the equations that constitute the public key, due initially to Shamir [19]. At Asiacrypt'98 [14], Courtois, Patarin and Goubin show that C^{*-} can be attacked, and if r is the number of removed equations, a factor of q^r appears in the attack. For various reasons it is conjectured that the security of C^{*-} does increase with at least q^r when removing equations [1], and the same is also conjectured for other multivariate cryptosystems[2]. When q^r is very big, e.g. 2^{80}, it is believed that C^{*-} is secure, we then call it C^{*--}, as a lot of equations are removed. It is possible to see that due to many equations removed, C^{*--} can only be used in signature, no longer in encryption.

From C^{*-}, in 2000, Courtois, Patarin and Goubin designed the Flash signature scheme, submitted to Nessie European call for cryptographic primitives, and also a special version of Flash called Sflash that manages to decrease the size of the public key[3]. Unfortunately at Eurocrypt'2002, Gilbert and Minier, showed that this very trick, used to decrease the size of the public key of Sflash, is insecure, and broke Sflash, see [6]. Since then the specification of Sflash has been revised, the new version of Sflash is in fact a version of Flash with a better choice of parameters.

Finally, it is important to note that the design of Flash and Sflash does not reduce to C^{*--}. There is difficulty in the design of multivariate signature schemes that comes from the fact that the systems of equations, have in general many solutions, and only the knowledge of the internal algebraic structure allows to find one of them, which is usually done by fixing some internal variables. If this process is not handled correctly, it might leak information about this internal structure, and eventually allow to recover the private key of Flash/Sflash. See [17] and [1].

Sflash is therefore the best solution that has been found so far to make digital signatures in a low-cost device such as smart card, USB token or a palm device. However, the security of an implementation of a cryptographic algorithm in such a device does not reduce to the security of the cryptographic algorithm itself. It is hard to protect a secret that is entirely in the hands of a potential attacker: the implementation should also have in mind possible side-channel attacks. In 1998, Kocher, Jaffe and Jun showed the feasibility of such attacks [11] using the power consumption of the device, and since then other side-channel attacks have been proposed. In this paper we will also describe, on top of our optimized implementation, a protection against side-channel attacks.

---

[2] For example see the experiments with Buchberger's algorithm applied to HFE-, presented in [2] (in these proceedings) or on slide 35 of [3].

[3] The main drawback of many multivariate cryptosystems.

2   Structure of the Smart Card

We consider a low-end smart card built on a 8-bit CPU core, an Intel 8051. It has no arithmetic or cryptographic coprocessor. The memory of this card is divided in three parts as follows:

- The *data*: 128 bytes which one can address directly in one CPU clock.
- The *xdata*: between 1 and 4 Kbytes, indirectly addressable in two CPU clocks.
- The *code*: between 4 and 64 Kbytes of unrewritable memory, indirectly addressable in two CPU clocks.
- Most smart card processors that are based on 8051 contain also between 2 and 128 Kkbytes of E^{2}PROM memory, that can be used to store keys.

As a comparison one could see the *data*, the *idata* and the *xdata* like the RAM of a classical PC, whereas the *code* would be the ROM. According to those considerations, we will try to store the most manipulated variables in the *data* in order to save as much time as possible in the computation.

3   Basis Structures and Variables Used in Sflash

A complete description of Sflash can be found in [17, 18]. The signature process consists mainly of a composition of three functions defined over the extensions of finite fields: $s^{-1} \circ f^{-1} \circ t^{-1}$, with two multivariate affine functions s, t and one univariate power function f, In this paper we concentrate on the implementation of the basic operations that are used in Sflash.

3.1   Main Structures

The algorithm mainly manipulates elements of the finite field $L = GF(128^{37})$, constructed as an extension of the base Galois field $K = GF(128)$. The field $K = GF(128)$ defined as $GF(2)[X]$ polynomials modulo $(X^7 + X + 1)$:
$$K = GF(2)[X]/(X^7 + X + 1)$$
Each element of K is written as 7 bits stored in one byte; the coefficient of X^i becomes the coefficient of 2^i, $i = 0..6$. The big field $L = GF(128^{37})$ is defined as follows:
$$L = K[X]/(X^{37} + X^{12} + X^{10} + X^2 + 1) \tag{1}$$
We also identify L with K^{37} and represent an element of L by 37 elements of K (the coefficients of X^i, $i = 0..36$), that in turn are written as 37 bytes, each of them using only 7 bits.

Our implementation uses two temporary variables called y and *temp*, that are structures containing an element of L, in the *data* zone of the smart card. This allows them to be easily accessible so that the computation is faster. We will also store another structure of type L, called x, in the *xdata* zone because at some moment we need to manipulate three elements of L, when using a function having two inputs and one output (we are not able to store this third one in the *data* as we need additional space in the *data* zone for something else).

3.2   The Private Key of Sflash

The secret parameters of the signature scheme are the two transformations from L to L, s and t, that are multivariate affine functions, *i.e.* they are affine when seen as functions from $K^{37} \to K^{37}$. We do not actually store s and t but their inverses s^{-1} and t^{-1}. We have $t^{-1} : x \mapsto T_m x + T_c$ and $s^{-1} : x \mapsto S_m x + S_c$ with T_m and S_m being two matrixes 37×37 and with T_c and S_c being the constant vectors[4]. All these are stored in either the *code* zone or the E^2PROM of the card.

We will also store the 80-bit secret string Δ in the *code* zone (or E^2PROM).

4   Fast Implementation of the Operations over the Fields

The Implementation of K:

1. Addition: Easy in characteristic 2 of $K = GF(128)$, the addition in $K = GF(128)$ is implemented by XORing the byte representations of the elements.

2. Multiplication: more work is required here. Since the multiplicative group K^* is cyclic, say generated by α, each element of K (but zero) can be seen as a power of α. Powers add when we multiply two non-zero elements: $\alpha^x . \alpha^y = \alpha^{x+y}$, and the multiplication by zero is obvious. In order to execute this operation, we store two tables of 127 bytes, one (named *expo* and stored in the *code* zone) giving the exponent of α corresponding to a given non-zero element of K, and the reciprocal operation (named *log* and also in *code*) giving the element of K corresponding to a given exponent of α.

The Implementation of L: Based on the definition of L in (1).

1. Addition: given two elements of L represented by two polynomials $a = \sum_{i=0}^{36} a_i X^i$ and $b = \sum_{i=0}^{36} b_i X^i$, their sum is computed by XORing the coefficients of the same degree:

$$c = a + b \overset{def}{=} \sum_{i=0}^{36} (a_i \oplus b_i) X^i$$

with $\oplus$ being the XOR operation.

2. Multiplication: It is costly, because we compute the product of two polynomials a and b which will be of degree 72, and then compute its euclidian reduction modulo the irreducible polynomial $X^{37} + X^{12} + X^{10} + X^2 + 1$ (as there are no trinomials for this field).
   (a) Build $c' = \sum_{i=0}^{72} c_i' X^i$, where $c_i = \sum_{l+k=i} a_l . b_k$.
   (b) Then reduce c' by $X^{37} + X^{12} + X^{10} + X^2 + 1$, the result c is the product $a.b$ in L.

---

[4] Actually these two constant vectors are not really secret as shown in [8]. Therefore one can choose s and t linear instead of affine, which reduces the size of the secret key.

3. Square: It is interesting to code the squaring operation in L independently, it can be done at least 5 times faster than a multiplication of an element by itself. The above multiplication algorithm requires a quadratic-time computation on the coordinates of the two operands (the building of c' in (a) above) whereas, to square an element a, we only have to compute:

$$a' = \sum_{i=0}^{36} a_i^2 X^{2i}$$

which is linear in the a_i, and then reduce a' modulo $X^{37}+X^{12}+X^{10}+X^2+1$, like in step (b) above.

The Affine Transformations s and t: They are computed as classical matrix multiplications, with additional XOR with the constant vector. As in each step of the matrix multiplication we have to compute several multiplications in K (one of the coordinates of the input with one of the matrix' coefficients), and regarding to how we compute such a multiplication (*cf* above), it will be faster if we store base α logarithms of the coefficients of the matrix.

5   How to Compute $A = f^{-1}(B)$ in Sflash ?

We need to compute $A = B^h$ in L, with:

$h = (128^{11} + 1)^{-1} \bmod (128^{37} - 1)$
$ = 1000000\ 1000000\ 1000000\ 0111111\ 0111111\ 0111111\ 0111111\ 1000000$
$ 1000000\ 1000000\ 1000000\ 0111111\ 0111111\ 0111111\ 1000000\ 1000000$
$ 1000000\ 1000000\ 0111111\ 0111111\ 0111111\ 0111111\ 1000000\ 1000000$
$ 1000000\ 0111111\ 0111111\ 0111111\ 0111111\ 1000000\ 1000000\ 1000000$
$ 1000000\ 0111111\ 0111111\ 0111111\ 1000000$

The cost of a classical "square and multiply" algorithm to carry on this power h would be, at least, 259 squaring and 145 multiplications ! The slowest operation is the multiplication in the field L (squarings are faster). Our best implementation of multiplication in L requires about 10 000 CPU cycles (which takes at least 2.4 ms on a 10 MHz smart card).

We need to find an addition chain for h involving as little multiplications as possible. We did not limit ourselves to finding a "classical" addition chain for h, but also privileged some special powers, namely 128 and 128^7 which, as we will see in the next part, are quite easy to compute. After numerous attempts we have found the following method:

- $\alpha \longleftarrow (B^2)^2$;
- $\beta \longleftarrow B \times \alpha$;
- $\gamma \longleftarrow (\alpha^2)^2$;
- $\delta \longleftarrow \beta \times \gamma$;
- $u \longleftarrow \delta^2 \times \delta$;
- $v \longleftarrow (\gamma^2)^2$;

- $t \longleftarrow ((v^{128})^{128})^{128} \times u;$
- $w \longleftarrow ((t^{128} \times t)^{128} \times t)^{128};$
- $x \longleftarrow ((w \times u)^{128})^{128^7};$
- $z \longleftarrow v^{128^7} \times w \times v \times x;$
- $A \longleftarrow (((z^{128^7})^{128^7})^{128} \times x)^{128^7} \times z.$

This method has a particularly low number of multiplications: 12, instead of 145 for "square and multiply".

5.1   Special Operations Involved in the Computation of f^{-1}:

We already described the implementation of the multiplication and the squaring. What remain, are the efficient implementations of $x \mapsto x^{128}$ and $x \mapsto x^{128^7}$. In $K = GF(128)$, those two operations are K-linear on L, so they can be seen fulfilled with a matrix multiplication. Moreover, due to the fact that the polynomial by which we reduced $(X^{37} + X^{12} + X^{10} + X^2 + 1)$ has only coefficients 0 and 1, the matrices involved are only made up of 0s and 1s, which allows us to store their coefficients on single bits.

The Function $x \mapsto x^{128^7}$: As the matrix used for the raising to the power 128^7 is fixed, we can also accelerate this computation by finding a "cheap" road in the matrix, which is related to the idea of the Gray code. The Gray code is an ordering of all binary n-bits words, such two consecutive words differ by only one bit, see [9] for example. This allows to compute all possible linear combinations over $GF(2)$ of some n vectors, with one XOR by combination, instead of $n/2$. We use an even better, specific solution that is adapted to the particular matrix that is fixed (even for two different private keys). Our goal is to compute:

$$y = M.x \; ; \quad \text{with } x, y \in K^{37} \text{ and } M \in \mathbf{M}_{37,37}(GF(2))$$

For this we divide the matrix in some $37 \times n$ submatrices for some small n. For each submatrix we look for a "cheap" road: each y_i is a XOR of different x_i, how to compute them minimizing the number of XORs as possible. For example we assume that the first submatrix begins with:

$$\begin{pmatrix} y_1 \\ y_2 \\ y_3 \\ y_4 \\ .. \end{pmatrix} = \begin{pmatrix} 0\,0\,1\,0\,1\,0\,0 \\ 0\,0\,1\,1\,1\,0\,0 \\ 0\,0\,0\,0\,1\,0\,0 \\ 0\,0\,1\,1\,0\,0\,0 \\ .\;.\;.\;.\;.\;.\;. \end{pmatrix} \cdot \begin{pmatrix} x_1\; x_2\; x_3\; x_4\; x_5\; x_6\; x_7\; ... \end{pmatrix}^T$$

We store $x_1, ..., x_n$ in separate registers. Let A be the main register. We first put $A \leftarrow x_5$. Then we XOR A with x_3: $A \leftarrow A \oplus x_3$ and then put $y_1 \leftarrow A$, now $y_3 = x_3 \oplus x_5$. Then we put $y_2 \leftarrow A \leftarrow A \oplus x_4$. Finally we do $y_4 \leftarrow A \leftarrow A \oplus x_5$, etc.. A "cheap" road should use about 1 XOR per y_i computed. We need to find the cheapest road in each submatrix and also to find the best n for such an operation. For our specific matrices 37×37 $n = 7$ seemed to be optimal and our best solution has been found with some computer simulations.

This technique allows to accelerate quite a lot (about 40 times !) the operation $x \mapsto x^{128^7}$, however it takes a lot of space in term of program code (0.7 Kbyte).

The Function $x \mapsto x^{128}$: It is useless to use the above technique to compute the power $128 = 2^7$. Doing 7 successive squarings is faster than a matrix multiplication, even if done in a clever way. It is also much cheaper in term of code size, not only we have no matrix to store, but we will mostly re-use the existing code. In addition to that, $x \mapsto x^{128}$ can be computed faster than doing seven squarings in a row. Indeed, seven squares will be a succession of squares in $GF(128)$ done position by position on 37 values, and a multivariate linear operation over $GF(128)^{37}$ that comprises expansion and modular reduction modulo the irreducible polynomial. It is easy to see that "position by position" squaring commutes with the multivariate linear part. Thus we may postpone all the 7 "position by position" squarings to the end, and then we realize that they are not needed, because in $GF(128)$ we have always $x^{128} = x$.

6   The Performance Data

To summarize, our implementation of Sflash requires:
- 2 matrix products to apply T_m and S_m.
- 12 multiplications in L.
- 7 squarings in L.
- 8 raisings to the power 128 in L.
- 5 raisings to the power 128^7.

From here we have two possible implementations of Sflash:

- A **fast** one, using the technique above to compute the power 128^7 which is quite fast but a bit large in term of code size:
  - RAM: 334 bytes (112 bytes of *data* and 222 bytes of *xdata*).
  - Code size (ROM): 3.1 Kbytes.
- A **slower** one, using a classical matrix product which is slower (but still acceptable) and have a shorter code:
  - RAM: 334 bytes (112 bytes of *data* and 222 bytes of *xdata*).
  - Code size (ROM): 2.5 Kbytes.

We have implemented the two versions of Sflash on two Intel 8051 CPU based components: an original Intel 8051 CPU and an Infineon SLE66 component without cryptoprocessor. The timings (without hashing) are the following:

Component	8051	8051	SLE66	SLE66	8051	8051	SLE66	SLE66
Frequency [MHz]	3.57	10	3.57	10	3.57	10	3.57	10
Code version	fast	fast	fast	fast	slow	slow	slow	slow
ROM size [kbytes]	3.1	3.1	3.1	3.1	2.5	2.5	2.5	2.5
Timings [ms]	750	268	164	**59**	1075	384	230	82

We see that on a smart card without any coprocessor and in usual conditions (10 MHz is today a normal frequency for a low-cost component such as SLE66) one can compute digital signatures in as little as 59 ms ! It is much less than for RSA or Elliptic Curves, even if a cryptographic co-processor is used (!), see the comparison in Section 8.

7   Protecting Sflash against Side-Channel Attacks

In the side-channel attacks, the adversary tries to recover the private key of
a signature scheme (or other useful information) given the information that
leaks from the intermediate data that appears during the computation, or from
the computation itself, see for example [11].

7.1   Protecting against SPA-Like Attacks

For Sflash, the computation is always the same, whatever the value of the private
key is. Moreover, all the computations in Sflash use full bytes of the private
key, making the dependency of power consumption on the key very complex to
exploit. This prevents SPA attacks known for unprotected implementations of
RSA, in which the power consumption allows to see the values of single bits of
the private key.

7.2   Protecting against DPA-Like Attacks

For DPA-like attacks, the protection boils down to masking the intermediate data. The signature of Sflash involves mainly the composition of 3 functions, t^{-1}, f^{-1} and s^{-1}. The best way to prevent an information leak (of any
type) is to mask completely the two intermediate values: the output of t^{-1} and
of f^{-1}. For this, we will use the homomorphic properties of the functions t^{-1}
and f^{-1} with regard to respectively the addition and the multiplication. Thus,
since t^{-1} is affine, its output is still masked additively (with another mask).
Similarly we may pass through f^{-1} with a multiplicative masking.

The proposed method for a secured implementation of Sflash is shown on
Figure (1).

7.3   Algorithmic Considerations

A. Computation of $f(\lambda)$: The function f is the following :

$$f : x \mapsto x^{128^{11}+1} = \left(\left(\left(\left(x^{128^7}\right)^{128}\right)^{128}\right)^{128}\right)^{128}\right) \cdot x$$

so we can compute $f(\lambda)$ with one raising to the power 128^7, 4 raisings to the
power 128 and one multiplication.

B. Computation of λ^{-1}: First of all we begin with remarking that $|L^*| =
128^{37} - 1$, so inverting an element of L can be done by raising it to the power
$128^{37} - 2$. Besides $128^{37} - 2 = (11...110)_2$ (*i.e.* 258 "1" followed by "0" in basis 2).
Thus we can compute λ^{-1} as follows:

- $z \longleftarrow \lambda$
- $z \longleftarrow z^2.z$ (i.e. $z = \lambda^{(11)_2}$ that we store)
- $z \longleftarrow z^{2^2}.z$ ($z = \lambda^{(1111)_2}$)

$x \longleftarrow$ hashed message to sign.
$r \longleftarrow$ random $\in L$.
$\lambda \longleftarrow$ random $\in L^*$.

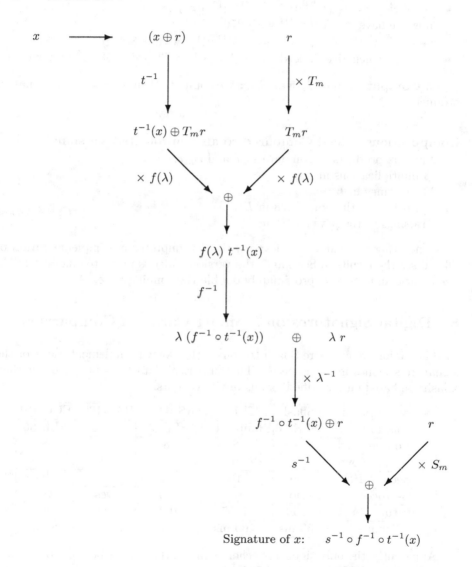

Fig. 1. A randomized masking method to protect Sflash against side-channel attacks

- $z \longleftarrow z^{2^4}.z$ $\hspace{2cm}$ $(z = \lambda^{(11111111)_2})$
- $z \longleftarrow (z^{128})^2.z$ $\hspace{2cm}$ $(z = \lambda^{(1111111111111111)_2})$
- $z \longleftarrow ((z^{128})^{128})^4.z$ $\hspace{1cm}$ $(z = \lambda^{(11111111111111111111111111111111)_2})$
- $z \longleftarrow ((((z^{128})^{128})^{128})^{128})^{2^4}.z$ $\hspace{1cm}$ $(z = \lambda^{(11...11)_2}$ with 64 "1")
- $z \longleftarrow z^{2^{64}}.z = (((z^{128^7})^{128})^{128})^2.z$ $\hspace{1cm}$ $(z = \lambda^{(11...11)_2}$ with 128 "1")
- $z \longleftarrow z^{2^{128}}.z = ((((z^{128^7})^{128^7})^{128})^{128})^{128})^{128})^4.z$
  (now we have $z = \lambda^{(11...11)_2}$ with 256 "1")
- $z \longleftarrow z^{2^2}.\lambda^{(11)_2}$ $\hspace{2cm}$ $(z = \lambda^{(11...11)_2}$ with 258 "1")
- $z \longleftarrow z^2$ which gives indeed $z = \lambda^{-1} = \lambda^{(11...110)_2}$ with 258 "1" and one "0".

C. Computation of $T_m r$ et $S_m r$: We compute them with a classical matrix product.

Computations Added Compared to an Unprotected Version:
- 2 matrix products to compute $T_m r$ and $S_m r$.
- 13 multiplications in L.
- 20 squarings in L.
- 17 raisings to the power 128 in L.
- 4 raisings to the power 128^7 in L.

Comparing to what we achieved with our (unprotected) implementation of Sflash, see the results in Section 6, the version which is protected against DPA-like attacks implies to approximately double the running time.

8   Digital Signatures on a Smart Card – a Comparison

In this section we compare Sflash to some other known implementations of the signature schemes in smart cards. The numerical data for schemes other than Sflash are based on unverified claims of the vendors.

cryptosystem	Sflash	NTRU-251	RSA-1024	RSA-1024	ECC-191
platform	SLE-66	Philips 8051	SLE-66	ST-19XL	SLE-66
word size [bits]	8	8	8	8	8
ROM size [Kbytes]	3.1	5			
speed [MHz]	10	16	10	10	10
co-processor	no	no	no	yes	yes
Signature Length	259	1757	1024	1024	382
Timings	59 ms	160 ms	many s	111 ms	180 ms

Apparently, the only signature scheme known that might be able to compete with Sflash is NTRUSign. An NTRUSign signature seems to be slower, but also about 6 times longer. Knowing that the communication ports of low-end smart cards are quite slow, at 9600 bit/s, an NTRUSign card would take additional 200 ms to transmit the signature.

9   Conclusion

In this paper we described a highly optimized implementation of the Sflash signature schemes on a low-cost smart card. Our fastest implementation of Sflash takes 59 ms on a 8051 based CPU at 10MHz. We also presented a method to protect this implementation against DPA-like attacks that requires about twice as much time.

Though the security of Sflash is not as well understood as for example for RSA, Sflash is apparently the fastest signature scheme known. It is suitable to implement PKI on low-cost smart card, token or palm devices. It allows also to propose secure low-cost payment/banking solutions.

References

[1]   Nicolas Courtois, *La sécurité des primitives cryptographiques basées sur les problèmes algébriques multivariables MQ, IP, MinRank, et HFE*, PhD Thesis, Paris 6 University, 2001, in French. Available at http://www.minrank.org/phd.pdf 268

[2]   Nicolas Courtois, Magnus Daum, Patrick Felke, *On the Security of HFE, HFEv- and Quartz*, PKC'2003, to appear in LNCS, Springer. 268

[3]   Magnus Daum, Patrick Felke, *Some new aspects concerning the Analysis of HFE type Cryptosystems*, Presented at Yet Another Conference on Cryptography (YACC'02), June 3-7, 2002, Porquerolles Island, France. 268

[4]   Magnus Daum, *Das Kryptosystem HFE und quadratische Gleichungssysteme über endlichen Körpern*, Diplomarbeit, Universität Dortmund, 2001. Available at daum@itsc.ruhr-uni-bochum.de

[5]   Jean-Charles Faugère, *Report on a successful attack of HFE Challenge 1 with Gröbner bases algorithm F5/2*, announcement that appeared in sci.crypt newsgroup on the internet on April 19th 2002.

[6]   Henri Gilbert, Marine Minier, *Cryptanalysis of Sflash*, EUROCRYPT'2002, LNCS 2332, Springer, pp. 288-298. 268

[7]   Michael Garey, David Johnson, *Computers and Intractability, a guide to the theory of NP-completeness*, Freeman, p. 251.

[8]   Willi Geiselmann, Rainer Steinwandt, Thomas Beth, *Revealing 441 Key Bits of SFLASH-v2*, Third NESSIE Workshop, November 6-7, 2002, Munich, Germany. 270

[9]   A page about the Gray code, http://www.nist.gov/dads/HTML/graycode.html 272

[10] Neal Koblitz, *Algebraic aspects of cryptography*, Springer, ACM3, 1998, Chapter 4: "Hidden Monomial Cryptosystems", pp. 80-102. 267

[11] Paul Kocher, Joshua Jaffe, Benjamin Jun, *Introduction to Differential Power Analysis and Related Attacks*. Technical Report, Cryptography Research Inc., 1998. Available at http://www.cryptography.com/dpa/technic/index.html 268, 274

[12] Tsutomu Matsumoto, Hideki Imai, *Public Quadratic Polynomial-tuples for efficient signature-verification and message-encryption*, EUROCRYPT'88, LNCS 330, Springer 1998, pp. 419-453. 267

[13] Jacques Patarin, *Cryptanalysis of the Matsumoto and Imai Public Key Scheme of Eurocrypt'88*, CRYPTO'95, LNCS 963, Springer, pp. 248-261. 267

[14] Jacques Patarin, Nicolas Courtois , Louis Goubin, *C*-+ and HM - Variations around two schemes of T. Matsumoto and H. Imai*, ASIACRYPT'98, LNCS 1514, Springer, pp. 35-49. 267, 268

[15] Jacques Patarin, Louis Goubin, Nicolas Courtois, *Quartz, 128-bit long digital signatures*, Cryptographers' Track RSA Conference 2001, San Francisco 8-12 April 2001, LNCS 2020, Springer, pp. 282-297.
Note: The Quartz signature scheme has been updated since, see [16].

[16] Jacques Patarin, Louis Goubin, Nicolas Courtois, *Quartz, 128-bit long digital signatures*, An updated version of Quartz specification. available at http://www.cryptosystem.net/quartz/ or http://www.cryptonessie.org 278

[17] Jacques Patarin, Louis Goubin, Nicolas Courtois, *Flash, a fast multivariate signature algorithm*, Cryptographers' Track RSA Conference 2001, San Francisco 8-12 April 2001, LNCS 2020, Springer, pp. 298-307. 267, 268, 269

[18] An updated version of Sflash specification. Available at http://www.cryptosystem.net/sflash/ or http://www.cryptonessie.org 267, 269

[19] Adi Shamir, *Efficient signature schemes based on birational permutations*, CRYPTO'93, LNCS 773, Springer, pp. 1-12. 268

A Practical Public Key Cryptosystem from Paillier and Rabin Schemes

David Galindo, Sebastià Martín, Paz Morillo, and Jorge L. Villar

Dep. Matemàtica Aplicada IV. Universitat Politècnica de Catalunya
Campus Nord, c/Jordi Girona, 1-3, 08034 Barcelona
{dgalindo,sebasm,paz,jvillar}@mat.upc.es

Abstract. We propose a practical scheme based on factoring and semantically secure (IND-CPA) in the standard model. The scheme is
obtained from a modification of the so called RSA-Paillier [5] scheme.
This modification is reminiscent of the ones applied by Rabin [22] and
Williams [25] to the well-known RSA cryptosystem. Thanks to the special properties of such schemes, we obtain efficiency similar to that of
RSA cryptosystem, provably secure encryption (since recovering plaintext from ciphertext is as hard as factoring) and indistinguishability
against plaintext attacks. We also construct a new trapdoor permutation based on factoring, which has interest on its own. Semantic security
of the scheme is based on an appropiate decisional assumption, named as
Decisional Small 2e-Residues assumption. The robustness of this assumption is also discussed. Compared to Okamoto-Uchiyama's scheme [18],
the previous IND-CPA cryptosystem in the standard model with one-
wayness based on factoring, our scheme is drastically more efficient in
encryption, and presents higher bandwith, achieving the same expansion
factor as Paillier or El Gamal schemes. We believe the new scheme could
be an interesting starting point to develop efficient IND-CCA schemes
in the standard model with one-wayness based on factoring.

Keywords: public-key cryptography, semantic security, factoring, standard model.

1 Introduction

Nowadays, two main hard arithmetic problems are used in public key encryption,
namely, the integer factorization problem and the discret logarithm problem.
Among all public key schemes, the only ones with existing commercial realizations are RSA or Rabin-Williams schemes, related to the factoring problem, and
El Gamal scheme, related to the discret logarithm problem. The hardness of these
problems ensures the cryptosystems are *secure*, in the sense of the infeasibility
of recovering the whole plaintext from the ciphertext. But the actual underlying goal of any encryption scheme is to guarantee that no partial information
about the the plaintext is revealed from the ciphertext in a complexity-theoretic
scenario. This notion is usually called *semantic security* or *indistinguishability of encryptions*. Depending on the capabilities allowed to the attacker, one

Y.G. Desmedt (Ed.): PKC 2003, LNCS 2567, pp. 279–291, 2003.

talks about indistinguishability against chosen plaintext attack (IND-CPA) or indistinguishability against chosen ciphertext attack (IND-CCA). The latter is considered as the right notion of security, although IND-CPA level is still maintained, since homomorphic cryptosystems can't achieve IND-CCA.

Up to now, we can find in the literature several settings for designing practical public-key IND-CCA schemes. The most popular is the so-called Random Oracle Model (ROM) [2], an idealized model of computation in which a cryptographic hash is considered as a *truly random* oracle accessible to both legitimate and illegitimate users. It turns out to be a very powerful primitive, and there exist several generic constructions (see [21] for instance), that provide IND-CCA schemes under standard computational assumptions. Although the ROM is a convenient setting, security proofs in this model are somewhat heuristic, since in real implementations hash functions are not truly random. This problem leads to a related approach, initiated by Canetti [4], with the aim of identifying useful and realizable properties of random oracles. There is a realization in this setting based on the factoring problem [16]. Another approach consists on building encryption schemes by means of integrating several cryptographic primitives, as symmetric cryptosystems, message authenticated codes and cryptographic hash functions. An instance in this model can be found in [1].

A different and appealing approach is used in [8] and [9]. In this setting, the security of the proposed IND-CCA schemes is only based on number-theoretic decisional assumptions. The technique used in [8] and [9] is to improve existing IND-CPA schemes under appropiate and widely accepted decisional assumptions, obtaining IND-CCA schemes based on the same assumptions and without significantly degrading their efficiency. There exist three different realizations in this setting, which are based on the Decisional Diffie-Hellman, Decision Composite Residuosity [19] and the classical Quadratic Residuosity assumptions respectively. It would be of great interest to construct IND-CCA schemes from the RSA and Rabin-Williams primitives in this model. A decisional assumption's candidate for the RSA scheme was proposed in the modification of Paillier scheme [5], although the proof of the equivalence between the one-wayness of this scheme and the RSA scheme has been presented very recently [6]. It is an open problem to study the validity of this new assumption and to develop an IND-CCA scheme from it. As far as we know, no decisional number-theoretic problem for the Rabin-Williams primitive has been proposed.

Our Results

In this paper we first construct a new trapdoor permutation based on factoring, which has interest on its own. Trapdoor permutations play an important role in cryptography. Many theoretic schemes use this object as a building block, in such a way that any trapdoor permutation can be easily transformed into IND-CCA ciphering (although very impractical), signature, or authentication schemes for instance. Despite this fact, few candidate trapdoor permutations are known, and fewer that are as secure as factoring (cf. [20]).

The new trapdoor permutation is obtained from a modification of RSA-Paillier's trapdoor permutation [5], which is reminiscent from the modifications applied by Rabin [22] and Williams [25] to RSA cryptosystem. Then, using this new function as a primitive, we design a new cryptosystem which is one-way under the intractability of factoring $n = pq$, with $p \equiv q \equiv 3 \bmod 4$, and IND-CPA under an appropiate number-theoretic decisional assumption. We summarize hereafter the main features of the proposed scheme:

- We take profit of the nice characteristics of Rabin schemes and overcome their drawbacks, by using the Rabin-Williams function to hide the randomness. More precisely, the encryption of a message $m \in \mathbb{Z}_n$ with randomness $r \in Q_n$ is defined as $E(r, m) = r^{2e} + mn \bmod n^2$, where e is an integer of small size.
- It is remarkable that the scheme allows to encrypt arbitrary messages with a very simple procedure, that does not depend further on the form of the message to be enciphered, which was the case for the previous Rabin based schemes. Besides, the efficiency is similar to that of plain RSA.
- The scheme is IND-CPA under the Decisional Small 2e-Residues assumption (DS2eR). We can also stablish a relation between the decisional assumption in RSA-Paillier scheme, the Quadratic Residuosity and the new DS2eR assumption.

Although the scheme is obtained by a simple modification of the RSA-Paillier scheme, this modification deeply influences the underlying mathematical structure. This was in turn the case of RSA-Paillier scheme respect to original Paillier scheme [19]. The main difference is that one-wayness of the new scheme is equivalent to factoring and independent of the size of the exponent e. Thus, the exponent e only affects the semantic security of the scheme.

We can also compare our scheme with the Okamoto-Uchiyama's scheme (OU) [18]. The one-wayness of OU is equivalent to factoring $n = p^2 q$, whereas in our case is equivalent to factoring $n = pq$, which is the classical factoring assumption. Our scheme is drastically more efficient in ciphering, since OU presents an encryption cost proportional to the lenght of the modulus n. Besides, our scheme presents a expansion factor 2, while OU's expansion factor is 3. However, OU scheme is homomorphic and more efficient in decryption than ours.

The main drawback of our scheme is that, as well as in the previous schemes with one-wayness equivalent to factoring, there exist a chosen ciphertext attack that completely breaks the scheme. In the ROM this problem can be solved by directly applying the technique in [21]. It remains an open problem to study the validity of the DS2eR assumption and to modify our scheme to achieve IND-CCA security under the DS2eR assumption in the standard model.

2   Some Previous Schemes and Related Trapdoor Permutations

In this section, we briefly recall some previous schemes and related trapdoor permutations, from which we will derive the new trapdoor permutation based on factoring, and the scheme we propose. We begin by fixing some notation.

If A is a non-empty set, then $x \leftarrow A$ denotes that x has been uniformly chosen in A, and $\mathtt{negl(k)}$ stands for a negligible function in a security parameter k. If n is an RSA modulus, i.e. $n = pq$ where p, q are different odd primes, then we denote by $\mathrm{RSA}[n, e]$ the RSA function with exponent e. The conjecture about the infeasibility of inverting the $\mathrm{RSA}[n, e]$ function on a randomly chosen input in $\mathbb{Z}_n^*$ will be referred as the $\mathrm{RSA}[n, e]$ assumption. If N is a positive integer, then Q_N stands for the set of quadratic residues modulo N. If D_1 and D_2 are two probability distributions, then $D_1 \approx D_2$ denotes that the distributions are polinomally indistinguishable [10]. It holds that if $\mathcal{A}$ is a probabilistic polynomial time (PPT) algorithm and $D_1 \approx D_2$, then $\mathcal{A}(D_1) \approx \mathcal{A}(D_2)$. Another useful property is that if g is a bijection such that g and g^{-1} can be computed in PPT, then $D_1 \approx D_2$ is equivalent to $g(D_1) \approx g(D_2)$.

Rabin Function

Let p, q be two different primes with equal length, $n = pq$. Rabin proposed in [22] a provably secure cryptosystem based on the modular squaring function

$$\mathbb{Z}_n^* \longrightarrow Q_n$$
$$x \longmapsto x^2 \bmod n.$$

It is well known that modular squaring is a trapdoor one-way function assuming that factorisation of large numbers is infeasible. However, modular squaring is a 4 to 1 function, so a ciphertext is not uniquely decrypted. In order to avoid this drawback and to speed up the decryption algorithm (i.e. the computation of square roots modulo n), the following proposal by Blum and Williams can be considered:

Blum-Williams Function

Let p, q be (different) primes with equal length, $p \equiv q \equiv 3 \bmod 4$, $n = pq$. The squaring function restricted to Q_n, i.e.

$$\mathcal{G}_n : Q_n \longrightarrow Q_n$$
$$x \longmapsto x^2 \bmod n$$

is a trapdoor one-way permutation if factoring large numbers is infeasible (see page 34 in [11]). Then, if we restrict the set of messages to Q_n, a ciphertext will be uniquely decrypted. However, this is not suitable for real applications, since it does not allow to encrypt arbitrary messages. To decrypt $c \in Q_n$ one has to compute $\mathcal{G}_n^{-1}(c)$, i.e. the element $s \in Q_n$ such that $s^2 = c \bmod n$. Let us briefly recall how to make this computation (see [24] for a nice account on this). Assume that we know the factorisation of $n = pq$, where $p \equiv q \equiv 3 \bmod 4$. We first compute the numbers $f = c^{\frac{p+1}{4}} \bmod p$ and $g = c^{\frac{q+1}{4}} \bmod q$, which are the square roots of c modulo p and modulo q that are quadratic residues to their respective modulus. Then, by using the Chinese Remainder Theorem, we obtain an $s \in Q_n$ such that $s^2 = c \bmod n$.

Rabin-Williams Function

Let p, q be (different) primes with equal length, $p \equiv q \equiv 3 \bmod 4$, $n = pq$ and e a public RSA exponent (i.e. an integer such that $\gcd(e, \lambda(n)) = 1$, where λ denotes Carmichael's function). The map

$$\mathcal{W}_e : Q_n \longrightarrow Q_n$$
$$x \longmapsto x^{2e} \bmod n$$

is also a trapdoor one-way permutation assuming that factoring large numbers is infeasible, since a perfect reduction to the Blum-Williams function inversion problem can be done as follows. Given $c = \mathcal{G}_n(x) = x^2 \bmod n$, x can be retrieved from $c^e \bmod n = x^{2e} \bmod n$ by inverting the Rabin-Williams function with some non-negligible probability.

RSA-Paillier Function

Catalano et al. proposed in [5] a mix of Paillier's scheme [19] with RSA scheme, in order to obtain an IND-CPA cryptosystem in the standard model with efficiency similar to that of RSA cryptosystem. It is based on the permutation

$$\mathcal{E}_e : \mathbb{Z}_n^* \times \mathbb{Z}_n \longrightarrow \mathbb{Z}_{n^2}^*$$
$$(r, m) \longmapsto r^e(1 + mn) \bmod n^2,$$

where p, q are distinct primes with the same length, $n = pq$, and $e \in \mathbb{Z}_n$ is such that $\gcd(e, \lambda(n^2)) = 1$. The encryption scheme $\mathcal{E}_e(r, m)$ with randomness $r \in \mathbb{Z}_n^*$ is semantically secure under the *Decisional Small e-Residues* assumption [5].

Sakurai and Takagi claimed in [23] that deciphering RSA-Paillier scheme with public exponent e is actually equivalent to inverting the original RSA$[n, e]$ function. However, Catalano, Nguyen and Stern found a flaw in the proof by Takagi and Sakurai, and they proposed in [6] an alternative proof of the claim in [23]. Therefore, RSA-Paillier scheme is the first semantically secure RSA-type scheme in the standard model.

3   New Trapdoor Permutation Based on Factoring

In this section we present a new length-preserving trapdoor permutation based on factoring, i.e. a length-preserving bijection that is one-way assuming that factoring large integers is hard. It is worthwhile to remark that as well as ours, all previous trapdoor permutations provably secure [1] are based on the factoring problem [20]. To the best of our knowledge, only two length-preserving provably secure trapdoor permutations exist, namely, the Blum-Williams permutation, and another one proposed by Gong and Harn in [12].

A New Trapdoor Permutation

Let p, q be primes, $p \equiv q \equiv 3 \bmod 4$, $n = pq$, e a positive integer such that $\gcd(e, \lambda(n)) = 1$ and

$$\mathcal{F}_e : Q_n \times \mathbb{Z}_n \longrightarrow Q_{n^2}$$
$$(r, m) \longmapsto r^{2e} + mn \bmod n^2.$$

Proposition 1. $\mathcal{F}_e$ is a well-defined length-preserving bijection.

Proof: From the Hensel-lifting, the set of quadratic residues modulo n^2 can be alternatively defined as $Q_{n^2} = \{x + yn \mid x \in Q_n, y \in \mathbb{Z}_n\}$. Then if $c = \mathcal{F}_e(r, m) = r^{2e} + mn \bmod n^2$, with $r \in Q_n$, $m \in \mathbb{Z}_n$, it is obvious that $c \bmod n = r^{2e} \bmod n \in Q_n$, which implies that $\mathcal{F}_e$ is well-defined.

To prove that $\mathcal{F}_e$ is bijective it suffices to show that it is injective, because, from the alternative definition of Q_{n^2}, we deduce that the sets $Q_n \times \mathbb{Z}_n$ and Q_{n^2} have the same number of elements. Let us suppose that $\mathcal{F}_e(r_0, m_0) = \mathcal{F}_e(r_1, m_1)$. Then $r_0^{2e} = r_1^{2e} \bmod n$, and since squaring and computing e-th powers modulo n, with $\gcd(e, \lambda(n)) = 1$, are bijections over Q_n, we conclude that $r_0 = r_1 \bmod n$. This implies $m_0 n = m_1 n \bmod n^2$, so $m_0 = m_1 \bmod n$.

Finally, $\mathcal{F}_e$ is length-preserving, since the natural bit representation of an arbitrary element either in $Q_n \times \mathbb{Z}_n$ or in Q_{n^2} has length $2\lceil \log_2 n \rceil$. □

In the sequel we prove that inverting $\mathcal{F}_e$ is as difficult as factoring the modulus n. We denote by $\mathcal{PRIMES}(k)$ the set of primes of length k which are congruent with 3 modulo 4.

Assumption 1 (Factoring assumption) *For every probabilistic polynomial time algorithm $\mathcal{A}$, there exists a negligible function* negl() *such that*

$$Pr\left[\begin{matrix} p, q \leftarrow \mathcal{PRIMES}(k/2), \ n = pq, \\ \mathcal{A}(1^k, n) = (p, q) \end{matrix} \right] = \texttt{negl}(k).$$

---

[1] We say a cryptographic scheme is provably secure if it is proven to be as secure as the underlying primitive problems (i.e., discrete logarithm or factoring problems).

Notice that the set $\mathcal{PRIMES}(k/2)$ is a subset of the set of all primes with length $k/2$. However, there is no evidence suggesting that the factoring problem is *easier* in $\mathcal{PRIMES}(k)$ than in the whole set.

Assumption 2 $\mathcal{G}_n$ *is one-way, that is, for every probabilistic polynomial time algorithm* $\mathcal{A}$, *there exists a negligible function* negl() *such that*

$$Pr\begin{bmatrix} p, q \leftarrow \mathcal{PRIMES}(k/2), \ n = pq, \\ r \leftarrow Q_n, \ c = r^2 \bmod n, \\ \mathcal{A}(1^k, n, c) = r \end{bmatrix} = \text{negl}(k).$$

Proposition 3 $\mathcal{G}_n$ *is one-way if and only if the Factoring Assumption holds.*
Proof: (see any basic book on cryptography, for instance [24]).

Assumption 4 $\mathcal{F}_e$ *is one-way, that is, for every probabilistic polynomial time algorithm* $\mathcal{A}$, *there exists a negligible function* negl() *such that*

$$Pr\begin{bmatrix} p, q \leftarrow \mathcal{PRIMES}(k/2), \ n = pq, \\ r \leftarrow Q_n, \ m \leftarrow \mathbb{Z}_n, \ c = \mathcal{F}_e(r, m), \\ \mathcal{A}(1^k, n, e, c) = (r, m) \end{bmatrix} = \text{negl}(k).$$

Proposition 5 *For all e such that* $\gcd(e, \lambda(n)) = 1$, $\mathcal{F}_e$ *is a trapdoor permutation if and only if the Factoring Assumption holds.*

Proof:
($\Rightarrow$) Let us suppose the Factoring Assumption does not hold. Then there exists a polynomial time algorithm that factors $n = pq$ with a non-negligible probability ε. Knowing p and q, one can compute $d \subset \mathbb{Z}_n^*$ s.t. $de \equiv 1 \bmod \lambda(n)$, since $\gcd(e, \lambda(n)) = 1$. For any $c \in Q_{n^2}$ we can also compute $r = \mathcal{G}_n^{-1}(c^d \bmod n) = \mathcal{G}_n^{-1}(r^2 \bmod n)$, and $m \in \mathbb{Z}_n$ from the equality $mn = c - r^{2e} \bmod n^2$. These values are such that $\mathcal{F}_e(r, m) = c$, so we can invert $\mathcal{F}_e$ on $c \leftarrow Q_{n^2}$ with non-negligible success probability ε, which implies that $\mathcal{F}_e$ is not one-way.

($\Leftarrow$) Let us suppose that $\mathcal{F}_e$ is not one-way for a certain e such that $\gcd(e, \lambda(n)) = 1$. The goal is to show that a probabilistic polynomial time algorithm that inverts $\mathcal{F}_e$ on a random input can be transformed into another algorithm that inverts Blum-Williams permutation $\mathcal{G}_n$. Assume then we are given a security parameter k, an integer n and $c \in Q_n$ with the distributions described in assumption 2. Let $c' = c^e + mn \bmod n^2$, where $m \leftarrow \mathbb{Z}_n$. Then, since c was uniformly chosen in Q_n and the map

$$Q_n \times \mathbb{Z}_n \longrightarrow Q_{n^2}$$
$$(c, m) \longmapsto c^e + mn \bmod n^2$$

is a bijection, we deduce that c' is uniformly distributed in Q_{n^2}. Let $(r, m') = \mathcal{A}(n, c')$, where $\mathcal{A}$ is the algorithm that inverts $\mathcal{F}_e$ on a random input with a non-negligible probability ε. If $\mathcal{A}$ gives the correct answer, then $c^e + mn = r^{2e} + m'n \bmod n^2$. Reducing this equality modulo n, we have $r^{2e} = c^e \bmod n$, which is equivalent to $c = r^2 \bmod n$, since $\gcd(e, \lambda(n)) = 1$. Then $\mathcal{G}_n^{-1}(c) = r$ with probability ε. $\square$

4   The New Scheme

Using the permutation $\mathcal{F}_e$ as a primitive, we are able to develop the following encryption scheme:

Key Generation

Given a security parameter ℓ, choose at random two primes p and q with $\ell/2$ bits such that $p \equiv q \equiv 3 \bmod 4$, and choose an integer $e > 2$ s.t. $\gcd(e, \lambda(n^2)) = 1$. Then the public key is PK=(n, e), where $n = pq$, and the secret key is SK=(p, q, d), where $d = e^{-1} \bmod \lambda(n)$.

Let us observe that in the definition of $\mathcal{F}_e$ in the previous section, the integer e must only satisfy the condition $\gcd(e, \lambda(n)) = 1$. Now we demand, in addition, that $e > 2$ and, since $\lambda(n^2) = n\lambda(n)$, that $\gcd(e, n) = 1$. The reason for this choice will become clearer when we study both one-wayness and semantic security of the scheme.

Encryption

To encrypt a message $m \in \mathbb{Z}_n$ we compute $c = \mathcal{F}_e(r, m)$, where r is randomly chosen in Q_n. The choice of the randomness in Q_n can be done, for instance, by selecting $s \leftarrow \mathbb{Z}_n^*$ at random, and computing $r = s^2 \bmod n$.

Decryption

To recover the message m from $c = \mathcal{F}_e(r, m)$, the randomness r is computed firstly, and, afterwards, m is easily obtained from

$$mn = c - r^{2e} \bmod n^2 .$$

To obtain r from c, we compute $t = RSA[n, e]^{-1}(c \bmod n) = c^d \bmod n$, and then $r = \mathcal{G}_n^{-1}(t)$, computed as explained in section 2.

5   Security Analysis

In this section we discuss the security properties of the encryption scheme, namely, its one-wayness and semantic security against passive adversaries. We show the scheme is one-way under the Factoring Assumption and semantically secure under an appropiate number-theoretic decisional assumption.

5.1   One-Wayness

In order to study the one-wayness of the scheme, we introduce a new computational problem which is closely related. Afterwards, we prove that the new computational problem is intractable if and only if the factoring problem is intractable. In fact, the new problem is the natural extension to our case of the questions dealt with in [23] and [6].

In [6], given an RSA modulus n and a public exponent e relatively prime to $\lambda(n)$, the following function from $\mathbb{Z}_n^*$ to $\mathbb{Z}_{n^l}^*$, for $l > 1$, is defined:

$$\textbf{Hensel-RSA}[n, e, l](r^e \bmod n) = r^e \bmod n^l \,,$$

and it is proven that the hardness of computing such a function is equivalent to the RSA $[n, e]$ assumption. With some slight modifications, the arguments in [6] can be applied to our encryption scheme. Let us consider the **Hensel-Rabin-Williams** function from Q_n to Q_{n^l} defined as

$$\textbf{Hensel-RW}[n, e, l](r^{2e} \bmod n) = r^{2e} \bmod n^l \,,$$

where $r \in Q_n$. The following proposition can then be stated

Proposition 6 *Given p, q (different) primes with equal length, $p \equiv q \equiv 3 \bmod 4$, $n = pq$ and e a public RSA exponent relatively prime to n, computing **Hensel-RW**[n, e, 2] on a random element $w \in Q_n$ is hard if and only if the function $\mathcal{W}_e$ is one-way.*

Proof.
($\Rightarrow$) If $\mathcal{W}_e$ is not one-way, then r can be computed from $r^{2e} \bmod n$ with non-negligible probability and therefore **Hensel-RW**$[n, e, 2](r^{2e})$ is trivially computed.

($\Leftarrow$) The adversary, who wants to invert the Rabin-Williams function on a random input $r^{2e} \bmod n$, calls an oracle twice for the **Hensel-RW**$[n, e, 2]$ on inputs r^{2e} and $r^{2e}a^{2e}$, where a is randomly chosen in Q_n. Assuming that ε is the probability that the oracle gives the right answer, the adversary knows $r^{2e} \bmod n^2$ and $\mu^{2e} \bmod n^2$, where $\mu = ar \bmod n$, with probability ε^2. Then, it follows that there exists $z \in \mathbb{Z}_n$ such that

$$ar = \mu(1 + zn) \bmod n^2. \qquad (1)$$

Raising this equality to the power $2e$ we obtain the equation $a^{2e}r^{2e} = \mu^{2e}(1 + 2ezn) \bmod n^2$, from which z can be computed, since the rest of values involved are known. The last step is the computation of r and μ from equation (1). This can be done by using lattice reduction techniques (see [6] for further details). $\square$

The   following   lemma   states   the   relation   between   computing **Hensel-RW**$[n, e, 2]$ function and the one-wayness of our scheme.

Lemma 7 *The encryption scheme described in section 4 is one-way if and only if computing* **Hensel-RW**$[n, e, 2]$ *on a random input is hard.*

Proof:
($\Rightarrow$) For a random ciphertext $c \leftarrow Q_{n^2}$, the message m is easily recovered from the **Hensel-Rabin-Williams** oracle since $mn = c - $ **Hensel-RW**$[n, e, 2](c \bmod n)$.

($\Leftarrow$) To compute **Hensel-RW**$[n, e, 2]$ on $c_0 \leftarrow Q_n$, it suffices to choose $m_0 \leftarrow \mathbb{Z}_n$, and submit $c_0 + m_0 n$ to the adversary that is able to invert the proposed cryptosystem with a non-negligible probability ε. (Note that m_0 is intended to match the exact probability distribution needed for the query to the adversary.) Since there exist uniques $r \in Q_n$ and $m \in \mathbb{Z}_n$ such that $c_0 + m_0 n = r^{2e} + mn \bmod n^2$, the adversary answers m with probability ε. Then, **Hensel-RW**$[n, e, 2](c_0) = c_0 + (m_0 - m)n \bmod n^2$. $\square$

The above arguments lead to the following theorem.

Theorem 8 *The encryption scheme described in section 4 is one-way if and only if the Factoring Assumption holds.*

Proof: From Lemma 7 and Proposition 6, one-wayness of our scheme is equivalent to one-wayness of the Rabin-Williams function, that is in turn equivalent to the Factoring Assumption. $\square$

At this point, we have to notice that, as the previous schemes with one-wayness based on factoring, there exists a chosen ciphertext attack that completely breaks our cryptosystem. This problem can be avoided by directly applying the construction in the random oracle model introduced by Pointcheval in [21]. Since this construction provides an IND-CCA scheme from any partial one-way function, assuming only the random oracles and the assumption under which the function is one-way, we can build the new scheme from the primitive

$$Q_n \times \mathbb{Z}_n \longrightarrow Q_{n^2}$$
$$(r, m) \longmapsto r^2 + mn \bmod n^2,$$

that is, taking $e = 1$. Thereby we obtain an IND-CCA scheme in the ROM based on factoring and highly efficient. This new scheme presents a *tight reduction* to the factoring problem, and it has a simpler description than some of the previous similar constructions [15, 3, 17].

5.2   Semantic Security

Now we describe the number-theoretic decisional assumption on which the semantic security of the scheme is based:

Decisional Small 2e-Residues Assumption (DS2eR)

Let p, q be randomly chosen ℓ-bit long primes, with $p, q \equiv 3 \bmod 4$, $n = pq$, and let e be an integer such that $\gcd(e, pq(p-1)(q-1)) = 1$. The following probability distributions are polinomially indistinguishable in the security parameter ℓ:

$$D_{2e-\text{multiple}} = (n, \ r^{2e} \bmod n^2) \text{ where } r \leftarrow Q_n, \text{ and}$$
$$D_{\text{random}} = (n, c) \text{ where } c \leftarrow Q_{n^2}.$$

Proposition 9 *The encryption scheme described in section 4 is semantically secure if and only if DS2eR assumption holds.*

Proof: Semantic security is equivalent to indistinguishability of encryptions, that is, for all $m_0 \in \mathbb{Z}_n$, the distributions

$$D_0 = (n, \ r^{2e} + m_0 n \bmod n^2) \text{ where } r \leftarrow Q_n \quad \text{and}$$
$$D = (n, \ r^{2e} + mn \bmod n^2) \text{ where } r \leftarrow Q_n, \ m \leftarrow \mathbb{Z}_n$$

are polynomially indistinguishable. It is easy to see that the map

$$Q_{n^2} \longrightarrow Q_{n^2}$$
$$c \longmapsto c - m_0 n \bmod n^2$$

is a polynomial time bijection. Then, $D_0 \approx D$ is equivalent to

$$(n, r^{2e} \bmod n^2) \approx (n, r^{2e} + m'n \quad \bmod n^2) \text{ where } r \leftarrow Q_n, m' \leftarrow \mathbb{Z}_n.$$

Note that the distribution on the left side is $D_{2e-\text{multiple}}$.
Besides, since $r^{2e} + m'n \bmod n^2 = \mathcal{F}_e(r, m')$, and $\mathcal{F}_e$ is a bijection, then D and D_{random} are identically distributed. $\square$

Once we have proved the equivalence between the semantic security of the scheme and DS2eR assumption, the question that immediately arises is the confidence we should have on this assumption. The decisional assumption in the RSA-Paillier scheme [5], named as DSeR assumption, is very similar to ours. In their case it is conjectured that it is infeasible to distinguish between a random element in $\mathbb{Z}_{n^2}^*$ and an element of the form $r^e \bmod n^2$, where $r \leftarrow \mathbb{Z}_n^*$, when the factorisation of n is unknown. As it is argued in [5], the better way we know to attack DS2eR assumption is to solve its computational version, that is, we answer the DS2eR problem by finding a solution of the equation $x^{2e} = c \bmod n^2$, with $c \in Q_{n^2}$. So we are adressed with the problem of finding small solutions of low degree polynomials. The best known way to do it is to apply the following result due to Coppersmith [7]:

Theorem 10 *Let N be an integer and let $f(x) \in \mathbb{Z}_N[x]$ be a monic polynomial of degree d. Then there is an efficient algorithm to find all $x_0 \in \mathbb{Z}$ such that $f(x_0) = 0 \bmod N$ and $|x_0| < N^{1/d}$.*

In our case, given the equation $c = x^{2e} \bmod n^2$, we must find a root $x < n$.

Coppersmith's result ensures this is efficiently computable (i.e. in polynomial time) for all $|x| < n^{2/2e} = n^{1/e}$. For all values x greater than this bound, at present there is no polynomial algorithm that solves this problem when the factorization of n is unknown. Then for any $e > 2$ the assumption seems to be valid with hardness depending on the size of exponent e.

Regarding decisional assumptions DSeR and DS2eR, we can establish the following interesting link.

Proposition 11 *If both Quadratic Residuosity [13] and DSeR assumptions hold, then the DS2eR assumption also holds.*

Sketch of the proof: If the Quadratic Residuosity assumption holds, then the probability distributions D_1 and D_2 obtained from $(r^e \bmod n^2, \; r \leftarrow Q_n)$ and $(r^e \bmod n^2, \; r \leftarrow \mathbb{Z}_n)$ are indistinguishable. Moreover, DSeR assumption implies that these distributions are indistinguishable from the distribution D_3 obtained from $(c \leftarrow \mathbb{Z}_{n^2})$. Finally, squaring D_1 and D_3 we conclude that $(r^{2e} \bmod n^2, \; r \leftarrow Q_n)$ is indistinguishable from $(c^2 \bmod n^2, \; c \leftarrow \mathbb{Z}_{n^2})$, that is uniformly distributed over Q_{n^2}. $\square$

Nevertheless, nowadays we have very little knowledge about the validity of this family of decisional assumptions, and more research is needed to evaluate their difficulty. We think this could enlighten on the design of IND-CCA encryption schemes in the standard model which one-wayness is based on the RSA or factoring problems.

Acknowledgements

We would like to thank Dario Catalano for sending us an early version of his paper [6] and the anonymous referees for their useful comments.

References

[1] M. Abdalla, M. Bellare and P. Rogaway. DHAES: An Encryption Scheme Based on the Diffie-Hellman Problem. *Submission to IEEE P1363a.* (1998) 280

[2] M. Bellare and P. Rogaway. Random Oracles are Practical: a Paradigm for Designing Efficient Protocols. *ACM CCS 93, ACM Press* (1993) 280

[3] D. Boneh. Simplified OAEP for the RSA and Rabin Functions. *CRYPTO' 01, LNCS* **2139** 275–291 (2001). 288

[4] R. Canetti. Towards realizing random oracles: Hash functions that hide all partial information. *CRYPTO' 97, LNCS* **1294** 455–469 (1997). 280

[5] D. Catalano, R. Gennaro, N. Howgrave-Graham and P. Q. Nguyen. Paillier's Cryptosystem Revisited. *ACM CCS '2001 ACM Press* (2001). 279, 280, 281, 283, 289

[6] D. Catalano, P. Q. Nguyen and J. Stern. The Hardness of Hensel Lifting: The Case of RSA and Discrete Logarithm. *To appear at Proceedings of ASIACRYPT'2002. LNCS* **2501** (2002). 280, 283, 287, 290

[7] D. Coppersmith. Finding a small root of a univariate modular equation. *EURO-CRYPT '96, LNCS* **1070** 155–165 (1996). 289

[8] R. Cramer and V. Shoup. A Practical Public Key Cryptosystem Provably Secure against Adaptive Chosen Ciphertext Attack. *CRYPTO' 98, LNCS* **1462** 13–25 (1998). 280

[9] R. Cramer and V. Shoup. Universal Hash Proofs and a Paradigm for Adaptive Chosen Ciphertext Secure Public-Key Encryption. *EUROCRYPT '2002, LNCS* **2332** 45–64 (2002). 280

[10] O. Goldreich. Foundation of Cryptography - Basic Tools. *Cambridge University Press* (2001). 282

[11] S. Goldwasser and M. Bellare. Lecture Notes on Cryptography. http://www-cse.ucsd.edu/users/mihir 283

[12] G. Gong and L. Harn. Public-key cryptosystems based on cubic finite field extensions. *IEEE Transactions on Information Theory* **45** (7) 2601–2605 (1999) 284

[13] S. Golwasser and S. Micali. Probabilistic encryption. *Journal of Computer and System Sciences* **28** 270–299 (1984). 290

[14] M. Joye and J. J. Quisquater. Cryptanalysis of RSA-type cryptosystems: a visit. *Network Threats, DIMACS Series in Discr. Math. ant Th. Comp. Sci., AMS* 21–31 (1998).

[15] K. Kurosawa, W. Ogata, T. Matsuo and S. Makishima. IND-CCA Public Key Schemes Equivalent to Factoring $n = pq$. *PKC' 01, LNCS* **1992** 36–47 (2001). 288

[16] S. Müeller. On the Security of a Williams Based Public Key Encryption Scheme. *PKC' 01, LNCS* **1992** 1–18 (2001) 280

[17] M. Nishioka, H. Satoh and K. Sakurai. Public Key Cryptosystems Based on a Modular Squaring. *ICISC'2001, LNCS* **2288** 81–102 (2001) 288

[18] T. Okamoto and S. Uchiyama. A New Public-Key Cryptosystem as Secure as Factoring. *EUROCRYPT-98, LNCS* **1403** 308–318 (1998) 279, 281

[19] P. Paillier. Public-Key Cryptosystems Based on Composite Degree Residuosity Classes. *EUROCRYPT '99, LNCS* **1592** 223–238 (1999). 280, 281, 283

[20] J. Patarin and L. Goubin. Trapdoor One-Way Permutations and Multivariate Polynomials. Extended version of the paper published at *ICICS' 97, LNCS* **1334** 356–368. 281, 284

[21] D. Pointcheval. Chosen-Ciphertext Security for any One-Way Cryptosystem. *Proc. PKC '2000 LNCS* **1751** 129–146 (2000). 280, 281, 288

[22] M. O. Rabin. Digitalized signatures and public key functions as intractable as factorisation. MIT/LCS/TR-212 *MIT Laboratory for Computer Science* (1979) 279, 281, 282

[23] K. Sakurai and T. Takagi. New Semantically Secure Public-Key Cryptosystems from the RSA-Primitive. *PKC 2002, LNCS* **2274** (2002). 283, 287

[24] H. C. A. van Tilborg. A Professional Reference and Interactive Tutorial. *Kluwer Academic Publishers SECS* **528** (1999). 283, 285

[25] Williams H. C. A modification of the RSA Public-Key Encryption Procedure. *IEEE Trans. Inf. Theory* Vol. IT-26, No.6, 726–729 (1980). 279, 281

A Lattice Based Public Key Cryptosystem Using Polynomial Representations

Seong-Hun Paeng[1] *, Bae Eun Jung[2], and Kil-Chan Ha[3] **

[1] Department of Mathematics, Konkuk University, Seoul, 143-701 Korea
shpaeng@konkuk.ac.kr
[2] ETRI, 161 Kajong-dong, Yusong-gu, Taejon, 305-350, Korea
bejung@etri.re.kr
[3] Department of Applied Mathematics, Sejong University, Seoul, 143-747 Korea
kcha@sejong.ac.kr

Abstract. In Crypto 97, a public key cryptosystem based on the closest vector problem was suggested by Goldreich, Goldwasser and Halevi [4]. In this paper, we propose a public key cryptosystem applying representations of polynomials to the GGH encryption scheme. Its key size is much smaller than the GGH system so that it is a quite practical and efficient lattice based cryptosystem.

Keywords: GGH cryptosystem, lattice based public key cryptosystem, polynomial representation

1 Introduction

In Crypto 97, Goldreich, Goldwasser and Halevi proposed a cryptosystem (GGH) using the closest vector problem (CVP) [4]. It is one of the most notable cryptosystem based on the complexity of lattices. The authors of the GGH published 5 numerical challenges for the security parameter $n = 200, 250, 300, 350, 400$, of which the public key sizes range from 330KBytes to 2MBytes. Nguyen solved all the GGH challenge except $n = 400$ [9]. For $n = 400$, the GGH is not practical since the key size is too large. It uses $n \times n$-matrices as a public key and a private key. Thus its key sizes are very large, so it is considered not to be practical. Almost every lattice based public key cryptosystem except for NTRU has an impractical key size. Micciancio suggested to express the public matrix as Hermitian normal form (HNF), whose key sizes are much smaller than those of the GGH system [8].

However, the GGH system has some advantages. For example, it seems to be asymptotically more efficient than RSA and ElGamal encryption schemes using modular exponentiations. Furthermore, it has a natural signature scheme. Currently, NTRU cryptosystem is the most efficient cryptosystem among lattice based PKC's. But in view of security, the GGH encryption scheme has an advantage. Attackers can find out only the message by known lattice attacks, i.e.

---

* Supported by the Faculty Research Fund of Konkuk University in 2002 and NSRI.
** Supported by NSRI.

the secret key of the GGH cannot be obtained by solving the shortest vector problem (or CVP) [9]. But in NTRU, the secret key of NTRU can be obtained by finding the shortest vector of NTRU-lattice.

In this paper, we propose a public key cryptosystem applying polynomial representations to the GGH scheme whose key size is practical. In section 2, we shortly review the GGH system and explain the security related to the choice of a secret parameter T. In section 3, we study various representations of polynomials by $n \times n$-matrices and their direct applications to the GGH system. In section 4, we suggest a public key cryptosystem using the representations in section 3. Also we study its parameter selection, security analysis and key sizes. Its key sizes are much smaller than HNF expression and comparable with NTRU. In Appendix A, we introduce a scheme whose key size is smaller than that of the scheme proposed in section 4.

2 Description of the GGH System

2.1 The GGH System

In this section, we describe the GGH cryptosystem briefly. First, recall the definitions related to lattice:

Definition 1. *Let B be a real non-singular $n \times n$-matrix. The orthogonality defect of B is defined as*

$$orth\text{-}defect(B) := \frac{\prod_i \|b_i\|}{|det(B)|},$$

where $\|b_i\|$ is the Euclidean norm of the i-th column in B.

Then orth-defect$(B) = 1$ if and only if B is an orthogonal matrix.

Definition 2. *Let B be a real non-singular $n \times n$-matrix. The dual orthogonality defect of B is defined as*

$$orth\text{-}defect^*(B) := \frac{\prod_i \|b_i^*\|}{|det(B^{-1})|} = |det(B)| \prod_i \|b_i^*\|,$$

where b_i^* is the i-th row in B^{-1}.

The GGH uses the closest vector problem (CVP). It is well known that CVP is an NP-hard problem. The GGH system is as follows:

Private key The private key is an $n \times n$-matrix R with a low dual-orthogonality-defect. It can be generated by $R' + kI$, where $R' = (R'_{ij})$ satisfies that $|R'_{ij}| \leq l$ and $k \approx \sqrt{n}l$ for some constant l.

Public key The public key is an $n \times n$-matrix B such that B generates the same lattice as R with a high dual-orthogonality-defect. Then $B = RT^{-1}$ for some $T \in GL(n, \mathbb{Z})$.

Encryption The message v is an element of $\mathbb{Z}^n$. The ciphertext is obtained as follows:

$$c = Bv + e$$

for an error vector $e = (\delta_1 \sigma, \cdots, \delta_n \sigma)$, where $\delta_i = -1$ or 1 and σ is a small constant, e.g. 4.

Decryption The deciphertext is obtained as follows:

$$v' = T\lceil R^{-1} c \rfloor,$$

where $\lceil v \rfloor$ denotes the vector in $\mathbb{Z}^n$ which is obtained by rounding each entry in v to the nearest integer.

Since T^{-1} is an integer matrix, we have

$$
\begin{aligned}
T\lceil R^{-1} c \rfloor &= T\lceil R^{-1}(RT^{-1}v + e) \rfloor \\
&= T\lceil T^{-1}v + R^{-1}e \rfloor \\
&= v + T\lceil R^{-1}e \rfloor.
\end{aligned}
\tag{2.1}
$$

If $\lceil R^{-1}e \rfloor = 0$, then decryption works. We denote the maximum of L_∞-norm of the rows in R^{-1} by $\gamma/\sqrt{n}$. If $\sigma = \lfloor (\gamma\sqrt{8\ln(2n/\epsilon)})^{-1} \rfloor$ for some small real number $\epsilon > 0$, then the probability of decryption error is bounded by ϵ, where $\lfloor a \rfloor = \max\{\, x \mid x \text{ is an integer, } x \leq a \,\}$.

2.2   Why Is $|\det(T)| = 1$ Needed?

Let L_R and L_B be the lattices generated by columns of R and $B = RT^{-1}$, respectively. In the GGH, L_R and L_B are the same lattices so that T is unimodular. Even if L_B is a sublattice of L_R (i.e. T^{-1} is an integer matrix and $|\det(T^{-1})| \geq 1$), the decryption works. But in this case, its security can be weakened. In this section, we discuss the reason why we should use R and B such that $L_R = L_B$ in view of security.

Assume that L_B is a sublattice of L_R, i.e. $|\det(T)| < 1$. For the embedding attack ([4], [9]), L_B is embedded in $\bar{L}_B$ as (4.7). (see Section 4.) Note that $\det(\bar{L}_B) = \det(L_B) = \det(R)\det(T^{-1})$. Then CVP for L_B is changed to the shortest vector problem (SVP) for $\bar{L}_B$ [4],[9].

Recall the definition of the gap of the lattice.

Definition 3. *The gap of a lattice L, G_L is the ratio between the second successive minimum (the smallest real number r such that there are two linearly independent lattice points of length at most r) and the length of a shortest non zero vector in L.*

The larger the lattice gap is, the easier it becomes to find the shortest vector [9]. For $\bar{L}_B$, $(e, 1)$ will be the shortest vector with high probability and the second successive minima will be similar to the norm of the column vector of R if $|\det(T^{-1})| = 1$. Hence, in the case of the GGH, the gap of $\bar{L}_B$ could be estimated.

In the case that $|\det(T^{-1})| > 1$, since L_B is a sublattice of L_R, such an estimate is invalid. Instead, we can consider the security analysis used in NTRU. Gaussian heuristics says that the expected size of the smallest vector in a random lattice of dimension $n + 1$ lies between

$$s_1 = \det(\bar{L}_B)^{1/n+1}\sqrt{\frac{n+1}{2\pi e}} = \det(T^{-1})^{1/n+1}\det(L_R)^{1/n+1}\sqrt{\frac{n+1}{2\pi e}}$$

and

$$s_2 = \det(\bar{L}_B)^{1/n+1}\sqrt{\frac{n+1}{\pi e}} = \det(T^{-1})^{1/n+1}\det(L_R)^{1/n+1}\sqrt{\frac{n+1}{\pi e}}.$$

Let $\lambda_1(\bar{L}_B)$ be the length of the shortest vector in $\bar{L}_B$. Since the second successive minima is expected to be larger than s_1, if we can find a vector b_1 such that $||b_1|| \leq s_1 = \frac{s_1}{\lambda_1(\bar{L}_B)}\lambda_1(\bar{L}_B)$, it will be the shortest vector. Hence the larger $\frac{s_1}{\lambda_1(\bar{L}_B)}$ is, the easier it is to find the shortest vector.

By LLL-algorithm, we can find a vector b_1 such that $||b_1|| \leq 2^{n/2}\lambda_1(\bar{L}_B)$. BKZ algorithm with block size β finds a vector of length at most $O(\beta^{n+1/\beta}\lambda_1(\bar{L}_B))$ [10]. Hence the larger β is, the higher the probability to find the shortest vector is. On the other hand, the run time of BKZ algorithm is exponential in the block size.

The authors of NTRU guessed the following conjecture based on experiments [5]:

Conjecture 1. For a given n-dimensional lattice L, let s_1 be $\det(L)^{1/n}\sqrt{\frac{n}{2\pi e}}$. The required time to find the shortest vector is $\exp(O(\frac{\lambda_1(L)}{s_1}n))$.

Based on this conjecture, the larger $|\det(T^{-1})|$ is, the easier it is to find the shortest vector in the embedded lattice $\bar{L}_B$. Hence it is an essential condition to use T^{-1} such that $|\det(T^{-1})|$ is small (especially 1). Assume that $n = 500$ and let t be the run time to find the shortest vector for the case that $|\det(T^{-1})| = 1$. If we choose T^{-1} such that $\det(T^{-1}) \approx 1.1^{500} = 5 \times 10^{20}$, then the run time to find the shortest vector will be $t^{0.91}$. But if we choose T^{-1} randomly in $M(n, \mathbb{Z})$, the probability to choose T^{-1} such that $|\det(T^{-1})| \leq 5 \times 10^{20}$ is almost 0.

3   Lattice Generated by Representations of Polynomial Rings

3.1   Representation of a Polynomial Ring

We introduce a representation of a polynomial ring as follows: We identify $c_{n-1}x^{n-1} + \cdots + c_0 \in \mathbb{Z}[x]/\langle r(x)\rangle$ with a vector $(c_0, \cdots c_{n-1}) \in \mathbb{Z}^n$, where $r(x)$ is a polynomial of degree n. Then we have the following representation of $\mathbb{Z}[x]/\langle r(x)\rangle$ into the set of $n \times n$ matrices with integer entries:

$$\begin{aligned}\Phi : \mathbb{Z}[x]/\langle r(x)\rangle &\to M(n, \mathbb{Z})\\ h &\mapsto \Phi(h), \ \Phi(h)(f) = h(x)f(x).\end{aligned} \tag{3.2}$$

$$(c_0, \cdots, c_{n-1}) \in \mathbb{Z}^n \xrightarrow{\quad \Phi(h) \quad} \Phi(h)(f) = (d_0, \cdots, d_{n-1}) \in \mathbb{Z}^n$$

$$f(x) = \sum_{i=0}^{n-1} c_i x^i \in \mathbb{Z}[x]/\langle r(x) \rangle \xrightarrow{\quad\quad\quad} h(x)f(x) = \sum_{i=0}^{n-1} d_i x^i \in \mathbb{Z}[x]/\langle r(x) \rangle$$

Let $\{1, x, x^2, \cdots, x^{n-1}\}$ be a basis of $\mathbb{Z}^n = \mathbb{Z}[x]/\langle r(x) \rangle$. Depending on the choice of $r(x)$, we can find various representations.

Example 1. Let $h(x)$ be $h_{n-1}x^{n-1} + \cdots + h_0$.
(1) If $r(x) = x^n - 1$, then we have a circulant matrix

$$\Phi(h) = \begin{pmatrix} h_0 & h_{n-1} & \cdots & h_2 & h_1 \\ h_1 & h_0 & \cdots & h_3 & h_2 \\ \vdots & \vdots & \ddots & \vdots & \vdots \\ h_{n-2} & h_{n-3} & \cdots & h_0 & h_{n-1} \\ h_{n-1} & h_{n-2} & \cdots & h_1 & h_0 \end{pmatrix}. \tag{3.3}$$

(2) If $r(x) = x^n - x - 1$, then we have

$$\Phi(h) = \begin{pmatrix} h_0 & h_{n-1} & \cdots & h_2 & h_1 \\ h_1 & h_0 + h_{n-1} & \cdots & h_3 + h_2 & h_2 + h_1 \\ \vdots & \vdots & \ddots & \vdots & \vdots \\ h_{n-2} & h_{n-3} & \cdots & h_0 + h_{n-1} & h_{n-1} + h_{n-2} \\ h_{n-1} & h_{n-2} & \cdots & h_1 & h_0 + h_{n-1} \end{pmatrix}. \tag{3.4}$$

3.2   Direct Applications of Polynomial Representations

From representations of polynomials, we can obtain various lattices as we see in the above example. We can apply these representations to the GGH scheme directly as follows: Let $r(x)$ be $x^n - 1$. Then we obtain a circulant matrix as Example 1 (1). If $f(x) = a_{n-1}x^{n-1} + \cdots + a_0 \in \mathbb{Z}[x]/\langle r(x) \rangle$ satisfies that $|a_0| \approx \sqrt{n}l$ and other coefficients are contained in $[-l, l]$, then the dual-orthogonal-defect of $R = \Phi(f)$ would be low. In order to apply $R = \Phi(f)$ to the GGH system, it is necessary to find g such that $T^{-1} = \Phi(g)$ and $|\det(T^{-1})|$ is small (especially 1). But it is difficult to find a sufficiently large class of g such that $|\det(T^{-1})| = 1$ (i.e. $\Phi(g)$ is invertible in $M(n, \mathbb{Z})$).

4   Cryptosystem : Scheme I

In this section, we propose cryptosystems using a representation of polynomials.

4.1   Key Generation

We will take the private and public key in polynomial rings. Let n be a prime number and p be a positive integer. Experimentally, we can verify that sufficiently many elements of $\mathbb{Z}_p[x]/\langle x^n - 1\rangle$ have their inverses. Intuitively, if p is a prime number, then $|\mathbb{Z}_p^*| = \phi(p) = p - 1$, so almost every element of $\mathbb{Z}_p[x]/\langle x^n - 1\rangle$ has its inverse, where ϕ is Euler phi function. Even if p is not a prime number, $\mathbb{Z}_p$ has sufficiently many invertible elements, so sufficiently many elements of $\mathbb{Z}_p[x]/\langle x^n - 1\rangle$ have their inverses.

First, we generate 4 polynomials

$$f_1, f_2, h_1, h_2 \in \mathbb{Z}[x]/\langle x^n - 1\rangle$$

for the private key, which have the following properties:

- $f_1(x) = \alpha_{n-1}x^{n-1} + \cdots + \alpha_0$ and $f_2(x) = \beta_{n-1}x^{n-1} + \cdots + \beta_0$, where $|\alpha_{i_0}|, |\beta_{j_0}| \approx \sqrt{2nl}$ for some i_0, j_0 and the other coefficients are contained in $[-l, l]$ (l will be set to be 1).
- The coefficients of h_1 and h_2 are contained in $[-l, l]$.

We make the private matrix R as follows:

$$R = \begin{pmatrix} \Phi(f_1) & \Phi(h_1) \\ \Phi(h_2) & \Phi(f_2) \end{pmatrix}.$$

Since the diagonal entries of $\Phi(f_1), \Phi(f_2)$ are about $\sqrt{2nl}$ and other entries are contained in $[-l, l]$, the dual-orthogonality-defect of R would be low by the same reason as the GGH.

In order to generate the public key, we choose $g \in \mathbb{Z}[x]/\langle x^n - 1\rangle$ such that the coefficients of g are contained in $(-p/2, p/2]$. Then g can be considered as an element of a ring $F = \mathbb{Z}_p[x]/\langle x^n - 1\rangle$. We take g which is invertible in F. Then there exist g_p and Q in $\mathbb{Z}[x]/\langle x^n - 1\rangle$ such that $gg_p - 1 = pQ \in \mathbb{Z}[x]/\langle x^n - 1\rangle$. We generate 4-polynomials $P_1, P_2, P_3, P_4 \in \mathbb{Z}[x]/\langle x^n - 1\rangle$ as follows:

$$\begin{aligned} P_1 &= f_1 g + h_1 Q, \\ P_2 &= p f_1 + h_1 g_p, \\ P_3 &= h_2 g + f_2 Q, \\ P_4 &= p h_2 + f_2 g_p, \end{aligned} \qquad (4.5)$$

which are expressed as

$$B = \begin{pmatrix} \Phi(P_1) & \Phi(P_2) \\ \Phi(P_3) & \Phi(P_4) \end{pmatrix}.$$

Then we have the following private key and public key:

- Private key : f_1, f_2, h_1, h_2 (i.e. R)
- Public key : P_1, P_2, P_3, P_4 (i.e. B)

4.2   Encryption and Decryption

Encryption   A message is $M = (m_1, m_2) \in (\mathbb{Z}[x]/\langle x^n - 1 \rangle)^2$. Then the ciphertext is

$$c = \begin{pmatrix} c_1 \\ c_2 \end{pmatrix} = B \begin{pmatrix} m_1 \\ m_2 \end{pmatrix} + \begin{pmatrix} e_1 \\ e_2 \end{pmatrix} = \begin{pmatrix} P_1 m_1 + P_2 m_2 + e_1 \\ P_3 m_1 + P_4 m_2 + e_2 \end{pmatrix} \in (\mathbb{Q}[x]/\langle x^n - 1 \rangle)^2$$

for an error vector $e = (e_1, e_2)$, where $e_i \in \{-\sigma, \sigma\}^n$ (σ will be set to be $1/2$).

Decryption   Let T be a matrix defined as follows:

$$T = \begin{pmatrix} \Phi(g) & pI \\ \Phi(Q) & \Phi(g_p) \end{pmatrix}^{-1}.$$

Then we decrypt as follows:

$$M = (m_1, m_2) = T \lceil R^{-1} c \rfloor.$$

Why decryption works?   As we see in the above, $2n \times 2n$-matrix R has also a low-dual-orthogonality defect. Furthermore, we have the following lemma:

Lemma 1. $\det(T) = 1$.

Proof. Since

$$\begin{pmatrix} \Phi(g) & pI \\ \Phi(Q) & \Phi(g_p) \end{pmatrix} \begin{pmatrix} \Phi(g_p) & 0 \\ 0 & I \end{pmatrix} \begin{pmatrix} I & 0 \\ -\Phi(Q) & I \end{pmatrix} = \begin{pmatrix} I & pI \\ 0 & \Phi(g_p) \end{pmatrix},$$

we obtain that

$$\det(T^{-1})\det(\Phi(g_p)) = \det(\Phi(g_p)),$$

which implies that $\det(T^{-1}) = 1$.   □

Also we can easily verify that

$$B = \begin{pmatrix} \Phi(f_1 g + h_1 Q) & \Phi(p f_1 + h_1 g_p) \\ \Phi(h_2 g + f_2 Q) & \Phi(p h_2 + f_2 g_p) \end{pmatrix} = R T^{-1}.$$

The decryption works by the same reason as the GGH scheme.

4.3   Security

Algebraic View In the GGH, we can have the equation $B = RT^{-1}$, where R and T are unknown. Then we have n^2 linear equations with $2n^2$ unknown variables. (In fact, we have an additional non linear equation $|\det(T)| = 1$.)

Assume that p is not a secret parameter. ¿From the equation (4.5), we have $4n$ equations with $5n$ unknown variables. For any subsets of equations of (4.5), the number of unknown variables $\geq$ the number of equations $+ n$. Hence if n is sufficiently large, we cannot obtain secret keys by solving equations algebraically.

Also note for each equation in (4.5), the lattice attack in NTRU is not applicable.

Gap of an Embedded Lattice and Selections of σ and l Nguyen attacked the GGH by the embedding attack [9]. To our knowledge, the embedding attack seems to be the most efficient attack to the GGH. So we select the parameter σ and l under the consideration of the embedding attack.

By the attack to the GGH system used in [9], the security of the system is not so closely related to the size of σ. Precisely, the linear equation $c = Bm + e$ can be reduced to

$$\bar{c} = \frac{c - Bm_{2\sigma}}{2\sigma} = Bm' + \frac{e}{2\sigma}, \tag{4.6}$$

where $m_{2\sigma}$ is the solution of

$$c + (\sigma, \cdots, \sigma) = Bm \pmod{2\sigma}.$$

So the error vector $\bar{e} = e/2\sigma$ is an element of $\{\pm 1/2\}^n$. Hence the choice of a large σ is not so essential condition for the security of the GGH scheme if $\sigma \geq 1/2$. Hence we take σ to be $1/2$.

The embedding technique builds the lattice $\bar{L}_B$ such that

$$\bar{L}_B = \begin{pmatrix} \mathbf{b_1} \ \mathbf{b_2} \ \cdots \ \mathbf{b_n} \ c \\ 0 \quad 0 \ \cdots \ 0 \ 1 \end{pmatrix}, \tag{4.7}$$

where $\mathbf{b_i}$ are the column vector of B and c is the ciphertext. If v is the closest vector to c, then one can hope that $c - v$ is the shortest vector in $\bar{L}_B$. Recall that the gap of lattice (Definition 4). By experiments, the smaller the lattice gap is, the larger block size for BKZ algorithm we need in finding the shortest vector (Table 7). For a lattice whose gap size is about 10, Nguyen found the shortest vector by BKZ algorithm with block size 20 in 300-dimensional lattice reduced by (4.6) [9]. In $\bar{L}_B$, the second successive minimum is smaller than the minimal norm of column vectors of R, which is smaller than $2\sqrt{nl}$. If $\sigma = 1/2$, then we have

$$G_{\bar{L}_B} \leq \frac{||2\sqrt{nl}||}{||\bar{e}||} \leq 2.83l.$$

So the smaller l is, the harder it is to find the shortest vector in $\bar{L}_B$. Hence, we take l to be 1. Experimentally, if $l = 1$, then the probability of decryption error is sufficiently small if $n \geq 30$ and $G_{\bar{L}_B} \leq 2.4$ which is much smaller than the gap of the reduced lattice of the GGH system. Since the gap of our lattice is smaller than 2.4, BKZ algorithm with block size 20 cannot find the shortest vector in $158 = 79 \times 2$-dimensional lattice in many cases (Table 5, Table 7). Note that the run time of BKZ algorithm is exponential in the block size.

Assuming that $k \approx O(n/G_{\bar{L}})$-block size is needed for BKZ algorithm in finding the shortest vector (Table 7), we have the following natural conjecture:

Conjecture 2. The run time to solve the shortest vector in $\bar{L}$ by a lattice reduction algorithm is about $\exp(O(n/G_{\bar{L}}))$.

Also note that the reduction of our lattice is not easier than non reduced GGH lattice as we see experimental results for low dimensions (Table 6). (We used the implementation of the GGH in http://theory.lcs.mit.edu/~cis/lattice/lattice.html.)

Selection of p In order to estimate the public key size, the bit size of p should be determined. If $p \geq 2^{80}$, then it can be regarded as a private parameter. But if p takes 10 bits, then p cannot be considered as a private parameter. If p is larger than 2^{80} and it is kept secret, then we have the following advantages in the security. First, even if an attacker obtains g, he cannot obtain g_p and Q. Second, the reduction time for 80-bit p is longer than that for 10-bit p. The run time of lattice reduction algorithm for 10-bit p is shorter than $1/6$ of that for 80-bit p (Table 5). It is a natural result since the run time of BKZ algorithm is proportional to $\log B$ where B is the maximal norm of input basis [10].

However, the bit size of p does not seem to be a critical point for the security. Instead, if we use small p, then the efficiency increase significantly. If we use a 10-bit p, then the key size is comparable to NTRU and its efficiency can be significantly increased.

By our limited and non-optimized experiments, the run time to find the shortest vector in $\bar{L}_B$ with 10-bit number p is longer than $e^{0.1n}$-seconds with Pentium III 866 MHz. (see Table 5.) Based on these experiments, we estimate the security for 10-bit number p as Table 1.

Remark 1. If we use a 10-bit integer p, then p cannot be considered as a secret key. Even if p is not a secret key, it would be better to keep p secret for increasing the security.

Key Sizes Let p be about 10-bit number. The coefficients of P_i will take about 18 bits for 514-dimensional lattice ($n = 257$). Then public key takes 2.3 KBytes.

Let p be about an 80-bit number. The coefficients of P_i will take 88 bits for 514-dimensional lattice ($n = 257$), the public key takes 11.3 KBytes, which is much smaller than the key sizes of both 200-dimensional GGH and 200-dimensional GGH using HNF expression [8].

4.4 Other Representations

Let $r(x)$ be $x^n - x - 1$. Then $r(x)$ is irreducible polynomial in $\mathbb{Z}_p[x]/\langle r(x) \rangle$. Hence every non zero element has its inverse [7]. Let $f_1, f_2, h_1, h_2, g \in \mathbb{Z}[x]/\langle x^n - x - 1 \rangle$ be defined by the same method except that $|\alpha_0|, |\beta_0| \approx \sqrt{8n}$ instead of $|\alpha_{i_0}|, |\beta_{j_0}| \approx \sqrt{2n}$ for some i_0, j_0. Then $\Phi(f_i)$ has a low dual-orthogonality-defect.

Table 1. Expected run time to find the shortest vector for Scheme I

n	expected run time
211	1.46×10^9-seconds$\approx$ 46-years
257	1.45×10^{11}-seconds$\approx 4.6 \times 10^3$-years
373	1.58×10^{16}-seconds$\approx 5 \times 10^8$-years
503	5.18×10^{21}-seconds$\approx 1.6 \times 10^{14}$-years

Table 2. Comparison of key sizes (KB) of Scheme I with the GGH

rank of B	10-bit p	80-bit p	GGH	GGH(HNF)
200	0.85	4.4	330	32
300	1.4	6.6	990	75
400	1.8	8.8	2370	140
500	2.3	11		
750	3.6	16.7		
1000	4.8	22.3		

The gap of the embedded lattice is smaller than 6. Our experiments say that the gap is about 4, which is larger than the gap for $r(x) = x^n - 1$. The larger the gap size is, the larger the dimension we need for the security is. As we see in Table 8, if we use $x^n - x - 1$ as $r(x)$, the shortest vector for $n = 79$ is found by BKZ algorithm with block size 10. When we use $x^n - 1$ as $r(x)$, we cannot find the shortest vector for $n = 79$ with block size 20. For the similar complexity of lattice generated by $x^{211} - 1$, we need $n \approx 400$ based on Conjecture 2, the public key size is about 18KBytes, which is also much smaller than the key sizes of both 200-dimensional GGH and 200-dimensional GGH using HNF expression but it is two times larger than the scheme with $r(x) = x^{211} - 1$.

When we use this representation, we have the following advantages: First, $\Phi(f_i)$ is more complicated. Second, if p is a prime number, then every non zero g is invertible in $\mathbb{Z}_p[x]/\langle r(x) \rangle$. But since it seems that there are no special lattice reduction algorithm for $r(x) = x^n - 1$, the scheme with $r(x) = x^n - 1$ is more efficient than that with $r(x) = x^n - x - 1$.

5   Conclusion

We proposed a lattice based public key cryptosystem using polynomial representations. The proposed cryptosystem is an improvement of the GGH system. Our scheme has the advantages of the GGH system written in the introduction. Furthermore, our scheme is practical in key sizes compared with the GGH.

It has not been proved that the security of our scheme is equivalent to that of the GGH scheme since our schemes use specific lattices generated by polynomial representations. Although the further research on the security of the proposed schemes is required, any serious weakness has not been found yet.

As we see in Section 3, 4 and Appendix A, we can make various lattices with representations of polynomials. By studying various representations and size of coefficients of polynomials, the key size might be decreased and the efficiency could be increased. Furthermore, the security of the cryptosystem is closely related to the choice of representations. (See Section 4.4.)

References

[1] D. Coppersmith, A. Shamir *Lattice Attacks on NTRU*, Advances in Cryptology-Eurocrypt '97, LNCS 1233 (1997), 52–61

[2] E. Fujisaki, T. Okamoto *Secure Integration of Asymmetric and Symmetric Encryption Schemes*, Advances in Cryptology-Crypto '99, LNCS 1666 (1999), 537–554 306

[3] C. Gentry *Key Recovery and Message Attacks on NTRU-Composite*, Advances in Cryptology-Eurocrypt '01, LNCS 2045 (2001), 182–194

[4] O. Goldreich, S. Goldwasser, S. Halevi *Public Key Cryptosystems from Lattice Reduction Problems*, Advances in Cryptology-Crypto '97, LNCS 1294 (1997), 112–131 292, 294

[5] J. Hoffstein, J. Pipher , J. Silverman *NTRU : a Ring Based Public Key Cryptosystem*, ANTS III, LNCS 1423 (1998), 267–288 295

[6] E. Jaumels, A. Joux *A Chosen-Ciphertext Attack against NTRU*, Advances in Cryptology-Crypto 2000, LNCS 1880 (2000), 20–35

[7] R. Lidl, H. Niederreiter *Introduction to Finite Fields and Their Applications*, Cambridge University Press, (1986) 300

[8] D. Micciancio *Improving Lattice Based Cryptosystems Using the Hermite Normal Form*, CaLC 2001, LNCS 2146 (2001), 126–145 292, 300, 305

[9] P. Nguyen *Cryptanalysis of the Goldreich-Goldwasser-Halevi Cryptosystem from Crypto '97*, Advances in Cryptology-Crypto '99, LNCS 1666 (1999), 288–304 292, 293, 294, 299

[10] C. P. Schnorr *A Hierarchy of Polynomial Time Lattice Basis Reduction Algorithms*, Theoretical Computer Science 53 (1987), 201–224 295, 300

[11] L. C. Washington *Introduction to Cyclotomic Fields*, Springer-Verlag, GTM 83 (1996)

Appendix A : Scheme II

In this section, we introduce a scheme whose key size is smaller than that of Scheme I.

Key Generation Let n be a prime number and p be a positive integer as Scheme I.

Private key First, we generate 9 polynomials

$$f_i, \; h_k \in \mathbb{Z}[x]/\langle x^n - 1 \rangle \; i = 1, 2, 3, \; k = 1, 2, \cdots 6$$

for the private key such that

- $f_1 = \alpha_{n-1}x^{n-1} + \cdots + \alpha_0$, $f_2 = \beta_{n-1}x^{n-1} + \cdots + \beta_0$ and $f_3 = \gamma_{n-1}x^{n-1} + \cdots + \gamma_0$ satisfy that $\alpha_{i_0} = \beta_{j_0} = \gamma_{k_0} \approx \sqrt{3n}$ for some i_0, j_0, k_0 and other coefficients are contained in $\{-1, 0, 1\}$.
- All coefficients of h_i's are contained in $\{-1, 0, 1\}$. Furthermore, $f_2 + h_4 = f_3 + h_6 = q \approx \sqrt{3n}$ for a positive integer q and $h_1 + h_2 = 0$.

The secret data are $\{f_1, f_2, f_3, h_1, h_3, h_5\}$. We make the private matrix R as follows:

$$R = \begin{pmatrix} \Phi(f_1) & \Phi(h_1) & \Phi(h_2) \\ \Phi(h_3) & \Phi(f_2) & \Phi(h_4) \\ \Phi(h_5) & \Phi(h_6) & \Phi(f_3) \end{pmatrix}.$$

In order to generate the public key, we choose $g \in \mathbb{Z}[x]/\langle x^n - 1\rangle$ such that the coefficients of g are contained in $(-p/2, p/2]$. Then g can be considered as an element of a ring $F = \mathbb{Z}_p[x]/\langle x^n - 1\rangle$. We take g which is invertible in F. Then there exist g_p and Q in $\mathbb{Z}[x]/\langle x^n - 1\rangle$ such that $gg_p - 1 = pQ \in \mathbb{Z}[x]/\langle x^n - 1\rangle$. We obtain that

$$\begin{aligned} P_{13} &= h_1 + h_2 = 0 \\ P_{23} &= f_2 + h_4 = q \\ P_{33} &= f_3 + h_6 = q \\ P_{31} &= h_5 g - f_3 Q \pmod{q} \\ P_{32} &= p h_5 + h_6 g_p \pmod{q}. \end{aligned} \tag{5.8}$$

Every coefficient of P_{31} and P_{32} is contained in $(-q/2, q/2]$. We define T_1, T_2 as follows:

$$\begin{aligned} T_1 &= q^{-1}(P_{31} - h_5 g + f_3 Q) \\ T_2 &= q^{-1}(P_{32} - p h_5 - h_6 g_p). \end{aligned} \tag{5.9}$$

Then we obtain

$$\begin{aligned} P_{11} &= f_1 g - h_2 Q + T_1 P_{13} = f_1 g - h_2 Q \\ P_{12} &= p f_1 + h_1 y_p + T_2 P_{13} = p f_1 + h_1 g_p \\ P_{21} &= h_3 g - h_4 Q + T_1 P_{23} = h_3 g - h_4 Q + q T_1 \\ P_{22} &= p h_3 + f_2 g_p + T_2 P_{23} = p h_3 + f_2 g_p + q T_2 \end{aligned} \tag{5.10}$$

Then we have the public matrix B as follows:

$$B = \begin{pmatrix} \Phi(P_{11}) & \Phi(P_{12}) & \Phi(P_{13}) \\ \Phi(P_{21}) & \Phi(P_{22}) & \Phi(P_{23}) \\ \Phi(P_{31}) & \Phi(P_{32}) & \Phi(P_{33}) \end{pmatrix} = \begin{pmatrix} \Phi(P_{11}) & \Phi(P_{12}) & 0 \\ \Phi(P_{21}) & \Phi(P_{22}) & q \\ \Phi(P_{31}) & \Phi(P_{32}) & q \end{pmatrix}.$$

Consequently, we have the following private key and public key:

- Private key : $f_1, f_2, f_3, h_1, h_3, h_5$ (i.e. R)
- Public key : $P_{11}, P_{12}, P_{21}, P_{22}, P_{31}, P_{32}$ (i.e. B)

Encryption and Decryption

Encryption A message is $M = (m_1, m_2, m_3) \in (\mathbb{Z}[x]/\langle x^n - 1\rangle)^3$. The ciphertext is

$$c = \begin{pmatrix} c_1 \\ c_2 \\ c_3 \end{pmatrix} = \begin{pmatrix} P_{11} m_1 + P_{12} m_2 + P_{13} m_3 + e_1 \\ P_{21} m_1 + P_{22} m_2 + P_{23} m_3 + e_2 \\ P_{31} m_1 + P_{32} m_2 + P_{33} m_3 + e_3 \end{pmatrix} = BM + e. \tag{5.11}$$

for an error vector $e = (e_1, e_2, e_3)$, where $e_i \in \{-1/2, 1/2\}^n$ for $i = 1, 2, 3$.

Decryption The deciphertext is

$$M = T\lceil R^{-1}c\rfloor$$

for

$$T = \left\{ \begin{pmatrix} \Phi(g) & pI & 0 \\ 0 & \Phi(g_p) & I \\ -\Phi(Q) & 0 & I \end{pmatrix} \begin{pmatrix} I & 0 & 0 \\ 0 & I & 0 \\ T_1 & T_2 & I \end{pmatrix} \right\}^{-1}. \tag{5.12}$$

We can easily check that $B = RT^{-1}$. By the same reason as the GGH and Scheme I, the decryption works.

We can prove that $|\det(T)| = 1$.

Lemma 2. $|\det(T)| = 1$.

Proof. From the equation

$$\begin{pmatrix} \Phi(g_p) & -pI & pI \\ -\Phi(Q) & \Phi(g) & -\Phi(g) \\ \Phi(g_pQ) & -\Phi(pQ) & \Phi(gg_p) \end{pmatrix} \begin{pmatrix} \Phi(g) & pI & 0 \\ 0 & \Phi(g_p) & I \\ -\Phi(Q) & 0 & I \end{pmatrix} = I,$$

we obtain that T^{-1} is invertible, so $|\det(T)| = 1$. □

Remark 2. In (5.12), if $g_1g_2g_3 - 1 = pQ$ generally, we obtain an invertible matrix

$$T^{-1} = \begin{pmatrix} \Phi(g_1) & pI & 0 \\ 0 & \Phi(g_2) & I \\ -\Phi(Q) & 0 & \Phi(g_3) \end{pmatrix}.$$

Note that

$$\begin{pmatrix} \Phi(g_2g_3) & -p\Phi(g_3) & pI \\ -\Phi(Q) & \Phi(g_1g_3) & -\Phi(g_1) \\ \Phi(g_2Q) & -\Phi(pQ) & \Phi(g_1g_2) \end{pmatrix} \begin{pmatrix} \Phi(g_1) & pI & 0 \\ 0 & \Phi(g_2) & I \\ -\Phi(Q) & 0 & \Phi(g_3) \end{pmatrix} = I.$$

In order to reduce the public key size, we replace g_3 by 1 and make modular reduction.

Security and Key Size In algebraic view, we can use the similar arguments on the security as Scheme I.

By our experiments, if we use an 80-bit number as p, the run time to find the shortest vector in $\bar{L}_B$ in Scheme II is about half of the run time for Scheme I. We guess that such results are obtained since the entries of B are smaller than that of Scheme I. If p is a 10-bit number, then the run time is shorter than $1/7$ similarly as Scheme I. Our limited experiments say that the run time of BKZ algorithm for the embedded lattice $\bar{L}$ is longer than $\exp(0.14n)$-seconds with Pentium III 866 MHz.

Based on our experiments (Table 5), we obtain the security for 10-bit number p as Table 3.

Table 3. Expected run time to find the shortest vector for Scheme II

n	expected run time
137	2.1×10^8-seconds$\approx$ 6.8-years
167	1.4×10^{10}-seconds$\approx$ 451-years
251	1.8×10^{15}-seconds$\approx 5.8 \times 10^7$-years
331	1.3×10^{20} seconds$\approx 4.2 \times 10^{12}$ years

Table 4. Comparison of key sizes (KB) of Scheme II

rank of B	10-bit p	80-bit p	Scheme I with 10-bit p
400	1.4	6.1	1.8
500	1.7	7.6	2.3
750	2.8	11.6	3.6
1000	3.8	15.4	4.8

By modular operations, coefficients of $P_{13}, P_{23}, P_{31}, P_{32}, P_{33}$ are smaller than q, which are relatively small numbers. If $n = 167$, the dimension of the lattice is 501, and the public key size is about 1.7 KBytes for 10-bit p and about 7.6KBytes for 80-bit p.

Remark 3. (1) Our lattice reduction programs used for experiments in Appendix D are not optimized. If the programs are optimized, then the expected run time to solve SVP in Table 1 and Table 3 will be decreased.
(2) Even if the key size of Scheme II is slightly smaller than that of Scheme I, Scheme I seems to be more secure than Scheme II when we use 10-bit p.

Appendix B : IND-CCA2

The GGH system encrypts as follows:

$$c = BM + e,$$

where M is a message and e is an error vector. But this encryption does not satisfy the indistinguishability and is insecure against adaptive chosen ciphertext attack.

Indistinguishability If one encrypts one of two messages M_1 and M_2 and obtain a ciphertext c, then an adversary can distinguish a plaintext as follows: if $||BM_i - c|| < ||BM_j - c||$, then M_i is a plaintext.
    In [8], the ciphertext for a message M is as follows:

$$c = B\phi + M,$$

where ϕ is a random vector in $\mathbb{Z}^n$ and $M \in \{-\sigma, \sigma\}^n$. In this case, an adversary distinguishes which of M_i is a message by checking which of $c - M_i$ is contained in $\text{Im}(B)$.

Adaptive Chosen Ciphertext Attack Given a ciphertext c of a message M, i.e. $c = BM + e$, if an adversary inputs the $c + BM'$ to the decryption oracle for some M', then the decryption oracle outputs $\bar{M}$. Then the adversary can find out the original message M by calculating $M = \bar{M} - M'$.

IND-CCA2 For the security against IND-CCA2, we can apply the Fujisaki-Okamoto scheme.[2] We denote $2n$ (resp. $3n$) by N for Scheme I (resp. Scheme II). Let $\mathcal{E}_K, \mathcal{D}_K$ be a symmetric encryption and a decryption from $\mathbb{Z}[x]/\langle x^n - 1 \rangle$ to $\mathbb{Z}[x]/\langle x^n - 1 \rangle$ with a key K, respectively. Also M, e, B, T and R are the same notations which appeared in 4.1 and 4.2. Let H, G be random oracles. Then $M' = H(e, M)$ and the ciphertext is obtained as follows:

$$c = c_1 || c_2 = (BM' + e) || \mathcal{E}_{G(e)}(M).$$

For the decryption, first we obtain $\bar{M}' = T\lceil R^{-1}c_1 \rfloor$ and $\bar{e} = c_1 - B\bar{M}'$. Second, we obtain a deciphertext $\bar{M}$ with the symmetric key $G(e)$. Finally, if $B(H(\bar{e}, \bar{M})) + \bar{e} = c_1$, then decryption oracle outputs $\bar{M}$, otherwise the decryption fails. Then the security against IND-CCA2 depends on one-wayness of the function $f(m) = Bm + e$.

Remark 4. We can simplify the above scheme as follows:

$$M' = \mathcal{E}_{h(e)}(M) \text{ and } c = BM' + e,$$

for a hash function h. The decryption is as follows: Compute

$$M' = T\lceil R^{-1}c \rfloor \text{ and } e = c - BM'.$$

If

$$e \notin \{-1/2, 1/2\}^N,$$

then the decryption fails. Otherwise, the decryption oracle outputs

$$M = \mathcal{D}_{h(e)}(M').$$

The security of this scheme has not been proved yet but this scheme prevents message expansion in Fujisaki-Okamoto scheme, trivial distinguishability and chosen ciphertext attack described in the above.

Appendix C : Experimental Results

We have the following data for the run time to find the shortest vector in $\bar{L}$. Our program is simply using BKZ algorithm in NTL 5.2, so it is not optimized.

Table 5. Run time ($r(x) = x^n - 1$, Pentium III 866)

n	Scheme	p's bit size	block size	run time (sec)	succeed
31	I	10	4	33.72	succeed
41	I	10	4	147.86	succeed
47	I	10	4	280.78	fail
47	I	10	10	280.67	succeed
59	I	10	10(prune 12)	1003.49	succeed
67	I	10	10(prune 12)	1568.89	fail
79	I	10	20(prune 12)	5602.56	fail
79	I	10	20	7691.87	fail
29	II	10	4	109.3	succeed
31	II	10	4	144.67	succeed
47	II	10	4	1098.9	succeed
47	II	10	10	1169.85	succeed
53	II	10	10(prune 12)	2222.35	fail
53	II	10	20(prune 12)	2373.22	fail
53	II	10	20	2544.43	succeed
59	II	10	25(prune 12)	4704.26	fail
59	II	10	25	4758.63	succeed
41	I	80	4	1388.57	succeed
41	I	80	10	1352.54	fail
47	I	80	4	2681.9	succeed
47	I	80	10	2747.15	succeed
47	I	80	10(prune 12)	2797.96	succeed
59	I	80	4	7421.31	fail
59	I	80	10(prune 12)	8066.63	succeed
67	I	80	10(prune 12)	15117.1	succeed
79	I	80	20(prune 12)	34736.1	succeed
29	II	80	4	952.35	succeed
31	II	80	4	1312.45	succeed
41	II	80	10	5036	succeed
47	II	80	4	10760	fail
47	II	80	10	9597.35	succeed
53	II	80	20(prune 12)	16952.8	succeed
53	II	80	10(prune 12)	17130.1	succeed

Table 6. Comparison of the key sizes for the non reduced GGH and Scheme I with 80-bit p (Pentium III 866)

dimension	block size(GGH)	run time (sec)	succeed	block size(Scheme I)	run time(sec)	succeed
94	4	561.51	succeed	4	280.78	fail
118	4	1768.06	succeed	4	7421.31	fail
118	10(prune 12)	1958.26	succeed	10(prune 12)	8066.63	succeed
158	4	7553.46	succeed	10		fail
158	20(prune 12)	16164.6	succeed	20(prune 12)	34736.1	succeed

Table 7. Run time of Scheme I($r(x) = x^n - 1$), SUN BLADE 1000 750MHZ (Experimentally, for $l = 1$, $G_{\bar{L}} \leq 2.4$. For $l = 3$, $G_{\bar{L}} \leq 6.8$ and for $l = 5$, $G_{\bar{L}} \leq 12$.)

n	Scheme	p's bit size	block size	l	run time (sec)	suceeed
67	I	10	20	1	769	fail
79	I	10	20(prune 12)	1	2218.57	succeed
67	I	80	4	1	3172.6	fail
67	I	80	4	3	3216.02	fail
67	I	80	4	5	3257.28	succeed
67	I	80	10	1	3276.23	fail
67	I	80	10	3	3319.16	fail
67	I	80	10	5	3373.16	succeed
67	I	80	20	1	3771.76	succeed
67	I	80	20	3	3662.1	fail
67	I	80	20	5	3754.34	succeed
79	I	80	4	5	6935.06	succeed
79	I	80	10	1	7053.14	fail
79	I	80	10	3	7151.54	fail
79	I	80	10	5	7137.82	succeed
79	I	80	20	1	8672.55	fail
79	I	80	20	3	8901.04	fail
79	I	80	20	5	9598.09	fail
79	I	80	20(prune 12)	1	8278.63	fail

Table 8. Run time of Scheme I($r(x) = x^n - x - 1$, $G_{\bar{L}} \leq 4.1$, Pentium III 866)

n	block size	run time (sec)	succeed
23	4	81.12	succeed
31	4	336.2	succeed
41	4	1337.66	succeed
47	4	2776.43	succeed
59	4	7543.8	succeed
59	10	8250.79	succeed
67	4	13632.1	succeed
67	10	13773.2	succeed
79	10	29102.3	succeed
79	10	29118.3	fail
89	10	51793.1	fail
89	20	63542.6	succeed

The Security of DSA and ECDSA
Bypassing the Standard Elliptic Curve Certification Scheme

Serge Vaudenay

Swiss Federal Institute of Technology (EPFL)
Serge.Vaudenay@epfl.ch

Abstract. DSA and ECDSA are well established standards for digital signature based on the discrete logarithm problem. In this paper we survey known properties, certification issues regarding the public parameters, and security proofs.
ECDSA also includes a standard certification scheme for elliptic curve which is assumed to guarantee that the elliptic curve was randomly selected, preventing from any potential malicious choice. In this paper we show how to bypass this scheme and certify any elliptic curve in characteristic two. The prime field case is also studied. Although this does not lead to any attack at this time since all possible malicious choices which are known at this time are specifically checked, this demonstrates that some part of the standard is not well designed. We finally propose a tweak.

DSA was published in 1994 following a long dynasty of digital signature schemes based on the ElGamal scheme [10, 11, 12]. Since then an extensive literature addressed security analysis, performances, and variants. Among the famous variants ECDSA was proposed in 1998. In this paper we aim to survey dedicated attacks and provable security. We also address the parameter validation issue. In particular we show that we may be able to maliciously choose an elliptic curve for ECDSA despite the standard validation scheme.

1 DSA and ECDSA

In order to define the notations, we first summarize the DSA as presented in ANSI X9.30 Part 1 [1] and FIPS 186 [5].

Public Parameters: integers p, q, g and a seed in order to validate q
  p is a prime of L bits (L is at least 512, at most 1024, and a multiple of 64)
  q is a prime of 160 bits and a factor of $p - 1$
  g is in $[1, p - 1]$ and of order q modulo p
Secret Key: integer x in $[1, q - 1]$
Public Key: $y = g^x \bmod p$

Y.G. Desmedt (Ed.): PKC 2003, LNCS 2567, pp. 309–323, 2003.

Signature Generation for M**:** generate $k \in [1, q-1]$ and compute

$$r = (g^k \bmod p) \bmod q$$
$$s = \frac{\text{SHA-1}(M) + xr}{k} \bmod q$$

If $r = 0$ or $s = 0$, try again. The signature is (r, s)

Signature (M, r', s') **Verification:** check that r' and s' are in $[1, q-1]$ and that

$$r' = (g^{\frac{\text{SHA-1}(M)}{s'}} y^{\frac{r'}{s'}} \bmod p) \bmod q$$

SHA-1 is not specified in FIPS 186 [5]. It is standardized in FIPS 180-1 [4] and the Part 2 of ANSI X9.30. The Appendixes of ANSI X9.30 [1] and FIPS 186 [5] however specify how public parameters, secret keys and k values shall be generated. They do not specify how the parameters validity should be checked. They simply say that the parameters must be transmitted in an authenticated way. Let us now summarize the ECDSA as presented in ANSI X9.62 [2].

Public Parameters: finite field $\mathbf{F}_q$ and a field representation choice, two parameters a and b which define an elliptic curve C over $\mathbf{F}_q$, a seed which validates C, a prime integer $n > 2^{160}$, and a point $G \in C$ of order n. Here q is either prime or a power of 2

Secret Key: integer d in $[1, n-1]$

Public Key: $Q = dG$

Signature Generation for M**:** generate $k \in [1, n-1]$ and compute

$$(x_1, y_1) = kG$$
$$r = \overline{x_1} \bmod n$$
$$s = \frac{\text{SHA-1}(M) + dr}{k} \bmod n$$

If $r = 0$ or $s = 0$, try again. The signature is (r, s)

Signature (M, r', s') **Verification:** check that r' and s' are in $[1, n-1]$ and that $r' = \overline{x_1} \bmod n$ for $(x_1, y_1) = u_1 G + u_2 Q$, $u_1 = \frac{\text{SHA-1}(M)}{s'} \bmod n$, and $u_2 = \frac{r'}{s'} \bmod n$

Here $\overline{x_1}$ is simply a way of converting a field element into an integer and SHA-1 is a hash function specified in FIPS 180-1 [4].

The signature is a pair of integers. The public key is a point on a curve. So ANSI X9.62 [2] needs to define a standard way for representing an integer, a point, and therefore a field element. In addition we need a standard way to represent the public parameters: the field representation, the curve definition, ... ANSI X9.62 [2] extensively defines all this.

Additionally, users need to check if the public parameters are valid as follows.

1. Check that q is an odd prime or a power of 2. In the latter case, check that the field representation choice is valid.

2. Check that a, b, x_G, y_G where $G = (x_G, y_G)$ lies in $\mathbf{F}_q$.
3. Check that seed certifies a and b. (This point will be discussed in Section 5.)
4. For q prime, check that $4a^3 + 27b^2 \bmod q \neq 0$. For q a power of two, check that $b \neq 0$.
5. Check that G lies in C.
6. Check that n is a prime greater than 2^{160} and $4\sqrt{q}$.
7. Check that $nG = \mathcal{O}$, the neutral element in C.
8. Check the MOV and anomalous condition for C.

The verifier further validates the public key by checking that $Q \neq \mathcal{O}$, $Q \in C$, and $nQ = \mathcal{O}$.

2 Dedicated Attacks

In this section we survey some known properties of DSA and ECDSA.

2.1 Signature Manipulation in ECDSA

Interestingly, the $(x_1, y_1) \mapsto \overline{x_1} \bmod n$ function does not use the information about y_1. We have two points in the elliptic curve with the same x_1 coordinate which happen to be opposite of each other. (Hence dropping y_1 looses one bit of information.) It means that replacing k by $-k \bmod n$ would lead to the same x_1 hence the same r. This manipulation replaces s by $-s \bmod n$. Hence we can replace any (r, s) signature by $(r, -s \bmod n)$ which is another valid signature for the same message.

The drop of one bit has the other consequence that one can choose his secret key in order to create a valid signature for two different messages simultaneously as pointed out by Stern et al. [24]. Indeed we can just compute r from a random k then select

$$d = -\frac{\text{SHA-1}(M_1) + \text{SHA-1}(M_2)}{2r} \bmod n.$$

2.2 Bleichenbacher Attack against the Pseudorandom Generator

The initial standard pseudorandom generator in DSA for k was simply a 160-bit pseudorandom number reduced modulo q. Bleichenbacher[1] observed that the probability of k in the $[0, 2^{160} - q]$ range have probability which is twice of the others. This leads to a bias

$$E\left(e^{\frac{2i\pi k}{q}}\right) \approx \frac{q e^{i\pi \frac{N-1}{q}}}{\pi N} \times \sin\left(\frac{\pi N}{q}\right)$$

where $N = 2^{160}$. Since $q \approx N$, this may be large depending on the $\frac{\pi N}{q}$ angle. Bleichenbacher actually used it in order to approximate the secret key more and more precisely with signatures. Based on that the standard was tweaked by basically replacing N by N^2. (See [6].)

The same remark holds for ECDSA with n instead of q (but the $\frac{\pi N}{n}$ angle is very small most of the time).

---

[1] Private communication.

2.3   Restart Attack

Assuming that the pseudorandom generator for k is deterministic and that one can reset the internal state of the generator, then we can break the scheme with signatures of two different messages: if the signer signs M_1 by generating k and we can reset it so that it generates the same k for M_2, we have a signature (r, s_1) for M_1 and a signature (r, s_2) for M_2. Hence we obtain that

$$x = -\frac{s_2\text{SHA-1}(M_1) - s_1\text{SHA-1}(M_2)}{r(s_2 - s_1)} \bmod q.$$

This attack model makes sense if we have a clone of the signer with the same initial state.

A similar attack holds for ECDSA.

3   Parameter Validation

In this section we survey some parameter certification issues.

3.1   Public Keys Certificate

Authentication of public keys is a well known problem. It can be solved by using certificates which are basically signatures of the public key by a certificate authority. Certificates then rely on the authentication of the certificate authority public key. This is still an important issue since there is no other mean than physical protection: when delivered, the public key needs to be manually authenticated, then physically protected in the memory.

We show in the next sections that we have similar issues for the public parameters.

3.2 p and q Validation

As pointed out by Vaudenay [25], one can choose p and q in DSA such that a collision on SHA-1 mod q is known. One simply take random $q = \text{SHA-1}(M_1) - \text{SHA-1}(M_2)$ until it is a 160-bit prime number and take random $p = aq + 1$ until it is a prime. With this choice one can forge a signature for M_2 with a signature of M_1.

In order to avoid this attack we generate p and q following a standard generator and use the initial seed as a certificate of good forgery. As specified in [5], q is generated by

$$q = (\text{SHA-1}(\text{seed}) \oplus \text{SHA-1}(\text{seed} + 1)) \vee 2^{159} \vee 1$$

until it is valid where $\oplus$ and $\vee$ denote the bitwise XOR and OR operations. This means that we take the XOR of two random values coming out from SHA-1 and we force the least and most significant bits to 1. The certificate for p and q is thus simply the seed.

As pointed out in [25], the attack still holds whenever

$$\text{SHA-1}(\text{seed}) = \text{SHA-1}(\text{seed}+1) \pm q$$

which occurs with probability $2 \times \frac{1}{4} \times \left(\frac{3}{4}\right)^{158} \times \frac{1}{4} \approx 2^{-68.6}$. (2 is for $\pm$, each $\frac{1}{4}$ is for a difference equal to 1 without carry bit, each $\frac{3}{4}$ is for a difference without carry bit).[2] Therefore it takes roughly 2^{80} trials in order to get a seed which satisfies the condition due to the additional overhead due to the primality tests. This is within the order of magnitude of the brute force attacks which are discussed in Sec. 4.1.

3.3 g Validation

As pointed out in [25], there is no similar certificate for g (resp. G). If we had no verification on g at all, we may have attacks against a given DSA signature verifier as follows. (Similar attacks hold for ECDSA.)

Replacing g by 0. If we can corrupt g in the memory of the verifier we can replace it by 0. Then any signature with $r = 0$ becomes valid for any public key.

Replacing g by 1. If we can corrupt g in the memory of the verifier we can replace it by 1. Then we can forge a signature for any message for a given public key y by picking random $r = (y^\alpha \bmod p) \bmod q$, then $s = \frac{r}{\alpha} \bmod q$.

Other replacement. One may want to check that g has an order of q which would thwart the last two attacks. However we can still replace g by a random power of y. In this case the attacker knows the discrete logarithm of y in this basis and can sign any message.

4 Provable Security

In this section we survey provable security results for DSA and ECDSA.

4.1 Necessary Conditions

Theorem 1. *Here are necessary security conditions for DSA (resp. ECDSA).*

1. *The discrete logarithm in the subgroup spanned by g (resp. G) is hard.*
2. *SHA-1 is a one-way hash function.*
3. *SHA-1 is a collision-resistant hash function.*
4. *The generator for k is unpredictable.*

As will be noticed later these conditions are "more or less" sufficient in some particular models.

---

[2] In [25] a probability of $2^{-68.16}$ was given but there was a computation error in the estimate.

Proof. Condition 1 is quite obvious: if the condition does not hold, we can just compute the discrete logarithm of the public key and obtain the secret key. (One need to randomize the public key by standard whitening techniques.) One should however notice that the discrete logarithm problem is not equivalent to computing the secret key. The legitimate signer indeed knows how to compute it but does not necessarily know how to solve the discrete logarithm problem.

Condition 2 comes from the existential forgery attack which enables forging (h, r, s) triplets where h plays the role of SHA-1(M): for DSA, one can just pick $r = (g^\alpha y^\beta \bmod p) \bmod q$ for random α and β, take $s = \frac{r}{\beta} \bmod q$, then $h = s\alpha \bmod q$. (A similar existential forgery attack holds for ECDSA.) With the triplet one can try inverting SHA-1 on h and get a valid signed message.

Condition 3 is trivial: if one can get a collision SHA-1(M_1) = SHA-1(M_2) then one can ask for the signature of M_1 (in a chosen message attack) then forge the signature for M_2.

If Condition 4 does not hold one can predict k then extract the secret key from s and r.   □

We can quantify the workload of brute force attacks: Shanks algorithm can break Condition 1 within a complexity $\Omega(\sqrt{q})$ (resp. $\Omega(\sqrt{n})$). Random search can break Condition 2 within 2^{160} computations. The birthday attack breaks Condition 3 within 2^{80} computations. One can also break Condition 4 within 2^{160} trials.

4.2   Brickell Model

In the Brickell model[3], we assume that both SHA-1 and the mod q (resp. $(x_1, y_1) \mapsto \overline{x_1} \bmod n$) function from the subgroup spanned by g (resp. G) behave like random oracles. (Note that it implies Conditions 2 and 3 of Theorem 1.) Under this assumption, Condition 1 and another assumption which may be stronger and Condition 4, one can formally prove that DSA (resp. ECDSA) is secure. We quote the result from [19]. The proof comes from the Forking Lemma techniques of Pointcheval and Stern [18] and is available in [19, 8]. The same result holds for ECDSA.

Theorem 2. *In DSA we assume that SHA-1 is replaced by a uniformly distributed random oracle H_1 and the computation of r is replaced by $H_2(g^k \bmod p)$ where H_2 is another uniformly distributed random oracle. We further assume that the pseudorandom generator for k is indistinguishable from a uniformly distributed random generator. Given an algorithm which given the public key y forges a valid (M, h, r, s) quadruplet in time $O(T)$, probability greater than ε, and $O(N)$ oracle accesses, we can make an algorithm which given y computes x within $O(N/\varepsilon)$ replays of the given algorithm.*

We notice that all conditions are necessary but for

- the one on the mod q (resp. $(x_1, y_1) \mapsto \overline{x_1} \bmod n$) function,

---

[3] This was presented as an invited talk at CRYPTO' 96 but unpublished. See [19, 8].

- the one on the pseudorandom generator (which is stronger than Condition 4),
- the random oracle model which is known to be controversial.

The condition on the mod q function is not very satisfactory for DSA. It may look better for ECDSA since the $x_1 \mapsto \overline{x_1}$ is arbitrary.

This model was later generalized by Yung et al. in [8] as the TEGTSS-I scheme.

4.3   Pointcheval-Vaudenay Model

The Pointcheval-Vaudenay result (see [19]) holds with more realistic assumptions for a variant of DSA which is included in the ISO/IEC 14888 [3] standard. In this variant SHA-1(M) is replaced by SHA-1($r|M$) as in the Schnorr signature [20, 21].

In the Pointcheval-Vaudenay result, SHA-1 still needs to behave like a random oracle. The hypothesis on the mod q (resp. $(x_1, y_1) \mapsto \overline{x_1} \bmod n$) function is replaced by a $O(\log q)$-collision freedom (resp. $O(\log n)$-collision freedom).[4] This means that all preimage sizes are bounded by $O(\log q)$ (resp. $O(\log n)$). This hypothesis is quite realistic (it actually holds for random functions with same range). Therefore all assumptions are realistic, but for the controversy on the random oracle model.

Theorem 3 (Pointcheval-Vaudenay [19, 8]). *We consider the Pointcheval-Vaudenay variant of DSA in which SHA-1(M) is replaced by SHA-1($r|M$). In this scheme we assume that SHA-1 is replaced by a uniformly distributed random oracle H. The function f over $\mathbf{Z}_q$ which maps k to $f(k) = (g^k \bmod p) \bmod q$ is assumed to be $O(\log q)$-collision free. We further assume that the pseudorandom generator for k is indistinguishable from a uniformly distributed random generator. Given an algorithm which given the public key y forges a valid (M, h, r, s) quadruplet in time $O(T)$, probability greater than ε, and $O(N)$ oracle accesses, we can make an algorithm which given y computes x within $O(N \log q \log \log q / \varepsilon)$ replays of the given algorithm.*

The key idea in the proof is in an improvement of the Forking Lemma which makes forks with $\Omega(\log q)$ branches instead of two.

This model was later generalized by Yung et al. in [8] as the TEGTSS-II scheme. As shown by Lee and Smart [15], the same variant and result can be made for ECDSA.

4.4   Brown Model

Brown [9] presented another proof model in which functions are no longer random oracles, but the underlying group operations are performed in a generic group. One property of generic group is that discrete logarithm is provably hard

---

[4] In this paper, t-collision free means that no t inputs collide on their outputs. It is stronger than collision resistance in the sense that collisions really do not exists.

which implies Condition 1 of Theorem 1. The best attack requires $\Omega(\sqrt{q})$ (resp. $\Omega(\sqrt{n})$) as proven by Shoup [22]. For DSA, it means that multiplications modulo p are assumed to be represented by a generic group, which is a wrong assumption since sieving algorithms can compute discrete logarithm in sub-exponential time. For ECDSA, it means that elliptic curve points addition is assumed to be represented by a generic group. It is quite natural for random elliptic curves as long as our understanding on the group structure is currently limited. For some special curves like Koblitz curves this hypothesis is not valid at all since some exponential can be computed faster than the regular square-and-multiply algorithm.

Brown also requires the assumption that the $(x_1, y_1) \mapsto \overline{x_1} \bmod n$ function is invertible, which is correct for ECDSA, but we have no similar property for DSA. (One would need that the mod q function of the subgroup spanned by g is invertible which is an open problem so far.) Hence the Brown model is meaningful for ECDSA with random elliptic curves only.

In this model Brown has shown that ECDSA is secure under Conditions 2 and 3 and undistinguishability of the generator for k. His proof was a little flawed, but fixable as pointed out by Stern et al. [24].

Theorem 4. *In ECDSA we assume that elliptic curve is replaced by a generic group of order n greater than 2^{160}. We assume that the $(x_1, y_1) \mapsto \overline{x_1} \bmod n$ function from the generic group to $\mathbf{Z}_n$ is invertible. We further assume that the pseudorandom generator for k is indistinguishable from a uniformly distributed random generator. Given an algorithm which given the public key y forges a valid (M, r, s) triplet in time $O(T)$, probability greater than ε, and $N = O(\sqrt{n}\varepsilon)$ oracle accesses, we can make an algorithm which inverts SHA-1 with a complexity of $O((T + N \log N)N/\varepsilon)$ or which finds a collision with complexity $O((T + N \log N)/\varepsilon)$.*

5   Elliptic Curve Validation

The proposed elliptic curve generator of ECDSA works as follows. It consists of selecting first a finite field, second a seed of a pseudorandom generator (denoted seed) which generates a j-invariant, and third the elliptic curve of required j-invariant over the field.

Curves over $\mathbf{F}_p$ with $p > 3$ Prime:
1. We choose a prime $p > 3$ and consider $\mathbf{F}_p$.
2. We generate a random bitstring c from seed.
3. We translate c into a field element.
4. We arbitrarily select a and b such that $a^3/b^2 = c \pmod{p}$ and take the elliptic curve defined by

$$y^2 \equiv x^3 + ax + b \pmod{p}.$$

We recall that in this case the j-invariant is

$$j = 6912 \frac{a^3/b^2}{4a^3/b^2 + 27} \bmod p = 6912 \frac{c}{4c + 27} \bmod p$$

hence j is fully validated by seed.

Curves over $\mathbf{F}_q$ of Characteristic 2:

1. We choose q a power of 2 and consider $\mathbf{F}_q$. We choose a representation of $\mathbf{F}_q$ (i.e. an irreducible polynomial).
2. We generate a random bitstring c from seed.
3. We translate c into a field element and call it b.
4. We arbitrarily select a and take the elliptic curve defined over $\mathbf{F}_q$ by

$$y^2 + xy = x^3 + ax^2 + b.$$

We recall that in this case the j-invariant is $j = \frac{1}{b}$ hence j is fully validated by seed.

Then the seed is kept as a certificate of good forgery. Users can check that seed validates the j-invariant of the curve. This certificate is assumed to convince that one hid no trapdoor in the specific choice of the curve.

5.1 Elliptic Curves with Same j-Invariant

As noticed, only j is validated from seed. The j invariant is however not a complete characteristic for the elliptic curve. One can replace an elliptic curve by its twist which has the same j-invariant but is not isomorphic. In the prime field case, we can replace (a, b) by $(u^2 a \bmod p, u^3 b \bmod p)$ where u is a non-quadratic residue in $\mathbf{F}_p$. In characteristic two fields, we can replace (a, b) by $(a + \theta, b)$ where θ is an element of trace 1 over $\mathbf{F}_2$, i.e. $\mathrm{Tr}(\theta) = 1$ where Tr is defined by

$$\mathrm{Tr}(\theta) = \theta + \theta^2 + \theta^{2^2} + \theta^{2^3} + \ldots + \theta^{\frac{q}{2}}.$$

Both curves have the same j-invariant. Although they are isomorphic in some extension field, they are not isomorphic in general over the chosen field. Therefore the exact choice of the curve is not certified by this scheme. This means that if users accept an elliptic curve with the field/seed certificate, they also implicitly accept its twist.

This property can easily be avoided by requiring that seed generates c together with an extra bit which is such that

- $\left(\frac{b}{p}\right) = (-1)^{\mathrm{bit}}$ for prime fields,
- $\mathrm{Tr}(a) = \mathrm{bit}$ for characteristic two fields.

In this case seed fully validates the elliptic curve up to an isomorphism.

5.2   Bypassing the Scheme in the Characteristic Two Case

In the standard validation scheme, the pseudorandom generator for c is used *after* the finite field choice, though it does not really use it. One can wonder what happens if we first generate c then choose the finite field. The characteristic two case is easy since the field representation choice is open, and basically free. Hence one can easily bypass the validation scheme as follows. We assume that we have an elliptic curve defined by

$$y^2 + xy = x^3 + ax^2 + b$$

over a given field $\mathbf{F}_q$ of characteristic two. We want to validate it by looking for a field representation and seed.

1. Pick seed at random.
2. Generate a bitstring c from seed.
3. Look for the field representation of $\mathbf{F}_q$ such that the string c represents the field element b. If not possible go back to step 1.

As shown in Appendix A, this works within less than $\log_2 q$ iterations on average for any b but $b = 0$ (for which the curve is singular) or $b = 1$ (which is quite relevant for Koblitz curves). Note that Step 3 simply consists of looking for roots of the polynomial equation $C(X) = b$ where $C(X)$ is defined by c. (See Appendix A.)

Therefore the pseudorandom generation of the elliptic curve provided in ANSI X9.62 [2] brings a very weak guaranty of honest elliptic curve generation.

5.3   Prime Fields Case

The prime field case do not offer any choice for the field representation. However we can still try to choose p after having generated c. At the time this paper is written we have no clue how to maliciously pick p so that the elliptic curve is weak. We let this as an open problem.

> *Given a random integer c, can we choose a prime p such that an elliptic curve over $\mathbf{F}_p$ whose j-invariant is $j = 6912\frac{c}{4c+27} \bmod p$ is flawed?*

As a challenge we propose

> *Given a random integer c, can we choose a prime p such that $j = 6912\frac{c}{4c+27} \bmod p$ is the j-invariant of an anomalous elliptic curve over $\mathbf{F}_p$?*

Anomalous elliptic curves over $\mathbf{F}_p$ are known to be weak.[5]

---
[5] See [23, 17].

5.4   A Possible Tweak for ECDSA

We recommend to update the validation scheme by concatenating the seed with p (resp. q and the field representation) in the generator and by generating an extra bit. Here is the tweaked scheme.

Curves over $\mathbf{F}_p$ with $p > 3$ Prime:
1. We choose a prime $p > 3$ and consider $\mathbf{F}_p$.
2. We generate a random bitstring c and bit from seed and p.
3. We translate c into a field element.
4. We arbitrarily select a and b such that $a^3/b^2 \equiv c \pmod{p}$ and $\left(\frac{b}{p}\right) = (-1)^{\text{bit}}$, and take the elliptic curve defined by a, b, p.

Curves over $\mathbf{F}_q$ of Characteristic 2:
1. We choose q a power of 2 and consider $\mathbf{F}_q$. We choose a representation of $\mathbf{F}_q$ (i.e. an irreducible polynomial).
2. We generate a random bitstring c and bit from seed, q, and the field representation choice.
3. We translate c into a field element and call it b.
4. We arbitrarily select a such that $\mathrm{Tr}(a) = \text{bit}$ and take the elliptic curve defined over $\mathbf{F}_q$ by a, b, q.

This way we are ensured that the elliptic curve was randomly selected up to an isomorphism.

6   Conclusion

We surveyed security properties of DSA and ECDSA.

- We have seen that, like for many cryptographic schemes, DSA and ECDSA are highly vulnerable when used in a poor way. For instance the pseudorandom generator must be cryptographically strong. We also need to care about cloning issues.
- We also investigated the parameter validation issue. Like the public key validation problem, parameter must be validated and securely stored. Otherwise one can hide trapdoors in p, q, or g (resp. G).
- DSA and ECDSA are provably secure in the random oracle model by assuming that the $k \mapsto r$ has nice properties. Slight variants of DSA and ECDSA benefit from stronger security proofs.

Finally, the standard elliptic curve validation scheme happens to provide weak guaranty for honest generation. While the prime field case is proposed as an open problem, the validation process is easy to bypass in the characteristic two case. Therefore we recommend to update the elliptic curve validation scheme as proposed in Section 5.4.

Acknowledgments

I would like to thank Japanese Government (IPA) for having proposed this work under the CRYPTREC project.[6] I would also like to thank Daniel Bleichenbacher for providing information on his attack and Franck Leprevost for helpful discussions.

References

[1] ANSI X9.30. Public Key Cryptography for the Financial Services Industry: Part 1: The Digital Signature Algorithm (DSA). American National Standard Institute. American Bankers Association. 1997. 309, 310

[2] ANSI X9.62. Public Key Cryptography for the Financial Services Industry: The Elliptic Curve Digital Signature Algorithm (ECDSA). American National Standard Institute. American Bankers Association. 1998. 310, 318

[3] ISO/IEC 14888. Information Technology — Security Techniques — Digital Signatures with Appendix. ISO/IEC, Geneva, Switzerland, 1998. 315

[4] Secure Hash Standard. *Federal Information Processing Standard* publication #180-1. U.S. Department of Commerce, National Institute of Standards and Technology, 1995. 310

[5] Digital Signature Standard (DSS). *Federal Information Processing Standards* publication #186-2. U.S. Department of Commerce, National Institute of Standards and Technology, 2000. 309, 310, 312

[6] Recommendations Regarding Federal Information Processing Standard (FIPS) 186–2, Digital Signature Standard (DSS). NIST Special Publication 800–XX. U.S. Department of Commerce, National Institute of Standards and Technology, October 2001. 311

[7] D. Bleichenbacher. Generating ElGamal Signatures without Knowing the Secret Key. In *Advances in Cryptology EUROCRYPT'96*, Zaragoza, Spain, Lectures Notes in Computer Science 1070, pp. 10–18, Springer-Verlag, 1996.

[8] E. Brickell, D. Pointcheval, S. Vaudenay, M. Yung. Design Validations for Discrete Logarithm Based Signature Schemes. In *Public Key Cryptography*, Melbourne, Australia, Lectures Notes in Computer Science 1751, pp. 276–292, Springer-Verlag, 2000. 314, 315

[9] D. R. L. Brown. The Exact Security of ECDSA. Technical Report CORR 2000–34, Certicom Research, 2000. http://www.cacr.math.uwaterloo.ca 315

[10] T. ElGamal. Cryptography and Logarithms over Finite Fields. PhD Thesis, Stanford University, 1984. 309

[11] T. ElGamal. A Public-key Cryptosystem and a Signature Scheme based on Discrete Logarithms. In *Advances in Cryptology CRYPTO'84*, Santa Barbara, California, U.S.A., Lectures Notes in Computer Science 196, pp. 10–18, Springer-Verlag, 1985. 309

[12] T. ElGamal. A Public-key Cryptosystem and a Signature Scheme based on Discrete Logarithms. *IEEE Transactions on Information Theory*, vol. IT-31, pp. 469–472, 1985. 309

[13] N. Koblitz. CM-Curves with good Cryptographic Properties. In *Advances in Cryptology CRYPTO'91*, Santa Barbara, California, U.S.A., Lectures Notes in Computer Science 576, pp. 279–287, Springer-Verlag, 1992.

---

[6] http://www.ipa.go.jp/security/index-e.html

[14] R. Lidl, H. Niederreiter. *Introduction to Finite Fields and their Applications*, Revised Edition, Cambridge University Press, 1994. 322

[15] J. Malone-Lee, N. P. Smart. Modifications of ECDSA. To appear in the proceedings of SAC'02. 315

[16] U. Maurer, S. Wolf. Lower Bounds on Generic Algorithms in Groups. In *Advances in Cryptology EUROCRYPT'98*, Espoo, Finland, Lectures Notes in Computer Science 1403, pp. 72–84, Springer-Verlag, 1998.

[17] J. Monnerat. Computation of the Discrete Logarithm on Elliptic Curves of Trace One — Tutorial. Technical report IC 200249, EPFL, 2002. http://lasecwww.epfl.ch 318

[18] D. Pointcheval, J. Stern. Security Arguments for Digital Signatures and Blind Signatures. *Journal of Cryptology*, vol. 13, pp. 361–396, 2000. 314

[19] D. Pointcheval, S. Vaudenay. On Provable Security for Digital Signature Algorithms. Technical report LIENS 96-17, Ecole Normale Supérieure, 1996. 314, 315

[20] C. P. Schnorr. Efficient Identification and Signature for Smart Cards. In *Advances in Cryptology CRYPTO'89*, Santa Barbara, California, U.S.A., Lectures Notes in Computer Science 435, pp. 235–251, Springer-Verlag, 1990. 315

[21] C. P. Schnorr. Efficient Identification and Signature for Smart Cards. *Journal of Cryptology*, vol. 4, pp. 161–174, 1991. 315

[22] V. Shoup. Lower Bounds for Discrete Logarithms and Related Problems. In *Advances in Cryptology EUROCRYPT'97*, Konstanz, Germany, Lectures Notes in Computer Science 1233, pp. 256–266, Springer-Verlag, 1997. 316

[23] N. P. Smart. The Discrete Logarithm Problem on Elliptic Curves of Trace One. *Journal of Cryptology*, vol. 12, pp. 193–196, 1999. 318

[24] J. Stern, D. Pointcheval, J. Malone-Lee, N. P. Smart. Flaws in Applying Proof Methodologies to Signature Schemes. In *Advances in Cryptology CRYPTO'02*, Santa Barbara, California, U.S.A., Lectures Notes in Computer Science 2442, pp. 93–110, Springer-Verlag, 2002. 311, 316

[25] S. Vaudenay. Hidden Collisions on DSS. In *Advances in Cryptology CRYPTO'96*, Santa Barbara, California, U.S.A., Lectures Notes in Computer Science 1109, pp. 83–88, Springer-Verlag, 1996. 312, 313

A   Number of Field Representations

Theorem 5. *Let ℓ be an integer. Let $q = 2^\ell$ and consider $\mathbf{F}_q$. Let $b \in \mathbf{F}_q$. Let $C(X) = c_0 + c_1 X + \ldots + c_{\ell-1} X^{\ell-1} \in_U \mathbf{F}_2[X]$ be a uniformly distributed random binary polynomial of degree at most $\ell - 1$. We consider the probability $\Pr$ that there exists an element $x \in \mathbf{F}_q$ of degree ℓ such that $C(x) = b$.*

- *For $b = 0$ or $b = 1$, we have $\Pr = 2^{-\ell}$.*
- *In other cases, we have $\Pr \geq \frac{1}{\ell}$ for $\ell \neq 6$, and $\Pr \geq \frac{1}{7}$ for $\ell = 6$.*

Given an element $x \in \mathbf{F}_q$ of degree ℓ, we know that $1, x, x^2, \ldots, x^{\ell-1}$ is a basis of $\mathbf{F}_q$ over $\mathbf{F}_2$ so we can choose the minimal polynomial $\mu_x(X)$ of x in order to represent $\mathbf{F}_q$ as $\mathbf{F}_2[X]/\mu_x(X)$. This way C represents b.

This theorem thus means that for any b which is neither 0 nor 1 and any bitstring C there is a probability greater than $\frac{1}{\ell}$ that there exists a representation of $\mathbf{F}_q$ in which C represents b.

Proof. When $b = 0$ or $b = 1$, we notice that $C(x) = b$ implies that x is a root of $C(X) - b$ which is a binary polynomial. When this polynomial is nonzero, this means that x is a root of a polynomial of degree less than ℓ, so x cannot have a degree of ℓ. Hence x exists only when $C(X)$ is identically equal to b which holds with probability $2^{-\ell}$. Let us now consider other cases.

Let A be the set of all $x \in \mathbf{F}_q$ of degree ℓ. For any $x \in A$, we know that $1, x, x^2, \ldots, x^{\ell-1}$ is a basis of $\mathbf{F}_q$ over $\mathbf{F}_2$. Thus we can represent b as a linear combination and obtain $b = C(x)$ for some polynomial $C(X)$ of degree less than ℓ. Hence to any $x \in A$ corresponds a unique polynomial which we denote $C_x(X)$.

For any polynomial $C(X) = c_0 + c_1 X + \ldots + c_{\ell-1} X^{\ell-1}$ in $\mathbf{F}_2[X]$ the values $x \in A$ such that $C_x(X) = C(X)$ are all roots of $C(X) - b$ which is a *nonzero* polynomial in $\mathbf{F}_q[X]$ of degree at most $\ell - 1$. Hence we have at most $\ell - 1$ values $x \in A$ which are mapped onto the same $C_x(X)$. Hence the number of $C(X)$ for which we have a solution is at least $\frac{|A|}{\ell-1}$ where $|A|$ is the cardinality of A. Thanks to the following lemma we obtain that $\Pr \geq \frac{1}{\ell-1}\left(1 - \frac{1}{\ell}\right) = \frac{1}{\ell}$ for $\ell \neq 6$. For $\ell = 6$ we have $\Pr \geq \frac{1}{5}\left(1 - \frac{11}{64}\right) \geq \frac{1}{7}$. $\square$

Lemma 1. *Let ℓ be an integer. Let $q = 2^\ell$ and consider $\mathbf{F}_q$. The number N of $x \in \mathbf{F}_q$ of degree ℓ is such that $N \geq q - \sqrt{q}\log_2 \ell$. For $\ell \neq 6$ we also have $N \geq q - \frac{q}{\ell}$ which is tighter for $\ell \leq 10$. For $\ell = 6$ we have $N = q - 11$.*

Proof. We proceed by upper bounding the number of x whose degree is less than ℓ. Let $\ell = p_1^{\alpha_1} \ldots p_r^{\alpha_r}$ be the factorization of ℓ. We assume that the p_is are pairwise different prime integers and that the α_is are non negative integers.

Let $x \in \mathbf{F}_q$ of degree $d < \ell$. The minimal polynomial $\mu_x(X)$ of x is an irreducible polynomial of $\mathbf{F}_2[X]$ of degree d whose roots are the conjugates of x. The $\mathbf{F}_2[X]/\mu_x(X)$ finite field contains the roots of $\mu_x(X)$ and is thus a subfield of $\mathbf{F}_q$ and d divides ℓ. We deduce that $x^{2^d} = x$. Since $d < \ell$ and d divides ℓ there must exists i such that d divides $\frac{\ell}{p_i}$. Raising to the power $2^{\frac{\ell}{p_i}}$ is equivalent to raising $\frac{\ell}{dp_i}$ times to the power 2^d. Hence x is a root of $X^{2^{\frac{\ell}{p_i}}} - X$. We deduce that the number of $x \in \mathbf{F}_q$ of degree $d < \ell$ is at most $\sum_{i=1}^r 2^{\frac{\ell}{p_i}}$. Since $p_i \geq 2$ we have $2^{\frac{\ell}{p_i}} \leq \sqrt{q}$. Similarly we have $r \leq \log_2 \ell$ so the number of elements of degree less than ℓ is at most $\sqrt{q}\log_2 \ell$.

In order to deduce a tighter bound we use the explicit number of irreducible polynomial of degree ℓ over $\mathbf{F}_2[X]$ which is

$$\frac{1}{\ell} \sum_{d \text{ divides } \ell} \mu(d) 2^{\frac{\ell}{d}}$$

where μ is the Mœbius function (see [14, pp. 84–86]). To each irreducible polynomial corresponds ℓ roots so we have

$$N = \sum_{d \text{ divides } \ell} \mu(d) 2^{\frac{\ell}{d}}$$

which leads us to

$$N = \sum_{\beta_1=0}^{1} \cdots \sum_{\beta_r=0}^{1} (-1)^{\beta_1+\cdots+\beta_r} \times 2^{\ell/(p_1^{\beta_1}\cdots p_r^{\beta_r})}.$$

We can check that $N \geq q - \frac{q}{\ell}$ for all $\ell \leq 10$ but $\ell = 6$ for which $N = 2^6 - 2^3 - 2^2 + 2^1 = 2^6 - 11$.

We easily demonstrate that for $\ell \geq 11$ we have $\sqrt{q} \log_2 \ell \leq \frac{q}{\ell}$ so $N \geq q - \frac{q}{\ell}$ holds for all ℓ but $\ell = 6$. $\qquad\square$

Side-Channel Attacks on Textbook RSA and ElGamal Encryption

Ulrich Kühn

Dresdner Bank, IS-STA 5, Information Security
D-60301 Frankfurt, Germany
ulrich.kuehn@dresdner-bank.com
ukuehn@acm.org

Abstract. This paper describes very efficient attacks on plain RSA encryption as usually described in textbooks. These attacks exploit side channels caused by implementations that, during decryption, incorrectly make certain assumption on the size of message. We highlight different assumptions that are easily made when implementing plain RSA decryption and present corresponding attacks.

These attacks make clear that plain RSA is a padding scheme that has to be checked carefully during decryption instead of simply assuming a length of the transported message.

Furthermore we note that the attacks presented here do also work against a similar setting of ElGamal encryption with only minimal changes.

Keywords: RSA encryption, ElGamal encryption, Side-channel attack.

1 Introduction

In general RSA is described as the modular exponentiation applied directly to a message M – plain RSA. Boneh, Joux and Nguyen [6] have shown that this method is insecure when the bit-length m of the encrypted message is fixed to a small amount of bits, say 64 bits, by giving a meet-in-the-middle attack that uses $2 \cdot 2^{m/2}$ modular exponentiations and $2^{m/2}m$ bits of memory; this result is independent of the size of the modulus. But if longer messages are involved, e.g. 128 bits or more in length, this method becomes impractical. Attacks against RSA encryption of messages with related or stereotyped content do not seem applicable when only random session keys of considerable size are encrypted as part of a hybrid encryption scheme (see Boneh [5] for an overview of attacks on RSA).

On the other hand, attacks using side channels caused by incorrect implementations have been presented by Bleichenbacher [3] against PKCS #1 v1.5 RSA block type 2 padding as well as by Manger [12] against PKCS #1 v2.0 (RSA-OAEP); here the adversary learns one bit of information about the resulting plaintext from a server that sends detailed error codes for different failures in the decryption process. The query complexities of these attacks essentially depend exponentially on the number of bits that the padded message is shorter

Y.G. Desmedt (Ed.): PKC 2003, LNCS 2567, pp. 324–336, 2003.

than the modulus; the attacks are efficient because for the PKCS #1 padding schemes these numbers are 16 resp. 8 bits for usual choices of the length of the modulus.

In this paper we present attacks that exploit side channels in plain RSA encryption and make use of the homomorphic property of RSA. The side channels result from implementation flaws in the decryption process, namely certain assumptions about the message being encrypted; we argue that these assumptions are easily made when implementing the decryption of plain RSA.

We model the decryption process in a server as an oracle that tests whether a given message is – under some equivalence relation specific to the oracle – equivalent to the original message that was given to the adversary as a challenge. The oracle-specific assumptions on the message are either that the relevant message bits (the session key) occur at certain positions or that the message has a specific, a-priori known (short) size when interpreted as an integer. The latter assumption is similar to the one used by Manger [12], but here we have to deal with messages that are a lot shorter than the modulus.

We present the *approximation attacks* that can very efficiently break the confidentiality of the messages using the oracles that assume positions of the message bits, provided that the size of the message is at most about one third of the size of the modulus. We also present the *divisibility attack* that works when the adversary can gain one bit of knowledge about the size of a (short) decrypted message. All our attacks are independent of the size of the modulus, they depend only on the size of the encrypted message.

Related to our attacks are the attacks of Bleichenbacher [3] and Manger [12], as all these attacks exploit side channels that result from incorrect implementations of the RSA decryption and unpadding process. The query complexity of Bleichenbacher's resp. Manger's attack e.g. for a message encrypted under a 1024-bit modulus is about one million resp. roughly a thousand queries; the approximation attacks need only 130 queries to reveal a 128-bit message, while an improved divisibility attack requires for example roughly 7000 queries and 2^{32} offline work with a probability of success of about one in 82 messages. It should be noted that our attacks do not work for PKCS #1 padded messages, while Bleichenbacher's and Manger's attacks effectively do not work in the setting of plain RSA.

The practical aspect of our attacks is that they exploit implementation errors one can easily step into. We found that the home banking system HBCI, an early version of the e-government protocol OSCI (the current specification uses PKCS #1 padding) and an early (now obsolete) version of PEM do apply plain RSA, and we are aware of implementations seemingly vulnerable to the approximation attacks.

The rest of this paper is organised as follows. Section 2 describes the different types of server oracles that are examined here, Sections 3 to 5 give attacks on each of these oracles, while Section 6 shows that nearly the same attacks might work against improperly implemented plain ElGamal encryption. Then Section 7 discusses the practical impact on the above-mentioned systems in more detail. Finally some conclusions are drawn.

2   Decryption Oracles

While we model our attacks in terms of oracles they should be viewed with a hybrid encryption setting in mind.[1] We further assume that redundancy to check for decryption errors is present. In the sequel we refer to the session key also as the *message* of the plain RSA encryption.

When a message M of fixed and a-priori known size is transmitted after encryption with plain RSA useful information might leak from the receiver, depending on the way the receiver reacts on the result of decryption. In the sequel we will refer to the receiver of the message as the server.

Throughout this paper we will use the following notation:

Notation. We denote the size of a value X measured in bits by $L(X)$. Let N be an RSA modulus, i.e. $N = PQ$ for two primes P and Q, and e resp. d the public resp. private exponent. When using modular reduction, we identify integers in the interval $[0, N)$ with the elements of $\mathbb{Z}_N$; elements of $\mathbb{Z}_N$ are represented by the least positive residue modulo N in the interval $[0, N)$. For y with $\gcd(y, N) = 1$ we use the notation $x/y \mod N$ to denote $x \cdot a \mod N$ with a being the inverse of y modulo N, i.e. the unique integer a, $0 < a < N$, such that $ay \equiv 1 \pmod{N}$.

Modeling the Oracles. Throughout this paper we will use the following definitions to refer to the oracles and the queries involved:

Definition. We model the server as an oracle $\mathcal{O}$, holding a secret $M_{\mathcal{O}}$ known only to the oracle. We assume that $M_{\mathcal{O}} < B$ for a fixed, publicly known bound $B = 2^b$, i.e. $M_{\mathcal{O}}$ has at most b bits. $\mathcal{O}$ has an associated public RSA-key (N, e) and a private exponent d. The adversary is given the public key (N, e) and the challenge ciphertext $C_{\mathcal{O}} = M_{\mathcal{O}}^e \mod N$.

The oracle answers a query $\mathcal{O}(C)$ either with success or failure, depending on whether the decrypted $M = C^d \mod N$ is equivalent to $M_{\mathcal{O}}$ with the equivalence relation depending on the oracle actually used. The oracle treats the query message $M = C^d \mod N$ after RSA decryption in one of the following ways, depending on the oracle-specific secret $M_{\mathcal{O}}$:

LSB-oracle: The oracle uses the least significant b bits of M, i.e. checks if $M \equiv M_{\mathcal{O}} \pmod{B}$.

---

[1] A payload is encrypted under a random session key using symmetric cryptography while the session key itself is encrypted with plain RSA; both ciphertexts are transmitted to the receiver. Some redundancy, i.e. a MAC or a digital signature is assumed to be present to distinguish between a correct and an incorrect decryption.

MSB-oracle: If $L(M) < L(B)$, then the oracle checks that $M = M_{\mathcal{O}}$. If M has $L(M) \geq L(B)$ bits, the most significant b bits of M (i.e. the value $\lfloor M/2^{(L(M)-b)} \rfloor$) are tested if they equal $M_{\mathcal{O}}$.

A variant checks if the most significant octets, words etc. of M, e.g. the most significant $\lceil \frac{b}{8} \rceil$ octets[2] of M equal $M_{\mathcal{O}}$, i.e. uses the value

$$\left\lfloor \frac{M}{2^{8(\lceil \frac{L(M)}{8} \rceil - \lceil \frac{b}{8} \rceil)}} \right\rfloor .$$

Size-checking oracle: The oracle checks that $M < B$, i.e. checks if M is conforming to the size assumption on the message.

Remark 1. Note that none of these oracles represents a correct implementation of the decryption process for plain RSA.

Remark 2. A server can be modeled as the size-checking oracle if it provides error codes that allow to distinguish between a message $M \geq B$ and a message $M < B$ that is incorrect for some other reason, i.e. does not yield a valid decryption of the payload in a hybrid encryption scheme. This oracle has been used in Manger's attack on RSA-OAEP [12], but his attack does not work efficiently if B is much shorter than the modulus.

3   Attacking the LSB-Oracle

The attack on the LSB-oracle is based on two crucial observations: First, encryptions of multiples of $M_{\mathcal{O}}$ of the form $M = (aB+1)M_{\mathcal{O}}$ result, as $M \equiv M_{\mathcal{O}}$ (mod B), in the oracle answering success whenever $M < N$; if a is too large (thus $M \geq N$) then the modular reduction in the RSA decryption is likely[3] to yield an incorrect message.

Second, if z is such that $zM_{\mathcal{O}} \approx N$, $zM_{\mathcal{O}} < N$, then $M_{\mathcal{O}} \approx \lfloor N/z \rfloor$ with a small margin of error. We will show below that an approximation of the most significant b plus a small constant number of bits of N are sufficient to work reliably. Therefore we call this kind of attack the *approximation attack*.

The idea of the attack is to use the homomorphic property of RSA to compute ciphertexts from the oracle's challenge (the encryption of $M_{\mathcal{O}}$) yielding multiples of $M_{\mathcal{O}}$. Furthermore the modular reduction in the RSA encryption / decryption operation indicates whether $M < N$ or not; this information is employed in

---

[2] Such a behavior can occur if the long integer package used for implementation returns numbers without leading zeros and the integer-to-octet-array conversion places the highest octets first into the array.

[3] The heuristic here is that if $M = (aB+1)M$ is only slightly larger than N, changes are wrapped by the modular reduction into the result of decryption and truncation. This assumption might not hold if N has a special form $N \equiv c$ (mod B) where the least significant $L(c)$ bits of the session key are ignored (e.g. a Triple-DES key where the parity bits are ignored has $c = 1$).

a (truncated) binary search to find the approximation $M = zM_{\mathcal{O}} \approx N$. Informally speaking, an additional copy of the original message is shifted towards the more significant bits as far as possible without making it bigger than the modulus and is subsequently padded out by other copies not shifted that far while still keeping the result below the modulus. This is basically done by binary search.

The attack algorithm works as follows, where the bound B is assumed to be known to all parties. Furthermore, it is assumed that $M_{\mathcal{O}} \neq 0$ and N is of size $L(N) > 3b + c$, where c is some small constant ($c = 3$ is sufficient).

Input: LSB-oracle $\mathcal{O}$ with public RSA-key (N, e), challenge $C_{\mathcal{O}} = M_{\mathcal{O}}^e \mod N$ derived from $M_{\mathcal{O}}$ with $0 < M_{\mathcal{O}} < B$; $M_{\mathcal{O}}$ is known only to $\mathcal{O}$.
Output: The message $M_{\mathcal{O}}$.

1. Set $z \leftarrow \max\{2^w | w > 0 \text{ and } 2^w < N/B\}$, $b' \leftarrow b$.
2. Compute the query $C = C_{\mathcal{O}}(2z+1)^e \mod N$; if $\mathcal{O}(C) = \mathsf{success}$, set $z \leftarrow 2z$, $b' \leftarrow b' - 1$ and repeat this step.
3. Set $y \leftarrow z/2$.
4. Do for $b' + 1$ times:
   (a) Compute the query $C = C_{\mathcal{O}}(z + y + 1)^e \mod N$; if $\mathcal{O}(C) = \mathsf{success}$, set $z \leftarrow z + y$.
   (b) Set $y \leftarrow y/2$.
5. Compute a candidate $\hat{M} \leftarrow \lfloor N/(z+1) \rfloor$ for $M_{\mathcal{O}}$ and return it.

To show the correctness of the attack algorithm we show that a partial approximation of N is sufficient.

Proposition 1. *Let N, b, $k < b$ be positive integers; let $B = 2^b$. If $N > 2^{b+k}$ then for each integer M, $0 < M < B$ there exists an integer z with*

$$N - zM < 2^{L(N)-1-k}, \tag{1}$$

i.e. an approximation of the most significant k bits of N by multiples of M is possible.

Proof. Equation 1 can be fulfilled if $0 < M < 2^{L(N)-1-k}$, as the points in the set $\{iM \mid i \in \mathbb{Z}\}$ have a distance of less than the error bound, and thus a point exists with the claimed property.

As Equation 1 has to hold for all $M < B$, this can be fulfilled if $B = 2^b \leq 2^{L(N)-1-k}$, thus $2^{L(N)-1-k-b} \geq 1$. As $N > 2^{L(N)-1}$, the claim follows.   □

Proposition 2. *Let N, b, $k < b$ be positive integers such that $N > 2^{b+k}$; let $B = 2^b$ and $M \in \{0, \ldots, B-1\}$. Let z be a positive integer such that $zM < N$ and $N - zM < 2^{L(N)-k-2}$, i.e. the most significant $k+2$ bits of zM and N match. With $M' := \lfloor N/z \rfloor$ the approximation error is bounded by $|M - M'| < 2^{b-k-1}$.*

Proof. The existence of such a z follows from Proposition 1. To prove the error bound, we use the first order Taylor expansion of $N/(z+x)$ at z with $x \geq 0$:

$$\frac{N}{z+x} = \frac{N}{z} - \frac{Nx}{\xi^2} \quad \text{with } \xi \in [z, z+x] \tag{2}$$

and thus

$$\delta(x) \stackrel{\text{def}}{=} \frac{N}{z} - \frac{N}{z+x} = \frac{Nx}{\xi^2} \le \frac{Nx}{z^2} \text{ , as } \xi \ge z. \tag{3}$$

From $M < B$ it follows that $z > N/B$, and as $x = (N - zM)/z$, we have $x < 2^{L(N)-k-2}/z$. Thus

$$\delta(x) < \frac{N2^{L(N)-k-2}B^3}{N^3} < \frac{B^3}{2^{k+1}N} < 2^{b-k-1}, \tag{4}$$

as $B = 2^b$, $N > 2^{L(N)-1}$ and $N > B^2$.   □

The condition $L(N) > 3b + c$ for the algorithm is necessary in order to have at all times the correct message being present as the b least significant bits plus the approximation using copies of $M_{\mathcal{O}}$ shifted to the more significant bits while the least significant bits of the shifted copies must not interfere with the most significant bits of $M_{\mathcal{O}}$ in the original position (as these bits are used by the oracle to check the equivalence).

The first two steps of the attack algorithm make sure that leading zero bits in $M_{\mathcal{O}}$ are taken care of, thus allowing to apply Proposition 2 using a modified bound $B' = 2^{L(M_{\mathcal{O}})}$. Step 4 is basically binary search with the condition that $M_{\mathcal{O}}(z + y + 1) < N$ during each iteration. The loop count makes sure that the error condition of Proposition 2 with $k = b$ is fulfilled; thus Step 5 results in $\hat{M} = M_{\mathcal{O}}$ as the approximation error is less than $1/2$.

The algorithm is very efficient as it uses only $b + 2$ queries, thus proving the intuition that the oracle leaks about one bit per query. Furthermore it should be noted that this attack is independent of the size of the modulus, as long as the condition for the size of B and N are fulfilled. The algorithm requires nearly no memory.

4   Attacking the MSB-Oracle

The MSB-oracle can be attacked with a similar method as the LSB-oracle in the last section. In the sequel we will be mostly concerned with the variant that uses the most significant $L := \lceil \frac{b}{8} \rceil$ octets of the decrypted query message M (see Section 2). An adaption to the situation where this is done for single bits or words is rather straight-forward.

Remark 3. In order for this attack to work it is necessary that the message $M_{\mathcal{O}}$ has full length in octets, i.e. $\lceil L(M_{\mathcal{O}})/8 \rceil = L$, as otherwise any shifted copy of $M_{\mathcal{O}}$ would result in the oracle reporting failure. A random message M is expected to have full length in octets in 255 out of 256 cases.

Roughly speaking, the essential observation is that any multiple of $M_{\mathcal{O}}$ of the form $M = (2^{8Lc} + z)M_{\mathcal{O}}$ for $z < 2^{8(L(c-1))}$, $c > 1$, results in the oracle reporting success whenever $M_{\mathcal{O}}$ has full length, i.e. consists of L octets. Then the bound 2^{8Lc} can be approximated by multiples of $M_{\mathcal{O}}$. Thus this is another instance of the approximation attack.

In order to use Proposition 2 with $k = b$ it is necessary to have slightly more than $8L$ bits in an approximation, thus we have to use at least one more octet. The attack algorithm approximates $2^{8(Lc+1)}$ for $c = 2$ by a multiple $zM_{\mathcal{O}}$ by binary search in the same way as N is approximated in Section 3. The attack algorithms works for $N > 2^{8(Lc+1)}B$.

Input: MSB-oracle $\mathcal{O}$ with public RSA-key (N, e), challenge $C_{\mathcal{O}} = M_{\mathcal{O}}^e \mod N$
     derived from $M_{\mathcal{O}}$ with $2^{8(L-1)} \le M_{\mathcal{O}} < 2^{8L}$; $M_{\mathcal{O}}$ is known only to $\mathcal{O}$.
Output: The message $M_{\mathcal{O}}$.

1. Set $f \leftarrow 2^{8(2L+1)}$, $z \leftarrow 2^{8(L+1)}$, $b' \leftarrow b$.
2. Compute the query $C = C_{\mathcal{O}}(f+z)^e \mod N$; if $\mathcal{O}(C) = \mathsf{success}$, set $z \leftarrow 2z$,
   $b' \leftarrow b' - 1$ and repeat this step.
3. Set $y \leftarrow z/2$.
4. Do for $b' + 1$ times:
   (a) Compute the query $C = C_{\mathcal{O}}(f+z+y)^e \mod N$; if $\mathcal{O}(C) = \mathsf{success}$, set
       $z \leftarrow z + y$.
   (b) Set $y \leftarrow y/2$.
5. Compute a candidate $\hat{M} \leftarrow \lfloor f/z \rfloor$ for $M_{\mathcal{O}}$ and return it.

The correctness of this attack algorithm can be seen in basically the same way as in the case of the LSB-oracle in Section 3, again using Proposition 2 with $k = b$.

The algorithm is as efficient as the one in Section 3, it uses only $b+2$ queries to retrieve the complete message $M_{\mathcal{O}}$, provided that $M_{\mathcal{O}}$ has the full length in octets; this is fulfilled for 255 out of 256 messages. Thus this oracle also leaks about one bit per query. Again, the algorithm needs virtually no memory.

Remark 4. A difficulty for the attack algorithm may arise if some bits of an RSA-encrypted session key are ignored, e.g. a Triple-DES key where the parity bits are ignored or corrected whenever they are incorrect. In this situation a cleared parity bit in the octet located at the least significant position will result in Step 2 in z being too big by a factor of 2; the reason is that the most significant set bit of $M_{\mathcal{O}}$ has to be shifted past this critical parity bit to lead to a negative result of the oracle query. This also happens in Step 4, thus leading to $\hat{M} = \lfloor M_{\mathcal{O}}/2 \rfloor$; therefore it is necessary to modify the last step of the attack algorithm as follows:

5'. Compute two candidates for $M_{\mathcal{O}}$ as $\hat{M}_1 \leftarrow \lfloor f/z \rfloor$ and $\hat{M}_2 \leftarrow \lfloor 2f/z \rfloor$,

which effectively leaves a single bit of entropy of the session key; this bit has to be determined by the adversary from other sources of redundancy like the parity bits or the symmetrically-encrypted message itself.

Interestingly, the fact that keys for Triple-DES employ odd parity results in the situation that all messages $M_{\mathcal{O}}$ have full length as a leading zero octet – which would have even parity – is impossible; thus all messages can be recovered by the attack.

5   Attacking the Size-Checking Oracle

Given the attacks in the previous sections one might try to fix the vulnerability by checking on the receiver's side that the decrypted message is below an a-priori fixed bound B. We show here that simply checking the size of the message after decryption may not be sufficient to prevent the attacks of this paper. When not done very carefully an implementation might actually implement a size-checking oracle leaking information to an adversary. This is a setting similar to that of Manger's attack on RSA-OAEP [12], although his attack cannot be applied efficiently in our situation here. This is due to the running time containing an expression exponential in N/B.

Definition 1. *(see [14]) A number n with factorisation $n = \prod_{i=1}^{k} p_i$ with p_i prime is called y-smooth if $p_i \leq y$ for $1 \leq i \leq k$.*

Definition 2. *(see [1]) A number n with factorisation $n = \prod_{i=1}^{k} p_i$ with p_i prime and $p_i \geq p_{i+1}$ is called semismooth with respect to y and z if $p_1 \leq y$ and $p_2 \leq z$. We also say in this case that n is (y, z)-semismooth.*

The next Proposition essentially allows to convert the size-checking oracle into an oracle that answers requests of the type "Does p divide the secret message M_O?", i.e. a test for divisibility. Therefore we call the attack based on this oracle the *divisibility attack*.

Proposition 3. *Let $B < N$, $x \in \{0, \ldots, B-1\}$ and a such that $1 \leq a < N/B$ and $\gcd(a, N) = 1$. Let $y = x/a \mod N$. Then $y \in [0, B)$ if and only if $a|x$.*

Proof. The claim is clear for $a|x$. Assume now $y \in [0, B)$. Then we have $ay \in \{0, a, 2a, \ldots, (B-1)a\}$. Furthermore, for $0 \leq t \leq (B-1)$ it is $ta < N$ as $a < N/B$, i.e. no wrap-around occurs when reducing modulo N. It follows that $ay = a\,y \mod N$ and thus $ay = x$. We find that $x \in \{aj|1 \leq j < B\}$, i.e. $a|x$. $\square$

The attack based on the oracle provided by Proposition 3 tries to extract a large smooth part of the message M_O and to find the rest of the message by other means, e.g. by offline search using brute force.

The attack algorithm is as follows:

Parameters: Fix a bound S for the smooth part of M_O and a bound T for the amount of offline work; both S and T may depend on the bound B.

Input: A size-checking oracle O with public RSA-key (N, e) and a challenge $C_O = M_O^e \mod N$ derived from M_O with $0 < M_O < B$; M_O is known only to O.

Output: If successful, the message M_O.

State variables: m', the currently known smooth part of M_O; c', the RSA encryption of M_O/m'.

1. Initialise $m' \leftarrow 1$, $c' \leftarrow C_\mathcal{O}$.
2. For each prime $p \leq S$ (assuming $\gcd(p, N) = 1$)
    (a) Compute the next query $C = c'/p^e \mod N$.
    (b) If $\mathcal{O}(C) = \mathsf{success}$ (i.e. $p \mid \frac{M_\mathcal{O}}{m'}$), set $m' \leftarrow pm' \mod N$, $c' \leftarrow c'/p^e$ mod N, and go to step 2a.
    (c) Otherwise, go to the next prime.
3. For each $m_t \leq T$ test if $c' = m_t^e \mod N$. If so, return $\hat{M} \leftarrow m_t m' \mod N$ as candidate for $M_\mathcal{O}$.
4. If the execution path arrives here, abort, as $M_\mathcal{O}$ cannot be recovered with these settings.

The correctness of the attack algorithm is based on an invariant that is maintained in Steps 1 and 2:

$$C = (m')^e c' \mod N. \tag{5}$$

During Step 2, m' resp. c' are modified if and only if Proposition 3 says that the decryption of c' is divisible by p. As a result of the loop the S-smooth part of $M_\mathcal{O}$ is extracted. Finally, Step 3 tries to find the non-S-smooth part of $M_\mathcal{O}$.

Selection of Parameters. The attack works for those messages $M_\mathcal{O}$ that are divisible by primes $p < S$ possibly except for a factor bounded by T. Thus the probability of success is given by the probability that a random message is of this form.

For certain choices of S and T this is related to the concept of semismooth numbers, as the attack works for all numbers that are (T, S)-semismooth. Therefore probabilities of semismoothness give a lower bound on the success probabilities of the attack (see [1, Table 1]). On the other hand, if $T < S^2$ this bound is also tight, as the non-S-smooth part m_t of $M_\mathcal{O}$ must be a prime in this case.

The following example indicates that an adversary can find the message with a non-negligible advantage:

Example 1. Assume that keys for 2-key Triple-DES with correct parity, i.e. keys with 128 bits but only 112 bits of entropy, are encrypted by plain RSA using a 1024-bit modulus. Thus, $B = 2^{128}$. Using $S = 2^{22}$ and $T = 2^{42}$ the bound provided by the semismoothness probability is tight. Experiments with $22 \cdot 2^{14} = 360448$ random 128-bit numbers with adjusted parity yielded 559 numbers being (T, S)-semismooth, representing a fraction of $0.155\% \approx 2^{-9.3}$.

Improvements. The attack can be improved by combining it with the approximation attack, namely by using Proposition 2 with $k < b$. We will first describe the method with general parameters and then give a concrete setting.

Assuming that an adversary is willing to invest the queries to the server to find all factors of $M_\mathcal{O}$ below S using the divisibility attack, and further assuming that for the resulting rest $\hat{M}$ (free of divisors $\leq S$) $\hat{M} < T = 2^t$ holds, Proposition 2 guarantees that $b - t - 2$ further bits of $\hat{M}$ can be found with a process similar to the approximation attacks of Sections 3 and 4 with $b - t$ queries, thus leaving $t - (b - t - 2) = 2t - b + 2$ bits to be found by brute force.

The probability of success is that of a random number $M_{\mathcal{O}} < 2^b$ being divisible by primes below S and leaving a non-S-smooth remainder below T.

In a concrete setting using $b = 128$ (thus $M_{\mathcal{O}} < 2^{128}$), $S = 2^{16}$ and $t = 79, T = 2^{79}$ results in less than 7000 queries (see [14, Table 3]) to find the small prime factors of $M_{\mathcal{O}}$, approximation of 47 bits of $\hat{M}$ using 49 queries and finding of 32 bits by brute force. The probability of success has been experimentally found (using 2^{16} random numbers) to be about $2^{-6.4}$ or 1 in 82 random messages. Many other trade-offs are possible.

6   Attacking ElGamal Encryption

In [8] ElGamal encryption of a message $M_{\mathcal{O}}$ is described as $C = (g^r, M_{\mathcal{O}} y^r)$ where $p, g, y = g^x$ is the public key, x the private key, and computation is done in $\mathbb{Z}_p$. Similar to the RSA case, for plain ElGamal encryption no further padding is applied to the message before encryption. Plain ElGamal encryption has been shown in [6] to be attackable under certain conditions on the order of the generator g and the bit-size b of the messages using $2 \cdot 2^{b/2}$ modular exponentiations.

As the message $M_{\mathcal{O}}$ is masked by multiplying with y^r there is basically the same multiplicative property as in RSA (this was also noted by Bleichenbacher [4]): Given $(g^r, M_{\mathcal{O}} y^r)$, the ciphertext $(g^r, zM_{\mathcal{O}} y^r)$ decrypts to $zM_{\mathcal{O}}$.

This implies that the attacks presented above do also work for plain ElGamal encryption after minor adaptions without changing the analysis. It should be noted that, given a susceptible implementation, the attacks do not depend on the choice of p or the generator g, provided that $L(p) > 3b + c$ for small c and $M_{\mathcal{O}} < B = 2^b$.

Remark 5. While in [8] ElGamal encryption is proposed with multiplication modulo p to blind $M_{\mathcal{O}}$ with y^r, it is also noted there that other reversible operations could be used, e.g. bitwise XOR. This would destroy the multiplicative property used here and thus make the attacks much harder or even impossible.

The same problem exists with ElGamal encryption based on any other group, e.g. elliptic curves, provided that the blinding value is combined with the message by modular multiplication without any other precautions.

7   Practical Impact

In the sequel we will discuss three systems that make use of plain RSA encryption. It should be noted that the assessment that these systems might be susceptible to the attacks given in this paper is based purely on theoretical analysis of the specification. Generally, any system using plain RSA might be susceptible to our attacks if the highlighted implementation issues are present.

Furthermore it should be noted that only the confidentiality of payload messages is in danger, not their integrity, if the integrity of the messages is properly protected, e.g. by a digital signature.

7.1   HBCI

The Home Banking Computing Interface (HBCI) [9] is a protocol for providing a means of online banking to a bank's customers. To ensure confidentiality of the messages HBCI employs two alternatives: one is based fully on Triple-DES and will be ignored here, the other uses a hybrid encryption scheme on which we will focus. The actual banking messages (including a digital signature) are encrypted with 2-key Triple-DES in CBC mode under a random session key that is generated anew for each banking message; this session key is encrypted using plain RSA. The length parameters given in [9] are a modulus size of 768 bits for RSA and session keys of 128 bits for Triple-DES (including the correct parity bits).[4]

While it is possible to implement the encryption scheme such that our attacks do not work, we are aware of implementations that may be vulnerable. To be more precise, we found implementations of the cryptographic functionality with freely available source code, and, according to a source code inspection, they implement the LSB- and the MSB-oracle.[5] On the other hand we have no example of an implementation instantiating a size-checking oracle.

Interestingly the HBCI specification [9, Sect. VI.2.2.1] explains very carefully how to generate session keys and how to format them for encryption, but does not specify how the decryption and session key extraction have to be done.

7.2   OSCI

Another system that might be vulnerable is the (now outdated) version 1.0 of the Online Services Computing Interface (OSCI) [7] which is a proposal for an

---

[4] The recently published draft of version 3.0 [10] specifies, besides the old method, encryption of the message key using PKCS #1 padding and longer RSA keys; thus our attacks do not apply in this case, but one has to guard against the attack of [3].

[5] One is an implementation of an HBCI-Client which retrieves the session key from the last 16 octets of the result of the RSA decryption; these are the least significant octets. While the attack does not seem to work against a client, the attack from Section 3 can reveal any intercepted message with only 130 queries to a server that uses the same method.

The other is a generic implementation, suitable both for server and client. Here the session key is retrieved from an octet array with the leading zeroes being removed; but the result is not checked if it is too long, while too short arrays are padded. Thus the session key is constructed from the most significant 16 octets resulting from the RSA decryption. Here the attack from Section 4 needs only 130 queries to a server for obtaining the plaintext of an intercepted message. Remark 4 applies here as the parity is automatically corrected when it is incorrect.

XML-based e-government protocol. This version uses basically the same crypto-graphic functionality as HBCI to conceal messages, although with longer RSA keys (1023 to 1024 bits). Thus, depending on the actual implementation, a server implementing this protocol might instantiate one of the oracles examined here. Again the specification explains in great detail how to encrypt but not in detail how to decrypt.

Note that the newer version 1.2 as specified in [13] uses PKCS #1 v1.5 padding as part of XML encryption so that the attacks of this paper do not apply, but instead an implementation has to be guarded against [3].

7.3   Early Version of PEM

A third system that used plain RSA to transport session keys is an early, now obsoleted version of the Privacy-enhancement for Internet electronic mail (PEM) as specified in [11]. An important difference to the other systems mentioned above is that with PEM no server is normally present; instead, a mail reader performs the decryption under human supervision, so persuading the user to answer more than 100 queries might be difficult. But as newer versions [2] do not use plain RSA anymore this possible vulnerability does no longer exist.

8   Conclusion

In this paper we have shown that the decryption oracles examined here all result in insecure implementations of the decryption process for plain RSA, effectively destroying the confidentiality of the messages. The oracles are the result of as-sumptions on the messages during decryption; these assumptions are easily made when implementing the decryption process, we even found examples of seemingly vulnerable implementations.

In order to protect oneself against our attacks one has to rigorously check the padding with zeroes and the size of the message – this avoids the approximation attacks – and furthermore make sure that an adversary cannot get any informa-tion on the size of the decrypted message from error codes etc., effectively avoid-ing the divisibility attack. Our attacks show that plain RSA is indeed a padding scheme, contrary to the common belief that it does not use any padding.

It should be noted that a decryption process has not only to deal with valid ciphertexts but also with ciphertexts that are not the outcome of the correspond-ing encryption process; thus the specification of the decryption has to contain more than just the reversal to the encryption process. Indeed, the decryption process has to be specified and implemented very carefully.

Acknowledgment

The author is thankful to the anonymous referees for their helpful comments. Thanks are also due to Stefan Lucks for helpful discussions.

References

[1] E. Bach and R. Peralta. Asymptotic semismoothness probabilities. *Mathematics of Computation*, 65(216):1701–1715, 1996. 331, 332

[2] D. Balenson. RFC 1423: Privacy enhancement for Internet electronic mail: Part III: Algorithms, modes, and identifiers, Feb. 1993. Obsoletes RFC1115 [11]. 335, 336

[3] D. Bleichenbacher. Chosen Ciphertext Attacks Against Protocols Based on the RSA Encryption Standards PKCS #1. In H. Krawczyk, editor, *Advances in Cryptology – CRYPTO '98*, volume 1462 of *Lecture Notes in Computer Science*, pages 1–12. Springer Verlag, 1998. 324, 325, 334, 335

[4] D. Bleichenbacher. Decrypting ElGamal messages. Message to ietf-open-pgp mailing list on imc.org, April 1999. http://www.imc.org/ietf-open-pgp/mail-archive/msg02431.html. 333

[5] D. Boneh. Twenty years of attacks on the RSA cryptosystem. *Notices of the AMS*, 46(2):203–213, February 1999. 324

[6] D. Boneh, A. Joux, and P. Q. Nguyen. Why Textbook ElGamal and RSA Encryption Are Insecure. In T. Okamoto, editor, *Advances in Cryptology – ASIACRYPT 2000*, volume 1976 of *Lecture Notes in Computer Science*, pages 30–43. Springer Verlag, 2000. 324, 333

[7] Bremen Online Services. OSCI – Online-Services-Computer-Interface. Candidate for Version 1.0, November 2000. http://www.bos-bremen.de/downloads/kap10_1.html. 334

[8] T. ElGamal. A public key cryptosystem and a signature scheme based on discrete logarithms. In G. R. Blakley and D. Chaum, editors, *Advances in Cryptology: Proceedings of CRYPTO 84*, volume 196 of *Lecture Notes in Computer Science*, pages 10–18. Springer-Verlag, 1985, 19–22 Aug. 1984. 333

[9] HBCI – Home Banking Computer Interface. Specification Version 2.2, May 2000. http://www.hbci.de/. 334

[10] HBCI – Home Banking Computer Interface. Draft Specification Version 3.0, July 2002. http://www.hbci.de/. 334

[11] J. Linn. RFC 1115: Privacy enhancement for Internet electronic mail: Part III — algorithms, modes, and identifiers, Aug. 1989. Obsoleted by RFC1423 [2]. 335, 336

[12] J. Manger. A Chosen Ciphertext Attack on RSA Optimal Asymmetric Encryption Padding (OAEP) as Standardized in PKCS #1 v2.0. In J. Kilian, editor, *Advances in Cryptology – Crypto 2001*, volume 2139 of *Lecture Notes in Computer Science*, pages 230–238. Springer Verlag, 2001. 324, 325, 327, 331

[13] OSCI Leitstelle. OSCI-Transport Version 1.2, June 2002. See http://www.osci.de/projekte/osci.html. 335

[14] H. Riesel. *Prime Numbers and Computer Methods for Factorization*. Birkhäuser, 2nd edition, 1994. 331, 333

On the Security of HFE, HFEv- and Quartz*

Nicolas T. Courtois[1], Magnus Daum[2], and Patrick Felke[2]

[1] CP8 Crypto Lab, SchlumbergerSema
36-38 rue de la Princesse, BP 45, 78430 Louveciennes Cedex, France
courtois@minrank.org
[2] Ruhr-Universität Bochum, Postfach 102148, 44780 Bochum, Germany
{Magnus.Daum,Patrick.Felke}@ruhr-uni-bochum.de

Abstract. Quartz is a signature scheme based on an HFEv- trapdoor function published at Eurocrypt 1996. In this paper we study "inversion" attacks for Quartz, i.e. attacks that solve the system of multivariate equations used in Quartz. We do not cover some special attacks that forge signatures without inversion.

We are interested in methods to invert the HFEv- trapdoor function or at least to distinguish it from a random system of the same size. There are 4 types of attacks known on HFE: Shamir-Kipnis [27], Shamir-Kipnis-Courtois [8], Courtois [8], and attacks related to Gröbner bases such as the F5/2 attack by Jean Charles Faugère [15, 16].

No attack has been published so far on HFEv- and it was believed to be more secure than HFE. In this paper we show that even modified HFE systems can be successfully attacked. It seems that the complexity of the attack increases by at least a factor of q^{tot} with tot being the total number of perturbations in HFE. From this and all the other known attacks we will estimate what is the complexity of the best "inversion" attack for Quartz.

Keywords: asymmetric cryptography, finite fields, multivariate cryptanalysis, Gröbner bases, Hidden Field Equation, HFE problem, Quartz, Nessie project.

1 Introduction

The HFE family of trapdoor functions, that have been proposed at Eurocrypt 96 [22] generalizes the previous Matsumoto-Imai cryptosystem called C^* from Eurocrypt 88 [20] broken by Patarin[1] in [21]. The HFE family consists of a so called basic HFE (also called the basic algebraic version of HFE) and modified versions, also called "combinatorial versions of HFE". These modified versions are built on a basic HFE adding the so called "perturbations" that are expected to make attacks harder, but still conserve the existence of the trapdoor.

---

* The work described in this paper has been partially supported by the French Ministry of Research under RNRT Project "Turbo-signatures".

[1] As was now made public also H. Dobbertin has independently found this attack in '93/94 being employed by BSI-Institute [private communication].

For example the Quartz signature scheme that has been submitted to the European Nessie call for cryptographic primitives uses (as a component) such a combinatorial version of HFE, called HFEv-. In this paper we will study the security of HFEv- and Quartz. We will cover all the "inversion" attacks on Quartz, that forge signatures by solving the system of equations that constitutes the public key. We are interested in inverting the HFEv- trapdoor function, not in recovering the secret key of Quartz[2]. In particular we study the "specific" attacks for Quartz (the contrary of "generic" attacks), i.e. attacks that do use the specific algebraic structure of Quartz due to the existence of a trapdoor. This amounts to see whether the public key of Quartz can be distinguished from a random system of multivariate quadratic equations (MQ). We will study the complexity of the best algorithms known to solve the system of equations of HFE and/or for general MQ systems of the same size. Our goal is also to estimate the security of Quartz given all the known attacks, including properties/attacks that have been conjectured.

There are other "generic" attacks for Quartz (working even if the public key were a random MQ system), that are not based on inversion, see [11]. These are not covered in this paper.

The paper is organized as follows: In the first part we attempt to cover all what is known about the security of HFE and HFEv-, including experimental and conjectured properties. Then we introduce solving polynomial systems with Gröbner bases algorithms, which seems to be the best way to attack HFE or HFEv- so far. We will make numerous simulations with Gröbner bases algorithms to see how the perturbations affect the security of HFE. We will show that perturbated systems can indeed be attacked. Finally we will use our best knowledge to evaluate the security of the trapdoor one-way function used in Quartz against all known "inversion" attacks.

Notations

We use exactly the same notations n, m, h, r, v as in the description of Quartz [25, 26]. h is the size of the extension field on which the internal HFE univariate polynomial is defined and d is the degree of the polynomial. v is the number of added so called "vinegar" variables, r is the number of removed equations and m the number of equations of the public key, i.e. the number of equations after the removal.

2   Known Attacks on HFE and Its Variants

Attacks on "Basic HFE"

At Crypto'99, Shamir and Kipnis presented a structural attack on HFE [27], that reduces the problem of recovering the secret key of HFE to a problem later

---

[2] The complexity to recover the secret key is obviously at least as much, and therefore we do not need to care about it.

called MinRank, see [8]. At the same time Courtois evaluated the complexity of the Shamir-Kipnis attack and presented two more efficient attacks, see [8].

All these attacks concern only the "basic HFE". They are subexponential. The original Shamir-Kipnis attack is in at least $n^{\mathcal{O}(\log_q^2 d)}$, see [8]. The same attack improved by Courtois, with a better method of solving the involved Min-Rank problem, gives $n^{3\log_q d + \mathcal{O}(1)}$, see [8]. Both attacks will recover the secret key. The direct attack by Courtois, that only inverts the trapdoor function without recovering the secret key, is much faster in practice. It requires only about $n^{\frac{3}{2}\log_q d + \mathcal{O}(1)}$ computations. Moreover, in [8, 10], a so called "distillation" attack is presented that asymptotically seems to give even about $n^{\frac{3}{4}\log_q d + \mathcal{O}(1)}$. However for values used in practice it did not give better results (except that it uses much less memory).

There are also attacks that apply general methods for solving polynomial systems (by computing Gröbner bases) and seem to be closely related to the direct attack described by Courtois [8, 10]. Recently Faugère has demonstrated a new, and very efficient attack on the basic HFE. With his new improved algorithm F5/2, he was able to break the so called "HFE Challenge 1" in 96 hours on a 833 MHz Alpha workstation with 4 Giga-bytes of memory, see [16, 15], instead of 2^{62} for the direct attack by Courtois from [8].

In [13] and on page 28 of [12] it is shown experimentally that the complexity of the Buchberger algorithm applied to HFE systems depends very strongly on the degree d of the hidden polynomial or rather on the value $\lceil \log_q(d) \rceil$, exactly as expected from the Courtois attacks [8, 10]. This observation was also confirmed by Faugère with F5/2 (private communication).

State of the Art on the Modified Versions of HFE

Until now no attacks have been published on HFE- or other modified versions of HFE, except two attacks on C^{*--} published in [24] and [17]. Though none of the above described attacks on HFE has been specifically designed to work on HFEv−, it is important to see that the direct attack by Courtois and all the Gröbner bases attacks can be applied to any system of equations, without adaptation. For the other attacks, it is not known if they can be extended or adapted. At first sight, from some simulations made by Courtois in [8, 10], it seems that his attack does not work at all, even if we apply one single perturbation "minus" on an HFE-system. From this, if all the known attacks on HFE have indeed a common ground, one might think that the modified "combinatorial" versions of HFE are much more secure than the original HFE, and even Faugère's attack (the fastest known today) will fail, i.e. the complexity will be largely increased. But the questions is, how much will it be increased?

Extrapolating from the complexity of two existing attacks on C^{*--} [24, 17], and having in mind some unpublished attacks on HFE- [10], Courtois conjectured that if *tot* is the total number of perturbations used, then the security of a multivariate scheme such as HFE will be increased by at least a factor of q^{tot}. In this formulation "at least" suggests that it is probably much more secure in many interesting cases.

In this paper we show that this optimistic view is not true. We will see that the Gröbner bases algorithms can solve systems modified with the "minus" perturbation, the "vinegar" perturbation and with the combination of both[3]. The perturbations are not an absolute weapon against these attacks. However we will see that the perturbations increase security, by some amount, and this amount seems to be indeed at least q^{tot}, but not much more. Thus the true question to be answered for Quartz, will be: Is the number of perturbations sufficient or not, to achieve the desired security level?[4]

3   General Methods for Solving Systems of Multivariate Polynomial Equations

The HFE family of cryptosystems is based on the hardness of the problem of finding a solution to a system of multivariate quadratic equations, the so called MQ problem, see [10]. It turns out that the best attacks known up to date for this MQ problem, such as the XL algorithm from Eurocrypt 2000 (see [7]), the aforementioned experimental attacks on HFE by Courtois, and the more advanced attack by Faugère on HFE, are all clearly related. They all can be seen as a way of manipulating the initial equations multiplied by some monomials, that are linearly combined. The language and the tools to deal with such situations are provided by the theory of Gröbner bases, a part of the computational algebraic geometry.

3.1   Solving Systems with Gröbner Bases Algorithms

In this section we describe very briefly some features of solving systems with Gröbner bases. A comprehensive treatment of this theory can be found in [4].

Given a system of m polynomial equations

$$p_i(x_1, \ldots, x_n) = y_i, \ i = 1, \ldots, m$$

with some $p_i \in GF(q)[x_1, \ldots, x_n], y_i \in GF(q)$, the classical way of solving such a system is to consider the ideal $I := (\tilde{p}_1, \ldots, \tilde{p}_m)$ generated by the polynomials $\tilde{p}_i := p_i - y_i$ and to compute the set of all common zeros of these polynomials over the algebraic closure, the so called variety of this ideal. This is done by computing a special ideal basis[5], a so called Gröbner basis[6]. A typical example for a Gröbner

---

[3] Precisely, an HFEv- that combines 4 "vinegar" perturbations and 3 "minus" perturbations is used in Quartz

[4] Unfortunately this question is critical in Quartz. Due to the very short signatures in Quartz, the total number of perturbations used is only 7 and $q^r = 2^7$. It is very different in Sflash that has $q^{tot} = (2^7)^{11} = 2^{77}$.

[5] An ideal basis is a set of generators for the $GF(q)[x_1, \ldots, x_n]$-module I.

[6] A Gröbner basis is defined with respect to a term ordering. A term ordering generalizes the monomial ordering of univariate polynomials and thus a polynomial division can be defined. A Gröbner basis has some special properties with respect to this division.

basis is $\gcd(\tilde{p}_1, \ldots, \tilde{p}_m)$, if the generators are univariate polynomials. Another well known example consists of the triangular system of linear polynomials which can be computed by Gaussian elimination provided that the generators are linear polynomials.

In general one usually computes a so called lexicographical[7] Gröbner basis of the ideal, which has a triangular structure, similar to that known from systems of linear equations after applying Gaussian elimination. More precisely for each $i = 1, \ldots, n$ there is at least one polynomial in the Gröbner basis with the property that it includes only monomials with variables $x_1, \ldots, x_i$. Therefore one can compute the common zeros by factoring one univariate polynomial, then substituting this partial solution into the polynomial(s) with two variables, and thus getting further univariate polynomials to factor and so on.

The classical algorithm to compute a Gröbner basis is the Buchberger algorithm, see for example [4]. In general this algorithm has double exponential worst case complexity. However in the setting of multivariate cryptography we are only interested in solutions over the base field $GF(q)$ and not in the algebraic closure. In this case the complexity can be cut down to single exponential worst case complexity just by adapting the inputted system:

Since the set of solutions of the equation $x^q = x$ is equal to $GF(q)$, the variety of the enlarged ideal $(\tilde{p}_1, \ldots, \tilde{p}_m, x_1^q - x_1, \ldots, x_n^q - x_n)$ consists just of those solutions of the original system which are lying in the base field. It can be shown that applying Buchberger algorithm to ideals of this form has single exponential worst case complexity (for this see [13] or [1]).

Due to Faugère there are some comparatively very efficient alternatives to the Buchberger algorithm for computing Gröbner Bases (the algorithms F4, see [14], F5 and recently F5/2, see [15, 16]).

3.2   The Special Case of Signing

The common drawback of the algorithms described above is that they compute the complete variety (i.e. the set of all the solutions) and are unable to profit from the fact that we only need one of the solutions. Indeed, in order to forge a signature for a given message in a HFEv- based signature scheme, it is enough to be able to compute at least one solution to a given system of equations[8].

In the case of HFEv- systems, with r perturbations of type "minus" and v of type "vinegar" we obtain a system with $n = h + v$ variables, and $m = h - r$ equations. Such a system has an expected number of about q^{r+v} solutions, and an algorithm that computes a Gröbner basis does too much work. There is however an obvious way to reduce the number of computed solutions. We will substitute $n - m = r + v$ of the variables with some arbitrary fixed values, and

---

[7] The lexicographical term ordering is the best suited for computing zeros.

[8] Some signature schemes based on HFEv- compute signatures using several inverses, i.e. they need to compute $F^{-1}(y)$ several times in a row for different y, with F being the public key. This allows shorter signatures, see [22, 10] or [11] for explanation. For example in Quartz there are 4 inverses [25, 26].

get a system with $m = h - r$ unknowns and as many equations, which will have about 1 solution on average. Such systems prove to be substantially easier to solve than the original system with many solutions. In Section 4 below we will apply this idea. It seems that fixing exactly $n - m$ variables is the optimal way to solve a system of equations with Gröbner bases, at least when $n > m$, see the Appendix A of the full version ([29]) for further discussion.

4   Applying Gröbner Bases to HFE

To study the effect of the perturbations "minus" and "vinegar" we did many simulations on HFEv- systems with different sets of parameters. We were especially interested in the question how much randomness is added by these perturbations. This is meant to indicate how much perturbations will be needed to produce an HFEv- system, that is indistinguishable from a random system of the same size (with no trapdoor).

The simulations were done using the `stdfglm` function of Singular for computing Gröbner bases (a fast and general implementation of the Buchberger algorithm, see [18]). They were run on a 1.5 GHz Pentium-4 PC, working under Windows 2000. We did simulations on HFE systems of degree $d \in \{5, 9, 17\}$ and on randomly generated systems, both with $h \in \{15, 19, 21\}$, $0 \leq r \leq 3$ and $0 \leq v \leq 5$. We only measured times for systems that have a solution, and systematically casted away systems that have no solution. Following the idea of fixing variables described in Section 3.2 and discussed in Appendix A of the full version ([29]), our simulations apply the following steps:

- Given an HFEv- system with $n = h + v$ unknowns, $m = h - r$ equations, choose $n - m = v + r$ variables to fix.
- Fix the $n - m = v + r$ variables with a set of values not chosen before and solve the resulting system with $m = h - r$ unknowns and equations using Buchberger algorithm (i.e. use the `stdfglm` function of SINGULAR).
- Repeat the fixing and solving until you find a solution to the initial system (one is enough).

5   Our Methodology

Cryptosystems of the HFE family have two independent security parameters: The extension degree h and the degree of the hidden polynomial d. Quite often they also have additional security parameters, for example v and r for HFEv- and Quartz. This makes the study of their security much more complex than for cryptosystems that basically have one security parameter such as RSA. It also makes the multivariate cryptographic schemes much more flexible than the usual schemes. For example one parameter (in our case h) can usually be small to achieve a cryptosystem that operates on small blocks (and e.g. allows short signatures), and the other parameters can be independently adjusted to achieve the desired security level.

5.1   Critical Parameters for Quartz

From the design of Quartz [25, 26], we see that the parameters h, v, r are more or less constrained by the requirement to have very short signatures. Thus the security of Quartz depends mainly on the degree d of the hidden HFE polynomial. As we have already explained in section 2, the complexity of the Gröbner bases algorithms applied to the basic HFE (and also of all other known attacks and for other versions of HFE) does depend very strongly on d. More precisely it depends on the value $\lceil \log_q(d) \rceil$. This is motivated (but not fully explained) by the Shamir-Kipnis attack from [27], and can be seen very distinctively in the Courtois attack [8]. For Gröbner bases algorithms this has been shown experimentally by Daum and Felke, in [12] (also in [13]) and independently confirmed by Faugère for his latest F5/2 algorithm (private communication).

6   The Simulations on HFEv-

Let T_{tot} be the total time (on average) needed by the above described algorithm to find at least one solution of a given system with n variables and m equations; for HFEv- we have $n = h + v$ and $m = h - r$.

Let N_{guess} be the number of guesses (and thus the number of invocations of the Buchberger algorithm) the algorithm had to make till the resulting system (after fixing variables) was solvable. It turns out that the time to solve any of the $N_{guess} - 1$ systems that have no solution and for the last system that has a solution are about the same. Therefore $T \overset{def}{=} \frac{T_{tot}}{N_{guess}}$ describes the average time spent by the Buchberger algorithm trying to solve one of the resulting systems (i.e. the initial system after fixing variables).

The Semantics of T: The value T measures the cryptographic quality of each single system with $n - m$ variables fixed. By construction it is independent of $n - m$ (for fixed m), and gives more precise results than just to measure the time of solving the last system. The time to find one solution to the whole system is usually between T and $1.6 \cdot T$, see Appendix A of the full version ([29]).

We define T_{rnd} as the value of T obtained for a random system of quadratic equations of (respectively) the same size. This is our reference time.

6.1   Randomness ∼ Security

The notions of security and randomness are very closely related in cryptography, and even more so for multivariate cryptosystems: The public key of an HFEv- system is a system of multivariate quadratic equations. Therefore breaking an HFEv- system means to solve an instance of the MQ-Problem. At present the hardest instances of the MQ problem we know are just random systems of quadratic equations. It is known that MQ is NP-complete, see [10], which guarantees worst case hardness, and moreover it seems that the problem is difficult on average and even most of the time. Moreover all the known algorithms for this problem are exponential, see for example [13] or [1] for the results on the complexity of the Buchberger algorithm. In [7] authors raise some hopes for a subexponential algorithm, that would be however very inefficient in practice.

Thus we expect that the complexity to break the HFEv- schemes is always less than to solve a random MQ system of the same size. Moreover, if we increase the parameter d of HFE systems to nearly q^n, the system does converge to a random MQ system. The same is also true for $v \to \infty$ in HFEv-.

We simply measure the time per guess relatively to a random system of the same size, i.e. we define

$$R = \frac{T}{T_{rnd}}.$$

Now we are ready to study how much randomness/security is added by various "perturbations" in HFE.

6.2   The Impact of the Perturbations "Vinegar" and "Minus"

Table 1 shows the times per guess (in seconds) needed for solving HFE systems with $h = 15$ and $d = 5$ perturbated with r times "minus" and v times "vinegar" operations. We also compute our randomness measure R as defined above.

From these values of R (and also the corresponding values in the tables given in Appendix C of the full version ([29])) we can deduce that using perturbations strongly increases the randomness of HFE systems, especially for low degrees d. Moreover we see that the amount of randomness added depends mainly on the total number $v + r$ of used perturbations, and is rather independent of whether one uses "minus" or "vinegar" or a mixture of both.

However if we consider the absolute times needed to solve (find one solution to) the perturbated systems there is an explicit difference between the effects of "minus" and "vinegar":

These times show that applying "minus" in many cases does not increase the absolute time needed to find one solution and may even decrease this time, whereas "vinegar" does increase the attack time. The same behaviour was observed when applying "minus" and "vinegar" to completely random systems.

Table 1. Absolute and relative times per guess for HFEv- systems with $h = 15, d = 5$

Times per Guess $T = T_{tot}/N_{guess}$:

	v					
	0	1	2	3	4	5
0	0,50	1,93	5,45	11,52	11,89	11,95
r 1	0,75	2,36	4,16	5,20	5,23	5,28
2	0,77	1,30	1,35	1,35	1,38	1,38
3	0,48	0,48	0,50	0,50	0,51	0,51

Ratios $R = T/T_{rnd}$:

	v					
	0	1	2	3	4	5
0	0,05	0,18	0,46	0,97	1,01	1,00
r 1	0,16	0,50	0,81	1,00	1,00	1,00
2	0,60	1,00	1,00	1,00	1,00	1,00
3	1,00	1,01	1,01	1,00	0,99	0,99

(see Appendix C of the full version ([29]) for similar results for different values of d and h)

There we observed that T_{rnd} is nearly independent of v but depends strongly on r. The explanation of this difference is very easy: "minus" in contrast to "vinegar" changes the size of the systems to solve for each guess, from h to $h - r$.

Eventually there are four main conclusions from these simulations:

1. The operations "minus" and "vinegar" are similar in terms of the amount of relative security or randomness added to pure HFE systems of low degree d.
2. For the absolute security they are different, and considering the total time of an attack, "minus" may even decrease the time needed to solve a system, as it decreases the size m of the system to solve after fixing $n - m$ variables. However "minus" still does increase the security against some other, very efficient attacks, for example Patarin's attack on Matsumoto-Imai (C^*) [21].
3. It is unclear, if this is still significant when $m \gg r + v$ as in Quartz.
4. It seems that for the total number of perturbations that can be used, it is more interesting to use as many as possible "vinegar" perturbations and as little as possible "minus" perturbations. However it is not advocated to use only "vinegar" perturbations, the mixture of both might be more secure against some other attacks.

6.3   Some Conclusions for Quartz

It is not directly clear how to quantify the influence of the perturbations in the case of Quartz due to the much bigger size of Quartz systems. It seems that $\log_2 d = \log_2 129$ is a very small degree with respect to the large value of $h = 103$ (as in Quartz). Thus the results of the simulations support the assumption that applying 4 perturbations of type "vinegar" and 3 perturbations of type "minus" will increase the complexity of the attacks. It would be probably better to use 7 perturbations of type "vinegar". However, it is easy to see that this is not possible with the given signature size and security requirements.

There are many constraints in the design of Quartz, and $h = 103$ cannot be easily changed: It is in fact chosen to be a prime, see [25, 26]. Thus with $h = 103$, $v = 7$ and $r = 0$ we get $n = h + v = 110$ and $m = 103$. Since m increases by 3, the length of the signatures would increase from 128 bits to 131. If we instead used $h = 101$ the signature length would be 129 bits, and for $h = 97$ which gives $m = 97$ the scheme would no longer achieve the required security level of 2^{80}, given the well known generic attack in $q^{\frac{4}{5}m}$, see [25, 26, 10, 11].

6.4   Quantitative Effect of "Vinegar" and "Minus"

In this section we will try to see if our simulations confirm (or not) the conjecture from Section 2 to the effect that the security of multivariate schemes with tot perturbations (for us $tot = r + v$) would be increased by (at least) a factor of q^{tot}. We see however that this behaviour can only continue until T achieves T_{rnd}, after that T will not grow anymore. From all our simulations we have the following conclusions:

1. The value R increases quite uniformly with $r + v$, i.e. it is nearly the same for a constant $r + v$ and the same h.
2. All our simulations show that the value R grows at least twice, each time $tot = r + v$ increases by 1, except when R is already very close to 1 and cannot grow anymore.
3. Thus our conjecture that the relative security of multivariate schemes with tot perturbations would be increased by at least a factor of q^{tot} can be said to be confirmed for $R << 1$.
4. Moreover, the smaller R is, the higher is the increase in R when $tot = r + v$ increases by 1. More precisely we see that:
   - For $h = 15$ and $d = 5$ R increases first 4 times, 3 times, 2 times, and then it achieves 1.
   - For $h = 15$ and $d = 9$ R increases first 3 times, 2 times, and then it achieves 1.
   - For $h = 15$ and $d = 17$ R increases first 2 times, and then it achieves 1.
   - For $h = 19$ and $d = 5$ R increases first 8 times, 2 times, 2 times, and then it achieves 1.
   - For $h = 19$ and $d = 9$ R increases first 6 times, 3 times, 2 times, and then it achieves 1.
   - For $h = 19$ and $d = 17$ R increases first 2 times, 2 times, and then it achieves 1.
   - For $h = 21$ and $d = 5$ R increases first 10 times, 12 times, 3 times, 2 times and then it achieves 1.
   - For $h = 21$ and $d = 17$ R increases first 3 times, 2 times, and then it achieves 1.
5. Very clearly, the more $R << 1$, the more is the increase in the relative security R when adding one perturbation. Thus we see that the increase in the relative security R is more significant when d is small, and for a fixed d, it is more significant for a bigger h.

7   Our Estimation of the Security of Quartz

In this section we will first look at the complexity of the best known attacks on HFE when applied to the particular instance of HFE that is a sub-component of the HFEv- that is used in Quartz, i.e. if we ignore the existence of the perturbations. Then we will try to extrapolate what (at best) is the complexity to solve the whole HFEv-.

Attacks on the Internal Sub-Component HFE

Let ω be the exponent of the Gaussian reduction. Though the best known algorithm for this problem is asymptotically in $T^{2.376}$, see [3], the best practical algorithm we know is Strassen's algorithm, see [28]. We will put $\omega = \log_2(7) = 2.807$.

Nobody has ever demonstrated a practical attack on HFE when $d = 129$ as in Quartz. For the so called HFE Challenge 1 described in the extended version of [22], we have $d = 96$ and two working attacks have been found by Courtois [8] and later Faugère [16]. Their behaviour is similar and we expect that Courtois' attacks give much worse results than Faugère's attack. The complexity of this latter attack has been estimated for $d = 96$ to be $\mathcal{O}(h^8)$ by Faugère [16]. In Appendix B of the full version ([29]) we estimate the constant to be about $1/4$. From this we extrapolated that for the basic HFE that can be seen inside the HFEv- used in Quartz, with $d = 129$ instead of $d = 96$ above, the complexity of Faugère's attack should be about $h^{10}/4$, see Appendix B of the full version ([29]) for more details.

Including the Conjectured Effects of the Perturbations

First of all, because of the effect of minus, see point 2 in Section 6.2, we have to use $(h - r)^{10}/4$ instead of $h^{10}/4$. Secondly, since in Quartz there are $tot = 7$ perturbations, following Section 2 and our simulation results in Section 6.4, this complexity should be multiplied by at least 2^7. Thus we obtain that the working factor (WF) needed to inverse a trapdoor one-way function HFEv- should be about:

$$WF(HFEv-) \approx 2^7 \cdot (h - 3)^{10}/4 = 2^7 \cdot 100^{10}/4 \approx 2^{71}$$

7.1 Our Estimation of the Security of Quartz

The above figure needs still to be multiplied by 4, because we need to do 4 iterated inversions of the trapdoor function in order to forge a Quartz signature. Moreover in the process of solving we fix $v + r$ variables and we need to repeat the solving process several times, until the system has a solution, 1.6 times on average[9], see Appendix A of the full version ([29]). Thus we have an additional factor of $4 * 1.6$ and we get:

$$WF(Quartz) \approx 2^{74}$$

We convert this to triple-DES operations as required in Nessie project. In order to have a fair comparison, one should implement the triple-DES on the same platform on which Faugère's attack has been implemented. The best optimized 64-bit implementation we are aware of, with improved Biham's bitslice technique, will give about $3 * 192 \approx 2^9$ CPU clocks for triple-DES, see [5]. Thus we get the following estimate:

$$WF(Quartz) \approx 2^{65} \text{ TDES computations.}$$

Remark: From Section 6.4, point 4, we see that the factor 2^{v+r} might be in fact bigger, then our complexity would increase.

---

[9] Indeed, Faugère's attack was applied to a system that had a solution.

8   Is It Necessary to Repair Quartz?

If in Quartz we had $d = 257$, we expect that the attack of Faugère should be in $\mathcal{O}(h^{12})$. Then our complexity will be multiplied by 100^2, i.e. we would get $WF(Quartz) \approx 2^{87}$ which is approximately $\approx 2^{78}$ TDES computations.

8.1   The Speed of Quartz

The best implementation of Quartz we are aware of has been programmed in C by Mehdi-Laurent Akkar for the Nessie project. For the usual Quartz with $d = 129$ (i.e. the revised standard version from [25, 26]), it takes less than 2 seconds to sign a message on a PC working at 2GHz. For $d = 257$ it takes about 6 seconds on average.

9   Conclusion

Quartz is a multivariate signature scheme based on an HFEv- trapdoor function. The interesting property of such functions is that they have two security parameters, and thus one of them can be adjusted independently of the other. Thus it is possible to build signature schemes in which the security is adjusted independently of the signature length. This suggests that in theory, it may be always possible to build a secure signature scheme with fixed signature length, but will it be practical ?

There are several subexponential attacks known for HFE, however no attacks on modified HFE cryptosystems (such as HFEv- used in Quartz) have been published so far. In this paper we showed that it is possible to successfully attack the modified systems by Gröbner bases techniques. From this we tried to evaluate the security of the Quartz signature scheme submitted to Nessie project. The results suggest that the parameter d probably needs to be increased which will accentuate the major drawback of Quartz: it's slowness.

This is currently the price to pay for such a short signature scheme. There are only two other short signature schemes known that give less than the 160 bits of the Weil-pairing scheme [2]. The first one is the McEliece scheme from Asiacrypt 2001, which is about as slow as Quartz and has a much bigger public key of about 1Mbyte instead of 71 Kbytes, see [6]. The second one is the degree 3 Dragon scheme (based on HFE) which seems quite fast, but also has a very big public key, see [23, 19]. It is possible that applying the same Gröbner bases computations to this scheme, the parameter d would have to be revised, and it would end up being quite slow, too.

References

[1] Boo Barkee, Deh Cac Can, Julia Ecks, Theo Moriarty, R. F. Ree: *Why You Cannot Even Hope to use Gröbner Bases in Public Key Cryptography: An Open Letter to a Scientist Who Failed and a Challenge to Those Who Have Not Yet Failed*, in Journal of Symbolic Computation 18, 1994, pp. 497-501 341, 343

[2] Dan Boneh, H. Shacham, and B. Lynn: *Short signatures from the Weil pairing*, Asiacrypt 2001, LNCS 2139, Springer, pp. 514-532. 348

[3] Don Coppersmith, Shmuel Winograd: *Matrix multiplication via arithmetic progressions;* J. Symbolic Computation (1990), 9, pp. 251-280. 346

[4] David Cox, John Little, Donal O'Shea: *Ideals, Varieties, and Algorithms,* Springer-Verlag, 1992 340, 341

[5] Francisco Corella: *A fast implementation of DES and triple DES on PA-RISC 2.0.* http://www.usenix.org/events/osdi2000/wiess2000/full_papers/corella/corella.pdf 347

[6] Nicolas Courtois, Matthieu Finiasz and Nicolas Sendrier: *How to achieve a McEliece-based Digital Signature Scheme;* Asiacrypt 2001, LNCS2248, Springer, pp. 157-174. Available at http://www.cryptosystem.net/mceliece/. 348

[7] Nicolas Courtois, Adi Shamir, Jacques Patarin, Alexander Klimov, *Efficient Algorithms for solving Overdefined Systems of Multivariate Polynomial Equations,* in Advances in Cryptology, Eurocrypt'2000, LNCS 1807, Springer-Verlag, pp. 392-407. 340, 344

[8] Nicolas Courtois: *The security of Hidden Field Equations (HFE);* Cryptographers' Track RSA Conference 2001, San Francisco 8-12 Avril 2001, LNCS2020, Springer-Verlag, pp. 266-281. 337, 339, 343, 347

[9] Nicolas Courtois: The HFE cryptosystem home page. http://www.hfe.info

[10] Nicolas Courtois: *La sécurité des primitives cryptographiques basées sur les problèmes algébriques multivariables MQ, IP, MinRank, et IIFE,* PhD thesis, Paris 6 University, 2001, in French. Available at http://www.minrank.org/phd.pdf. 339, 340, 341, 343, 345

[11] Nicolas Courtois: *Generic Attacks and the Security of Quartz,* PKC 2003, in these proceedings. A preliminary version was presented at the second Nessie workshop, Royal Holloway, University of London, September 2001. 338, 341, 345

[12] Magnus Daum, Patrick Felke: *Some new aspects concerning the Analysis of HFE type Cryptosystems;* Presented at Yet Another Conference on Cryptography (YACC'02), June 3-7, 2002, Porquerolles Island, France. 339, 343

[13] Magnus Daum: *Das Kryptosystem HFE und quadratische Gleichungssysteme über endlichen Körpern,* Diplomarbeit, Universität Dortmund, 2001. Available from daum@itsc.ruhr-uni-bochum.de 339, 341, 343

[14] Jean-Charles Faugère: *A new efficient algorithm for computing Gröbner bases (F4),* Journal of Pure and Applied Algebra 139, 1–3 (1999) pp. 61-88. See www.elsevier.com/locate/jpaa 341

[15] Jean-Charles Faugère: *Computing Gröbner basis without reduction to 0,* technical report LIP6, in preparation, source: private communication. Also presented at the Workshop on Applications of Commutative Algebra, Catania, Italy, 3-6 April 2002. 337, 339, 341

[16] Jean-Charles Faugère: *Report on a successful attack of HFE Challenge 1 with Gröbner bases algorithm F5/2,* announcement that appeared in sci.crypt newsgroup on the internet on April 19th 2002. 337, 339, 341, 347

[17] Henri Gilbert, Marine Minier: *Cryptanalysis of SFLASH,* Eurocrypt 2002, LNCS 2332, pp. 288-298, Springer. 339

[18] G.-M. Greuel, G. Pfister, and H. Schönemann. SINGULAR 2.0.3. A Computer Algebra System for Polynomial Computations. Centre for Computer Algebra, University of Kaiserslautern (2001), www.singular.uni-kl.de. 342

[19] Neal Koblitz: "Algebraic Aspects of Cryptography"; Springer-Verlag, ACM3, 1998, Chapter 4: "Hidden Monomial Cryptosystems", pp. 80-102. 348

[20] Tsutomu Matsumoto, Hideki Imai: "Public Quadratic Polynomial-tuples for efficient signature-verification and message-encryption", Eurocrypt'88, Springer-Verlag 1998, pp. 419-453. 337

[21] Jacques Patarin: "Cryptanalysis of the Matsumoto and Imai Public Key Scheme of Eurocrypt'88"; Crypto'95, Springer-Verlag, pp. 248-261. 337, 345

[22] Jacques Patarin: "Hidden Fields Equations (HFE) and Isomorphisms of Polynomials (IP): two new families of Asymmetric Algorithms"; Eurocrypt'96, Springer Verlag, pp. 33-48. The extended version can be found at http://www.minrank.org/hfe.ps 337, 341, 347

[23] Jacques Patarin: *La Cryptographie Multivariable*; Mémoire d'habilitation à diriger des recherches de l'Université Paris 7, 1999. 348

[24] Jacques Patarin, Nicolas Courtois , Louis Goubin: "C*-+ and HM - Variations around two schemes of T. Matsumoto and H. Imai"; Asiacrypt 1998, Springer-Verlag, pp. 35-49. 339

[25] Jacques Patarin, Louis Goubin, Nicolas Courtois: *Quartz, 128-bit long digital signatures*; Cryptographers' Track Rsa Conference 2001, San Francisco 8-12 April 2001, LNCS2020, Springer-Verlag.
Note: The Quartz signature scheme has been updated since, see [26]. 338, 341, 343, 345, 348

[26] Jacques Patarin, Louis Goubin, Nicolas Courtois: *Quartz, 128-bit long digital signatures*; An updated version of Quartz specification available at http://www.cryptosystem.net/quartz/ 338, 341, 343, 345, 348, 350

[27] Adi Shamir, Aviad Kipnis: "Cryptanalysis of the HFE Public Key Cryptosystem"; Crypto'99. Can be found at http://www.minrank.org/hfesubreg.ps 337, 338, 343

[28] Volker Strassen: *Gaussian Elimination is Not Optimal;* Numerische Mathematik, vol 13, pp 354-356, 1969. 346

[29] Nicolas Courtois, Magnus Daum and Patrick Felke: *On the Security of HFE, HFEv- and Quartz;* Cryptology ePrint Archive, Report 2002/138. Available at http://eprint.iacr.org. 342, 343, 344, 347

Generic Attacks and the Security of Quartz[*,**]

Nicolas T. Courtois

CP8 Crypto Lab, SchlumbergerSema
36-38 rue de la Princesse, BP 45, 78430 Louveciennes Cedex, France
courtois@minrank.org

Abstract. The signature scheme Quartz is based on a trapdoor function G belonging to a family called HFEv-. It has two independent security parameters, and we claim that if d is big enough, no better method to compute an inverse of G than the exhaustive search is known. Such a (quite strong) assumption, allows to view Quartz as a general construction, that transforms a trapdoor function into a short signature scheme. The main object of this paper is the concrete security of this construction. On one hand, we present generic attacks on such schemes. On the other hand, we study the possibility to prove or justify the security with some well chosen assumptions. Unfortunately for Quartz, our lower and upper security bounds do not coincide. Still the best attack known for Quartz is our generic attack using $\mathcal{O}(2^{80})$ computations with $\mathcal{O}(2^{80})$ of memory. We will also propose an alternative way of doing short signatures for which both bounds do coincide.

Keywords: Asymmetric cryptography, finite fields, Hidden Field Equations (HFE), MQ, HFEv-, short signatures, Quartz, Flash, Sflash, Nessie.

1 Introduction

The shortest signature scheme known in the "classical cryptography" is based on Weil pairing and achieves 160 bits with the security of 2^{80} [1]. Only recently schemes with signatures shorter than 160 bits have been proposed. These new schemes belong to the multivariate cryptography. Quartz, proposed for standardisation in the European Nessie project, achieves signatures of 128 bits with a claimed security level of 2^{80}. The McEliece-based signature scheme CFS gives signatures of about 80 bits [4] but has a substantially bigger public key than Quartz. Both Quartz and McEliece have features that make them a unique choice for some applications, while remain excluded from other applications. It seems that, see [4], the security of McEliece signatures can be proven in the random oracle model and the lower and upper bounds coincide with respect to two well known problems. In the present paper we will try to see what are the

---

[*] The work described in this paper has been supported by the French Ministry of Research under RNRT Project "Turbo-signatures".

[**] An early version of this paper has been presented at the second Nessie workshop, September 2001, Royal Holloway University of London.

Y.G. Desmedt (Ed.): PKC 2003, LNCS 2567, pp. 351–364, 2003.

lower and upper bounds on the security of Quartz, based on some well-chosen (but plausible) assumptions.

The paper is organized as follows: First we overview the hardness properties that are believed to hold for such multivariate trapdoor functions as HFEv- and we formulate the Assumption 2.0.2 which is the basis of all our subsequent security considerations. In the section 3 we study generic attacks on such meta signature schemes. Then in the Section 4 and in the Appendix we study if the security of Quartz can be proved, or justified, based on our Assumption 2.0.2. Finally we give our conclusions.

2   Multivariate Quadratic Trapdoor Functions

In this paper we study a security of signature schemes based on multivariate quadratic trapdoor functions $GF(q)^n \rightarrow GF(q)^m$. For example for Quartz, described in [13], we only need to know that it uses a trapdoor quadratic function of type HFEv-, with $n = 107$ variables and $m = 100$ equations over $GF(2)$. The HFEv- cryptosystem has an important second security parameter d that can be adjusted independently of m and n, so that all structural attacks disappear, and all attacks that remain are generic attacks that behave as if G was random without any trapdoor:

Theorem 2.0.1 (Generic Attack on a Trapdoor Function).
Let $G : GF(q)^n \rightarrow GF(q)^m$ be an efficiently computable function. For all $0 \leq T \leq q^m$ there is an adversary that computes an inverse of G for a random $y \leftarrow GF(q)^m$ with success probability of about:

$$\varepsilon \approx T/q^m.$$

For HFEv-, it is believed that if the parameter d is sufficiently high, then we have a sort of converse of this Theorem, as follows:

Critical Assumption 2.0.2 (Strong One-Wayness of HFEv-).
Let G a random public key $G \leftarrow \text{HFEv}^-(q, n, m)$ with $m \approx n$, $n \geq m$ and $m \leq 100$. For any Adversary A running in T CPU clocks, given random $y \leftarrow GF(q^m)$, the probability that A outputs some $x = G^{-1}(y)$ is at most:

$$\varepsilon \leq T/q^m.$$

This assumption is a consequence of the current state of knowledge in multivariate cryptography. A full and detailed explanation of this assumption is quite long and appears in the extended version of this paper.

In the remaining part of this paper we will study the upper and lower bounds that may be given for the security of Quartz (and also of other multivariate signature schemes), given, on one hand this (very strong) assumption, and on the other hand, using the generic attack above.

3   Feistel-Patarin Construction

3.1   Generic Threats

The classical way to compute digital signatures with a trapdoor function $G : GF(q)^n \to GF(q)^m$ is to compute a hash H, and the signature is given as:

$$\sigma = G^{-1}(H)$$

As a direct consequence of 2.0.1, such a signature can be forged in the square root of exhaustive search. This attack is generic: it does not depend on G. We produce a lists of $q^{m/2}$ $G(\sigma_i)$ and a list of $q^{m/2}$ hashes of different messages (or different versions of the same message). Then we expect to be able to produce at least one valid pair (message, signature), which is an existential forgery.

Remark: This generic attack is not an issue for most well-known signature schemes such as RSA, DSA, McEliece etc. It is because for all these functions there already exists an attack in the square root of exhaustive search (or less) and the parameters have already been chosen sufficiently large to avoid it. The situation is somewhat different for multivariate quadratic schemes such as HFE. For several such schemes, there is no attack known noticeably smaller than the exhaustive search. Therefore if the signature is computed as $\sigma = G^{-1}(H)$ for a scheme such as HFE or HFEv-, $q^{m/2}$ should be at least 2^{80} and it implies that the signatures should have at least 160 bits. For this reason, when it comes to shorter signatures, multivariate quadratic schemes usually compute a signature in different, somewhat strange way.

3.2   Removing Existential Forgeries

We assume $m = n$ (this condition will be relaxed later). How to compute a signature using a trapdoor function ? On one hand, the owner of the private key should use the computation of $G^{-1}()$ at least once, so that he will be the only person to be able to compute a signature. On the other hand, the verification should be in the implicit form $\text{Verif}(\sigma, H)$ in order to avoid meet-in-the middle attacks. On the Figure 1 we show an example of such a construction derived from the Feistel scheme, in which the hash is divided in two pieces and the signature is computed as (cf. Fig. 1):

$$H(M) = (H_1(M), H_2(M))$$
$$\sigma = H_1 \oplus G^{-1}(H_2 \oplus G^{-1}(H_1))$$

Now, the meet-in-the middle attack fails: we can still produce two lists of candidate messages and candidate signatures, but we are unable to detect which signature correspond to which message by just sorting two lists. It is necessary to run the verification algorithm on each pair (message, signature) and it gives a complexity of q^m.

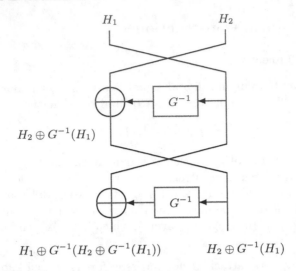

Fig. 1. 2-round Feistel applied to signature generation

Security: Clearly, the Feistel-based (meta) signature scheme described above is better than the (ordinary) signature scheme, but still not perfect. In [10] Patarin explains that that a signature can still be forged in $q^{\frac{2m}{3}}$ instead of $q^{\frac{m}{2}}$ previously. For this, we precompute $q^{\frac{2m}{3}}$ values $f(X)$ for some $q^{\frac{2m}{3}}$ values for X. It allows to compute an inverse of G with probability $q^{-\frac{m}{3}}$. Thus one can compute two consecutive inverses with probability $q^{-\frac{2m}{3}}$. Then, given $q^{\frac{2m}{3}}$ messages we are able to forge a signature of (about) one of them. In general we have:

Theorem 3.2.1 (Generic Attack on Signature Schemes).
Let $G : GF(q)^n \rightarrow GF(q)^m$. Any deterministic signature scheme that combines K inverses and message hash values can be broken in $q^{\frac{K}{K+1}m}$.

Proof. We precompute $q^{\frac{K}{K+1}m}$ values $f(X)$ for some $q^{\frac{K}{K+1}m}$ values for X. It allows to compute an inverse of G with probability $q^{-\frac{1}{K+1}m}$ and thus to compute iteratively K inverses with probability $q^{-\frac{K}{K+1}m}$. Thus with $q^{\frac{K}{K+1}m}$ messages we are able to forge a signature. □

Remark: For a function $G : GF(q)^n \rightarrow GF(q)^m$ the complexity is $q^{\frac{K}{K+1}m}$ with $q^{\frac{K}{K+1}m}$ of memory. It is in fact the best known attack against Quartz and gives 2^{80} computations with 2^{80} of memory.

It is obvious that when K grows, the complexity of the attacks tends to q^m of the exhaustive search. Unfortunately using the Feistel structure cannot easily be extended to more rounds: we will not have enough information to verify the signature anymore. Still the formula it gives can be generalized and in many different ways:

$$\sigma \leftarrow 0$$
$$\textbf{for } i = 1 \textbf{ to } K \textbf{ do}$$
$$\{$$
$$\qquad \sigma \leftarrow \sigma \oplus H_i(M)$$
$$\qquad \sigma \leftarrow G^{-1}(\sigma)$$
$$\}$$
$$\textbf{return } \sigma$$

Fig. 2. Basic Feistel-Patarin scheme with K inverses

3.3   Extending to any Number of Inverses

For example we may consider the following (cf. Fig. 2):

$$H(M) = (H_1(M), H_2(M), \ldots, H_K(M))$$

$$\sigma = G^{-1}(H_K \oplus \ldots \oplus G^{-1}(H_3 \oplus G^{-1}(H_2 \oplus G^{-1}(H_1)) \ldots)$$

We call it the Feistel-Patarin signature scheme, though it has little to do (now) with the original Feistel scheme.

3.4   Extending to $m \neq n$

We need to generalize the above construction to trapdoor functions with input and output spaces of different sizes $G : GF(q)^n \rightarrow GF(q)^m$, and $m \neq n$. In this paper we limit to $m \leq n$, see [5] for the case $m > n$. The adaptation consists of cutting off and publishing the additional $(m - n)$ symbols obtained in every round, as they are a necessary ingredient in the signature verification process. It makes signatures somewhat longer. More precisely we do the following (Fig. 3):

This is precisely used in Quartz with $K = 4$, as represented on Fig. 4.

$$\sigma \leftarrow 0$$
$$\textbf{for } i = 1 \textbf{ to } K \textbf{ do}$$
$$\{$$
$$\qquad \sigma \leftarrow \sigma \oplus H_i(M)$$
$$\qquad U \in G^{-1}(\sigma)$$
$$\qquad \sigma \leftarrow U_{1 \rightarrow m}$$
$$\qquad X_{i1}|| \ldots ||X_{i(n-m)} \leftarrow U_{(m+1) \rightarrow n}$$
$$\}$$
$$\textbf{return } \sigma||X_{11}|| \ldots ||X_{K(n-m)}$$

Fig. 3. Generalized Feistel-Patarin with $m \leq n$

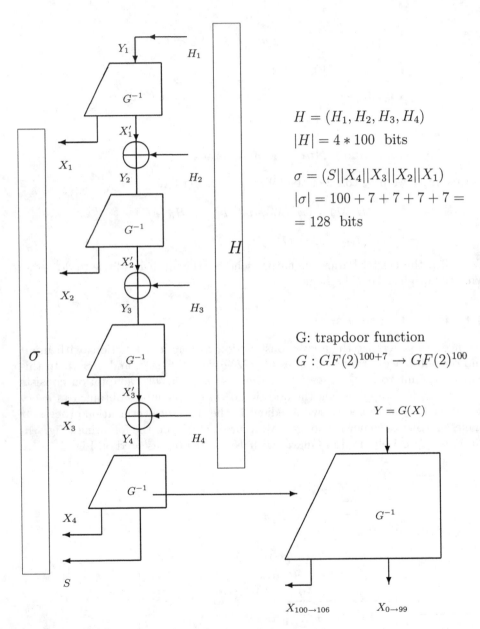

$$H = (H_1, H_2, H_3, H_4)$$
$$|H| = 4 * 100 \text{ bits}$$

$$\sigma = (S||X_4||X_3||X_2||X_1)$$
$$|\sigma| = 100 + 7 + 7 + 7 + 7 =$$
$$= 128 \text{ bits}$$

G: trapdoor function
$$G : GF(2)^{100+7} \rightarrow GF(2)^{100}$$

Fig. 4. Signature generation in Quartz

3.5   The Signature Length

The signature length in the generalized Feistel-Patarin construction is:

$$|\sigma| = (\, m + K(n-m)\,) \cdot \log_2(q)\ \text{bits}$$

Given the Theorem 3.2.1, the signature length at a given security level 2^{SF} is:

$$|\sigma| = \left\lceil \frac{K+1}{K} \cdot SF \right\rceil + K(n-m)\log_2(q)\ \text{bits}$$

We note that the length decreases for small K, and then it increases. Therefore at some point the signature is the shortest. In Quartz the minimum is $|\sigma| = 128$ bits, achieved for both[1] $K = 3$ and $K = 4$.

4   Is It Possible to Prove the Security of Quartz ?

We established lower bounds for the attacks on signature schemes such as Quartz. The question is now whether these lower bounds are also upper bounds, and more importantly, can the perfect correspondence between the generic attack 2.0.1 and the Assumption 2.0.2, be extended to Quartz ? This problem is studied in this section, and in more details in the Appendix. Though several open problems remain, we will prove several interesting results about the security of Quartz, Flash and Sflash.

We restrict to no-message attacks. The goal is to prove that an adversary cannot compute a valid pair (message, signature) given the public key. We assume the random oracle model with Q being the number of queries. It is a very powerful tool for security proofs. It allows an immediate reduction for a signature scheme of the form $G^{-1}(h)$: if the adversary computes a valid pair (message, signature) for some h taken out of the Q oracle answers, then we can transform this adversary into a machine that computes $G^{-1}(h)$ for one out of Q given values. This remains true not only for Q random values, but also for with probability very close to 1 to any set of chosen Q values. Indeed our reduction must behave exactly in the same way as with truly random values, provided that this set cannot be distinguished from random (which is in most cases easily achieved).

Thus we get machine that given some Q random (or chosen, but randomly looking values), outputs $G^{-1}(h)$ for one of them. By injecting a chose value into a list of length Q, we get a a machine able to invert G with probability at least $1/Q$. However from the Assumption 2.0.2 we know that this success probability cannot be bigger than T/q^m, and thus $1/Q \le T/q^m$. Reading the oracle takes time and thus we have $Q \le T$. Combining these two equations gives: $T \ge Q \ge q^m/T$ and thus $T \ge q^{m/2}$. A signature cannot be forged in less than $q^{m/2}$ for no-message attacks.

---

[1] The reasons for which the $K = 4$ has been chosen, and not $K = 3$, is that the authors wanted some internal value, namely $h = m + r$ to be a prime, with $m = \left\lceil \frac{K+1}{K} \cdot 80 \right\rceil$ and $r = 3$, see [14, 13].

We note that this argument applies also to Sflash [15, 16] and shows that if it satisfies our (quite strong) Assumption 2.0.2, then a signature cannot be forged in less than 2^{91}, again only for no-message attacks.

It also applies for the first G^{-1} in Quartz: its entry is given entirely by the oracle, see Fig. 4. A Quartz signature cannot be forged in less than 2^{50}, quite disappointing compared to the claimed security level of 2^{80}.

Now let us assume that in a signature scheme, several inverses G^{-1}, say K inverses, are computed for several H_i, such that all the H_i are independent parts of an output of one single application of a hash function. Then an adversary that can do an existential forgery, is able, with probability $1/Q$, to solve the inversion problem simultaneously for K independent instances H_i. Our Assumption 2.0.2 says that the probability of finding an inverse is at most T/q^m. It is therefore legitimate to think that the probability to compute K inverses in parallel will [2] be at most $(T/q^m)^K$. The adversary does with probability $1/Q$ something that can only be done with probability $(T/q^m)^K$. Thus, we get $1/T \geq 1/Q \geq (T/q^m)^K$. This gives $T \geq q^{\frac{K}{K+1}m}$. We obtain a lower bound that is the exact converse of our generic attack 2.0.1 !

From this one might think that it is possible to prove the security of Quartz and obtain an upper and a lower bound that coincide, thus achieving the exact security level of 2^{80} for no-message attacks. Unfortunately our argument does not apply to Quartz, the entries of the three other G^{-1} functions are not given by the random oracle, see Fig. 4. We are here at the heart of the problem of short signatures. Is it possible to have a signature scheme for which a lower bound on an attack can be proven that is more than $q^{\text{signature size}/2}$? The answer is yes and in Section A.4 we show a very surprising way to compute signatures, in which the signer does compute G^{-1} for two independent values H_1 and H_2, but in which the signature length is only the size of one $G^{-1}(H_i)$.

5   Conclusion

Quartz is based on a trapdoor function G that belongs to a family called HFEv-. It has two independent security parameters and if d is sufficiently large, there is no better method known to compute inverses of G, than simple guessing. We formalized this, and we studied what kind of security can be achieved by a general class of (short) signature schemes, under this assumption and in the

---

[2] It is not a consequence of our Assumption 2.0.2 and requires an additional assumption (cf. Assumption A.2.1 in the Appendix). It does not contradict any known attacks for Quartz. We need to assume that K is small. We may deduce this result, assuming that the only way to compute K inverses is to use the best algorithm to compute one inverse K times. For example the owner of the private key can compute 1 inverse with probability 1, and K inverses with probability at most $1^K = 1$, even here there is no contradiction. For the algorithms that does not contain the private key, we expect it to be true, because it seems that the only thing they can do to find solutions is to guess them, and our assumption is obviously true for any algorithm that is just guessing.

random oracle model. On one side we studied generic attacks on such signature schemes and gave exact lower security bounds. On the other side, we studied the security reductions that could give security upper bounds under some well chosen assumptions. Unfortunately for Quartz, our lower and upper bounds do not coincide. We also proposed a new method for computing short signatures for which the two bounds do coincide, however it is less general than the scheme of Quartz.

In practice it seems that Quartz, though lacking a tight security reduction, is still a correct way to achieve short signatures. The best attack known for Quartz is our generic attack using $\mathcal{O}(2^{80})$ computations with $\mathcal{O}(2^{80})$ of memory. In practice memory is very expensive and the fastest "memoryless" attack known requires as much as 2^{100} computations.

References

[1] Dan Boneh, H. Shacham, and B. Lynn: *Short signatures from the Weil pairing*, Asiacrypt 2001, LNCS 2139, Springer, pp. 514-532. 351
[2] Nicolas Courtois: *The security of Hidden Field Equations (HFE)*; Cryptographers' Track Rsa Conf. 2001, LNCS2020, Springer-Verlag, pp. 266-281.
[3] N. Courtois, L. Goubin, W. Meier, J.-D. Tacier: *Solving Underdefined Systems of Multivariate Quadratic Equations*; PKC 2002, LNCS 2274, Springer, pp. 211-227.
[4] Nicolas Courtois, Matthieu Finiasz and Nicolas Sendrier: *How to achieve a McEliece-based Digital Signature Scheme*; Asiacrypt 2001, LNCS2248, Springer, pp. 157-174. 351
[5] Nicolas Courtois: *La sécurité des primitives cryptographiques basées sur les problèmes algébriques multivariables MQ, IP, MinRank, et HFE*, PhD thesis, Paris 6 University, 2001, in French. 355
[6] Michael Garey, David Johnson: *Computers and Intractability, a guide to the theory of NP-completeness*, Freeman, p. 251.
[7] S. Goldwasser, S. Micali and R. Rivest: *A Secure Digital Signature Scheme*; Siam Journal on Computing, Vol. 17, 2 (1988), pp. 281-308.
[8] Neal Koblitz: *Algebraic aspects of cryptography*; Springer-Verlag, ACM3, 1998, Chapter 4: "Hidden Monomial Cryptosystems", pp. 80-102.
[9] Jacques Patarin: *Hidden Fields Equations (HFE) and Isomorphisms of Polynomials (IP): two new families of Asymmetric Algorithms*; Eurocrypt'96, pp. 33-48.
[10] Jacques Patarin: *La Cryptographie Multivariable*; Mémoire d'habilitation à diriger des recherches de l'Université Paris 7, 1999. 354
[11] Jacques Patarin, Louis Goubin, Nicolas Courtois, + papers of Eli Biham, Aviad Kipnis, T.T. Moh, et al.: *Asymmetric Cryptography with Multivariate Polynomials over a Small Finite Field*; known as "orange script", compilation of different papers with added materials. Available from Jacques.Patarin@louveciennes.tt.slb.com
[12] Jacques Patarin, Nicolas Courtois, Louis Goubin: *C*-+ and HM - Variations around two schemes of T. Matsumoto and H. Imai*; Asiacrypt 1998, pp. 35-49. *Unbalanced Oil and Vinegar Signature Schemes*; Eurocrypt 1999, Springer-Verlag.
[13] Jacques Patarin, Louis Goubin, Nicolas Courtois: *Quartz, 128-bit long digital signatures*; Cryptographers' Track Rsa Conference 2001, San Francisco 8-12 April 2001, LNCS2020, Springer. See [14] for the updated Quartz specification. 352, 357

[14] Jacques Patarin, Louis Goubin, Nicolas Courtois: *Quartz, 128-bit long digital signatures*; An updated version of Quartz specification. available at `http://www.cryptosystem.net/quartz/` 357, 359

[15] Jacques Patarin, Louis Goubin, Nicolas Courtois: *Flash, a fast multivariate signature algorithm*; Cryptographers' Track Rsa Conference 2001, LNCS2020, Springer. 358, 362

[16] An updated version of Sflash specification. Available at `http://www.cryptosystem.net/sflash/` 358, 362

[17] D. Pointcheval, J. Stern: *Security arguments for Digital signatures and Blind Signatures*; Journal of Cryptology, Vol.13(3), Summer 2000, pp. 361-396. *Efficient signature schemes based on birational permutations*;

[18] Nicolas Courtois, Adi Shamir, Jacques Patarin, Alexander Klimov, *Efficient Algorithms for solving Overdefined Systems of Multivariate Polynomial Equations*, Eurocrypt'2000, LNCS 1807, Springer-Verlag, pp. 392-407.

[19] Adi Shamir, Aviad Kipnis: *Cryptanalysis of the HFE Public Key Cryptosystem*; Crypto'99.

A   Black-Box Reductions For No-Message Attacks

In this section we study the security of some signature schemes based, as in Quartz on computation of one or several inverses $y \mapsto G^{-1}(y)$, provided that the trapdoor function G is difficult to inverse, as specified by the Strong One-wayness Assumption 2.0.2. We limit ourselves to no-message attacks, i.e. for the usual case with the adversary trying to forge a valid pair (message, signature) given (only) the public key (and no signature oracles). We need to build a black-box reduction, from the forger, to a machine that solves some difficult problem. It is done for a scheme that is similar to Quartz, but not identical: the signature is longer and it does not involve chaining of the G^{-1} as in Quartz. Later we will see if the result can be extended to Quartz.

A.1   The Black-Box Reduction

First of all, it is easy to prove the security of the usual signature scheme $\sigma = G^{-1}(H(M))$ in the random oracle model. The point is that the value $H(M)$ on which the trapdoor function G is inverted, is produced by the hash function. It does not only mean that it is completely random, and therefore G is inverted on random y, but also that the value may in fact be **chosen** by the random oracle, and as long its probability distribution is indistinguishable from random source, the adversary cannot say the difference. Therefore the adversary may as well be used to compute inverses of some **chosen** values: we have a black-box reduction that is achieved by replacing the random oracle by a given source (if it is random-looking).

Similar black-box reduction works for signature schemes that compute several inverses and we have the following:

Theorem A.1.1 (Security Reduction for Signatures Scheme that Compute Inverses of Hashed Values). Let G be a trapdoor one-way function. Assume that a signature scheme satisfies:

- it computes $G^{-1}(H_i)$ for some K values $H_i \in GF(q)^m$,
- all the H_i are independent parts of a (single) output of a hash function:

$$H(M) = (H_1, H_2, \ldots, H_K).$$

- all the K values $G^{-1}(H_1), .., G^{-1}(H_K)$ can be completely recovered in the signature verification,

If an attacker having (only) the access to the public key is able to compute a valid pair (message, signature) with probability ε, in random oracle model, and with Q queries to the hashing oracle.
Then it can be then transformed into a machine than given a random K-tuple $(y_1, y_2, \ldots, y_K)$ will with probability ε/Q output all the K inverses: $(G^{-1}(y_1), G^{-1}(y_2), \ldots, G^{-1}(y_K))$.

Proof. In the adversary's interaction with the hash oracle, the oracle gives a random and independent K-tuple $(H_1^{(i)}, H_2^{(i)}, \ldots, H_K^{(i)})$ each time it is called for $i = 1..Q$. We replace a randomly chosen K-tuple by $(y_1, y_2, \ldots, y_K)$. Since both lists are random and independent, even a computationally unbounded adversary cannot distinguish between two situations. Consequently the result will be the same: he will, with probability ε output, a valid pair (message, signature), and with probability ε/Q it will contain the inverse of the chosen K-tuple.

A.2   Security Arguments

It turns out that our Strong One-wayness Assumption 2.0.2 is not enough.

Assumption A.2.1 (Super-Strong One-Wayness of HFEv-).
Let K be a small integer. Let G a random public key $G \leftarrow \text{HFEv}^-(q, n, m)$ with $m \approx n$, $n \geq m$ and $m \leq 100$. For any Adversary A running in T CPU clocks, given random K-tuple $(y_1, \ldots, y_K) \leftarrow GF(q^m)^k$, the probability that A computes all the inverses $x_i = G^{-1}(y_i)$ with probability ε' is upper-bounded by:

$$\varepsilon' \leq (T/q^m)^K.$$

It is not a consequence of the Assumption 2.0.2. There may be algorithms that compute all K inverses $x_i = G^{-1}(y_i)$ faster than applying K times, the best algorithm to compute one inverse. Cf. also the footnote 2, p. 358.

Theorem A.2.2. Let K be a small integer. Let G be a trapdoor one-way function $G : GF(q)^n \to GF(q)^m$ with $m \leq n$. Assume that G satisfies the Assumption A.2.1. Assume that in a signature scheme, given a valid (pair message, signature), K inverses $G^{-1}(H_i)$ can be computed, with $H(M) = (H_1, H_2, \ldots, H_K)$. We assume that H is a random oracle. Let A be an Adversary, having (only) the access to the public key, running in time T, and able to compute a valid pair (message, signature) with a success probability ε. Then:

$$T \geq \varepsilon^{\frac{1}{K+1}} \cdot q^{m \cdot \frac{K}{K+1}}.$$

Proof. From Theorem A.1.1, we obtain a machine that inverts G in parallel for K random values $y_1, \ldots, y_K$ and with probability $\varepsilon' = \varepsilon/Q$. Following our Assumption, the attacker is able to do with probability ε/Q something that can only be done with a probability at most $(T/q^m)^K$. Thus:

$$\varepsilon/Q \leq (T/q^m)^K.$$

Finally, since the oracle queries take time, we have $Q \leq T$ and obtain:

$\varepsilon/T \leq \varepsilon/Q \leq (T/q^m)^K$, from this we get $T^{K+1} \geq \varepsilon(q^m)^K$, and finally

$$T \geq \varepsilon^{\frac{1}{K+1}} \cdot q^{m \cdot \frac{K}{K+1}}.$$

$\square$

Corollary A.2.3. Let G be a trapdoor one-way function $G : GF(q)^n \rightarrow GF(q)^m$ with $m \leq n$. Assume that the only method known for to obtain $G^{-1}(y_i)$ for some values y_i is to guess them and apply G. Assume that in a signature scheme, given a valid pair (message, signature), K inverses $G^{-1}(H_i)$ are be computed, with $H(M) = (H_1, H_2, \ldots, H_K)$. Let A be an Adversary having (only) the access to the public key and running in time T that is able to compute a valid pair (message, signature). Then, under the random oracle assumption,

$$T \geq q^{m \cdot \frac{K}{K+1}}.$$

We obtained an exact, tight converse of the Theorem 3.2.1. It gives the exact security level of the described signature schemes (but not for Quartz).

A.3   Applications, $K = 1$, Consequences on Flash and Sflash

All well known signature schemes constructed as $\sigma = G^{-1}(H)$ satisfy the assumption of the signature scheme we used in Theorems A.1.1 and A.2.2. However that trapdoor functions they use, for example RSA encryption, admit attacks asymptotically much faster than the exhaustive search, and therefore **do not** satisfy our very strong hardness Assumption 2.0.2 used in Theorems A.2.2.

Currently the only convincing trapdoor functions that seem to satisfy our Strong One-wayness Assumption 2.0.2 are multivariate cryptographic trapdoor functions. For example the signature scheme Flash and Sflash [3], submitted to European call for cryptographic primitives [15, 16], use a trapdoor function $G : GF(q)^{37} \rightarrow GF(q)^{26}$ with respectively $q = 256$ for Flash and $q = 128$ for Sflash. Thus by the Theorem A.2.2 and the converse given by the Theorem 3.2.1 we have:

Corollary A.3.1 (Exact Security of Flash and Sflash). If the trapdoor function used in Flash/Sflash satisfies the Strong One-wayness Assumption 2.0.2, the security of these respective signature schemes [15, 16] against no-message attacks is exactly:

$$q^{m/2} = 2^{104} \text{ for Flash } \quad \text{and } 2^{91} \text{ for Sflash.}$$

---

[3] We refer here to the updated version of Sflash that is very similar to Flash, see [16].

A.4 Applications with $K \geq 2$, Differential Signature Scheme

It is trivial to construct a signature scheme for which the Theorem A.2.2 applies, for any small K, and based on any trapdoor function. For this we need just to compute in parallel K signatures $\sigma_i = G^{-1}(H_i)$ and the signature will be given by a K-tuple $\left(G^{-1}(H_1(M)), \ldots, G^{-1}(H_K(M))\right)$. Unfortunately such a signature will be K times as long as when $K = 1$.

Differential Signatures It is highly non-trivial to construct a signature scheme for which the Theorem A.2.2 applies, but with shorter signatures. For $K = 2$, it is possible to have a complete signature compression. For example we may compute the signature as follows:

$$\boxed{\sigma = F^{-1}(H_2) - F^{-1}(H_1)}$$

This surprising signature scheme has a non-trivial verification procedure. The signature compression is based on the fact that the two values $x = F^{-1}(H_1)$ and $x + \sigma = F^{-1}(H_2)$ can be completely recovered given their difference σ, as the equation $F(x+\sigma) - F(x) = H_2 - H_1$ becomes linear in the x_i after σ, H_1 and H_2 are known (the degree 2 terms will just cancel out). This scheme is called the "Differential Signature" scheme. It is not completely generic: it works only when G is a Multivariate Quadratic (MQ) function and only for $K = 2$.

Example: For example we may use the differential signature scheme with the following set of parameters for HFEv-: q=2, h=127, r=7, v=1, d=257, n=128, m=120. For these parameter values[4], we have:

Corollary A.4.1. Let $\varepsilon = 1$, $m = 120$, $n \geq m$, $K = 2$. Then the exact security of the differential signature scheme for no-message attacks is

$$Security = 2^{\frac{2}{3}m} = 2^{80}.$$

This follows immediately from Theorems A.2.2 and 3.2.1. The differential signature scheme allows, unlike Quartz, to have digital signatures of 128 bits with proven exact security of 2^{80} (for no-message attacks).

A.5 Application to Quartz and Similar Schemes

Unfortunately, in the construction used in Quartz as represented on Fig. 4 and more generally for generalized Feistel-Patarin with $K > 1$, only one of the values for which we have to compute the inverse G^{-1} is given by the hashing oracle. Our reduction, the Theorem A.1.1, cannot be applied for $K = 4$. We may however apply the Theorem A.1.1 and thus A.2.2 with $K = 1$, only considering the first inverse, that is indeed given by the random oracle. This shows that the security of this scheme is at least $q^{m/2}$, which is not very satisfactory, knowing that the the Theorem 3.2.1 gives an attack in $q^{m\frac{K}{K+1}}$. Concretely, our lower bound for the security of Quartz under the Assumption 2.0.2 is 2^{50}, and the upper bound is 2^{80}. They do unfortunately not coincide.

---

[4] We note that $h = 127$ is a prime as in Quartz (though yet no attacks are known when it isn't).

B   Chosen-Message Security

The chosen-message security of schemes such as Quartz remains an open problem. In the extended version of this paper, available from the author, it is shown that, for some special trapdoor function, and without an additional assumption, they are not in general secure against such attacks. However, it is conjectured that if the signature is computed in deterministic way, with random coins being derived from the message by a pseudo-random generator using an additional secret key, such schemes should be secure also against this (the most general) class of attacks. Such a solution is used in Quartz.

Author Index

Lecture Notes in Computer Science

For information about Vols. 1–2476

please contact your bookseller or Springer-Verlag

Vol. 2516: A. Wespi, G. Vigna, L. Deri (Eds.), Recent Advances in Intrusion Detection. Proceedings, 2002. X, 327 pages. 2002.

Vol. 2517: M.D. Aagaard, J.W. O'Leary (Eds.), Formal Methods in Computer-Aided Design. Proceedings, 2002. XI, 399 pages. 2002.

Vol. 2518: P. Bose, P. Morin (Eds.), Algorithms and Computation. Proceedings, 2002. XIII, 656 pages. 2002.

Vol. 2519: R. Meersman, Z. Tari, et al. (Eds.), On the Move to Meaningful Internet Systems 2002: CoopIS, DOA, and ODBASE. Proceedings, 2002. XXIII, 1367 pages. 2002.

Vol. 2521: A. Karmouch, T. Magedanz, J. Delgado (Eds.), Mobile Agents for Telecommunication Applications. Proceedings, 2002. XII, 317 pages. 2002.

Vol. 2522: T. Andreasen, A. Motro, H. Christiansen, H. Legind Larsen (Eds.), Flexible Query Answering. Proceedings, 2002. XI, 386 pages. 2002. (Subseries LNAI).

Vol. 2525: H.H. Bülthoff, S.-Whan Lee, T.A. Poggio, C. Wallraven (Eds.), Biologically Motivated Computer Vision. Proceedings, 2002. XIV, 662 pages. 2002.

Vol. 2526: A. Colosimo, A. Giuliani, P. Sirabella (Eds.), Medical Data Analysis. Proceedings, 2002. IX, 222 pages. 2002.

Vol. 2527: F.J. Garijo, J.C. Riquelme, M. Toro (Eds.), Advances in Artificial Intelligence – IBERAMIA 2002. Proceedings, 2002. XVIII, 955 pages. 2002. (Subseries LNAI).

Vol. 2528: M.T. Goodrich, S.G. Kobourov (Eds.), Graph Drawing. Proceedings, 2002. XIII, 384 pages. 2002.

Vol. 2529: D.A. Peled, M.Y. Vardi (Eds.), Formal Techniques for Networked and Distributed Sytems – FORTE 2002. Proceedings, 2002. XI, 371 pages. 2002.

Vol. 2531: J. Padget, O. Shehory, D. Parkes, N. Sadeh, W.E. Walsh (Eds.), Agent-Mediated Electronic Commerce IV. Proceedings, 2002. XVII, 341 pages. 2002. (Subseries LNAI).

Vol. 2532: Y.-C. Chen, L.-W. Chang, C.-T. Hsu (Eds.), Advances in Multimedia Information Processing – PCM 2002. Proceedings, 2002. XXI, 1255 pages. 2002.

Vol. 2533: N. Cesa-Bianchi, M. Numao, R. Reischuk (Eds.), Algorithmic Learning Theory. Proceedings, 2002. XI, 415 pages. 2002. (Subseries LNAI).

Vol. 2534: S. Lange, K. Satoh, C.H. Smith (Ed.), Discovery Science. Proceedings, 2002. XIII, 464 pages. 2002.

Vol. 2535: N. Suri (Ed.), Mobile Agents. Proceedings, 2002. X, 203 pages. 2002.

Vol. 2536: M. Parashar (Ed.), Grid Computing – GRID 2002. Proceedings, 2002. XI, 318 pages. 2002.

Vol. 2537: D.G. Feitelson, L. Rudolph, U. Schwiegelshohn (Eds.), Job Scheduling Strategies for Parallel Processing. Proceedings, 2002. VII, 237 pages. 2002.

Vol. 2538: B. König-Ries, K. Makki, S.A.M. Makki, N. Pissinou, P. Scheuermann (Eds.), Developing an Infrastructure for Mobile and Wireless Systems. Proceedings 2001. X, 183 pages. 2002.

Vol. 2539: K. Börner, C. Chen (Eds.), Visual Interfaces to Digital Libraries. X, 233 pages. 2002.

Vol. 2540: W.I. Grosky, F. Plášil (Eds.), SOFSEM 2002: Theory and Practice of Informatics. Proceedings, 2002. X, 289 pages. 2002.

Vol. 2541: T. Barkowsky, Mental Representation and Processing of Geographic Knowledge. X, 174 pages. 2002. (Subseries LNAI).

Vol. 2544: S. Bhalla (Ed.), Databases in Networked Information Systems. Proceedings 2002. X, 285 pages. 2002.

Vol. 2545: P. Forbrig, Q, Limbourg, B. Urban, J. Vanderdonckt (Eds.), Interactive Systems. Proceedings 2002. X, 269 pages. 2002.

Vol. 2546: J. Sterbenz, O. Takada, C. Tschudin, B. Plattner (Eds.), Active Networks. Proceedings, 2002. XIV, 267 pages. 2002.

Vol. 2548: J. Hernández, Ana Moreira (Eds.), Object-Oriented Technology. Proceedings, 2002. VIII, 223 pages. 2002.

Vol. 2549: J. Cortadella, A. Yakovlev, G. Rozenberg (Eds.), Concurrency and Hardware Design. XI, 345 pages. 2002.

Vol. 2550: A. Jean-Marie (Ed.), Advances in Computing Science – ASIAN 2002. Proceedings, 2002. X, 233 pages. 2002.

Vol. 2551: A. Menezes, P. Sarkar (Eds.), Progress in Cryptology – INDOCRYPT 2002. Proceedings, 2002. XI, 437 pages. 2002.

Vol. 2552: S. Sahni, V.K. Prasanna, U. Shukla (Eds.), High Performance Computing – HiPC 2002. Proceedings, 2002. XXI, 735 pages. 2002.

Vol. 2553: B. Andersson, M. Bergholtz, P. Johannesson (Eds.), Natural Language Processing and Information Systems. Proceedings, 2002. X, 241 pages. 2002.

Vol. 2554: M. Beetz, Plan-Based Control of Robotic Agents. XI, 191 pages. 2002. (Subseries LNAI).

Vol. 2555: E.-P. Lim, S. Foo, C. Khoo, H. Chen, E. Fox, S. Urs, T. Costantino (Eds.), Digital Libraries: People, Knowledge, and Technology. Proceedings, 2002. XVII, 535 pages. 2002.

Vol. 2556: M. Agrawal, A. Seth (Eds.), FST TCS 2002: Foundations of Software Technology and Theoretical Computer Science. Proceedings, 2002. XI, 361 pages. 2002.

Vol. 2557: B. McKay, J. Slaney (Eds.), AI 2002: Advances in Artificial Intelligence. Proceedings, 2002. XV, 730 pages. 2002. (Subseries LNAI).

Vol. 2558: P. Perner, Data Mining on Multimedia Data. X, 131 pages. 2002.

Vol. 2559: M. Oivo, S. Komi-Sirviö (Eds.), Product Focused Software Process Improvement. Proceedings, 2002. XV, 646 pages. 2002.

Vol. 2560: S. Goronzy, Robust Adaptation to Non-Native Accents in Automatic Speech Recognition. Proceedings, 2002. XI, 144 pages. 2002. (Subseries LNAI).

Vol. 2561: H.C.M. de Swart (Ed.), Relational Methods in Computer Science. Proceedings, 2001. X, 315 pages. 2002.

Vol. 2566: T.Æ. Mogensen, D.A. Schmidt, I.H. Sudborough (Eds.), The Essence of Computation. XIV, 473 pages. 2002.

Vol. 2567: Y.G. Desmedt (Ed.), Public Key Cryptography – PKC 2003. Proceedings, 2003. XI, 365 pages. 2002.

Vol. 2569: D. Gollmann, G. Karjoth, M. Waidner (Eds.), Computer Security – ESORICS 2002. Proceedings, 2002. XIII, 648 pages. 2002. (Subseries LNAI).

Vol. 2572: D. Calvanese, M. Lenzerini, R. Motwani (Eds.), Database Theory – ICDT 2003. Proceedings, 2003. XI, 455 pages. 2002.

Vol. 2575: L.D. Zuck, P.C. Attie, A. Cortesi, S. Mukhopadhyay (Eds.), Verification, Model Checking, and Abstract Interpretation. Proceedings, 2003. XI, 325 pages. 2003.